MOON HANDBOOKS®

HAVANA

young boy and Cadillac
Eldorado, Santiago de
las Vegas

© CHRISTOPHER P. BAKER

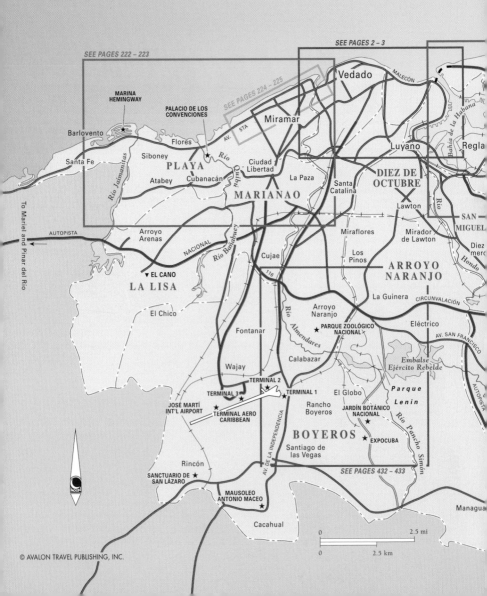

METROPOLITAN
HAVANA

SEE PAGES 222 – 223

SEE PAGES 2 – 3

SEE PAGES 224 – 225

Vedado

MALECÓN

MARINA
HEMINGWAY

PALACIO DE LOS
CONVENCIONES

Miramar

Barlovento

Florés

Río Quibú

Bahía de la Habana

Santa Fe

Siboney

Ciudad
Libertad

Luyano

Regla

Río Jaimanitas

PLAYA

Atabey   Cubanacán

La Paza

Santa
Catalina

DIEZ DE
OCTUBRE

SAN
MIGUEL

Arroyo
Arenas

MARIANAO

Lawton

Diez
merc

AUTOPISTA

NACIONAL

Río Batabuey

Cujae

Miraflores

Mirador
de Lawton

Hondo

To Mariel and Pinar del Rio

LA LISA

EL CANO

Los
Pinos

ARROYO
NARANJO

El Chico

Fontanar

116

Río Almendares

La Guinera

CIRCUNVALACIÓN

Arroyo
Naranjo

Eléctrico

PARQUE ZOOLÓGICO
NACIONAL

AV. SAN FRANCISCO

Wajay

Calabazar

Embalse
Ejército Rebelde

TERMINAL 2

Parque
Lenin

AUTOPISTA

TERMINAL 3

TERMINAL 1

El Globo

JOSÉ MARTÍ
INT'L AIRPORT

TERMINAL AERO
CARIBBEAN

Rancho
Boyeros

JARDÍN BOTÁNICO
NACIONAL

Río Pancho Simón

Rincón

BOYEROS

EXPOCUBA

AV. DE LA INDEPENDENCIA

SANCTUARIO DE
SAN LÁZARO

Santiago de
las Vegas

SEE PAGES 432 – 433

Manague

MAUSOLEO
ANTONIO MACEO

Cacahual

Managua

0   2.5 mi

0   2.5 km

MOON

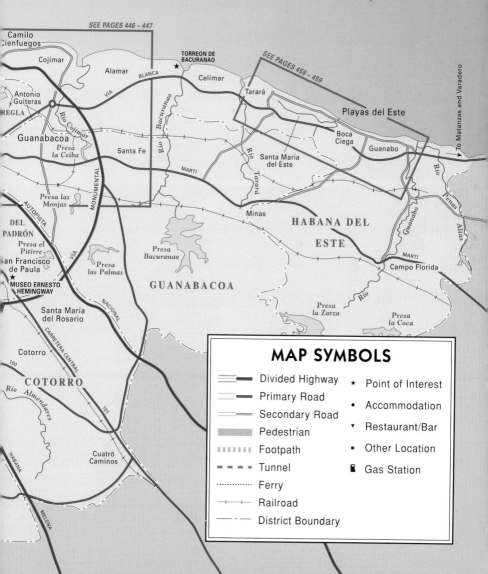

STRAITS OF FLORIDA

SEE PAGES 446 – 447

SEE PAGES 458 – 459

Camilo Cienfuegos

Cojímar

Alamar

BLANCA

VIA

TORREON DE BACURANAO ★

Celimar

Tarará

To Matanzas and Varadero

Antonio Guiteras

REGLA

Río Cojímar

Guanabacoa

Presa la Ceiba

Santa Fe

Río Bacuranao

MARTÍ

Río Tarará

Playas del Este

Boca Ciega

Guanabo

Santa María del Este

Río Guanabo

Río Peñas Altas

Presa las Monjas

MONUMENTAL

Minas

HABANA DEL ESTE

DEL PADRÓN

AUTOPISTA

Presa el Pitirre

an Francisco de Paula

VIA

Presa las Palmas

Presa Bacuranao

GUANABACOA

MARTÍ

Campo Florida

★ MUSEO ERNESTO HEMINGWAY

Santa María del Rosario

NACIONAL

Presa la Zarza

Río

Presa la Coca

Cotorro

CARRETERA CENTRAL

100

COTORRO

Río Almendares

101

HABANA

Cuatro Caminos

MELENA

MAP SYMBOLS

▬▬▬ Divided Highway	★ Point of Interest
▬▬ Primary Road	• Accommodation
▬▬ Secondary Road	▾ Restaurant/Bar
▬▬ Pedestrian	▪ Other Location
▥▥▥ Footpath	🯄 Gas Station
▪ ▪ ▪ Tunnel	
·········· Ferry	
┼─┼─┼ Railroad	
─·─·─ District Boundary	

La Milagrosa,
Cementerio Colón

MOON HANDBOOKS®

HAVANA

SECOND EDITION

CHRISTOPHER P. BAKER

AVALON
TRAVEL

Contents

© CHRISTOPHER P. BAKER

Introduction 1

Inhabited by a cultured, civilized, and sensual people, this is the most exhilarating (and occasionally exasperating) city between Miami and Montevideo. Havana's mysteries and contradictions will fascinate you—this may well be the destination of the new millennium. Visit now . . . before it loses its magic.

Planning Your Trip 73

While it isn't illegal to travel to Cuba from the United States, the laws are specific. Here are all the details—how to get there, when to go, and what to take.

Habana Vieja—The Old City

The finest collection of Spanish colonial buildings in the Americas lines Habana Vieja's cobbled streets. Stroll the tree-lined Prado, hang out in Hemingway's old haunts, and people-watch in quintessentially Cuban plazas.

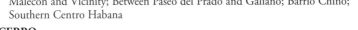

Centro Habana and Cerro

Although its once-regal mansions are now dilapidated, this area features shopping along Calle San Rafael and in Cuatro Caminos, the country's largest farmers market. Not to be missed is the Malecón—Havana's seafront drive and undisputed social gathering spot.

Malecón and Vicinity; Between Paseo del Prado and Galiano; Barrio Chino; Southern Centro Habana

Vedado and Plaza de la Revolución

Hilly Vedado is Havana at its middle-class best, with the University of Havana, historic Plaza de la Revolución, and prime restaurants and hotels, such as the lavish Hotel Nacional. Walking La Rampa will lead you to cinemas, nightclubs, art deco buildings, and the best ice cream in the city at Parque Coppelia.

Playa (Miramar and Beyond) 220

With their luxurious residences and new apartment buildings, Playa and Miramar are the face of Cuba's quasi-capitalist makeover—and possibly its future. The shoreline along 1ra Avenida and the famed Tropicana nightclub in Marianao are must-sees.

Accommodations 237

Tourist hotels, villas, casas particulares—find the right kind of accommodation for you, in your price range, and in the best location for your ideal experience.

Peso Hotels; Tourist Hotels; Aparthotels; Villas, Apartments, and *Protocolos; Casas Particulares;* Staying with Cuban Friends

Food 265

You can eat well in Cuba. Here you'll learn the best places to eat and drink, what to order . . . and what to avoid.

Cuban Dishes; Breakfast; Peso Eateries; *Paladares;* Fast Food; Cafés, Bakeries, and Ice Cream

Entertainment and Recreation 297

Music and dance are the pulsing undercurrent of Cuban life. With a rich art tradition, plus golf, sailing, swimming, fishing, baseball—there's always something to see and do, day and night.

Festivals and Events; Folk Music and Dance; Cabarets *(Espectáculos);* Discotheques and Dancing; Jazz and Salsa Venues; Rap, Hip-Hop, and Reggae Venues; Rock Venues; Tango and Flamenco; Bars; Cinema; Theater, Classical Music, and Dance; Museums and Galleries

SPORTS AND RECREATION 331

Shopping 340

What comes to mind when you think of Cuba? Cigars, of course—and rum. Find out where to buy the highest quality Cuban merchandise.

Antiques; Arts and Crafts; Open-Air Markets; Cigars; Rum and Liquors

Information and Services 358

Unclear on the nuances between dollars and pesos? Want to call home or mail a package? Need to know what kind of electrical adapter to bring? Get all the practical details here.

Money; Communications; Media; Embassies and Consulates; Travel Agencies; Tourist Information; Health Issues; Safety and Related Issues; Practicalities

Transportation 401

Whether you're navigating the airport, renting a car, mastering the public bus system, catching a ciclotaxi *or* cocotaxi, *bicycling your way around, or meeting up with a tour, find out everything you need to know to get to and around Havana.*

Arriving in Havana; Getting into Town; Getting Around Havana; Exploring Beyond Havana; Departing Cuba

Exploring Suburban Havana

Venture beyond the city to check out the national zoo, Parque Lenin, ExpoCuba, Hemingway's former home, charming provincial towns, botanical gardens, and the popular beaches of Playas del Este.

Resources

Maps

ABOUT THE AUTHOR
Christopher P. Baker

© CHRISTOPHER P. BAKER

Christopher P. Baker was born and raised in Yorkshire, England. He received a B.A. (Honors) in Geography at University College, London, during which he participated in two Sahara research expeditions and an exchange program at Krakow University, Poland. Later he earned Master's degrees in Latin American Studies from Liverpool University and in Education from the Institute of Education, London University. He began his writing career in 1978 as contributing editor on Latin America for *Land & Liberty*, a London-based political journal. In 1980 he received a Scripps-Howard Foundation Scholarship in Journalism to attend the University of California, Berkeley. Since 1983, he has made his living as a professional travel writer, photographer, lecturer, and tour guide. His stories and photography have appeared in publications as diverse as *Newsweek, National Geographic Traveler,* BBC's *World Magazine, National Wildlife, Islands, Elle, The Los Angeles Times, Saveur,* and *Writers' Digest.* His other books include the best-selling *Moon Handbooks Cuba* and *Moon Handbooks Costa Rica,* plus *Mi Moto Fidel: Motorcycling Through Castro's Cuba,* winner of both the Lowell Thomas Award for Best Travel Book and the North American Travel Journalist Association's Grand Prize. His photo-essay book *Island Classics: Cars of Cuba* was published in 2003. He has also authored guides to Jamaica, California, Nevada, and the Bahamas, Turks and Caicos. He has also written for the National Geographic Society, Time-Life, the Discovery Channel, and Writer's Digest.

Baker has escorted group tours to New Zealand, Hong Kong, Korea, England, and Cuba. He has been profiled in *USA Today;* appears frequently on radio and television talk shows and as a guest-lecturer aboard cruise ships throughout the Caribbean and farther afield; and has been privileged to address the National Press Club, the World Affairs Council, and the National Geographic Society as a faculty member of *Live from National Geographic.* Baker is a member of the Society of American Travel Writers and National Writers Union. He has been honored with numerous awards for outstanding writing, among them the prestigious Lowell Thomas Travel Journalism Award (five times, including Best Travel News Investigative Reporter) and the 1995 Benjamin Franklin Best Travel Guide award for *Moon Handbooks Costa Rica.* In 1998, the Caribbean Tourism Organization named him Travel Journalist of the Year. He lives in California.

To Jorge Coalla Potts, Marisel, and Jessica

Preface

Winston Churchill, approaching Havana by sea in 1895, wrote that he felt "delirious yet tumultuous. . . . I felt as if I sailed with Long John Silver and first gazed on Treasure Island. Here was a place where anything might happen. Here was a place where something would certainly happen. Here I might leave my bones."

Countless writers have commented on the exhilarating sensation that engulfs visitors in this most beautiful and beguiling of Caribbean cities. The potency of Havana's appeal is owed to a quality that "runs deeper than the stuff of which travel brochures are made. It is irresistible and intangible," wrote Juliet Barclay. Arnold Samuelson, recalling his first visit to Havana in 1934, says taking in the city is as if "everything you have seen before is forgotten, everything you see and hear then being so strange you feel . . . as if you had died and come to life in a different world." Havana's ethereal mood, little changed today, is so pronounced that it finds its way into novels. "I wake up feeling different, like something inside me is changing, something chemical and irreversible. There's a magic here working its way through my veins," observes Pilar, a Cuban-American character from New York who returns to Havana in Cristina García's novel *Dreaming in Cuban.*

Set foot once in Havana and you can only succumb to its enigmatic allure. It is impossible to resist the city's mysteries and contradictions. Walking the city's streets you sense you are living inside a romantic thriller. You don't want to sleep for fear of missing a vital experience. Before the Revolution, Havana had a reputation as a place of intrigue and tawdry romance. The whiff of conspiracy, the intimation of liaison, is still in the air. Havana, now Communist but still carnal, is peopled in fact as in fiction by characters from the novels of Ernest Hemingway and Graham Greene.

Your first reaction is of being caught in an eerie colonial-cum-1950s time warp. Fading signs advertising Hotpoint and Singer appliances evoke the decadent decades when Cuba was a virtual colony of the United States. High-finned, chrome-spangled dowagers from the heyday of Detroit are everywhere, conjuring images of dark-eyed temptresses and men in Panama hats and white linen suits. "Nick and I are in one of the weirdest places on earth, weird not so much because it is stuck in the fifties," wrote Isadora Tattlin in *Cuban Diaries,* "but because it is *open, staffed,* and *routine.* It is one of the weirdest places on earth, but it is at the same time familiar, as if a nuclear missile really *did* hit [my] school and forty-year-olds now climb out from under their desks, blinking at what's left."

All the glamour of an abandoned stage set is here, patinated by age. For foreign visitors, it is heady stuff.

HAVANA REDUX

In the 1950s, Cuba was North America's premier playground. Tens of thousands of *yanquis* flocked to Havana each year, lured by tourist brochures selling gambling and "glamorous, lissome Latin lasses, black-eyed señoritas, langorously, enticingly swaying." North Americans arrived by plane or aboard the *City of Havana* ferry from Key West to indulge in a few days of sun and sin. They went home happy, unaware of General Batista's reign of terror or that behind the scenes revolutionary forces were at work.

On New Year's Eve 1958, Castro & Co. triumphed and the tourist business succumbed, says Rosalie Schwartz, "to uncertainty, inconvenience, and unpleasantness."

Eager to reassure tourists, in October 1959 Fidel Castro spoke to the American Society of Travel Agents (ASTA) convention, held that year in Havana's old Blanquita Theater (now the Karl Marx). "We have sea," said Castro. "We have bays, we have beautiful beaches, we have medicinal waters in our hotels, we have mountains, we have game and we have fish in the sea and the rivers, and we have sun. Our people are noble, hospitable, and, most important, they hate no one. They love visitors—so much in fact that our visitors feel completely at home."

Normal relations with the United States still existed back then, and U.S. ambassador Philip Bonsai also lauded Cuban tourism at the ASTA convention: "Cuba is one of the most admirable countries in the world from the point of view of North American tourism and from many other points of view."

Despite good intentions, the convention proved a last hurrah. Even as the delegates departed, five major steamship companies eliminated their stops in Havana. Shortly afterward, Cuba spun off into the Soviet orbit and the doors slammed shut to tourists. Lack of revenue doomed the city's hotels, restaurants, and bars, and the city sank into decay.

But time has a way of coming full circle. Castro's view of tourism has shifted profoundly since the demise of the Soviet Union. Cuba has put a polish on Havana's old tourist haunts and invested heavily in jazzing up its hotels and tourist infrastructure, and is extending its hand to the rest of the world. Five decades after Castro took power, Havana is enjoying cult status again. Hip, happenin' Havana—the most exhilarating and exasperating city between Miami and Montevideo—may well be the destination of the new millennium.

About 1.7 million foreign visitors arrived in Cuba in 2001, including more than 160,000 U.S. citizens, most of whom traveled legally. The rest circumvented U.S. travel restrictions to worship at the shrine of '50s kitsch and savor a frisson of the forbidden (they did so by entering Cuba through Canada, Mexico, Jamaica, or the Bahamas). Cubans play their part by abstaining from stamping passports, so Uncle Sam need never know. Most *yanquis* harbor the misguided impression that it's illegal for U.S. citizens to travel to Cuba. It's not; it's merely illegal to spend dollars there. In any event, no U.S. tourist has ever been prosecuted merely for visiting Cuba. (For more information see the Planning Your Trip chapter.)

HAVANA'S LURES

One of the great historical cities of the New World, Havana (pop. 2.2 million—one-fifth the total population of Cuba) is made for tropical tourism. It has a flavor all its own, a surreal and sensual amalgam of colonialism, capitalism, and Communism. The city is a far cry from the Caribbean backwaters that call themselves capitals elsewhere in the Antilles. It is obvious, as you walk tree-lined boulevards and raucous, eerily Neapolitan streets, that Havana was wealthy to a degree that most Caribbean cities were not—and not too long ago. Havana is a city, notes architect Jorge Rigau, "upholstered in columns, cushioned by colonnaded arcades."

The Spanish colonial buildings pushed hard up against the Atlantic are handsome indeed. They come in a spectacular blend of styles—from the neoclassic aristocratic homes and baroque palaces to the bold, modern art deco and art nouveau buildings.

At the heart of the city is enchanting Habana Vieja (Old Havana), a living museum that contains the finest collection of Spanish colonial buildings in all the Americas. Baroque churches, convents, and castles that could have been transported from Madrid or Cádiz still reign majestically over squares embraced by the former palaces of Cuba's ruling gentry. Ernest Hemingway's house—Finca Vigía—in the suburb of San Francisco de Paula is one of dozens of museums dedicated to the memory of great men and women. And although many of the older monuments—those of Cuba's

UNITED STATES–CUBA SISTER CITIES

Mobile, Alabama, was the first U.S. city to establish fraternal ties with a city in Cuba. Mobile and Havana launched the first formal sister cities link in October 1993 when Mobile's mayor and city council and Havana's mayor signed a twinning agreement. For more information, contact Society Mobile–La Habana, 2507 Myrtle St., Mobile, AL 36607, 251/473-8775, jashinault@aol.com.

Similarly, the Washington, D.C.–Havana Sister City Project, 202/541-9433, bshango@juno.com, a recognized member of the US–Cuba Sister Cities Association (320 Lowen-hill St., Pittsburgh, PA 15216, 412/563-1519, fax 412/563-1945, uscsca@aol.com, www.USCSCA.org) is "a coalition for peace and social justice comprised of D.C.-based groups seeking to establish and promote mutually respectful relations between these two capital cities," through the "official twinning of our two cities through our respective local governments and work to establish people-to-people cultural exchanges in areas such as education, health & science, art, sports, youth development, etc."

"politically incorrect" heroes—were pulled down, they were at least replaced by numerous monuments to those on the "correct" side of history.

Street names may have been changed, but balmy city streets with walls of faded tropical pastels still smolder gold in the waxing sun. By day, magnesium sunlight gleams on the chrome of old American autos and filters through stained-glass *mediopuntos* to dance on the cool marble floors. And time cannot erase the sound of the "jalousies above the colonnades creaking in the small wind from the sea," in the words of Graham Greene.

Havana's greatest, most enigmatic appeal is that you sense you are living inside an unfolding drama. Novelist Bob Shacochis thought it like "a Latin woman, beautiful but exhausted, dancing through the perfumed night with a gun in her hand." The city is still intoxicating, still laced with the sharp edges and sinister shadows that made Spanish poet Federico García Lorca write to his parents, "If I get lost look for me in Cuba," and that made Hemingway want "to stay here forever."

Still, an open-minded visitor is torn two ways: Havana is both disheartening and uplifting. You'll most probably fall in love with the city, while being thankful you don't have to live in it.

Forty years of negative media reports have led many visitors to expect the worst—a fossilized shell of a city with a population cowed and sullen, their lips glued shut in fear. Those who see only the negatives—the overwhelming decay and dishevelment, the inept bureaucracy, the shortages and suffocating restraints that make life a misery for many locals—fail to see the smiling children or healthy, educated youth eager to challenge you to a game of chess, discuss Voltaire, or whisk you off for a bit of romance. Havana is inhabited by a cultured, civilized, and sensual people.

You'll be particularly impressed by the human values: the Cubans' kindness, hospitality, and a system of mutual helpfulness belie any equation of poverty with vice and unhappiness. *Habaneros* you have met only moments ago will invite you into their homes, where rum and beer are passed around and you are lured to dance by narcotic rhythms. It is hard to believe that the U.S. government's Trading with the Enemy Act is directed at these compellingly warm-hearted people. How often have I teared up and cried, laughed, flirted, danced, as it were, with the enemy?

There is nothing depressing about the *habaneros,* only the situation in which the majority are forced to live their lives.

FADED GLORY

Havana has been "a city in lamentable decline" for more than a century, but policies since the Revolution have only hastened its tragic decay. Havana aches with pathos and penury, combining all the sultry sadness and sun-washed spontaneity of Naples and New Orleans. Even Esteban Lazo, the mayor of Havana, has admitted that "the Revolution has been hard on the city." The sultry seductress of prerevolutionary days needs a million gallons of paint—political humorist P. J. O'Rourke has written that "half an hour in Havana is enough to cure you of a taste for that distressed look so popular in Crate & Barrel stores." However, one can take comfort in the fact that the best of the buildings are still standing and haven't been swept away by a gaudy wave of tourist hotels, shopping malls, and marinas. Colonial-era villages are also scattered throughout Greater Havana, engulfed by the metropolis but still rich in historical character.

Soon after Castro took power his government announced a policy emphasizing rural development over urban improvement. The countryside had long been neglected, and a significant portion of the rural population lived in abject poverty. But the triumphs of the Revolution in the countryside could not stem migration to the cities, particularly Havana, which suffered ongoing neglect and impoverishment. Little new construction has taken place in the past 40 years—except in the suburbs, where melancholic "internationalist" apartment housing and other Communist carbuncles reflect Cuba's gravitation into the Soviet orbit.

Habana Vieja, the colonial core that is a vast reservoir of historic attractions, is in the midst of a dramatic, decade-old restoration that will impress and astonish. Scores of mansions in Vedado and Miramar are being restored to haughty grandeur and turned into posh boutiques, restaurants, and offices for Cuban and foreign corporations. Many *habaneros* insist that the "new" Havana is a kind of Disneyland with a false frontage, although the improvements have finally begun to extend beyond the tourist zones, and the beginning of community-oriented restoration is now taking place.

The decade since the collapse of Cuba's Soviet benefactor has been desperate—Cuba lived on Soviet largesse for four decades, while its own economy stagnated. Fortunately, Havana has begun to return to some semblance of normality. The notorious *apagones* (power outages) that plagued the city nightly in the early 1990s are now brief, albeit still frequent, inconveniences. Gasoline is again available, if not plentiful, and reports of Havana's transport system having come to a virtual standstill are now outdated.

A FUTURE REALITY

Travelers visiting Havana today do so at a fascinating, historic moment, as Cuba is emerging from its exclusively Marxist cocoon. In the quest for survival, Cuba has been forced to turn back to the capitalist model it once eschewed. A new Cuba is taking shape based on a homespun paradigm of state-controlled Communist-cum-quasi-capitalist economy—a "market dictatorship" dubbed *capitalismo frío,* or cold capitalism—that relies on tourism to restore economic growth while avoiding political reform and social upheaval.

The tourism boom has the hallmarks of a Faustian bargain. In the 1960s, the Castro government scorned tourism for its attendant bourgeois decadence—the gambling, prostitution, live sex acts, and drugs. Beginning in the early 1990s, things began coming full circle. An economic elite of *masetas* (rich Cubans) is once again visible. Prostitution is back. Corruption is once again evident, as are beggars. Even drugs have returned, albeit in minuscule quantities.

Every day, too, there are more and more taxis, Internet cafés, fast food emporiums, and shops stocked with Western items. A creeping commercialization is taking hold of the city. Once Fidel goes, things will probably change beyond recognition. *The time to visit Havana is now . . . before it loses its magic.*

It doesn't take great imagination to envision how Havana could again become, in Somerset Maugham's piquant phrase, "a sunny place for shady people." The city's demimonde continues to bubble beneath the surface, just waiting for someone to marshal it. What makes Havana so fascinating won't last forever. As the foreign influence spreads, the more Havana may be "spoiled," changing the face of the Malecón and creating a Havana skyline as hazy as Cuba's future.

But no matter what, there'll still be impassioned poetry, *santería,* salsa, and sunny days on diamond-dust beaches trolled by sultry *habaneras* in tiny *tanguitas.* Whatever the temperature, there'll be a fresh breeze blowing, carrying the city's aroma—a combination of sea air, tobacco, mildew, and mimosa—through cobbled colonial plazas. There'll be *mojitos* to enjoy in the Bar Dos Hermanos and the world's finest cigars to smoke fresh from the factory as you rumble down the narrow streets in a chrome-spangled 1955 Cadillac to the rhythm of the rumba on the radio.

Introduction

THE EARLY COLONIAL ERA

The Spanish Arrival

On the evening of October 27, 1492, Genovese explorer Christopher Columbus first set eyes on the hazy mass of Cuba, at the time inhabited by peaceable Taíno Indians. The explorer voyaged along the north coast for four weeks, touching land at various points and finally dropping anchor on November 27 in a perfectly protected harbor near today's Gibara, in eastern Cuba.

In 1509, King Ferdinand gave Christopher Columbus's son, Diego, the title of Governor of the Indies with the duty to organize an expedition to further explore Cuba. In 1511, four ships from Spain arrived carrying 300 settlers under Diego Columbus and his beautiful wife, María de Toledo (grandniece of King Ferdinand). Also on board was the new governor of Cuba—a tall, portly, blond soldier named Diego Velásquez de Cuellar, looking very dashing in a great plumed hat and a short velvet cloak tufted with gold. A young Hernán Cortés was also on board; he would later set sail from Havana for Mexico to subdue the Aztecs.

Velásquez founded the first town at Baracoa in 1512, followed within the next few years by six other crude *villas*, whose mud streets would eventually be paved with cobblestones shipped

Catedral de la Habana

© CHRISTOPHER P. BAKER

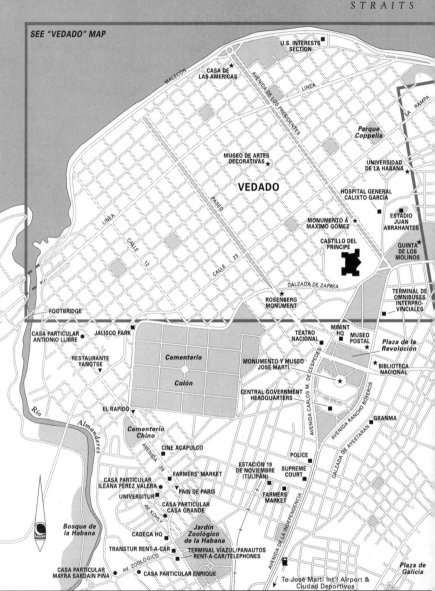

VEDADO TO BAHÍA DE LA HABANA

STRAITS

SEE "VEDADO" MAP

U.S. INTERESTS SECTION

MALECÓN

CASA DE LAS AMÉRICAS

AVENIDA DE LOS PRESIDENTES

LINEA

LA RAMPA

Parque Coppelia

MUSEO DE ARTES DECORATIVAS

VEDADO

PASEO

UNIVERSIDAD DE LA HABANA

HOSPITAL GENERAL CALIXTO GARCÍA

LINEA

CALLE 12

CALLE 23

MONUMENTO Á MAXIMO GÓMEZ

CASTILLO DEL PRINCIPE

ESTADIO JUAN ABRAHANTES

QUINTA DE LOS MOLINOS

CALZADA DE ZAPATA

ROSENBERG MONUMENT

TERMINAL DE OMNIBUSES INTERPROVINCIALES

FOOTBRIDGE

To Miramar

CASA PARTICULAR ANTIONIO LLIBRE

JALISCO PARK

RESTAURANTE YANGTSE

Cementerio

Colón

TEATRO NACIONAL

MININT HQ

MUSEO POSTAL

Plaza de la Revolución

BIBLIOTECA NACIONAL

MONUMENTO Y MUSEO JOSÉ MARTÍ

AVENIDA CARLOS M. DE CÉSPEDES

CENTRAL GOVERNMENT HEADQUARTERS

Río

Almandares

EL RÁPIDO

Cementerio Chino

AVENIDA 26

CINE ACAPULCO

AVENIDA RANCHO BOYEROS

GRANMA

CALZADA DE AYESTARÁN

CASA PARTICULAR ILEANA PÉREZ VALERA

FARMERS' MARKET

PAIN DE PARIS

POLICE

ESTACIÓN 19 DE NOVIEMBRE (TULIPAN)

SUPREME COURT

UNIVERSITUR

AV KOHLI

CASA PARTICULAR CASA GRANDE

FARMERS' MARKET

Bosque de la Habana

CADECA HQ

Jardín Zoológico de la Habana

AVENIDA DE LA INDEPENDENCIA

TRANSTUR RENT-A-CAR

AV. ZOOLÓGICO

TERMINAL VÍAZUL/PANAUTOS RENT-A-CAR/TELEPHONES

CASA PARTICULAR MAYRA SARDAÍN PIÑA

CASA PARTICULAR ENRIQUE

To José Martí Int'l Airport & Ciudad Deportivos

Plaza de Galicia

M INTRODUCTION

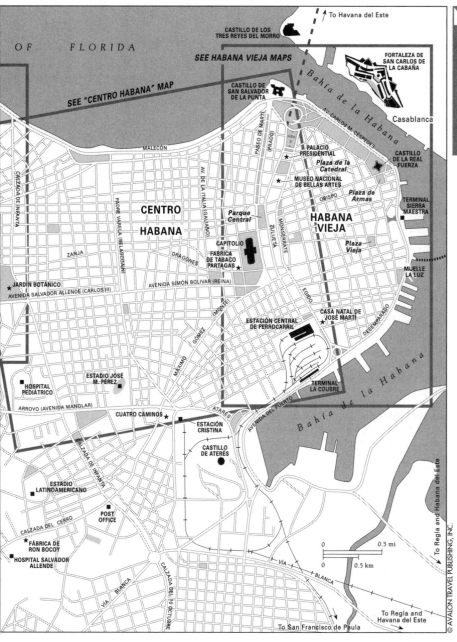

from Europe as ballast aboard the armada of vessels now bound for the Americas. Humble little San Cristóbal de la Habana began life in July 1515 as the westernmost of Velásquez's seven cities, founded by one of Velásquez's deputies, Pánfilo de Narváez.

Foundation of a City

Fledgling Havana was first located on the south coast, where Batabanó stands today. The name came from the Taíno, who named this western part of the island for their local chief, Habaguanex. The site for this roughhewn settlement was an unmitigated disaster. Within four years, the settlers had moved to the north coast, where they erected rough huts at the mouth of the Río Chorrera (now Almendares). The swampy site was also ill-chosen, and the occupants were tormented by plagues. A few years earlier, the expeditionary Sebastián de Ocampo had discovered a more promising site—Puerto de Carenas, so named because the site was ideal for careening ships—a few kilometers farther east. On November 25, 1519, the date of the second founding of San Cristóbal de la Habana, the settlers moved to the shore of this flask-shaped, deep-water bay surrounded by rolling hills and hidden within a cliff-hung narrow channel.

The first houses stood facing the sea in a row between the present sites of the Plaza de Armas and the Plaza de San Francisco. Initially, life was extremely spartan, and for several decades the town was composed entirely of shacks. But Puerto de Carenas' proximity to the deep channel between Cuba and the shallow seas of the Bahamas was highly advantageous, and the township grew quickly.

The Spaniards had set out in search of spices, gold, and rich civilizations and were not on a holy mission. Medieval Spain had a penchant for foreshortening its cultural lessons with the sword and musket ball; thus, the indigenous island cultures—considered by the Spaniards to be a backward, godless race—were subjected to the Spaniards' ruthless and mostly fruitless quest for silver and gold.

Although the Spanish found little silver and gold in Cuba, they had greater luck in Central and South America, whose indigenous cultures flaunted vast quantities of precious metals and jewels. When Mexico and Peru were conquered, the quantities rose to astronomical heights. Cuba was set to become a vital stopover and the hub of trade and shipping for galleons and traders carrying the wealth of the Americas back to Spain.

The Key to the New World

Throughout the 16th century, an ever-increasing number of ships called in Havana's port as the New World began to yield its riches. In 1526, a royal decree declared that ships had to travel in convoy to Spain—the Crown had a vested interest in protecting the wealth from pirates; it received one-fifth of the treasure—and Havana's sheltered harbor, at the gateway to the Gulf of Mexico, was the logical gathering point. Havana gained such prominence that in July 1553 the governor of Cuba, Gonzalo Pérez de Angulo, moved the capital (and his residence) there from Santiago de Cuba in the east of the island. The port city of Havana earned the title "key to the New World."

Havana's fortunes were further bolstered in 1564 when a Spanish expedition reached the Philippines. The next year, it discovered the northern Pacific trade winds that for the next 250 years propelled ships laden with treasures from Asia to Acapulco, from where the booty was carried overland to Veracruz, on the Gulf of Mexico, and loaded onto ships bound for Havana. Here, a great armada was assembled for the dangerous passage to Europe. Every spring and summer, all the ships returning from the Americas crowded into Havana's harbor before setting off for Spain in armed convoys. Perfumes, pearls, silks, and ivories passed through the city. To these shipments were added silver from Bolivia, alpaca from Peru, and rare woods from Central America, plus Cuban tobacco, leather, fruit, meats, hides, and precious hardwoods. The forests surrounding the city were felled for the needs of the shipbuilding industry (the city was renowned for building the best galleons in the Indies) and also for the raising of cattle and planting of tobacco—and later, sugar—for sale in Europe. The fleet of 1583 had to leave one million pesos behind because there was no more room in the ships' holds.

To provision the treasure fleet (the *flota*, usually consisting of 30 to 90 vessels), an aqueduct was built to bring water down to the harbor. Fruit and vegetables came from small holdings outside Havana. And the citizens made soup and *tasajo* (salted meat) from the vast quantities of crabs and tortoises that overran the city. The reeking city overflowed with drunken sailors, packs of wild dogs, cutthroats, and whores—at night, few citizens dared venture out unless heavily armed.

At the end of the century, Havana had already assumed what historian Hugh Thomas called its "semi-criminal, maritime, and cosmopolitan character." Nonetheless, it was still a small town of about 3,500 permanent residents. The town was dirty and smelly—today's Calle O'Reilly was then known as Sumidero, or sewer; and Calle Teniente Rey was Basurero, or rubbish dump. When it rained, the streets ran with mud.

"Black Gold" and Piracy

Cuba's indigenous Taíno culture was quickly choked by the stern hand of Spanish rule—condemned so that Jehovah and Mammon might triumph over the local idols. The 16th century witnessed the extinction of the Taíno race. Those Taíno not put to the sword or worked to death in mines and plantations fell victim to exotic diseases. Within 100 years of Columbus's landfall, virtually the entire indigenous Cuban population had perished. Spain turned to West Africa to supply its labor. By the end of the 16th century, an incredibly lucrative slave trade had developed. Treasure ships bound for Europe returned to Cuba with their holds full of "black gold." Havana was the major conduit and the New World's unrivaled emporium of human flesh. After being herded into ships, slaves were shackled below and endured the most deplorable conditions at sea. They arrived in Havana diseased and half-starved, and after being sold were shipped to Cuban plantations or other colonies of the Americas to be worked as beasts of burden, blasting and pummeling stone for gold and cutting sugarcane beneath the searing sun.

Havana—Pearl of the Antilles—grew inordi-nately rich on the proceeds. The wealth from sugar and slavery grew exponentially, adding to that from the Spanish treasure fleets. Landowners, slave traders, and merchants were in their heyday. Even slaves showed off jeweled earrings and pearl bracelets. The Spanish Crown heavily taxed exports and prohibited *criollos* (Cuban-born Europeans) from trading with any nation but Spain. In 1740, Spain formalized the monopoly on all imports and exports by creating the Real Compañía de Comercio, which bought Cuban products cheaply and sold necessities from Europe at inflated prices. Forbidden to manufacture anything, the *criollos* had to buy even such ordinary items as cutlery, cloth, and paper directly from Spain. A separate monopolistic agency—La Factoria—had been created in 1717 to control tobacco trading. Cuban tobacco was purchased at a low fixed price. A rebellion in 1708 by tobacco growers in Havana province was brutally crushed by Spanish troops.

The usurious monopoly on goods fostered smuggling. Havana was a center for contraband on a remarkable scale: the goods of the hinterlands, especially precious leathers and timber, flowed out from the harbor, while slaves and the fineries of Europe flowed in. The Spaniards tried to regulate both smuggling and illegal slaving, but these activities were so profitable and official corruption so great that they resisted control.

Defending the City

Cuba was a plump plum ripe for plucking—a treasure chest without a lid. French corsairs and English pirates preyed mercilessly on cities and plantations across the island. In 1537, Havana itself was raided when two shiploads of French pirates came ashore and torched part of the town. Three Spanish ships that arrived after the pirates had left were cajoled into giving chase; alas, they lost their nerve and when they encountered the French, turned tail. They were in turn pursued by the pirates, who called once again on the city and, not content with the fat ransom offered, again looted the town. One year later, French pirate Jacques de Sores arrived and demanded a ransom. When a bid by the Spaniards to retake the city faltered, de Sores put its inhabitants to the sword before razing the city. News traveled fast, and as the surviving *habaneros* struggled to rebuild their city, other pirates arrived to cart off whatever de Sores had been unable to carry.

In 1558, work began on a fortress—the Castillo de la Real Fuerza—to protect the harbor. Military engineers were sent from Spain and the city's free slaves and mulattoes had their freedom revoked and were ordered to aid in construction. Work was so slow, however, that in 1561 a pirate ship sailed into the harbor in pursuit of a galleon groaning under the weight of a hold full of silver. (To save his ship, the captain threw his cargo of 100,000 *ducados* overboard). The fortress was completed in 1582, and the governor of Cuba set up residence within. The island's governors lived here until 1762.

Notwithstanding the fortress, daring foreigners—most notably the English privateer John Hawkins and his nephew, Francis Drake—were perpetual thorns in the sides of the Spanish, whose galleons they seized at random. Drake's reputation preceded him, and when he arrived off Havana with a fleet of 14 ships on May 29, 1586, intent on testing the fortress's mettle, the citizenry "shook like rabbits frozen before the approach of a stoat." Drake's fleet, however, was laid low by fever and, after firing a few desultory shots, departed. The citizens wisely chose to add another castle on the *morro* (headland) across the harbor mouth. Work began in 1589 on the Castillo de los Tres Reyes del Morro and another fortress—Castillo de la Punta—that could catch enemy ships in a withering crossfire. As added defense, a massive chain could now be drawn across the harbor channel at night. Additional small fortresses were built at the mouth of the Río Chorrera and at Cojímar, to the east.

As the 17th century progressed, the pirates became highly organized, able to muster small armies. They were soon encouraged and eventually licensed by the governments of France, Holland, and England to prey upon Spanish shipping and ports as a prelude to challenging Spanish dominance in the Americas.

In 1587, King Philip of Spain determined to end the growing sea power of England and amassed a great armada to invade her. This proved a fateful error. The British Navy destroyed the armada in the English Channel, breaking the power of Spain in the Old World. The humbling defeat left Spain impotent. In 1634, a royal decree proclaimed that Havana was "the key to the New World and bulwark of the West Indies." A new coat of arms for the city was bestowed in 1665 showing the three castles. In 1662, however, Havana's defenses proved hollow when Henry Morgan, a stocky Welshman and leader of the Buccaneers (a disciplined group of pirates operating under British license from Port Royal in Jamaica), ransacked Havana, pilfered the cathedral bells, and left with a taunt that the Spanish weren't equal to the stone walls that Spain had built: "I could have defended Morro Castle with a dog and a gun," said Hawkins.

Building for Posterity

While the British went out to their colonies to grow rich and return, the Spanish went to grow rich and stay. They brought a permanence of design and planning to their New World cities that other colonial powers never achieved. "The Spanish built cities where they settled, but the English just let cities grow. The poorest street of Havana had dignity compared to the shanty towns of Kingston," wrote Graham Greene.

Havana rose to such prominence that in 1607 it officially became the island's capital. By this time, Havana was an immensely prosperous city on a par with European counterparts and became even more so as the tobacco industry prospered from European noses, which reverberated with satisfied sneezes induced by Cuban snuff. All this wealth found its outlet in stone. Spanish ships unloaded builders and craftsmen, hired to help citizens display their earnings—legitimate and ill-gotten alike—in an outpouring of architectural sophistication. These Andalusian craftsmen brought with them a Moorish aesthetic, which they translated into a unique "tropical synthesis of column, courtyard, and chiaroscuro," wrote Juliet Barclay.

Life was lived ostentatiously by those with the means. Wealthy merchants and plantation owners erected beautiful mansions graced with baroque

LIFE IN EARLY HAVANA

Colonial Havana was a colorful place. Life coursed through Havana's plazas: peasants leading mules bearing baskets of fruit and vegetables, farmers adding to the great crush as they drove cattle and pigs to market, acrobats and clowns doing tricks for handouts, musicians serenading, lottery-ticket sellers bearing down on anyone who looked as if they deserved some good luck that day, water vendors hawking foul-smelling water, and goats being milked door-to-door.

Carriages (called *volantas*) with light bodies suspended as if in midair between enormous wheels, raced around the streets, each pulled by a well-groomed horse ridden by a *calesero* (postilion) in resplendent livery. The *volanta* was usually kept in the hall of the house and entered by the home's vast arched doorway. The rank and wealth of Havana nobility was displayed by the horses' distance from the body of the carriage. The higher the rank, the longer the shafts, so those with the most prodigious length had great difficulty negotiating tight corners. Two carriages traveling in opposite directions found it impossible to pass and provided "the occasion of much hard swearing," recorded Samuel Hazard. Many of the street signs embedded in the walls of Habana Vieja still bear a hand in a frilly cuff pointing the way for passing *caleseros*.

The city must have resembled a grand operatic production, especially at night, with the harbor, crosshatched by masts and spars, shining under the glint of soft moonlight, and on Sundays, when coquettish *habaneras* wearing white ball gowns and necklaces of giant *cocuyos* (fireflies) gathered for the brilliant masked balls. Traveler Maturin Ballou recorded how the women were "passionately fond of dancing, and tax the endurance of the gentlemen in their heroic worship of Terpsichore." Adds Juliet Barclay in her marvelous book, *Havana: Portrait of a City:* "The *Criollo* stalked about, exchanging stately salutations and lifting an eyebrow at the parvenu, who, with one eye on his own wife and the other on everyone else's, sought introductions."

By day, the female citizenry—at least the well-to-do—spent most of their time indoors (to walk the streets was considered a social solecism). Here, eligible maidens stared through the *rejas* (wooden grills) and looked out wistfully upon life itself passing by. Occasionally they went shopping, hidden from view in *volantas* to which the goods were brought for inspection. Havana's cloistered beauties could receive visitors, however, during which formalities were as starched as the collars of the gentlemen who came to visit.

While *habaneras* wiled away their days indoors, wealthy menfolk spent most of their days in idle splendor: gambling, dallying with their mistresses, enjoying the thrill of a bullfight or the Valla de Gallos, where cockerels were tormented into a frenzy then released to fight to the death. The gentry also frequented brothels, of which Havana had several hundred, concentrated along Calles Teniente Rey and Habana. Like chaste virgins, prostitutes by law were resigned to life behind bars. While husbands philandered, many of their wives found solace in religion, although, claims Barclay, "not necessarily in the traditional sense," for "many of them were visited by Holy Fathers, who went ostensibly to hear confession but frequently gave further cause for it."

Amid the splendor, Havana had its sordid side. It was a "villainously odiferous" city, and many fastidious Northerners, who flocked there for the winter sun and a taste of exoticism, commented on the offensive olfactory cocktail. The cacophony of noises also preyed upon their fragile sensibilities—even late at night, when the arguing, partying mobs were sound asleep, the bells in the churches and castles rang the quarter-hours, while the stomping boots and stentorian cries of *serenos* (street watchmen) caused insomniacs to contemplate murder with their nocturnal cries of "All serene!"

In fact, there was no shortage of murder. Life was extremely hard, of course, for many citizens and to survive, the desperate and cutthroat evolved entrepreneurial skills worthy of Sweeney Todd—during the 19th century, a gang of sausage manufacturers grew wealthy kidnapping plump *negros* for the mincer; their sausages, sold as prime meat, were highly popular until their deeds were eventually discovered.

stonework painted in every conceivable combination of pastel colors, "all shimmering and quivering in the hot, glowing air." Inside, they were fitted with every luxury in European style.

By the late 1600s, Spanish baroque had reached Havana—many of the elaborate stone doorways of mansions such as the Casa de la Obra Pía were crafted in Spain and shipped to Havana. Frilly baroque replaced the more imposing *mudéjar* (Moorish) style characterized by marble floors, panels of porcelain tiles, iron rails, lofty ceilings with open rafters, and massive windows grated like dungeons. Havana was, in contrast with today's time-worn, paint-starved city, gaily colored, with the incandescent light of the tropics dancing on walls and shining through stained-glass *ventrales* of Prussian blue, Hansa yellow, and blood red.

Most households in Havana were also maintained by slaves—often in great numbers. The slave trade through Havana had multiplied astronomically as sugar began to dominate the slave-based agricultural economy, contributing even vaster sums to Havana's coffers.

The 17th and 18th centuries also saw a surge of pious energy and ecclesiastical construction as the ever-powerful bishops brought their influence to bear in statuary and stone. Most notable of the "builder-bishops" was Diego Evelino de Compostela, a vigorous ecclesiastic who arrived from Spain in November 1687. In short order, he initiated the Convento de Belén, Convento de Santa Clara de Asís, Iglesia Santa Teresa de Jesús, and Iglesia del Santo Ángel Custodio. He was so revered by the citizens of Havana that when he died in 1704, a guard had to be posted to stop them from taking pieces of his clothing and body. Compostela's work was continued by an equally dynamic bishop, Gerónimo Valdés, who founded the University of Havana. The wealth of the Americas helped fill the churches and convents with silver and gold.

Havana's streets had evolved in an orderly grid pattern, with plazas and plazuelas between them. Eventually, Havana's city walls went up, beginning in 1674 under Captain General Don Francisco Orejón y Gastón. The walls replaced weak wooden barricades. They took a century to build, measuring 10 meters high and 1.4 meters thick, with sentry boxes and nine entry gates. They ran along the edge of the bay and on the landward side along today's Calles Egido, Monserrate, and Zulueta.

The British Take Over

By the turn of the 18th century, Havana, which by then numbered about 40,000 inhabitants, was the third-largest city in the New World, after Mexico City and Lima. It was also heavily fortified. Various governors and the citizenry had been resting on their laurels for decades, had grown lazy, and were ill-prepared to repel a well-organized attack. Its citizens must have felt few qualms for the future when, on January 4, 1762, George III of England declared war on Spain. Some years before, the British governor of Jamaica, Charles Knowles, had been hosted on an official visit to Havana and spent much of his time reconnoitering the city's defenses. Knowles was consulted by England's military leaders, and a plan was drawn up for an attack on Havana. It was an audacious scheme that would shake Havana, and Cuba, to the core.

Though the city was heavily defended, its Achilles' heel was the Cabaña, a long ridge overlooking Morro Castle and Havana's harbor. On June 6, a British fleet of 28 warships and 145 transport ships carrying 11,000 troops arrived off Cojímar, a small cove about 12 miles east of the city. The next day, the troops put ashore and Havana erupted in panic. Every fit man in Havana was summoned to fight, and 9,000 foreign seamen in harbor were coerced into the city's defense. The Spanish—encumbered by what Juliet Barclay terms "Governor de Prado's bovine serenity" —scuttled three ships in the harbor mouth, ineptly trapping their own warships inside the harbor. Meanwhile, the governor's order to evacuate all women and children managed to block all the streets to troop movement. That night, when British scouts appeared atop the Cabaña, the Spanish warships began blasting the ridge, causing their own troops to flee and permitting British troops to take the ridge and begin preparations for a siege of Havana. The castle governor, Captain Luís de Velasco, knowing that his position was hopeless, sent an emissary to the city requesting instructions from the Capitán General as to whether he should surrender. The vague reply left him no choice but to fulfill his military honor and hold out until the last man.

Meanwhile, the British entrenched and a six-week bombardment of the Morro Castle ensued. On July 29, British sappers blew an enormous hole in the seaward side of the Morro, which was swiftly captured and topped by the flag of St. George. The British commander, George Keppel, Count of Albemarle—himself a person with more influence at court than military prowess—remarked that "Spanish sloth and stupidity is unaccountable." However, the British had not had it all their own way; they lost thousands of troops to heat and sickness, and had to call on reserves from North America.

Though the British had dammed the aqueduct that supplied the city with water, Havana held out. On August 3, after the governor had refused to surrender, British cannonballs began to rain down on the city. At two o'clock on August 13, 1762, the surrender flag fluttered over Havana. British Admiral Sir George Pocock permitted the Spanish troops to depart, then took over the city. Pocock received a reward of £122,697 for taking Havana.

The Spanish Crown—which jealously guarded its trade monopoly—had treated Cuba as a colonial cash cow to milk dry as it pleased. The British were more enlightened, and immediately lifted trade restrictions and opened the island up to free trade to foreign vessels, including unrestricted trade in slaves. Foreign merchants flocked, and Cuba witnessed surging prosperity as a trading frenzy ensued. Overnight, Havana became what Abbé Guillaume Raynal called the "boulevard of the New World." To his discredit, however, Keppel seemed equally bent on milking Havana. He imposed usurious levies upon the citizens and Catholic Church, creating a bitter loathing for the British—after the British commandeered Iglesia San Francisco de Asís for Protestant worship, the church was never again used for service by Havana's citizens.

The *habaneros* were relieved of further indignation on February 10, 1763, when England

and Spain signed the Treaty of Paris, ending the war and allowing England to exchange Cuba for Florida—sugar planters in Jamaica had pressured England to cede back to Spain what would otherwise become a formidable rival for the British sugar market. On July 6, the last British troops departed Havana.

The Spanish lost no time in rebuilding their forts, and between 1764 and 1774 constructed Fortaleza de San Carlos de la Cabaña, the largest fortress in the Americas, atop the Cabaña ridge. The British invasion ensured that Havana fortunes and fortifications would never again be neglected by Spain.

THE LATE COLONIAL ERA
Havana Comes of Age

Meanwhile, Spain had acquired a more enlightened king, Charles III. The boom spawned by the brief British incursion was encouraged a decade later when the newly independent United States began trading directly with Cuba. The North Americans' collective sweet tooth fostered the rapid expansion of sugar plantations in Cuba. Vast fortunes were being made in sugar—and therefore also in slaves. Wealthy Cuban and U.S. slave merchants funded planting of new lands in sugar by granting loans for capital improvements. Land planted in sugar multiplied more than tenfold by the turn of the 18th century. For the first time, sugar outstripped tobacco in importance. Havana reaped the benefits as wealth continued to pour into the city. The planters themselves, however, weren't as a rule wealthy men. Their estates were deeply mortgaged to various port merchants, who were normally Spaniards, Americans, or Europeans, but rarely Cubans. "The slave-owners are but go-betweens, who secure the profits of the slave-trade for the merchants," wrote Anthony Trollope.

Cuba's slave population had been slow to develop compared to that of neighboring Caribbean islands. The short tenure of British rule in 1765, however, sent the slave trade soaring. British slave traders established themselves in Havana and remained thereafter to control and profit in the booming trade. Between 1791 and 1810, more

SLAVE SOCIETY

Black slavery in Cuba began in 1513 with the arrival of slaves from Hispaniola, and wasn't abolished until 1886. At the peak of the trade, in the 1840s, slaves formed about 45 percent of Cuba's population. Only about one-third, however, worked the plantations. Most were domestics who lived in the cities.

In 1713, the Treaty of Utrecht, which ended the War of the Spanish Succession, had granted the British sole rights to the Spanish-American slave trade, with Britain agreeing to supply 144,000 slaves to the Spanish West Indies over a period of 30 years. The trade grew throughout the century: as many as 2,000 slaving ships a year called into Havana annually during the 1830s.

Britain had by then abolished the trade and in 1817, at Britain's behest, Spain had agreed to end its slave trade, but slaving continued. Slavery was too profitable to quell, with *habaneros* from the governor down to the harbormaster profiting immensely from bribes. The British sent representatives to Havana to ensure that Spain complied with its agreement, but, says Juliet Barclay, "they might as well have tried to catch mercury in a sieve" (one British naval ship, the *Romney,* was manned entirely by free blacks). Slaving ships operated under the noses of the British, and Spanish authorities claimed ignorance. To outwit the British navy, the slave traders merely adopted foreign flags; others simply unshackled their cargo and tossed the incriminating evidence overboard.

The majority of slaves that were shipped to Cuba came from highly developed West African tribes such as the Fulani, Hausa, and Yoruba. They came mostly from Senegal, Gambia, and Guinea at first, and later from Nigeria and the Congo. After being rounded up and herded to African ports, slaves were loaded onto ships, where they were scientifically packed like sardines. Space meant profit. Chained together body to body in the airless, dark, rancid hold, they wallowed in their own excrement and vomit on the nightmare voyage across the Atlantic. Dozens died from sickness and starvation.

Once ashore, the Africans were herded into *barracones* (rough shelters) to be stored until sold to plantation owners or to work in Havana's grand mansions or on civic construction projects. To avoid the expense of advertising, the Havana *barracones* were located near the governor's summer palace at the western end of Paseo (now Avenida Salvador Allende), where citizens out for a stroll could view the merchandise like zoo-goers. No attention was paid to family relationships. Parents, children, and siblings were torn asunder forever.

Slaves organized themselves into *cabildos,* social groups defined according to tribal origin, and members held meetings at which they played music and performed religious rites drawn from their African heritage. Contemporary *santería* is derived from these rites. The Spanish authorities even granted slaves their own celebration, the sacred *Día de los Reyes,* on January 6. A colorful ceremonial procession was permitted to take to the streets, ending in Plaza de Armas, where the slaves engaged in a pandemonium of singing and dancing before the governor and his entourage. Victor Patricio Landaluze's representations of 19th-century life, which hang in

than 100,000 slaves arrived, and countless more undocumented slaves were brought in illegally. A royal decree in 1818 opened Cuba's ports to free trade; the sudden explosion in the sugar trade and production saw more than 500,000 slaves imported in the ensuing decade. By 1840, slaves constituted 45 percent of the population.

Havana grew more elegant and sophisticated year by year and by 1760 was already larger than New York or Boston. The first university had been established in 1728. The first newspaper appeared in 1763, and the postal service in 1764. Cuba's citizenry was growing vastly wealthy on trade with North America, with the difference

Havana's Palacio de Bellas Artes, vividly portray how Africans were regarded at the time, as do the series of 19th-century cigarette labels on display in Havana's national library.

House slaves, while treated poorly, experienced better conditions than slaves in the country, where plantation life was exceedingly cruel. Nonetheless, many Havana homes still have rings in the walls where recalcitrant slaves were chained. Other slaves were sent to a special whipping place near the Punta, where trained experts meted out any punishment that the slave owner found too onerous to personally give, and the streets outside the punishment building echoed the screams within.

Understandably, rebellion was always around the corner. The first slave revolt occurred in 1532 in Oriente. A few years later, Havana was sacked by slaves in the wake of an attack by French pirates. Other slaves chose to run away and flee to the mountains. While runaways on other islands developed fiercely independent communities, such as the Maroons of Jamaica, Cuba's *cimarrones* tended to be independent; runaways often captured and sold other runaways. To track down runaways, the authorities used posses of *ranchadores,* cruel white peasants with specially trained hunting dogs. When a slave was caught, it was standard procedure to cut off one ear as a warning to other slaves.

Nonetheless, slaves had the legal right to buy their own and their relatives' freedom. For example, slaves could keep a percentage of whatever fee their masters charged for hiring them out as labor and apply it towards buying their manumission. In fact, free blacks formed a significant part of Havana's populace: "In no part of the world, where slavery exists, is manumission so frequent as in the island of Cuba," noted Alexander von Humboldt. Once free, they could even own and sell property. Many free blacks set up small businesses or worked as artisans, while women hired out as domestics. Some rose to positions of wealth and prominence, and there evolved a significant slave-owning black middle class. All in all, slaves fared better in Cuba than on neighboring islands. Anthony Trollope, comparing Cuba to Jamaica, wrote that "a present healthy condition is cared for, but long life is not regarded." The estates in Cuba were "on a much larger scale, in much better order, overlooked by a larger proportion of white men, with a greater amount of skilled labor. The evidences of capital were very plain in Cuba; whereas, the want of it was frequently equally plain in our own island."

It was common for white men to take a black mistress, and their offspring (*rellollos* of creole parentage) usually received their freedom. Havana's free mulattas soon found their way to Europe and North America, where their combination of African exoticism and grace and Spanish hauteur found favor with discerning males. Occasionally, a black mistress would be particularly favored and treated well, although there were limits to their upward mobility. Any mulatta who had ideas of rising above her station usually ended up caught short, as with Cecilia Valdés, the beautiful heroine of the marvelous, tragic, and eponymous novel by Cirilo Villaverde about a mulatta who cherishes the idea of rising to become accepted by Havana's upper social stratum, but whose ambition ends in a violent denouement.

that now much of the prosperity flowed back to Cuba, changing the face of Havana.

Late colonial Havana benefited from repeated urban renewal plans intended to lend a powerful public face to Spain's cherished island. Following the return of Cuba to Spain in 1763, the new Spanish governor, the Marqués de la Torre, initiated a public works program. Havana attained a new focus and rigorous architectural harmony, with a more comprehensive approach to urban planning following a grid pattern dictated by the New Laws of the Indies. The elegant Paseo de Extramuros (later renamed the Paseo del Prado) was laid as the first boulevard outside the city walls, great warehouses went up along the harbor front, and most of the streets—which had by now been given the names they possess today—were cobbled. The first gas lighting arrived in 1768, along with a workable system of aqueducts. Until 1790, when night fell, darkness kept most Cubans off the streets, except those who were up to no good. That year, street lamps went up throughout the city.

Havana's oldest plaza—the Plaza de Armas—was reconstructed, with a fine park and a grandiose governor's residence (the Palacio de los Capitanes Generales) and other grand *palacios* lining each side. The Plaza de Viejas, dating back to 1584, emerged afresh as a fashionable quarter with galleried palaces. And a baroque cathedral and ornate merchant's palaces were erected in the Plaza de Ciénaga (today's Plaza de la Catedral), formerly a swampy area that earlier in the century had functioned as a fish market. The elaborately contoured facade of the Havana Cathedral, completed around 1777, epitomized the peak of Spanish baroque. On January 15, 1796, the *San Lorenzo* sailed into Havana harbor, bringing what were thought to be the ashes of Christopher Columbus from Santo Domingo, after the island had passed into the hands of France. The coffin, swathed in black velvet, was laid to rest in the new cathedral and remained there until 1899, when it was returned to Spain.

Havana owes much of its modern face to Governor Miguel Tacón y Rosique, an ultra-conservative monarchist named governor in 1843. He conceived an integrated urban expansion plan and initiated a brisk program of redesign in which old facades were realigned and "set to the rhythmic cadence of columned *portales* running for blocks at a time," wrote Rachel Carey. Tacón ordered the streets cleaned, drove out criminals, and whipped the idle and unemployed into action. He built fountains and a great theater (a precursor to today's Gran Teatro), paved the streets and erected street signs, and created a fire brigade and Havana's first police force. Tacón also supported the first railroad in the Spanish colonies, linking Havana with Bejucal in 1837—Havana's first railroad station opened that year. The Prado Militar—today known as Avenida Salvador Allende—was laid out, knifing east–west to permit rapid troop deployment into the city from the Castillo del Príncipe in the event of revolt.

Tacón also commissioned a governor's country house—the Quinta de los Molinos—midway along the length of the Prado Militar, which became a ceremonial avenue popular for fashionable perambulation by the social elite. The ancient, uncovered aqueduct that carried water from the Río Almendares to the city center was covered, increasing the water purity. Later, 400 springs nine miles south of Havana were enclosed, and an aqueduct and storage facility increased the water supply.

Tacón had a rival: the Conde de Villanueva, the *criollo* administrator of the royal estates, who was bent on outdoing Tacón in civic construction as an expression of disaffected *criollo* pride. We owe the Templete, the neo-baroque Gran Teatro on Parque Central, and the contemporary face of the Prado to this feud.

By the mid-1800s, Havana had achieved a level of modernity that surpassed that of Madrid.

The City Bursts Its Seams

Havana was by now a densely populated city, but its 55,000 citizens were trapped *intramuros* (within the city walls). New buildings were going up, and the city was bursting with uncontainable energy. Soon not a square centimeter was left for building within the city walls, and affluent families had begun moving to the city outskirts in search of healthier surroundings. A rapid expansion of residential districts *extramuros* (beyond the city walls) began with El Cerro, a cool, hilly region immediately southwest of the old city.

In 1863, the city walls came tumbling down—less than a century after their completion. Urban green spaces were introduced in Vedado, a new upscale district laid out in 1859 behind the shore west of Habana Vieja. It became the first city quarter with strips of planted greenery between sidewalk and street. The city's eternal nemesis, an inadequate water supply, was resolved by a Cuban engineer, Don Francisco de Albear, who in 1856 began work on an aqueduct to take water from the fast-flowing Vento springs on the left bank of the Río Almendares. Graceful boulevards pushed westward—part of a planned redesign of the city aided by the city's first formal building codes, passed in 1861—into the surrounding hills and countryside, lined with a parade of *quintas* (country houses) fronted by classical columns. The baroque bowed out, as architects harked back further to the heyday of Greece, utilizing neoclassicism in their public edifices to convey a sense of cultural achievement and dignity.

The upper classes abandoned their inner-city *palacios,* many of which gradually deteriorated into slums called *cuarterías.* By mid-century, the early colonial quarter contained many crowded, low-class rental buildings called *solares.* Richard Henry Dana Jr. recorded: "The drive, by way of Calzada de Jesús del Monte, takes one through a wretched portion, I hope the most wretched portion, of Havana, by long lines of one-story wood and mud hovels, hardly habitable even for Negroes."

War

Spain continued to rule Cuba badly. Spain's colonial policy, applied throughout its empire, was based on exploitation, with power centralized in Madrid and politics practiced only for the spoils of office and to the benefit of *peninsulares.* Spain's monopoly laws encouraged the migration to Cuba of a kind of Spanish carpetbagger. Native *criollos* resented the corrupt *peninsulares,* who denied them self-determination. No Cuban could occupy a public post, set up an industry or business, bring legal action against a Spaniard, or travel without military permission. And onerous new taxation on income and property imposed in 1867 added further salt to the wound. Unquenchable animosity had arisen between the Spaniards and *criollos,* firing the wars of independence that were to tear Cuba asunder during much of the ensuing century By the early 19th century, a new generation of young Cuban intellectuals and patriots began to make their voices heard. Nationalist feelings ran high. On October 10, 1868, a lawyer, poet, and planter named Carlos Manuel de Céspedes freed the slaves on his plantation at La Demajagua, near Manzanillo, in Oriente province. He raised the *Grito de Yara* (Shout of Yara), a cry of liberty that resounded around the island. The Ten Years War erupted.

Havana's intellectual elite were *criollo* nationalists whose illicit writings and speeches for the cause of independence brought a wave of repression to the city streets. Spanish volunteers were recruited as a militia. Once arrived, the Volunteers—what Claudia Lightfoot describes as "an ersatz army of hand-picked bullies" —were given a virtual carte blanche to terrorize the people of Havana. Spanish authorities in Havana meted out harsh sentences against anyone who declared himself against Spain. La Cabaña became a jail, and many famous nationalist figures, including José Martí, a young *criollo* writer and thinker born in 1854 who would later lead the independence movement, were imprisoned here. The walls of the Foso de los Laureles, the moat of La Cabaña, resounded to the crack of the firing squad as scores of *criollos* were shot for treason.

Meanwhile, Cuba's commercial development had broadened and a large middle class had developed. While Havana matured, the surrounding countryside was being laid waste by war, and many wealthy, land-owning *habaneros* were forced to sell their crippled estates to U.S. citizens. The war ended in February 1878 with the signing of the Treaty of Zanjón, which freed those slaves who had fought on either side, but maintained slavery as an institution (it was finally abolished only on October 7, 1886). Cubans were granted a small amount of say in the Spanish Court, but it was a wholly unsatisfactory peace.

Spain clung to its colony with despairing strength and the support of many wealthy *criollos* concentrated in western Cuba, who feared that abolitionist sentiments in Europe would lead to the abolition of slavery in Cuba. They looked to the United States for support. Public sentiment in the United States favored the Mambí (the Cuban freedom fighters). The U.S. public hungered for information about the war, feeding sales of newspapers. The *New York World* and *New York Journal* owned, respectively, by Joseph Pulitzer and William Randolph Hearst started a race to see which newspaper could first reach one million subscribers. The press took on the job of inflaming Yankee patriotism and fanning war fever based on fabrication and lies. While Hearst's hacks made up stories from Cuba, the magnate himself worked behind the scenes to orchestrate dramatic events. He sent artist Frederic Remington to Cuba in anticipation of the United States entering the war. At one point, Remington wired Hearst: "There will be no war. I wish to return." Hearst hastily replied: "Please remain. You furnish the pictures and I'll furnish the war."

Remember the Maine!

Responding to public pressure, President McKinley had sent the USS *Maine* to Havana, ostensibly to protect U.S. citizens living there. The U.S. government had long coveted Cuba and found its pretext when the warship mysteriously exploded in Havana harbor on February 5, 1898, killing 258 people. No one knows whether this was the work of the Spanish, Cuban nationalists, or United States (as the Castro government claims), or, more likely, merely an accident, but Hearst had his coup and rushed the news out in huge red headlines, beating the *World* to one million sales. He blamed the Spanish, and so did the public. His *New York Journal* coined the phrase "Remember the Maine, to hell with Spain." The paper belabored the jingoistic phrase day after day. The reaction in the United States was furious; it was taken for granted that Spain was responsible. (The hulk of the *Maine* lay in the harbor until 1912, when the rusting symbol of *norteamericano* interference in Cuban affairs was raised, hauled far out to sea, and sunk.)

Other North Americans were eager to test their mettle, too, especially the army and navy, which hadn't seen action in more than three decades and had modern equipment to put to the test. Theodore Roosevelt, then Assistant Secretary of the Navy, also fanned the flames, seeing the venture as "good for the navy."

Thus, on April 25, 1898, Congress declared war against Spain. U.S. forces also invaded Puerto Rico, Guam, and the Philippines, which they captured in one day. On July 17, Spain surrendered. The Spanish flag was lowered and the Stars and Stripes raised, ending one of the most foolishly run empires in the world. In an act of gross arrogance, U.S. military leaders refused to invite the Mambí to the victory ceremony and parade. The Cuban people have never forgotten the slight.

The U.S. military occupation formally began on January 1, 1899, when 15 infantry regiments, one of engineers and four of artillery, arrived to "pacify" Cuba. For the first, but not the last time, U.S. troops occupied Havana. Officers who spoke no Spanish, had never lived in a hot country, and had no notion of Spanish or Cuban history and ideals found themselves in charge of a tired, starving people and a devastated land wrecked by war. "It would have been a poor boon to Cuba to drive the Spaniards out and leave her to care for herself, with two-thirds of her people unable to read and write, and wholly ignorant of the art of self-government," stated Secretary of War Elihu Root. Although the U.S. military administration swiftly initiated far-reaching reforms—including setting up schools, starting a postal system, establishing a judiciary and civil service, and eradicating the yellow-fever epidemics then common in Havana—Cuba ended the century as it had begun—under foreign rule.

THE REPUBLICAN ERA (1898–1959)
Into the 20th Century

On Ascension Day (May 20) 1902, the Stars and Stripes was lowered and the lone-star flag of Cuba rose into the sunny sky of Havana. The city broke out in a three-day spree of rejoicing. But Washington granted Cuba its independence at the end of a short leash. Even the Cuban Constitution was written by Washington in 1901, ushering in a period known as the Pseudo-Republic. "It's not the republic we dreamed of," said general and war hero Máximo Gómez.

The opening years of the Cuban republic were a time of great opportunity. The economy was in shambles and everything was up for grabs. Cuba witnessed a great influx of capital as U.S. companies invested in every major industry—tobacco, railroads, utilities, mining, and, above all, sugar. Several thousand U.S. citizens settled, bringing their North American style and sensibilities to the city. Cuba became a giant Monopoly board controlled by Uncle Sam. Havana witnessed a postwar boom and expanded markedly during the early 1900s, when Cuba received a surge of immigrants from the West Indies, the United States, and Europe. Rising land values fostered a frenzied real estate boom, setting the stage for the development of Havana's periphery.

Havana's residential expansion had hitherto moved outward from the ancient core along routes that had originally followed its topography. Housing occupied ridges and hills, avoiding flood-prone valleys. By the mid-19th century, Chinese immigrants had occupied the marshy lowlands, which they drained and planted with market gardens to supply the *habaneros*. As the city expanded, land values rose and the Chinese were squeezed out. A massive public works project initiated in 1907 moved millions of tons of earth into the valleys, which were raised for residential development. Surveyors laid out the roads that would link Habana Vieja with the rapidly expanding areas of Vedado, Cerro, Vista Alegre, and other suburbs beyond the Río Almendares, where the middle classes were building dwellings in eclectic, neoclassical, and revivalist styles.

As early as the mid-19th century, wealthy Spanish officials and sugar planters had built fine summer homes in Marianao, about eight miles west of the city center, laying down streets on the breeze-swept land that rose inland of the shore. A railroad had been laid in 1863, and a paved road in 1864. General Fitzhugh Lee, son of the Civil War hero and the region's U.S. military governor during the occupation, also found Marianao to his liking. He had established his headquarters here in a Spanish nobleman's abandoned home, with views across luxuriant gardens and, beyond, a bucolic landscape edging down to the sea. Lee set up Camp Columbia atop Marianao's heights as headquarters of the occupation troops, fueling a new prosperity for the region. Electricity and new water supplies were extended westward, local merchants soon followed, and Marianao experienced a rapid expansion.

By 1900, water pipes had been laid to supply water tanks that had been built under most buildings, and Havana could boast a clean water supply throughout the city. The aqueduct begun by Don Francisco de Albear in 1856 had taken four decades to complete, but proved outstanding enough to win a gold medal at the Paris Exhibition; today it still brings water into the city center. But only one-eighth of the city had sewers—most houses were served by cess-pools, which were occasionally drained and the contents dumped into the harbor. Although fresh water flowed from hotel faucets, passengers aboard ships arriving in Havana harbor were greeted by the gut-wrenching smell of sewage. Disease was rife—and bad for tourism. In 1907, therefore, the Cuban government initiated far-reaching public works that included new highways and sewers. By 1920, US$55 million had been spent on these projects, and more than 265 miles of sewer pipes and storm drains had been built, with a pumping station that bilged human waste into the sea at Cojímar, several miles east of the city.

All these fine public works, of course, benefited government officials and their civilian cronies immensely. Nonetheless, the crowded narrow streets and tight, shade-giving colonial quarters of older sections gave way to broad sidewalks and shaded porches facing onto broad lawns. The city began to spread out, too, its perimeter enlarged by grid extensions (*ensanches*) incorporating parks, boulevards, and civic spaces. By 1910, uncrowded neighborhoods lined the city's western edge, including seaside communities beyond the Río Almendares. "Havana's physical reaching out from cramped quarters to openness symbolized the optimism of a generation," wrote Rosalie Schwartz. The capital city—jewel of the Caribbean—wore a new luster, and "a healthful and pleasurable city unfolded before the tourists' eyes."

Meanwhile, many colonial mansions disappeared, leveled by the wrecking ball and replaced by banks and other commercial establishments. Many once-grand colonial homes were subdivided and rented to less affluent *habaneros* who could not afford the upkeep, while the real estate boom sponsored further spatial fragmentation, turning homes that once belonged to single families into beehives. The communities of *solares* expanded, the humble, unsanitary dwellings crowded within patios and back lots of buildings and hidden from the street. Some *solares* were in *ciudadelas,* small cities—virtual rabbit warrens—within the city, in independent buildings erected inside the enclosed grounds of a large urban unit. One such configuration was the Arco building in Vedado, looking like a fortress, with three structures of six stories appropriately detached from the city by a moat. Havana's population explosion also fostered speculative housing developments for the poorer classes, built by poorly paid bricklayers working without architectural designs; the tenement houses that sprang up throughout Havana were called *casas de vecindad.*

Discontent among the poorer classes found its outlet in frequent violent demonstrations that prompted U.S. intervention. When an August 1906 uprising in Pinar del Río province spread to Havana, President Estrada asked for U.S. marines to help quash this "Little August War." U.S. troops occupied Cuba for 28 months, during which time U.S. Secretary of State William Taft ran the island as governor of a provisional government before turning the country over to an appointee of President Theodore Roosevelt. In 1912, U.S. troops were again rushed to Havana when an outlawed Afro-Cuban party demonstrated against injustice toward blacks; the U.S. response was to arrest and execute the party's leaders. Marines again poured into Havana in 1917 when workers called a general strike, the "Cambelona Uprising." This time the troops remained until 1923.

The Roaring Twenties

Following the end of World War I, Cuba experienced a renewed building boom fed by a rush from high sugar prices. The peak of the sugar boom—the "dance of the millions"—lasted from 1915 to 1920, when the price of sugar climbed to 22.5 cents a pound. Sugar money paid for the plush mansions then blossoming in Havana's Vedado district as the older residential areas settled into a period of decay.

Havana received electric lights, and electric trams reached into the suburbs. The Malecón

was laid out. In the older city, the Presidential Palace (now the Museum of the Revolution) went up in 1920, melding vaguely classical allusions with Spanish colonial overtones, its interior appointments by the New York firm of Tiffany. Stylistically, architects stuck with the classical canon well into the Republican period, though by the late 19th century the beaux arts style was popular and North American influences were now obvious—General Leonard Woods had reorganized the school of architecture along U.S. lines. In the early 20th century, many of the financial buildings that went up in Habana Vieja took on the look of Wall Street. The art deco style then prevalent in Miami influenced other buildings, utilizing the geometrical terra-cotta motifs and vertical setbacks popular in North American skyscrapers.

Although sugar profits crashed in 1921 and again in 1929, the building boom didn't end. Desperate suppliers of construction materials extended credit, and real estate bargain hunters took advantage to build on land they had purchased. Apartment blocks went up all over Havana, with cafés and corner stores at ground level. Meanwhile, many of the once-fashionable houses along the Prado and in Habana Vieja were converted for commercial use, while many cherished old buildings were demolished because their ground space increased in value beyond that of the standing structure.

Most of the investors were local, led by Carlos Miguel de Céspedes and his partners, José Manuel Cortina and Carlos Manuel de la Cruz (the "Three C's"). With an eye to forging a tourism boom, their Compañía Urbanizadora Playa de Marianao developed residential lots in Marianao and pushed for the legalization of gambling. Céspedes and his Cuban buddies had a vested interest: they were partners in a tourism-related gambling concession. Marianao was set to become Havana's tourist mecca. At the time, it was already a local amusement center that at night resounded to the heartbeat and songbeat of Africa from rows of café hovels and smoky, low-roofed dance halls where the poor of Havana went for rumba entertainment after dark. The middle-class blacks had their own sophisticated cultural organizations, such as Club Atenas. In the Cuba of the time, "only the poor and déclassé, the sporting elements, and gentlemen on a spree danced the rumba," recalls Frederic Remington.

Céspedes was now President Machado's Public Works Secretary and the Cuban official most responsible for boosting Cuba's tourism industry. Hand in hand with wealthy Cuban investors, he promoted the expansion of the Miramar area west of the Río Almendares. They built streets and highways, and financed homes within reach of both the downtown area and the socialites' clubs and tourist facilities—such as the new Marianao country club. Private clubs proliferated during the Republican era. The Lyceum Lawn Tennis Club and Vedado Tennis Club dated from the pre-WWI years, followed by the Havana Yacht Club (founded in 1888, though the clubhouse dates from 1924). Predominantly utilized by the Cuban upper crust, architecturally they combined a North American beaux arts style with a conservative expression of tradition quite aristocratic in scope.

These facilities were farther west, in the fashionable new residential districts accessible by a lovely landscaped boulevard called La Quinta (Fifth Avenue). Wealthy *yanquis* and *cubanos* built their posh mansions side by side in these western suburbs, where Havana's Oriental Park racetrack opened in 1915. Marianao and the adjacent area called Country Club—now called Cubanacán— were significant for evolving in a "garden-city" tradition, with winding tree-lined streets and enormous park like lots. In 1919, much to the chagrin of the U.S. Congress, the Cuban congress passed a bill legalizing casinos. Wealthy business folk flocked to play golf at the Havana Country Club and gamble at Marianao's Oriental Park racetrack and Grand Nacional Casino. The Club became the place to be, and Country Club Park became the most exclusive address in town— Havana's Beverly Hills. Here were built the architecturally distinctive homes of the Cuban elite, who danced the *danzón* and Charleston at afternoon teas on the country club terrace and found new pleasure in golf at Bowman's Biltmore Yacht and Country Club. Completed in 1928 behind a fine beach on the shorefront of Cubanacán, its

2,000-acre lot stretched along five miles of shore and offered fine views of the Straits of Florida. Billed as the "world's grandest resort," Bowman's boasted its own casino, seafront hotel and marina blasted from the coral foreshore. To serve the middle classes, a bathing pavilion with 1,000 cabanas was also added at La Playa, the public beach on the Cubanacán shore. The poorer classes found their pleasures along the Malecón, where square baths called the Elysian Fields had been carved into the shoreline rocks. It was "delicious to while away hot afternoons under the striped awnings . . . wriggling one's toes in the white sand and shells, and splashing in the gentle swirl of the waves," wrote Juliet Barclay. "Visitors to the city were fond of what the Habaneros considered the lunatic pursuit of sea bathing all year round."

President Gerardo Machado (1925–33) and Céspedes envisioned Havana as a model modern city on the grand European theme using a city beautification plan based on Jean-Claude Nicolas Forestier's beaux arts scheme. Forestier, an internationally acclaimed landscape designer who had reshaped Paris, led an interdisciplinary team of Cuban designers who would pay homage to Havana's history while reshaping the city. They created landscaped malls, tree-lined avenues, parterres, and a gigantic park at the heart of a new metropolitan center. In 1926, Machado signed off on a master enlargement plan for the capital, financed by new real estate and luxury taxes, and bonds issued by Chase Manhattan Bank in New York.

Machado's fall from power in 1933 left much of the plan unfulfilled, but not without leaving behind some notable achievements. These included giving the Paseo del Prado its modern face, with a double aisle of laurel trees; remodeling and extending the Malecón west to the Río Almendares and east to the docks along the newly constructed Avenida del Puerto; conceiving an acropolis-like structure and classically inspired tiered staircase for the University of Havana; and planning new hotels for Vedado. Also, in 1929 a Central Post Office had been added, and that same year, the ribbon was cut on the statuesque Capitolio, a symmetrically massed structure some 692 feet long that is perhaps Havana's greatest symbol of classical ceremony, an appropriate place for the legislature to take its seats. The Capitolio was begun in 1912 under President Mario Menocal (1912–20) on the site of a partially built presidential palace. Redesigned during the Machado years and completed only after the initial dome had been blown off with dynamite, it soaked up 25 percent of the US$50 million national budget.

Cuba was far and away the richest tropical country anywhere, with a per capita income equivalent to that of Ireland, two-thirds that of Britain, and half that of the United States. Most of the wealth was concentrated in Havana. The city truly was the Pearl of the Antilles and soon vied with Florida for the title of America's Riviera.

While Havana was developing a reputation for libertine pleasures, it was also a cultured city with rapidly expanding middle and upper classes.

Yankee Doodle Comes to Town

The U.S. Congress gave Cuban tourism a major boost on July 1, 1919 when it enacted Prohibition. Within months of the United States going dry, John Bowman, New York hotelier and father of the Biltmore hotel chain, purchased Havana's Hotel Sevilla (built in 1908). He pumped half a million dollars into the hotel and reopened it in 1920 as the most lavish hotel in Havana.

Cuba beckoned from tourist posters and brochures, and U.S. magazines outdid themselves in purple prose full of sultry mahogany-colored maidens and sensuous men. Havana "is hot, it is 'wet,' it is, in its easy tropical way, Wide Open," wrote Bruce Bliven, in unabashed style. Tourism promoters also began to boost Cuba's African heritage, and Regla, the working-class *barrio* across the harbor, received gawkers seeking out the sight of near-naked, dark-skinned Cubans dancing to rhythms "more savage than the beat of tom-toms."

As Prohibition and a wave of morality swept through the United States, Yankees flocked to Havana, where those who chose to could wallow up to their noses in cocaine and sex. At least 20 steamships arrived in Havana's commodious harbor weekly from U.S. ports—so lucrative was the New York–Havana route that P&O ordered

THE BITE

Following the War of Independence, Washington firmly wanted to establish a stable, democratic government in the U.S. tradition. Alas, Uncle Sam—who, in writing the Cuban Constitution, had copied the U.S. Constitution almost verbatim—chose an Anglo-Saxon system unsuited to the Cuban mentality; the centuries of corruption and graft could not be eradicated overnight. Despite Washington's better intentions, Cuban politics swiftly sank into a spiral of corruption and graft (called *la mordida*—the bite—in Spanish). Cubans sought political office to get rich—an idea heartily endorsed by powerful U.S. business interests, which also profited—and the U.S. government was constantly influenced to support this or that Cuban who had given, or would give, opportunities to U.S. investors or who had borrowed from North American banks. Year by year, Cuba became more corrupt.

Each Cuban president forged new frauds of his own, handing out sinecures (which the Cubans called *botellas*—milk bottles given to babies) to cronies. Through successive administrations, Cuban politics sank deeper into iniquity. Despite its hopes for a better system, Washington discouraged any changes in the status quo where the country's efforts at political and economic reform threatened North American investors. "Dollar diplomacy" it was called (a term coined by President Howard Taft). When U.S. economic interests were threatened, Uncle Sam sent in troops. Dollar diplomacy was blind to the corruption, state violence, and poverty plaguing the country. The sordid system would last six decades, until a bearded young rebel came down from the mountains to oust the ancien régime.

a 700-passenger steamer for the passage to compete with Cunard and the Ward Line. Passengers escaping the snows of New York for Havana's winter sunshine paid as little as US$40 one-way, first-class, with meals.

In ensuing decades, Havana attracted the good and the bad in equal measure. Prostitution was rampant (it had always been present in Cuba's major port city), and the 1928 edition of *Terry's Guide to Cuba* told readers how to find houses where voyeurs could witness live sex or, in Havana's officially nonexistent "indecorous quarter," procure "teenagers who ranged in color from peach to coal" roaming the streets alongside ebony antiques. Guidebooks even lured tourists with accounts of tong wars and murky opium dens in Havana's Chinese quarter, where narcotics were sold openly on Dragones Street. Nightclub revues enhanced Havana's reputation for salacious sensuality. "Nights of Hollywood" were "nights of pleasure," proclaimed Club Hollywood, which touted a "gorgeous revue" of "15 girls." The Rex Dancing Club proclaimed that it had "200 girls."

When U.S. naval vessels entered Havana harbor, the narrow harbor mouth beneath Morro Castle was "jammed with rowboats full of clamoring prostitutes," recalls one sailor. Havana, wrote Juliet Barclay, was filled with "milkshakes and mafiosi, hot dogs and whores. Yanqui Doodle had come to town and was having martini-drinking competitions in the Sevilla Bar."

By the mid-1920s, when Havana's population reached about 250,000, some 80,000 tourists called on Cuba each year to realize their dreams of romance and adventure. When Havana's first scheduled airline service began in 1931, socialites and the working class alike hopped a plane for Havana to sidestep propriety and class barriers. They hoped to find youthful self-expression and nourish their human frailties with swarthy gigolos and dusky maidens at a time when "scandalizing one's parents and pastors became the thing to do" and sex appeal "signaled a willingness . . . to pluck a new personality from under the apron or the pinstriped suit," suggests Rosalie Schwartz. Hollywood, too, helped bolster the image of a Latin mystique. Who could resist Rudolf Valentino's smoldering eyes or the come-hither look of Marlene Dietrich personifying the "sexual danger" of a cabaret dancer. Havana offered new frontiers at a time when old ones had been tamed.

The city's hotels were jammed with curious sightseers who scattered their dollars throughout the city, filling the cash boxes of nightclubs and casinos—more than US$400 million flowed

in from U.S. tourists in 1926. Tourism revenues sifted through the economy, multiplying as dollars turned over many times in the local economy, through restaurants, taxi services, souvenir sellers, and prostitution. Tourists called the shots. Havana's traditional Carnaval was even changed to meet their expectations, moving the Mardi Gras Lenten season forward, increasing the number of days to enhance the tourist season, and adding imported theatrical pageantry to the sensuous music and dance of Afro-Cuban *comparsas.*

Big Trouble in Havana

Like his predecessors, Machado and his cronies were corrupt men susceptible to *la mordida* (bribes—literally, "the bite"). Although he sponsored Cuba's economic development and was responsible for magnificent enhancements to Havana, he gradually became a tropical Mussolini: at the end of his democratic four-year term—Machado had manipulated the phony 1928 election, triggering a wave of opposition—he announced that the demands of government called for a six-year term, and he himself would fill it. The dictator was unwilling to accommodate opposition. However, it blossomed during the Great Depression, which coincided with the collapse of Cuba's one-crop sugar economy and wrought misery throughout the country.

Machado responded to mounting antigovernment demonstrations with an iron fist. Thousands of Cubans were imprisoned, tortured, and executed as Machado's sense of self-importance mounted. Labor leaders and students were murdered by operatives of his Partido de la Porra death squads (including a female unit)—while his Sección de Expertos (secret police) tortured suspected opponents. When fellow students protested, he closed the universities. Havana was mired in deep unrest and violence, including assassinations and random bombings. Carleton Beals, a journalist who visited Havana in 1932 against a backdrop of chaos, wrote: "Beneath the tropical opulence of Cuba, hidden in the tangled jungle of her present cruel political tyranny, are the fangs of bitter discontent. . . . Outwardly Havana was a tomb. In reality it was a boiling cauldron." Beals blamed Machado and an American policy toward Cuba that "helped drive her to despair and ruin." Machado in fact remained in power because he was supported by powerful U.S. economic interests.

In July 1933, a Havana radio falsely announced that Machado had resigned. Delighted citizens took to the streets with the rallying cry, "Long live free Cuba!" Machado's police taught them the truth by mowing them down, killing 20 people. Finally, in the summer of 1933, a general strike brought the whole country to a halt. On August 11, Machado fled the country carrying a suitcase full of gold.

Tourism was barely affected: free-spending foreigners staying at the newly opened Hotel Nacional above the Malecón saw only a prosperous and exotic city with modern amenities, and went home to spread the good news.

The Post-Machado Years

The post-Machado era witnessed a series of ineffectual presidents in rapid succession. Only the army could reestablish control. A few weeks after Machado fled, a 32-year old sergeant named Fulgencio Batista y Zaldívar effected a *golpe* (coup) called the Sergeant's Revolt. Havana's university students signed on, and one of their own professors—Dr. Ramón Grau San Martín—became president. Grau's leftist leanings and the radical reforms he swiftly enacted, however, proved untenable for Washington, which persuaded Batista to force him aside. Supported by the United States, the upstart sergeant wielded control behind a veil of stooge presidents—six presidents served between 1934 and 1940—whom he selected and deposed in succession. With the U.S. blessing, Batista suppressed the far right as well as extreme leftist elements.

President Roosevelt advised the Cubans to expand tourism, but to forsake gambling and cabarets in favor of more culturally uplifting attractions. "In Roosevelt's view," wrote Rosalie Schwartz, "a country concerned with its wellbeing had to attract responsible persons, using entertainment compatible with human dignity." A new breed of civic-minded businessmen had similar thoughts and put its shoulder into constructing and enhancing cultural facilities

throughout the capital, substituting museums for Monte Carlo. A vast new park—Bosque de la Habana—was even laid out. Although sporadic violence broke out in 1935, tourists continued to respond to Havana's many allures.

The outbreak of World War II burst Havana's tourist bubble, but *habaneros* had again arrived at a relative calm. In 1940, a new constitution reflected more enlightened attitudes toward civil liberties, workers' rights, and public welfare. That year, Batista put away his marionettes and ran for the presidency on a progressive platform. Cuban voters gave him a four-year term (1940–44) in what was perhaps the nation's first clean election. In 1944, following a fairly benign term, Batista retired to Florida, leaving his country in the hands of men who permitted their administrations to again sink into chaos and unbridled corruption (there had, of course, been plenty of corruption under Batista; it was simply a matter of degree). Street demonstrations, assassinations, and bombings were once more daily events on the streets of Havana.

As the end of World War II approached, the United States sponsored tourism as an economic development strategy, and Havana—what the *Washington Times* called a "prodigious pastel Paradise"—was a beneficiary. War-ravaged Europe would be unable to absorb the outpouring of U.S. production. Washington needed to promote rapid market expansion and looked to Latin America. Tourism, it figured, would put dollars in the hands of Latin Americans, who would then buy U.S. goods. High-volume, low-cost air travel would be facilitated by the entry into the commercial market of thousands of wartime aircraft. Backed by Roosevelt, a bullish Pan American World Airways founded the Intercontinental Hotel Corporation—the "hotel chain with wings."

Despite FDR's vision, Havana faced new competition from Mexico, the Bahamas, and other destinations with exotic treats—primarily beaches—that the city couldn't offer. Havana's hotels also were looking a bit tattered. Hotel developers feared Cuba's newly empowered and militant labor unions, and therefore shunned Cuba. In the immediate postwar years, Cubans spent more money abroad than tourists brought in.

GENERAL FULGENCIO BATISTA

Fulgencio (christened Rubén) Batista y Zaldívar was born out of wedlock and into dire poverty in 1901 at Veguitas, near Banes, a backyard region of Oriente. His father was a sugar field worker (and the son of an indentured Chinese laborer); his mother was black. He enlisted and became a professional soldier and, after learning stenography, was promoted to sergeant.

Batista—an insecure, "fiery little bantam of a fella"—rose to the top during a *golpe* in 1933, when Fidel Castro was only seven. He became chief of staff of the army and, as such, took over the government. The general brutally suppressed the opposition and began a 25-year tenure as the most powerful man in Cuba. He ruled through a series of puppet presidents before winning the 1940 presidential election himself. Batista was himself a puppet, whose puppeteers lived in Washington.

Batista ruled during a period of prosperity and was at first popular with the masses, perhaps because of his lowly origins but also because he enacted progressive social reforms and a new, liberal constitution that favored labor. He also began massive civic construction works that enhanced the face of Havana. Despite, this he was blackballed by the social elite for being mulatto and gradually became despised by the masses because his government was immensely corrupt.

In 1944, Batista retired to Florida, having accumulated US$20 million during his 11-year tenure. He missed the limelight, however, and, after working out a deal with the Mafia, returned to Cuba venal and gluttonous. In March 1952, he pulled off his second coup. Batista oversaw an economic boom for Cuba that included major civic works for Havana. But the general had come back to power to commit grand larceny hand in hand with the mob. Corruption rose to new heights during his time in office. He met growing opposition to his rule with increasing brutality and terror.

Eventually, at midnight on New Year's Eve 1958, Batista fled Cuba with a group of followers. He settled in Spain, where he lived a princely life until his death in 1973. The poor cane cutter died as one of the world's wealthiest men—he had milked Cuba of almost US$300 million.

Desperate to lure tourists, in 1948, newly elected President Francisco Prío reopened the doors to gambling. At the time, only the Tropicana, Jockey Club, and Casino Nacional had gaming licenses, but the Sans Souci and Montmartre cabarets soon added casinos. The ploy worked. Cuban developers rushed to put up new hotels in anticipation of a rush of Yankee vacationers, although it wasn't until the mid-1950s that an infusion of foreign capital built Havana's Las Vegas-style hotel-casino with which prerevolutionary Havana will always be associated. By 1950, a rare era of puritanical zeal swept through the government. It briefly closed the casinos and cracked down on houses of prostitution, but hoteliers and nightclub owners convincingly argued that their financial success relied on the casinos, forcing the government to relent.

By 1958, 80 flights a week served Havana from Miami alone in high season. Everything that tourists had enjoyed in the 1920s emerged afresh with new vigor: a greater variety of restaurants—from the kosher menu at Moishe Pipik's and the Russian food at Boris's to the pedestrian fare at Woolworth's food counter—livelier bars, and racier nightclubs such as the Tropicana, which had opened in 1939 as Havana's most spectacular show with the most lavishly costumed, most statuesque Cuban showgirls. An open-air theater in the gardens of a mansion that had once housed the U.S. ambassador, the Tropicana quickly eclipsed all other nightclubs and drew international stars such as Josephine Baker, Carmen Miranda, and Nat "King" Cole, putting on elaborate productions with spectacular theatrical settings. The Tropicana was so lavish—it needed to pull in US$5,000 nightly to break even—and popular that a "Tropicana Special" flew nightly from Miami for an evening of entertainment that ended in the nightclub's casino.

By the late 1950s, more than three-quarters of total investment in Cuban construction was earmarked for Havana. The city was overcrowded, and dozens of new neighborhoods sprang up, aided by the 1952 Law of Horizontal Property that encouraged investment in apartment projects and rental houses on tiny lots measuring only four meters across and 30 meters deep. On the eve of the Revolution, about 75 percent of Havana's housing units were rentals. Needless to say, the boom led to deteriorating construction standards. Much of Havana's modern face is a legacy of this era, including La Rampa, the sloping boulevard that rises from the Malecón to the heart of Vedado.

The Heyday of Sin

In 1952, Batista became bored by retirement and again put himself up as a presidential candidate in the forthcoming elections. When it became clear that he wouldn't win, he upended the process with a bloodless *golpe*. One of the candidates for congress whose political ambitions were thwarted was a dashing young lawyer with a predilection for stylish suits and baseball. His name was Fidel Castro, a 25-year-old who had risen to great prominence as the most outspoken critic of corrupt government and was being hailed as an incorruptible future president.

Batista had lingered too long in Miami with *mafiosi* and returned spoiled with ambition and greed. Mobsters began to take over the hotels and casinos with Batista's blessing—for a cut of the proceeds, of course—and Cuba sank into a new round of corruption: "From the very beginning, every public works contract, of which there were many, brought its 30 percent commission to various secretaries and assistants of the President and thence to Batista's bank account," wrote Hugh Thomas.

Havana will always be primarily associated with sin—the Babylon of the Caribbean—and the pre-Fidel mobsters who seared the city into our consciousness. In truth, the period of mobsters and sin was very short-lived, spanning the few years immediately prior to the Revolution. "A few years of profitable frivolity ensured [Havana's] lasting reputation as the premier pleasure

island of the time and the rallying cry and a focal point for antigovernment rebels," wrote Schwartz.

The line between legitimate business and organized crime began to blur in the early-1950s as Batista actively promoted Havana's latest tourism boom. He launched a frenetic era of hotel construction hand in hand with mobster-genius Meyer Lansky, whom he appointed as his gambling supervisor. Economically, building a new breed of casino-hotels made sense. Cuba's share of Caribbean tourism had fallen from 43 percent in 1949 to 31 percent in 1951, and with new competition from neighboring islands, the country needed to put a polish on its attractions. Casino-hotels had built Las Vegas and could do so for Cuba, too. Batista promised to issue a casino license for investors willing to put up one million dollars for hotel construction, with a portion of the casino proceeds to be designated for charity. A hotel boom followed, with room capacity doubling between 1955 and 1958.

Lansky, a bootlegger and a Batista friend from the days of Prohibition, had bought an early interest in the Montmartre casino—displaced American mobsters became partners in four of Havana's five casinos. Lansky had long since mastered the art of professional casino operation and, with maximum profits in mind, shared Batista's desire to ensure that foreign tourists had a good time. He set up a school for casino employees and ensured that the casinos ran an honest game. Batista regulated the casinos to make certain that tourists weren't being cheated; the tourist commissioner even sent troops into the casinos to put an end to crooked games. Lansky also headed an investor group of Prohibition-era friends and built the sumptuous Havana Riviera on the Miramar seafront under the watchful eye of the Banco Desarrollo Económico y Social (Bandes), a public financial institution that the Cuban government set up in 1955 to fund economic development and oversee foreign investment. The government, which permitted 24-hour gambling and no limit on wagers, got more than its fair share of the proceeds; a gambling license cost US$25,000, but US$250,000 was expected under the table. Even Batista's wife got 10 percent of the proceeds from Trafficante's five casinos; she would roll up to casinos in her sleek black limousine and sit in the back while the bagman collected her weekly take.

The Riviera opened in December 1957 to general fanfare, with the casino at the core of operations—it pulled in three dollars for every two spent on hotel rooms, restaurants, shops, and cabaret. That month, the 250-room Hotel Capri also opened with its own casino and fancy nightclub, as well as a rooftop swimming pool, where guests could watch an underwater show through specially constructed windows. The Hotel Nacional also gained a Las Vegas-type casino and cabaret. Casinos opened at the old Sevilla-Biltmore Hotel and the new Hotel Comodoro, in Miramar. Several smaller hotels also popped up in Vedado, including the 32-story Hotel Habana Libre, built by Hilton but owned by the culinary workers' union's pension fund with a casino franchise leased to the Mob for one million dollars a year. Hilton's neon-lit name emblazoned across the skyline of Havana imparted new stature to Cuba's capital city.

Cuba's capital city had everything. It had opera. It had baseball and ballroom dancing. Havana's many museums and theaters hosted major cultural productions: a symphony orchestra and an internationally acclaimed ballet company had been formed, and the ultra-modern, air-conditioned Blanquita Theater was added in 1949 to accommodate 7,000 patrons, with a parking lot for more than 1,000 cars (the stage could also be lowered to form a skating rink).

What really made the city so popular was that it also had sex. "The first thing every secretary, schoolteacher, and nurse wants to see when they come here is *la exhibición*," recorded mobster lawyer Frank Ragano. *Las Exhibiciones*—live sex shows—were visited by tens of thousands of tourists. The majority were family types who ostensibly came to Havana for its cultural attributes, perhaps finding titillation along the way much as latter-day tourists do when they visit Amsterdam's Rosse Buurt or New Orleans' Bourbon Street.

North Americans arrived by plane or aboard the *City of Havana* ferry from Key West to indulge in a few days of sun and sin, with 10,000 prostitutes in the city to service their needs—there were about 270 brothels in Havana in the late 1950s. "In the transitional era between the clumsy groping of the drive-in movie and the boastful sexuality of the hot tub, Cuba offered tourists an acceptable way to succumb to temptation without scandalizing the neighbors," wrote Schwartz. They went home happy, unaware that behind the scenes, chaos and corruption were rife.

Cuba's tourism boom worked in Batista's favor, bringing in millions of dollars that spread throughout the economy and creating thousands of jobs across the spectrum, from hotel maids to urban migrants peddling souvenirs from streetside stalls—"fully ninety percent of Havana's lighted storefronts had signs in English," claims Tom Miller. And the Mob-run syndicates invested their profits in banking, hotels, restaurants, real estate, and scores of other legitimate businesses, employing tens of thousands of *habaneros* directly or indirectly.

But Cuba's military leader also accomplished fine deeds. Batista initiated plans for the nation's economic welfare and attempted to reconfigure Havana's public profile with a modernist plan for redevelopment. One of his first acts was to appoint a National Planning Board, which commissioned a modernist plan by Cuban architect José Luís Sert that owed its inspiration to Frenchman Le Corbusier and envisioned a Havana of "superblocks" intersected by green corridors.

The government issued US$350 million in bonds to finance public works programs, including construction of a long-awaited tunnel beneath Havana harbor. Batista fixed up the roads, expanded the airport at Rancho Boyeros, enforced sanitation codes for restaurants, and set up a special police force to protect against tourist abuse. A fine arts museum was established. Havana acquired skyscrapers such as the 35-story Focsa building, a minimalist design typical of the postwar era. It boasted its own garage, power plant, school, and restaurant, epitomizing a trend toward luxury that the 1959 revolution cut short. Government ministries were moved to a new center of construction, the Plaza de la República (today the Plaza de la

THE MOB IN HAVANA

For three decades, the Mafia had dealings in Cuba, and though it never had the run of the house as claimed, prerevolutionary Havana will forever be remembered for its presence.

During U.S. Prohibition (1920–33), mobsters such as Al Capone had contracted with Cuban refineries to supply molasses for their illicit rum factories. When Prohibition ended, the Mob turned to gambling. The Mafia's interests were represented by Meyer Lansky, the Jewish mobster (as a Jew he could never be a full member of the Mafia) from Miami who arrived in 1939 and struck a deal with Fulgencio Batista, Cuba's strongman president. Lansky described Batista to national crime syndicate boss Salvatore "Lucky" Luciano as "the best thing that ever happened to us." Lansky, acting as lieutenant for Luciano, took over the Oriental Park racetrack and the casino at Havana's Casino Nacional, where he ran a straight game that attracted high rollers. The Cuban state was so crooked, the Mob didn't even need to break the law (Lansky had brilliant business acumen and was as skilled in making money disappear without a trace as he was in bringing it in).

World War II effectively put an end to the Mob's business, which was relatively small scale at the time. Lansky returned to Florida, followed by Batista in 1944 when he lost to Ramón Grau in the national election. Lansky's aboveboard operation soon withered in the Mob's absence, replaced by rigged casinos, and Havana's gambling scene developed a bad reputation: Cuban casinos rented space to Cuban entrepreneurs who, says Stephen Williams, ran "wildly crooked games with the only limit to their profit being the extent of their daring."

Meanwhile, following the war, the United States deported Luciano to Italy. In 1946, he moved to Cuba, where he intended to establish a gambling and narcotics operation and regain his status as head of the U.S. Mob. He called a summit in Havana's Hotel Nacional. The meeting—the biggest since Chicago in 1932—was immortalized in *The Godfather,* and the official cover, records Alan Ryan, "was that it was meant to honor a nice Italian boy from Hoboken called Frank Sinatra," who went down to Havana to say thanks. The United States, however, pressured Grau to deport Luciano back to Italy. Before leaving, Luciano named Lansky head of operations in Cuba.

The Mob's presence in Cuba was given a boost when Florida voters declined to legalize gambling and the state's casinos were closed down, followed by a federal campaign to suppress the Mob. Mobsters decided Cuba was the place to be. A new summit was called at Batista's house in Daytona Beach, attended by Cuban politicians and military brass. A deal was struck: Batista would return to Cuba, regain power, and open the doors to large-scale gambling. In return, he and his crooked pals would receive a piece of the take. A gift of US$250,000 (personally delivered by Lansky) helped convince President Grau to step aside, and on March 10, 1952, Batista again occupied the Presidential Palace. New laws were quickly enacted to attract

Revolución), completed in 1959 inland from Vedado. The Palace of Justice, National Library, and National Theater surrounded the trapezoidal plaza, pinned by a 450-foot modernist monument to José Martí.

Although the benefits may have been lopsided, Batista's government undoubtedly spurred economic growth and fueled a period of renewed prosperity in a society frustrated by long years of economic stagnation due mostly to Cuba's ties to a dormant sugar economy. Havana of the late 1950s was a wealthy and modern city on a par with Buenos Aires and Montevideo. The city's financially comfortable middle class had developed a taste for American TV and cars, went to Coney Island and the newly developed beach resorts on weekends, and enjoyed the same restaurants, bars, and cabarets as tourists. "The future looks fabulous for Havana," said Wilbur Clarke, the croupier who operated the Hotel Nacional casino, little knowing what the course of history had in store.

investment in hotels and casinos, and banks were set up as fronts to channel money into the hands of Cuban politicos.

North American crime figures became a familiar sight in Havana. Four "families" ruled the roost. The first, headed by Cuban-Italian Amleto Batistti, controlled the heroin and cocaine routes to the United States and an emporium of illegal gambling from Batistti's base at the Hotel Sevilla. The "family" of Amadeo Barletta organized the "Black Shirts" in Havana. The third family, headed by Tampa's Mafia boss, Santo Trafficante Jr., operated the Sans Souci casino-nightclub, plus the casinos in the Capri, Comodoro, Deauville, and Sevilla-Biltmore Hotels. Watching over them all was Lansky, who ran the Montmartre Club and the Club Internacional of the Hotel Nacional.

Corruption and self-enrichment occurred on a colossal scale. Organized crime became one of the three real power groups in Cuba (the others being Batista's military regime and American business), although there was never any doubt that Batista was in control, and he kept the Mob on a tight chain. Anything was permissible: gambling, pornography, drugs. Nonetheless, Lansky again cleaned up the gambling to attract high-stakes gamblers from the States. No frivolities were allowed. Games were regulated, and cardsharps and cheats were sent packing. Casinos were extensively renovated, and cocaine and prostitutes were supplied to high rollers. John F. Kennedy occasionally popped down to Havana for sexual excitement. In 1957, Mob boss Santo Trafficante claims to have set JFK up with a private party, supplying three gorgeous prostitutes in a special suite in the Hotel Comodoro, which Trafficante owned, in the hope that it would put Kennedy in his debt. Unbeknownst to the young senator from Massachusetts, the room had a two-way mirror, and Trafficante and casino owner Evaristo Garcia watched the antics—but neglected to film them.

The tourists flocked. Lansky's last act was to build the ritziest hotel and casino in Cuba—the US$14 million Hotel Riviera and Gold Leaf Casino, which opened on December 10, 1958. Within three weeks, on New Year's Eve, the sold-out floor show at the Riviera's Copa Room nightclub had 200 no-shows. Batista and his crooked henchmen had fled the country.

Ironically, Trafficante and the mob had considered Castro "a joke" but were hedging their bets for all eventualities by secretly funding the rebels as well as Batista. To no avail. Once Castro took power, the casinos were closed down (only after they had paid their employees), and, in June 1959, Lansky, Trafficante, and other "undesirable aliens" were kicked out of Cuba. Said Lansky: "I crapped out."

For the full scoop on the Mafia's involvement in Havana, read *The Mob,* an autobiography by mob lawyer Frank Ragano.

The Gathering Storm

While tourism pumped millions of dollars into the Cuban economy, rebels charged that it had corrupted the country. Gambling, they claimed, soaked up precious dollars that should be used for socially beneficial programs. By 1957, when "tourism appeared to have fulfilled its economic promise," suggests Schwartz, "Cuban rebels escalated their challenge to Fulgencio Batista's government and began to hurl the island's Las Vegas image like a grenade at the leaders who had fashioned it." Fidel Castro and other rebels effectively propagandized the underworld connections in a moralistic, nationalist call to arms. Casinos became the rallying call of the rebels, eager to mobilize popular discontent. The U.S. media picked up the scent and published a series of accusatory articles linking Mob ties to Havana's casinos. The stories were prompted by the murder of New York mobster Albert Anastasia in 1957. Although ties with Cuba were never proved, Havana was tarred and feathered with speculative accusations that bore the precedent of history and would be difficult to remove.

History has exaggerated the scale of the problem. As Schwartz points out: "Foreign gamblers introduced neither gangsterism nor vice to the island, nor did they necessarily corrupt righteous islanders." Nor did the Mob move in and take over. Batista might have brought big-time casinos to Cuba, but Cubans still ran the show. When it came to extortion rackets and payoffs, the Mob was playing ball with seasoned veterans, not second-stringers. Havana's policemen, for example, made daily rounds of the brothels and gambling houses, where they collected a "tax" (Cubans called it el forrajeo), and the payments climbed up the chain of command. The deadly rivalries and rampant corruption of the times—gangsterismo, a term for the assassinations and street violence that marked the politics of the period—had brutalized Cuban politics long before the Mob arrived. Castro and his generation of student rebels became radicalized during the mid-1940s and early 1950s, when student and political activities settled their ideological differences with guns—there were 64 political assassinations on the streets of Havana during Grau's 1944–48 administration. Castro himself was accused of assassination and went into hiding. "The machine gun in the big car became the symbol not only of settling scores but of an approaching change of government," wrote Hugh Thomas.

As radical opposition to Batista found its violent outlet on the streets, he struck back. In the escalating conflict, the police and military became increasingly heavy-handed. General opposition to Batista's authoritarian rule was mounting. Many Cubans were disgusted by the depth of depravity into which Havana had sunk, made more sordid by the poverty and destitution endemic in the slums of Havana. Batista's rule became so widely hated that it united the Cuban people. He got himself "elected" president in November 1954. But it made no difference. He maintained his empire with a brutal police force. Neither Washington nor Batista understood the revolutionary forces at work.

Almost immediately following Batista's golpe, Castro had begun to plot the dictator's denoue-ment. The rebel possessed a vision of his place in Cuba's future that seemed preordained. He was also ruthlessly focused. He organized the Movement, later known as MR-26-7, for Movimiento Revolucionario 26 Julio, and ran it with military discipline. Soon the Movement was an army in training. Castro launched his revolution on July 26, 1953 with an attack on the Moncada barracks in Santiago de Cuba. It collapsed in a hail of bullets, and Castro was sentenced to 15 years in jail. In May 1955, Batista bowed to mounting public pressure and freed Castro.

When the train carrying Castro reached Havana, he was hoisted aloft by a huge crowd and carried through the streets. He immediately launched his anti-Batista campaign. Castro was banned from making public addresses, and newspapers that printed his articles were shut down. But the public was with him. When police brutally beat students who took their demonstration onto the baseball field at Havana stadium, the scene was broadcast on national television and helped turn the tide in Castro's favor. A year later, Havana's pro-Batista mayor was booed out of the stadium by a crowd chanting "Viva Fidel!"

On July 7, 1955, Castro boarded a flight to Mexico to prepare a guerrilla army in exile. On December 2, 1956, Castro and 81 men came ashore. While his Rebel Army nibbled away at Batista's troops in the Sierra Maestra mountains, a war of attrition spread throughout the countryside and cities. In Havana, Batista's henchmen were assassinated; army posts, police stations, and public utilities were destroyed; and a terror campaign was enacted to scare away tourists. The urban terrorism was mostly the work of José Antonio Echevarría's Revolutionary Directorate—the militant arm of the University of Havana's student federation—which targeted Havana, while Castro's Twenty-Sixth of July Movement fomented rebellion in Oriente (the two groups had signed a pact that gave free rein to the other), but both groups planted phosphorus bombs in hotels, movie houses, nightclubs, and other prominent public places, claims Schwartz. Exploding bombs occasionally rocked the hubbub of Havana's streets. Political terrorists were at work, bent on undermining the tourism boom.

Says Schwartz: "Cuba became a holiday paradise in the midst of a political hell."

On March 13, 1957, an attack on the presidential palace in Havana by almost 100 members of the Student's Revolutionary Directorate—acting independently of Castro—failed (35 students died in the attack). Batista met the increasing storm with increasingly brutal violence. In Havana, Batista's secret police tortured suspected opposition members and hung them from trees. The leader of the opposition Ortodoxo Party was murdered and his body dumped on the grounds of the Havana Country Club. In the countryside, night fell with a blackness made more menacing by the awareness of mysterious forces at work.

The international media was paying attention to Havana's turmoil, especially after a U.S. tourist got in the way of a bullet during a gun battle on the streets of Habana Vieja. Although a general strike called by Castro failed—even when more than 100 Cubans were killed by police on the streets, most workers stayed on the job—he was winning the media battle. As bombings of buses, major shopping districts, and theaters escalated, Cubans thought it wise to stay home. So did foreigners. "Castro's bombs were frightening away the tourists," wrote Graham Greene in *Our Man in Havana*.

Prompted by the mounting crisis and foreign pressure, Batista set a date for new elections in 1959. Buoyed by Cuba's economic prosperity, Batista also opened a peace offensive, restoring constitutional guarantees and encouraging political parties to organize for the coming elections. But it was too late. "The President's regime was creaking dangerously towards its end," wrote Greene. For Castro, the scent of victory was in the air. His rebel armies were closing in on Havana.

At midnight on New Year's Eve, 1958, Batista and his closest supporters boarded a plane for the Dominican Republic. Batista intended to leave Captain Ventura, his evil police chief, behind, but Ventura arrived at the airfield and held Batista at gun point, forcing him to remove some of his baggage to make room for him. Two days later, the Rebel Armies of Camilo Cienfuegos and Che Guevara entered Havana.

While jubilant citizens celebrated Batista's ouster, scores of others went on a rampage of looting and general destruction.

THE REVOLUTIONARY ERA

On January 3, 1959, the triumphant guerrilla army began a five-day Romanesque victory march to Havana, with crowds cheering Castro atop a tank, all of it televised to the nation. Castro, ever the grand showman, arrived in Havana on January 9—the city had by then settled down—to a tumultuous welcome. That night, Castro bathed in spotlights while delivering his victory speech before the nation. Two white doves suddenly appeared, and one miraculously flew down to rest on his shoulders—a stupefying event that fulfilled an Afro-Cuban superstition (doves in *santería* mythology represent life) and granted Castro the protection of the gods. It was "one of those rare, magical moments when cynics are transformed into romantics and romantics into fanatics," wrote photojournalist Lee Lockwood.

Castro—now the "Maximum Leader"—set up his headquarters in the recently opened Havana Hilton, while croupiers worked the first floor. An official democratic government under President Manuel Urrutia ostensibly ruled from the Presidential Palace while Castro—as Prime Minister—moved cautiously but vigorously behind the scenes to solidify his power under the guise of establishing a pluralist democracy. He was intent from day one on turning the old social order upside down. In retail shops, new signs spelled the future: "The Customer Is Always Right Except When He Attacks the Revolution." Castro was about to embark on a grand social revolution that would remake the country entirely, from the bottom up.

In 1959, Havana was a highly developed city—one of the most developed in Latin America—with a large wealthy class, a prospering middle class, and a vigorous culture. The island's per capita rankings for automobiles, literacy, and infant mortality (32 per 1,000 live births) suggest that it was comparatively advanced in socioeconomic terms. It had a mature market economy and banking sector, more cars per capita than

Italy, and shops full of produce cheap enough for mass consumption. About one-fifth of Cuba's 6.5 million population lived in Havana, where most of Cuba's wealth and facilities were concentrated. But tens of thousands of *habaneros* also lived without light, water, or sewage. Poverty was endemic, and thousands of citizens lived by begging and prostitution. Ernest Hemingway knew the ubiquitous destitution that American tourists of his day rarely saw while carousing in cabarets and casinos: "the nose-snot of children, the shuffle of untreated syphilis, sewage in the old beds of brooks . . . scale on the backs of old men's necks." Hemingway lived in the suburb of San Francisco de Paula. To get there he had to drive through the *barrio* of Luyano, a shantytown so blighted by poverty that in *Islands in the Stream,* the protagonist Thomas Hudson carried drink to fortify himself against the shock when passing through.

One of the first acts of the government was to close the strip clubs, casinos, and brothels. It was a highly unpopular move. Thousands of Cuban workers faced unemployment if the casinos were closed down. They joined hands with vested interests and demanded—successfully—that the casinos be reopened. Castro soon saw the light: Casinos helped pay off the negotiated loans that the inexperienced new government had inherited. Says Rosalie Schwartz: "The contribution of American tourists, projected to reach six billion dollars a year by 1964, appeared as economic redemption to revolutionaries in need." A new tourism commission—the Instituto Nacional de Industriales Turísticas—was founded with experienced staff at its head, and a commitment of US$200 million made to a four-year development program. Havana even hosted the annual convention of the American Society of Travel Agents (ASTA) in October 1959, and Oriental Park—Havana's racetrack—opened its horse-racing season with a big media splash.

Wholesale change, however, was already being felt in the city as the revolutionary government set itself to redressing social needs that had long been neglected. On March 6, 1959, all rents in Cuba were reduced by 50 percent. Electricity, gas, and public transport fees were dramatically lowered, as were other fees. Price controls were instituted on goods sold on the free market. The government poured money into health care. And Castro set up special schools for the indigent; the blind, deaf, and mute; and ex-prostitutes.

Castro was everywhere in Havana, speaking before huge crowds in an ingenious exercise he called "direct democracy," by which he utilized his incredibly manipulative powers to gauge and shape the public mood. Havana's new government was wherever Castro happened to be at the time. President Urrutia genuinely attempted to establish a democratic government and had established an unusually gifted cabinet. On July 13, 1959, Urrutia denounced the growing Communist trend. Castro, who had emasculated and replaced José Miró Cardona (a moderate lawyer) as prime minister, in turn resigned. He followed this with a typically brilliant gambit. He understood that the key to the Revolution was Cuban sentiment. At the time of Urrutia's resignation, Castro had arranged for peasants to be brought to Havana to celebrate the attack on Moncada. Castro then appeared on TV and denounced Urrutia, selling the Revolution direct to the masses. The streets of Havana erupted in calls for the President's resignation and pleas for Castro's return. He had carried out the world's first televised coup d'état. On May 1, 1960, Castro reneged on his promise to hold elections within one year: the "people," he proclaimed, had declared them unnecessary, rationalizing the suspension of the Constitution and refusal to seek a popular mandate.

On March 4, 1960, *Le Coubre,* a French freighter carrying Belgian armaments for Cuba, exploded in Havana harbor, killing more than 80 Cubans. Castro blamed the CIA. If true, the CIA had managed to rally the Cuban people around Castro at a time when he was facing increasing domestic opposition. During the funeral ceremonies, Castro responded with a new battle cry: *"¡Patria o Muerte!"*—Fatherland or Death! Recalls Nobel Laureate Gabriel García Márquez: "The level of social saturation was so great that there was not a place or a moment when you did not come across that rallying cry of anger, written on everything from the cloth shades on the sugar mills to the bottom margins of official documents. And it was repeated endlessly for days and months on radio and television stations until it was incorporated into the very essence of Cuban life."

The Revolution was turning ugly. Gun-toting street thugs and unemployed youngsters had joined Castro's urban militia. Angry blacks and *guajiros* (peasants) shouting revolutionary slogans roamed the streets. *Prensa Libre* and other independent publications were forced to close. Repression was making itself felt. The atmosphere was tense. Counter-revolutionary groups also became active. Bombs once more exploded on the streets of Havana. Political denunciations had created a climate of fear as accusations by loyal *fidelistas* led to arrests in the middle of the night. Fusillades rang out once again in the Foso de los Laureles as summary tribunals headed by Che Guevara—the "supreme prosecutor"-sent hundreds of Batista supporters to the firing squads. Scores of innocent people, fingered by *chavatos* (informers) were also shot; Guevara dismissed the murders as "a revolutionary process of justice at the service of future justice." No exact figures are known of how many were executed in the wave of revolutionary retribution.

Castro's fiery speeches had turned distinctly anti-American. Tourists got the message, dooming Havana's hotels, restaurants, and other businesses to bankruptcy. Havana's former hot spots gathered dust. Apart from a handful of Russians, the beaches belonged to the Cubans throughout the 1960s and '70s, when tourism contributed virtually nothing to the nation's coffers.

In the Wake of the Bay of Pigs

In the predawn hours of April 15, 1961, Cuban exiles trained by the CIA bombed Campamento Libertad airfield in Cubanacán, in western Havana, as a prelude to the Bay of Pigs invasion. The strike destroyed most of Cuba's tiny air force. Next day, standing at the corner of Avenida 23 and Calle 12, Castro gave a fiery funeral speech in honor of those Cubans killed and claimed that the attack happened because the United States couldn't forgive Cuba for having created a "socialist revolution" under its nose. It was the first time that Castro had uttered the dreaded word.

The Bay of Pigs fiasco consolidated support for

plaque commemorating Castro's annoucement on April 16, 1961, that Cuba is socialist

Castro and solidified his regime, enhanced by the unanimous distaste among Cubans for the all-encompassing U.S. trade embargo enacted in October 1960. But the sordid CIA debacle also provoked a wave of repression. Castro ordered the arrest of anyone considered disloyal to the revolution. Havana's bohemian middle-class sectors were suddenly sealed off. Armed with lists, the revolutionary police swept the city, arresting, in the words of Carlos Franquí, "homosexuals, vagrants, suspicious types, intellectuals, artists, Catholics, Protestants, practitioners of voodoo . . . prostitutes and pimps." Detainees were made to wear uniforms stitched with a large P on the back, much like Jews had been branded in prewar Nazi Germany.

In September 1961, Castro created the Committees to Defend the Revolution (CDRs). The inhabitants of every block in Havana (and the rest of Cuba) formed a committee to ensure the implementation of revolutionary decrees and perform the grassroots vigilante work of the State Security apparatus.

In October 1962, Havana's ports were sealed off and a curfew enacted as Soviet missiles were brought into Cuba. They were a public secret that everyone knew, including Cuban exiles leaving for Florida. Their discovery by a U-2 spy plane triggered the Cuban Missile Crisis, which Cubans refer to as the Caribbean Crisis. The population of Havana went on combat alert, prepared to face down the atomic bomb with rifles. In *Return to Havana,* Maurice Halperin recalls living in Havana in October 1962: "Unbelievably, the popular mood was defiance. *'¡Patria o Muerte!'* Castro shouted, and the masses seemed almost eager to take on the Yankees. There was an air of celebration in the city . . . Havana was throbbing."

Jean-Paul Sartre and Simone de Beauvoir reported that "Havana has changed; no more nightclubs, no more gambling, and no more American tourists. On every side, in the streets, the militia was drilling. . . "

A Tragic Progression

As time unveiled the Communist nature of the Castro regime, a mass exodus of the wealthy and the middle class began, inexorably changing the face of Havana. Miami received a flood of unhappy exiles. At first, these were composed of corrupt elements escaping prosecution—pimps, politicos, thugs, assassins, henchmen, political hacks and their accomplices, *mafiosi,* and the thousands of underlings that support a corrupt regime. Then the reforms extended to affect the middle classes. An Urban Reform Law was passed, canceling existing leases and mortgages, and reducing rents to 10 percent of tenants' incomes, payable now to the state. The rental revenues that had been a prime source of income for Havana's middle classes were choked off; tens of thousands of families with their income tied up in real estate lost it all. Although rent payments could now be amortized toward the nontransferable purchase of a house, few buildings passed into private ownership. Says Rachel Carey: "Thousands of tenants did not keep up with rent payments. . . . [C]ourts did not evict." Castro's government became Havana's principle, and lousiest, landlord. It took the cash and divested itself of further responsibility: tenants were made responsible for the upkeep of properties.

Inevitably, the trickle of émigrés turned into a flood. About 250,000 Cubans left by 1963, most of them white, urban professionals—doctors, teachers, engineers, technicians, businesspeople, architects, and others with entrepreneurial skills—ensuring Havana's inevitable decay as entrepreneurship and know-how were replaced by socialist ineptitude and turmoil. Many of Castro's revolutionary cohorts also began to desert him. Later, intellectuals and homosexuals were persecuted, and they, too, joined the flood.

Those who were forced to leave Cuba had to leave their possessions behind. Their houses were confiscated—"donated to the Revolution" is the official verbiage. "We did not take anyone's house," Fidel said on August 24, 1998, "They went on extended vacation." The houses were given to loyal *fidelistas* and citizens in need of housing, while others became schools, medical facilities, and social centers for the elderly and disadvantaged. Havana faced a tremendous housing shortage. Festering slums and shanty towns marred the suburbs, and the new government ordered them razed. Concrete high-rise apartment blocks were erected on the city's outskirts, notably in Habana del Este.

Unfortunately, about 90 percent of Cuba's architects had already fled Cuba. While a few individuals found room to express their creativity in stone, the move to centralized industrial planning under the Ministry of Construction soon eclipsed the independent mind. It was replaced with a utilitarian doctrine that defaced the Havana landscape with mass-produced, prefabricated concrete modules: the Soviet *gran panel* (involving in-place casting) was introduced to Cuba in 1963, joining the Yugoslavian IMS, which relied on precast columns and slabs, post-tensioned during installation. Everyone agrees that these trial-and-error prototypes were failures, but they continued being used until the Soviet Union itself collapsed. Meanwhile, the Presidential Palace and Capitolio—ultimate symbols of the "sordid era"—were turned into museums, while the new government moved into new ministry buildings surrounding the Plaza de la Revolución.

That accomplished, the Revolution turned its back on the city and gave its attention instead to the countryside. Says Claudia Lightfoot: "Fidel was never really enamored of Havana, as his support base came overwhelmingly from the peasant classes mainly in the east of the island. Despite the fact that most of the wealthy had fled the city almost overnight, he was distrustful of the capital. He had inherited a largely Americanized cityscape representing sophistication, corruption, intellectuals, and possible dissent." Resources were diverted away from Havana. Left to deteriorate, thousands of older homes collapsed (currently, almost 100 important colonial houses a year collapse according to one estimate), forcing their occupants into temporary jerry-built shelters that eventually became permanent. Meanwhile, "pragmatism invaded tall rooms," says Nancy Stout, "forcing them to yield their height to additional sleeping quarters popularly labeled *baracoas*." The city was relayered horizontally as tens of thousands of migrants poured into Havana. The poor peasant migrants predominantly came from Oriente and were shipped in at first by the Castro government to

show support for the radical land reforms, bolstering the city from Fidel's natural base of support. Many were encouraged to settle, changing the city's demographic profile, as most of the immigrants were black. Some estimates suggest that as many as 400,000 *palestinos,* immigrants from Santiago and the eastern provinces, live in Havana. The "Palestinians" are not liked by a large segment of *habaneros*; many of Havana's policemen are *palestinos* who still live in Oriente and commute weekly to work.

Havana's aged housing and infrastructure, much of it already decayed, have ever since suffered benign neglect.

Mismanaging the Economy

Cuba's infant socialism was living off the fat accumulated by Cuban capitalism. By 1968, the Cuban economy was coming apart at the seams. To make matters worse, that year Castro nationalized the entire retail trade still in private hands. More than 58,000 businesses—from corner cafés and ice cream vendors to auto mechanics—were eliminated in the "Great Revolutionary Offensive." As a result, even the most basic items disappeared from Havana's shelves. Socialism had nationalized wealth but, says Guillermo Cabrera Infante, it "socialized poverty," too. Havana's population was learning to do without. Even Santa Claus had disappeared from Havana's streets at Christmas.

In an attempt to alleviate the difficulties Cuba was facing, in 1974 Castro created the system of *poder popular* (popular power) based on elected local assemblies designed to improve public administration through limited decentralized power. The organs of *poder popular,* still in use today, also serve as forums for citizens' grievances and deal with problems such as garbage collection (with limited success) and the operation of day-care centers. They are not autonomous bodies, however, and the Communist Party closely monitors their performance.

A brief attempt to abandon a sugar-based economy and to industrialize failed, so Castro switched tack and mobilized the entire workforce to achieve a record 10-million-ton sugar harvest by 1970. To achieve the goal, tens of thousands of "voluntary" workers left their jobs in Havana and headed to the countryside. Holidays were abolished. Every inch of arable land was turned over to sugar. Nonetheless, the effort was a failure, leaving the economy in chaos; production everywhere had been severely disrupted and output declined.

Cuba was kept afloat by massive amounts of Soviet aid. In the wake of the Yankees came the Russians, or *bolos* (balls), as the Cubans called them. Rough-hewn and poorly dressed, to the Cubans they acted like peasants. "The women were fat and wore long peasant dresses and headscarves, and the men, ill-fitting suits of poorquality cloth. They sweated heavily in Cuba's heat, but used no deodorant, and to the finicky Cubans, the Russians smelled bad," reports John Anderson. (Alas, by now the Cubans themselves had to make do without deodorant.)

Beneath the triumphalist rhetoric, severe shortages were being felt on the streets. Rising discontent found an outlet in 1980 when 12 Cubans walked through the gates of the Peruvian embassy in Havana and asked for asylum. When the Peruvians refused to hand them over, Castro removed the embassy guards. Within 72 hours, 11,000 Cubans had sought shelter in the embassy. When the foreign press gave the case prominence, Castro decided to allow them to leave. He also seized the opportunity to empty his prisons of dissidents, hardened criminals, homosexuals, and other "antisocial elements." And many innocent "counter-revolutionaries" were coerced to leave. They were joined by tens of thousands of ordinary citizens who had had enough of "socialist paradise." Local CDRs organized hate campaigns against anyone who had the temerity to seek to leave. The Cuban government called them *escoria* (scum), much as Joseph Goebbels called Jews *Ungeziefer* (vermin). Thus, Castro disposed of more than 120,000 critics and disaffected in what is known as the Mariel Boatlift, after the port 45 kilometers west of Havana.

In 1989, the Berlin Wall collapsed, and the Communist dominoes came tumbling down. Goods began to disappear from Havana's shelves. When East German powdered milk ceased to arrive, Cuba eliminated butter; when Czechoslovakian malt no longer arrived, Cuban beer disappeared. Soaps, detergents, deodorants, toilet paper, clothing—everything vanished.

THE SPECIAL PERIOD

You know, when the Soviet Union was paying, it was kind of a party here. The problem is, the party's over.

A character in Martin Cruz Smith's
Havana Bay

In January 1990, Castro declared that Cuba had entered a "Special Period in a Time of Peace." He also announced a draconian, warlike austerity plan. A new slogan appeared on Havana's walls: *"¡Socialismo o muerte!"* (Socialism or death!). Tensions simmered and boiled over on April 21, 1991, when clashes erupted in Havana between *roqueros* (rock-music fans) and police—the first act of spontaneous rebellion since 1959.

Then, on August 18, 1991, on the last day of the highly successful Pan-American Games in Havana (which Cuba won with 140 gold medals), the Soviet Union began its dizzying unraveling. Subsidies and supplies to Cuba virtually ceased. The same year, General Manuel Noriega was ousted in Panama—Cuba's main source for Western goods. Cuba was cast adrift, a lone socialist island in a capitalist sea.

With the umbilical cords severed, Cuba's economy slipped into a coma. The lights went out on the Revolution—literally. After the last Soviet tanker departed, in June 1992, the government began electricity blackouts. There was no air-conditioning, fans, refrigeration, or lights. There was no fuel for transportation. Buses and taxis gave way to *coches*— homemade, horsedrawn carts. Everywhere, human and animal labor replaced oil-consuming machinery.

Without oil or electricity to run machines, or raw materials to process, or spare parts to repair machinery, factories closed down. State bureaucracies began transferring laid-off workers to jobs in the countryside. By the end of 1994, half of Havana's industrial factories had shut down.

Lunch breaks were eliminated so that office workers could leave early to save on electricity. Power outages further disrupted industrial production. Between 1990 and 1994, the economy shrank 34 percent, according to the Cuban government; it was most likely far higher. Once-full nightclubs, restaurants, and hotels all closed. Gaiety on the streets was replaced with a forlorn melancholy. Traffic ground to a halt.

Without their fans or air-conditioners, people couldn't sleep. The *apagones* (blackouts) could last for hours, and ugly and previously unknown incidents began to occur. Crime rose swiftly, and envy and anomie filled the vacuum left by the collapse of the egalitarian promise. Holdups became common. In the rough-and-tumble suburb of Cerro, so many *bodegas* (bars) were robbed that the authorities rigged the area to avoid *apagones.*

Harvests simply rotted in the fields for want of distribution, undermining one of Castro's bedrock promises—that all Cubans would have enough to eat. People accustomed to a government-subsidized food basket guaranteeing every person at least two high-protein, high-calorie meals a day were stunned to suddenly be confronting shortages in almost every staple. The scarcities were manifest in long lines for rationed goods, a phenomenon that had nearly disappeared by the mid-1980s. A kind of line organizers' mafia evolved, selling *turnos* (places) in *la cola* (the queue). *Habaneros* spent their days standing and waiting.

Havana went from down to destitute. Even cigarettes were rationed—to three packs a month. Cubans had to resort to simulating hamburger meat from banana peels and steaks from grapefruit rinds. Many *habaneros* began rearing chickens, pigs, and even *jutías* (ratlike native rodents), while the most desperate resorted to eating rats. Black marketeers were said to be melting condoms and passing the rubber off as cheese on pizzas. Havana's population faced malnutrition on a massive scale. Beggars and *buzos*—people who live off garbage bins—resurfaced.

When state-owned restaurants closed, unauthorized restaurants in private homes—*paladares*—began offering a black-market supply of meals cooked from food "borrowed" by staffers at tourist hotels or purchased from enterprising farmers who sold surplus produce.

Cuba's number one priority was to increase food production. Ground zero in the battle was the fertile agricultural land around Havana, where large tracts of land were switched from export crops to food crops. Vacant land, such as that along roadsides, was cultivated. Vegetable gardens—previously a rare sight—sprouted in the urban centers. Legions of "volunteers" and laid-off workers were shipped from Havana to the countryside to help boost production. However, the massive mobilization of cityfolk to farmlands failed to meet basic needs. Tensions in Havana ran high.

Riots erupted on the streets of Havana, invoking a new wave of repression. While dissidents were being rounded up and jailed, the growing reformist movement found an unexpected ally in Raúl Castro, Fidel's younger brother, who argued for deregulating key sectors of the economy. Fidel—who was now nicknamed *"NiNi"*—"neither nor," as is neither electricity, nor food, nor water, nor anything else—was seen little in pubic during this period; partly, it is suggested, because many Cubans were planning his murder.

In 1993, possession of the dollar was legalized. Private enterprise was also permitted, and enterprising *bisneros* popped up everywhere, mending shoes, tire punctures, and cigarette lighters. The legal availability of dollars eased life for those Cubans who had access to greenbacks, and farmers markets eased life for those without.

Throughout all of this, the exigencies of the Special Period drove the government to revive Cuba's moribund tourism industry, with Old Havana as the natural focus.

Trouble All over Again

On August 5, 1994, crowds gathered along the Malecón in response to a rumor that a major exodus was to be permitted and that a flotilla of boats was en route from Florida. When police attempted to clear the boulevard, a riot ensued. Passions were running dangerously high, and two police officers were killed and 35 people injured. Castro saw a chance to defuse a dangerous situation and benefit at the same time. He declared that Cuba would no longer police the U.S. borders: if the United States would not honor its agreement to allow people to migrate legally, then Cuba would no longer try to prevent anyone from going illegally. The United States was hoisted on its own petard as thousands of *balseros* fled Cuba on makeshift rafts. During the three weeks following Castro's declaration, at least 20,300 Cubans were rescued at sea and shipped to Guantánamo naval base in eastern Cuba. Perhaps as many drowned—a tragic twist on Castro's cry: *"¡Socialismo o muerte!"*.

Meanwhile, a Miami-based volunteer group called Brothers to the Rescue had been operating rescue missions. When the flood of *balseros* stopped, pilots of the organization began buzzing Havana and dropping "leaflets of a subversive nature." On February 24, 1996, two Brothers to the Rescue Cessnas were shot down by Cuban jet fighters, killing both pilots and resulting in a wave of anti-Castro sentiment in Miami and Washington that permitted Sen. Jesse Helms to steer a piece of draconian anti-Cuban legislation—the Helms-Burton Bill—into law. (Castro may have planned the whole affair. In May 1999, U.S. federal agencies had finally pieced together the events leading to the shooting down of the two Brothers to the Rescue planes in 1996. U.S. Attorney General Janet Reno issued indictments against 14 Cuban agents, including several spies rounded up in Miami plus "MX," the code name for the head of Havana's Directorate of Intelligence, and charged them with actively working to provoke the incident in a plot called Operación Alacrán—Operation Scorpion.)

On the domestic front, Havana again felt the pinch as Cubans poured into the city. Lacking the resources to build new housing—and with water, electricity, and transportation services stretched to the limit—a law was passed in May 1997 banning such migration.

About the same time, a series of bombs planted by right-wing-sponsored exiles exploded in Havana's tourist zones with the aim of scaring off a new wave of tourists. The campaign claimed the life of an Italian businessman when a bomb exploded in September 1997 at the Chateau Miramar. The Cubans arrested the culprits: two

Salvadorans reputedly working on behalf of the Cuban-American National Foundation, a leading anti-Castro organization in the United States. The Salvadorans received the death sentence.

CLOSING THE MILLENNIUM

In January 1998, Pope John Paul II made a highly publicized four-day visit to Cuba and delivered a sermon to half a million Cubans in the Plaza de la Revolución. For the occasion, Castro declared Christmas an official holiday, and festive lights went up in the streets for the first time in decades. Buildings along his route were given a quick facelift; and the scaffolding along the Malecón briefly came down for his passing. The pontiff denounced the U.S. embargo as immoral but also appealed for greater political and economic liberty in Cuba, raising cheers from the crowd that were drowned out by piped-in music. The most vociferous dissidents were surrounded by plainclothes police dressed in Red Cross bibs and "disappeared" into Red Cross trucks.

Meanwhile, serious crime such as muggings returned to the streets of Havana. An armored van was even robbed by armed youths in Guanabacoa (an unprecedented occurrence), and two Italian tourists were killed in September 1998 during an armed robbery. Havana developed a significant drug problem, with cocaine and crack sold openly on the street and at discos. Thousands of young Cuban women had also turned to quasi-prostitution as *jineteras,* spawned by the city's overt sexuality and a boomlet of tourists. Low-level corruption among police and government officials was becoming obvious, and a local Mafia was beginning to develop.

The government sensed that it was losing control. When two Cuban *jineteras* died of cocaine overdoses in December 1998, Havana's discos and bars were closed down, and thousands of young men and women were arrested on the streets, accused of prostitution and pimping.

In January 1999, President Clinton announced that he was easing the trade embargo, permitting more cash to be sent to Cuban individuals and nongovernmental organizations. Castro called the move a "fraud" and later that month announced the Law for the Protection of Cuba's National Independence and Economy. This draconian bit of legislation signaled a harsh crackdown throughout Havana. That month, several thousand police from an elite National Brigade were deployed on street corners throughout the city to round up prostitutes and petty hustlers. Hundreds of *jineteras* and innocent bystanders were arrested, as were scores of other hustlers. At least 10 convicted criminals were executed, and, in June 1999, dozens of high officials within the tourism and business sectors were fired for corruption.

The police remain on the streets 24 hours a day. The policy is officially "a battle against that which means disorder, crime, disrespect for authority, illegal business, and lack of social control." Drug traffickers now face the firing squad (drugs have gone underground but are still available; some areas, notably the Sitio area of Centro, south of Salvador Allende, are said to be trafficking centers), and prostitutes face a 24-year jail term. Thankfully, the permanent police presence has cleared the streets of petty thieves and other hoodlums.

Castro got a break in March 1999 when the Baltimore Orioles came to Havana and beat the Cuban Sugar Kings, the national baseball team, 3–2 in the first meeting of a U.S. professional club and a Cuban squad since March 1959. The 50,000-seat stadium was filled with loyal fans of Castro; only party members were invited to attend the game. On May 3, the Cubans got their revenge in Oriole Park, trouncing the Baltimore team 12–6 in a game that had all Havana glued to the TV.

Cuba saw the millennium in with a new battle with Uncle Sam, this one over a five-year-old boy, Elián González, saved by the U.S. Coast Guard after his mother and 10 other people drowned when their boat sank en route from Cuba to Florida during Thanksgiving 1999. Elián, plucked from his inner tube, launched a continuing soap opera. Miami's anti-Castro Cubans and right-wing politicians turned the child into a poster boy for the American Way of Life—a "new Dalai Lama," thought Wayne Smith—and demanded that the boy remain in the United States against the Cuban father's wishes and in defiance of an Immigration and Naturalization Service (INS) order. Castro, who routinely denies permission for the children of Cuban exiles to join their parents abroad, responded by demanding the "kidnapped" boy be returned and turned the issue into an anti-American crusade by organizing "Free Elián" protests and summoning Cubans to attend the nationwide rallies—some teenagers sang their own muffled version of the protest chant, "Elián, our friend! Cuba is with you!" chanting, "Elián, our friend! Take us with you!"

The population of Havana—in fact, of the entire country—was mobilized for mass demonstrations. In January 2000, Castro vowed that protests would last "10 years, if necessary," while the case wound through the Florida courts. In Havana, a new plaza was laid out in front of the U.S. Interests Section, and a US$2 million stage—the José Martí Anti-Imperialist Platform—was erected for rallies to denounce Uncle Sam. While CNN newscasts aired bloated reports about spontaneous passions in Havana, I watched trucks with loudspeakers cruise the streets, summoning loyalists to the demonstrations. Schoolchildren and workers were bused in for these government-orchestrated yet almost festive occasions. Meanwhile Elián's crazed custodians refused to hand him over to his loving father when the latter arrived in the United States in April 2000 to collect his son. In a dawn raid, the INS grabbed Elián and reunited him with his father, who is happily reconciled with life in Cuba. The Cuban government even created a website for Elian: www.elian.cu/elian0.htm.

When the dust had settled, Castro attended a rally and announced: "This is just the beginning. There are 160 more municipalities to rally, and many more issues." A new crackdown on government opponents was initiated.

The Past Few Years

In July 2001, a mass demonstration attended by as many as one million Cubans took part was arranged to protest the jailing of five Cuban spies in Miami. Later that year, Fidel fainted at the podium while giving a televised speech. The mobile phones of foreign journalists covering the event were immediately cut and police immediately appeared outside the houses of dissidents to forestall "trouble."

Following the September 11, 2001, attacks on the United States, tourism to Cuba plummeted. Cuba was dealt a double whammy shortly thereafter when Hurricane Michele swept past Havana in November 2001, causing the evacuation of thousands of residents living in unstable homes. At least 179 homes collapsed during the storm. Meanwhile, in February 2002, thousands of *habaneros* were involved in a campaign to combat an outbreak of dengue fever. Workers, students, and activists were mobilized in a vast fumigation drive.

In March 2002, 22 asylum seekers hijacked a bus and crashed through the gates of the Mexican Embassy in Havana. Police moved in swiftly to prevent others from flooding the embassy grounds, while massed supporters—"rapid action brigades"—where shipped in to chant for Fidel.

The highlight of 2002 was a five-day visit by President Jimmy Carter to Havana . . . the first visit by a U.S. president to Cuba since Calvin Coolidge in 1928. Although Carter traveled as a private citizen, the highly publicized visit had massive political repercussions. Just days before Carter's arrival, dissidents delivered to the National Assembly a petition called Proyecto Varela containing 11,020 signatures demanding sweeping reforms in Cuba. Amazingly, Fidel permitted Carter to address the nation live on TV, without interruption or editing. Carter denounced the U.S. embargo, as Fidel no doubt had wished, but focused primarily on the call for greater freedoms in Cuba and mentioned Proyecto Varela by name . . . the first time most Cubans learned of the organization. No hard feelings: later, Fidel and Carter went to an exhibition game at Estadio Latinoamericano.

Three weeks later, with Carter safely off the island, Castro sought to stamp out the Varela germ by organizing the largest demonstrations in years. Fidel led several hundred thousand *habaneros* on a march past the US Interests Section to affirm the Cuban peoples' unwavering commitment to socialism and the existing constitution. The Castro regime then pulled out of its hat a petition of more than eight million signatures, it claimed, calling for a resolution to amend the constitution to make it "eternal" and "untouchable." Signing wasn't voluntary, however; the government had knocked on everyone's door, with the understanding that serious consequences would follow for those who didn't sign.

Government

The Cuban Constitution, adopted in 1975, defines the independent republic as a "socialist state of workers and peasants and all other manual and intellectual workers." Fidel Castro Ruz is head of both state and government. The constitution names Castro as first secretary of the Communist Party, president of the Republic, chairman of the State Council, chairman of the Council of Ministers, and commander in chief of the armed forces—he is normally referred to as Comandante-en-Jefe, or Commander in Chief. His younger brother, Raúl, is first vice president of both the Council of State and the Council of Ministers, the second secretary of the Communist Party, defense minister, and General of the Army.

All power and initiative are in the hands of the Communist Party (*Partido Comunista de Cuba,* or PCC), which controls the labyrinthine state apparatus. There are no legally recognized political organizations independent of the party. Steering the party is the Comité Central (Central Committee), whose members are selected by Castro. At the base of the PCC chain is the party cell of 10 members organized at work and educational centers. Policy emanates from Castro, who has used his own charismatic qualities and inordinate tactical skills to consolidate almost hegemonic authority. The PCC has no program—Castro defines the flavor of the day.

The highest-ranking executive body is the

Council of Ministers, whose Executive Committee administers Cuba on a day-to-day basis. The council is accountable to the National Assembly of People's Power, which "elects" the members at the initiative of the head of state. However, it is mostly a rubber-stamp legislature and meets only twice annually. The Council of State is modeled on the Presidium of the former Soviet Union and functions as the Executive Committee of the National Assembly when the latter is not in session.

GOVERNMENT BY PERSONAL WHIM

Cuba is really a *fidelista* state, one in which Marxist-Leninism has been loosely grafted onto Cuban nationalism, then tended and shaped by one man. The Cuban leader likes to leave his development choices wide open, allowing a flexible interpretation of the correct path to socialism. Ideological dogma is subordinated to tactical considerations. Castro's emotions, what Castro biographer Tad Szulc calls his *caudillo* temperament (that of a modernizing but megalomaniacal political strongman), are powerful factors in his decision-making.

Castro makes decisions about the minutest aspects of life in Cuba: for example, Fidel chooses who will be Miss Cuba each year, and decided that nurses should wear trousers, not skirts, because a nurse in a skirt leaning over a patient, he suggested impishly, might cause a man lying in a bed behind her to have a heart attack. Even decisions more minor than these are delayed until they have received Castro's blessing.

LOCAL GOVERNMENT

The country is divided into 14 provinces and 169 municipalities (*municipios*), dominated by the city of Havana (a separate province). Havana is governed by an Assembly of Delegates of People's Power, representing state bodies at the local level. The Assembly is headed by Esteban Lazo, the First Secretary of the Communist Party of Havana, a position equivalent to City Mayor.

MASS ORGANIZATIONS

Citizen participation in building socialism is manifested through a number of mass organizations controlled by the PCC. Prominent among them are the Federation of Cuban Women, the Confederation of Cuban Workers, the Organization of Small Farmers, and the Union of Communist Youth. Although ostensibly representing their members' interests, the bodies subordinate these to national goals.

THE JUDICIARY

Courts are a fourth branch of government and are not independent. The judiciary is not charged with protecting individual rights but rather, according to Article 121 of the Constitution, with "maintaining and strengthening socialist legality." Interpretation of the Constitution is the prerogative solely of the National Assembly, not the courts.

The highest court in the land is the People's Supreme Court in Havana. Its president and vice president are appointed by Castro; other judges are elected by the National Assembly. There are seven courts of appeal, 14 provincial courts, and 169 municipal courts for minor offenses. The provinces are divided into judicial districts with courts for civil and criminal cases.

A STATE OF ACQUIESCENCE

Castro has engineered a state where an individual's personal survival requires a display of loyalty and adherence to the Revolution. Cubans have to voice—or fake—their loyalty. To become *integrado* (integrated) is essential to get by, as the government maintains a file on *every* worker, a labor dossier that follows him or her from job to job. Transgressions are reported in one's dossier. If "antisocial" comments are noted, the worker may be kicked out of his or her job, or blackballed. Cuban citizens can hardly make a move without accounting for it to the authorities.

A margin of public criticism is allowed, to vent political pressure. The headiest steam is periodically allowed to leave for Florida on rafts and inflated inner tubes. Otherwise, jail or "spontaneous" acts of repudiation by gangs of "citizens" quickly silence the dissident and serve to put others on notice.

Most Cubans have accommodated themselves to the parameters of permissible behavior set out years ago. The hardcore opponents left for Miami long ago. Most of the rest go along. Wrote James Michener, "Perhaps only the kindness of the climate prevents the smoldering of revolt that might accompany the same conditions in a cold and relentless climate."

COMMITTEES FOR THE DEFENSE OF THE REVOLUTION

The linchpins in maintaining the loyalty of the masses and spreading the Revolution at the grassroots level are the *Comités para la Defensa de la Revolución* (CDRs), created in 1960 as neighborhood committees designed to protect the Revolution from internal enemies. There are 15,000 CDRs in Havana, and 100,000 throughout the island. Every block has one.

On one hand, the CDRs perform wonderful work: they collect blood for hospitals, take retired people on vacations, discourage kids from playing hooky, organize graduation parties, and patrol at night to guard against delinquency. But they are also the vanguard in watching and snitching on neighbors—the CDRs are under the direction of MININT, the Ministry of the Interior, which handles most aspects of state security. Anyone nay-saying the Revolution, mocking Castro, or dealing on the black market (economic crimes are political crimes, seen as a security threat to the state) is likely to be reported by the block warden, a loyal revolutionary or self-serving sycophant who records what he or she hears from colleagues and neighbors.

People face harsh retribution if they cross the line into political activism. In 1991, Rapid Response Detachments were formed, ostensibly made up of volunteers from local CDRs but under the purview of MININT, to deal with public expressions of dissent. This they do through distasteful pogroms called *actos de repudios,* beating up dissidents, much as did Hitler's *Blockwarts.* Like Nazi

street gangs, the brigades are said to be a spontaneous reaction of outraged Cubans.

FIDEL CASTRO

Whatever you think of his politics, Fidel Castro is unquestionably one of the most remarkable and enigmatic figures of this century, thriving on contradiction and paradox like a romantic character from the fiction of his Colombian novelist friend Gabriel García Márquez.

Fidel Castro Ruz, child prodigy, was born on August 13, 1926 at Manacas *finca* near Birán in northern Oriente, the fifth of nine children of Ángel Castro y Argiz. Fidel's father was an émigré to Cuba from Galicia in Spain as a destitute 13 year old. In Cuba, he made money from the presence of the American-owned United Fruit Company and became a wealthy landowner who employed 300 workers on a 26,000-acre domain; he owned 1,920 acres and leased the rest from the United Fruit Company, to whom he sold cane. Fidel's mother was the family housemaid, Lina Ruz González, whom Ángel married after divorcing his wife. Fidel weighed 10 pounds at birth—the first hint that he would always be larger than life. The early records of his family are sketchy, and Castro, who seems to have had a happy childhood, likes to keep it that way— much as he attempts to suppress the notion that he comes from a well-to-do family.

As a boy Fidel was extremely assertive, rebellious, and combative. He was a natural athlete and grew especially accomplished at track events and baseball. He was no sportsman, however; if his team was losing, he would often leave the field and go home. Gabriel García Márquez has said, "I do not think anyone in this world could be a worse loser." (In December 1999, Castro withdrew the Cuban boxing squad from the world amateur boxing championship in Houston because he disagreed with some of the referees' decisions.) It became a matter of principle to excel—and win—at everything. His Jesuit teachers identified what Richard Nixon later saw in Castro: "that indefinable quality which, for good or evil, makes a leader of men." His school yearbook recorded that he was *excelencia* and predicted that "he will fill with brilliant pages the book of his life."

Star Rising

Fidel enrolled in Havana University's law school in October 1945, where he immediately plunged into politics and gained the limelight as a student leader. Castro earned his first front-page newspaper appearance following his first public speech, denouncing President Grau, on November 27, 1946. In 1947, when the foremost political opposition figure, Edward Chibás, formed the *Ortodoxo* party, Castro, at the age of 21, was sufficiently well known to be invited to help organize it. He stopped attending law school and rose rapidly to prominence as the most outspoken critic of the Grau government, including as head of his own revolutionary group, Orthodox Radical Action.

The period was exceedingly violent: armed gangs roamed the campus, and Fidel never went anywhere without a gun. As organizer of the street demonstrations calling for Grau's ouster, Castro was soon on the police hit list, and several attempts were made on his life. In February 1949, Fidel was accused of assassinating a political rival. After being arrested and subsequently released on "conditional liberty," he went into hiding.

He remained determined to stay in the limelight, however. In March, he flew to Bogotá to attend the Ninth Inter-American Conference, where foreign ministers were destined to sign the charter of the Organization of American States. Soon enough, Castro was in the thick of student demonstrations opposing the organization as a scheme for U.S. domination of the hemisphere. One week later, while he was on his way to meet Jorge Eliécer Gaitán (the popular leader of the opposition Progressive Liberal Party), Gaitán was assassinated. Bogotá erupted in spontaneous riots—the *Bogotazo*. Castro was irresistibly drawn in and, arming himself with a tear-gas shotgun and police uniform stolen from a police station, found himself at the vanguard of the revolution—with a police detachment under his command. Inevitably, Castro again made headline news.

On October 12, 1949, Castro married a pretty philosophy student named Mirta Díaz-Balart, and they honeymooned for several weeks in the United States. Fulgencio Batista even gave the couple US$1,000 for their honeymoon; Castro's father-in-law was Batista's attorney. The couple divorced in 1954. Back home, Castro was once again in the thick of political violence. Gangsterism had soared under President Prío. In November, Fidel gave a suicidal speech in which he denounced the gangster process, admitted his past associations with gangsterism, then named all the gangsters, politicians, and student leaders profiting from the "gangs' pact." Again in fear for his life, Fidel left Cuba for the United States.

He returned four months later to cram for a multiple degree. In September 1950, Castro graduated with the title of Doctor of Law—in the press, Fidel is often referred to as Dr. Castro. He then began a law practice, concentrating on "lost causes" on behalf of the poor. Most of his legal work was offered pro bono.

Congressional Candidate

By 1951, Castro was preparing for national office. Fulgencio Batista, who had returned from retirement in Florida to run for president, even asked to receive Castro to get the measure of the young man who in January 1952 shook Cuba's political foundation by releasing a detailed indictment of President Prío. Castro's campaign was far ahead of its time. The imaginative 25-year-old utilized mass mailings and stump speeches with a foresight and veracity theretofore unknown. His personal magnetism, his brilliant speeches, and his apparent honesty aroused the crowds, who cheered him deliriously.

Castro was certain to be elected to the Chamber of Deputies. It was also clear that Batista was going to be trounced in the presidential contest, so at dawn on March 10, 1952, he effected a *golpe* (military coup) and, the next day, moved back into the presidential palace he had vacated eight years before.

Says Tad Szulc: "Many Cubans think that without a coup, Castro would have served as a congressman for four years until 1956, then run for the Senate, and made his pitch for the presidency in 1960 or 1964. Given the fact that Cuba was wholly bereft of serious political leadership and given Castro's rising popularity . . . it would appear that he was fated to govern Cuba—no matter how he arrived at the top job."

The rest, as they say, is history.

A Communist Caudillo

At 30 years old, Castro, a disgruntled lawyer turned revolutionary who craved Batista's job, was fighting in the Sierra Maestra. At 32, he had had it. He was determined not to let go... the last in a long line of self-proclaimed Cuban redeemers who have reneged on their promise. When he came down from the mountains, he was considered a "younger, bearded version of Magwitch: a tall outlaw emerging from the fog of history to make Pips of us all," wrote Guillermo Cabrera Infante, a brilliant novelist who, like thousands, supported Castro but later soured on him: "The outlaw became a law unto himself." Fidel used the Revolution to carry out a personal *caudillista* coup (a *caudillo* is a strongman leader). "Communist or not, what was being built in Cuba was an old-fashioned personality cult," wrote John Anderson.

Castro has since led Cuba through four decades of "dizzying experience." He has outlasted nine U.S. presidents, each of whom predicted his imminent demise and plotted to hasten it by fair means or foul. He shows no sign of relinquishing power and has said he will never do so while Washington remains hostile—a condition he thrives on and works hard to maintain. Castro—who knew he could never carry out his revolution in an elective system—is consummately Machiavellian: masking truth to maintain power. Says Infante, "Castro's real genius lies in the arts of deception and while the world plays bridge by the book, he plays poker, bluffing and holding his cards close to his olive-green chest." "He has lied all his life, although he does not see his 'lies' as lies," suggests biographer Georgie Ann Geyer. "Often the first person he deceived was himself," adds historian Hugh Thomas.

Castro may genuinely believe that disease, malnutrition, illiteracy, economic inadequacy, and dependence on the West are criminal shames and that a better social order can be created through the perfection of good values. One never knows, as *everything* with Castro has a political motive. "Political ideas are worthless if they aren't inspired by noble, selfless sentiments," he has said. "I am sure that all the people could be happy—and for them I would be ready to incur the hatred and ill will of a few thousand individuals, including some of my relatives, half of my acquaintances, two-thirds of my professional colleagues, and four-fifths of my former schoolmates." Says Gabriel García Márquez: "He has the nearly mystical conviction that the greatest achievement of the human being is the proper formation of conscience and that moral incentives, rather than material ones, are capable of changing the world and moving history forward."

Despite the turn of events, Castro clings to the thread of his dream: "I have no choice but to continue being a Communist, like the early Christians remained Christian . . . If I'm told 98 percent of the people no longer believe in the Revolution, I'll continue to fight. If I'm told I'm the only one who believes in it, I'll continue."

Nonetheless, he is far from the saint his ardent admirers portray.

A Hatred of Uncle Sam

Castro turned to Communism mostly for strategic, not ideological, reasons—Graham Greene determined that Castro was "an empirical Marxist, who plays Communism by ear and not by the book," but his bitterness towards the United States undoubtedly also shaped his decision. He has been less committed to Marxism than to anti-imperialism, in which he is unwavering: he has chosen, suggests Geyer, a "classic Massada posture of eternal and suicidal confrontation against the Americans." He has cast himself in the role of David versus Goliath, in the tradition of José Martí, who wrote "my sling is the sling of David." Castro sees himself as Martí's heir, representing the same combination of New World nationalism, Spanish romanticism, and philosophical radicalism. His trump card is Cuban nationalist sentiment.

Castro's boyhood impressions of destitution

in Holguín province under the thumb of the United Fruit Company and, later, the 1954 overthrow of the reformist Árbenz government in Guatemala by a military force organized by the CIA and underwritten by "Big Fruit," had a profound impact on Castro's thinking. Ever since, Castro has viewed world politics through the prism of anti-Americanism. During the war in the Sierra Maestra, Castro stated, "When this war has ended, a much bigger and greater war will start for me, a war I shall launch against them. I realize this will be my true destiny."

He brilliantly used the Cold War to enlist the Soviet Union to move Cuba out of the U.S. orbit, and was thus able—with Soviet funds—to bolster his stature as a nationalist redeemer by guaranteeing the Cuban masses substantial social and economic gains while exerting constant energy and creativity to maintain an antagonistic relationship against the United States. Though the Cold War is over, he appears like Napoleon on St. Helena, thought Wendy Gimbel, a prisoner of his own fantasies, "playing on the floor with his tin soldiers, recreating his victories in battles ended long ago."

Castro, however, has no animosity towards North Americans. His many close personal contacts range from media maverick Ted Turner to actor Jack Lemmon and even the Rockefeller clan.

Many Talents

Castro has a gargantuan hunger for information. An avid speed-reader with a prodigious memory, he never forgets facts and figures, a remarkable asset he nourished at law school, where he forced himself to depend on his memory by destroying the materials he had learned by heart. There is a sense of perfection in everything he does, applied through a superbly methodical mind and laser-clear focus. He has astounding political instincts, notably an uncanny ability to predict the future moves of his adversaries—it goes without saying that Castro is a masterly chess player. Castro's "rarest virtue," says his intimate friend Gabriel García Márquez, "is the ability to foresee the evolution of an event to its farthest-reaching consequences."

Castro is also a gambler of unsurpassed self-confidence. His daring and chutzpah are attributed by some observers to his stubborn Galician temperament—that of an anarchist and born *guerrillero* (guerrilla fighter). He has stood at the threshold of death several times and loves to court danger. For example, in 1981, he chose to run to the Mexican port of Cozumel in a high-speed launch just to see whether the U.S. Navy—then patrolling the Gulf of Mexico to stop Cuban arms shipments to Nicaragua—could catch him.

Above all, Castro has an insatiable appetite for the limelight, and a narcissistic focus on his theatrical role: the one thing that infuriates Fidel is to be ignored. Says Mead: "Castro needs international celebrity the way a fire needs oxygen." His vanity is so monumental that on one of his rare visits to see his illegitimate and ignored daughter, Alina, he asked if she wanted to see a movie. She wanted to see *The Godfather*, but instead her father treated her to a screening of a film about his triumphal tour of Eastern Europe. His beard is also more than a trademark; he likes to hide his double chin. Likewise, he wears false teeth, and his long fingernails are lacquered and filed. He never laughs at himself unless he makes the joke. And he assiduously avoids singing or dancing—he is perhaps the only male in Cuba who has never been seen to dance.

He nurtures his image with exquisite care, feigning modesty to hide his immense ego. "I am not here because I assigned myself to this job . . . I am here because this job has been thrust upon me," Castro told journalist Ann Louise Bordach in 1994. He sees himself as a leader of vast international significance. He also claims that his place in history does not bother him: "All the glory in the world can fit into a kernel of corn." Yet in the same breath he likens himself to Jesus Christ, one of his favorite allusions—the reason Castro didn't object to pictures of Jesus next to him, went a joke during the Pope's visit to Cuba in 1998, is because he thought it was another picture of himself. Castro has carefully cultivated the myth of Fidel the Christ-like redeemer figure. "He had the 'Jordan River' syndrome," Cuban psychiatrist Dr. Rubén Darío Rumbaut told Geyer, "If people came to him, they would be purified." Adds journalist Michael Paterniti, of

Fidel's loquacious speeches: "He keeps you there until he thinks you've been saved. He is convinced of his power to convince."

Castro's revolutionary concept has been built on communicating with the masses (whom he sees and treats as his "children"), and he conducts much of his domestic government through his frequent public speeches, usually televised in entirety. He understood at an early stage that he and television were made for each other. Castro—"one of the best television actors in the world"—is masterfully persuasive, an amazingly gifted speaker who holds Cubans spellbound with his oratory textured in rich, gilded layers, using his trademark combination of flattery and enigmatic language to obfuscate and arouse. Says the *Wall Street Journal:* "Say this for Fidel: the man knows spin."

His speeches often last for hours. Fidel's loquaciousness is legendary. When he and Raúl were imprisoned together on the Isle of Pines in 1954, Raúl complained that his elder brother "didn't let me sleep for weeks . . . he just talked day and night, day and night." He is not, however, a man of small talk; he is deadly serious whenever he opens his mouth. He also listens intently when the subject interests him; he is a great questioner, homing immediately in on the heart of the matter.

Adored or Hated?

A large segment of Cubans see Castro as a ruthless dictator who cynically betrayed the democratic ideals that he used to rally millions to his banner. To Miami exiles especially, *El Líder* is just a common tyrant. Nonetheless, Castro retains the admiration of many among the Cuban people to whom he was and remains a hero. There persists an adulation for *El Máximo* or *El Caballo* (the horse—an allusion to the Chinese belief that dreams represent numbers to place bets on, and that the horse is number one). Traveling through Cuba you'll come across families who keep a framed photograph of him, though many do so to keep in Fidel's good books. You'll even hear of women offering themselves to Fidel, "drawn by his power, his unfathomable eyes."

Cubans' bawdy street wisdom says that Castro has various domiciles—a sane precaution in view of the CIA's numerous attempts on his life—so that he can attend to his lovers. Certainly, many highly intelligent and beautiful women have dedicated themselves to Castro and his cause. But Fidel saves his most ardent passions for the Revolution, and the women in his life have been badly treated, as *Havana Dreams,* the biography of his former lover, Naty Revuelta, reveals. Delia Soto del Valle, Castro's wife of 30-odd years and with whom he has five sons, is rarely seen in public, and never with her husband. The average Cuban in the street knows virtually nothing of the private life of their secretive leader. The Cuban media are prohibited from reporting on Castro's personal life, and photos of his wife—a former schoolteacher from Trinidad—and their children have never been published in Cuba. They live relatively austerely and secluded, far from the limelight in a two-house complex in Jaimanitas; they travel with tight security whenever they venture out.

Castro is a "dilettante extraordinaire" in esoteric pursuits, notably gourmet dining (but not cigars; Fidel quit smoking in 1985). His second love is deep-sea fishing. He is also a good diver and used to frequently fly down to spearfish at his tiny retreat on Cayo Piedra, where he dined on an offshore barge and slept in a rustic old caretaker's home while guests relaxed more luxuriously in a modern guesthouse.

Castro retains the loyalty of millions of Cubans, but he is only loyal to those who are loyal to him. His capacity for Homeric rage is renowned, and it is said that no official in his right mind dares criticize him. Paradoxically, he can be extremely gentle and courteous, especially towards women, in whose company he is slightly abashed. Cubans fear the consequences of saying anything against him, discreetly stroking their chins—an allusion to his beard—rather than uttering his name. He feels that to survive he must be "absolutely and undeviatingly uncompromising." In 1996, his biographer Tad Szulc wrote, "He is determined not to tolerate any challenge to his authority, whatever the consequences." You are either for the Revolution or against it. Castro does not forget, or pardon.

Beneath the gold foil lies a heart of cold steel—Castro's former mentor at the Colegio de Belén, Father Armando Llorente, noted that he "had the cruelty of the Gallego . . . The Spaniard of the north is cruel, hard." Thus, while he has always shown solicitude for those who have served him or the Revolution, he demands, for example, that loyalists sever personal ties with family members who have turned their backs on Cuba. His policies have divided countless families, and Castro's family is no exception. His sister, Juanita, left for Miami in 1964 and is an outspoken critic of her brother's policies; and his tormented daughter, Alina Fernández Revuelta, fled in disguise in 1993 and vilifies her father from her home in Miami. Castro's long-suffering former wife, Mirta Díaz-Balart, lives in Spain.

Castro denies that a personality cult exists. Yet Castro lives, suggests Szulc, "bathed in the absolute adulation orchestrated by the propaganda organs of the regime." Although there are no streets or public edifices named for him, monuments, posters, and billboards are adorned with his quotations and face. His visage is the banner of the daily newspaper, *Granma,* while the front page of newspapers and the lead item on the evening television news are devoted to Castro's public acts or speeches. At school gatherings and public rallies around the country, stooges work the crowds with chants of "Fi-del! Fi-del!" And the historical record has been rewritten to reflect his monumental and pervasive will.

Given his innate conviction of destiny and unquenchable thirst to lead, the indefatigable Cuban leader, who turned 76 in 2002 and has outlasted all other leaders of his time, could be around for many years.

Doctors say Castro maintains a mostly vegetarian diet and works out every day on an exercise bicycle. And his family is renowned for longevity. But rumors persist of ill health, including a recent, undisclosed stroke. Castro is clearly ailing, if not dying. At times he seems gaunt and pale, his speech seems incoherent and faltering, and he now increasingly walks with aides supporting his arms. His fainting spell in 2001 was the first hint that his end is coming.

CHE GUEVARA AND THE "NEW MAN"

Ernest "Che" Guevara was born into a leftist middle-class family in Rosario, Argentina, in 1928. He received a medical degree from the University of Buenos Aires in 1953, then set out on an eight-month motorcycle odyssey through South America that had a profound influence on his radical thinking.

In 1954, he spent a brief period working as a volunteer doctor in Guatemala and was on hand when the Árbenz government was overthrown by a CIA-engineered coup. Guevara helped organize the leftist resistance, and his experience left him intensely hostile to the United States. He fled Guatemala and went to Mexico where, in November 1955, he met Fidel Castro and, seeing in him the characteristics of a "great leader," joined the revolutionary cause.

The two had much in common. Guevara was a restless soul who, like Castro, was also daring and courted danger. They were both brilliant intellectuals: Guevara wrote poetry and philosophy and was probably the only true intellectual in Cuba's revolutionary leadership. Each had a relentless work ethic, total devotion, and an incorruptible character. Although the handsome, pipe-smoking rebel was a severe asthmatic, with an acute allergic reaction to mosquitoes, Che also turned out to be Castro's best field commander, eventually writing two books on guerrilla warfare that would become standard texts for Third World revolutionaries. He commanded the Third Front in the Sierra Escambray and led the attack that on December 28, 1958 captured Santa Clara and finally toppled the Batista regime. It was Che Guevara who took command of Havana's main military posts on New Year's Day 1959.

Shaping the Revolution

The revolutionary regime declared Guevara a native Cuban citizen as an act of gratitude, rendering him legally entitled to hold office in Cuba. Che (the word is an affectionate Argentinian appellation, literally "you" but colloquially meaning "pal" or "buddy") became head of the National

Bank of Cuba and Minister of Finance and, in 1961, Minister of Industry. He also led the tribunals that dispensed with scores of Batista supporters—Guevara never flinched from pulling the trigger himself—and was instrumental in the general repression that was meant to crush "counter-revolutionaries." To U.S. officials, says biographer Jon Lee Anderson, he was "the fearsome Rasputin of the regime." His mystical influence on others attracted to him a crowd of fanatically loyal disciples, *los hombres del Che.* (Once, Che—a notoriously bad driver—rammed a car from behind. The driver leaped out, swearing, but seeing Che he turned craven: "Che, Comandante! What an honor it is to have been struck by you!" he exclaimed, caressing his dent.) Nonetheless, he narrowly escaped an assassination attempt on February 24, 1961, outside his home on Calle 18 in Miramar.

Guevara supervised the radical economic re-

Che . . . revolutionary icon

forms that swept through Cuba and embraced the Soviet Union with innocent fervor as a bulwark for the coming break with the United States. He negotiated the trade deals with the Soviet Union and COMECON countries—Soviet representative Alexandr Alexiev said, "Che was practically the architect of our relations with Cuba."

Meanwhile, Guevara's grand ambition was to export peasant revolution around the world: Che "had become the high priest of international revolution," says Anderson. "Stealthily, Che was setting up the chessboard for his game of continental guerrilla warfare, the ultimate prize being his homeland." He worked ceaselessly to goad a conflict between the Soviet Union and United States. The forces he helped set in motion in Latin America created a dark period of revolutionary violence and vicious counter-repression throughout the continent.

Creating the "New Man"

Guevara was a "complete Marxist"—though born into a bourgeois family, he developed an obsessive hatred of bourgeois democracy—who despised the profit motive and U.S. interests. He believed that the "selfish motivations" that determine behavior in a capitalist system would become obsolete when collective social welfare became the stated goal. Che set out his thoughts in an essay, "Man and Socialism in Cuba," in which he explained the difference in motivation and outlook between people in capitalist and socialist societies. He believed that the notion of material value lay at the root of capitalist evil. Man himself became a commodity. Meanwhile, liberty eroded moral values: individualism was selfish and divisive and essentially detrimental to social development. At the heart of the revolution was the elimination of individualism.

To build socialism, a new ethos and consciousness must be built. By removing market forces and profit or personal gain, replacing these with production for the social good and planning instead of market "anarchy," a new individual would emerge committed to a selfless motivation to help shape a new society. Castro agreed with Guevara—though probably for Machiavellian, not philosophical, motives—and a revolution to create the New Man was launched. It called for collective spartanism shaped by Castro's personal belief in sacrifice. Che set the example and lived up to his own severe dictates: he was unrelentingly moralistic. He became austere and deadly serious, casting aside his trademark humor. He "brutalized his own sensitivities," said his father. If he could do it, so could others.

The government moved to censure work for personal benefit. Bonuses and other financial incentives were replaced with "moral incentives"; consumerism was replaced by the notion of "collective and individual satisfaction" from work. Private enterprise and trade were banned. Ideological debate was quelled. Apathy was frowned on. And psychological and other pressures bore down on anyone who refused to go along with the new values imposed from above.

For many Cubans, the idea of the New Man struck a resonant chord, because the Revolution came from the people themselves, not against their will or in spite of them (that is, unless you were one of the unfortunates whose business or property were being seized). This nourished the concept of collective responsibility and duty, subordinating liberty for the common good. There was nothing the believers wouldn't do. The state didn't even need to ask. "No one worked from eight to five," a 59-year-old woman told reporter Lynn Darling. "You worked around the clock. The horizons were open. We had a world to conquer, a world to give to our grandchildren."

Over time, an intrinsic sense of egalitarianism and dignity was nourished and seeped into the Cuban persona, as many individuals strove to embody the New Man ideal (not everyone agreed: more than a million Cubans opted to leave rather than suffer the crushing suppression of individual freedoms). Cubans spread their spirit throughout the Third World, helping the poor and the miserable.

Fall from Grace

However, Guevara was greatly at odds with Castro on fundamental issues. Castro's scheme to institutionalize the Revolution hand-in-hand with the Soviets, for example, ran counter to Guevara's beliefs—Guevara considered the Soviet Union as rapacious as the capitalists.

Although they were intellectual equals, in many ways Che Guevara and Fidel Castro were unmatched. Where Castro was pragmatic, Guevara was ideological. And Guevara was fair-minded toward Cubans critical of the Castro regime, unlike Castro. Guevara gradually lost his usefulness to Fidel's revolution. His frankness eventually disqualified him, forcing him into suicidal exile.

Guevara left Cuba in early 1965. He renounced all his positions in the Cuban government as well as his honorary Cuban citizenship. Guevara apparently severed his ties with Cuba voluntarily, although the reasons have never been adequately explained.

Death and Eternal Glory

Che was convinced that revolution was the only remedy for Latin America's social inequities ("revolution cleanses men") and advocated peasant-based revolutionary movements. He fought briefly in the Congo with the Kinshasa rebels before returning in secret to Cuba. He reemerged in 1966 in Bolivia, where he unsuccessfully attempted to rouse the Bolivian peasantry to revolutionary passions . . . reflecting his ambition, in his own words, "to create another Vietnam in the Americas" as a prelude to another—and, he hoped, definitive—world war in which socialism would be triumphant. Che was betrayed to the Bolivian Army Rangers by the peasants he had hoped to set free. He died on October 9, 1967, ambushed and executed along with several loyal members of the Cuban Communist Party.

Critics claim that he was abandoned by Castro, who may have foreseen the benefits that would derive from Che as martyr. Castro has since built an entire cult of worship around Che. He has become an icon, exploited as a "symbol of the purest revolutionary virtue" and lionized for his glorious martyrdom and lofty ideals. Che Guevara became the official role model of the *hombre nuevo*, the New Man. The motto *seremos como Che* ("we will be like Che") is the official slogan of the Young Pioneers, the nation's youth organization.

His image is everywhere. The photographer Korda shot the famous image that will live to eternity—"The Heroic Guerrilla"—showing Guevara wearing a windbreaker zippered to the neck, in his trademark black beret with five-point revolutionary star, his head tilted slightly, "his eyes burning just beyond the foreseeable future," wrote Tom Miller.

Che has been turned into a modern myth the world over. He became a hero to the New Left radicals of the 1960s for his persuasive and purist Marxist beliefs. He believed in the perfectibility of man, although his own mean streak and manically irresponsible actions are glossed over by leftists. The ultimate tribute perhaps came from the French philosopher Jean-Paul Sartre, who honored Guevara as "the most complete man of our age."

In 1997 Che's remains were delivered to Cuba and interred in Santa Clara.

The Habaneros

The population of Havana is approximately 2.2 million, or 19.9 percent of Cuba's population, which on December 31, 2001, totaled 11,243,358 inhabitants (the last census was undertaken in 1981; however, the Cuban government has a firm grasp on who's who and where). The people of Havana are called *habaneros* (*habaneras* for women).

Their lives are so surreal that society is not easy to fathom. *Habaneros* "adore mystery and continually do their damnedest to render everything more intriguing. Conventional rules do not apply," notes author Juliet Barclay. Adds author Pico Iyer: "When it came to ambiguity, Cuba was the leader of the pack. An ironist can have a field day."

THE ETHNIC MIX

The 1993 census reported that, officially, about 66 percent of the population are "white," mainly of Spanish origin. About 12 percent are black, and 22 percent are mulattoes of mixed ethnicity. In reality, the percentage of mulattoes is far greater, and certainly more than 50 percent of the population.

Havana's population has grown markedly darker since the Revolution. More than two million Cubans have left the island since 1959. The vast majority were urban and white (98 percent of Miami's Cuban-exile community is white), and the vacuum drew in thousands of blacks from the countryside.

Race Relations

Slavery has burdened many countries of the Americas with racial and social problems still unresolved today. But Cuba has gone further than any other to untangle the Gordian knot. Cuban society is more intermixed than any other on earth, and racial harmony is evident everywhere on the streets of Havana.

Despite slavery, by Caribbean norms Cuba has been a "white" society, whose numbers were constantly fed by a steady inpouring of immigrants from Spain. After emancipation in 1888, the island was spared the brutal segregation of the American South. There was significant mobility and opportunity. To be sure, a color code prevailed, with the whites at the top and the pure-blooded blacks at the bottom. But the caste system was much more subtle and flexible than that of the United States and other Caribbean islands, such that citizens of all colors mingled freely and a significant black middle class evolved, with its own social clubs, restaurants, and literature. However, many blacks in Havana lived as described by Ernest Hemingway in *Islands in the Stream:* "The lean-to was built at a steep slant and there was barely room for two people to lie down in it. The couple who lived in it were sitting in the entrance cooking coffee in a tin can. They were Negroes, filthy, scaly with age and dirt, wearing clothing made from old sugar sacks."

Jim Crow came to Cuba with the boom in Yankee tourism in the 1920s and '30s, and legal racial segregation gradually became the norm in Washington's Caribbean protectorate. Capitalist Cuba eventually boasted "whites only" clubs, restaurants, schools, hotels, beaches, recreation centers, and housing areas, as well as discrimination in job

BRINGING JIM CROW TO CUBA

Cuban society has been triple-tiered in social color terms. At the base are the pure-blooded blacks. In the middle, the mixed bloods. At the top, the whites and near-whites. But these lines have never been as tightly drawn as in the other Caribbean islands. "The British islands are the worst in this respect. The Latin Islands are more careless concerning racial matters," observed black writer Langston Hughes, in the 1920s. He also thought Havana's color lines to be "much more flexible than that of the United States, and much more subtle. There are no Jim Crow cars in Cuba, and at official state gatherings and less official carnivals and celebrations, citizens of all colors meet and mingle." Nonetheless, a separate culture had developed, and Havana had its own black social clubs and fine restaurants for the black middle classes.

Unfortunately, American tourists who began flocking in the 1920s and '30s brought Southern racial prejudice to their winter playground. To court the approval of racially bigoted yankees, hotels that were formerly lax in their application of color lines began to discourage even mulatto Cubans. The Biltmore club, which had taken over the city's only wide, clean stretch of beach, now charged a dollar for the privilege of its use (no small sum in those days) and introduced a color bar as well, although mulatto plutocrats and policemen still mingled there. Later, in the 1950s, even President Batista would be blackballed by the Havana Yacht Club because he was mulatto. Havana society of the time, wrote Hugh Thomas, was "one in which relations between black and white were of an extreme, if tolerant complexity, endogamy combined with joint preoccupation with Afro-Cuban cults as well as left wing politics. The prejudices which kept blacks from the new luxury hotels of the late 1950s were still things of the future."

know that although he was president, as a mulatto he was not welcome.

In the late 1950s, Cuba's revolutionary government outlawed institutionalized discrimination and vigorously enforced laws to bring about racial equality. Castro said: "We can't leave the promotion of women, Blacks, and mestizos to chance. It has to be the work of the party: we have to straighten out what history has twisted."

There is no doubt that the Cuban government has achieved marvelous things. By replacing the social structures that allowed racism to exist, the Revolution has made it virtually impossible for any group to be relegated forever to racial servitude. As a whole, Afro-Cubans are far healthier, better educated, and more skilled and confident than blacks in Brazil, Colombia, Panama, Jamaica, Haiti, or the urban underclass of the United States. Hence, blacks are, on the whole, more loyal to Castro than whites.

The social advantages that opened up after the Revolution have resulted in the abolition of lily-white scenes. Mixed marriages no longer raise eyebrows. Everyone shares a Cubanness. Black novelist Alice Walker, who knows Cuba well, has written, "Unlike black Americans, who have never felt at ease with being American, black Cubans raised in the Revolution take no special pride in being black. They take great pride in being Cuban. Nor do they appear able to feel, viscerally, what racism is." (A negative perspective is offered by Carlos Moore, an Afro-Cuban writer who left Cuba in 1963, in his *Castro, the Blacks, and Africa,* Center for Afro-American Studies, University of California, Los Angeles, 1988, available through www.cubabooks.com.)

AfroCuba Web, www.afrocubaweb.com, offers information on all things related to Afro-Cuban affairs.

Behind the Veil

The Revolution has achieved what appears to be a truly color-blind, multiracial society. Yet there are still cultural barriers and subtle and not-so-subtle discrimination. Some social venues attract an almost exclusively white crowd, while others are virtually all-black affairs. Most Cuban blacks still work at menial jobs and earn, on average, less

hiring. By the 1940s, racism had become so endemic among the elite that when dictator Fulgencio Batista—who was a mixture of white, black, and Chinese—arrived at the exclusive Havana Yacht Club, they turned the lights out to let him

than whites. The most marginal Havana neighborhoods still have a heavy preponderance of blacks. Blacks are notoriously absent from the upper echelons of government—an exception is Esteban Lazo—aka King Kong—the black First Secretary of the Communist Party of Havana, a position equivalent to City Mayor. Blacks are virtually absent on the professional model scene and, until recently, nowhere to be seen in tourist promotion materials. And blacks suffer a disproportionate degree of harassment from the police. They're also far more likely to come up against tourist apartheid, such as being prevented from entering hotel lobbies. Tourism apartheid isn't so obvious in Havana, but in the provinces, official apartheid policy that bars Cubans from mingling with tourists—usually relegated to specific restaurants and nightclubs—is most frequently applied when the Cuban is black.

Nor has the Revolution totally overcome stereotypical racial thinking and prejudice. Racist comments can still be heard, and many Cuban mulattoes prefer to define their racial identity with whites rather than with blacks—prior to the Revolution, it was common for mulattoes with lighter skin to be referred to as *más adelantados*—more advanced.

At the other extreme, the State is not about to permit any organizations specifically representing the interests of blacks—when black Communist Walterio Carbonell tried to organize a Cuban branch of Black Power, he was condemned to hard labor.

Still, most racial references—and Cuba is full of them—are well-meaning (see Cuban Spanish in the Resources).

CHARACTER, CONDUCT, AND CUSTOMS

Cubans are somewhat schizoid. In the four decades since the Revolution, most *habaneros* have learned to live double lives. One side is spirited, inventive, irrepressibly argumentative and critical, inclined to keep private shrines at home to both Christian saints and African gods, and profits however possible from the failings and inefficiencies of the state. The other side commits

SPANISH SURNAMES

Spanish surnames are combinations of the first surname of the person's father, which comes first, and the mother's first surname, which comes second. Thus, the son of Ángel Castro Argiz and Lina Ruz González is called Fidel Castro Ruz.

After marriage, women do not take their husbands' surnames; they retain their maiden names.

A single woman is addressed as *señorita* if less than 40 years old, and *señora* if above 40.

to being a good revolutionary and to cling to the state and the man who runs it. Hence, Havana is a divided society populated by two sets of people: revolutionary stalwarts and those who long for the return of their individual liberty. Both groups, however, hold an innate Cubanness in common, and in many regards the distinctions are blurred.

The Cubans' value context, their philosophical approach to life differs markedly from North American or northern European values. Thus, attempts to analyze Cuba through the North American value system is bound to be wide of the mark. For example, most North Americans don't understand what the "Revolution" means. When Cubans speak of the Revolution, they don't mean the toppling of Batista's regime, Castro's seizure of power, or even his and the country's conversion to Communism. They mean the ongoing process of building a society where everyone supposedly benefits and the individual lives motivated by concern for fellow beings before himself. Their philosophical framework is different. Most Cubans, regardless of their feelings for Castro, take varying degrees of pride in the achievements of the Revolution, and, at least until the onset of the Special Period, many *habaneros* were happy to accept the sacrifice of individual liberties for the sake of improving equality. Those who did not were jailed, or chose exile or sullen silence.

Most *habaneros* hold a broad view of "democracy," based on a commitment to social justice and equality. The idea that democracy includes every person's right to culture and guaranteed health care and education—the twin jewels in the revolutionary crown—is deeply ingrained in their consciousness. This has less to do with an innate Cuban characteristic than with four decades of indoctrination in *fidelismo,* whose tenets call for puritanism, morality, and revolutionary loyalty.

As such, most *habaneros* are not concerned with the accumulation of material wealth, although this is changing. Unlike North Americans, they are not individual "consumpto-units." Instead, they find gratification in developing their strengths and, in rising to the challenges of love, restraint, and raising children. Most Cubans are more interested in sharing something with you than getting something from you. Cubans call each other *compañero* or *compañera,* which has a cozy sound of companionship. They are unmoved by talk of your material accomplishments. It is more important that everyone has more than the basic minimum—more important, too, to live life. Four decades of socialism have not changed Cubans' hedonistic culture. Only the scale of the dreams have changed.

Although it puts onerous restrictions on individual liberty, Castro's government has attempted to maximize its human potential, and despite several obvious failings, its education system is justifiably a source of national pride. It is a joy to hear throughout the city the intelligent voices of an educated and evocatively philosophical people. In general, *habaneros* are highly knowledgeable, often displaying an astonishing level of intellectual development and erudition. Their conversations are spiced with literary allusions and historical references thanks to the extraordinary success of the literacy campaign initiated after the revolution. On the downside, the hyper-educated population is hard pressed to find books, and the panorama is severely circumscribed: only politically acceptable works are allowed.

Cuban women are astute and self-assured, and Cuban men are sentimental. The struggles of the past four decades have fostered a remarkable sense of confidence and maturity. As such, there's no reserve, no emotional distance, no holding back. *Habaneros* engage you in a very intimate way. They're not afraid of physical contact; they touch a lot. They also look you in the eye; they don't blink or flinch but are direct, assured, and free of social pretension. They're alive and full of *chispas* (spark) and emotional intensity.

The economic crisis and demise of socialism elsewhere in the world has fostered an identity crisis; even the most dedicated Communists admit their fears about the future, particularly that a loss of values, morals, and solidarity is eroding the principles of the "New Man"—Che Guevara's dream of an individual inspired by noble virtue, willing to sacrifice his or her individual whims for the social good and the common well-being of neighbors and community. There is perhaps no more exemplary benefit of the Revolution than the incredible value system that has infused Cuban society and individuals with gracious and noble virtues. "All of a sudden money is necessary. As always money crushes everything in its path. Thirty-five years spent constructing the new man. And now it's all over. Now we've got to make ourselves into something different, and fast," wrote Pedro Juan Gutiérrez in *Dirty Havana Trilogy* (see Suggested Reading). The *jineteras,* the petty thieves on the streets, the children who are now taught to beg: all these things are the result of Cuba's poverty. The New Man— one of the Revolution's greatest gifts—is slowly dying. "The world is poorer for the loss of that intangible, optimistic, altruistic spirit," says Saul Landau. Indeed it is.

Social Divisions and Family Life

The Revolution destroyed the social stratification inherited from Spanish colonial rule. Distinct delineations among the classes withered away. Not that prerevolutionary Cuba was rigid—it was unusual in Latin America for its high degree of social mobility. For example, Castro's father was a poor farm laborer when he emigrated from Spain but rose to become a wealthy landowner in Cuba. Havana boasted a huge middle class that lived a characteristically North American middle-class way of life. As an agrarian-populist movement pitted against Havana-based "bourgeois" interests, *fidelismo* warred against the middle class and destroyed it, or chased its away. The old privileged class has been replaced by a *nueva clase* of senior Communist Party members who enjoy benefits unavailable to other Cubans; the old underclass has been replaced by a class of outcasts who do not support the revolutionary government and have therefore been deprived of social benefits.

Habaneros lack the social caste system that makes so many Europeans walk on eggshells. There is absolutely no deference, no subservience. *Habaneros* accept people at face value and are slow to judge others negatively. They are instantly at ease, and greet each other with hearty handshakes or kisses. Women meeting for the first time will embrace like sisters. A complete stranger is sure to give you a warm *abrazo* (hug). Even the most fleeting acquaintances will offer you a meal or go out of their way to help you. As a foreigner, you'll meet with the warmest courtesies wherever you go, although this is nothing new: last century, Anthony Trollope reported that "they welcome you with easy courtesy; offer you coffee or beer; assure you at parting that their whole house is at your disposal; and then load you—at least they so loaded me—with cigars." There is a profound spirituality to the Cubans, who give love because they have little else to give.

Habaneros are uncommonly generous, extremely courteous and gracious, and self-sacrificing to a fault. They can't understand why foreigners are always saying, "Thank you!" Doing things for others is the expected norm. Cubans rarely say "thank you" when they receive gifts—which you, the wealthy foreigner, may be expected to provide.

The city's social life revolves around the family and, to a lesser degree, friends and neighbors. Cubans are a gregarious people, and foreigners are often amazed by the degree to which Cubans exist in the public eye, carrying on their everyday lives behind wide-open windows visible to the streets as if no one were looking. To Cuban passersby, this is nothing remarkable, but foreigners can't resist satisfying their curiosity and taking a gander at what might be happening inside.

Many families are torn by divided feelings towards the Revolution and Castro and don't even talk with one another. The worst divisions, fired by true hatred, are found among family split between those who departed for Miami and those who stayed. *Se fue* (he/she left) and *se quedó* (he/she stayed) carry profound meaning. Every year tens of thousands plot their escapes to Miami, often without telling their relatives, and sometimes not even their spouse. Cubans thus tend to evolve speedy relationships and/or grasp at opportunity. "All the Cubans' experience tells them that there is no time to go slow, that pleasures and love must be taken fast when they present themselves because tomorrow . . . *se fue*," wrote Lightfoot.

Cuban Curiosity

A sense of isolation and a high level of cultural development have filled *habaneros* with intense curiosity. One reason why so many Cubans ask foreigners *"¿Qué hora es?"* is to strike up a conversation—another reason is that they really do need to know the time in a country where time stopped years ago. They will guess at your nationality and quiz you about the most prosaic matters of Western life, as well as the most profound. Issues of income and costs are areas of deep interest, and you may be questioned in intimate detail. Sexual relations arouse equally keen interest (Cubans discuss sex forthrightly), and Cubans of both genders are often eager to volunteer their services to help guide Cupid's arrow.

If you tell them you are a *yanqui,* most Cubans light up. They are genuinely fond of U.S. citizens and keen to discuss international affairs and philosophies, although the minority who remain ardent revolutionaries still harbor suspicions. *Habaneros* want to know about the outside world and resent being kept in the dark by their government. They watch Hollywood movies and often converse with a surprising mix of worldly wise erudition and naiveté in a nation where only information endorsing a virulently anti-U.S. posture makes the news. They often will pepper you with questions.

Although *habaneros* thrive on debate, they hesitate to discuss politics openly, except behind closed doors, and only then when it is felt you can be trusted. Then, the vitriol felt for the system and you-know-who comes pouring out. Although *his* name is never used, the silent reference is usually communicated by the gesture of a hand stroking a beard. Only rarely will someone open up to you publicly with sometimes unexpected frankness—in which case you should be cautious!

Humor

Despite their hardships, Cubans have not lost the ability to laugh. Their renowned humor is called the "yeast for their buoyant optimism about the future." Stand-up comedy is a tradition in Havana's nightclubs, and *chistes* (jokes) race around the city.

Habaneros turn everything into a *chiste,* most of which are aimed at themselves. Their penetrating black humor spares no one—the insufferable bureaucrat, *jineteras,* the Special Period. There are no sacred cows. Not even Castro (perhaps *especially* not *El Jefe*) is spared the barbs. Other favorite targets of scorn are Russian-made Lada cars and Hungarian buses, which every Cuban agrees are all lemons and which the Hungarian government stopped making after selling the fleet to Cuba—hence, no spare parts. The biggest source of jokes is the system, which most urbanites believe is a failure. Thus:

Question: "How can we be sure Adam and Eve were Cuban?"

Answer: "Because they went without clothing, didn't have any shoes to wear, were prohibited from eating apples, but were told they were living in paradise."

Like the British, Cubans also boast a great wit. They lace their conversations with double entendres and often risqué innuendo. Even the Spanish-speaking foreigner is often left behind by subtle inflections and Cuban idioms.

Many *habaneros* are alternately sad and high-spirited. Suicide is said to be the second leading cause of death in Cuba. Conditions are often heartbreaking, yet most Cubans don't get beaten down. They never seem to lose their sense of humor, reminding writer Pico Iyer of a statement by the 18th-century Englishman Oliver Edwards: "I have tried in my time to be a philosopher, but I don't know how, cheerfulness was always breaking in."

The Nationalist Spirit

Cubans are an intensely passionate and patriotic people united by nationalist spirit and love of country. They are by culture and tradition politically conscious. The revolutionary government has tapped into this and has engaged in consciousness raising on a national scale—primary school children not only lisp loyalty to the flag daily at school . . . they recite their willingness to *die* for it. Cubans are nationalists before they are socialists or even incipient capitalists. They had not expected socialism from the Revolution, but those who were not forced into exile or otherwise devastated could accept it, not simply because so many benefited from the Revolution but because, as Maurice Halperin suggests, "it came with nationalism, that is, an assertion of economic and political independence from the United States, the goal of Cuban patriots for a half century." This reality provides Cubans with a different perspective and viewpoint on history.

That said, Cubans aren't fully sure who they are, suggests Claudia Lightfoot: "The country dissects itself under a microscope trying to define the elements that constitute *cubaní, cubanidad, cubanismo*—Cubanness."

Labor and the Work Ethic

Cubans are distinct from all their Caribbean neighbors in one important respect. They combine their southern joy of living with a northern work ethic and an intellectual ability that makes them unique achievers. Through the centuries, Havana has received a constant infusion of the most energetic Spanish people in the Caribbean, what author James Michener calls "a unique group, one of the strongest cultural stocks in the New World": the wealthier, better-educated, and most motivated colonizers fleeing rebellion and repression and invasion. The entrepreneurial spirit isn't dead, as evidenced by the success of *paladares* (private restaurants), and the brief flourishing in the mid-1990s of self-employed, makeshift entrepreneurs. Those entrepreneurs (*cuenta propistas*) have since virtually

HOW HABANEROS FEEL ABOUT THE REVOLUTION

The fall of the Berlin Wall and the disintegration of the Soviet Bloc brought expectations of a Ceausescu-like ending for Castro. Why, then, have Cuba's internal and external crises not produced Castro's downfall? The U.S. State Department and right-wing Cuban-Americans sow the field with stories of a "one-party monopoly," "40 years of brainwashing," and the "grip of fear" imposed on Cubans by "the police state." True enough. However, these assessments don't take into account the unifying power of national pride, the very real achievements of the Revolution, and above all, Castro's unique charisma and the Machiavellian way he is able to shape *habaneros'* minds like a hypnotist.

Many of the same Cubans who complain about harrowing privation and the ubiquitous and oppressive presence of the state in almost the same breath profess loyalty to Castro. Those with a hate-hate relationship are resigned to sullen silence, prison, or exile. Most Cubans, however, have a love-hate relationship with *el máximo*, although no one in his or her right mind would dare express their negative feelings openly for fear of the consequences.

Tangible Gains

Those Cubans who support the Revolution do so because they believe they are better off than many residents of neighboring countries beset by true poverty (many among the Party faithful do so, of course, because they're the beneficiaries of the system, which created its own social elite with access to cars and other privileges). Cuba has invested 40 years of resources to protect all members of society from illiteracy and ill health, as the Cuban government is at pains to remind them, notwithstanding the dour shortages of food and medicines. Nowhere do you find, as you do in many Latin American and Caribbean cities, hordes of child beggars sniffing glue (though if there were glue to be had, it might be different).

For loyalists, defending the system is a knee-jerk reaction. The party faithful are so defensive of their system that, says Isadora Tattlin, "if you mention material hardship, they will launch right into education and health care, as if no other country in the world offered free education and health care." One often wonders how many of them believe what they're saying (many do, of course, as Cubans are kept unaware that several other Latin American and Caribbean nations —such as Costa Rica and even Paraguay—have surpassed Cuba in many regards). Tattlin, who, as the wife of a high-placed foreign businessman, hosted Fidel and many dozens of Cuban officials during a four-year stint in Havana, felt that for the loyalists to admit failure would be too much pain to bear: "They cannot have their pride offended; that is the most important thing."

Even in hardship, many Cubans see the glass as half full. They appreciate life for what it offers, not for what it lacks; for what it has given the people, not for what it has taken away or can no longer provide, especially in the countryside, where support for the Revolution is strongest.

Wholesale Discontent

Most *habaneros,* however, see the glass as half-empty. Since the onset of the Special Period, Cuba has found it impossible to sustain its cradle-to-grave benefits. The social gains of the Revolution were achieved three decades ago thanks to Soviet largesse, which was taken for granted. Today, a majority of Cubans—especially city dwellers—are tired of the inefficiencies, the endless hardships, the growing inequalities, the sacrifices to satisfy Castro's pathological battle with Uncle Sam. How, for example, can the government explain the US$60,000 Mercedes tourist taxi when local pharmacies lack medicines?

The surreal contradictions of contemporary life are absurdly tragic. Says Claudia Lightfoot: "*Habaneros* are asked to live on a tiny peso wage, but pay out in dollars; praise the free medical service but buy medicines on the black market; despise capitalism while watching the well-heeled capitalists pass through town; and above all, deride the U.S. government when most of them have family in *la yuma* and long to join them."

Forty-odd years of Communism has created palpable discontent. *Habaneros* are pained by their own poverty and the political posturing to disguise it. The people are tired of deprivation. The mood on the streets is now one of frustration and restlessness. Support for the Revolution is highly tenuous. *Habaneros* are increasingly anxious for a return to the market economy and a chance to control and improve their own lives. They are tired of being answerable to the state for their every move. They feel like they are on a yo-yo; any brief liberalization is always followed by a yank on the string. *Habaneros* are forced to break the law constantly to survive. They live under enormous stress of being caught for the slightest transgression and are tired of having to look over their shoulder for the secret police in the shadows. It is disconcerting to see police harassment of pedestrians on the street; dozens are arrested daily this way quite literally for being in the wrong place at the wrong time, or for being unable to account for a few extra loaves of bread. Tourists who pass briefly through Cuba usually don't witness this Nazi-like side of the state.

Not surprisingly, a significant majority of citizens hate the government spies, informers and cronies, and others among the party faithful. Says Catherine Moses: "Because of the resentment Cubans harbor toward these individuals, the choice for them truly may be socialism or death, as Fidel's downfall could lead to violent retribution against them."

Feelings toward Fidel?

While support for Castro remains strong in the countryside, the majority of *habaneros* long ago lost faith in *El Jefe*. While his hold on power seems as strong as ever, his hold on hearts and minds has faded, made more tenuous by the petty and persistent persecution that impinges on Cubans' daily lives.

On one side, a majority of *habaneros* hate Castro for the turmoil and hardship he has wrought in their lives. On the other, Castro's spell over his people, his ability to manipulate the mood, has been such that many Cubans, to an astonishing degree, have separated their discontent with the situation from the man in charge. "No matter how strong and conflicted our emotions about Fidel may be, there is an erotics to his domination," wrote Ruth Behar. "Women deny it at their peril. Men, too, but in a different way, not daring to admit that

© CHRISTOPHER P. BAKER

waving the flag

(continued on next page)

HOW HABANEROS FEEL ABOUT
THE REVOLUTION (cont'd)

they could be seduced by a more macho man." Even the disaffected have tended not to speak with hatred, as East Germans did of Erich Honecker. They usually speak of Castro with the anger a son feels for an overbearing father who can't get with the times. His heart is in the right place, they say, but his head isn't. For the silent majority of Cubans today Fidel is, at the very least, a bore (when he comes on the TV, many *habaneros* turn off the sound but leave the picture on so that they know when he's finished).

Most *habaneros* say that things cannot go on as they are: "We must have change!" But when you ask them how change will come, most roll their eyes and shrug. Politically, the majority of the city's population—those not firmly committed to the political apparatus—are weighed down with passivity. Silence, congruity, and complicity—pretending to be satisfied and happy with the system—are cultural reflexes that have been called indicative of cultural decay. As James Michener wrote of Havana, perhaps "Only the kindness of the climate prevents the smoldering of revolt that might accompany the same conditions in a cold and relentless climate."

disappeared, driven out of business by crippling taxation and state harassment; the number of licensed self-employed persons plunged from 208,346 in 1995 to 112,929 by mid-2000, and it has fallen further since then, though the numbers working illegally in the black market has swelled. The Cuban government likes to present the self-employed as "a breeding ground for the subversive work of the enemy," and as a parasitic nouveau riche . . . but, says Catherine Moses, "this class of conspicuous consumers is usually thought of by peso-earning Cubans as being comprised of the privileged children of high-level Party officials."

The vast majority of *habaneros* work for the state. At some stage, most citizens must participate in "volunteer" brigades, in which urban workers, university students, and even schoolchildren are shipped to the countryside to toil in the fields. Few *habaneros* sign up these days out of a sense of duty. Most do so out of fear of recrimination or because volunteer workers get an *estímulo* (reward), such as priority listing for scarce housing. There are moral as well as material rewards—perhaps a week at Varadero, or the right to buy a refrigerator—for other workers. Wages are given according to a salary scale of 22 levels, with the top level getting six times that of the lowest (the average salary is about US$14 per month). Though paid slightly more, doc-

tors, engineers, and lawyers are not a separate "class" as they are in the United States, Europe, or even the rest of the Caribbean. Life is little different for those who earn 250 pesos (US$10) a month and those who earn 850 (US$34). Highly trained professionals share the same struggles as unskilled workers. (Pensioners get between 100 and 200 pesos monthly.) Such wages don't go far in contemporary Cuba: "You get paid in pesos, but life's sold in dollars," is a local refrain, reflecting reality in a society where the Communist state has deprived labor of its dignity by devaluing it financially.

The degree of anomie is great. Many *habaneros* ask their doctor friends to issue *certificados* (medical excuses) so that they can escape the boredom of employment that offers little financial reward and little hope of promotion. So many teachers have left their profession to work in tourism, where they can earn tips and put food on the table, that tourism companies are now forbidden from hiring teachers—one hotel in Playas del Este is staffed with so many teachers that it is known as "Little Lenin," for the Lenin High School, where many of its employees once taught.

Socio is the buddy network that shields citizens from the demands of the state. *Pinche* and *mayimbe* are their high-level contacts, those who help them get around the bureaucracy, such as the doctor who writes a false note to relieve someone of "voluntary" work in the countryside.

Simple Pleasures

Havana has no *fiesta* tradition. The populace is too industrious for that—too busy playing volleyball or baseball or making love while the other half whiles away the long, hot afternoons at the cinema or eating ice cream at Coppelia park or playing dominoes in the cool shade of arcaded balconies.

Havana's nocturnal pleasures are simple: movies, *trovas* (musical soirées), discos, cheap rum, and sex. For the vast majority of *habaneros*, those without money, life is reduced to making do and making out, with the frequent highlight of a *cumbancha*, the Cuban equivalent of a party that might go on all night, with plenty of saucy rumba and saucier females to dance the hip-shaking rumba with. *Habaneros* move sinuously to Latin rhythms under bare light bulbs that cast shadows on garishly painted cinder block walls, while others gather around the TV to watch *telenovas* (soap operas) and state-prescribed programs. In the early 1990s, *habaneros* rigged their roofs with *parábolas*—improvised parabolic antennas of aluminum, wire netting, or an empty sunflower oil can—that pointed at the Hotel Habana Libre, which was linked to a satellite and distributed U.S. television signals to other hotels. The government tolerated the *parábolas* briefly during the hardest years of the Special Period, when tensions were running high. As conditions improved, the dishes were ordered removed. For good measure, the government coded the signals.

But Havana's intellectual tradition also runs deep. The city is intensely cultured. *Peñas*, theater openings, art exhibits, reasoned debate on every subject are the grist of the well-educated, who spring from all walks of life. This potlatch of cultural expression is one of the triumphs of the Revolution, a tribute to Cuba's success, "rising above the gray patina of Havana's buildings . . . and adding proper weight to the scale of things," thought C. Peter Ripley.

Nonetheless, throughout the city, life for the majority can appear melancholy. Many are the *habaneros* relegated to neighborhoods where pleasures are reduced to the rum speakeasy and to

© CHRISTOPHER P. BAKER

playing dominoes

courting couples murmuring in darkened doorways while destitute neighbors rock on their porches or sit on their doorsteps into the wee hours, waiting for something to happen.

SEX AND GENDER
Sexual Mores

Cuba is a sexually permissive society. As journalist Jacobo Timerman wrote, "Eros is amply gratified in Cuba and needs no stimulation." *Habaneros*—men and women alike—emanate a joyous eroticism that transcends the hang-ups of essentially puritanical Europe or North America. They are sensualists of the first degree. Judging by the ease with which couples neck openly, wink seductively at strangers, and spontaneously slip into bed, the dictatorship of the proletariat that transformed Eastern Europe into a perpetual Sunday school has made little headway in Cuba.

"'We Cubans,'" noted one *habanera*, "have been able to elevate eroticism into national genius." The Cuban revolution counted on this genius to lend its social experiment a unique flavor. "It would be, said Guevara, 'a revolution with *buchango* [pizzazz],'" wrote Lois Smith and Alfred Padula in *Sex and Revolution: Women in Socialist Cuba.*

Their mature attitude, unfettered by shame or guilt, is a direct result of state policy that has brought serious sex education to the masses, challenging many traditional taboos and myths, though in regard to sexual freedom, the party argued that this "does not imply licentiousness, which degrades the beauty of relations between men and women." The state may promote the family, but *habaneros* have a notoriously indulgent attitude toward casual sex that has defied the efforts of the regime to control it. Seduction is a national pastime pursued by both sexes—the free expression of a high-spirited people confined in an authoritarian world. After all, Cubans joke, sex is the only thing Castro can't ration.

Male and female, old and young alike insist that promiscuity is a natural attribute. Few Cubans disapprove. You're *expected* to enjoy sex . . . and as much of its as you can handle, regardless of gender orientation.

In *Chronicles of the City of Havana,* Uruguayan journalist Eduardo Galeano tells the following story:

One day at noon, guagua *[bus] 68 screeched to a halt at an intersection. There were cries of protest at the tremendous jolt until the passengers saw why the bus driver had jammed on the brakes: a magnificent woman had just crossed the street.*

"You'll have to forgive me, gentlemen," said the driver of guagua *68, and he got out. All the passengers applauded and wished him luck.*

The bus driver swaggered along, in no hurry, and the passengers watched him approach the saucy female, who stood on the corner, leaning against the wall, licking an ice cream cone. From guagua *68, the passengers followed the darting motion of her tongue as it kissed the ice cream while the driver talked on and on with no apparent result, until all at once she laughed and glanced up at him. The driver gave the thumbs-up sign and the passengers burst into a hearty ovation.*

Promiscuity is rampant. So are extramarital affairs. Love is not associated with sex. And both genders are unusually bold. Men and women let their eyes run slowly over strangers they find attractive. *Ojitos* (long glances), often accompanied by uninhibited comments, betray envisioned improprieties. Even the women murmur *piropos* (courtly overtures) and sometimes comic declarations of love. "Dark-eyed Stellas light their feller's panatelas," Irving Berlin once wrote of Cuba. And how!

Teenagers become sexually active at an early age: girls at 13 on average, boys at 15, according to Cuba's National Center for Sex Education, which dispenses sex counseling to youths, along with condoms and birth control pills (considered to be tools of liberation for women). More than 160,000 abortions are performed free of charge each year, one-third on teenagers. About two-thirds of births are out of wedlock.

Feminism and Machismo

Castro set an ambitious and ambiguous goal of "full sexual equality." Today, according to Saul Landau, Cuba is the only "unisex" country in the world. A United Nations survey ranks Cuba among the top 20 nations in which women have the highest participation in politics and business. Women make up 50 percent of university students and 60 percent of doctors—a review of the University of Havana yearbooks shows that women were also well represented *before* the Revolution—although they are still poorly represented in the upper echelons of government.

Cuba's solid achievements in the past four decades reflect Castro's own faith in the equal abilities of women, and the belief that the Revolution cannot be called complete until women share full opportunities. Equality of the sexes is also given legal guarantees through the Cuban Family Code, which even stipulates that the male must share household duties.

The Spanish heritage is patriarchal—under the Spanish Civil Code, which was extended into the Cuban Republic, a husband had exclusive rights to property, finances, and, legally, the obedience of his wife and children. The Revolution has broken down the strict Spanish pattern, but it still colors family life. Prejudices and stereotypical behaviors still exist. Male machismo continues, and pretty women walking down the street are often bombarded with comments ranging from *piropos* to forthright invitations to sex. Although the sexes may have been equalized, the Revolution has not been able to get the Cubanness out of *habaneras* who, regardless of age, still adore coquetry. The Cuban philosophy is that bodies are to be displayed, looked at, enjoyed, and indulged.

Few *habaneras* simply put on a dress and go out. Instead, they make a great show of expressing their bodily beauty. "Cuban women don't walk, they sway," Naty Revuelta, one of Castro's former mistresses and the mother of his daughter, has said. "When they walk, everything is in motion, from the ankle to the shoulder. The soldiers had a terrible time in the beginning, trying to teach them to march in the militia. They just couldn't get the sway out of them." Even the most ardent revolutionaries still paint their faces and attempt a toilette to heighten the femme fatale effect, as in their preference for minimalist and tight-fitting clothing. Female officials still routinely shorten and take in their uniforms to show their legs and outline their backsides.

Overt appreciation of the female form may seem sexist to politically correct North Americans, but in Cuba, rear ends have a value and meaning much more significant than in other cultures. Cuban literature overflows with references to *las nalgas cubanas* (the Cuban ass), usually plump and belonging to a well-rounded mulatta. Tom Miller synthesizes the long-standing fascination with *el culo* (the butt) in his marvelous travelogue, *Trading with the Enemy.* "I found enough material to keep a culophile busy for months."

Mulattas and *negras* are particularly revered among Cuban males for their perceived sexuality—*quemar petróleo* (to burn diesel fuel) is the colloquial term for sexual relations with a black woman. White Cubans have always had an appreciation for black beauty and have never been shy about saying so. Most Cuban love songs have always had a risqué quality, with lyrics praising the charms of *mi negra* (my black girl), *mi morena* (my dark girl), my chocolate sweetie, or my mulatta beauty, plainly described as such in racial terms. Interracial sexuality is the central theme, for example, of Cuba's most famous novel, Cirilo Villaverde's *Cecilia Valdés.* Today no less than in the past, the married white *habanero* is likely to maintain a mulatta mistress, who is probably married herself—even José Martí abandoned his wife and was consoled by a mistress. And male tourists are constantly quizzed by taxi drivers, bar staff, and even party functionaries as to whether or not they've experienced sex with a mulatta girlfriend. "*¡Son calientes!*" (They're hot!) they'll say matter-of-factly. Havana's mulattas seem determined to prove them right.

Of course, these stereotypes belie the ongoing debate within Cuba about the "correct" role of women, led by the **Cuban Federation of Women** (Federación de Mujeres Cubanas, Paseo #250, Havana, tel. 830-6043), headed by Vilma Espín, former wife of Raúl Castro and known as the First Lady of Cuba. The Federation was

PERMISSIVE, AND THEN SOME!

"What effect is dollarization having on families and society?" asked one of [the journalists]. Said Maruetti [a Cuban economist], looking bureaucratically oblivious, "Number One: foreign investment. Two: intensive development of tourism. Three: opening to foreign trade." Sis had been out hitchhiking and someone made a foreign investment in her. It's all part of Cuba's intensive development of tourism. And, boy, is she open to foreign trade.

P. J. O'Rourke

Before the Revolution, Batista's Babylon offered a tropical buffet of sin: Castro declared that there were 100,000 prostitutes in Havana, about ten times the true figure. In 1959, the revolutionary government closed down the sex shows and porn palaces and sent the prostitutes to rehabilitative trade schools, thereby ostensibly eliminating the world's oldest trade. Prostitution reappeared, however, within a few years of the Triunfo. Fred Ward recorded in 1977 how "a few girls have been appearing once again in the evenings, looking for dates, and willing to trade their favors for goods rather than money." He thought it "more a comment on rationing than on morals."

Jineteras—the word comes from *jinete*, or jockey—have always been part of the postrevolutionary landscape, especially at embassy functions. The Cuban government, claims Guillermo Cabrera Infante, has always made "state mulattas" available to foreign dignitaries—as a foreign diplomat quipped, "Cubans are better suited to make their living in bed than anyone else on earth"—and even maintains a "discreet house of select prostitutes" in Jaimanitas, according to journalist Pedro Alfonso. Critics even claim that in the early 1990s, the Cuban government sponsored the island's image as a cheap-sex paradise to kick-start tourism. Tourism-related "prostitution" was soon proliferating beneath a general complacency, with girls as young as 13 hanging around outside the Hotel Habana Libre. The situation reached its nadir when Rumbos, a Cuban tourist company, was stung by allegations of exporting "dancing girls" to Latin America, while in 1999 a Mexican company, Cubamor, was accused of operating organized sex tours with official connivance. (Osmany Cienfuegos, Cuba's Minister of Tourism, fell from grace in the scandal.)

The Government's Response

Castro told *Time* magazine, "The state tries to prevent it [prostitution] as much as possible. It is not legal in our country to practice prostitution, nor are we going to legalize it. Nor are we thinking in terms of turning it into a freelance occupation to solve unemployment problems. [Laughter.] We are not going to repress it either," he stated, while also boasting that Cuba had the healthiest and best-educated prostitutes in the world.

However, the Cuban government was clearly stung by an avalanche of foreign media reports on the subject. In 1996, Cuban women were barred from guest rooms in tourist hotels, and the police initiated a crackdown. Then, in January 1999, thousands of young women were picked up on the streets and jailed, while anyone without an official Havana address was returned to their homes in the countryside. Hundreds of innocent females have been jailed—falsely accused of prostitution—without recourse.

Nonetheless, sexual relations between tourists and Cubans continue. Many cabaret showgirls operate a kind of prostitutes' guild. *Jineteras* continue to work the major tourist discos and bars with the complicity of the staff (and perhaps even that of the State). On the streets, perfumed mulattas in high heels still smile invitingly, while langorous Lolitas in tiny *tanguitas* sashay along the beaches blowing kisses at unaccompanied foreign males. Cuban males, too, tout themselves as gigolos and are warmly received by foreign females seeking (predominantly black) Cuban lovers.

Like everything in Cuba, the situation is complex and needs some explaining.

A Chance to Get Ahead—and Get Away

The women who form intimate relationships with tourists are a far cry from the uneducated prostitutes of Batista days. Most are ordinary Cubans who would laugh to be called *jineteras*. A study by the Federation of Cuban Women (FMC) has shown that even among *jineteras*, "Most have the benefit of extensive educational opportunity compared to the lot of their sisters before the Revolution. Most are not ashamed [and] few have low self-esteem. . . . With very few exceptions, they don't need to practice commercial sexual relations to survive. Instead, what motivates these women . . . is the desire to go out, to enjoy themselves, go places where Cubans are not allowed to go." They're seeking a *papiriqui con guaniquiqui* (a sugar daddy) as a replacement for a paternalistic government that can no longer provide. Says writer Coco Fusco, "On the street these women are seen as heroic providers whose sexual power is showing up the failures of an ailing macho regime."

A pretty *cubana* attached to a generous suitor can be wined and dined and get her entrance paid into the discos, drinks included, to which she otherwise wouldn't have access. Many women hook up with a man for the duration of his visit in the hope that a future relationship may develop. No small number succeed in snagging foreign husbands. Their dream is to live abroad—to find a foreign boyfriend (usually considerably older) who will marry them and take them away.

It happens all the time . . . especially for good-looking *negras de pelo* (black women with straight hair). "'Italian and German men are *locos* for *negras y mulatas de pelo,*'" says Lety, in Isadora Tattlin's *Cuban Diaries*. "'*Ay,* being *una negra de pelo* in Cuba is as good as having a visa to Canada or western Europe, guaranteed. And being *una negra* with blue eyes'—Lety shakes her fingers again, like they have been scalded— 'when the girl turns fourteen, people say, '*el norteño* is coming, *chica,* pack your bags!'"

In a society where promiscuity is rampant and sex on a first date is a given, any financial transaction—more in one night in *fula* (dollars) than she can otherwise earn in a month's salary in worthless pesos—is a charitable afterthought to a romantic evening out. Thus, educated and morally upright Cuban women—doctors, teachers, accountants—smile at tourists passing by on the street or hang out by the disco doorways, seeking affairs—*lucha un yuma*—and invitations to be a part of the high life. Says the *New York Times* (in a review of *Dirty Havana Trilogy;* see Suggested Reading), "He lives off the earnings of one of his girlfriends who is a prostitute, but then again most of the women who inhabit Pedro Juan's world pick up the occasional trick when the opportunity presents itself." Not too many parents seem to mind. In fact, many a *mamá* has prepared a bed for her daughter and partner, reflecting how morally unburdened in issues of sex is Cuban popular culture.

The Congress of the FMC agreed that the rise in "prostitution" has a lot to do with Cuban youth's permissive attitudes towards sex. It recognized *jineterismo* as an expression of a moral crisis and stressed the need to emphasize the role of the family, to help dissuade young women who have discovered the megaton power of their sexuality from living it out to the fullest.

Sex is legal at the age of 16 in Cuba but under Cuban and international law, foreigners can be prosecuted for sex with anyone under 18.

The **Center for Responsible Tourism,** 1765-D Le Roy Ave., Berkeley, CA, 94709, CRTourism@ aol.com, publishes a leaflet, *What You Should Know About Sex Tourism Before You Go Abroad,* dealing with sex with minors.

If you know of anyone who is traveling to Cuba with the intent of sexually abusing minors, contact the U.S. Customs Service, International Child Pornography Investigation and Coordination Center, 45365 Vintage Park Rd., Suite 250, Sterling, VA 20166, 703/709-9700, icpicc@customs.sprint.co.

founded to rouse women to be good revolutionaries but in recent years has devoted more effort to women's issues and rights, particularly the fight against a rising tide of teenage pregnancy. Likewise, a nongovernmental organization called **Association of Women Communicators,** (MAGIN, Calle 11 #160 e/ K y L, Vedado, Havana, tel. 832-3322, fax 33-3079), organizes workshops designed to build self-esteem and develop a greater understanding of the concepts of gender and feminism.

The Cubans themselves have yet to produce a book-length analysis of women's status in postrevolutionary Cuba. For that, refer to the excellent *Sex and Revolution: Women in Socialist Cuba,* by Lois Smith and Alfred Padula (Oxford University Press, 1996, www.cubabooks.com).

Homosexuality

Cuban gays must find it ironic that the heart of the homosexual world is Castro Street in San Francisco. It is assuredly not named in *el jefe's* honor, as gays—called "queens," *(maricones), mariposas* (butterflies), *pájaros* (birds), *patos* (ducks) or *gansos* (geese) in the Cuban vernacular (and *tortillera,* for "dykes")—were persecuted following the Revolution. Castro (who denies the comment) supposedly told journalist Lee Lockwood that a homosexual could never "embody the conditions and requirements of . . . a true revolutionary."

Castro says that such prejudices were a product not of the Revolution but of the existing social milieu. "We inherited male chauvinism—and many other bad habits—from the conquistadores," he told Tomás Borge in *Face to Face with Fidel Castro* (Ocean Press, 1992). "That historical legacy . . . influenced our attitude toward homosexuality." It is also true that at the onset of the Revolution, the gay rights movement had not yet been born in the United States, and the same prejudices that the revolutionaries inherited about homosexuals were prevalent elsewhere in the world. Thus, gays and lesbians met with "homophobic repression and rejection" in Cuba, just as they did in the United States. In Cuba, however, it was more systematic and brutal.

The pogrom began in earnest in 1965; homosexuals were arrested and sent to agricultural work and reeducation camps called UMAP (Units for Military Help to Agricultural Production). Echoing Auschwitz, over the gate of one such camp in Camagüey was the admonition: "Work Makes You Men." Many brilliant intellectuals lost their jobs because they were gay, or accused of being gay through anonymous denunciation. Homosexuality was also considered an aberration of nature that could weaken the family structure. Hence homosexuals were not allowed to teach, become doctors, or occupy positions from which they could "pervert" Cuban youth.

Although UMAP camps closed in 1968, periodic purges occurred throughout the 1970s and early '80s. Many homosexuals left—or were forced to leave—on the Mariel Boatlift. (Julian Schnabel's acclaimed 1999 movie *Before Night Falls,* based on the life of the gay writer Reinaldo Arenas, chronicles the brutality of the period.) However, by the mid-1980s, Cuba began to respond to the gay rights movement that had already gained momentum worldwide. Officially, the new position was that homosexuality and bisexuality are no less natural or healthy than heterosexuality. In 1987, a directive was issued to police to stop harassment. The 1994 Oscar-nominated *Fresa y Chocolate,* which deals with the persecution of gays in Cuba and the government's use of informers, was officially approved by Cuba's Film Institute—headed by Alfredo Guevara, a homosexual and close confidante of Castro—offering proof that the government was exorcising the ghost of a shameful past.

However, persecution and discrimination continue. Gay organizations, magazines, and clubs are banned, and in 1997 police initiated a new crackdown that made headlines when French designer Jean Paul Gaultier was arrested along with some 800 other people during a raid of the El Periquitón nightclub. The attendees were fined 30 pesos and had to sign statements promising not to frequent "places of perversion."

Gay Cuba, by Sonja de Vries, looks candidly at the treatment of gays and lesbians in Cuba since the Revolution. You can order copies from Frameline, 346 Ninth St., San Francisco, CA 94103, 415/703-8654, fax 415/861-1404;

distribution@frameline.org, www.frameline.org. Also check out *Machos, Maricones, and Gays: Cuba and Homosexuality,* by Ian Lumsden (Philadelphia, PA: Temple University, 1996) for a study of the relationship between male homosexuality and Cuban society.

LIFE IN HAVANA

Havana's physical decrepitude and the miscellaneous hardships of daily life faced by most people are so pervasive that one of the first things almost every visitor to Havana asks is, "How on earth do the *habaneros* get by?"

On the eve of the Revolution, Havana was a highly developed city with more millionaires than anywhere south of Texas, and more Cadillacs per capita than any other city on earth. It had a rapidly evolving capitalist infrastructure and an urban labor force that had achieved "the eight-hour day, double pay for overtime, one month's paid vacation, nine days sick leave, and the right to strike." On the other hand, *habaneros* who drove Cadillacs and otherwise lived a well-to-do middle-class life were as remote culturally as they were economically from the mass of their countrymen. In 1950, a World Bank study team reported that 40 percent of urban dwellers and 60 percent of rural dwellers were undernourished. For the nation as a whole, more than 40 percent of Cuban people were illiterate; only 60 percent had regular full-time employment. The city orphanage in Havana even had a drop chute with flaps to facilitate the abandonment of babies by mothers who couldn't afford to bring them up.

The Revolution immeasurably improved the material and spiritual condition of millions of Cubans, eliminating the most abject poverty while destroying the middle and wealthy urban classes, emasculating individualism, and imposing a general paucity, if not poverty, on millions of others. A life was destroyed for every one that was raised up. But at least everyone had the bare essentials. The government provided five crates of beer as a wedding present, and birthday cakes for kids under 10. Everyone enjoyed two two-week vacations a year at the beach. But things changed for the worse overnight when the benefi-

icence of the Soviet Union ended following the latter's collapse. The Soviets had propped up the moribund Cuban economy with subsidies of US$3 billion annually; on the eve of the collapse, 84 percent of Cuba's trade was with the Soviet Union and Eastern Europe.

The early 1990s were devastating for a population accustomed to a much higher standard of living. In 1991, when Castro told his people that they were entering a "special period," he was warning them that their society was about to experience a special kind of collapse, and they were about to feel a special kind of pain. The Cuban economy has since bounced back from disastrous collapse, much thanks to tourism, but the average *habanero* still feels plenty of pain.

Habaneros will tell you that life is a *lucha* (struggle). Havana's citizens are focused on issues of everyday survival. Every morning, people prepare to cobble together some kind of normalcy out of whatever the situation allows them. Cubans are masters at making the best of a bad situation. *Resolver* (to resolve, to overcome obstacles with ingenuity, spontaneity, and humor) and *conseguir* (to get or obtain) are two of the most commonly used verbs on the island. For many people, the socialist dream has turned into a nightmare. Socialist equality looks dismal as you contemplate the aged and impoverished walking around inconsolably as if they'd been castrated—*jaca* is the local term—and at a loss over their lives, ruminating over what has gone terribly wrong with a Revolution that held greater promise. Often, especially in work places, you come across people in a state of catatonia. "It's very active in Cuba, this random time-standing-still, people-being-paralyzed thing. It's like in fairy tales: some people frozen or turned to stone," wrote Isadora Tattlin.

Thousands of *habaneros* live, to greater or lesser degree, like Pedro Juan, the protagonist in the brilliant novel *Dirty Havana Trilogy,* who is forced to become a gigolo, a pimp, and a black marketeer, picking up incremental income wherever he can and finding relief from the repetitiveness of daily life in elemental hedonism . . . "Rum, women, marijuana, a little rumba whenever possible."

The Bare Essentials

Row upon row of citrus trees grow just 30 miles from Havana, but it is nearly impossible to find an orange for sale. Vast acres of state farms and cooperatives go unfarmed, while cultivated land is poorly tended. What happens to the food produced is a mystery. Hospitals, schools, and work canteens get priority, but almost nothing reaches the state groceries. Almost 40 percent of produce is stolen as it passes through the dysfunctional distribution system known as *acopio*). The *campesinos* (farm workers) do okay. But many *habaneros* go without. The *libreta*—the ration book meant to supply every Cuban citizen with the essentials—provides, at best, sufficient for perhaps 10 days per month. Cubans must pick up their rations from the *bodega* on the first of the month, because by the next day there may not be anything left.

A certain amount of staples is allowed per person from the state grocery store per month—six pounds of rice, 11 pounds of beans, four ounces of coffee, four ounces of lard—but only when available. Candles, kerosene, and matches all appear in the *libreta* but are hardly ever in stock. Nor are cooking oil, household detergent, or soap—the items whose lack is most direly felt. (*Habaneros* are notoriously toilet-conscious. Even the poorest *habanero* manages to keep fastidiously clean. It has been said that "to take away their soap would be Castro's greatest folly. Almost anything else can be tolerated, but take away their soap and the regime would fall!") Conversations are laced with an obsession for items that many *habaneros* haven't seen in years.

Much of the food supplied by the state you wouldn't feed to your cat. (Not that there are many of those anyway; cats are only now making a comeback on the streets of Havana, most of their forebears having ended up in the cooking pot during the early 1990s. Dogs fared better, although hundreds were put out on the street to fend for themselves because their owners could no longer feed them.) For example, *picadillo* is second-grade ground meat mixed with soybean, hailed by bureaucrats as a "meatsome mass." Worse than that, says Humberto Werneck, is the *pasta de oca,* a "culinary enigma which is thought to contain the viscera of geese, none of them noble like the liver from which the famous paté is made."

The U.S. embargo probably worsens the situation by denying the export of U.S.-made goods to Cuba. In actuality, there's no shortage of U.S. products in Havana, from Marlboro cigarettes to Nikes and Coca-Cola, imported through Mexico or other countries. *El bloqueo*—the blockade, as the Cuban government refers to the embargo—is an embargo only in name. In May 2002, President Carter pointed out live on Cuban TV that Cuba can trade with more than 100 countries and can buy medicines—and many other goods—cheaper from Mexico and other countries than it could from the United States. Thousands of cars—including US$60,000 Mercedes taxis—and buses are imported each year from Europe and Asia, and there's no shortage of electronic goods, imported foodstuffs, clothing, and household miscellany, or of all the necessary furnishings to stock tourist hotels. And the pharmacies serving foreigners are full of medicines manufactured in and imported from Caribbean and Central American countries; local pharmacies do not stock imported medicines, suggesting that this is a purposeful decision of the government.

The real problem is that Cubans are paid in pesos but anything worth buying—including basic necessities—is sold by Cuban state enterprises for U.S. dollars, usually at extortionate prices. The average monthly wage is about 350 pesos—about US$14 at black market exchange rates—yet meat in the *mercados agropecuarios* (the independent farmers market created in 1993 to resolve the food crisis) can cost 25 pesos a pound, and black beans nine pesos. Fortunately, rent and utilities are so heavily subsidized that they are virtually free.

A few years ago, a peso income had some value. Today it is virtually worthless. Life has become organized around a mad scramble for dollars. The lucky ones have access to family cash, known as *fula,* sent from Miami—social obligations dictate that if you make money, you are expected to support family members—or donated by a foreign lover and benefactor. By some estimates, as much as US$1 billion a year is sent to Cuba from relatives living abroad.

Much of the cash coming from Florida is smuggled in by *caballos* ("horses"), often in creative schemes that come a cropper, such as the one conceived by an unfortunate Cuban in Miami who answered his brother's plea for *fula*. As told by Humberto Werneck, the latter was disappointed to receive only a pair of shoes—and one size too small at that. He sold them to a stranger and then almost went mad when he later discovered that his clever brother had hidden US$1,000 in each shoe.

Cuban economists reckon that only about 25 percent of the population has regular access to dollars. The rest, including the professionals (doctors, engineers, architects, white-collar workers), have experienced downward mobility, replaced by a new breed of upper class—black marketeers, part-time prostitutes, waiters, and entrepreneurs, and anyone with philanthropic family abroad. Without access to U.S. dollars, Cubans must rely on their wits and faith—Cubans joke about getting by on *fe,* Spanish for faith, but today an acronym for *familia extranjera*—family abroad. The majority of Cubans must simply *buscar la forma* (find a way).

The Black Market and Resolviendo

Habaneros survive by *resolviendo*—the Cuban art of barter, the cut corner, the gray market where much of Cuba's economy operates. Most *habaneros* rely on *los bisneros* (the underground economy), doing business illegally. The black market, known as the *bolsa* (exchange), resolves the failings of the state-controlled economy. For four decades, it has touched all walks of life. Gas station attendants sell gasoline "stretched" with kerosene—siphoning off the good stuff to sell on the black market—while store managers routinely set aside part of the state-supplied stock to sell on the *bolsa*. Meanwhile, illegal vendors surreptitiously knock on neighborhood doors selling eggs and other essentials often stolen from state stores, carrying out their trade *sotto voce* for fear of being caught. Even otherwise loyal Revolutionaries are forced to break the law to survive.

Habaneros are maestros at inventing to get around shortages. Barter is common. So are time payments, verbal contracts for future delivery,

and a hundred variations on the theme. Those with a few dollars might buy scarce products and then barter them to other Cubans with no link to the dollar economy. One neighbor might bring another canned goods in exchange for fish. A third may get his car engine fixed in exchange for peanut butter. And many Cubans live off swindles, or *trampas.*

Habaneros are also the world's best recyclers. The *libreta,* for example, provides only four cigars and six packets of cigarettes monthly. During the worst years of the early 1990s, even cigar and cigarette butts were recycled to make *tupamaros,* hand-crafted cigarettes rolled in a rustic oversized roller. To save energy, crafty *habaneros* have rigged their bicycles with engines taken from chain saws and even fumigators.

Many front and backyards, rooftop *azoteas,* and even household quarters have been turned into chicken coops and pig sties. Havana households often share living quarters with a pig, as depicted in the movie *Fresa y Chocolate,* in which a pig is seen being pushed up the stairs of a tenement. Raising a pig inside remains illegal, so many of the urban pigs are mute—they've had their vocal chords slit—a practice so common that it, too, was mentioned on celluloid, in *Adorable Lies.*

Cubans have learned to laugh about their hardships. Nonetheless, having sacrificed for the Revolution for more than four decades, many Cubans are exhausted. It's a remarkable testament to the enduring spirit of the people (and to the efficiency of the State Security apparatus and the power the system holds over people's lives) that they have been able to withstand the upheavals without grave social and political consequences. But then, there's always *La Yuma*—the United States (from the 1957 film *3:10 to Yuma* starring Glenn Ford and Van Heflin)—beckoning just 90 miles away . . . a handy safety valve.

Housing Conditions

Until the Revolution, government expenditures were concentrated mostly in and around Havana. The provinces were neglected, rural housing was basic, and many towns had few sewers, electricity, plumbing, or paved roads. Since the Revolution,

¡SE PERMUTA!

Cubans can swap (*permutar*) their houses without state approval but cannot sell them without government say-so. Cash transactions involving houses are illegal, and for those that are approved, the government has the right to acquire the property at a sharp discount (nice houses in good neighborhoods are often taken by the government for the *nomenclatura*—political elite—or for offices).

The laws are full of quicksand. For example, only houses of similar sizes may be swapped. And some neighborhoods have had their populations "frozen" by law, so that if a family of four wants to move out, no more than four may move in. And, claims the *Washington Post*, if one of the swapping parties flees Cuba illegally within five years of the deal, his or her former house may be seized, which effectively screws those who moved in.

Since there's no such thing as classified ads or websites for real estate, *habaneros* hang signs outside their homes announcing *se permuta* ("For swap"), or hang out on the Paseo del Prado, where an informal house swap meet takes place and a sweat-stained notebook that passes for a multiple listings service gets passed around (the government *does* keep a computerized clearinghouse of properties on the swapping block, but it's woefully incomplete and outdated). A swap can take years to arrange, after which the government must approve it . . . another year or so. A few greased palms along the way can help.

As with everything in Cuba, home owners find a way to get around the law by posing a house purchase transaction entirely as barter, while cash changes hands beneath the table . . . assuming you have the cash. Not surprisingly, a new breed of real estate broker—a "barter agent"—has emerged. Houses located in areas with few or no *apagones* (blackouts), such as those close to hotels or hospitals, are most highly prized.

The difficulties add new dimensions to Havana's surreal theater. Divorced couples are often forced to remain together, as are families divided by irreconcilable feuds. "Surgeon Guillermo Oceguerra Fuste and his ophthalmologist wife divorced almost a year and a half ago. They both have new loves in their lives," wrote the *Washington Post*. "But because of Cuba's acute housing shortage and socialist laws, they still share the same apartment . . . Life there is often like a stiff stage play, and they must pursue their new love lives elsewhere."

the government has concentrated its energies on developing the countryside and replacing urban shantytowns with apartment housing.

Most housing built since the Revolution (in both town and country) is concrete apartment block units of a standard Bulgarian design—the ugly Bauhaus vision of uniform, starkly functional workers' housing, which had the advantage of being cheap to build and, in theory, easy and cheap to maintain. Most were jerry-built by unskilled volunteer labor, adding salt to the wound of the aesthetic shortfall. Most have not been maintained. And do they ever need it!

Today, virtually every house in Havana has electricity, although a large percentage do not have running water; it is normal for certain areas to have their water supply cut off for much of the

day because demand outstrips supply. Households are metered separately for use of electricity. Payments for this are made directly to state authorities. By law, no renter can pay more than 10 percent of his or her salary in rent. However, almost 80 percent of Cubans own their own homes. "Mrs. Thatcher's vision of a homeowners' society come true in communist Cuba," Martha Gellhorn notes, wryly. "Rents pile up like down payments year after year, until the sale price of the flat is reached, whereupon bingo, you become an old-fashioned capitalist owner." Those who owned houses before the Revolution have been allowed to keep them; those who fled Cuba forfeited their property to the state.

Buying or selling homes, however, is illegal (see the Special Topic "¡Se Permuta!"). In any event, people are tied to their official address by the *libreta*, which is allocated to a specific address rather than an individual. In 2000, the government began a crackdown against "irregularities" in properties. More than 1,400 *habaneros* have since had their houses confiscated because the government deemed them too fancy, or for illegal renting or purchase, and other supposed abuses. Among them are unlucky foreigners who've bought homes illegally in the name of Cuban girlfriends.

Conditions vary markedly. There *are* many fine, well-kept houses. Most of Havana prerevolutionary housing, however, has deteriorated to a point of dilapidation—while the effort to restore Habana Vieja is well underway, poorer peripheral neighborhoods continue to decay. In certain areas, conditions are truly depressing. Many *habaneros* cling tenaciously to family life behind crumbling facades festooned with makeshift wiring and inside tottering buildings that should have faced the bulldozer long ago. Many buildings have fallen masonry and piles of plaster on the floor, unpainted walls mildewed by the tropical climate, and stairs so dilapidated one is afraid to step onto them. Once-pleasant strolls in Cerro and Habana Vieja have become obstacle courses over piles of rubble and beneath wooden braces propping up one building after another. Many people live in *solares*, entire communities of crowded, low-class, run-down apartments that pre-date the Revolution by decades; or *ciudadelas*, large mansions converted into multiple dwellings. Others exist on rooftop *azoteas*, prominent in the Centro and Cerro districts; the pressure for urban housing has left an epidemic of ungainly additions. The blight is acute in Vedado . . . an archetypal 1920s "City Beautiful." Far from prying eyes, an entire *azotea* subculture has evolved, and it is here that much of Havana's illicit activity takes place, including illegal *paladares* and speakeasies. And thousands of *habaneros* live in shanty dwellings tucked into ravines and hillsides, or hidden behind more substantial housing, surrounded by garbage and leaking sewage, as sordid as those that infest Mexico City or tumble down the hills of Rio de Janeiro. Castro has admitted that 300,000 people

in Havana live in slum conditions and that only 50 percent of inhabitants have proper sewage. Officially, half of Havana's housing is rated "poor" to "bad." Squatting is common, and homelessness has begun to appear. To halt the growth of shanty dwellings, in 1977 the government attempted a partially effective remedy: it restricted migration to Havana.

The government claimed to have built 45,000 housing units nationwide in 2001, but that appears to be an exaggeration and falls far short of what is needed. "The powers that be call it 'housing redistribution.' The redistributed call it 'living like sardines,'" wrote Gutiérrez. The housing shortage is so critical that many *habaneros* live in a partitioned room, often divided into several tiny cubicles for individual family members. In many cases, the high-ceilinged rooms of old colonial buildings have been turned into two stories by adding new ceilings and wooden staircases to form *barbacoas* (barbecues). Several generations are often crowded together unwillingly; there is simply nowhere for the offspring to go—many adult "children" are even forced to share the same bed as their parents. The stress that this creates is immense.

Interiors often belie the dour impression received on the street. Rooms everywhere are kept spick-and-span and furnished with typically Cuban decor: family photos, kitschy ceramic animals, plastic flowers, and other effusive knick knackery—and frequently a photo of Castro, Guevara, or Camilo Cienfuegos, if only to keep in with the government. Always there is a large refrigerator (Russian or prerevolutionary Yankee) and at least one TV, and the lucky ones with access to *fula* (dollars) usually have a VCR and perhaps some other electronics—though only the *very* few trusted loyalists have access to a computer. And usually there's a *perrito* (a small dog), as Cubans are animal lovers.

Supplies for repairs are virtually impossible to find. Nails? Paint? Forget it. Everything has to be foraged. Why is there no paint? Because the centralized planning process has always been intent on meeting production quotas, not on allocating resources for maintenance and repair. Spare parts aren't ordered to maintain sewers or electrical boxes, so everything is jerry-rigged and/or deteriorates without hope of repair. Until 1993, it was illegal for Cubans to freelance as electricians, plumbers, or construction workers, so everyone relied on the state, which gave home and public utility repair low priority—in recent years, freelancer entrepreneurs have again been squeezed out of business by a control-obsessed Communist bureaucracy. For four decades, *habaneros* have been denied access to pots of paint, whitewash, and chemical treatments to prevent molds and mildews, so that the latter abound. When walking the streets of Habana Vieja, it is common to pass an open doorway that delivers a lungful of mildew, quite horrible to breathe—Cuba, apparently, has the highest rate of asthma in the world due to the dust and mold, reports Tattlin. And most elevators are rickety, deathly contraptions—in 2000, an elevator in the Focsa building plunged 20-odd stories, killing its occupants. "This elevator is a cruder, simpler piece of junk," wrote Gutiérrez, "Very dark, because the neighbors steal the light bulbs, with a permanent stink of urine, filth, and the daily vomit of a drunk who lives on the fourth floor."

Anyone who wants to repair or remodel a home (a constant necessity) must prove that all building materials were purchased from the state. Yet what little there is for sale in state stores is sold at vastly inflated prices. Black-market cement and other items—most of it stolen from government sources—sell at a fraction of official prices. Hence, merely to fix a falling-down wall can lead to a home being confiscated. Meanwhile, municipal administration is a disaster. When telegraph poles fall down, no one moves them; when sidewalks collapse, no repairs are made; when pavements buckle, they go unattended.

CHILDREN AND YOUTH

One of the simplest pleasures for the foreign traveler is to see smiling children in school uniforms so colorful that they reminded novelist James Michener of "a meadow of flowers. Well nourished, well shod and clothed, they were the permanent face of the land." And well behaved, too. You almost never hear a child crying in Cuba, nor even a parent scolding their children.

Children are also treated with great indulgence by the state. The government has made magnificent strides to improve the lot of poor children (it also attempts exemplary care of the elderly). And it teaches youngsters magnificent values. In the Communist Party youth group, for example, the Young Pioneers learn the virtues of public service doing duty collecting litter and other noble works. Once, when asked about the sister who turned her back on the Revolution, Castro told TV interviewer Barbara Walters, "We have the same mother and father, but different ideas. I am a committed socialist. She is an enemy of socialism and that is why she says [bad] things about me. But let me tell you. I have five million brothers and sisters, and between us we have millions of children. We love these children." There is no doubt he is sincere, although Castro is also a master at using Cuba's children as a political tool.

About 35 percent of Havana's population is below 16 years of age. Throughout Havana, you'll come across bright-eyed children laden with satchels, making their way to and from school in pin-neat uniforms colored according to their grades. Younger ones (*pioneros*) wear short-sleeved white shirts, light-blue neckerchiefs, and maroon shorts or skirts; secondary school children (*alumnos de secundaria*) wear white shirts, red neckerchiefs, and mustard-yellow long pants or miniskirts all the way up to...12th grade. The neckerchiefs show that they are Pioneers, similar to Cub and Boy Scouts.

There's a school in Havana every few blocks, usually indicated by a small bust of José Martí in the forecourt. In 2002, construction of 33 new schools and rehabilitation of 28 deteriorated schools was prioritized, and classes for the 2002–03 year were slated to yield one teacher for every 20 students. Today, the literacy rate is 96.7 percent according to UNICEF statistics—about the same as Argentina and Costa Rica; the equivalent for Haiti is 50 percent, and for Jamaica 94.52 percent—which show that the average Cuban child receives about 11.3 years of schooling, the same as Mexico and Panama (the

TURNING SWEET FIFTEEN

Four decades of socialism have killed off many traditional celebrations, but not *las fiestas de quince,* the birthday parties celebrating a girl's fifteenth birthday, marking her coming of age. There is nothing like a *quince* party (a direct legacy of a more conservative Spanish era) for a young *cubana.*

Parents will save money from the day the girl is born to do her right with a memorable fifteenth, the day on which the *quinceañera* may openly begin her sexual life without family recrimination. A whole arsenal might be involved, from the hairdresser and dressmaker (a special dress resembling wedding gowns or a knock-'em-dead Scarlett O'Hara outfit is de rigueur) to the photographer and the classic American car with chauffeur to take the young woman and her friends to the party (usually featuring a feast of not-so-adult ice-cream, sponge cake, and soft drinks).

The Revolution put a damper on this bourgeois celebration, which originated among Spain's upper classes as a "coming out" party to announce a young maiden's attaining adulthood. But the *fiesta de quince* refused to die, and actually came back whole-hog. Today's *quince* is as kitschy as it comes. On the day in question, the young girls are dolled up with lashings of mascara and lipstick, a fancy hairdo, and that oh-so-tantalizing, albeit slightly vulgar, "coming out" costume. She is bustled inside, say, a convertible Cadillac Fleetwood, and paraded through town with balloons trailing behind. In Havana, the party typically heads to the Palacio de los Capitanes Generales, where the young ladies flash coquettish smiles for the camera.

U.S. equivalent is 15.9; that of the U.K. is 16.6; that of Jamaica is 10.9). School is compulsory to age 15 (ninth grade). Children may then choose to continue three years of pre-university study (called *pre*) or attend technical schools. Anyone who has ever visited a Cuban classroom will remark on the enthusiasm displayed by willing, lively pupils. However, schoolchildren are constantly monitored for their "political soundness," and their ability to move up into institu-

tions of higher education and to otherwise succeed depends on their displaying loyalty to the Revolution and, reflecting the education they receive, to the battle against U.S. "imperialism."

Occasionally, Havana's secondary schoolchildren ship out to spend time working in the countryside, where they live in boarding schools attached to 1,250-acre plots of arable land and fulfill José Martí's dictum: "In the morning, the pen—but in the afternoon, the plow." Thus, most intermediate-level children attend a rural boarding school (*escuela del campo*) for at least some of their education: time is divided equally between study and labor, the latter most often in citrus plantations, where the kids bring in the harvest. Here, too, unintended by the state, children learn to be lovers. Promiscuity is a staple in the fields.

Cuban youth have grown up in a mature Revolution—more than 65 percent of the Cuban population was born after the Revolution, and every child is sworn in at the age of six to become a Communist pioneer. The older generation has attempted to make the Revolution, has faced down the threat of U.S. invasion, and witnessed astounding social achievements—all through collective endeavor. Although there is respectful communication between generations, clashes are becoming more common. Where their parents use "we," Havana's youth use "I"—I want to do so and so. The majority are bored by the constant calls for greater sacrifice and tired of being treated as if they were stupid. They want to enjoy life.

Havana's youth are in a confusing limbo where neither the socialist role model nor its complete rejection is appropriate to the current circumstances. Young people growing up in the current era of hardship and economic opening are not necessarily abandoning revolutionary principles. But the ideas many are adopting alarm the authorities. As the quest for U.S. dollars tightens its grip, an increasing number of Cuban youth are asking, "What's the point in studying?" A worrisome number of students are dropping out of class or playing truant. Many realize they can get further through their own work and initiative, and are going into business for themselves as *jineteros* and *cuenta propistas* (entrepreneurs), making a buck doing anything from driving taxis to repairing tire punctures. In recent studies to ascertain high-school students' goals, almost every student stated a desire to work as a *cuenta propista* or with tourists.

The government worries that the increased association with tourists helps foster nonconformism, such as the growing number of long-haired youths—*roqueros* and *frikis*—who sport ripped jeans and would look at home at a Metallica concert.

Cuban youth show a marked preference for anything North American, especially clothing. They wouldn't be caught dead in a *guayabera,* the traditional tropical shirt favored by older men; instead, young women dress in the latest fashion—halter tops, Lycra bodysuits, diaphanous blouses, miniskirts, tight jeans, flared pants, and platform shoes. Young men follow suit, though more conservatively, and as well as their budgets allow. Consumerism is capturing the imagination of Havana's youth, spawned by the notion that the only way to advance is by making money.

More and more, youth feel there is no future in Cuba. "We can't wait forever," they say. Many still look up to Castro as a hero, but the vast majority of youth today see him as a dour father figure who can't get with the times.

Cuban youth are served by their own state newspapers, such as *Pionero* and *Juventud Rebelde (Rebel Youth),* which mix intelligent articles with paternalistic pabulum.

¡Cuba Va! is a splendid hour-long documentary released in 1993 in which Cuban youth express their fears and hopes; US$95; Cuba Va Video Project, 12 Liberty St., San Francisco, CA 94110, 415/282-1812, fax 415/282-1798.

Also see the Special Topic "Where To Take The Kids" in the Entertainment and Recreation chapter and the Notes for Travelers with Children section in the Information and Services chapter.

RELIGION

Cuba is officially an atheist country, and proselytizing is illegal. Nonetheless, a recent government survey found that more than half of all Cubans are *creyentes,* believers of one sort or another.

Christianity

Habaneros have traditionally been lukewarm about Christianity, mostly because the Catholic Church sided with the Spanish against the patriots during the colonial era. After independence, the constitution therefore provided for separation of church and state, depriving the former of its political influence and state support.

Later, the Catholic Church had a quid pro quo with the corrupt Machado, Grau, and Batista regimes—"you keep out of our business and we'll keep out of yours." When the Revolution triumphed, many of the clergy left for Miami along with the rich to whom they had ministered.

The Catholic Church has since been a focus of opposition. Hence, although the Castro regime has never banned the practice of religion, the church was allowed to engage in only marginal social activities. Church attendance came to be considered antisocial. Religious education was eliminated from the school curriculum. Practicing Catholics were banned from the Communist Party. Religious believers declined from more than 70 percent of the population to less than 30 percent, and church attendance plummeted. Churches had to close down due to disrepair, and many priests resorted to holding services in private homes.

In 1986, Castro performed an about face: religion was no longer the opiate of the masses. In 1990, he admitted that believers had been unjustly treated. That year, for only the second time in more than 30 years, radio and television stations began transmitting religious music and songs. The following year, the Communist Party opened its doors to believers, and security agents disappeared from churches. It was a timely move, co-opting the shifting mood. Church attendance has since skyrocketed, as has the number of seminarians.

Pope John Paul II's emotionally charged visit to Cuba in January 1998 was an extraordinary event that boosted the influence of the Catholic church in Cuba and reignited an expression of faith among the Cuban people. In December 1997, Castro had declared Christmas a holiday as a goodwill gesture to the Pope, three decades after it was canceled; Christmas trees appeared in the stores for the first time in many years, and in 1999 even Santa Claus was to be seen acting as doorman outside Havana's Hotel Meliá Cohiba. An ensuing display of goodwill towards the church was reflected in an open-air celebration involving tens of thousands of Cuban Protestants in Plaza de la Revolución in June 1999, with Fidel Castro in attendance. Protestants are estimated to number about 300,000, with about 23 distinct churches represented.

Despite increased tolerance of the church, harassment continues. In April 1999, for example, the Communist Party arranged noisy street demonstrations to march outside Cathedrals while Mass was being held over Easter Week and even ordered crucifixes removed from funeral cars donated by Italy. In December 1999, the Pope, disappointed with the meager progress since his visit, urged Castro to respect human rights and display "a more generous opening."

Despite the increased expression of faith in recent years, a huge percentage of *habaneros*—perhaps the majority—remain atheistic, or at least agnostic, and bring to their dialectic an unusually rigid investigative rationale by which to reach their conclusions about the purported existence of a god. A far larger percentage, however, are superstitious and believe to lesser or greater degree in *santería*. Even devout Catholics will have a *limpieza* (ritual *santería* cleansing) performed to hedge their bets in times of need.

Santería

It's said that if you scratch a Cuban, Catholic or non, you'll find a *santería* believer underneath. Even Castro, a highly superstitious person, is said to be a believer; many loyalists link him to the warrior god Changó, which they imagine helps account for his political longevity and escapes from countless assassination attempts. To help support their suspicions, they point to some interesting facts. Castro triumphed on January 1, a holy day for the *orishas*. The red and black flag of the revolutionaries was that of Eleguá, god of destiny. Then, on January 9, 1959, as Castro addressed the nation from Camp Columbia, two doves suddenly flew over the audience and circled the brightly lit podium; miraculously, one of the doves alighted on Castro's shoulder, touching off an explosion from the ecstatic onlookers: *"Fi-del! Fi-del! Fi-del!"* In *santería*, doves are symbols of Obatalá, the Son of God. To Cubans—and perhaps Castro himself—the event was a supreme symbol that the gods had chosen him to guide Cuba.

Santería, or saint worship, has been deeply entrenched in Cuban culture for 300 years. Then, as now, its roots have been in the Regla and Guanabacoa districts, across Havana harbor. The cult is a fusion of Catholicism with the *Lucumí* religion of the African Yoruba tribes of modern-day Nigeria and Benin. Since slave masters had banned African religious practice, the slaves cloaked their gods in Catholic garb and continued to pray to them in disguise.

Thus, in *santería*, Catholic figures of virtue are avatars of the Yoruban *orishas*, the spiritual emissaries of Olorún (God). These divine beings, or guardian spirits, of African animism are worshiped in secretive and complex rituals that may feature animal sacrifices along with chanting, dancing, and music. Metaphorically, *orishas* change their identity—even their gender—at midnight: by day, adherents may pray in front of a figure of Santa Barbara and at night worship the same figure as Changó. As sociologist Nelson Valdés notes, Cubans live comfortably with this paradox. There are about 400 gods in the pantheon, but only about 20 are honored in daily life.

© CHRISTOPHER P. BAKER

santería doll, Bosque de la Habana

Almost every home in Havana has a *bóveda*, or "spirit altar," with a statue of a *santería* god and a glass of water and other miscellany to appease the spirits of the dead. And walking Havana's streets, you'll see believers clad all in white, having just gone through their initiation rites as *santeros* or *santeras*.

A follower of *santería* may choose at any stage in life to undertake an elaborate initiation that will tear the follower away from his or her old life and set their feet on *La Regla de Ocha*—the Way of the Orishas. During this time, the *iyawó*—an initiate or "bride" of the *orishas*—will be possessed by, and under the care of, a specific *orisha* who will guide the initiate to a deeper, richer life for the rest of his or her time in this world. Initiations are highly secret and involve animal sacrifice (usually pigeons and roosters). The rites are complex. They include having to dress solely in white and stay indoors at night for a year, though exceptions are made for employment. And an *iyawó* may not touch anyone or permit him—or herself to be touched, except by the most intimate family members . . . or, this being Cuba, by lovers.

It is thought that the *orishas* control an individual's life—a string of bad luck will be blamed on an *orisha*—and must therefore be placated. The gods are believed to perform all kinds of miracles on a person's behalf and are thus consulted and besought. They're too supreme for mere mortals to communicate with directly. Hence *babalawos* (priests) act as go-betweens to honor the saints and interpret their commands . . . for a fee. *Babalawos* use divination to interpret the *obi* and *ifá*—oracles—and solve everyday problems, notably those related to health, using coconut pieces of dried shells and seashells.

Santería is a sensuous religion. It lacks the arbitrary moral prescriptions of Catholicism—the *orishas* let adherents have a good time. The gods themselves are fallible and hedonistic philanderers, such as the much feared and respected Changó (or Santa Barbara), god of war, fire, thunder, and lightning. Changó's many mistresses include Oyá (or Santa Teresa, patron saint of the ill and dead, and guardian of cemeteries) and Ochún (the Virgen de la Caridad del Cobre),

BRIDE OF THE ORISHAS

Miss Cuba appeared, dressed all in white. She hurried toward me wraithlike in the dark, the moonlight shining full upon her white turban, blouse, shawl, and calf-length skirt that billowed around her sleek legs, now adorned in white stockings. Copper and bronze amulets glinted upon her arms, and she wore many necklaces— collares—of colorful beads. Marleni—for that was her name—was a santera, a follower of the Santería religion; dressed thus, I knew that she lived at this moment in a high state of grace.

"Hola, Cristóbal," she said, her big brown eyes beaming widely, her whole pretty face lit up with a sublime mixture of innocence and joy. Our smiles ricocheted.

She took my hand, and I sensed once again the simplicity with which in Cuba desire can strike flaming miracles from charming scenes of tropical naiveté . . .

We hailed an illegal taxi—a '53 Ford with blackened windows—tucked ourselves in the back seat, and rode hand in hand back to Vedado through dimly lit streets. On a dark, narrow lane off Infanta, a policeman suddenly leaped into our path and frantically waved down the jalopy. A man lay bleeding in the street, he explained to the driver. The policeman wanted to bundle him into the car and commandeer it for a trip to the hospital.

"¡Ay, mi Dios!" Marleni exclaimed. She leaned forward and spoke through the driver's window: "¡Estoy de santera. ¡No se puede!"

The policeman, a young black man, looked aghast, then waved us on and ran off to look for another car.

"What did you tell him?" I asked, astounded.

"I am not myself," she replied. "I am Santa Teresita, the patrona de los muertos." The patron saint of the dead. "If he had put that man in the car, I might have killed him."

I felt a chill run down my spine, and pondered what my last few hours in Cuba had in store.

Christopher P. Baker, Mi Moto Fidel: Motorcycling Through Castro's Cuba

the sensuous black goddess of pleasure who loves to dance and make love, and whom many Cuban women identify as the *orisha* of love in an erroneous syncretism with Venus. This fits well with the sensualist Cuban psyche.

Each saint has specific attributes. Changó, for example, dresses in red and white and carries a scepter with double-headed axe. Thus, followers of Changó wear collars decorated with red and white plastic beads. Ochún wears yellow; thus her followers wear yellow and white beads. Eleguá (Saint Anthony), the guardian of highways and the crossroads to the future, wears red and black; his beads correspond. Obbatalá (the Virgen de la Merced), goddess of peace and creation, dresses in white. Yemayá (the Virgen de Regla), goddess of the sea and of motherhood, wears blue and white. Each saint also has his or her own dance, as well as an "altar," such as the ceiba tree in the northeast corner of Havana's Plaza de Armas, where offerings (fruits, rum-soaked cakes, pastries, and coins) are strewn near its trunk. At other altars, caged pigeons and chickens await their fate at the end of a knife. Devout *santeros* even keep a collection of vases in their bedrooms in which one's personal orisha, plus Obbatalá, Yemayá, Ochún, and Changó live . . . in that hierarchical order.

Homage is paid to *orishas* on specific saint's days. For example, Ochún is honored on September 18.

Following the Revolution, the government stigmatized *santería* as *brujería* (witchcraft). Castro's dogma of scientific Communism and his need to emasculate rival sources of power translated into an attempt to convert *santería* into a folkloric movement. Religious rites were restricted. As Marxism lost its appeal in the late 1980s, *santería* bounced back, offering relief from the "propagandistic realism" of the socialist world. The desperate conditions of the Special Period caused millions to visit their *babalawos*. The Castro government began to co-opt support for the faith (not least, perhaps, as a counterpoint to the rising power of the Catholic Church) by supporting the *babalawos*. Reportedly, many *babalawos* have been recruited by MININT, for they above all know people's secrets.

You can arrange to visit a *babalawo* through state agencies such as Rumbos (Línea #60, esq. M, Vedado, tel. 66-2113 or 204-9626, fax 33-3110) or on your own. One such is Eberardo Marero, Calle Ñico López #60, e/ Coyola y Camilo Cienfuegos, Regla. There are several others in Regla. Ask around.

African Cult Religions

Other spiritualist cults exist in Cuba. The most important is the all-male *Abakua* secret mutual protection society that originated in Nigeria, appearing in Cuba in the early 19th century. It still functions among the most marginalized black communities, where it is known as *naniguismo*. The first duty of an adherent is to protect a fellow member. Membership is restricted to "brave, virile, dignified, moral men" who contribute positively to their communities. Nonetheless, it is extreme and involves worship of ancestral devil figures, called *diablitos* or *iremes,* where dancers appear dressed from head to toe in hooded woven Hessian costumes. Members use a system of writing called *anaforuana* with symbols employed for religious powers.

Palo Monte (known also as *reglas congas*) also derives from West-Central Africa and is a spirit religion that harnesses the power of the deceased to control supernatural forces. Adherents (called *paleros*) use ritual sticks and plants to perform magic. Initiates receive small incisions in their body into which magical substances are inserted. A three-legged cauldron called a *nganga* is used as a form of altar, containing all the natural elements of the world, plus the dead person's spirit.

Planning Your Trip

U.S. Law and Cuba Travel

Contrary to popular belief, U.S. law does *not* prohibit U.S. citizens from visiting Cuba. However, to visit Cuba legally you must either spend no money there, or qualify for a license issued by the U.S. Treasury Department in order to buy goods (a meal at a hotel, for example) or services (an airline ticket, tour package, or hotel room). In order to apply, you need a good reason. Except as specifically licensed by the Office of Foreign Assets Control (OFAC), payments in connection with any other travel to Cuba are prohibited, whether travelers go directly or via a third country such as Mexico, Canada, or a Caribbean island.

U.S. citizens and any person in the United States are subject to these restrictions, regardless of citizenship. Under these restrictions, spending money relating to Cuban travel is prohibited unless the traveler is licensed. The regulations change frequently and are open to interpretation by the understaffed office—interpretation often shifts with the political breeze.

U.S. universities and nongovernmental organizations may apply for two-year travel permits to Cuba that will permit any of its members to travel to Cuba.

To determine if you or your organization qualifies for a **general license** (which does not require prior government authorization) or a **specific license** (which does require prior

Plaza Vieja

government authorization), contact the Licensing Division, Office of Foreign Asset Control (OFAC), U.S. Department of the Treasury, 1500 Pennsylvania Ave. NW, Washington, D.C. 20200, 202/622-2520, fax 202/622-1657, http://www.treas.gov/offices/enforcement/ofac/sanctions/. Request the *Cuban Assets Control Regulations.* Alternately, check with the U.S.–Cuba Trade and Economic Council, 30 Rockefeller Plaza, New York, NY 10112-0002, 212/246-1444, fax 212/246-2345, www.cubatrade.org, which stays abreast of the latest regulations. Relevant information is contained within the Code of Federal Regulations (CFR)—31 CFR Part 515.

The Office of Cuban Affairs (OCA), Department of State, Washington, D.C. 20520, 202/647-9273, fax 202/736-4476, www.state.gov, establishes the policies by which the OFAC interprets the regulations by which laws are enforced.

CURRENT REGULATIONS

Below is a list of the current regulations at press time.

Who Is an "Individual Subject to United States Law"?

An individual subject to U.S. law includes: any individual, wherever located, who is a citizen or resident of the United States; any person who is within the United States (a non-U.S. citizen in transit at an airport, for example); any corporation organized under the laws of the United States or of any state, territory possession, or district of the United States; any corporation, partnership, or association, wherever organized or doing business, that is owned or controlled by an individual or individuals subject to U.S. law. Non-U.S. citizens who have H-1 visas are generally considered to be subject to U.S. law.

General Licenses

The following categories of travelers are permitted to spend money for Cuban travel without the need to obtain special permission from OFAC, nor are they required to inform OFAC in advance of their visit to Cuba:

Official Government Travelers: U.S. and foreign government officials, including representatives of international organizations of which the United States is a member, who are traveling on official business.

Journalists: Individuals who are regularly (full-time) employed by a news-gathering organization (television network, television station, television production company, radio station, newspaper, newsletter, magazine, video production company, and so on), and persons regularly employed as supporting broadcast or technical personnel. Travelers are advised to have company identification (with photograph), business card, and/or a letter from the company confirming full-time employment.

Warning: Note that if you travel as a journalist, the Cuban government requires that you be issued a journalist's visa, not a tourist card. This usually takes at least three weeks for approval, but usually much longer.

Persons Visiting Close Relatives: People with close relatives in Cuba may visit them in circumstances of humanitarian need. This authorization is valid only once every 12 months.

"Fully Hosted" Travelers: Individuals subject to U.S. law traveling on a "fully hosted" basis can travel without a specific license so long as they do not spend any funds of their own while in Cuba. This includes travel on a prepaid, all-inclusive tour package. Funds used to make payments for hotels, meals, ground transportation, sundries, and other items must originate from (a) an entity within Cuba, (b) an entity within another country, or (c) an individual within another country. The use of indirect transfers is not permitted. A "fully hosted" traveler may pay for transportation only if aboard a non-Cuban carrier such as Mexicana, Air Jamaica, Lacsa, or Iberia. Travelers whose expenses are covered by a person not subject to U.S. jurisdiction may not bring back any Cuban origin goods, except for informational materials (like books, magazines, and posters) and an unlimited amount of artwork. Gifts from Cuban nationals may be brought into the United States, but the gift must remain with the U.S. Customs Service at the point of entry; the traveler subject must then request a license from the OFAC to take possession of the gift.

"Fully hosted" travelers are subject to increased scrutiny. The OFAC states that a letter from an individual or entity not subject to U.S. law—or a letter from a U.S.-based law firm—confirming that the individual was "fully hosted" will not be accepted as "proof" that a visit was "fully hosted." "Fully hosted" travelers are now required to produce receipts for all daily expenses within Cuba which demonstrate that all of the expenses were paid by an individual or entity not subject to U.S. law, and to submit a signed letter to that effect.

Amateur or Semiprofessional Athletes: Athletes are allowed to enter Cuba when traveling to participate in athletic competition held under the auspices of an international sports federation.

Full-Time Professionals: Individuals whose travel transactions are directly related to noncommercial, academic research and whose research will comprise a full work schedule in Cuba and has a likelihood of public dissemination; plus full-time professionals whose travel transactions are directly related to attendance at professional meetings or conferences that do not promote tourism or other commercial activity involving Cuba or the production of biotechnological products.

Students and Academic Employees: These individuals, when affiliated with an academic institution that has been issued a specific license, may engage in travel transactions so long as travel is for participation in a structured educational program; noncommercial academic research; formal course study; teaching in a Cuban academic institution; educational exchange involving formal study; or preparation of such educational activities. Secondary school students may be accompanied by "a reasonable number of adult chaperones." Such travelers must carry a letter from the licensed institution stating the institution's license number and as of 2003, students have to show that travel is for academic course work.

Travelers Affiliated with Religious Institutions: Religious groups that hold a specific license may engage in travel transactions without seeking OFAC authorization so long as travel is under the auspices of the institution and that a full-time program of religious activity is pursued in Cuba.

Specific Licenses

A specific license requires written government approval. Applicants should write a letter to OFAC stating the date of the planned visit and the length of stay; the specific purpose(s) of the visit; plus the name(s), title(s), and background(s) of the traveler. OFAC is notoriously slow: allow two or three months. For OFAC information regarding Specific Licenses, call 202/622-2480 or 305/810-5140.

U.S. academic institutions may apply for a license (good for two years) permitting its students and employees to make travel transactions in Cuba. Religious organizations can apply for a similar license permitting individuals affiliated with that organization to make such transactions. Special licenses are also issued by OFAC on a case-by-case basis authorizing travel transactions by persons in connection with the following travel categories:

Humanitarian Travel: Persons traveling to Cuba to visit close relatives in cases involving hardship more than once in a 12-month period; persons traveling to Cuba to accompany licensed humanitarian donations (other than gift parcels); or persons traveling in connection with activities of recognized human rights organizations investigating human rights violations. In early 2003, the list of licensable humanitarian activities was enlarged to include construction projects, educational training, journalism, and other criteria.

Freelance Journalists: Persons with a suitable record of publication who are traveling to do research for a freelance article. Licenses may be issued for multiple trips.

Professional Research and Meetings: Persons engaging in professional research or attending professional meetings that do not meet the general license requirements.

Educational Research: Travel in connection with educational activities that are not related to an academic institution's specific license, including educational exchanges that promote people-to-people contact.

Religious Activities: Travel in connection with religious activities that are not related to a religious institution's specific license.

Private Foundations or Research or Educational Institutions: Persons traveling to Cuba on behalf of such institutions to collect information for noncommercial purposes.

Export, Import, or Transmission of Informational Materials: Persons traveling to engage in exportation, importation, or transmission of informational materials.

Licensed Exportation: Individuals traveling to engage in activities directly related to marketing, sales negotiation, delivery, or servicing of exports of health care products or other exports that may be considered for authorization (this has included the fields of artwork, communications, entertainment, and telecommunications; register trademarks and patents; organize and participate in trade shows; authorize consumer credit cards to be valid for use; and provide travel services and provide air transportation services).

Others: Persons attending public performances, clinics, workshops, and exhibitions.

What You May Spend

Licensed travelers are authorized to spend up to the State Department Travel *Per Diem* allowance (www.state.gov/www/perdiems/index.html), which was US$158 per day for Cuba in 2002. This allowance covers accommodation, food, and transportation, and necessary incidentals. Exemptions to the US$158 per day authorization can be requested from OFAC. "Fully hosted" travelers are not subject to spending limits while within the Republic of Cuba. Journalists also may spend more than $158 daily (the amount is unspecified) to cover expenses incurred in the reporting of a story. There is no restriction on the amount that may be spent on informational materials; such expenditure is not counted in the daily allowance.

Money may be spent only for purchases of items directly related to travel such as hotel accommodations, meals, and goods personally used by the traveler in Cuba, or for the purchase of US$100 worth of Cuban merchandise to be brought into the United States as accompanied baggage. Purchases of services related to travel, such as non-emergency medical services, are prohibited.

Licensed travelers (except fully-hosted travelers) may return from Cuba with up to US$100

worth of Cuban products (such as cigars, rum, T-shirts, and crafts) for their personal use. For cigars, the U.S. Customs Service permits up to 100 cigars, but the total value must not exceed US$100. For example, if a traveler returns with 100 cigars that cost US$1 each, the traveler would not be permitted to bring any other Cuban products (such as rum). Travelers should retain a receipt showing the amount paid for all Republic of Cuba-origin products.

Qualified Travel Service Providers

U.S. law states, "U.S. travel service providers, such as travel agents and tour operators, who handle travel arrangements to, from, or within Cuba must hold special authorizations from the U.S. Treasury Department to engage in such activities."

OFAC licenses companies as authorized Travel Service Providers (TSPs), who are legally entitled to make commercial travel arrangements to Cuba. Some TSPs are also Carrier Service Providers (CSPs) licensed to operate their own charters to Cuba. See the Special Topic "Licensed Carrier Service Providers" for information on individual companies. As of March 2003, the Treasury Department began to close what it sees as a "loop hole" and no new licenses or renewals of existing ones were to be granted.

OFAC also issues TSP licenses to certain companies and organizations permitting them to offer pre-packaged group tours. A surprisingly wide range of tours are offered, spanning the spectrum from salsa and music study to Jewish heritage tours.

TSPs can only make reservations for individual travel for licensed travelers. You must obtain approval before proceeding with a reservation. Qualified travelers should begin preparations two months in advance of their travel date.

However, referring to other travel agencies and tour operators (i.e., non-TSPs), "It is possible to provide travel services to U.S. persons legally able to travel to Cuba for family visits, professional research, or news gathering," says Michael Krinsky, a partner in the law firm of Rabinowitz, Boudin, Standard, Krinsky and Lieberman, which represents the Cuban government in the United States.

U.S. travel agencies can also provide services to third countries, from where a traveler makes his or her own arrangements for travel to and within Cuba. They may also be able to provide services, such as travel arrangements to Jamaica, where a component includes an excursion to Cuba. Treasury Department regulations do not "show a clear penalty against travel agents who book travel this way." *Travel agents should double-check the regulations,* however, with the U.S. Department of the Treasury, or with Krinsky, 740 Broadway, New York, NY 10003, 212/254-1111, fax 212/674-4614, mkrinsky@igc.apc.org.

Visas for Licensed Travelers

All licensed travelers to Cuba must have a visa from the Cuban government prior to reserving their flight. TSPs can assist you in acquiring your visa (TSPs typically charge about US$35 for the visa, and often an additional fee for preparing the documents). There are two different forms: one for those born in Cuba and one for those born outside Cuba. Allow 30 days for processing.

Cubans and Cuban-Americans: Anyone who permanently left Cuba after December 31, 1970, must have a valid Cuban passport—people born in Cuba who left Cuba permanently before that date don't need a Cuban passport. If you don't have a Cuban passport and you left Cuba after December 31, 1970, you must contact the Cuban Interests Section in Washington, D.C. (2639 16th St. NW, Washington, D.C. 20009, 202/797-8518, fax 202/797-8521, cubaseccion@igc.apc.org) to get the required paperwork. Cubans who left Cuba permanently prior to 1959 can acquire a slightly less expensive 359 Visa, acquired directly from the Cuban Interests Section.

Illegal Travel

About 170,000 U.S. citizens visited Cuba in 2002. The majority did so legally, while about 22,000 slipped in through third countries and spent freely without a license (surprise: U.S. citizens constitute the third largest source of tourists to Cuba, behind Canadians and Germans). Until recently, the U.S. government basically turned a blind eye to these travelers, but in 2001 the Bush administration sought to tighten control of un-

sanctioned travel. Between 1994 and 1999, OFAC threatened to fine 379 people for illegal transactions. (Trading with Cuba illegally is good for a fine up to US$55,000, but most demands for fines have been US$7,500 or so.) In 2001, there was a significant increase in the numbers of people receiving letters from OFAC threatening and attempting to levy fines; perceived offenders first receive a questionnaire and, if the Feds believe the law has been broken, a "pre-penalty notice" listing the amount of the proposed fine.

Since May 1998, persons subject to U.S. jurisdiction who travel to Cuba without a license bear a "presumption of guilt" and may be required to show documentation that all expenses incurred were paid by a third party not subject to U.S. law.

However, the U.S. Government has never brought this regulation to court, hence, the only fines they've ever collected are from people who upon receiving the "pre-penalty" notice "voluntarily" paid the fine. To date, the government has used the regulation as a threat and deterrent and appears unwilling to test its constitutionality in court. Anyone receiving a pre-penalty notice can kill the action dead by requesting a hearing.

How to Defend the Right to Travel: If you ask for a hearing, your case will most likely be put aside to gather dust. As of press time *no* hearings had been held and *not a single person has been prosecuted.*

The **National Lawyers Guild,** 126 University Place, New York, NY 10003, 212/627-2656, fax 212/627-2404, nlgno@nlg.org, has a website with two response forms to OFAC notices; see www.nlg.org/Cuba. The NLG also has a Cuba subcommittee that can aid in defending against "these restrictions and enforcement actions." Contact Art Heitzer, 606 W. Wisconsin Ave., Suite 1706, Milwaukee, WI 53203, 414/273-1040, aheitzer@igc.org. The NLG maintains a database of lawyers willing to provide such representation. If you choose to pay the fine requested in the pre-penalty notice, you can negotiate the amount.

The **Center for Constitutional Rights,** 666 Broadway, New York, NY 10012, 212/614-6464, fax 212/614-6499, ccr@igc.apc.org, publishes *Advice for Travelers to Cuba* and also provides representation free of charge.

PLANNING YOUR TRIP

Getting There

BY AIR

About 40 airlines service Cuba. The majority of flights arrive at Havana's José Martí International Airport.

Many airlines operate a summer and winter timetable. Information below is based on winter (high season) schedules.

Cuba's national airline is **Cubana de Aviación,** www.cubana.cu, which handles 30 percent of all traffic into Cuba and generally offers lower fares than competing airlines. Cubana has been upgrading its fleet of late and now has 309-passenger DC-10s and new A-320s that serve Europe and Mexico, and offer Business Class and First Class (*Clase Tropical*) service. However, the workhorses in the stable remain uncomfortable and poorly maintained Soviet-made aircraft. The airline is poorly managed: its attitude toward scheduled departures is cavalier; it is notorious for disposing of passengers who arrive after the scheduled check-in time; nonsmoking regulations are rarely enforced; and its safety record is rated as the worst in the world (crashes occurred in Cuba in 1997, 2000, and 2002, and in Ecuador in 1998). Says one tour operator: "The horror stories we hear from clients will make your hair stand on end."

From the United States

At press time, no scheduled commercial flights were permitted between the United States and Cuba. Nor can any U.S. airline, tour operator, or travel agent make arrangements for flights to Cuba without a license from the U.S. Treasury Department.

At press time, Bahamasair was planning to introduce four scheduled flights weekly to Havana

PLANNING YOUR TRIP ONLINE

The e-commerce boom makes it easy to plan and arrange your trip to Cuba online.

Cubalinda.com Inter-Active Travel, info@cubalinda.com, www.cubalinda.com, a U.S.-owned but Cuban-based entity, offers an interactive travel emporium featuring information and reservation services for travel to Cuba, including air reservations. Clients get invoiced by email; payment is made by bank transfer to an account in Germany (for U.S. citizens), or direct to Cuba for transactions originating outside the United States. Electronic tickets are issued. The company was planning to introduce direct credit card payments online, including for U.S. credit cards. The site also lists information on accommodation and "a global offer of practically everything a foreigner can do in Cuba," including 21 activities. Also see Travel Agencies in the Information and Services chapter.

Tour & Marketing, in Spain, Los Cristianos, Arona, Tenerife, tel. 922/752233, fax 922/752153, offers complete travel services at www.gocubaplus.com. The company, which is based in the British Virgin Islands, has an office in Havana at Hotel Viejo y el Mar, Suite 6005, Marina Hemingway, tel. 204-6827, fax 204-3546. U.S. citizens should check out www.uscubatravel.com, or call voicemail: 800/863-3293 (the call will be returned). It offers a "pre-paid" ticket service for flights from Mexico City, Tijuana, Cancún, Nassau, Grand Cayman, as well as cities in Europe. Other services include: accommodations, excursions, city tours, car rentals, and airport transfers.

The Cuban government runs its own interactive website, **CubaSi.cu,** with a competent search engine and reservation ability for flights, hotels, and car rental. **Blue Ocean Tours,** info@blue oceantour.com, has its own interactive tourism website: www.blueoceantour.com.

Also see the section By Organized Tour in this chapter.

LICENSED CARRIER SERVICE PROVIDERS (CSPs)

Airline Brokers Company, 3971 SW 8 St., Miami, FL 33134, 305/871-1260, fax 305/447-0965, tfre97a@prodigy.com, operates charters from Miami on Monday, Wednesday, Friday, and Saturday.

C&T, 305/445-6422, operates charters from Miami on Monday, Thursday, and Sunday.

Cuba Travel Services, 310/772-2822, mz@lato cuba.com, www.cubatravelservices.com, specializes in flights from Los Angeles and operates charters on Friday.

Gulfstream, 305/871-0526, www.gulfstream air.com, operates charters from Miami on Monday, Wednesday, Friday, and Saturday. They also operate one flight a week to Havana exclusively for staff of the U.S. Interests Section.

Marazul Charters, 7311 Bergenline Ave., N Bergen, NJ 07047, 201/861-9950, fax 201/861-9954, www.marazulcharters.com, operates charters from New York on Saturday and Sunday, and from Miami on Friday and Sunday. Its affiliate, **Marazul Tours,** Tower Plaza Mall, 4100 Park Ave., Weehawken, NJ 07087, 201/840-6711 or 800/223-5334, fax 201/319-9009, info@marazultours.com, www.marazultours.com, offers dozens of specialist tours and arranges travel for licensed travelers.

Transair Travel, 2813 McKinley Place NW, Washington, D.C. 20015, 202/362-6100, fax 202/362-7411, blubic@aol.com.

Wilson International Services, 4919 SW 75 Ave., Miami, FL 33152, 305/662-6842, offers charters from Miami on Monday, Wednesday, and Friday.

Xael Charters, 4714 SW 74 Ave., Miami, FL 33155, 305/265-5011, offers charters from Miami on Wednesday and Friday.

Tico Travel, 161 E. Commercial Blvd., Ft. Lauderdale, FL 33334, 954/493-8426 or 800/493-8426, fax 954/493-8466, tico@gate.net, www.destinationcuba.com, makes reservations and was planning on introducing its own charter flights from Miami.

PLANNING YOUR TRIP

from Nassau, Thursday–Sunday (US$198 round-trip introductory fare) with connecting flights from Miami, Orlando, and Fort Lauderdale, using Boeing 737s. Unlicensed travelers will be able to take the flights. Reservations are being handled by the **Havana Flying Club,** 416/921-4102 or 877/488-0388, fax 416/969-8916, www.havanaflying club.com, or online via www.cubalinda.com.

Thousands of U.S. citizens take advantage of the many scheduled commercial airline services to Cuba from other countries. The *most* popular routes are through Canada, the Bahamas, Mexico, or Jamaica. As described in this chapter, there are a number of airlines, tour operators, and travel agencies that can provide travel arrangements via a third country.

It is *essential* to have completely separate tickets and reservations for your travel into and out of Cuba from any third country: under existing U.S. law, citizens showing an airline reservation that includes an onward flight to Cuba will be refused boarding on the flight out of the United States. However, you can reserve your ticket with a foreign carrier such as Air Jamaica (which serves Cuba from its North American gateways) but you have to pay for the Jamaica–Cuba leg upon arrival in Jamaica.

You can also search online with ticketing agencies such as www.travelocity.com, www.expedia.com, or www.orbitz.com and purchase a ticket to a third country gateway using a secure server to pay by credit card (compare quotations at different sites, as they vary, even for the same flight). Note, however, that you *cannot* purchase a ticket that involves a portion for travel to Cuba through a U.S. online company, even if you're a foreign citizen whose flight won't touch the United States. A website where you *can* book and pay online is www.cubalinda.com. Cubalinda.com makes reservations from its Havana office and prepays the tickets. The traveler picks up the ticket from the airline in the gateway city airport, such as Cancún. More information is available in the Special Topic "Planning Your Trip Online."

The following U.S. carriers fly to countries where you can connect to flights to Cuba: **American**

COURIERS WANTED

Conchord Cayo Hueso, P.O. Box 2306, Key West, FL 33045, tel./fax 305/294-0205, jitters@aol.com, www.geocities.com/conchordcayohueso, is licensed by OFAC to run food, medicine, and other humanitarian aid to the Cuban people using volunteers ("members") responsible for transporting up to 10 kilos (22.5 pounds) of donated material. Travelers are legally permitted their daily allowance, and may return with up to US$100 of Cuban merchandise. Most couriers fly, but boaters are also used. To become a courier, you have to join CCH as a member (US$50).

Cuba AIDS Project, c/o Byron L. Barksdale, M.D., Pathology Services, P.C., 500 West Leota St., Ste. 200, P.O. Box 1289, North Platte, NE 69103-1289, cubaids@aol.com, www.cubaon line.org, (also see the Special Topic "Cuba's War on AIDS" in the Information and Services chapter) also approves travelers for licensed travel to deliver medicines, medical books, and humanitarian supplies to the Monserrate Church in Centro Habana. Trips are limited to 10 days. You can't use the rest of the time for vacation, however, but are supposed to follow a regimen of people-to-people contacts. The Project also needs donations for travel and lodging expenses for Cuban physicians to come to the USA for professional reasons.

Airlines, 800/433-7300, www.aa.com; **Continental,** 800/231-0856, www.continental.com; **Delta Airlines,** 800/221-1212, www.delta.com; **Northwest,** 800/225-2525, www.northwestair lines.com; **TWA,** 800/892-4141, www.twa.com; **US Airways,** 800/428-4322, www.usairways.com.

For discount tickets, try **Airfares For Less,** 954/565-8667, www.airfares-for-less.com; **Cheap Airlines,** 800/852-2608, www.cheapairlines.com, or **Discount Airfares,** www.discount-airfares.com.

Non-licensed travelers should also refer to the sections on getting to Cuba from Canada, Mexico, and the Caribbean.

International specialists in low fares include **STA Travel,** 800/781-4040, go@statravel.com, www.statravel.com, or **Council Travel,** 888/268-6245, globotron@counciltravel.com, www.coun ciltravel.com, which have offices worldwide.

Licensed Charters and Service Providers: About two dozen companies—called Carrier Service Providers (CSP)—are authorized to fly direct charters to Cuba from the United States—see the Special Topic "Licensed Carrier Service Providers" for a list. Charter operators are only authorized to carry properly documented passengers as permitted by the U.S. Treasury Department. Individuals who are hosted by the Cuban government are barred from taking these flights and must travel on a non-Cuban carrier from outside the United States. CSPs and licensed Travel Service Providers (TSPs, which can make arrangements for travel to Cuba, but are not licensed to offer their own charter service) may also make reservations for authorized or fully-hosted travelers on flights between third countries and Cuba, including Cuban carriers for authorized travelers, but excluding fully-hosted travelers.

Licensed charter flights operate to Havana from Miami twice daily (the number leaps to as many as 10 daily during Christmas and Easter) and at press time typically cost US$299–329 round-trip, US$195–225 one-way; children under 12 US$175–180 round-trip, US$115–120 one-way. In addition, scheduled charter flights depart Los Angeles (about US$750 round-trip), and New York's John F. Kennedy airport (about US$629 round-trip). Atlanta was to be added, with charter service operated by Delta; and New Orleans and Fort Lauderdale are vying. Flights are operated by such airlines as American, Continental, and United, so you're in good hands. And the government fixes prices, which are the same for the First Class section as the back of the plane.

By Private Aircraft: Owners of private aircraft, including air ambulance services, who intend to land in Cuba must obtain a temporary export permit for the aircraft from the U.S. Department of Commerce prior to departure.

You must contact the **Instituto de Aeronáutica Civil de Cuba**, Calle 23 #64, e/ Infanta y P, Vedado, tel. 33-4445, fax 33-3082, at least 10 days prior to arrival in Cuba and at least 48 hours before an overflight.

From Canada

Most flights from Canada serve Cuba's beach resorts rather than Havana. Toronto-based charter tour operators are the driving force of the trade. You might find cheap airfares—about C$400 round-trip—through **Travel Deals**, 416/236-0125, or **Wholesale Travel Group**, 416/366-0062 or 877/970-3600, www.wholesaletravel.com. **Canadian Universities Travel Service** (Travel Cuts), 416/614-2887 or 800/667-2887 in Toronto, 604/717-7800 in Vancouver, www.travel cuts.com, sells discount airfares to students and has 25 offices throughout Canada.

A. Nash Travel Inc., 5865 McLaughlin Rd., Unit 2B, Mississauga, Ontario L5R 1B8, 905/755-0647 or 800/818-2004 ext. 221, fax 905/755-0729, jkrytiuk@nashtravel.com, www .nashtravel.com, has been recommended as a Cuba specialist.

Scheduled Flights: **Cubana**, 1240 Bay St., Suite 800, Toronto, 416/967-2822, fax 416/967-2824, sales@cubanatours.com, has departures weekly using an A-320 from Montreal (thrice weekly) and Toronto (four times weekly) to Havana; from about C$500 in low season and C$700 in high season (the flights are operated by TransAer International Airlines, with Irish crew). You can usually get rates lower than Cubana's published fares by booking with Canadian tour agencies. American Airlines even gives 1200 "AAdvantage Frequent Flyer Miles" if you book with **Canadian Airlines** to Cuba, which uses Cubana as a regional partner to operate the flight.

Air Canada, 800/247-2262, www.aircan ada.ca, flies three times weekly from Toronto to Havana. **Lacsa**, 800/225-2272 or 888/261-3269, www.grupotaca.com, flies to Havana four times weekly from Toronto, with continuing service to Costa Rica.

Air Jamaica, 416/229-6024 or 800/526-5585,

www.airjamaica.com, offers connecting flights to Havana through Montego Bay, Jamaica, departing Toronto.

Charter Flights: **Air Canada Vacations**, 514/422-5788, www.aircanadavacations.com, a division of Air Canada, offers air-hotel packages. Tickets are issued only via travel agencies.

Similar air-hotel packages are offered by companies that charter **Air Transat**, 514/987-1616, fax 514/987-9750, www.airtransat.com. Such companies advertise in the travel sections of leading newspapers, such as the *Toronto Globe & Mail* and *Montreal Gazette*.

From Europe

Direct air service to Cuba is available from most Western European countries. The cheapest fares are usually on direct flights, but you can also find cheap fares via Caribbean destinations or Miami, from where you can take a flight to the Bahamas and then to Cuba. Note that if flying aboard a U.S. carrier, you must have your ticket for the Cuban portion issued on a separate ticket stock, and you must make your reservation for the Cuba leg separately.

Flight times between Europe and Cuba average about nine hours.

From Belgium: Once-a-week **Cubana**, Avenue Louise Nr. #3-1050, Bruxelles, BTE 7, tel. 02/640-0810, flights serve Havana from Belgium (about US$590).

From Ireland: Russian carrier **Aeroflot** tel. 06/47-2299, in London 020/9241-1857, infres @aeroflot.co.uk, www.aeroflot.ru, flies from Shannon to Havana non-stop on Saturdays (Apr.–June, and Oct.) and Mondays (July-Sept.). The flight has generous legroom, but no in-flight movies . . . so bring a good book.

From France: Havana is served by **Air France**, tel. (0802) 80-28-02, www.airfrance.com.fr, from Paris's Charles de Gaulle airport on Tuesday, Thursday, Friday, and Saturday in summer and daily in winter (from €751 round-trip in summer, 30-day APEX economy). **Air Europa**, www.aireuropa.com, flies between Paris and Havana on Saturdays (from about €625). **AOM**, tel. (0803) 00-12-34, www.air-liberte.fr, flies to Havana from Paris Orly on Monday and Friday.

CUBANA OFFICES OUTSIDE CUBA

Cubana and its tour entity, Sol y Son, have the following offices worldwide:

Europe

Berlin: Frankfurter Tor 8-A, 10234 Berlin, tel. 030/293-6300, fax 030/294-7763, cu.alcala@t-online.de

Brussels: Avenue Louise Nr. #3-1050, Bruxelles, BTE 7, tel. 02/640-0810

Las Palmas: Calle Galicia #29, Las Palmas de Gran Canaria, tel. 928/272-408, fax 928/272-429

Madrid: (Cubana) Princesa 25, 28008 Madrid, tel. 091/542-2923 or 758-7751, fax 091/559-3690, cubanamad@deico.es; (Sol y Son) Calle Miguel Ángel #4, Puerta 10, 28010 Madrid, tel. 091/308-0592, fax 091/308-7271, ventasmad@solyson-sa.es

Milano: Via Appia Nouva 45, Scala B, 00182 Roma, tel. 06/4877-1330 or 06/700-0714, fax 06/700-1670, cubana.aviacion@flashnet.it

Moscow: (Cubana) Karovij Val 7, Corpus 1, Seccion 5, Moscow, tel. 095/237-1901, fax 095/237-8391, cubmow@cityline.ru; (Sol y Son) Korojvy Val, Bldg 7, Section 5, Moscow, tel. 095/931-9964, fax 095/237-8394, sol-y-son@mtu-net.ru

Paris: (Cubana) 41 Boulevard Du Montparnasse, 75006 Paris, tel. 01/53-63-23-23, fax 01/53-63-23-29, comercial.cubana@wanadoo.fr; (Sol y Son) 41 Blvd. du Montparnasse, 75006 Paris, tel. 01/53-63-39-39, fax 01/53-63-39-36, www.voyagessolyson.fr

Rome: (Cubana) Via Appia Nouva 45, Scala B, 00182 Roma, tel. 06/4877-1330 or 06/700-0714, fax 06/700-1670, cubana.aviacion@flashnet.it; (Sol y Son) Via Gaeta #16, Roma 00985, tel. 06/4470-2320, fax 06/49-1877, solyson@libero.it

Canada

Montreal: (Cubana) 4 Place Ville Marie #1535, Montreal, Quebec H3B 2B5, 514/871-1222, fax 514/871-1227, cubana@qc.aira.com; (Sol y Son) 620 St Jacques, Suite 30, Montreal, Quebec H3C 1C7, 514/861-2897, fax 514/871-1227, vara playa@qc.aira.com

Toronto: 1240 Bay St., Suite 800, Toronto, Ontario M5R 2A7, 416/967-2822, fax 416/967-2824, cubanasales1@home.com

Cubana, 41 Boulevard du Montarnasse, 75006 Paris, tel. 01/53-63-23-23, fax 01/53-63-23-29, comercial.cubana@wanadoo.fr, flies from Lyon via Paris Orly airport on Monday, with additional twice-weekly service from Orly.

Good online resources for discount airfares include www.travelprice.fr, www.anyway.fr, and (for students) www.wasteels.fr.

From Germany: A Cubana, Fankfurter Tor 8 A, 10243 Berlin, tel. 030/294-7763, fax 030/294-7763, cu.alcala@t-online.de, DC-10 flies to Havana from Berlin via Frankfurt on Sunday. **LTU,** tel. (0211)941-8888, fax (0211)941-

8881, service@ltu.de, www.ltu.de, flies to Havana and Holguín from Berlin on Fridays.

Kubareisen, Lindwurmstr. 207, 80337 München, tel./fax: 089/7479-1064, info@cubareisen.com, www.kubareisen.com, specializes in flights to Cuba.

From Italy: Air Europe, tel. 800/454-0000, fax 079/285-4490, www.aireurope.it, flies from Milan to Havana on Sunday (about €750 roundtrip). **Cubana,** Via Appia Nouva 45, Scala B, 00182 Roma, tel. 06/4877-1330 or 06/700-0714, fax 06/700-1670, cubana.aviacion@flashnet.it, flies from Rome three times weekly using a DC-10.

Mexico, Central America, and Caribbean

Cancún: Jabalí #225, Local H, Cancún, tel. 98/877-210, fax 98/877-373, cubana@cancun.novenet.com.mx

Kingston: 22 Trafalgar Road #11, Kingston 10, Jamaica, tel. 876/978-3410, fax 876/978-3406, cubana@cwjamaica.com

Mexico City: Homero #613, esq. Temistocles, Colonia Polanca, 11650 Mexico DF, tel. 05/250-6355, fax 05/255-0835, reservaciones@cubanamexico.com

Nassau: Nassau International Airport, tel. 242/377-8752, fax 242/377-3460

Panama City: Avenida Justo Arosemena, e/ 41 y 42, Unicentro, Bella Vista, Ciudad de Panama, tel. 507/227-2291, fax 507/272-2241

San José: Edificio Edicol, Sabana Sur, San José, tel. 506/290-5095, fax 506/290-5101, solyson@sol.racsa.co.cr

Santo Domingo: Avenida Tiradentes esq. 27 de Febrero, Plaza Merengue, Local 209, Dominican Republic, tel. 809/227-2040, fax 809/227-2044, cubana.aviacion@codetel.net.do

South America

Bogotá: Carrera 18 #76-76, Bogotá, tel. 01/610-1676, fax 01/610-5800, solyson@colomsat.net.co

Buenos Aires: Sarmiento 552, e/ Florida y San Martín, Buenos Aires, tel. 114/326-5291, fax 114/326-5294, cubana@tournet.com.ar

Caracas: Avenida Andrés Bello, e/ 1ra transversal y Avenida Francisco de Miranda, Los Palos Grandes, Caracas, tel. 212/286-7475, fax 212/286-9126, cubana@intercon.net.ve

Lima: Jirón Tarata #250, Miraflores, Lima 18, tel. 012/241-0554, fax 012/241-0554, solyson@mail.cosapidata.com.pe

Quito: Avenida de los Shyris #32-14, Edificio Torre Nova, Quito, Ecuador, tel. 02/22-7463, fax 02/22-7454, cubana@hoy.net

Santiago de Chile: Avenida Fidel Oteiza #1971, Providencia, Santiago de Chile, tel. 02/274-1819, fax 02/274-8207, cubanascl@entelchile.net

São Paulo: Rua da Consolação #232, Conjunto 1009, Centro, São Paulo, Brazil, tel. 011/214-4571, fax 011/255-8660, cubanabrasil@uol.com.br

PLANNING YOUR TRIP

Lauda Air, Strada Provinciale 52, 21010 Vizzola Ticino, Italy, tel. (0331) 75931, fax (0331) 230-467, www.lauda.it, flies charters from Milan on Wednesday.

From the Netherlands: Havana is served by **Martinair,** tel. 20/60-11-767, fax 20/60-11-303, www.martinair.com, from Amsterdam on Thursday via Cancún, and Sunday direct.

From Russia: Russian carrier **Aeroflot,** Kosmodamianskaya 52/5, Moscow, tel. 095/753-5555 in Moscow, tel. 812/118-5555 in St Petersburg, www.aeroflot.ru, flies from Moscow to Havana via Shannon. **Cubana,** Karovik Val 7, Section 5, Moscow, tel. 095/237-1801, fax 095/237-8391, cubmow@cityline.ru, operates a DC-10 once a week from Moscow on Wednesday, with a stopover in Madrid.

From Spain: Havana is served by **Cubana,** Princesa 25, 28008 Madrid, tel. 91/542-2923 or 758-7751, fax 91/559-3690, cubana mad@deico.es, from both Madrid and Barcelona once weekly using a DC-10, and from Santiago de Compostela and Las Palmas, Calle Galicia #29, Las Palmas de Gran Canaria, tel. 928/272-408, fax 928/272-429, using an Ilyushin. **Iberia,** tel. 01/587-8785, www.iberia.com, flies to Havana from Madrid, daily (€1,017 round-trip in summer). **Air Europa,** tel. 971/178-100 or 902/401-501, www.air-europa.com, flies from Madrid to Havana daily (€899 round-trip in summer). And **Spanair,** tel. 902/131-425, www.spanair.com, was planning to add service.

Good online resources for discount airfares include www.travelprice.es and (for students) www.barceloviajes.es and www.tuiviajes.com.

From Switzerland: Havana is served by **Cubana,** tel. 22/919-8975, fax 22/919-8976, geneva@aviareps.com, from Geneva on Fridays.

From the UK: The main carrier is now **Air Jamaica,** tel. 020/8570-7999, www.air jamaica.com, which flies to Havana direct from Heathrow on Mondays, with connecting service to Montego Bay. It also flies between Heathrow and Montego Bay, with connecting service to Havana. Typical APEX fares for 2002 averaged about £475 in low season, £750 in high season.

Kuoni, (01306) 74002 or (01306) 744442 (Caribbean desk), (0161) 832-0667 (Manchester), www.kuoni.co.uk, launched a year-round charter service from Gatwick to Havana in 2001, departing Mondays.

British Airways, tel. 020/8897-4000, www.britishairways.co.uk, initiated direct flights to Havana from Heathrow in Spring 1999, but canceled them in 2001; it's worth checking to see if they've been reinstated. Alternately, you can fly direct with British Airways from Heathrow to Nassau, the Bahamas, then connect with a Cubana flight. Likewise, **Cubana** closed its London office and reduced its Gatwick–Havana flights in 2001 to once weekly, on Saturdays, using a DC-10 (£435 in mid-2002), with a stop in Holguín.

Go, British Airways' budget wing, has cheap connecting service to other European destinations, as does **Virgin Express,** tel. 020/7744-0004, which connects with Madrid, where you can catch flights to Havana. London–Havana fare quotes for mid-2002 were from £513 via Madrid (Iberia); from £525 through Amsterdam (Martinair); from £529 via Paris (Air France).

Captivating Cuba, Centre London West, Twickenham, Middlesex, TW1 3SZ, tel. 020/8255-6000, www.captivating-cuba.co.uk, is the UK's largest tour agency handling air traffic to Cuba. **Cuba Holidays 4 Less,** 14 Greville St., London EC1N 8SB, tel. 020/7400-7051, cuba@travel4less.co.uk, www.cuba-holidays 4less.co.uk, specializes in airfares to Cuba. Also try **Journey Latin America,** 12 Heathfield Terr., London W4 4JE, tel. 020/8747-3108, fax 020/8742-1312, flights@journeylatinamerica .co.uk, www.journeylatinamerica.co.uk; **Regent Holidays,** 15 John St., Bristol BS1 2HR, tel. (0117) 921-1711, fax (0117) 925-4866, regent@ regent-holidays.co.uk, www.cheapflights.co.uk; and **Trailfinders,** 215 Kensington High St., London W8 7RG, tel. 020/7937-5400, www.trail finders.co.uk. **STA Travel,** 86 Old Brompton Rd., London SW7, tel. 020/7361-6262, www .statravelco.uk, specializes in student fares. STA also has offices throughout the UK. Alternately, try **Council Travel,** 28A Poland St., London W1V 3DB, tel. 020/7437-7767.

Good online resources for discount tickets include www.ebookers.com, www.cheapflights. co.uk, and www.bridgetheworld.com; and for charter flights, **Charter Flight Centre,** www.char terflights.co.uk, and **Dial a Flight,** www.diala flight.co.uk.

You may be able to save money by buying your ticket through a "bucket shop," which sells discounted tickets on scheduled carriers. Bucket shops advertise in London's *What's On, Time Out,* and leading Sunday newspapers.

From the Caribbean

From the Bahamas: Bahamasair, tel. 242/377-5505 or 800/222-4262, www.bahamasair.com, was planning to introduce four weekly flights between Nassau and Havana. Reservations are being handled by the **Havana Flying Club,** 416/921-4102 or 877/488-0388, fax 416/969-8916, www.havanaflyingclub.com, or online via www.cubalinda.com. **Cubana,** tel. 242/377-8752, fax 242/277-3460, offers a daily charter flight to Havana from Nassau. The flight times change frequently but were as follows at press time for the outbound flight to Havana: Mon.–Thurs. 3:45 P.M., Fri. 4 P.M., Sat. at 1 P.M., and Sun. at 6:15 P.M. (about US$189 round-trip, plus US$20 visa and US$10 ticket tax).

You may have more luck making a reservation through any of several tour agencies in Nassau, most of which also offer Cuba air-hotel packages. These include **Cuba Tours,** P.O. Box N-1629, Nassau, Bahamas, tel. 242/325-0042, fax 242/325-3339—its office is at Southland Shopping Centre, East St., Suite #3; **Havanatur Nassau,** Wongs Plaza, Madeira St, Nassau, tel. 242/326-8544, fax 242/394-6753, havanatur@mail.botelnet.bs; **Bahatours,** P.O. Box N-7078, Nassau, Bahamas, tel. 242/361-8060 or 361-6510, fax 242/361-1336; and **Majestic Travel,** tel. 242/328-0908, fax 242/326 1995, holidays@majesticholidays.com, www.majesticholidays.com. Majestic Travel has vans at the airport that offer free transfers to the office and back to the airport; if you plan to depart for Cuba the same day, be sure to allow two or three hours in Nassau for the transaction at their office.

Booking your ticket is awkward. Most agencies selling Cuban tickets don't accept credit card reservations and require you to pay a deposit in advance through a Western Union wire transfer or by certified check, which has to be mailed. You can pick up your ticket at the various company offices in Nassau, but most will also deliver the ticket to the airport for pick-up. None of these companies send confirmations unless you urge them. You should *demand* confirmation of your reservation and receipt of payment.

Returning from Cuba, you pass through Bahamian immigration (there is no in-transit lounge). Bahamian Customs go "on notice" when the Cubana flight arrives and may search your bags—although they're really interested in Bahamian nationals with bags stuffed full of cigars. The departure terminal for flights to the United States is to the left of the exit from the arrivals hall—you have to pay a US$15 departure tax, despite your brief stay in the Bahamas. You must pass through U.S. Immigration and Customs here. U.S. officials may ask you outright if you've been to Cuba, or where you stayed in the Bahamas and how long. If they discover that you've been to Cuba, expect to have your Cuban purchases confiscated.

Cubana, also flies on Fridays between Freeport and Havana (US$189 one-way, US $219 round-trip).

From the Cayman Islands: Havana is served weekly by **Cubana,** departing Grand Cayman (US$190 one-way, US$225 round-trip).

From the Dominican Republic: Charter flights with **Cubana,** Avenida Tiradentes y 27 de Febrero, Santo Domingo, tel. 809/227-2040, fax 809/227-2044, cubana.aviacion@codetel.net.do, serve Havana from Santo Domingo on Thursday (via Santiago de Cuba) and Sunday. **Aero Continente Dominicana** inaugurated thrice-weekly flights between Santo Domingo and Havana in August 2002.

From Jamaica: Air Jamaica, tel. 305/670-3222 or 800/523-5585 in the United States, www.airjamaica.com; in Jamaica, tel. 888/359-2475 (islandwide) or 876/922-3460 (Kingston) or 876/940-9054 (Montego Bay), flies from Montego Bay to Havana on Mondays and Thursdays using an Airbus A-320 (about US$356–376 round-trip depending on season); and daily via **Air Jamaica Express** (same contact information). **Cubana,** tel. 876/953-2600 (Kingston) ceased flights between Jamaica and Cuba in 2000 under a code-sharing agreement with Air Jamaica.

Caribic Vacations, 69 Gloucester Ave., Montego Bay, Jamaica, tel. 876/953-9878 or 876/979-6073, fax 876/979-3421, caribcuba @hotmail.com, www.caribicvacations.com, offers Cubana charter flights from Montego Bay to Havana on Friday and Sunday (US$190 round-trip, including Cuban visa). It also offers air-hotel packages to Havana.

Tropical Tours, tel. 876/979-3565 (Montego Bay), 876/920-3770 (Kingston), fax 876/952-0340, tropical-destinations@cwjaimaica.com, also offers charters to Havana from Montego Bay and Kingston. **Adventure Tours,** tel. 971-3859, fax 876/979-6363, www.cubaonweb.com, and **New InterCaribe Tours,** tel. 876/931-4919, fax 876/931-5184, intercaribe@colis.com, also offer package excursions.

From Elsewhere: Cubana operates service between Havana and Curaçao, Martinique, Guadeloupe, and Sint Maarten.

From Central America

Grupo Taca, 1600 NW LeJeune Rd. #20,

Miami, FL 33126, tel. 305/870-7500 or 800/
225-2272, 506/296-0909 in the United States,
www.grupotaca.com, has flights from El Salvador to Havana four times weekly (US$449
round-trip), with connecting flights from Costa
Rica and Guatemala to San Salvador at no extra
cost. Grupo Taca has a LatinPass (mail@latin-
pass.com, www.latinpass.com) permitting multiple stops at cities throughout the Americas,
including Havana. The cost varies according to
number of cities and their zone.

Cubana, Edifio Edicol, Sabana Sur, San José,
tel. 506/290-5095, fax 506/290-5101, solyson@
sol.racsa.co.cr, flies from Costa Rica to Havana on
Thursday and Sunday (US$499). Numerous
travel agencies and tour operators offer package
tours from Costa Rica.

COPA, Ave. Justo Arosemena y Calle 39,
Zona 1, Panamá, tel. 507/217-2672, in the USA
800/359-2672, www.copaair.com, flies to Havana from Panama City daily for about US$509.

From Mexico: The national carrier **Mexicana,** tel. 05/448-0990, in the USA 800/531-
7921, www.mexicana.com, flies from Mexico
City to Havana daily, with additional twice weekly flights via Mérida (about US$450 round-trip).
Cubana, Homero #613, esq. Temistocles,
Colonia Polanca, 11650 México D.F., tel. 05/
250-6355, fax 05/255-0835, reservaciones@
cubanamexico.com, also offers service from Mexico City twice weekly using a DC-10 (US$362
round-trip).

Allegro Airlines, tel. 800/903-2779, operates a charter from Tijuana; and **Viñales Tours,**
Oaxaca 95, Col. Roma, 06700 México, D.F.,
tel. 52/5242-4200 or 800/202-2937, fax 52/
5242-4249, www.vinalestours.com, operates seasonal charter flights from Tijuana and Guadala-
jara using Mexicana, for whose scheduled flights
it also offers significant discounts.

Far more popular among U.S. travelers are
the flights from Cancún. **Cubana,** Jabalí #225,
Local H, Cancún, tel. 98/877-210, fax 98/877-
373, cubana@cancun.novenet.com.mx, flies daily
from Cancún to Havana for about US$150 one-
way, US$192 round-trip, plus US$25 tax. These
flights on antiquated Russian jets are not for the
weak-hearted. A better alternative is Mexicana

Airlines' subsidiary **Aerocaribe,** Ave. Cobá #5,
Plaza América Local B, Cancún, tel. 98/842-
000, fax 98/841-364, in the United States call
Mexicana, 800/531-7901. They fly from Cancún
to Havana twice daily for about US$180 one-
way, US$297 round-trip.

Note that for the return leg on flights
to/from Mexico, you must obtain your tourist
card for Mexico *before* arriving at Havana airport, where tourist cards are *not* issued. Fortunately, these are handed out on the flight
just before arriving in Mexico. Or you can obtain one from the Mexican embassy at Calle
12 #518, Miramar, Havana, tel. 33-0856. It's a
good idea to reconfirm your outbound flight 48
hours before departure.

Numerous Mexican tour operators specialize
in Cuba. These include **Viajes Divermex,** Av.
Cobá #5, Centro Comercial Plaza América, Cancún, Quintana Roo, México CP 77500, tel.
998/884-5005, fax 998/884-2325, divermex@
cancun.com.mx; **Tip's Travel,** Tuxpan #74, Col.
Roma Sur, México D.F., CP 06760, tel. 5574-
5898, fax 5264-1767, ttarvel@netservice
.com.mx; **Taíno Tours,** Avenida Coyoacán
#1035, Col. del Valle, CP 03100, México D.F.,
tel. 66/559-3907, fax 66/559-3951, taino@
pceditres.com, www.pceditores.com/taino; or
Ignacio Comonfort #9330, Local 8, Zona Río,
Tijuana, Baja California 22320, tel. 66/24-0129
or 84-9453, fax 66/84-7077, calveira@hot
mail.com, offers Cuba charters.

From South America

Lan Chile, tel. 02/562-2000, in the USA
800/735-5526, www.lanchile.com, flies to Havana from Santiago de Chile for about US$950
round-trip. **Cubana,** Avenida Fidel Oteiza
#1971, Providencia, Santiago de Chile, tel.
02/274-1819, fax 02/274-8207, cubanascl@entel
chile.net, flies from Santiago de Chile to Havana twice weekly.

Tame, tel. 02/223-1921, fax 02/255-4905,
www.tame.com.ec, flies to Havana from
Guayaquil and Quito on Thursday (from about
US$390 round-trip). **Cubana,** tel. 02/22-7463,
fax 02/22-7454, cubana@hoy.net, flies to Havana from Quito.

Aeropostal, tel. 02/708-6211 or 800/284-6637, in the USA 888/912-8466, www.aeropostal.com, flies to Havana from Caracas daily for about US$250 round-trip. Cubana, tel. 02/286-8639, fax 02/286-7319, cubana@intercon.net.ve, also flies from Caracas.

Cubana also has service to Havana from Buenos Aires, Argentina, and Montevideo, Uruguay, tel. 114/326-5291, cubana@tournet.com.ar; Rio de Janeiro and São Paulo, Brazil, tel. 11/214-4571, cubanabrasil@uol.com.br; Bogotá, Colombia, tel. 01/610-1676, solyson @colomsat.net.co; and Lima, Peru, tel. 12/241-0554, solyson@mail.cosapidata.com.pe.

From Asia

Cubanacán and JAL (Japanese Air Lines), JAL Plaza, 1st Floor, Yurakucho Denki Bldg., 1-7-1 Yurakucho Chiyoda-ku, tel. 03/100-0006, www.jal.co.jp, offer a weekly charter flight between Tokyo and Havana using Boeing 747s. Otherwise you can take JAL to Paris and connect with an Air France flight.

Otherwise, travelers fly via Europe or the United States. Flying nonstop to Los Angeles, then to Mexico City, Tijuana, or Cancún is perhaps the easiest route. Alternately, fly United or Malaysia Airlines to Mexico City (20 hours) and catch a flight the next day to Havana (three hours). A round-trip economy ticket is about HK$16,000, depending on the agent. Hong Kong is a good source for discount plane tickets.

From Macau, you can fly with Iberia nonstop to Madrid and then on to Havana.

STA Travel, 800/781-4040, go@statravel.com, www.statravel.com, is a good resource for tickets and has branches in Hong Kong, Tokyo, Singapore, Bangkok, and Kuala Lumpur.

From Australia and New Zealand

The best bet is to fly to Los Angeles or San Francisco and then to Cuba via Mexico or Jamaica. Air New Zealand (in Sydney, tel. 02-9223-4666; in Auckland, tel. 09-366-2400), Delta Airlines (in Sydney, tel. 02-9262-1777; in Auckland, tel. 09-379-3370), Qantas (in Sydney, tel. 02-9957-0111; in Auckland, tel. 09-357-8900), and United Airlines (in Sydney, tel. 02-9237-8888; in Auckland, tel. 09-307-9500), offer direct service between Australia, New Zealand, and California. Round-trip fares from Sydney at press time ranged from A$2,545 to A$2,750.

A route via Buenos Aires or Santiago de Chile and then to Havana is also possible.

Specialists in discount fares include STA Travel, in Sydney, tel. 02/9212-1255 or 800/637444, www.statravel.co.au; in Auckland, tel. 09/309-9723, www.statravel.co.nz, which has regional offices throughout Australia and New Zealand.

Another good online resource for discount airfares is www.flightcentre.com.au.

BY SEA

By Cruise Ship

Havana is destined to become one of the biggest ports of call in the world once the U.S. embargo is lifted. The embargo has restricted the cruise industry's access to Cuba. No U.S. company can operate cruises to Cuba, and because foreign-owned vessels cannot dock in the United States within six months of visiting Cuba or carrying Cuban passengers or goods, most foreign cruise companies have shunned Cuba.

Nonetheless, several foreign cruise ships feature Havana on their itineraries . . . and it's *entirely legal* for *any* U.S. citizen to partake of these cruises without breaking the law under the provisions of fully-hosted travel, as described in the section U.S. Law and Cuba Travel at the beginning of this chapter. The Cuban government, you see, supplies a shore excursion at no cost to U.S. passengers and the in-transit visa used, which allows up to 48 hours in Cuba, means that no port fees apply. This, of course, assumes that you don't spend a dime ashore . . . but you wouldn't do that now, would you? U.S. citizens can also book these all-inclusive cruises through licensed travel providers.

However, of the several companies that have launched regular scheduled cruises to or from Cuba, none has stood the test of time. It's worth checking with those listed below as having been discontinued in case they've been reinstated.

The website www.cruisehavana.com purports to keep a current list of Cuba related cruises, but at last visit the site did not have links to its various pages. **Cruiseserver,** www.cruiseserver.net, is a good source and includes passengers' reviews of cruises to Cuba.

Spain's **Festival Cruises,** www.festivalcruises.com, began operating cruises in 2001 using its *Mistral,* with Havana as the mother port. Week-long Havana–Havana itineraries stop at Calica (Mexico), Montego Bay (Jamaica), Grand Cayman, and Isla de la Juventud (Cuba). Passengers can embark—and disembark a week later—in either Calica or Montego Bay. A second vessel, the 900-passenger *Bolero,* began similar cruises in late 2002. Festival is represented in the USA by **First European Cruises,** 95 Madison Ave., Suite 1203, New York, NY 10016, 888/983-8767, fax 212/779-0948, reser@first-european.com; and in the UK by Cruise International Ltd., 5th Floor, Victory House, 99/101 Regent St., London W1R 7HB, tel. 020/7734-0005, fax 020/7734-9459, festival@festival-uk.com.

England's **Fred Olsen Cruise Lines,** tel. (01473) 742424, cruiselines@fredolsen.co.uk, www.fredolsencruises.co.uk, featured Havana on its 2002–2003 Caribbean cruises using the *Black Prince* in winter.

Another British company, **Sun Cruises,** 300 Princess Rd., Manchester M14 7QU, tel. (0161) 232-2800, fax (0161) 232-2865, www.suncruises.co.uk, operates the 1,200-passenger *Sundream* (formerly Royal Caribbean's *Song of the Sea*) on 14-night cruises from Montego Bay, with calls in Havana and Santiago de Cuba, December–March.

Germany's **Hapag Lloyd,** www.hapag-lloyd.com, also features Havana on its peak-season programs using the *Europa.*

Germany's **Aida Cruises** (a subsidiary of P&O Princess Cruises), info@aida.de, www.aida.de, occasionally features Havana on cruises aboard the *Aida,* which offers regular Caribbean itineraries from the Dominican Republic.

The 425-passenger *Riviera 1,* formerly sailing from Cancún, initiated service from Jamaica, departing Montego Bay, each Friday on three-day cruises calling in Havana and Isla de la Juventud. You can stay over and catch the following week's cruise back to Mexico.

West Indies Cruises, 877/818-2822, fax 905/238-6177, initiated Cuba cruises aboard the *Valtur Prima* in 2000, sailing from Montego Bay, Jamaica, every Friday on seven-night cruises to Grand Cayman, Calica (Mexico), and Havana. At press time cruises had been discontinued.

Havana's **Terminal Sierra Maestra,** Avenida San Pedro, tel. 862-1925, is a natty conversion of the old Customs building. Passengers step through the doorways directly onto Plaza de San Francisco, in the heart of Havana. At last visit, the facility was being expanded to accept five cruise ships at one time.

By Freighter

At least two freighters that operate regular schedules between Europe and Cuba take paying passengers. **Hamburg-Süd Reiseagentur GMBH,** Ost-West 59, 20457 Hamburg, tel. 040/370-5155, fax 040/370-5242, www.hamburg-sued-reiseagentur.de, books passage aboard the M/V *Melbridge Pride* (with one double and three single cabins) and M/V *Melbridge Pearl* (with one double, one single, plus the Owner's Cabin). Both ships depart Rotterdam for Havana on 42-day round-trip voyages that feature five ports of call.

In the U.K., book through **Strand Cruise & Travel Centre,** Charing Cross Shopping Concourse, the Strand, London WC2N 4HZ, tel. 020/7836-6363, fax 020/7497-0078. U.S. citizens can book through **Freighter World Cruises,** 180 S. Lake Ave., #335, Pasadena, CA 91101, 626/449-3106 or 800/531-7774, fax 626/449-9573, www.freighterworld.com.

By Ferry

No ferry service currently connects Cuba with any international port. In 2002 efforts were launched to introduce fast-ferry service between Fort Myers and Key West and Havana for licensed travelers only; for updates contact **Fast Cats Ferry Service,** 239/337-2235, info@fastcats.org, or **Citizen Diplomats,** tourdecana.aol.com. Florida East Coast Railroad has plans to reinstate ferry service to Cuba once the embargo is lifted . . . but don't hold your breath. And there were rumors that a Mexican railroad was planning to operate rail ferries to western Cuba from the port of Coatzacoalas.

By Private Vessel

Cuba offers a warm reception to visitors arriving by sea. No advance permission is required. However, it is wise to give at least 72 hours advance warning by faxing complete details of your boat, crew, and passengers to the harbormaster's office at Marina Hemingway, fax 204-3104. Anyone planning on sailing to Cuba should obtain a copy of Simon Charles's *Cruising Guide to Cuba.*

The U.S. State Department advises that "U.S. citizens are discouraged from traveling to Cuba in private boats" and permits such travel "only after meeting all U.S. and Cuban government documentation and clearance requirements." Nonetheless, scores of sailors—including U.S. citizens in U.S.-registered vessels—sail to Cuba each year without incident and without breaking the law (which for U.S. citizens means spending no money there).

All persons subject to U.S. law aboard vessels, including the owner, must be an authorized traveler to engage in travel transactions in Cuba. If you are not an authorized traveler, you may not legally purchase meals, pay for transportation, lodging, dockage, or mooring fees, and you may not bring any Cuban-origin goods back to the United States. Any payments to the Marina Hemingway International Yacht Club would be considered a prohibited payment to a Cuban national and therefore in violation of the regulations. Ostensibly, you'll need to find a non-U.S. citizen to pay your berth fees, and presumably you will cater yourself with food brought from the United States. Get the picture? Most U.S. skippers I've spoken with have had no problems when they return to the United States—as long as they don't have their holds full of Cuban cigars. However, the onus is upon you to prove that you did *not* spend money.

Vessel owners are prohibited from carrying travelers to Cuba who pay them for passage if the owner does not have a specific license from OFAC authorizing him or her to be a Service Provider to Cuba.

At the present time, the United States and Cuba do not have a Coast Guard agreement. Craft developing engine trouble or other technical difficulties in Cuban territorial waters cannot expect assistance from the U.S. Coast Guard. Cuba's territorial waters extend 12 miles out. Although Cuban authorities have usually proven to be helpful to yachters in distress, there are reports of corruption among Cuban officials involving foreign yachters, some of whom have had their vessels impounded as collateral against the cost of rescue or salvage.

Yacht Charters and Crewing: U.S. citizens should refer to Treasury Department regulations regarding chartering vessels for travel to Cuba. Charter companies in the Bahamas may permit travel to Cuba. Try **Nassau Yacht Haven**, tel. 242/393-8173, fax 242/393-3429, www.nassau yachthaven.com.

Traveling with Private Skippers: It's possible to find private skippers sailing to Havana from Florida, New Orleans, and other ports along the southern seaboard, as well as from the Bahamas. Be flexible. Pinpointing exact vessel departure dates and times is nearly impossible, especially in winter. A nasty weather front can delay your departure as much as a week or more. As Ernest Hemingway wrote, "Brother, don't let anybody tell you there isn't plenty of water between Key West and Havana."

If you don't arrange a return trip with the same skipper, you'll find yachts flying the Stars and Stripes at Marina Hemingway in Havana. There'll usually be a skipper willing to run you back to Florida, but it can take days, or weeks, to find a skipper.

Vessel owners are prohibited from carrying travelers to Cuba who pay them for passage if the owner does not have a specific license from OFAC authorizing him or her to be a Service Provider to Cuba. Transporting "friends sharing expenses" does not require a Treasury license, and there's nothing illegal if passengers don't spend money in Cuba. However, skippers are responsible for their passengers and crew while in Cuba, and each person may be required to sign an affidavit that he/she will not be spending any money in Cuba. Also, once in Cuba skippers may not be allowed to leave for the USA without their entire manifest of crew and passengers (this seems arbitrary, however). If a skipper asks for money, legally you must

VOLUNTEER PROGRAMS

Cuba welcomes volunteer teams to work for 20-day stints in both Havana and the countryside. Most are socialist "solidarity" groups, and have a pronounced "down with U.S. imperialism" posture, but will also appeal to anyone wishing to contribute to the human community, make new friends, and learn some invaluable life lessons. Contact the Havana-based **Instituto Cubano de Amistad con los Pueblos** (Cuban Institute of Friendship with the Peoples), ICAP, Calle 17 #301 e/ H y L, Vedado, tel. 832-8017.

U.S. law prohibits U.S. citizens from receiving remuneration for work in Cuba. You are permitted to work in Cuba if fully hosted.

In the USA: The **American Friends Service Committee,** Human Resources, 1501 Cherry St., Philadelphia, PA 19102, 215/241-7000, fax 215/241-7275, afscinfo@afsc.org, www.afsc.org, is a Quaker organization which in the past has offered youth from the United States and other countries a chance to engage with Cuban youth on three-week summer programs. The program was not offered at press time but may be resurrected. The program involves summer work camps and conferences in which Christians and Communists come together. Participants should be between 18 and 28 years old and fluent in Spanish.

The **Center for Cuban Studies,** 124 W. 23rd St., New York, NY 10011, 212/242-0559, fax 212/242-1937, cubanctr@igc.org, www.cubaupdate.org, offers *La Abeja Obrera* (the worker bee) "solidarity work projects" in which volunteers help Cuban work brigades (*microbrigadistas*) in Víbora Park and La Güinera districts. Typical projects include building access ramps for the disabled, hauling dirt, installing door jambs, revitalizing old parks, painting murals, and the like. No prior construction experience is required. Two-week trips cost US$1,100 including round-trip airfare from New York.

IFCO/Pastors for Peace, 620 West 28th St., Minneapolis, MN 55408, 612/670-7121 or 612/378-0062, fax 612/870-7109 or 612/378-0134, p4p@igc.apc.org, www.ifconews.org, delivers humanitarian aid to Cuba through the annual "U.S.–Cuban Friendshipment Caravan." The caravan moves through, and gathers aid in, 150 cities from the West Coast to Washington, D.C., before traveling to Canada or Mexico, where the aid is shipped to Cuba. Volunteers can participate in the caravans, which openly defy the embargo and deliver aid to Cuba *without* a license. The organization also operates Work Brigades in which volunteers work to help construct houses. And research trips are offered in which participants live in a working-class *barrio* in Havana as fully hosted guests.

Send a Piana to Havana, 39 E. 7th St. #3, New York, NY 10003, blt@igc.org, www.sendapiana.com, arranges annual brigades of piano tuners and technicians to restore

---

decline. Consider negotiating a free passage; of course, diesel fuel is expensive, so you may feel charitably inclined.

In the United States, a humanitarian organization called **Conchord Cayo Hueso,** P.O. Box 2306, Key West, FL 33045, tel./fax 305/294-0205, jitters@aol.com, www.geocities.com/conchordcayohueso, has about 55 registered vessels on call to carry humanitarian aid under license from the Treasury Department. CCH runs an online "coffeehouse" (US$50 membership) that brings vessel owners and prospective

travelers together. Note, however, that they do *not* take ordinary citizens looking for a way to sneak into Cuba.

Maps and Charts: British Admiralty charts, U.S. Defense Mapping Agency charts, and Imray yachting charts can be ordered from **Bluewater Books & Charts,** 1481 SE 17th St., Ft. Lauderdale, FL 33316, 954/763-6533 or 800/942-2583, fax 954/522-2278, nautical-charts@bluewaterweb.com, www.bluewaterweb.com.

You can also order detailed National Oceanic & Atmospheric Administration charts from

PLANNING YOUR TRIP

clapped-out Cuban pianos and help train Cuban tuners (US$1,200). Participants stay in dormitory-like accommodations.

The **U.S.–Latin American Medical Aid Foundation,** 605 Harthan St., Austin, TX 78703, 888/669-1400, fax 512/457-0055, www.medaid.org, provides opportunities for individuals to travel to Cuba to hand deliver licensed medical supplies.

Volunteers for Peace, c/o International Work Camp, 1043 Tiffany Rd., Belmont, VT 05730, 802/259-2759, fax 802/259-2922, vfp@vfp.org, www.vfp.org, occasionally takes participants from around the world to work alongside Cubans and assist with community development.

Cross Cultural Journeys, P.O. Box 1369, Sausalito, CA 94666-1369, 415/332-0682 or 800/353-2276, info@crossculturaljourneys.com, www.crossculturaljourneys.com, also offers volunteer programs, while the **Venceremos Brigade,** P.O. Box 7071, Oakland, CA 94601-0071, 415/267-0606, vbsfbay@yahoo.com, www.venceremosbrigade.org, offers "workcamp brigades" for committed leftists, as does the **Brigada Antonio Maceo,** P.O. Box 248829, Miami, FL 33124, a Cuban-American organization.

Similar tours are offered by **Witness For Peace,** 1229 15th St., NW, Washington, D.C. 20005, 202/588-1471, fax 202/588-1472, witness@witnessforpeace.org, www.witnessfor peace.org, in which participants work alongside Cubans to assist with community development. The three-week trips are hosted by the Cuban Institute for Friendship with the People (ICAP) but coordinated by people in local communities.

In the UK: Caledonia Languages Abroad, Clock House, Bonnington Mill, 72 Newhaven Rd., Edinburgh, EH6 5QG, tel. (0131) 621-7721, fax (0131) 621-7723, www.caledo nialanguages.co.uk, offers volunteer work programs at the Centro Estudiantil, a youth center for children 4–18. Applicants ideally should have skills in storytelling, performing arts, puppetry, ecology, library studies, computer training, or arts and crafts.

The **Cuban Solidarity Campaign,** c/o Red Rose Club, 129 Seven Sisters Rd., London N7 7QG, tel. 020/7263-6452, fax 020/7561-0191, www.cuba-solidarity.org.uk, offers work brigades, including visits to hospitals and schools. Participants work in construction and agriculture.

The **Cuba Organic Support Group** (COSG), 58 Broad Lane, Coventry, CV5 7AF, tel. 024/7667-3491, supports the organic movement in Cuba through fund-raising, speakers, publicity and the promotion of "Gardening Brigades" to Cuba.

In Australia: The **Southern Cross Brigade,** P.O. Box 1051, Collingwood, Victoria 3066, tel. 03/9857-9249, fax 03/9857-6598, offers volunteer work programs.

NOAA, Riverdale, MD 20737-1199, 301/436-8301 or 800/638-8972, distribution@noaa.gov, www.chartmaker.ncd.noaa.gov.

In Havana, **Tienda de las Navegantes,** Calle Mercaderes #115, e/ Obispo y Obrapía, Habana Vieja, tel. 861-3625, fax 33-2869, sells nautical charts, including a "Chart Kit" containing maps of the entire Cuban coast (charts I and VII cost US$40; charts II, III, and VI cost US$45; charts IV and V cost US$35). Open Mon.–Fri. 8 A.M.–5 P.M., Sat. 8 A.M.–1 P.M.

Marina Hemingway: Private yachts and motor cruises berth at Marina Hemingway, Avenida 5ta y Calle 248, Santa Fe, tel. 204-1150, fax 204-1149, comercial@prto.mh.cyt.cu, 15 kilometers west of downtown. The marina is a self-contained village and duty-free port with accommodations, restaurants, and complete services. U.S. dollars are preferred, but all convertible currencies are accepted, as are credit cards (except those issued in the United States). You can register your credit card and charge everything to your account while berthed.

The harbor coordinates are 23° 5'N and 82°

29'W. You should announce your arrival on VHF Channel 16, HF Channel 68, and SSB 2790—expect a long wait for the reply. Arriving and departing skippers should watch for snorkelers and surfers near the narrow entrance channel.

You must clear Immigration and Customs at the wharf just inside the entrance channel. If you plan to dock for less than 72 hours, visas are not required (your passport will suffice). For stays of 72 hours or longer, you'll need a tourist card (US$20), issued at the marina. The harbormaster's office will facilitate your entry and exit (tel. 204-1150, ext. 2884), and visa extensions can also be arranged for US$25. Be patient!

U.S. citizens and other skippers under U.S. jurisdiction should be sure to obtain a letter from the marina office stating that you were a guest of the marina and that you paid no docking or other fees.

The marina has four parallel canals—each one kilometer long, 15 meters wide, and six meters deep—separated by "Intercanales" with moorings for 100 yachts. Docking fees, which include water, electricity, and custodial services, cost US$.35 per foot per day. Gasoline and diesel are available 8 A.M.–7 P.M. (tel. 204-1150, ext. 450), a mechanic is on hand, and your boat can be hauled out.

The marina has a tourism information center (8 A.M.–8 P.M., tel. 204-1150, ext. 733, or tel. 204-6336) and harbormaster's office in Complejo Turístico Papa's, the main service area at the end of channel B. The 24-hour medical post is here (ext. 737), as are a 24-hour Laundromat (ext. 451), bathrooms with showers, soda bar, and TV lounge, storage room (security boxes can be rented), ship chandler (or *avituallamiento*, ext. 2344), plus a beach-volleyball court and tennis courts. The post office (open 24 hours; ext. 448) is at the entrance of Intercanal C, where you'll also find the Hemingway International Nautical Club (ext. 701), which offers fax and telephone facilities, bar, and a quiet reading room. The shopping mall is at the east end of Intercanal B (ext. 739). The marina even has a scuba diving center (ext. 735) at Complejo Turístico Papa's at the west end of Intercanal B, where jet-skis can be rented (8:30 A.M.–4:30 P.M.).

FRIENDSHIP AMBASSADORS

If people get together, so eventually will nations.

President Eisenhower

Forget hotels. Stay with a Cuban family (or host one) and become a citizen diplomat.

Friendship Force, 34 Peachtree St., NW, Suite 900, Atlanta, GA 30303, www.friendshipforce.org, is an Atlanta-based program that puts people from opposite cultures together to prove that "friendship, trust and mutual respect can help break down international barriers," in the words of President Jimmy Carter, who helped co-found the project with Wayne Smith, who later became Carter's top diplomat in Havana. The organization's Bridgebuilders home-stay program links "volunteer ambassadors" who travel to other countries to live with host families, or serve as host families themselves. Cuba was added to the list of exchange countries in 1998.

People to People Ambassadors, 110 S. Ferrall St., Spokane, WA 99202-4800, 509/534-0430 or 800/669-7882 ext. 422, fax 509/532-3556, kristiw@ambassadorprograms .org, www.ambassadorprograms.org, was initiated by President Eisenhower to develop personal exchanges and individual, firsthand experiences of other cultures on the premise that while people of different cultures are very different, our values, goals, and day-to-day issues are the same. The organization offers group trips that focus on learning about specific aspects of Cuban culture, such as law and medicine.

Servas, 11 John St. #505, New York, NY 10038, 212/267-0252, helpdesk@servas.org, www.servas .org, an international, non-governmental, interracial peace association, works in a similar fashion to build understanding, tolerance, and world peace. It operates through a network of Servas hosts around the world who open their doors to travelers, while open-minded travelers who truly want to get to know the heart of the countries they visit are placed with hosts abroad. Servas had 16 host families in Cuba at press time. It has offices around the world.

Rental cars are also available (ext. 87), as are microbuses and taxis (ext. 85).

BY ORGANIZED TOUR

Tours from the United States

U.S. citizens can legally travel to Cuba by qualifying for certain organized tours with nonprofit organizations and other entities that arrange trips with government licenses in hand. Most programs are "study" tours that provide an immersion in particular aspects of Cuban life. Other trips are operated under the legally sanctioned philosophy of "people-to-people" exchange. Pretty much anyone can sign up for these trips. A large percentage are heavily politicized, left-leaning "solidarity" tours.

Uncle Sam permits participants to arrive one day before and stay one day after the end of the tour.

Unfortunately, in March 2003 the Bush administration announced new restrictions. No new licenses or renewals were to be issued for educational trips unrelated to academic study.

Center for Cuban Studies, 124 W. 23rd St., New York, NY 10011, 212/242-0559, fax 212/242-1937, cubanctr@igc.org, www.cubaupdate.org, a "solidarity" organization, offers regular "Cuba Update Trips," plus week-long to 10-day trips focusing on education and health care, urban issues, welfare, African roots of Cuba Culture, Jewish heritage, sexual politics, architecture and preservation, and cultural events such as the Havana Film Festival.

Cross-Cultural Solutions, 47 Potter Ave., New Rochelle, NY 10801, 914/632-0022 or 800/380-4777, fax 914/632-8494, info@crossculturalsolutions.org, offers people-to-people exchange programs, including to the Havana Jazz Festival.

Cuba Cultural Travel, 234 East 17th St., Suite #113, Costa Mesa, CA 92627, 949/646-1229, fax 949/646-1204, management@cubaculturaltravel.com, www.cubaculturaltravel.com, arranges group tours in the fields of art, architecture, dance, education, music, photography and film, and religion. It's also a specialist in taking law groups to Cuba.

Cuba Now, 1244 S. 4th St., Louisville, KY 40203, 502/479-3666, fax 502/459-4908, cubanow@mindspring.com, www.cubanow.org, specializes in tours focusing on historical preservation, architecture, and sustainable development. It also plans customized tours for licensed travelers.

Cuba Travel USA, P.O. Box 161281, Austin, TX 78716, 512/347-8952, fax 512/306-1278, info@cubatravel.com, www.cubatravelusa.com, offers tours and arranges travel.

Global Exchange, 2017 Mission St. #303, San Francisco, CA 94110, 415/255-7296, fax 415/255-7498, info@globalexchange.org, www.globalexchange.org, sponsors "solidarity" study tours, including health care, art, culture and education, religion, Afro-Cuban culture, women's issues, and music and dance. It also has bicycle tours.

Havana Flying Club, 416/921-4102 or 877/488-0388, fax 416/969-8916, www.havanaflyingclub.com, offers joint Bahamas–Cuba tour packages for unlicensed travelers.

Last Frontier Expeditions, 4823 White Rock Circle, Suite H, Boulder, CO 80301-3260, 303/530-9275, Bob@cubatravelexperts.com, www.cubatravelexperts.com, offers packages for cigar lovers, classic car enthusiasts, plus sports-related events, and birding, fishing, and cultural tours.

Island Travel & Tours, 2111 Wisconsin Ave. NW, Suite 319, Washington, D.C. 20007, 202/342-3171 (east coast), 619/749-6068 (west coast), or 866/488-8687, fax 202/342-3308, info@islandtraveltours.com, www.islandtraveltours.com, arranges travel to Cuba for licensed individuals and groups.

Marazul Tours, Tower Plaza Mall, 4100 Park Ave., Weehawken, NJ 07087, 201/840-6711 or 800/223-5334, info@marazultours.com, www.marazultours.com and www.marazulcharters.com, organizes special-interest tours and individual travel for those with OFAC licenses.

National Geographic Expeditions, P.O. Box 65295, Washington, D.C. 20035-5265, 888/966-8687, www.nationalgeographic.com/ngexpeditions, offers an 11-day "Discover the Soul of Cuba" tour (US$4,490) that features three days in Havana, plus an 11-day photography expedition, with departures January–April.

TOUR OPERATORS ABROAD

Foreign tour operators are increasingly being corralled into working through Cuba's state-run Havanatur, which has offices worldwide. The following are accredited agencies:

Argentina

Bapro, Juan Domingo Perón #725, 10mo. Piso, 1038 Buenos Aires, tel. 11/4326-3690, fax 11/4328-2887, cristinab@baprotur.com.ar

Havanatur Argentina, Maipú #464, piso 10, e/ Corrientes y Lavalle, Buenos Aires, tel. 11/4394-6263, fax 11/4322-6074, eduardohav@tour net.com.ar

Bahamas

Havanatur Nassau, Wong Plaza, Madeira St., Nassau, tel. 242/326-8643, fax 242/356-2773, havanatur@mail.batelnet.bs

Belgium

Havanatur Benelux, Avenue Louis 335, Brussels 1000, tel. 02/6274990, fax 02/6274998, director@havanatour.be

Canada

Caribe Sol, 818 Rue Sherbrooke E., Montreal, Quebec H2L 1K3, 514/522-6868, Fax: 514/522-6858

Hola Sun Holidays, 146 W. Beaver Creek Rd., Unit 8, Richmond Hill, Ontario L4B 1C2, 905/882-0136, fax 905/882-5184, ops@hola sun.com

Chile

Havanatur Chile, Providencia 2330, e/ Suecia y Bucanero, Santiago de Chile, tel. 02/233-0844, fax 02/234-1276, gerencia@havanatur.cl

Colombia

Havanatur Colombia, Calle 52 #19-19, Santa Fe de Bogotá, tel. 01/347-1858, fax 01/347-1871, havanaco@andinet.com

France

Havanatour Paris, 24 Rue Quatre-Septembre, 75002 Paris, tel. 01/44-51-50-80, fax 01/42-65-18-01, groupes1@havanatour.fr

Germany

Tropicana Touristik, Kantstrasse 10.60316, Frankfurt, tel. 69/943-3970, fax 69/9433-9711, 113025.2035@compuserve.com

Plaza Cuba, P.O. Box 318135, San Francisco, CA 94131, 510/848-0911, plazacuba@yahoo.com, www.plazacuba.com, offers a variety of music and dance study courses in Cuba, including to the Havana Jazz Festival and spanning Afro-Cuban folkloric forms through cha-cha-cha, mambo, rumba, salsa, and the hip-swiveling *despolote*. Chucho Valdés, Juan Formell, Changuito, and legendary flautist Richard Esqués are among the faculty who provide one-on-one tuition. Imagine learning guitar from Eric Clapton, and you have the idea.

WorldGuest, 8 75th St., North Bergen, NJ 07047, 201/861-5059, fax 201/861-4983, cuba2002@worldguest.com, www.worldguest.com, operates cultural exchange-study programs that include "Cuba's Colonial Heritage—Havana" and "Havana circa 1958."

In addition, dozens of colleges, universities, and cultural organizations operate tours to Cuba. Also see the Special Topic "Jews in Havana" in the Habana Vieja chapter for organizations that specialize in Jewish heritage tours.

Tours from Canada

Canadians primarily book inexpensive beach vacation packages, and most of the many travel and tour operators cater to this market. Havana-based tours are few.

Leading Cuba specialist travel agencies include **USA Cuba Travel,** 527 Beaverbrook Court, Suite 222, Fredericton, New Brunswick, Canada E3B 1X6, 506/459-3355 or 877/462-8221, information@usacubatravel.com; and **Cuban Adventures,** 877/282-2386, info@cuban adventures.com.

Italy

Havanatur Italia, Via Merchiorre Gioia 114, 20125 Milano, tel. 02/676-0691, fax 02/667-1361, havanatur@havanatur.it

Mexico

Taino Tours, S.A., Ave. Coyoacán #1035, e/ Matías Romero y Pilares, Col del Valle, México, D.F., tel. 05/559-3909, fax 05/559-3973, tainot@prodigy.net.mx

Viajes Divermex, Ave. Coba #5, Centro Comercial Plaza América (local B-6), Cancún, Quintana Roo, tel./fax 98/875487, divermex@cancun.com.mx

Netherlands

Havanatour Holanda, Holpfeing 19, 3032 AC, Rotterdam 119-31-10, tel. 10/411-2444, fax 10/411-4749, jorge@havanatour.ne

Portugal

Guama Portugal, Rua de São Nicolau 119, 1100 Lisbon, tel. 01/347-4505, fax 02/3474501, guama.port@mail.telepac.pt

Spain

Guama, S. A., Paseo de La Habana 28, Primero Izquierda 28036, Madrid, tel. 91/411-2048, fax 91/564-3918, 101475.154@compuserve.com

Switzerland

Travelway, S. A., Rue Chantepoulet, 1-3 BP 2242, 1211 Geneva, tel. 22/908-3839, fax 22/908-3838, travelway@span.ch

Turk and Caicos

Cuban Connection, 240 Pebble Beach Blvd. Suite 712, Providenciales, tel. 800/645-1179, fax 941/793-7157, cubanconnection@yahoo.com

UK

Havanatur UK, 3 Wyllyotts Place, Potters Bar, Herts. EN6 2HN, tel. (01707) 665570, fax (01707) 663139, IvonneRamirez@havanatour.co.uk

Venezuela

Ideal Tours, Torre Capriles, P.B. Locales 10 y 11, Plaza de Venezuela, Caracas 1050, tel. 02/7930037, fax 02/7828063, idealtours@cantv.net

Friendship Tours, 12883-98th Ave., Surrey, BC V3T 1B1, tel. 604/581-4065, fax: 604/581-0785, friendship@home.com, www.cubafriendship.com, offers "solidarity" tours.

San Cristóbal Travel, 331 Elmwood Drive, Suite 4171, Moncton, New Brunswick E1A 1X6, 866/886-2822, fax 506/855-9057, www.sancristobaltravel.com, offers group tour packages and customized trips for individuals.

Vacation Culture Cuba, 5059 Saint-Denis, Montreal H2J 2L9, 514/982-3330 or 888/691-0101, fax 514/982-2438, info@culturecuba.com, www.culturecuba.com, specializes in cultural trips, including to Carnaval and Jazz Fest, plus Spanish and salsa courses.

Air Transat Holidays, www.airtransatholidays.com, offers air-hotel packages.

Tours from the UK

Captivating Cuba, Centre London West, Twickenham, Middlesex, TW1 3SZ, tel. 020/8255-6000, www.captivating-cuba.co.uk, specializes in holidays to Cuba and offers a wide range of trips, including tours for cigar-lovers in conjunction with **Peter Lloyd,** 25 Terrace Rd., Aberystwyth SY23 1NP, Wales, tel. (07710) 511575, www.aelloyd.com. **Cubanacán UK,** Skylines Village, Unit 49, Limeharbour, London E14 9TS, tel. 020/7537-7909, arranges tours.

Exodus 9 Weir Rd., London SW12 0LT, tel. 020/8675-5550, www.exodus.co.uk, offers 14-night "Best of Cuba" packages combining Havana with the Bay of Pigs, Trinidad, and Santiago de Cuba (from £1,579). **Explore Worldwide,** 1 Frederick St., Aldershot, Hants GU11 1LQ, tel.

STUDYING IN CUBA

Thousands of people every year choose to study in Cuba, be it for a month-long dance course or five-year all-expenses-paid medical training. Needless to say, you'll need a solid grasp of and ear for Spanish to do this. Bring as many supplies as you think you'll need, as course materials and academic supplies are scant. Be prepared for *very* basic living conditions and food regimen if signing up for a long-term residential course.

Universitur, Calle 30 #768, e/ Av. Kohly y 41, Nuevo Vedado, tel. 55-5577, fax 55-5978, agencia@universitur.get.tur.cu, www.universitur.cu, arranges study visits for foreigners at centers of higher learning that span a wide range of academic subjects. It also arranges working holidays and runs a summer school at the University of Havana, with more than 100 study options. It specializes in Spanish language courses.

Student Visas: You can study in Cuba using a tourist visa for up to three months (you can ask for an extension—*prórroga*—for a further three months). Longer study courses, however, require a student visa. If possible, try to register well ahead of time for your course; the relevant institution will then process the paperwork, permitting you to apply for a visa (US$80) through a Cuban consulate. If you begin the process *after* arriving in Cuba, you'll need six passport photos, your passport and tourist card, plus a license certificate for the *casa particular* where you'll be staying.

For study at the University of Havana (Universidad de la Habana), contact the Dirección de Posgrado, Calle J #556, e/ 25 y 27, Vedado, tel. 832-4245, dpg@comuh.uh.cu. To register for short-term (usually two- to four-week) study programs—such as language and Cuban culture courses—you can simply show up at 9 A.M. on the first Monday of the month.

Academic Exchanges with the United States

The **Cuba Exchange Program,** School of Advanced International Studies at Johns Hopkins University, 1740 Massachusetts Ave. NW, Washington, D.C. 20036, 202/663-5732, fax 202/663-5737, and **MacArthur Cuba Scholarly Exchange,** Center for Latin American Studies, University of Chicago, 5848 S. University Ave., Chicago, IL 60637, 773/702-8420, fax 773/702-1755, clas@uchicago.edu, offer Cuba exchange programs for scholars.

Interlocken International Camp, RR2, Box 165, Hillsborough, NH 03244, 603/478-3166, fax 603/478-5260, mail@interlocken.org, www.interlocken.org, offers four-week-long Cuban Friendship Exchange programs at the **U.S.–Cuba Youth Camp,** where U.S. and Cuban high school students spend time together in Havana and Ciego de Ávila province.

Student Exchange between Cuba and America (SECA), 21 Pinehurst Circle, Madison, WI 53717, 617/869-9080, info@seca.org, www.seca.org, has an exchange program between students in Madison, WI, and Camagüey, but also works to establish student exchanges on behalf of schools and sister-city associations. It offers an educational summer program in Havana for U.S. high school and college students.

The Arts, Music, and Dance

The **Cátedra de Danza,** 5ta Calle #253, e/ D y E, Vedado, tel. 832-4625, fax 33-3117, bnc@cubarte.cult.cu, www.balletcuba.cu, part of the Ballet Nacional de Cuba (BNC), offers month-long intensive ballet courses for intermediate- and advanced-level professionals and students (US$250 monthly). It also offers courses in modern dance, plus a children's vocational workshop for 5–16-year-olds.

The **Centro Nacional de Conservación, Restauración y Museología,** Calle Cuba #610, e/ Sol y Luz, tel. 861-3335, fax 33-5696, offers residential courses for urban planners, conservationists, and architects at the Convento de Santa Clara in Habana Vieja. They average US$300 for 12 days.

Folcuba, Calle 4 #103, e/ Calzada y 5ta, Vedado, tel./fax 55-3823, offers dance classes from cha-cha-cha to rumba, taught by professionals from Cuba's foremost folkloric troupe, the Conjunto Folclórico Nacional. Courses begin the first Monday in January and July and cost US$250–350.

The Instituto Superior de Arte, Calle 120 #11110, e/ 9na y 13, Cubanacán, tel. 208-0288 or 208-8075, fax 33-6633, isa@cubarte.cult.cu, offers courses spanning the art world, including music, dance, theater, and visual arts. Besides short-term courses, it also accepts foreigners for full-year study beginning in September (from US$2,500 for tuition), for which applicants must sit an entrance exam.

The Unión de Escritores y Artistas de Cuba, Calle 17 #351, esq. H, Vedado, tel. 832-4551, fax 33-3158, uneac@cubarte.cul.cu, offers a series of courses in the arts and Cuban culture, focusing on music.

The Taller Experimental de Gráfica, Callejón del Chorro #6, Plaza de la Catedral, Habana Vieja, tel. 862-0979, fax 204-0391, tgrafica@cubarte.cult.cu, offers month-long (US$250) and three-month (US$500) courses in engraving and lithography.

From the USA: The Bridge for Historic Preservation, 1206 Amberwood Blvd., Kissimmee, FL 34741, 407/847-7892, fax 407/847-2986, www.connect2cuba.org, offers educational programs for people with a serious interest in historic architecture and preservation.

Center for Creative Education (CCE), 3588 Main St., Stone Ridge, NY 12484, 854/687-8890, fax 854/687-4590, ccedrums@aol.com, www.ccedrums.org, offers programs in Afro-Cuban music and dance.

Plaza Cuba, P.O. Box 318135, San Francisco, CA 94131, 510/848-0911, plazacuba @yahoo.com, www.plazacuba.com, specializes in cultural workshops in Cuba, where tour participants can learn to dance salsa, merengue, and other Cuban favorites like a pro.

Learn-to-dance package tours in Havana are also offered by Global Exchange, 2017 Mission St. #303, San Francisco, CA 94110, 415/255-7296, fax 415/255-7498, info@global exchange.org, www.globalexchange.org.

From Canada: The Eleggua Project, 7171 Torbram Rd., Suite 51, Mississauga, ON L4T 3W4, 800/818-8840, fax 905/678-1421, cancuba@pathcom.com, www.pathcom.com/~cancuba, offers a series of courses in Afro-Cuban culture, plus music and dance.

Voyage Culture Cuba, 5059 Saint-Denis Laurier, Montreal, Quebec H2J 2L9, 514/982-3330 or 800/691-0101, fax 514/982-2438, info@culturecuba.com, www.culturecuba.com, offers study tours in music and dance.

Culture

The arts promotion entity ARTEX, Avenida 5ta #8010 esq. 82, Miramar, tel. 204-2741, fax 204-5846, sponsors courses in the arts and literature, including courses at the Cuban School of Ballet (La Escuela Cubana de Ballet) and Instituto Superior de Arte.

Paradiso: Promotora de Viajes Culturales, Calle 19 #560 esq. C, Vedado, tel. 832-6928, fax 33-3921, paradis@turcult.get.cma.net, www.ceniai.inf.cu/paradiso, arranges visits and participation in cultural courses and programs, from children's book publishing to theater criticism, plus festivals such as the International Benny Moré Festival and the International Hemingway Colloquium.

The Universidad de la Habana, Avenida de la Universidad, esq. J, Vedado, tel. 878-3231, or 878-1506 (International Relations), has two- to four-week courses in Cuban culture beginning the first Monday of every month.

SPANISH LANGUAGE COURSES

There's no shortage of Spanish language tuition in Cuba. Most courses offer options from beginner to advanced and include at least a modicum of workshops or lectures on Cuban culture. Classes are best arranged from abroad via one of the following organizations:

The **Universidad de la Habana,** tel. 832-4345 or 55-2352, fax 33-3127, dpg@comuh.uh.cu or dpi@reduniv.edu.cu, offers Spanish language courses of two weeks (US$200) and one month (US$300), plus "Spanish and Cuban Culture" courses of four to six months (US$800 to US$1,280). Courses begin the first Monday of every month. Accommodations are also available (US$400 per month including breakfast and dinner); contact Jorge Domínguez, tel. 204-0908, etea@fec.uh.cu.

The **Centro de Idiomas y Computación José Martí** (José Martí Language and Computer Center for Foreigners), Calle 16 #109, Miramar, tel. 202-9338, fax 204-4846, ice@ceniai.inf.cu, offers four levels of tuition from basic to specialized, each either "intensive" (20–100 hours) or "regular" (120–160 hours). Courses cost US$130/200/300/330 for one/two/three/four weeks of study. Several of the organizations listed in this section place students at this institution. **Cubamar Viajes,** Paseo #306, Vedado, tel. 33-3111, cubamar@cubamar.mit.cma.net, markets courses at Centro de Idiomas y Computación José Martí to foreigners.

You can also sign up for two-week to four-month Spanish language and Cuban culture courses offered by **Universitur,** described earlier.

From the USA: Try **Global Exchange,** 2017 Mission St. #303, San Francisco, CA 94110, 415/255-7296, fax 415/255-7498, info@globalexchange.org, www.globalexchange.org, which offers a Spanish language school with the University of Havana that includes private tutors and group classes plus cultural activities. Two-week and month-long courses are offered monthly.

From Canada: Cuba specialist **Voyage Culture Cuba,** 5059 Saint-Denis Laurier, Montreal, Quebec H2J 2L9, 514/982-3330 or 800/691-0101, fax 514/982-2438, info@culturecuba.com, www.culturecuba.com, offers courses at the University of Havana.

From the UK: The **School of Latin American Spanish,** Docklands Enterprise Centre, 11 Marshalsea Rd., London SE1 1EP, tel. 020/7237-2197, offers seven-week regular and intensive summer language courses in Cuba. **Caledonia Languages Abroad,** Clock House, Bonnington Mill, 72 Newhaven Rd., Edinburgh, EH6 5QG, tel. (0131) 621-7721, fax (0131) 621-7723, www.caledonialanguages.co.uk, also offers courses.

(01252) 760000, fax (01252) 760001, www.explore.co.uk, has a similar program.

Journey Latin America, 12 Heathfield Terr., London W4 4JE, tel. 020/8747-3108, fax 020/8742-1312, flights@journeylatinamerica.co.uk, www.journeylatinamerica.co.uk, offers seven-night breaks in Havana (from £782, including airfare). JLA also has an office at 12 St Ann's Square, Manchester M3 7HW, tel. (0161) 832-1441, fax (0161) 832-1551, man@journeylatinamerica.co.uk.

Kuoni, (01306) 74002 or (01306) 744442 (Caribbean desk), (0161) 832-0667 (Manchester), www.kuoni.co.uk, has packages beginning at £914 for six days, or £1,040 for 13 days. **Regent Holidays,** 15 John St., Bristol BS1 2HR, tel. (0117) 921-1711, fax (0117) 925-4866, regent@regent-holidays.co.uk, www.cheapflights.co.uk, specializes in customizing tours for independent travelers but also has package tours.

Other tour companies offering Cuba tours include **Caribbean Connection,** Concord House,

Canal St., Chester CH1 4EJ, tel. (01244) 355300, fax (01244) 355419, cc@itc-uk.com; **Caribbean Expressions,** 104 Belsize Ln., London NW3 5BB, tel. 020/7431-2131, www.expressionsholidays.co.uk; **Cuba Connect,** tel. 020/7263-6452, office@cuba-solidarity.org.uk, www.cubaconnect.co.uk; **Cuba Welcome,** DRCA Business Centre, Charlotte Despard Avenue, Battersea Park, London SW11 5HD, tel. 020/7498-7671, fax 020/7498-8333, www.cubawelcome.com; and **Interchange,** 27 Stafford Rd., Croydon, Surrey CR0 4NG, tel. 020/8681-3612 fax 020/8760-0031, www.interchange.co.uk.

Windsor & Neate Travel, 107 Bartholomew St., Newbury, Berkshire, RG14 5ED, tel. (01635) 528-355, fax (01635) 580-074, travel@windsorneate.co.uk, www.photographyholidays.co.uk, offers photography tours to Havana.

For other companies, see the **Association of British Travel Agents** website—www.abtanet.com—as well as the travel sections of leading newspapers, plus *Time Out,* and *What's On* in London.

Tours from Europe

In Germany, contact **Kubareisen,** Lindwurmstr. 207, 80337 München, tel./fax: 089/7479-1064, info@cuba-reisen.com, www.kubareisen.com. In Italy, try **Cuba Italturist,** tel. 02/535-4949, fax 02/535-4901, in Milan. In Switzerland, try **Carib Tours,** Malzastrasse 21 / Postfach, Zurich 8036, tel. 01/466-5656, fax 01/466-5600, carib@rbm.ch.

Also see the Special Topic "Tour Operators Abroad."

Tours from Australia and New Zealand

Caribbean Bound, 379 Pitt St., Suite 102, Sydney 2000, NSW, tel. 02/9267-2555, www.caribbean.com.au; and **Caribbean Destinations,** tel. 03/9614-7144 or 800/354-104, fax 03/9614-7155, mardi@caribbeanislands.com.au, www.caribbeanislands.com.au; and **Oxfam Community Aid Abroad,** 156 George St., Fitzroy Victoria 3065, tel. 03/9289-9444, fax 03/9419-5895, enquire @caa.org.au, www.caa.org.au, offers tours to Cuba.

Ocean Travel, 546 Queensberry St., N. Melbourne, Victoria 3051, tel. 03/9326-4280, info@cubatravel.com.au, www.cubatravel.com.au, offers "solidarity" tours.

New Zealand's **Innovative Travel,** 247 Edgeware, Christchurch, tel. 03/365-3910, fax 03/365-5755, specializes in the Caribbean.

STUDYING TO BE A DOCTOR

The Cuban **Ministerio de Salud Pública** (Ministry of Public Health), Calle 23 #201, Vedado, tel. 55-5532, offers free scholarships for disadvantaged and minority students from the United States to train as doctors at the Latin American School of Medical Sciences, 20 miles west of Havana. Courses last six years. The Cuban government pays a US$5 monthly stipend, and provides a shuttle into Havana on weekends. All students at the school are foreign; Cuban medical students train elsewhere. (At press time, a majority of the U.S. students had reportedly dropped out due to the living conditions; six-to-a-room dormitories lack hot water, air-conditioning, and toilet seats.) Applications should be requested through the Cuban Interest Section, 2630 16th Street NW, Washington, D.C. 20009, 202/797-8518, ext. 109, or online at www.afrocubaweb.com/infomed/med scholarships.htm.

PLANNING YOUR TRIP

Visas and Other Paperwork

Tourist Visas

A valid passport is required for entry. Tourists must also enter Cuba with a tourist card (visa), issued by tour agencies such as Havanatur and at the ticket counter of the airline or charter company providing travel to Cuba. In some cases, tourist cards are issued at an airport upon arrival within Cuba. They cost US$25 (CAN$36 in Canada, or £15 in the U.K.), but commercial agencies sometimes charge US$35 or more. No tourist visa is required for a stay of less than 72 hours.

Citizens of Japan, Malaysia, Peru, and Singapore need a visa to enter Cuba obtainable from Cuban consulates. For other foreign visitors, including U.S. citizens, a tourist visa will suffice. Russian citizens do not need a tourist card for stays of 30 days or less.

In 2001, the Cuban government extended the period in which foreigners may stay in Cuba. Your initial tourist visa is now good for 30–90 days, and you can request a 30–90-day extension, or *prórroga,* which costs US$25, payable in stamps purchased from branches of the Banco de Comercio and Banco Financiero Internacional. To request a *prórroga,* you must visit the **Ministerio de Imigración,** Calle 20, e/ 3ra y 5ta, Miramar; open Mon.–Fri. 8:30 A.M.–1 P.M. and 2–3 P.M. Arrive early! Extensions can also be obtained at Marina Hem-

CUBAN CONSULATES/EMBASSIES ABROAD

Australia: P.O. Box 1412, Marouba, NSW 2035, tel. 02/9311-4611, fax 02/9311-1255

Austria: Himmelhofgasse 40a-c A-1130, Vienna, tel. 01/877-8198, fax 01/877-8198

Canada: (Embassy) 388 Main St., Ottawa K1S 1E3, 613/563-0141, fax 613/540-0068, cuba@embacuba.ca, www.embacu.ca; (Consulate) 5353 Dundas St. W., Suite 401, Etobicoke, Ontario M9B 6H8, 416/234-8181, fax 416/234-2754; (Consulate) 1415 Avenue des Pins Ouest, Montreal, Quebec H3B 1B2, 514/843-8897, fax 514/982-9034

Belgium: Robert Jonesstraat 77, 1180 Brussels, tel. 02/343-0020, fax 02/343-9195

China: 1 Xiushui Nanjie, Beijing 100600, tel. 10/6532-2822, fax 10/6532-1984, www.emb online.net/cuba

France: 16 rue de Presles, 75015 Paris, tel. 01/45-67-55-35, fax 01/45-66-80-92

Germany: (Embassy) Stavange Strasse 20, 10439 Berlin, tel. 30/9161-1810; (Consulate) Kennedyallee 22-24, D-53175 Bonn, tel. (0228) 3090, www.cubainfo.de

Italy: Via Arco #4, 20121 Milan, tel. 02/866167, fax 02/866166; Via Licinia 7, 00153 Rome, tel. 06/571-7241

Mexico: Presidente Masarik 554, Colonia Polanco, Mexico 5 DF, CP11560, tel. 55/5280-8039, www.embacuba.com.mx

Netherlands: Mauritskade 49, Den Haag, 2514 HG, tel. 070/360-6061, fax 070/364-7586; Stationsplein 45, 3013 AK, Rotterdam, tel. 10/206-7333, fax 10/206-7335

Portugal: Rua Pero Covilha 14, Lisbon 1400, tel. 01/213-015-317, fax 01/213-011-895, emb aixada.cuba@netcabo.pt

Spain: Conde Peñalver #38, piso 6, Madrid 28006, tel. 91/401-6941, fax 91/402-1948

Switzerland: Gesellschaftsstrasse 8, 3021 Bern, tel. 031/302-2111 or 031/302-9830

United Kingdom: (Embassy) 167 High Holborn, London WC1V 6PA, tel. 020/7240-2488, fax 020/7836-2602; (Consulate) 15 Grape St., London WC2H 8DR, tel. 020/7240-2488, fax 020/7836-2602

U.S.: (Interests Section) 2639 16th St. NW, Washington, D.C. 20009, 202/797-8518, fax 202/797-8512, cubaseccion@igc.apc.org; (Consulate) 2630 16th St. NW, Washington, D.C. 20009, 202/797-8609, fax 202/986-7283.

ingway for people arriving by private vessel. Immigration officials don't look kindly on tourists staying in *casas particulares*. To ease your being issued a *prórroga,* consider telling the official that you'll be traveling around the island staying at state hotels (thereby you won't need to name a lodging in Havana).

Don't list your occupation as journalist, police, military personnel, or government employer, as the Cuban government is highly suspicious of anyone with these occupations. "Consultant" is a far safer gambit.

Cuban embassies post "Migratory Regulations for Travellers and Consular Services" on their websites. U.S. citizens should refer to the Cuban Embassy in Canada: www.embacuba.ca.

Non-Tourist Visas

Journalists must enter on a journalists' D-6 visa (US$60). Ostensibly these should be obtained in advance from Cuban embassies, and in the United States from the **Cuban Interests Section,** 2630 16th St. NW, Washington, D.C. 20009, 202/797-8518, fax 202/797-8521, cubaseccion@igc.apc.org. However, processing can take months while your credentials are vetted. If you enter on a tourist visa and intend to exercise your profession, you must register for a D-6 visa at the **Centro de Prensa Internacional,** Calle 23, e/ N y O, Vedado, tel. 832-0526, fax 33-3836 (open 8:30 A.M.–5 P.M.). Ask for an Acreditación de Prensa Extranjera (Foreign Journalist's Accreditation). You'll need to supply passport photos, which you can have taken at the Photo Service store adjacent to the press center. Here, the process of getting a journalist's visa can be done in a day . . . although you might not get your passport back for a week!

A commercial visa is required for individuals traveling to Cuba for business. These must also be obtained in advance from Cuban embassies, or the Cuban Interests Section in Washington, D.C.

If you wish to enter using a tourist visa and then, while within Cuba, change your visa status, contact the **Ministerio de Relaciones Exteriores** (Ministry of Foreign Affairs; MINREX),

Calle Calzada #360, e/ G y H, Vedado, tel. 55-3537 or 55-3260, fax 33-3460, cubaminrex @minrex.gov.cu, www.cubaminrex.cu, which handles immigration issues relating to foreigners.

Are U.S. Citizens Welcome?

The Cubans have no restrictions on U.S. tourists. On the contrary, they welcome U.S. visitors with open arms. The Cubans are savvy—they stamp your tourist card, not your passport. The U.S. government recommends that its citizens arriving in Cuba register at the **U.S. Interests Section,** Calzada between L & M Streets, Vedado, tel. 33-3551/59, fax 33-1084, Public Affairs Office: 33-3967, fax 33-3869, Visa Information phone numbers: 33-4400/02, 33-0552/54, InfoUnit Havana@state.gov.

Cuban Émigrés

U.S. citizens of Cuban origin are required to enter and leave Cuba with Cuban passports. You will also need your U.S. passport to depart and enter the United States. No visa is required, but an entry permit (US$100) valid for a 21-day stay is necessary. It's issued by tour agencies or the Cuban Interests Section or any other Cuban embassy or consulate. Cuban émigrés who have "not demonstrated any hostile attitude toward Cuba and who do not have a criminal record in their country of residence" can obtain a Multiple Entry Travel Visa (*vigencia de viaje*) good for two years and entry to Cuba as many times as desired for periods of up to 90 days. A nonrefundable deposit of US$50 is required, plus a US$150 fee payable upon receipt of the permit. You'll need a valid Cuban passport, six passport pictures, and proof that you do not have a criminal record.

Uncle Sam permits Cuban-Americans to visit Cuba only once per year and only for reasons of extreme family hardship.

Cuba does not recognize dual citizenship for Cuban citizens who are also U.S. citizens; Cuban-born citizens are—according to the U.S. State Department—thereby denied representation through the U.S. Interests Section in the event of arrest.

DEALING WITH OFFICIALDOM

Cuba has an insufferable bureaucracy, as portrayed in Tomás Gutiérrez Alea's trenchant black comedy *Death of a Bureaucrat*. Sometimes it's enough to make you tear out your hair! The island is riddled with Catch-22s, and working with government ministries (I almost wrote "mysteries") can be a perplexing and frustrating endeavor. Behind every office door is a desk or counter, behind which is a woman—preferably middle-aged and the very "cornerstone of bureaucracy"— whose job it is to keep people out. Civil servants in Cuba are always civil but usually servants only to their master, in the words of Guillermo Cabrera Infante. Very few people have the power to say, "Yes," but everyone is allowed to say, "No!" Finding the person who can say "Yes" is the key.

Ranting at Cubans gets you nowhere. Getting apoplectic with stone-faced Cuban officialdom only results in "negatives given more positively, broader and more regretful smiles, a rueful elevation of palms, eyes, and shoulders." Logical arguments count for little; charm, even romantic *piropos* (affectionate epithets) or a gift of chocolate, seems to work better.

Bribery and Corruption

Cuba is one of the few places in the Third World where you can get yourself into serious trouble by offering a bribe. Castro's government has differed greatly from other countries receiving billions of dollars in foreign aid—most of which has ended up in officials' pockets. It also ended overt corruption, where an elite ruling class plundered the national treasury.

That said, Cuban society functions thanks to all manner of craft and graft; the system's failings cause otherwise upright, honest people to do unscrupulous things. The integrity of Cuban officials extends only so far. Even many loyal functionaries rely on a greater or lesser degree on the black market to augment their salaries or put food in their pantries. And the reemergence of a dollar-based market economy has fostered a rapid rise in corruption.

Occasionally tourists get shaken down for money, although most corruption relates to black-market activities that are hardly likely to affect you.

Police

The **Policía Nacional Revolucionario** (PNR, National Revolutionary Police) are a branch of the Ministry of the Interior. Their presence is ubiquitous. Uniformed Cuban policemen perform the same functions as uniformed police officers in other countries, although with less professionalism than you may be used to. During a span of one week in Havana in August 2002, I witnessed policemen standing idly by while drunks brawled in the street . . . got no response when I reported a naked man masturbating in public 200 yards away . . . got more shrugged shoulders when I reported being mugged . . . was hit up for a bribe by a policeman attempting to write a *multa*—fine—for an entirely spurious infraction . . . and was pulled over by a policeman who wanted me to give him and his police buddies a ride.

Above all, the PNR exists to enforce revolutionary purity. You may witness petty harassment of everyday Cubans on the streets, and even be subject to such harassment yourself. Cuban policemen tend to treat foreigners with disdain—they've been trained to be paranoid about Western imperialists! Hence, never attempt to photograph police officers or military figures without their permission.

You should carry a copy of your passport and tourist card at all times to verify your identity. If you are stopped by policemen wanting to search you, insist on it being done in front of a neutral witness— *"solamente con testigos."* If at all possible, do *not* allow an official to confiscate or walk away with your passport. Don't panic! Tell as little as circumspection dictates— unlike priests, policemen rarely offer absolution for confessions.

Never pay a policeman money. If a policeman asks for money, get his name and badge number and file a complaint with the Ministry of Foreign Relations.

OTHER DOCUMENTATION AND CONSIDERATIONS

All tourists may be required to demonstrate an outbound ticket and adequate finances for their proposed stay upon arrival. Cuban immigration authorities do not require travelers to show proof of immunizations or an international vaccination card.

The law requires that you carry your passport or tourist card with you at all times during your stay. It's a good idea to make photocopies of *all* of your important documents, including your passport, and keep them separate from the originals, which you can keep in your hotel safe along with other valuables. It's wise, too, to take half a dozen passport-size photographs.

Cuban officials are paranoid about incursions into the country by CIA agents, right-wing Cuban exiles, and other "antisocial" characters. Immigration officials are also sensitive to your appearance and are often overly zealous in grilling incoming tourists. If you look like you'd be a "bad influence," you might be turned around and put on the next plane home.

When to Go

Havana's climate—generally hot and moist (average relative humidity is 78 percent)—is semi- or subtropical. There are only two seasons: hot and wet (May–Oct.), and warm and dry (Nov.–April). Early spring and late autumn are preferable. The winter period, November–April, is the busy season, and many hotels in Havana can be fully booked, especially during Christmas, New Year's, and Easter. Most hotels charge lower rates in the summer low season (*temporada baja*).

The newspaper *Granma* prints a weather forecast, as does *Cartelera,* the weekly tourist news-paper. Cuban TV newscasts feature weather forecasts (in Spanish). The **Instituto de Meteorología** (Meterological Institute), meteoro@ceniai.inf.cu, www.met.inf.cu, provides weather information online in Spanish.

TEMPERATURES

Havana's mean annual temperature is 25.2°C (77°F), with an average of eight hours of sunshine per day throughout the year. Temperatures in January average 22°C (67°F), rising (along

HAVANA'S CLIMATE

Average Temperatures

Temperatures are listed in degrees Celsius.

Jan.	Feb.	Mar.	Apr.	May	June
22°	22.5°	23°	25°	26°	27°

Days with Rainfall

6	4	4	4	7	10

July	Aug.	Sept.	Oct.	Nov.	Dec.
28°	28°	27.5°	26°	24°	22.5°

Days with Rainfall

9	10	11	11	7	6

NATIONAL HOLIDAYS

January 1 . . . . . . Liberation Day (Día de la Liberación)
January 2 . . . . . . Victory Day (Día de la Victoria)
January 28 . . . . . José Martí's birthday
February 24 . . . Anniversary of the Second War of Independence
March 8 . . . . . . International Women's Day (Día de la Mujer)
March 13 . . . . . Anniversary of the students' attack on the presidential palace
April 19 . . . . Bay of Pigs Victory (Victoria del Playa Girón)
May 1 . . . . Labor Day (Día de los Trabajadores)
July 26 . . . . National Revolution Day (anniversary of the attack on the Moncada barracks)
July 30 . . . . Day of the Martyrs of the Revolution
October 8 . . . . . Anniversary of Che Guevara's death
October 10 . . . . Anniversary of the First War of Independence
October 28 . . . . Memorial day to Camilo Cienfuegos
December 2 . . . Anniversary of the landing of the *Granma*
December 7 . . . Memorial day to Antonio Maceo

with humidity) to an average of 27.2°C (81°F) in July. Midwinter temperatures occasionally fall below 50°F when severe cold fronts sweep down into the Gulf of Mexico, and visitors to Havana will be glad for a sweater and jacket.

The island is influenced by the warm Gulf Stream currents and by the North Atlantic high-pressure zone that lies northeast of Cuba and gives rise to the near-constant *brisa,* the local name for the prevailing northeast trade winds that caress Havana year-round. Indeed, despite its more southerly latitude, Havana, wrote Ernest Hemingway, "is cooler than most northern cities in those months [July and August], because the northern trades get up about ten o'clock in the morning and blow until about five o'clock the next morning." Summer months, however, can be insufferably hot and humid.

RAINFALL

Rain falls an average of 85–100 days a year, totaling an annual average of 132 centimeters (52 inches). Almost two-thirds falls during the May–October wet season. Summer rain is most often a series of intermittent showers (or dramatic, short-lived deluges) interspersed with sunshine, but lingering downpours and storms

that last two or three days are common. When it rains hard, pools of water collect in the streets, waves crash over the Malecón, power snaps off, telephone lines go down, one or more buildings collapse, and taxis are impossible to find.

December, and February through April are the driest months (known as *La Seca*), although heavy winter downpours can occur when cold fronts sweep south from North America.

HURRICANES

Cuba lies within the hurricane belt. August–October is hurricane season, but freak tropical storms can hit Cuba in other months, too. Most hurricanes that strike Cuba originate in the western Caribbean during October and move north over the island. Most recently, Hurricane Lili battered the island in October 1996; in September 1998, Hurricane George blasted Havana; Hurricane Michelle—the largest storm to hit Cuba in 50 years—struck western Cuba in October 2001; and Hurricanes Isidora and Iris walloped western Cuba in rapid succession in October 2002.

The **National Weather Service,** 1325 East-West Hwy., Silver Spring, MD 20910, www .nws.noaa.gov, provides updated weather forecasts and hurricane warnings.

What to Take

Pack light! A good rule of thumb is to lay out everything you wish to take—then cut it by half. Try to limit yourself to one bag (preferably a sturdy duffel or garment bag with plenty of pockets), plus a small day pack or camera bag.

Most important, don't forget your passport, airline tickets, traveler's checks, and other documentation. You'd be amazed how many folks get to the airport before discovering this "minor" oversight.

Leave your posh jewelry at home—it invites theft.

Toiletries are expensive in Cuba. Take all the toiletries you think you'll need, including some toilet paper or tissues, a towel, and face cloth.

Bring any specific medications you think you'll need. If you bring prescription drugs, be sure the druggist's identification label is on the container. Women should pack extra feminine hygiene products—those you don't use will make good gifts for Cuban women.

It can be buggy in Cuba; bug spray is a good thing to have with you. And don't forget the sunscreen!

Writing materials are hard to come by: take pens, pencils, and notepads (these make great gifts to children). An English/Spanish dictionary is handy and makes a good parting gift.

COPING WITH THE CLIMATE

Cuba is mostly hot and humid, and you'll want light, loose-fitting shirts and pants. It can get chilly in midwinter, especially at night. Pack a sweater and/or a jacket, which you'll need to cope with the bone-chilling air-conditioning in buses and many restaurants. Pack items that you can layer and which work in various combinations—preferably darker items that don't show the inevitable dirt and stains you'll quickly collect walking the streets of Havana. Note, though, that dark clothes tend to be hotter than light clothing, which reflects the sun's rays.

Three T-shirts, two dressier shirts, a couple of tank tops, a sweater, a sweatshirt, a pair of Levi's, plus a pair of jeans or cotton-polyester safari-style "cargo" pants and a pair of dress pants, two pairs of shorts, swimming trunks, and a sleeveless photographer's jacket with heaps of pockets suffice for me (and that's usually for a month or more). Women may wish to substitute blouses and skirts—and might consider following Cuban fashion by packing shorter versions of the latter.

Denim jeans take forever to dry when wet. Ideally, everything should be drip-dry, wash-and-wear.

Pack plenty of socks and undergarments—you may need a daily change. Wash them frequently to help keep athlete's foot and other fungal growths at bay.

In the wet season, a small fold-up umbrella is best—they're impossible to find in Havana. Raincoats are heavy and tend to make you sweat. Breathable Gore-Tex rainproof jackets work fine. A hooded poncho is also good. Make sure it has slits down the side for your arms and that it is large enough to carry a small day pack underneath.

HOW DRESSY?

Cubans do not stand on ceremony, and most travelers will not need dressy clothes. *Habaneros* dress informally but always very neatly—they rarely go out in the evening without first changing into fresh clothes. Even Cuban businesspeople and officials dress informally, often with a *guayabera* shirt worn outside the trousers, even at official functions.

Still, pack a pair of slacks and a dressy shirt for discos or the fancier restaurants. A jacket and tie or cocktail dress is entirely unnecessary, although the past few years have seen a creeping trend toward business suits among Cuba's business elite.

Shorts are acceptable wear in Havana for men, but save shorter-style runner's shorts for the beach. Women can get away with just about any skimpy item, following in the footsteps of their Cuban counterparts, although you're sure to attract attention from males.

A pair of lightweight sandals or low-heeled walking shoes are de rigueur. Sneakers will do double-duty for most occasions. High heels for women? Sure, they're all the rage among *ha-* *baneras,* although maneuvering the cobblestones and potholes in heels will be a challenge.

Health Concerns Before You Go

Dental and medical checkups are advisable before departing home, particularly if you intend to travel for a considerable time, partake in strenuous activities, or if you have an existing medical problem. Take any medications, including prescriptions for eyewear; keep prescription drugs in their original bottles to avoid suspicion at customs. If you suffer from a debilitating health problem, wear a medical alert bracelet.

A basic health kit is a good idea. Pack the following as a minimum in a small plastic container: alcohol swabs and medicinal alcohol, antiseptic cream, Band-Aids, aspirin or painkillers, diarrhea medication, sunburn remedy, antifungal foot powder, calamine and/or antihistamine, water-purification tablets, surgical tape, bandages and gauze, and scissors.

Information on health concerns can be answered in advance of travel by **Intermedic,** 777 3rd Ave., New York, NY 10017, 212/486-8900; the **Department of State Citizens Emergency Center,** 202/647-5226, travel.state.gov/medical .html; and the **International Association for Medical Assistance to Travelers** (IAMAT), 417 Center St., Lewiston, NY 14092, 716/754-4883, info@iamat.org, www.iamat.org. In the UK, you can get information, inoculations, and medical supplies from the **British Airways Travel Clinic,** 156 Regent St., London W1B 5LB, tel. 020/7439-9584.

An invaluable pocket-size book is *Staying Healthy in Asia, Africa, and Latin America,* published by Avalon Travel Publishing, www.moon.com, which is packed with first-aid and basic medical information.

VACCINATIONS

No vaccinations are required to enter Cuba unless visitors are arriving from areas of cholera and yellow fever infection (mostly Africa and South America), in which case they must have valid vaccinations.

Epidemic diseases have mostly been eradicated throughout the country—for example, Cuba is the only country to have totally eliminated measles.

Consult your physician for recommended vaccinations. At the least, you should consider vaccinations against tetanus and infectious hepatitis, although infectious hepatitis (hepatitis A) is reported only infrequently in Cuba. The main symptoms are stomach pains, loss of appetite, yellowing skin and eyes, and extreme tiredness. Hepatitis A is contracted through unhygienic foods or contaminated water (salads and unpeeled fruits are major culprits). A gamma globulin vaccination is recommended. The much rarer Hepatitis B is usually contracted through unclean needles, blood transfusions, or unsafe sex.

Also see Health Issues in the Information and Services Chapter.

TRAVEL INSURANCE

Travel insurance is highly recommended. Travelers should check to see if their health insurance or other policies cover medical expenses while abroad—and specifically in Cuba. Traveler's insurance isn't cheap, but it can be a sound investment. Travel agencies can sell you traveler's health and baggage insurance, as well as insurance against cancellation of a prepaid tour.

International

If you're concerned about things going wrong, consider purchasing insurance through **Assist-Card,** 15 Rue du Cendrier, 1201 Geneva, Switzerland, tel. 202/738-5852, fax 202/738-6305, www.assist-card.com, which offers travel assistance with everything from tracking lost luggage and finding medical, legal, and technical services to emergency transfers and repatriation, which you can request 24 hours a day. Insurance premiums cost from US$45 for five days to US$285 for 90 days for the basic package, and from

US$135 to US$1,143 for the top-line package. Assist-Card has Regional Assistance Centers worldwide, including in Cuba (even for U.S. citizens), c/o Asistur, tel. 867-1315 or 33-8920, cuba@assist-card.com. There is also a center in the United States, 305/381-9959 or 800/874-2223, fax 305/375-8135, usa@assist-card.com.

Asistur also represents about 160 insurance and assistance companies of 40 countries.

In the United States

Some U.S. insurance programs guarantee coverage for Cuba. These include **American Express**, P.O. Box 919010, San Diego, CA 92190, 800/234-0375, www.americanexpress.com; **Travelers**, 1 Tower Square, Hartford, CT 06183, 203/277-0111 or 800/243-3174, www.travelers.com; and **TravelGuard International**, 1145 Clark St., Stevens Point, WI 54481, 715/345-0505 or 800/826-4919, www.travelguard.com.

The **Council on International Education Exchange** (CIEE), www.ciee.org, offers insurance to students.

In the UK

The **Association of British Insurers**, 51 Gresham St., London BC2V 7HQ, tel. 020/7600-3333, www.abi.org.uk, provides advice for obtaining travel insurance. Inexpensive insurance is offered through **Endsleigh Insurance**, tel. 020/7436-4451, www.endsleigh.co.uk; and **STA Travel**, tel. 020/7361-6262, www.sta.com.

In Australia

AFTA, tel. 02/9956-4800, www.afta.com.au, and **Travel Insurance on the Net**, www.travelinsurance.com.au, are good resources.

In Cuba

You can obtain insurance in Cuba through **Asistur**, seguro@asist.sid.cu, in association with the Cuban insurance agency, **Aseguradora del Turismo La Isla S.A.**, Calle 14 #301 esq. 3ra Avenida, Miramar, tel. 204-7490, fax 204-7494, laisla@laisla.get.cma.net, www.cuba.cu/laisla. The basic package covers up to US$400 of baggage, US$7,000 in medical expenses, US$5,000 for repatriation, and more.

The Cuban agency **ESEN**, 5ta Calle #306, e/ C y D, Vedado, tel. 832-2500, fax 33-8717, esen@esen.com.cu, www.esen.com.cu, also offers medical insurance for foreign travelers (US$10 per US$1,000 of treatment). **ESICUBA** (Seguros Internacionales de Cuba), Calle Cuba #314, e/ Obispo y Obrapía, tel. 57-3231, fax 33-8038, esicuba@sic.get, offers travelers' insurance, although most of its policies are oriented toward the needs of companies, not individuals. Both ESEN and ESICUBA are independent companies, although the Cuban government is the major shareholder. They're rated by Insurance Solvency International and reinsured through Lloyd's of London and other major insurers.

Habana Vieja — The Old City

Evocative Habana Vieja (4.5 square km) is colloquially defined by the limits of the early colonial settlement that lay within fortified walls. Today, the legal boundary of Habana Vieja includes the Paseo de Martí (Prado) and everything east of it. The vast majority of sites of interest are concentrated here. Don't underestimate how much there is to see in Habana Vieja. At least three days are required, and one week isn't too much.

The original city developed along a polynuclear axis that extended roughly north–south from Castillo de la Real Fuerza to Plaza Vieja. Here are the major sites of interest, centered on two plazas of great stature: the Plaza de Armas and the smaller but more imposing Plaza de la Catedral. Each square has its own unique flavor, which seems to change with the hours and light—melancholic in the rain, bustling and alive in the sun, and "voluptuous when a hot midnight is illuminated by lamps and vibrates with guitar music and the muffled heartbeat of an African drum," thought Juliet Barclay. The plazas and surrounding streets shine after a complete restoration, their structures newly painted and seeming like confections in stone.

The area east of Avenida de Bélgica and southwest of Plaza Vieja, between Calles Brasil and Merced, was the great ecclesiastical center of

loggia of the Palacio de los Capitanes Generales

HABANA VIEJA HIGHLIGHTS

You could spend two or three days strolling the streets of Habana Vieja (Old Havana) and be mesmerized at every turn. It's a given that you'll visit **La Bodeguita del Medio** and **El Floridita** to pay homage to Papa (Ernest Hemingway) with a *mojito* in one hand and a daiquirí in the other. Then what? Here's my list of top must sees and dos:

Cámara Oscura. This simple reflective "camera" beams a revolving image over the rooftops of Havana onto a dish, providing an intriguing, magnified panorama and an introduction to what's where in the city.

Capitolio. Cuba's former congressional building is a stunner both inside and out.

Fábrica de Tabaco Partagás. A visit to this cigar factory is a must for an appreciation of how the world's finest cigars are made.

Fortaleza de San Carlos de la Cabaña. Largest fortress in the Americas, superbly restored with cannons in situ, excellent historical museum, and marvelous views over the city. Every night, soldiers in 18th-century period costume reenact the *canoñazo,* when a cannon is fired to commemorate the signal to close the city gates.

Maqueta de la Habana Vieja. A detailed 1:500 scale model of Habana Vieja.

Museo de Bellas Artes. A fabulous art collection housed in two sections and displaying the works of renowned international and Cuban artists spanning the centuries.

Museo de la Ciudad de La Habana. Housed in the former Spanish governor's palace, this collection of resplendent colonial relics recalls the ostentation of the era.

Museo de la Revolución. This former presidential palace now tells the tale of the Revolution. For the Castro government's take on events leading up to and during the Revolution, this is the place.

Museo de Ron. Take a guided tour inside a replica rum factory to learn the secrets of how Cuba's fine rums are made.

Plaza de la Catedral. The heart and soul of old Havana, this compact plaza will steal your heart. Visit by both day and night.

colonial Havana and is replete with churches and convents. The much deteriorated (mostly residential) southern half of Habana Vieja is given short shrift by most visitors. However, city fathers have chosen the path of restoration, rather than demolition; the restoration project is finally taking hold in the area. Take care with your possessions when walking this area.

Habana Vieja was not entirely spared modern expansion. During the 1950s numerous buildings went up that are today considered eyesores within their particular urban context, particularly in the "banking district" around the intersection of Calles Cuba and Aguiar. Fortunately, they are few and far between and as a whole, the neighborhood escaped the thoughtless, utilitarian real estate developments that have eradicated much of the early treasures of such

cities as Lima. There are no fast-food joints, no glitzy advertisements, no billboards or Golden Arches. Nor have the working class inhabitants been forced out by gentrification.

Habana Vieja is a living museum—as many as 60,000 people live within the confines of the old city wall—and suffers from inevitable ruination brought on by the tropical climate, hastened—notwithstanding the restoration project —since the Revolution by years of neglect. The grime of centuries has been soldered by tropical heat into the chipped cement and faded pastels. Beyond the restored areas, Habana Vieja is a quarter of sagging, mildewed walls and half-collapsed balconies festooned with laundry seemingly held aloft by telegraph cords and electrical wires strung across streets in a complex spider web. The narrow streets reverberate with the

HABANA VIEJA

HABANA VIEJA: SIGHTS

FORTALEZA DE SAN CARLOS DE LA CABAÑA

SEE "PARQUE HISTÓRICO MILITAR MORRO – CABAÑA" MAP

SEE "HABANA VIEJA: THE CORE" MAP

B A H Í A   D E   L A   H A B A N A

TUNEL DE LA HABANA

Plaza de San Francisco

Plaza de Armas

CASTILLO DE LA REAL FUERZA

MERCADERES

Plaza de la Catedral

SAN IGNACIO

CALLE

TACÓN

Parque Luz Caballero

FUENTE DE NEPTUNO

LA NIÑA (HARBOR CRUISE)

(AV. DEL PUERTO)

Parque Cespedes

PARQUE DIVERSIONES

PARQUE ANFITEATRO

CESPEDES

MANUEL DE

ANFITEATRO DE LA HABANA

CUBA

OBRAPIA

BOLSA DE LA HABANA

LAMPARILLA

BANCO CENTRAL DE CUBA

ROYAL BANK OF CANADA

O'REILLY

★ BANCO DE CRÉDITO Y COMERCIO

HABANA

IGLESIA SAN FELIPE DE NERI

BANCO NACIONAL

OBISPO

CASA DEL CONDE DE LA REUNIÓN ★

Parque Cervantes ★

CASA NATAL DE ★ FELIX VARELA

LIBRERÍA LA INTERNACIONAL

INFOTUR ■

Platuela de Supervielle

EL CASTILLO DE ATANE/POLICE

BANCO FINANCIERO DEL COMERCIO

TEJADILLO

DE

DIOS

JUAN

SAN

LA MODERNA TELECORREO ■

HARRIS BROTHERS ■

CASA CULTURAL DE FELIX VARELA

LIBRERÍA LA INTERNACIONAL

EMPEDRADO

COMPOSTELA

AGUACATE

VILLEGAS

AV. DE LAS MISIONES

MUSEO NACIONAL DE BELLAS ARTES (CUBAN SECTION)

EDIFICIO BACARDI ■

INFOTUR ■

LIBRERÍA LA POESÍA

Parque Central

MONUMENTO AL GENERAL MÁXIMO GÓMEZ

AV. CARLOS

PEÑA POBRE

PALACIO PEDROSO ■

AGUIAR

CUARTELES

BALUARTE DE ANGEL ★

IGLESIA DEL SANTO ★ ANGEL-COSTUDIO

MUSEO DE LA MÚSICA ★

PROVINCIAL ASSEMBLY

Plaza 13 de Mayo

SAU-100 TANK ■

MUSEO DE LA REVOLUCIÓN ★

GRANMA MEMORIAL

MUSEO NACIONAL DE BELLAS ARTES (INTERNATIONAL SECTION)

CASTILLO/MUSEO DE SAN SALVADOR DE LA PUNTA

CARCEL DE LA HABANA ★

Parque de los Mártires ★

CAPDEVILA

SPANISH EMBASSY ■

FABRICA DE TABACO LA CORONA

CINE FAUSTO ■

COLON

CARCEL

AGRAMONTE (ZULUETA)

CENTRO CULTURAL ASTURIANAS ★

MUSEO DE BOMBEROS ★

MONUMENTO DE ESTUDIANTES DE MEDICINA

MONUMENTO A JUAN CLEMENTE ZENEA

AV. ANTONIO MACEO (MALECÓN)

SAN LAZARO

GENIOS

REFUGIO

CONSULADO

MARTI (PRADO)

CENTRO ANDALUZ ■

Parque de los Enamorados ★

CAPDEVILA

ACADEMIA DE GIMNASIO/ESCUELA NATIONAL DE BALLET ■

ASISTUR ■

PALACIO DE MATRIMONIA ■

FOTO PRADO ■

PISCINA HOTEL SEVILLA ■

PASEO

DE

CENTRO CULTURAL DE ARABES ■

MUSEO NACIONAL DE BELLAS ARTES (INTERNATIONAL SECTION)

MONUMENTO A JOSÉ MARTÍ

TROCADERO

CRESPO

SAN

ANIMAS

VIRTUDES

AMISTAD

INDUSTRIA

NEPTUNO

SAN MIGUEL

RAFAEL

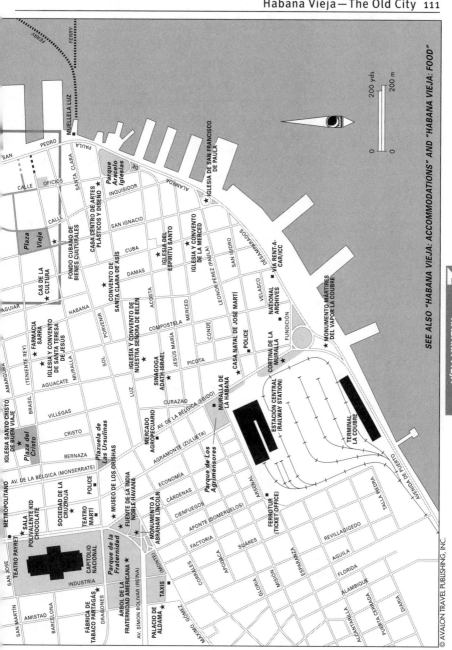

SEE ALSO "HABANA VIEJA: ACCOMMODATIONS" AND "HABANA VIEJA: FOOD"

HABANA VIEJA

© AVALON TRAVEL PUBLISHING, INC.

GETTING YOUR BEARINGS

La Ciudad de la Habana (the City of Havana) lies 150 kilometers (93 miles) due south of Florida, on the northwest coast of Cuba, the largest of the Caribbean islands at 114,524 square kilometers (44,218 square miles). The city lies just south of the Tropic of Cancer and looks out upon the Straits of Florida at the eastern perimeter of the Gulf of Mexico.

Havana is built on the west side of a sweeping bay with a narrow funnel entrance—Bahía de la Habana—but extends about 20 kilometers to the west and south of the bay. The city slopes gradually inland from the shore. The core is divided into three main regions of tourist interest: Habana Vieja, Centro Habana (Central Havana), and Vedado and Plaza de la Revolución.

East of Havana, a chain of hills runs parallel to the shore inland of the rocky coast. The coast is indented with coves. About 15 kilometers east of the city, a series of long, white sand beaches—the Playas del Este—prove tempting on hot summer days. The shore west of the city is mostly rocky with a few beaches of modest appeal.

Since the main sights are so spread out, it is best to explore Havana in sections, beginning with Habana Vieja, where the vast majority of historical sites are located and the narrow streets lend themselves to perambulation. All touristed areas are patrolled by police, who since 1999 have stood on virtually every other corner on a 24-hour basis.

Don't restrict your wanderings to daylight hours. There is always life on the streets, 24/7, though the life at 2 P.M. is different than that of 2 A.M.

To savor the quintessential Havana experience, it's a good idea to immerse yourself in a neighborhood. Hang out with the locals and become one with the local community.

Municipios and Districts

The metropolitan area of Havana—a sprawling city—covers 740 square kilometers (286 square miles) and incorporates 15 *municipios* (municipalities), subdivided into distinct districts. The urban center mostly lies west and south of the harbor, and encompasses almost 15,000 *manzanas* (blocks). Like all fine cities, Havana is a collection of neighborhoods, each with its own distinct character that owes much to the date that each developed.

La Habana Vieja (Old Havana) lies immediately west of the harbor, and with neighboring **Regla** across the harbor, dates from the 16th and 17th centuries, though most structures are of the 17th and 18th centuries. This is the most important section for sightseeing, where the museums, palaces, and plazas are concentrated. **Parque Histórico Militar Morro-Cabaña,** facing Habana Vieja on the north side of the harbor channel, features two castles-turned-museums.

Centro Habana, west of Habana Vieja, and **Casablanca,** a fishing village facing Havana to the north (and part of the *municipio* of Regla) date from the 18th century. They were the first residential areas outside the ancient city walls. Sightseeing attractions are relatively few.

honking of horns, as well as salsas, rumbas, and "feeling" songs emanating from open windows, inside which eerie neon lights glimmer, illuminating ceramic figurines, girlie posters (a favorite household decoration), and velveteen pictures of cats and dogs enjoying human pursuits.

You'll frequently find humble and haughty side by side, since for most of the colonial period, areas were socially mixed. Slaves lived in separate quarters or their masters' mansions. Merchants lived above their warehouses, where the slaves also lived. The best stores in colonial days were along Calles Obispo and O'Reilly, seething Asian bazaars that were once covered in colorful awnings that softened the sun's glare. They were Aladdin's caves of European fineries, incense, crystal and china, muslin and ribbons, and *piña* cloth, a silky gauze made of pineapple fiber and dyed in radiant colors. Obispo is still the commercial lifeline connecting Centro Habana with Habana Vieja.

Cerro and **Diez de Octubre,** which includes La Vibora district, lie south of Centro Habana and date from the 19th century. Sites of interest are few in these now-decrepit residential districts.

Plaza de la Revolución, west of Centro and Cerro, comprises **Vedado,** the modern heart of the city, and **Nuevo Vedado** to the south, blending neighborhoods of the 19th and 20th centuries. Plaza de la Revolución extends west from Centro to the Río Almendares. Most businesses, hotels, and nightclubs, are located in Vedado, as are many of the city's best *casas particulares* (private room rentals). The Universidad de la Havana, Cementerio Colón, and Plaza de la Revolución are among the prime sites.

Playa extends west of the Río Almendares and includes, in order, the districts of Miramar and (to its south) Buena Vista, with once glamorous Cubanacán, and Flores, Siboney, Atabey, and Santa Fe beyond. These areas date from the late 19th and early 20th centuries. Most embassies are here, as are many excellent restaurants and modern deluxe hotels.

La Lisa and **Marianao** lie south of Playa and are suburban, residential *municipios* offering little of touristic interest. Marianao, however, boasts Havana's most spectacular nightclub: the Tropicana.

Boyeros, Arroyo Naranjo, and **Cotorro** form the southern suburbs. These expansive *municipios* combine historic villages, such as Santiago de las Vegas and San Francisco de Paula (site of the Museo de Hemingway), with modern industrial enclaves. The national zoo, botanical garden, and a major recreational park are also here.

Guanabacoa, east of Regla, is an 18th-century town known for its ecclesiastical attractions and as a center for *santería* and Afro-Cuban music.

La Habana del Este extends east from the harbor for some 30 kilometers along the shore as far as the beaches of the Playas del Este. Between the city and Playas del Este are the post-revolutionary urban enclaves of **Ciudad Camilo Cienfuegos, Ciudad Panamericano,** and **Alamar,** and the 18th-century fishing village of **Cojímar.**

Introductions to the City

Several sites offer general overviews to Havana, good for getting your bearings. They are described in more detail in the appropriate travel chapters.

Maqueta de la Habana in Miramar, Calle 28 #113, e/ Avenida 1 y 3, tel. 204-2661 or 202-7303, features a 1:1,000-scale model of Havana that will give you an idea of the city's layout.

Maqueta de la Habana Vieja, Calle Mercaderes #114, has a 1:500-scale model of Habana Vieja.

Cámara Oscura, near Plaza Vieja in Habana Vieja, features a camera that revolves through 360° and projects a vista of the entire city.

Monumento y Museo José Martí, near the Plaza de la Revolución in Vedado, is pinned by a 109-meter-tall tower with a *mirador* (lookout) offering a bird's-eye view of the entire city.

ORIENTATION

Habana Vieja is roughly shaped like a diamond, with the Castillo de la Punta its northerly point. Its western boundary, Paseo de Martí (colloquially called the Prado) runs south at a gradual gradient from the Castillo de la Punta to Parque Central and, beyond, Parque de la Fraternidad, from where Avenida de Bélgica runs southeast, tracing the old city wall to the harbor front at the west end of Desamparados. East of Castillo de la Punta, Avenida Carlos Manuel de Céspedes (Avenida del Puerto) runs along the harbor channel and curls south to Desamparados.

The maze of narrow one-way streets is purgatory for anyone with a motor vehicle, so *walk.* In any event, the main plazas and the streets between them are barred to traffic by huge artillery shells in the ground.

ADDRESSES

Addresses are normally given as locations. Thus, the Havanatur office is at Calle 6 e/ 1ra y 3ra, Miramar, Havana, meaning it is on Street 6 between (*e/* stands for *entre*, between) First and Third Avenue (1ra Avenida y 3ra Avenida).

Street numbers are occasionally used. Thus, the Hotel Inglaterra is at Prado #416 esq. San Rafael, Habana Vieja, at the corner (*esq.* stands for *esquina*, or corner) of Prado and Calle San Rafael, in Old Havana (Habana Vieja).

Piso refers to the floor level (thus, an office on *Piso 3ro*, or *Piso tercero*, is on the third floor). Sometimes *alto* (upper floor) is used, or *bajo* (lower floor), or *sótano* (basement).

Much of Havana is laid out on a grid pattern with parallel streets (*calles*) running perpendicular to avenues (*avenidas*). Some areas, such as Vedado and Miramar, however, have even-numbered *calles* (north-south) running perpendicular to odd-numbered *calles* (usually east-west), with the main boulevards called *avenidas*.

Note that many (but not all) streets have at least two names: one predating the Revolution (and usually the most commonly used colloquially) and the other a postrevolutionary name. For example, the Prado is the old (and preferred) term for the Paseo de Martí. On maps, the modern name takes precedence, with the old name often shown in parentheses. Locals, however, usually prefer the old name.

New Name	Old Name
Agramonte	Zulueta
Aponte	Someruelos
Avenida Andrés	San Miguel
Avenida Antonio Maceo	Malecón
Avenida de Bélgica	Egido
Avenida Camilo Cienfuegos	Dolores
Avenida Carlos M. Céspedes (Habana Vieja)	Avenida del Puerto
Avenida de España	Vives
Avenida de la Independencia	Avenida Rancho Boyeros
Avenida de Italia	Galiano
Avenida de los Misiones	Monserrate
Avenida Salvador Allende	Carlos III
Avenida Simón Bolívar	Reina
Brasil	Teniente Rey
Capdevila	Cárcel
Enrique Barnet	Estrella
Leonor Pérez	Paula
Máximo Gómez	Monte
Padre Varela	Belascoaín
Paseo de Martí	Prado (Paseo del Prado)
Progreso	San Juan de Dios
San Martín	San José
Vía Blanca	Marina

La Punta to Parque de la Fraternidad

LA PUNTA

Castillo de San Salvador de La Punta

This charming fortress, Avenida Carlos M. de Céspedes, esq. Prado y Malecón, guards the entrance to Havana's harbor channel, at the northwest apex of Habana Vieja—an appropriate point from which to begin your perambulation. Small and low-slung, it sits at the base of the Prado. The fortress was initiated in 1589 directly across from the Morro Castle so that the two fortresses might catch invaders in a crossfire. A great chain was slung between them each night to secure Havana harbor; you can still see the cannons embedded in the reefs and to which the chain was attached. Originally, the fortress stood upon an outcrop that jutted out into the harbor channel. Its site remains pivotal, and from the plaza overlooking the channel (a favorite spot for trysting lovers at night), you may revel in the sweeping vista westward along the Malecón toward the statuesque facade of the Vedado district.

In 2002, the castle gates were reopened following a complete restoration. Today the castle contains the **Museo de San Salvador de la Punta,** displaying treasures from the golden age, when the riches of the Americas flowed to Spain. The air-conditioned Sala de Tesoro gleams with gold—gold bars, gold chains, gold coins, gold toothpicks, gold brooches the size of platters—surrounded by precious item of silver and jewels, bronze astrolabes, pewter dishes, rosary beads, clay pipes, silver reals ("pieces of eight"), and

TOURIST INFORMATION OFFICES

Infotur, oficturi@ofitur.mit.tur.cu, www.info tur.cu, the government tourist information bureau, has offices at Calle Obispo #360 e/ Bernazas y Villegas, tel. 33-3333 or 62-4586, infobisp @teleda.get.cma.net; at the corner of Calle Obispo and San Ignacio, tel. 63-6884; and in the Terminal de Cruceros (Cruise Terminal).

even an enema syringe—plucked from the seabed by divers of Carisub, the Cuban government's marine archaeology organization. Alas, the labels are in Spanish only. Another *sala* (room) has naval uniforms, swords, pistols, and model ships spanning three centuries. And, of course, there's no shortage of cannon, sabers, and muskets. Open Wed.–Sun. 10 A.M.–5:30 P.M. Entrance costs US$5 (cameras cost US$2).

Parque de Mártires and Parque de los Enamorados

The parkland, immediately south of the castle, on the south side of Avenida de Carlos M. Céspedes, at the base (and east) of the Prado is divided in two by Avenida de los Estudiantes.

Parque de los Enamorados (Park of the Lovers), on the north side of Avenida de los Estudiantes, features a statue of an Indian couple, plus the **Monumento de Estudiantes de Medicina,** a small Grecian-style temple shading the remains of a wall used by Spanish colonial firing squads. Here on November 27, 1871, eight medical students met their deaths after being falsely accused of desecrating the tomb of a prominent loyalist, Gonzalo Castañón. A trial found them innocent, but enraged loyalist troops—the Spanish Volunteers—held their own trial and shot the students. Elevated to the pantheon of revolutionary martyrs, the students are commemorated with a national holiday each November 27.

Parque de Mártires (Martyr's Park), on the south side of Avenida de los Estudiantes, occupies the ground of the former Tacón prison, built in 1838. Horrible mutilations were performed on common criminals and Cuban nationalists charged with conspiracy and treason. Nationalist hero José Martí was imprisoned here in 1869–70 and never recovered from the hard labor he was forced to perform. The prison was designed to hold 2,000 people, with separate divisions according to sex, race, and social status. It was demolished in 1939, and the park dedicated in memory of all those who suffered for their ideals. Preserved for posterity were two of

RECOMMENDED WALKING TOUR 1

Begin at **Parque Central**, taking in the **statue of José Martí** at its center and the **Hotel Inglaterra** and **Gran Teatro** on its western side. Head south to the **Capitolio**, taking time to explore inside.

Continue south to **Parque de la Fraternidad**, passing the **Fuente de la India** and **bust of Abraham Lincoln**, and scores of old Yankee cars serving as taxis.

Head to the northwest corner of the park, timing your arrival at the **Fábrica de Tabaco Partagás** for a tour of the cigar factory.

Return to Parque Central and walk north, taking in the length of the **Prado**, calling in at the **Hotel Sevilla**. Past the **Parque de los Mártires**, cross the Avenida Carlos M. Céspedes (be careful crossing this awkward junction) for the view along the **Malecón** toward Vedado. Browse the **Museo de la Plata**, in the **Castillo de la Punta**.

Return to the Parque de los Mártires, and visit the **Monumento de Máximo Gómez.** Walk the central median of **Plaza 13 de Mayo** to the **Palacio Presidencial**, where you should visit the **Museo de la Revolución** and **Granma Memorial.**

Follow Agramonte (Zulueta) south one block to the Cuban section of the **Museo de Bellas Artes.** Return to Parque Central via Agramonte and visit the international section of the **Museo de Bellas Artes.**

the punishment cells and the chapel used by condemned prisoners before being marched to the firing wall.

PASEO DE MARTÍ (PRADO)

Paseo de Martí, colloquially known as the Prado, is a kilometer-long tree-lined boulevard that slopes southward, uphill, from the harbor mouth and Castillo de San Salvador de la Punta to Parque Central. The Prado is a smaller but no less courtly version of Barcelona's La Rambla and a splendid place to linger and watch Havana's life unfold.

The beautiful boulevard lay *extramura*, outside the old walled city of San Cristóbal de la Habana, and was initiated by the Marquis de la Torre in 1772 and completed in 1852, when it had the name Alameda de Isabella II. Until the end of the last century, it was Havana's most notable thoroughfare, what Anthony Trollope called "the public drive and fashionable lounge of the town—its Hyde Park, the Boise de Boulogne, the Cascine, the Corso, the Alameda." The mansions of aristocratic families rose on each side, with spacious portals for carriages, and it was a sign of distinction to live on Prado Promenade. The *paseo* (the daily carriage ride) along the Prado was one of the more important social rituals of the times, with five bands positioned at regular intervals to play to the colorful parade of *volantas*. In time, the Prado lost its luster as the rich moved into exclusive new neighborhoods. During the "sordid era," the Prado and the area immediately west of it—the infamous Colón borough of Centro Habana—became famous for sleazy shows and gambling houses such as La Central, where President Prío held "his infamous nights of white powder and tall showgirls."

French landscape artist Forestier remodeled the Prado to its present form in 1929. It is guarded by eight bronze lions. Its central median is an elevated walkway. An ornate wall borders the path, with alcoves inset into each side containing marble benches carved with scroll motifs. At night it is lit by old brass gas lamps with big globes atop dark green wrought-iron lampposts in the shape of griffins. Schoolchildren sit beneath the shade trees, listening attentively to history or literature lessons presented alfresco. Midway down the Prado, between Calle Colón and Refugio, the laurel trees provide a shady gathering place for those seeking apartments or homes for swap or rent.

Up and down the Prado you'll see tiled mosaics reflecting the Moorish style that has influenced Havana's architecture through the centuries, including the mosaic mural of a Nubian beauty on the upper wall of the **Centro Cultural de Árabe** (between Refugio and Trocadero), and the façade of the former Hotel Regis on the corner of Refugio, combining art nouveau and arabesque flourishes. The most stunning example, however, is the lobby of the **Hotel Sevilla,** Calle Trocadero #55, tel. 860-8560, which is like entering a

GRAHAM GREENE—OUR MAN IN HAVANA

No contemporary novel quite captures the tawdry intrigue and disreputable aura of Batista's Havana than does Graham Greene's *Our Man in Havana*, published in 1958, on the eve of the revolutionary triumph, and set amid the torrid events of Havana in 1957.

The comic tale tells of Wormold, an English vacuum-cleaner salesman based in Havana and short of money. His daughter has reached an expensive age, so when approached by Hawthorne, he accepts the offer of £300 a month and becomes Agent 59200/5, MI6's man in Havana. To keep his job, he files bogus reports based on Lamb's *Tales from Shakespeare* and dreams up military apparatuses from vacuum-cleaner parts. Unfortunately, his stories begin to come disturbingly true, and Wormold becomes trapped by his own deceit and the workings of a hopelessly corrupt city and society.

Graham Greene (1904–91) was already a respected author when he was recruited to work for the Foreign Office, serving the years 1941–43 in Sierra Leone, in Africa. In the last years of the war, he worked for the British Secret Service dealing with counterespionage on the Iberian Peninsula, where he learned how the Nazi Abwehr (the German Secret Service) sent home false reports—perfect material for his novel, in which he also poked fun at the British intelligence services. He traveled widely and based many of his works, including *Our Man in Havana*, on his experiences. He visited Havana several times in the 1950s and was disturbed by the mutilations and torture practiced by Batista's police officers and by social ills such as racial discrimination: "Every smart bar and restaurant was called a club so that a negro could be legally excluded." But he confessed to enjoying the "louche atmosphere" of Havana and seems to have savored the fleshpots completely. "I came there . . . for the brothel life, the roulette in every hotel. . . . I liked the idea that one could obtain anything at will, whether drugs, women or goats," he later wrote.

Castro condoned *Our Man in Havana* but complained that it didn't do justice to the ruthlessness of the Batista regime. Greene agreed: "Alas, the book did me little good with the new rulers in Havana. In poking fun at the British Secret Service, I had minimized the terror of Batista's rule. I had not wanted too black a background for a light-hearted comedy, but those who had suffered during the years of dictatorship could hardly be expected to appreciate that my real subject was the absurdity of the British agent and not the justice of a revolution." Nonetheless, Castro permitted the screen version, starring Alec Guinness as Wormold, to be filmed in Havana in 1959.

Greene returned to Cuba in the years 1963–66. Although initially impressed by Castro's war on illiteracy (he called it "a great crusade"), he later soured after witnessing the persecution of homosexuals, intellectuals, and Catholics. Perhaps for this reason, the author isn't commemorated in Cuba in any way.

Moroccan medina. It was inspired by the Patio of the Lions at the Alhambra in Granada, Spain. The hotel opened in 1908 with the novelty of telephones and private baths in every room. It became a place of repose and merriment for fashionable society. The gallery walls are festooned with black-and-white photos of famous figures who have stayed here, from singer Josephine Baker (who was refused at the Hotel Nacional because she was black) and boxer Joe Louis to Al Capone,

who took the entire sixth floor for himself and his bodyguards (Capone occupied Room 615). The top story restaurant is a magnificent exemplar of neoclassical decor . . . perfect for sampling a Mary Pickford (rum, pineapple juice, and grenadine), invented here.

The Sevilla was the setting for the comical intrigues of Wormold in Graham Greene's *Our Man in Havana*. Greene also had Wormold and Hasselbacher sup at the Wonder Bar, two blocks south at the corner of Paseo and Virtudes, where a remnant of the bar called **La Maravilla** (The Wonder) still stands.

Another resplendent building worth a browse is the **Casa de los Científicos,** Prado #212, esq. Trocadero, tel. 862-4511, the former home of President José Miguel Gómez, first president of the Republic, on the west side of the Prado, now a hostel run by the Ministry of the Environment and offering the benefit of superlative if albeit slightly chipped detail. It has fabulous stained-glass work, and an intriguing chapel where locals come to pray and make offerings. Climb to the rooftop observation tower for a bird's-eye view of the Prado.

Habana Vieja's **Palacio de Matrimonio,** Prado #306, esq. Ánimas, tel. 862-5781, is where a majority of wedding ceremonies are performed. The palace, which boasts a magnificent neo-baroque façade, was built in 1914 for the Association of Spanish Immigrants with an ornate stuccoed interior that at last visit was in a desperate state of disrepair. Open Tues.–Fri. 10 A.M.–5 P.M., and Sat.–Sun. 4–5:30 P.M.

Also note the **CineFausto,** a simple yet powerful rectangular modernist building with an ornamental band on its upper facade harking back to art deco. Immediately south, budding gymnasts train for potential Olympic careers in the **Academía de Gimnástico,** Prado #207, e/ Colón y Trocadero. Visitors are occasionally welcomed inside this converted old mansion to see preteens practicing on the ropes and vaulting horses, surrounded by fluted columns and a baroque stucco ceiling. It was featured in the movie, *Buena Vista Social Club,* with Ruben González at the piano. It's open Monday–Friday 8:30 A.M.–5:30 P.M. and Saturday 8A.M.–noon. At press time, the building was being renovated and will eventually house the **Escuela Nacional de Ballet** (National School of Ballet), tel. 862-7053.

The bronze **statue of Juan Clemente-Zenea** (1832–71), at the base of the Prado, honors a patriotic poet shot for treason in 1871.

PARQUE CENTRAL

For travelers and Cubans alike, spacious **Parque Central** is ground zero, the social epicenter of

Gran Teatro, Parque Central

© CHRISTOPHER P. BAKER

Habana Vieja. Buses arrive and depart from the busy square, a center for Havana's social life, as it was during the city's heyday beginning in the late 19th century. Its position is pivotal. From here, the Prado continues south past the Capitolio to Parque de la Fraternidad. Calle Obispo slopes one kilometer east to Plaza Armas and the heart of the old city.

The park—bounded by the Prado (Paseo de Martí), Neptuno, Agramonte, and San Martín—is paved in pink slabs and presided over by stately royal palms, poinciana, and almond trees shading a **statue of José Martí,** poet, lawyer, writer, revolutionary fighter, and Cuba's foremost national hero, killed in combat in 1895. It was erected on the 10th anniversary of his death. Sculpted by José Vilalta de Saavedra and inaugurated in 1905, this was the first such monument built in his honor in Cuba and was made of Carrara marble. Baseball fanatics gather near the Martí statue at a point called *esquina caliente*

THE ROYAL PALM

The indisputable symbol of Cuba is the ubiquitous *Rostonea regia,* the majestic royal palm (*palma royal* in Spanish), which grows singly or in great elegant clumps and graces the Cuban capital at every turn. Its smooth gray trunk, which can tower 25 meters, resembles a great marble column with a curious bulge near the top. Long leaves droop sinuously from the explosive top, blossoming afresh with each new moon.

Even found on the national emblem and protected by law, the royal palm is as useful as it is stately. Its fronds (*pencas*) make good thatch, and the thick green base—the *yagua*—of the *penca,* being waterproof, also makes an excellent roof or siding material. The trunk itself makes excellent timber. Bees favor palm honey; and pigs seem to like the seeds, which are used for pig feed. Humans devour the delicious, succulent palm-heart (*palmito*) from the center of the trunk. And birds love its black fruit and carry the seeds (*palmiche*) all over the country.

("hot corner") to discuss and argue the intricacies of *pelota* (baseball).

The park is surrounded by hotels of historic import. The ocher-colored **Hotel Plaza,** Calle Agramonte #267, tel. 860-8583, built as a triangle in 1909, sits on the northeast face of the square. Immediately west, the facade of the **Hotel Parque Central,** Calle Neptuno e/ Agramonte y Prado, commands the north side of the park, blending historic components into a controversial contemporary guise. And the old **Hotel Telégrafo,** reopened in 2002 after a complete restoration, graces the northwest side of the park.

Much of the action happens in front of the **Hotel Inglaterra,** Paseo de Martí #416, tel. 860-9595, which opened as a café on the west side of the square in 1843; the hotel opened in 1856 and is today the oldest Cuban hotel still extant. The Café Louvre, in front of the hotel, was known in colonial days as the Acera del Louvre and was a focal point for bohemian society and for rebellion against Spanish rule. A plaque outside the hotel entrance honors the "lads of the Louvre sidewalk" who died for Cuban independence. Today the café, beneath the shady *portico,* provides a splendid vantage point for watching the toing and froing—note the ceramic tiles in the tables, designed in 1998 by Cuba's leading poets and artists. Inside, the hotel boasts elaborate wrought-ironwork and exquisite *mudéjar* (Moorish)-style detailing, including arabesque archways and *azulejos* (patterned tile). A highlight is the sensuous life-size bronze statue of a Spanish dancer—*La Sevillana*—in the main bar.

Immediately south of the Inglaterra is the exquisitely detailed **Gran Teatro,** Paseo de Martí #452, e/ San Rafael y Neptuno, tel. 862-9473 or 861-3077, built in 1837 as the Teatro Tacón, and in its time considered by some to be the finest theater in the world. Operatic luminaries such as Enrico Caruso and Sarah Bernhardt performed here. The current neo-baroque structure dates from 1915, when a social club—the Centro Gallego—was built around the old Teatro Tacón for the Galician community. The theater was renamed Gran Teatro. Its exorbitantly baroque facade drips with caryatids, and it has four towers, each tipped by an angel of white marble reaching gracefully for heaven. The entire edifice is crumbling dangerously, however, and at last visit much of the upper-story detail was held in place only by netting. It still functions as a theater for the National Ballet and Opera. Patrons still settle into the plush velvet seats of the main auditorium—the exquisitely decorated 2,000-seat Teatro García Lorca, featuring a painted dome and huge chandelier. Smaller performances are hosted in the 500-seat Sala Alejo Carpentier and the 120-seat Sala Artaud. Entrance costs US$2 with a guided tour that permits you to watch classes of classical ballet and even flamenco. To learn something of Cuban ballet and theater culture, pop into the **Buró de Información Cultural,** tel. 863-6690, in the lobby to the left; open Mon.–Sat. 9:30 A.M.–5 P.M.

HABANA VIEJA

SPANISH COMMUNITY CENTERS

During the 19th century, various Spanish communities were formed to represent the interests of groups from specific provinces. These national groups built lavish palaces as social centers, and vied with each other to build the grandest structure in the architectural métier of the moment. This rivalry blessed Havana with the neo-baroque Centro Gallego (today's Gran Teatro) and neo-classical Centro Asturia (today's Museo de Bellas Artes), facing each other on Parque Central; and the Plateresque Spanish Casino, with a ballroom decorated with escutcheons representing all the Spanish provinces.

Another, less imposing, theater, the **Teatro Payret,** Prado, esq. San Martín, built in 1878, faces the square from the south. Today it functions as a much-deteriorated cinema. Next to it is the **Sala Polivalente Kid Chocolate,** Prado, e/ San Martín y Brasil, Habana Vieja, tel. 862-8634, a sports stadium where you can watch basketball, boxing, and the like.

Museo Nacional de Bellas Artes (International Section)

On the southeast side of the square, the building with a tower at each of its corners is the **Centro Asturiano,** erected in 1885 but rebuilt in Renaissance style in 1927 following a fire. Until recently it housed the postrevolutionary People's Supreme Court, where a questionable version of justice was dispensed. The beautiful building is lavishly decorated with neoclassical motifs. An architectural highlight is the stained-glass window above the main staircase showing Columbus's three caravels.

The international section of the National Fine Arts Museum, Calle San Rafael, e/ Zulueta y Monserrate, tel. 861-3858 or 862-0140, musna@cubarte.cult.cu, www.museonacional.cult.cu, moved here in 2001 and is displayed on five floors covering 4,800 square meters. The museum banks 47,268 individual pieces, many in storage. The collection is separated by nationality. On the bottom floor *(Planta Baja)* are

works from the United States and Latin America, as well as contemporary 20th-century paintings and sculptures. The third floor is divided between Spanish and Asian works. The fourth floor displays *arte antiguo,* a large stamp collection, and French works of art. And the fifth floor is divided into sections covering British, Dutch, German, and Italian artists. Many of the great masters—including Goya, Murillo, Rubens, and Velásquez, as well as various Impressionists—are represented, as are English greats such as Reynolds, Gainsborough, and Turner. The museum also boasts Latin America's richest trove of classical antiquities, including Roman, Greek, and Egyptian statuary and artworks (not least a sarcophagus), including a sizeable display of Grecian ceramics.

It features a cafeteria and gift store selling art books, prints, posters, and reproductions from the collection, and there's a 248-seat theater where cultural activities are hosted.

Open Tues.–Sat. 10 A.M.–6 P.M. and Sun. 9 A.M.–1 P.M.; entrance US$5. You can arrange for guided tours.

CALLE AGRAMONTE (ZULUETA)

Calle Agramonte, more commonly referred to by its colonial name of Zulueta, parallels the Prado and slopes gently upward from Avenida de los Estudiantes to the northeast side of Parque Central. Traffic runs one-way uphill.

On the north side of Avenida de los Estudiantes (Cárcel) is the **Monumento al General Máximo Gómez.** This massive monument of white marble supported by classical columns dominates the waterfront at the base of Agramonte. The monument, erected in 1935, honors the Dominican-born hero of the Cuban wars of independence who led the Liberation Army as commander-in-chief. Although a foreigner, Gómez dedicated himself to the cause of Cuban independence and displayed Napoleonic brilliance in his tactics. He survived the war and died in Havana on June 17, 1905. Generalissimo Gómez (1836–1905) is cast in bronze, with his bare head aloft, reining in his horse. Designed and made by sculptor Aldo Gamba, its base contains three reliefs depicting the *Patria,* the People, and Freedom.

The access road to the Havana harbor tunnel that leads to Parque Morro, as well as to Playas del Este, Matanzas, and Varadero, curls and nose-dives beneath the monument.

The ornate building at the base of Agramonte, on the west side of Cárcel, is the **Spanish Embassy.** Wealthy businessman Dionisio Velasco was the former owner of the mansion—one of the most flamboyant of Havana's structures in art nouveau style.

Plaza 13 de Mayo (named to commemorate the ill-fated attack of the Presidential Palace by student martyrs on March 13, 1957) was laid out by French landscaper Forestier. It expands as a green swathe on the south side of Avenida de los Estudiantes and slopes gently upwards toward the former Presidential Palace. Before the Revolution it was a major gathering site for political rallies. At its southern end, fronting the former Presidential Palace, on Refugio, is a **SAU-100 Stalin tank,** illuminated at night on its lofty pedestal. It was supposedly used by Fidel Castro himself at the Bay of Pigs,

according to the plaque—history books suggest the claim is an exaggeration.

Museo de la Revolución

The ornate building facing north over Plaza 13 de Mayo was initiated in 1913 to house the provincial government. Before it could be finished (in 1920), it was earmarked as the Palacio Presidencial (Presidential Palace), and Tiffany's of New York was entrusted with its interior decoration. It was designed by Belgian Paul Belau and Cuban Carlos Maruri in eclectic style, with a lofty dome. It was from here that a string of corrupt presidents, ending with Fulgencio Batista, spun their webs of dissolution.

Following the Revolution, the three-story palace was converted into the Museum of the Revolution, Calle Refugio #1 e/ Agramonte y Monserrate, tel. 862-4091; open Tues. 10 A.M.–6 P.M. and Wed.–Sun. 10 A.M.–5 P.M.; entrance US$4 (cameras US$5 extra). The marble staircase in the foyer leads upstairs to a massive lobby with a fabulous mural ceiling. Beyond lie vast salons, notably the Salón de los Espejos (the Mirror Room), a replica of that in Versailles (replete with

SAU-100 tank and Museo de la Revolución

CASTRO'S SHIPWRECK

Shortly after midnight on November 25, 1956, Castro and his revolutionaries set out from Tuxpán, Mexico, sailing without lights for Cuba. The 1,235-mile crossing was hellish. Their vessel, the *Granma,* had been designed to carry 25 passengers. Battered by heavy seas and with a burden of 82 heavily armed men and supplies, the vessel lurched laboriously toward Cuba, which Castro had planned to reach in five days. Batista's army and navy were on alert. Castro figured they would not patrol far from shore, hence he planned a route 170 miles offshore, beyond reach of Cuban surveillance.

In the violent seas, the men, packed in like sardines, became seasick. The boat rose and dropped beneath them. In the open, the drizzle began to turn into a cold, penetrating rain. Castro smelled victory, but to the men on the slippery decks the smell in the air was vomit. Then one engine failed and the boat slowed, falling two days behind schedule. Castro ordered rationing: for the last two days there was neither water nor food—which may have been just as well.

At dawn on December 2, the ship ran aground at low tide, two kilometers south of the planned landing site, at Playa Las Coloradas. Two hours later, just after dawn, Castro stood on *terra firma* alongside 81 men, with minimal equipment, no food, and no contact with the Movement ashore. "This wasn't a landing," Che Guevara later recalled. "It was a shipwreck."

The motley group set out toward the safety of the Sierra Maestra none too soon. Within two hours of landing, *Granma* had been sighted and a bombardment of the mangroves began. Batista's military commander foolishly announced to the press that the rebels had been ambushed and captured or killed, "annihilating 40 members of the supreme command of the revolutionary 26th of July Movement—among them its chief, Fidel Castro." The United Press bureau sent the news around the world. Meanwhile, the exhausted, half-starved rebels moved unseen and unscathed.

On December 5, however, the rebels were betrayed by their guide and ambushed by Batista's troops. Only 16 of the survivors eventually managed to meet up, including Fidel and Raúl Castro and Che Guevara.

Thinking that the danger was over, Batista canceled his search-and-destroy missions and withdrew his forces. On December 13, Castro's meager force finally made contact with a peasant member of the 26th of July Movement, and with that, word was out that Castro had survived. That day, 20 peasants joined the rebel army. Aided by an efficient communications network and intense loyalty from the Sierra peasants, the rebel unit was passed from homestead to homestead as they moved deeper into the mountains, and safety.

paintings by Armando Menocal and other notable Cuban painters), and the Salón Dorado (the Gold Room), decorated with yellow marble and gold leaf and highlighted by its magnificently decorated dome and canvases by Esteban Valderrama and Mariano Miguel González mounted on 18-carat gold sheets. The building contains many other fine works of art.

Rooms are divided chronologically, from the colonial period to the modern day. You follow the route room by room through the mazelike corridors. Detailed maps describe the battles and progress of the revolutionary war. Hundreds of

guns and rifles are displayed alongside grisly photos of dead and tortured heroes. The Moncada Room displays the bloodstained uniforms of the rebels who attacked the Moncada barracks in Santiago in 1953. Another section is dedicated to the revolutionaries who died in an assault on the palace on March 13, 1957 (Batista escaped through a secret door to a secure apartment reachable only by a private elevator, frustrating an action that turned into a bloody debacle). A room labeled "El Triunfo de la Revolución" bears the red flag of MR-26-7 and other revolutionary groups along with a photo of an ecstatic Castro.

Che Guevara is there in the form of a lifelike statue, sweating, rifle in hand, working his way heroically through the jungle. Don't miss Ronald Reagan satirized alongside other notable adversaries of the Cuban state in the museum's *Rincón de los cretinos* ("Corner of Cretins"). A hand-painted cutout of Batista bears a sign: "Thank you, cretin, for MAKING the Revolution." That of Ronald Reagan has a sign that reads: "Thank you, cretin, for STRENGTHENING the Revolution." Another of George Bush dressed like a Roman emperor reads: "Thank you, cretin, for CONSOLIDATING the Revolution."

The **Sala de la Gesta Boliviana del Che y Sus Compañeros,** to the right of the entrance, celebrates the ill-fated efforts of Che to inspire a revolution in Bolivia.

At the rear, in the former palace gardens, is the **Granma Memorial,** preserving the vessel that brought Castro, Guevara, and other revolutionaries from Mexico to Cuba in 1956. The *Granma,* a surprisingly muscular launch that embodies the powerful, unstoppable spirit of the revolutionary movement, is encased in an impressive glass structure—a simulated sea—with a roof held aloft by great concrete columns, rather like Lenin's tomb. It's surrounded by vehicles used in the revolutionary war: armored vehicles, the bullet-riddled "Fast Delivery" truck used in the student commandos' assault on the Presidential Palace in 1957, and Castro's green Land Rover with *Comandancia General Sierra Maestra* stenciled in red on the door. There's also a turbine from the U-2 spy plane downed during the missile crisis in 1962, plus a naval Sea Fury and a T-34 tank.

You can take photos of the exhibits from the street, but to get closer to the *Granma,* you must enter the museum through the main entrance.

Museo Nacional de Bellas Artes (Cuban Section)

Cuba's most important art museum, the National Fine Arts Museum, is housed in the concrete Palacio de Bellas Artes, Calle Trocadero, e/ Zulueta y Monserrate, tel. 863-9042 or 861-2332, musna@cubarte.cult.cu, www.museonacional.cult.cu. The museum first opened in 1913, although the contemporary soberly classical structure dates from 1954 and stands on the site of the former Colón market. Following the Revolution it gradually deteriorated, although pieces were constantly added. A three-year reorganization of the museum was completed in 2001 along with a refurbishment of the structure that has turned it from an ugly duckling into a well-lit swan of modern design. From the atrium garden, ramps lead up to two floors spanning 7,600 square meters and exhibiting more than 1,200 works that offer a complete spectrum of Cuban art.

The museum contains a fabulous collection of Cuban paintings, engravings, sketches, and sculptures dating back several centuries and laid out according to eight themes in 24 *salas* (galleries). Works representing the vision of early 16th- and 17th-century travelers merge into colonial-era pieces, early 20th-century Cuban interpretations of leading international movements, such as Impressionism and Surrealism, thence into the dramatic works spawned by the Revolution. Rotating exhibits display the works of Cuba's leading contemporary artists, such as Zaida del Río, Roberto Fabelo, and Alexis "Kcho" Leyva. The greats are also represented: from colonial era virtuosos such as Nicolas de la Escalera and Victor Patricio Landaluze, to Rene Portocarrero, Amelia Palaez, Wilfredo Lam and other modern masters.

Much of the artwork was seized from the private collections of Cubans forced to flee the island, hoping to be able to return soon thereafter. These include the possessions of the Bacardí family, and of Fulgencio Batista. The catalog credits the origin of several such works.

Open 10 A.M.–6 P.M. Tues.–Sat., and 9 A.M.–1 P.M. Sun.; entrance US$5. You can book a guide for guided tours by calling the telephone number above.

Also see Museo Nacional de Bellas Artes (International Section) in the Parque Central section earlier in this chapter.

Other Sights

One block north of Parque Central, at the corner of Agramonte and Animas, a mosaic on the paving (on the west side of the street) announces your arrival at **Sloppy Joe's,** "a high-ceilinged, bottle-encrusted, tile-floored oasis" commemorated as Freddy's Bar in Hemingway's *To Have and Have Not.* The bar, formerly La Victoria, became an institution among partying tourists during U.S. Prohibition after an inebriated journalist sought a US$50 loan, was rebuffed by the owner, and wrote a vengeful editorial accusing the owner of running an unsanitary place, claiming it should be called "Sloppy Joe's." There's no such thing as bad publicity, and the crafty owner changed the name. Dedicated drinkers flocked and continued to do so through the decades. At last visit, the near-derelict building remained shuttered, its interior a dusty shambles, awaiting the restoration now sweeping Habana Vieja. It is slated to be restored as a bar and (possibly) a hotel.

Across the way is the old Cuartel de Bomberos fire station, slated in due course to house the **Museo de Bomberos** (Museum of Firemen), Calle Agramonte #257, e/ Neptuno y Animas, tel. 862-7762. The museum will exhibit turn-of-the-century firefighters' uniforms plus vintage fire engines, including a 1901 horse-drawn machine made by Shand, Mason & Co., London.

Immediately west of the Museo de la Revolución is the three-story green facade of the **Fábrica de Tabaco La Corona,** Calle Agramonte #106, e/ Refugio y Colón, tel./fax 862-6173, dating from 1888, when this cigar factory was built by the American Tobacco Company. Today it is officially called the Miguel Fernández Roig, but colloquially as La Corona. A favorite on the tourist circuit, it provides a splendid background of the intricacies of cigar manufacture, as well as a heady experience thanks to the cigar aromas. Odalys Lara, a well-known Cuban TV presenter, acts as *lector* (reader). It's open to the public Monday–Saturday 7 A.M.–5 P.M.

AVENIDA DE LOS MISIONES (MONSERRATE)

Avenida de los Misiones, or Monserrate as everyone knows it, parallels Agramonte one block to the east (if driving, Monserrate is one-way downhill) and follows the space left by the ancient city walls after they were demolished last century. A semi-derelict watchtower—**Baluarte de Ángel**—erected in 1680 still stands in front of the Presidential Palace at Refugio and Monserrate as a lone reminder of the fortified wall that once surrounded Habana Vieja.

At the base of Monserrate, at its junction with Calle Tacón, is the **Museo y Archivo de la Música,** Calle Capdevila #1, tel. 861-9846 and 863-0052, housed in the sober Casa de Pérez de la Riva, which was built in Italian Renaissance style in 1905 and for a short time served as a jail. The museum traces the evolution of Cuban music since early colonial days; it displays many antique instruments, including a collection of venerable pianos and the huge collection of drums once owned by Fernando Ortiz, a renowned Africanist. In a separate room, you can listen to old scores drawn from the record library. The museum also hosts concerts. Open Mon.–Sat. 10 A.M.–5:45 P.M. Entrance costs US$2.

Immediately to the south, three governmental buildings face onto the Plaza 13 de Mayo: the **Comité Nacional de UJC** (the Union of Communist Youth), the **Asemblea Provincial de Poder Popular** (Havana's local assembly), and the **Organización de Pioneros José Martí** (the Communist youth pioneers, Cuba's equivalent of Boy Scouts with a political twist).

Immediately east of the Presidential Palace is the **Iglesia del Santo Ángel Custodio,** sitting atop a rock known as Angel Hill. There's a virginal purity to this shimmering white church with its splendid exterior. Actually, the lavishly gothic facade is on Compostela, to the rear of the church, which was founded in 1687 by builder-bishop Diego de Compostela. The tower dates from 1846, when a hurricane toppled the original, while the facade was reworked in neo-gothic style in the mid-19th century. It's immaculate yet simple within: gray marble floor, modest wooden gothic altar, statues of saints all around, pristine stained-glass windows. Cuba's national hero, José Martí, was baptized here on February 12, 1853. The church has appeared in several movies and was the setting for both the opening scene and the tragic marriage scene that ends in the violent denouement on the steps of the church in the 19th-century novel *Cecilia Valdés*, by Cirilo Villaverde. A bust of the author stands in the *plazuela* outside the main church entrance on the corner of Calles Compostela and Cuarteles.

From the main entrance, continue along Cuarteles one block to a junction known as **Las Cinco Cuarteles de El Ángel** (Five Corners of the Angel). Here you can admire an agglomeration of ancient houses, some with beams of round trunks that attest to their age.

Monserrate continues south three blocks to **Plazuela de Supervielle,** commemorating Dr. Manuel Fernández Supervielle, mayor of Havana during the 1940s. His principal election promise—to resolve the city's ongoing water supply problem—went unfulfilled (the allocated money ended up in private pockets), causing him to commit suicide. One block north, at the corner of Empedrado, is the headquarters of the Museo Nacional de Bellas Artes, in the restored 18th-century **Edificio Antonio Rodgríguez Morey,** a former barracks for Havana's militia.

The plazuela is shadowed on its north side by the **Edificio Bacardí,** Monserrate #261, esq. Neptuno, a uniquely inspired building that was formerly the headquarters of the Bacardí rum empire. Designed by Cuban architect Esteban Rodríguez and finished in December 1929, this magnificent art deco edifice is clad in Swedish granite and local limestone and is to Havana what the Empire States Building is to New York. Terra-cotta of varying hues accents the design, with motifs showing Grecian nymphs and floral patterns. It is crowned by a Lego-like pyramidal bell tower topped in turn by a wrought-iron, brass-winged gargoyle . . . the famous Bacardí motif. The building is difficult to appreciate at street level; to better admire it, nip inside the Hotel Parque Central or Hotel Plaza, where it is best seen from the *azotea* (rooftop). The lobby is festooned with photographs of famous personages, including members of the Bacardí family. To the right, up the stairs, is a bar with black wood paneling with gold diamond relieves, mirrors highlighted by the square art deco ceiling lights, and wall lights etched with the famous Bacardí bat. The floor is a true gem of art deco

tilework. (At last visit water leakage had caused severe damage and the bar was closed for repair). For a tip the staff may take you up to the rooftop *mirador* for a bird's-eye view of Havana.

One block south brings you to **Plazuela de Albear,** a tiny plaza with a bust of Francisco de Albear, who last century engineered the Malecón and Havana's first water drainage system (still in use). Here, too, is . . .

El Floridita

This famous restaurant and bar, tel. 867-1300, at the corner of Monserrate and Calle Obispo, has been serving food at this location since 1819, when it was called Pina de Plata. Its name was later changed to La Florida, and then, more affectionately, El Floridita. It is haunted by Ernest Hemingway's ghost. The novelist's seat at the dark mahogany bar is preserved as a shrine (a chain prevents anyone from sitting on it). His bronze bust watches over things from its pedestal beside the bar, where Constante Ribailagua once served frozen daiquirís to the great writer—Hemingway immortalized both the drink and the venue in his novel *Islands in the Stream*—and such illustrious guests as Gary Cooper, Tennessee Williams, Marlene Dietrich, and Jean-Paul Sartre. Back then, Floridita had eleven broad doors open to the street, but in 1948 they were closed in so that air-conditioning could be installed—Hemingway briefly forsook the bar in disgust.

El Floridita was recently spruced up for tourist consumption with a 1930s art-deco polish. Waiters hover in tux jackets and bow ties. You expect a spotlight to come on and Desi Arnaz to appear conducting a dance band, and Papa to stroll in as he would every morning when he lived in Havana and drank with Honest Lil, the Worst Politician, and other real-life characters from his novels. "When we went to the Floridita bar in those days it wasn't like Orson Welles entering the lobby of the Grand Hotel, as Hotchner described Papa's public excursions in later years," recalls Hemingway's son, Gregory. "It was just a nice bar where my father knew the staff and could drink with us and his friends." They've overpriced the place for the package tourist crowd.

But, what the hell—sipping a daiquirí at El Floridita is a must.

Rum authority Francisco Campoamor's book, *The Happy Child of Sugar Cane,* tells the tale of El Floridita.

A separate entrance on Calle Obispo leads upstairs to the **Casa del Ron y Tabaco,** where free rum samples are given.

PARQUE DE LA FRATERNIDAD AND VICINITY

Paseo de Martí (Prado) runs south from Parque Central three blocks, where it ends at the junction with Avenida Máximo Gómez (Monte), on the south side of **Parque de la Fraternidad,** Havana's largest, most bustling, tree-shaded square. The streets around the park are a major start and drop-off point for urban buses and peso taxis, which congregate in vast numbers, forming a veritable auto museum of vintage Americana.

Parque de la Fraternidad was laid out in 1892

Fuente de la India Noble Habana

© CHRISTOPHER P. BAKER

on an old military drill square, the Campo de Marte, to commemorate the fourth centennial of Columbus's discovery of America. In olden times, a bull ring also stood here, and the plaza was a setting for the city's festivities. By the mid-1850s, it was the site of the city's railway station, terminating the railway that ran along today's Zanja and Dragones. The current layout by Forestier dates from 1928, with a redesign to celebrate the sixth Pan-American Conference, held in Havana that year.

The most important site in the park is the **Árbol de la Fraternidad Americana** (the Friendship Tree), planted at its center on February 24, 1928 to cement goodwill between the nations of the Americas. Each delegate to the conference brought soil from his or her home country. Busts of oustanding American leaders such as Simón Bolívar as well as a **statue of Abraham Lincoln** look out over the comings and goings.

Another monument of interest is the **Fuente de la India Noble Habana,** in the middle of the Prado, 100 meters south of Parque Central. The fountain, erected in 1837, is surmounted by a Carrara marble statue of *La Noble Havana,* the legendary Indian queen after whom the province is named. She is coyly clad in fringed drapes, a feather headdress, and palm leaves. In one hand she bears a cornucopia, in the other a shield with the arms of Havana. Four great fishes lie at her feet and spout water when the tap is turned on.

The **Teatro Martí,** Calle Dragones, esq. Agramonte, one block east of Parque de la Fraternidad, began life in 1884 as the Teatro Irijoa and it was here in 1901 that the Constitution for the Republic was signed. It fell into virtual ruin following the Revolution but at press time a full restoration was nearing completion. (The fortresslike building immediately east is a police station.) Around the corner, the **Sociedad de la Cruz Roja,** Agramonte, e/ Muralla y Brasil, is housed in an exquisite classical building looking like a piece of ancient Greece transplanted, with thick Corinthian columns holding aloft a bas-relief pediment.

The former **Hotel Saratoga,** Prado, esq. Dragones, was also nearing restoration as a deluxe hotel at last visit.

To its south, and opened in 2001, is the **Museo de los Orishas,** Prado #615, e/ Dragones y Monte (Máximo Gómez), tel. 863-5953, dedicated to telling the tale of *santería* and, specifically, of the various *orishas* (gods) of this Afro-Cuban religion. This small upstairs museum (in the Asociación Cultural Yoruba de Cuba) features 31 life-size clay statues of the most important *orishas* by Cuban artist Lázaro Valdés. Each has a backdrop displaying the specific attributes associated with that *orisha*. Open daily 9 A.M.–5 P.M. Entrance costs an overpriced US$10; children under 12 free.

Worth checking out, too, is the **Palacio de Aldama,** Calle Amistad #510, e/ Reina y Estrella, on the park's far southwest corner, is a grandiose mansion considered one of Havana's finest. It was built in neoclassical style in 1844 for a wealthy Basque, Don Domingo Aldama y Arrechaga, with a facade decorated with a wide Doric portico lined by Ionic columns and a wrought-iron balcony; and an interior of colored marbles and murals of scenes from Pompeii. Unfortunately, when the owner's nationalist feelings became known it was ransacked and the interior defaced in 1868 by the archly promonarchist Spanish Volunteers militia. Today, duly restored, it houses the **Instituto de la Historia del Movimiento Comunista y de la Revolución Socialista de Cuba** (Institute of the History of the Communist Movement and the Socialist Revolution), tel. 862-2076. Hardcore lefties might get a thrill. The garden courtyard features ornamental fountains. Open Mon.–Fri. 8 A.M.–4:30 P.M.

Capitolio Nacional

This fabulous building, Paseo de Martí e/ San Martín y Dragones, tel. 860-3411, on the north side of Parque de la Fraternidad and one block south of Parque Central, dominates Havana's skyline. It was built between 1926 and 1929 as Cuba's Chamber of Representatives and Senate and was obsequiously designed after Washington's own Congress building, reflecting the United States' expanding influence in the early 1900s (it cost US$20 million, much of which disappeared in graft). The 692-foot-long edifice is supported by flanking colonnades of Doric columns, with semicircular pavilions at each end of the building. The lofty stone cupola rises 61.75 meters, topped by a replica of 16th-century Florentine sculptor Giambologna's famous bronze Mercury in the Palazzo de Bargello. The dome—inspired by the Parisian Pantheon—sits not in the center of the structure, but forward near the front portico. The pristine, recently restored building is constructed of local Capellania limestone, hinting at the overwhelming opulence and beauty within.

A massive stairway—flanked by neoclassical figures in bronze by Italian sculptor Angelo Zanelli and representing Labor and Virtue—leads steeply up to a 40-meter-wide entrance portico with three tall bronze doors. The doors are sculpted with 30 bas-reliefs that depict important events of Cuban history up to the Capitolio's inauguration in 1929. You can have your

HABANA VIEJA

© CHRISTOPHER P. BAKER

Capitolio Nacional

HAVANA'S VINTAGE AMERICAN CARS

Magnificent finned automobiles cruise grandly down the street like parade floats.
I feel like we're back in time, in a kind of Cuban version of an earlier America.

Cristina García, Dreaming in Cuba

Fifties nostalgia is alive and well on the streets of Havana. Stylish Chevrolets, Packards, and Cadillacs weave among the sober Russian-made Ladas and Moskovitches, their large engines guzzling precious gas at an astonishing rate. Automotive sentimentality is reason enough to visit Havana—the greatest living car museum in the world.

American cars flooded Havana for 50 years. During Batista's days, Cuba probably imported more Cadillacs, Buicks, and DeSotos than any other nation in the world. Then came the

© CHRISTOPHER P. BAKER

photo taken at the base of the stairs by any of several official photographers whose antique cameras sit atop wooden tripods.

Inside, facing the door is the **Estatua de la República** (Statue of the Republic), a massive bronze sculpture (also by Zanelli) of Cuba's Indian maiden resembling the Statue of Liberty and representing the Cuban Republic. At 17.54 meters (56 feet) tall, she is the world's third-largest indoor statue (the other two are the gold Buddha in Nava, Japan; and the Lincoln Memorial, Washington, D.C.). Weighing 49 tons, her

voluptuous figure gleams sensuously after a recent cleaning. In the center of the floor is a 24-carat diamond that marks kilometer 0—the point from which all distances on the island are calculated. The diamond, alas, is a replica (rumor has it that the original is kept securely in Fidel's office). Above your head is the dome with its gilt-covered, barrel-vaulted ceiling carved in refulgent relief.

The stunning, 394-feet-long **Salón de los Pasos Perdidos** (Great Hall of the Lost Steps), so named because of its acoustics (the sound of

HABANA VIEJA

Cuban Revolution and the U.S. trade embargo. In terms of American automobiles, time stopped when Castro took power.

Still, relics from Detroit's heyday are everywhere, ubiquitous reminders of that period in the 1950s when American cars—high-finned, big-boned, with the come-hither allure of Marilyn Monroe—seemed tailor-made for the streets of prerevolutionary Havana.

Imagine. A '57 Packard gleams in the lyrical Cuban sunlight. Nearby, perhaps, sits a 1950 Chevy Deluxe, a '57 Chevrolet Bel Air hardtop, and an Oldsmobile Golden Rocket from the same year, inviting foreigners to admire the dashboard or run their fingers along a tail fin. More numerous are staid Chrysler New Yorker sedans, Ford Customlines, and Buick Centuries.

Lacking proper tools and replacement parts, Cubans constantly are adeptly cajoling one more kilometer out of their battered hulks. Their intestinally reconstituted engines are monuments to ingenuity and geopolitics—decades of improvised repairs have melded parts from Detroit and Moscow alike. (Russian Gaz jeeps are favorite targets for cannibalization, since their engines were cloned from a Detroit engine.)

One occasionally spots a shining example of museum quality. The majority, though, have long ago been touched up with house paint and decorated with flashy mirrors and metallic stars, as if to celebrate a religious holiday. Some are adorned with multicolored flags to invoke the protection of Elegguá or another *santería* god.

The mechanical dinosaurs are called *cacharros*. Normally, the word means a broken-down jalopy, but in the case of old Yankee classics, the word is "whispered softly, tenderly, like the name of a lost first love," says Cristina García.

Classic Car Meets: Havana boasts several classic car clubs. The **Club de Automóvil de la Habana** meets the second Saturday each month at La Ghiraldilla, Avenida 222 y Calle 35, La Coronela. The **Club de Autos Clásicos** meets each third Saturday of the month in Plaza de Armas. The annual **Exhibición de Coches Clásicos** (Classic Car Show), tel. 861-5868, fax 66-9281, tamara@cultural.ohch.cu, is held each March.

Resources: Christopher P. Baker's *Island Classics: Cars of Cuba* is a lavishly illustrated coffee-table book, available wherever books are sold.

Classic American Cars of Cuba is a 42-minute video (see Suggested Viewing in the Resources).

Tours: Colorado-based **Last Frontier Expeditions,** 4823 White Rock Circle, Suite H, Boulder, CO 80301-3260, 303/530-9275, Bob@cubatravelexperts.com, www.cubatravelexperts.com, offers a classic car tour that includes a classic car rally.

your footfalls seems to retreat behind you), is made almost entirely of marble, inlaid with patterned marble motifs, with bronze bas-reliefs and green marble pilasters all around and massive lamps on tall carved pedestals of glittering copper. Renaissance-style candelabras dangle overhead from the arched ceiling decorated with glorious frescoes. Two long lateral galleries that make up the Great Hall lead from this entrance vestibule. The semicircular Senate chamber and the former Chamber of Representatives at each end are quite stunning. Former congressional offices line

the hallway and offer their own jaw-dropping decor, and there's a mahogany paneled former congressional library.

French landscaper Forestier realized that the Capitolio sits almost apologetically sideways on to the Gran Teatro. He planned to level Calle Brasil to create an imposing boulevard leading to the Capitolio from the harbor, but the Revolution forestalled the plans.

The Capitolio is open daily 9 A.M.–7 P.M. Entrance is US$3. Guided tours are offered (US$1). A breeze-swept veranda café serves sandwiches and refreshments and offers grand views down over the Prado.

In 1960, the Capitolio became the headquarters of the **Academía de Ciencias** (Academy of Sciences). The library—the **Biblioteca Nacional de Ciencias Naturales**—is on the ground floor on the Capitolio's south side (open Mon.–Sat. 8 A.M.–5 P.M.).

Fábrica de Tabaco Partagás

A highlight of any visit to Havana is a visit to the Partagás Cigar Factory (officially named Fábrica Francisco Pérez Germán), Calle Industria #502, e/ Dragones y Barcelona, tel. 862-0086 or 878-4368, behind the Capitolio and one block east of the Dragon Gate. The exterior of this four-story structure is built in a classical Spanish style with cream walls and chocolate brown pilasters and other detailing, capped by a *remate superior,* a roofline of baroque curves topped by lions and bearing in large block letters the words "1845 PARTAGÁS REAL FÁBRICA DE TABACOS," proudly testifying that it has been making cigars here for more than 150 years. The three-story structure was built in 1845 to house the Vilar y Vilar Cigar Factory, one of the main cigar factories of the 19th century, when the Partagás cigar firm first occupied the site. An interior patio is surrounded by colored glass windows.

Here you may see Cuba's premium cigars being hand-rolled for export; the best rollers sit at the front of the workshop, where they make the largest brands while a *lector* reads from the daily newspaper and from novels as has been done since 1866, although today the reading is broadcast by loudspeaker throughout the factory. The factory specializes in full-bodied cigars such as the spicy, strongly aromatic La Gloria Cubana, Ramón Allones, the Montecristo, and, of course, the Partagás, one of the oldest of the Havana brands, started in 1843 by Catalan immigrant Don Jaime Partagás Ravelo. Partagás was murdered in 1868—some say by a rival who discovered that Partagás was "smoking" his wife—and his ghost is said to haunt the factory. Partagás turns out five million cigars a year, among them no fewer than 40 types of Partagás brand (many machine-made and of inferior quality). The factory's showroom displays a cigar measuring 50 inches.

The humidor to the right of the entrance has a "secret" air-conditioned lounge, replete with plump leather lounge chairs, TV, coffee bar, and its own humidor.

Guided tours are offered daily at 10 A.M. and 2 P.M. (US$10). It offers a "Big Habanos Smoke" every Friday at 7 P.M. (US$20 including buffet, cocktails, and music).

The Historic Core

AVENIDA CARLOS M. DE CÉSPEDES AND THE HARBOR CHANNEL

Throughout most of the colonial era, sea waves washed up on a beach that lined the southern shore of the harbor channel, known as the Playa de las Tortugas for the marine turtles that came ashore to lay eggs. The beach bordered what is today Calle Cuba and, eastward, Calle Tacón, which runs along the site of the old city walls forming the original waterfront. In the early 19th century, the area was extended with landfill, and a broad boulevard—**Avenida Carlos Manuel de Céspedes** (Avenida del Puerto)—was laid out

along the new harbor front, with a wide, shady park separating it from Calle Tacón.

The park is divided in two: to the west is **Parque Anfiteatro**, with an open-air theater in Greek fashion and a *parque de diversiones* (children's fairground); to the east is **Parque Luz Caballero**, pinned by a statue of José de la Luz Caballero, "teacher of Cuban youth, 1800–62." Caballero was a philosopher sympathetic to the cause of independence; José Martí called him the "father of *cubanía.*"

Overlooking the harbor front at the foot of Empedrado is the **Fuente de Neptuno** (Neptune Fountain), erected in 1838. This is the embarkation point for 45-minute harbor cruises (popular with Cubans, who pay five pesos) aboard the *Havana Princess* (see Discotheques & Dancing, in the Entertainment and Recreation chapter).

Calle Cuba

Calle Cuba extends east from the Monumento de Máximo Gómez and the foot of Monserrate. At the foot of Calle Cuarteles, is the **Palacio de Mateo Pedroso y Florencia,** Calle Cuba #64, a magnificent mansion built in Moorish style for nobleman Don Mateo Pedroso (a slave trader and former mayor) around 1780. Pedroso's home—a profusion of patterned tiles and foliate door arches—was a center for Havana's social life well into the 19th century. It well displays the typical architectural layout of period houses, with stores on the ground floor, slave quarters on the mezzanine, and the owner's dwellings above. Today, duly restored, it houses the **Palacio de Artesanía,** tel. 33-8072, with craft shops, boutiques, and a bar where you can soak up live music and soothing rum while enjoying a pronounced whiff of the *Arabian Nights.* Folkloric and other entertainment is offered at night and on weekends.

Cuba turns inland two blocks east at **Plazuela de la Maestranza,** where a remnant of the old city wall is preserved. It features a **watchtower,** or *baluarte.* Waves once beat against this sentry box, now landlocked since construction of the Avenida del Puerto. During the British attack on Havana in 1762, this section of wall bore the brunt of the assault on the city, fired on from the heights of El Morro and La Cabaña after the English had taken those fortresses.

Calle Tacón

Immediately east of Cuba, in the triangle formed by the junction of Cuba, Tacón, and Chacón, is a little medieval-style fortress. **El Castillo de Atane** that today houses a police headquarters, as it has since it was built in 1941 for the former Havana Police Department. It's only a pseudo-colonial confection.

The jewel in the crown is the **Seminario de San Carlos y San Ambrosio,** e/ Chacón y Empedrado, a massive seminary running the length of Tacón east of El Castillo de Atane. It was established by the Jesuits in 1721 and ever since has been a center for young men studying for an ecclesiastical career—José de la Luz Caballero and Félix Varela, two renowned Cuban intellectuals, both graduated here. The seminary was built in an irregular polygon shape during the second half of the 18th century, featuring a three-story gallery and a massive mahogany banister with elaborate carvings. Its dramatic baroque facade amazingly dates from the 1950s, when it was remodeled in neo-baroque style like the Havana cathedral. Alas, the seminary is normally closed to public viewing. That said, by ringing the doorbell (to the right of the main entrance), visitors are often welcomed to peruse the courtyard. And each first Sunday of October, the doors swing open and the public is admitted for the one day a year.

A large artisans' market takes up the length of Tacón directly in front of the seminary, where an excavated site shows the foundations of the original seafront section of the city walls—here called the **Cortina de Valdés.**

Tacón ends at a tiny *plazuela* at the foot of Empedrado, where a bevy of colorful old fishing boats that could have fallen from a painting by Hockney sit on the cobbled curbside. Horse-drawn open-air cabs called *calezas* gather here, offering guided tours to tourists.

Between Empredado and Plaza de Armas

South of the junction with Empedrado, a narrow extension of Tacón leads to Plaza de Armas, with three houses collectively called "Los Tacones."

The restored mansion (dating from 1759) on the corner—**Casa de Martín Aróstegui**—houses **Bar y Restaurante D'Giovanni,** Calle Tacón #4. Its fabulous inner courtyard is graced by three tiers of balustraded balconies. Note the stunning wall mural in the entranceway painted by anonymous Italian artists.

Casa de Juana Carvajal, Calle Tacón #12, e/ O'Reilly y Empedrado, next door, is also worth a visit. The beautiful mansion (first mentioned in documents in 1644) was inherited in 1700 by a mulatta (Juana) whose owner, Doña Lorenza de Carvajal, had granted her freedom

HABANA VIEJA

HABANA VIEJA: THE CORE

BAHÍA DE LA HABANA

AVENIDA CARLOS M. DE CÉSPEDES (AVENIDA DEL PUERTO)

CLUB LOS MARINOS

MONUMENT TO CUBAN SEAMEN

APARTOTEL SAN PEDRO

HOTEL SANTA ISABEL

BAR EL GLOBO

CASA DEL CAFÉ

TABERNA DEL GALEÓN

CASA DE LA COMEDIA

MUSEO DE ESCLAVOS

BODEGÓN ONDA

HOSTAL EL COMENDADOR

HOSTAL VALENCIA

EL TEMPLETE

ENNA

BIBLIOTECA PROVINCIAL DE LA HABANA

CASERÓN DE TANGO

JUSTIZ

EL MIRADOR DEL BAHÍA

MUSEO NACIONAL DE HISTORIA NATURAL

MUSEO NUMISMÁTICO

OFICIOS

CASTILLO DE LA REAL FUERZA/MUSEO DE CERÁMICA

Plaza de Armas

MONUMENTO CARLOS M. DE CÉSPEDES

OBISPO

CAFÉ LA MINA/ RESTAURANTE CUBANO

RESTAURANTE AL MEDINA

CASA DEL ÁRABE

CAFÉ TORRELAVEGA

OBRAPÍA

CASA DE OSWALDO

LA GIRALDILLA

PALACIO DEL SEGUNDO CABO/INSTITUTO CUBANO DEL LIBRO

O'REILLY

MONUMENTO M. DE CÉSPEDES

CASA DEL AGUA LA TINAJA

BARBERÍA DE PLAZA DE ARMAS

MUSEO DE PLATA

CASA DE BENITO JUÁREZ

HABANA 1791

CASA DE LOS ABANICOS

CASA DE LA MINIATURA

CAFÉ/RESTAURANTE DON GIOVANNI

GABINETE DE LA ARQUEOLOGÍA

COLECCIÓN HABANA

TACÓN

LA PAPELERÍA

HABANOS S.A. (HQ)

BAÑOS S.A. (HQ)

PALACIO DE LOS CAPITANES GENERALES

AMBROSERÍA

MUSEO DE ASIA

TIENDA DE LAS NAVEGANTES

TORRE DE MARFIL

CASA DE ÁFRICA

CASA DE LA OBRA PÍA

HORSE-DRAWN COACHES

TRANSAUTO

DOMINICA

MERCADERES

MUSEO DE LA CIUDAD DE LA HABANA

UNIVERSITY OF HAVANA BELL

HOTEL AMBOS MUNDOS

MAQUETA DEL CENTRO HISTÓRICO

MUSEUM OF TOBACCO/ CASA DEL TABACO

MUSEO Y FARMACIA TAQUECHEL

TELEPHONE

TAXIS

CRAFTS MARKET

Parque Luz Caballero

TACÓN

EMPEDRADO

CASA DE LOMBILLO

POST OFFICE

CASA DEL MARQUÉS DE ARCOS

CASA DEL CONDE DE BAYONA/MUSEO DE ARTE COLONIAL

PALADAR LA LUZ

MUSEO DE AUTOMÓVILES

RESTAURANTE LA LUZ

PANADERÍA SAN JOSÉ

INFOTUR

CORTINA DE VALDÉS

CATEDRAL DE LA HABANA

Plaza de la Catedral

CENTRO WILFREDO LAM

EL BODEGUITA DEL MEDIO

CALLEJÓN DEL CHORRO

CASA DE LOS MARQUESES DE AGUAS CLARAS/RESTAURANTE EL PATIO

CASA DE BAÑOS/GALERÍA VÍCTOR MANUEL

TALLER EXPERIMENTAL DE LA GRÁFICA

PALADAR DOÑA EUTEMIA

CASA DE DULCE MARÍA

SAN IGNACIO

PALADAR LA MONEDA CUBANA

CAFÉ PARIS

CAFÉ O'REILLY

O'REILLY

OBISPO

MUSEO DE FINANZAS/ BANCO NACIONAL DE CUBA

CUBA

HOTEL FLORIDA

CREMERÍA EL NARANJAL

SEMINARIO DE SAN CARLOS Y SAN AMBROSIO

FUNDACIÓN ALEJO CARPENTIER

SAN IGNACIO

HABANA VIEJA

TERMINAL
SIERRA MAESTRA
(CRUISE TERMINAL)

CUSTOMS

DOS
HERMANOS ★

MUSEO DE RON ★

SAN PEDRO

Garden

Parque
Humboldt

de Gales

CARPINETTI

Plaza de
San Francisco

FUENTE DE LOS
LEONES ★

IGLESIA Y CONVENTO
DE SAN FRANCISCO
DE ASIS/
MUSEO DE ARTE
RELIGIOSO ★

COCHE
PRESIDENCIAL
MAMBÍ

LA LONJA
DEL COMERCIO ■

EL MERCURIO ■

BARAT

CADECA

POST
OFFICE ■

AGENCI SAN
CRISTÓBAL/HABAGUANEX ■

BANCO FINANCIERO
INTERNACIONAL ■

OFICIOS

ANTIGUA
CÁMARA DE
REPRESENTANTES ■

CASA
ALEJANDRO
VON HUMBOLDT ●

CAFÉ
DEL ORIENTE ▼

STATUE OF
CABALLERO DE PARÍS ★

CASA
CARMEN MONTILLA ★

ESTUDIO GALERÍA
LOS OFICIOS ★

CAFÉ LA
MARINA ▼

SOL

UNITED COLORS
OF BENETTON ■

HOSTAL LOS
FRAILES ▼

AQUARIUM ■

MURALLA

CASA DE LA
POESÍA ★

PALACIO
VIENNA HOTEL ★

Bolívar

CASA DE LIBERTADOR
SIMÓN BOLÍVAR ★

ARMERÍA 9
DE ABRIL ■

Parque
Ruminahui

HOSTAL CONDE
DE VILLANUEVA ■

CAFÉ HABANA ▼

MESÓN DE
LA FLOTA ■

PUBLIC
TOILETS ■

MERCADERES

TABERNA
BENY MORÉ ★

CÁMARA
OSCURA ★

FOTOTECA/
SALÓN NACIONAL
DE FOTOGRAFÍA ■

MUSEO DE
NAIPES ■

INQUISIDOR

HOSTAL RAQUEL ●

SAN IGNACIO

APARTOTEL/
RESTAURANTE SANTO
ÁNGEL ■

Plaza
Vieja

FOUNTAIN

FONDO CUBANO
DE BIENES CULTURALES/
CASA DE LOS CONDES
DE JARUCO ★

MURALLA

LAMPARILLA

AMARGURA

Plazuela de
San Francisco
el Nuevo

CASA DE LAS
HERMANAS CÁRDENAS/
CENTRO DE DESARROLLO
DE ARTES VISUALES ★

CASA DEL CONDE DE
SAN ESTÉBAN DE
CAÑONGO ■

CASA DEL CONDE
DE CASA LOMBILLO ★

OBRAPRIA

CUBA

MUSEO DE CIENCIAS
CARLOS FINLAY/ANTIGUA ACADEMIA DE
CIENCIAS MÉDICAS,
FÍSICAS, Y NATURALES ★

IGLESIA Y CONVENTO
DE SAN AGUSTÍN ★

CASA DE CULTURA
MUNICIPAL ★

BRASIL (TENIENTE REY)

AGUILAR

BRASIL (TENIENTE REY)

0   50 yds

0   50 m

© AVALON TRAVEL PUBLISHING, INC.

RECOMMENDED WALKING TOUR 2

At Parque Central, begin at the **Hotel Plaza,** then head east on Neptuno one block to the **Plazuela de Supervielle** and after admiring the **Edificio Bacardí,** follow Monserrate north, downhill, to the **Iglesia Santo Ángel Custodio.**

Head east on Cuarteles two blocks to **Cinco Caminos,** then north along Habana to the **Museo de Música.** Follow Calle Tacón east past remains of the *murallas* (old city walls) to the **Palacio Pedroso** (Palacio de la Artesanía) and pop in to enjoy whatever music may be being hosted. Continue east past the **Seminario de San Carlos** to the end of Tacón and turn right into **Plaza de la Catedral.**

Browse the Plaza, including the **Catedral** and the **Casa del Conde de Bayona,** being sure to stop in for a *mojito* at **La Bodeguita del Medio,** half a block west on Empedrado.

Exit the plaza along San Ignacio and turn left onto O'Reilly. Two blocks brings you to **Plaza de Armas.** A clockwise tour takes in the **Palacio del Segundo Cabo,** the **Castillo de la Real Fuerza, El Templete,** the **Hotel Santa Isabel,** the **Casa de Ron,** the **Museo de Ciencias Naturales,** and the **Museo de la Ciudad** in the **Palacio de Capitanes Generales.**

Return to Parque Central along **Calle Obispo,** calling in at the **Hotel Ambos Mundos** to see Hemingway's room (#501), and **Farmacia Taquechel.**

household items from the early colonial years. It's open Tuesday–Saturday 9 A.M.–5 P.M., Sunday 9 A.M.–1 P.M. Entrance costs US$1.

PLAZA DE LA CATEDRAL

You'll find yourself returning again and again to this exquisite cobbled square dominated by the intimate but imposing and decadently baroque 18th-century "Columbus Cathedral"—and, on the other three sides, by aristocratic mansions.

This was the last square to be laid out in Habana Vieja, for it occupied a lowly quarter where rainwater drained and refuse collected and rotted, infecting the city (it was originally known as the Plazuela de la Ciénaga—Little Square of the Swamp). A cistern was built here in 1587, and only in the following century was the area drained for construction. Its present texture dates from the 18th century, before which it served as a fish market and cattle watering station.

The square is Habana Vieja at its most quintessential, the atmosphere enhanced by mulattas in traditional costume who will happily preen and pose for your camera (for a small fee). Be sure to visit by night also, when the setting is enhanced by the soft glow of wan lanterns and the plaza is moody and dreamy. Every Saturday night, the plaza is the venue for **Noches en la Plaza de la Catedral,** when tables are laid out in the square, dinner is served, and you get to witness a folkloric *espectáculo* with a stunning backdrop.

Catedral de la Habana

This splendid edifice, on the north side of the plaza, is the maximum exemplar of Cuban baroque. Known colloquially as Catedral Colón and Catedral de San Cristóbal, it is officially called the Catedral de la Virgen María de la Concepción Inmaculada, tel. 861-7771, or Virgin of the Immaculate Conception, whose statue is installed in the High Altar. The cathedral was initiated by the Jesuits in 1748. The order was kicked out of Cuba by Carlos III in 1767, but the building was eventually completed in 1777 and altered again in the early 19th century by Bishop José Díaz de Espada, who found many of the elements not to his liking. Thus the original

(Doña Lorenza's own daughter had brought disgrace upon herself by becoming pregnant and was shuttled off to a convent). The mansion's most remarkable feature is a series of eccentric floor-to-ceiling murals depicting life in bold Technicolor as it was lived in Havana centuries ago. The murals, painted between 1763 and 1767, were revealed during a recent restoration from beneath 26 layers of paint and whitewash. Duly restored, the building now houses the **Gabinete de la Arqueología** (the Archaeological Department of the Office of the City Historian), tel. 861-4469. It displays pre-Columbian artifacts, plus a miscellany of ceramics and other

Catedral de la Habana

baroque interior is gone, replaced in 1814 by a new classical interior.

The cathedral's baroque facade is adorned with clinging columns and rippled like a great swelling sea; Cuban novelist Alejo Carpentier thought it "music turned to stone." The facade, which derives from Francisco Borromini's 1667 San Carlo alla Quattro Fontane in Rome, is so simple yet magnificent that a royal decree of December 1793 elevated the church to a cathedral because "the beautifully carved stones of the church . . . are clamoring from their walls for the distinction of cathedral."

On either side of the facade are mismatched towers (one fatter and taller than the other) containing bells supposedly cast with a dash of gold and silver, which is said to account for their musical tone. The eastern bell tower can be climbed; it's not officially open to tourists but for a small tip, Marcelino the *campanero* (bell ringer) might

lead you up the timeworn stairs so that, like Quasimodo, you may run your fingers over the eight patinated bells of different sizes and peer down over the square. Take care up here, as nobody thinks to clean up the debris underfoot, and there are no guardrails. Marcelino even led me into the organ loft (also littered with debris), where I lay on a bed of dust and snapped photos down over the nave.

Columns divide the rectangular church into three naves, with a marble floor, two side aisles supported by great pillars, and eight chapels off to the side (the oldest, the Chapel of Nuestra Señora de Loreta, consecrated in 1755, predates the conversion of the original church into a cathedral). The interior remains in excellent condition, although the magnificent murals (the work of renowned Italian painter Guiseppe Perovani) above the main altar are badly deteriorated. The neoclassical main altar is very simple and made of wood; the original gilt baroque altar was replaced in 1820. More impressive is the chapel immediately to the left, with several altars, including one of Carrara marble inlaid with gold, silver, onyx, and carved hardwoods. Note, too, the wooden image of Saint Christopher, patron saint of Havana, dating to 1633 and originally composed of 170 pieces. The original was too heavy to carry in processions, so a sculptor was commissioned to reduce its size; unfortunately, his hand was uneven and there is a noticeable disproportion between head and body. Artist Jean-Baptiste Vermay, who was born in France around 1790, moved to Havana, and died—along with 8,000 other citizens—in the cholera epidemic of 1833, is also represented.

The Spanish believed that a casket that had been brought to Havana with due pomp and circumstance from Santo Domingo in 1796 and resided in the cathedral for more than a century held the ashes of Christopher Columbus. Casket and ashes—a "pile of dust and a bit of bone"—were returned to Spain in 1899. All but the partisan *habaneros* now believe that the ashes were those of Columbus's son Diego. The *Gran Almirante,* the stone statue of Columbus that stood outside the cathedral, is gone also, transferred to Spain with the casket (Graham Greene, in *Our Man From Havana*, thought it looked "as though it had been formed through the centuries under water, like a coral reef, by the action of insects").

At last visit, the cathedral was officially open Monday–Saturday 10:30 A.M.–2 P.M., Sunday 9 A.M.–noon. However, more often than not it is closed except for Mass (Mon., Tues., Thurs., and Fri. at 8 P.M., Sat. at 5:30 P.M., and Sun. at 10:30 A.M.).

Casa de los Marqueses de Aguas Claras

This splendid old mansion, on the northwest side of the plaza, was built during the 16th century by Governor General Gonzalo Pérez de Angulo and has since been added to by subsequent owners. Today a café occupies the *portico,* while the inner courtyard, with its fountain and grand piano amid lush palms and clinging vines, houses the Restaurante La Fuente del Patio. The restaurant extends upstairs, where members of the middle classes once dwelled in apartments. Sunlight pouring in through stained-glass *mediopuntos* saturates the floors with shifting fans of red and blue. Novelist Enrique Fernández, writing in 1994, recalled being able to look down from his grandmother's balcony and watch "the goings on in the plaza: the fruit vendors and bootblacks, the elegant men and women in white linen going into the restaurant (which was far too pricey for the second-floor tenants), and at the garishly dressed Americans buying stuffed baby alligators in the tourist shops that festooned the other two *palacios.*" You can still steal out onto the rickety balconies to look down on the colorful action; when the crowds disappear, note the patterned cobbles.

Casa del Conde de Bayona

For the best view and photos down over the square, ascend the steps to the upper level of Casa del Conde de Bayona, the simple two-story structure that faces the cathedral on the south side of the square. Dating from 1720, it's a perfect example of the traditional Havana merchant's house of the period, with side stairs and an *entresuelo* (mezzanine of half-story proportions)

tucked between the two stories and used to house servants and slaves. It was built in the 1720s for Governor General Don Luís Chacón, and later passed to Pancho Marty, a former smuggler-turned-entrepreneur. In the 1930s, it housed the Havana Club Bar, which gave out free rum for promotion and was used by Graham Greene as the setting for Wormold's meeting with Captain Segura (based on Batista's real-life police chief, Ventura) in *Our Man in Havana.* Today it houses the **Museo de Arte Colonial,** Calle San Ignacio #61, tel. 862-6440, which recreates the lavish interior of an aristocratic colonial home. The museum is an Aladdin's cave of colonial furniture, glass, porcelain, Baccarat crystal, ironwork, musical instruments, and other sumptuous artifacts from the colonial period. One room is devoted to the stunningly colorful stained-glass *vitrales* and *mediopuntos* unique to Cuba. There's even an array of chamberpots—handy if you get taken short. Open daily 9 A.M.–7 P.M.; entrance costs US$2 (cameras cost US$2, guides cost US$1).

Other Sights

On the southwest corner is the **Callejón de Chorro,** a tiny cul-de-sac where the original cistern was built to supply water to ships in the harbor. The *aljibe* (cistern) marked the terminus of the Zanja Real (the "royal ditch," or *chorro*) a covered aqueduct—completed in 1592—that brought water from the Río Almendares, some 10 kilometers away. A small sink and spigot are all that remain. The **Casa de Baños,** Calle San Ignacio #56, which faces onto the squares, looks quite ancient but was built this century in colonial style on the site of a 19th-century bathhouse erected over the *aljibe.* Today the Casa contains the **Galería Victor Manuel,** tel. 861-2955, which sells exquisite quality arts. Open daily 9:30 A.M.–9 P.M.

At the far end of Callejón de Chorro is the **Taller Experimental de la Gráfica,** tel. 862-0979, tgrafica@cubarte.cult.cu, where you can watch professional artists making prints; be sure to visit the art gallery up the stairs to the right. Open Mon.–Fri. 9 A.M.–4 P.M..

On the plaza's east side is the **Casa de Conde de Lombillo.** Built in 1741, this former home of a slave trader still houses a small post office (Cuba's first), as it has since 1821. Note the mailbox set into the outside wall; it is a grotesque face—that of a tragic Greek mask—carved in stone, with a scowling mouth as its slit that looks like it might take your fingers or at least spit back your letter. The building now houses historical lithographs, plus an exhibition portraying the restoration project for Habana Vieja. Open Mon.–Fri. 9 A.M.–5 P.M., Sat. 9 A.M.–1 P.M. Free.

Casa de Lombillo adjoins the **Casa del Marqués de Arcos,** built in the 1740s for the royal treasurer. At last visit the Casa del Marqués de Arcos was still undergoing restoration intended to turn this beautiful former colonial mansion into a hotel—the Hotel Casa del Marqués de Arcos—in traditional style. The two houses are fronted by a wide *portico* supported by thick columns; the *portico,* gives the impression that the building faces onto the square. Actually, what you see is the rear of the mansion; the entrance is on Calle Mercaderes. The building facing the entrance is graced by the **Mural Artístico-Histórico,** by Cuban artist Andrés Carrillo, portraying the building as it appeared during the 19th century, complete with famous intellectual and other figures in resplendent formal attire.

CALLE EMPEDRADO

Cobbled Calle Empedrado leads west from the north side of the Plaza de la Catedral. Although it was paved as late as 1821, Empedrado was the *first* street in Havana to be cobbled. Prior to that the city streets were little more than muddy lanes.

Anyone with an interest in art should call in at the **Centro Wilfredo Lam,** Calle San Ignacio #22, esq. Empredado, tel. 861-2096 and 861-3419, wlam@artsoft.cult.cu, immediately west of the cathedral, in the restored former mansion of the Counts of Peñalver. The center, named for the noted Cuban artist, displays works by Lam, other Cuban artists, and artists from throughout the Third World (primarily Latin America). The cultural institution studies, researches, and promotes contemporary art from around the world. It sponsors workshops and the biennial Havana Exhibition, in which up-

CUBA'S PICASSO

Wilfredo Lam, a Cubist and student of Pablo Picasso, was one of the greatest painters to emerge from Cuba during this century. His heritage was a mixture of Cuban, African, and Chinese blood. He was born in 1902, in Sagua La Grande, and studied at Havana's San Alejandro School of Painting. In 1936, he traveled to Paris and developed close ties with the Surrealists. Picasso took Lam under his wing and offered the young Cuban his studio to work in. Lam lived briefly in Marseilles before returning to Havana. In 1956, he returned to Europe, although he continued to visit Cuba periodically. He died in Paris on September 11, 1982.

Lam's work distills the essence of Afro-Antillean culture. He broke with the traditional rules and created his own style using the myths, rituals, customs, and magic of his background to explore a world of Caribbean negritude. His most important works are considered to be *La Silla,* painted in 1941, and *La Jungla,* painted in 1943. Many of his etchings, sketches, and canvases are exhibited in Havana's Museo de Bellas Artes. His *La Manigua,* painted in Haiti in 1956, hangs in the Museum of Modern Art in New York. And one of his paintings, *La Mañana Verde,* sold at Sotheby's in 1995 for US$965,000. You can even walk on his work, which is inset on the sidewalks of Calle 23 (La Rampa) in Vedado.

and-coming artists have a chance to exhibit. It also features a library on contemporary art, a large music store, and a collection of 1,250 art pieces. Open Mon.–Fri. and alternate Sat. 8:30 am.–4:30 P.M. Entrance costs US$2.

La Bodeguita del Medio

No visit to Havana is complete without at least one visit to Ernest Hemingway's favorite watering hole at 207 Calle Empedrado, tel. 862-6121, half a block west of the cathedral. This neighborhood hangout—Hemingway's "little shop in the middle of the street"—was originally the coachhouse of the mansion next door (that of the Condesa de la Reunión). Later it was a bodega, a mom-and-pop grocery store where

Spanish immigrant Ángel Martínez served drinks and food over the counter. According to Tom Miller in *Trading with the Enemy,* Martínez hit upon a brilliant idea: he gave writers credit. The writers, of course, wrote about their newfound hangout, thereby attracting literati and cognoscenti from around the world. (After the Revolution, Martínez stayed on as manager.)

You enter La Bodeguita through a saloon-style swinging door. The bar is immediately on your right, with the restaurant behind—note the beautiful tilework along the passageway wall. The bar is usually crowded with tourists. Troubadors move among the thirsty *turistas.* Between tides, you can still savor the proletarian fusion of dialectics and rum. The house drink is the US$3 *mojito,* the rum mint julep that Hemingway brought out of obscurity and turned into the national drink. However, the Bodeguita's *mojitos* are insipid, about as bad as you'll find in Havana.

The rustic wooden bar is carved with names. Miscellaneous bric-a-brac adorns the walls: posters, paintings, and faded black-and-white photos of Papa Hemingway, Carmen Miranda, and other famous visitors. The walls look as if a swarm of adolescents has been given amphetamines and let loose with crayons. The most famous graffiti is credited to Papa: "Mi Mojito En La Bodeguita, Mi Daiquirí En El Floridita," he supposedly scrawled on the sky-blue walls. Errol Flynn thought it "A Great Place to Get Drunk." They are there, these ribald fellows, smiling at the camera through a haze of cigar smoke and rum. Stepping from La Bodeguita with rum in your veins, you may feel an exhilarating sensation, as if Hemingway himself were walking beside you through the cobbled streets of this most literary of Havana's terrain.

Other Sights

The **Casa del Conde de la Reunión,** Calle Empedrado #215, 50 meters west of La Bodeguita, was built in the 1820s, at the peak of the baroque era. The trefoil-arched doorway opens onto a *zaguán* (courtyard) surrounded by rooms that Alejo Carpentier, Cuba's most famous novelist (and a dedicated revolutionary), used as the main setting for his novel, *El Siglo de las Luces* (The Enlightenment). Note the exquisite *azule-*

statue of Miguel de Cervantes, Plazuela de San Juan de Dios

jos (painted tiles) that decorate the walls. A portion of the home, which houses the Centro de Promoción Cultural, is dedicated to his memory as the **Fundación Alejo Carpentier,** tel. 861-5500. One entire wall bears a display under sloping glass of Carpentier's early works. His raincoat is thrown stylishly over his old desk chair, suggesting that the novelist might return home at any moment. The novelist's widow dedicated his posthumous royalties to establish and maintain the museum. Open Mon.–Fri. 8:30 A.M.–4:30 P.M. Entry is free.

Two blocks west, you'll pass **Plazuela de San Juan de Dios,** e/ Calles Habana y Aguiar, a small plaza centered on a white marble monument erected in 1906. The life-size facsimile of Miguel de Cervantes, author of *Don Quixote,* sits in a chair, book and pen in hand, looking contemplatively down upon rose bushes, lending the plaza its colloquial name: Parque Cervantes.

ALEJO CARPENTIER

Alejo Carpentier (1904–80) is acclaimed as Cuba's greatest latter-day writer. Carpentier (his name is pronounced in the French manner) was born in Havana to a French father and Russian mother. In 1927, he was imprisoned by the dictator Machado but escaped and fled Cuba for Paris on a false passport. He returned to Cuba in 1937 but in 1946, during the violent excesses of the Batista era, he fled Cuba again for Venezuela, where he wrote his best novels. Carpentier was also a gifted musicologist, and in 1945 published a seminal work called *Music in Cuba.*

When the Castro revolution triumphed, the gifted novelist and revolutionary returned as an honored spiritual leader. He was named head of the state publishing house. Alas, say some critics, Carpentier became a bureaucrat and sycophant; under his influence, the National Printing Press even reworked *Moby Dick* to make it palatable to the socialist masses (Captain Ahab, Ishmael, and Queequeg were still there, but "you couldn't find God in the labyrinth of the sea," wrote Guillermo Cabrera Infante).

In 1966, Carpentier was appointed ambassador to Paris, where he died in 1980.

He is known for his erudite and verbally explosive works that were seminal in defining the surreal Latin American magic-realist style. His first novel, *Ecué-Yamba-O,* about Afro-Cuban life, was published in 1933. A favorite is "Journey Back to the Source," a brilliant short story chronicling the life of Don Marcial, Marqués de Capellanías, but told chronologically backward from death to birth.

PLAZA DE ARMAS

The most important plaza in Habana Vieja, and the oldest—originally laid out in 1519—is this handsome square at the seaward end of Calles Obispo and O'Reilly, opening onto Avenida del Puerto to the east. Plaza de Armas, ground zero in Havana's history, was the early focus of the settlement and later became its administrative center, named Plaza de Iglesia for the church that once stood here. The church was demolished in 1741 after it was destroyed when an English warship, the ill-named HMS *Invincible,* was struck by lightning and exploded, sending its main mast sailing down on the church. The square derived its contemporary name following a dispute in 1581 between the Cuban governor, Gabriel Luján, and Diego Quiñones, governor of the Castillo de la Real Fuerza, who competed for command of the castle garrison. Luján won the day by taking over the square for military exercises: hence, Plaza de Armas.

The plaza seems still to ring with the cacophony of the past, when military parades, extravagant fiestas, and musical concerts were held under the watchful eye of the governor, and the gentry would take their formal evening promenade. The lovely tradition has been revived on Sunday, when musical concerts are sometimes offered at night. By day (Mon.–Sat.) the plaza hosts a secondhand book fair and is ringed by stalls selling well-thumbed antiquarian books.

At its heart is **Parque Céspedes,** a verdant park shaded by palms and tall kapok (ceiba) trees festooned with lianas and epiphytes. At its center stands a white marble **statue of Manuel de Céspedes,** hero of the Ten Years' War, with a tall palm at each corner. The park is lit at night by beautifully filigreed lamps.

It is still rimmed by four important buildings constructed in the late 18th century. The following are described in clockwise order around the plaza, beginning on the west side, with "cobblewood" laid instead of stone to soften the noise of carriages and thereby lessen the disturbance of the Capitanes Generales' sleep.

Palacio de los Capitanes Generales

Taking up the west side of the square is the somber yet stately Palacio de los Capitanes Generales,

© CHRISTOPHER P. BAKER

El Templete, Plaza de Armas

fronted by a cool loggia, shadowed by a facade of Ionic columns supporting nine great arches.

The palace was completed in 1791 and became home to 65 governors of Cuba between 1791 and 1898 (Spain's stern rule was enforced from here) and, after that, the U.S. governor's residence during Uncle Sam's occupation and, in 1902–20, the early seat of the Cuban government. Between 1920 and 1967, it served as Havana's city hall. Originally the parish church—La Parroquial Mayor, built in 1555—stood here. The holy structure was demolished when the mast and spars of the *Invincible* came through the roof—an unfortunate "act of God."

The palace is a magnificent three-story structure surrounding a courtyard (entered from the plaza), which contains a statue of Christopher Columbus by Italian sculptor Cucchiari competing for the light with tall palms and a veritable botanical garden of foliage. Don't be alarmed by any ghoulish shrieks—a peacock lives in the courtyard. Arched colonnades rise on all sides, festooned with vines and bougainvillea. Several afternoons each week, an orchestra plays while pretty girls in crinolines flit up and down the majestic staircase, delighting in the ritual of the *quince,* the traditional celebration of a girl's 15th birthday. On the southeast corner, you can spot a hole containing the coffin of an unknown nobleman, one of several graves from the old Cementerio de Espada. A church that once stood here was razed to make way for the palace; note the plaque—the oldest in Havana—commemorating the death of Doña María de Cepero y Nieto, who was felled when a blunderbuss was accidentally fired while she was praying—another unfortunate "act of God".

Today, the palace houses the **Museo de la Ciudad de La Habana** (City of Havana Museum), Calle Tacón #1, e/ Obispo y O'Reilly, tel. 861-2876. The entrance is to the side, on Calle Obispo. The great flight of marble stairs leads to high-ceilinged rooms as gracious and richly furnished as those in Versailles or Buckingham Palace. The Salón del Trono (Throne Room), made for the King of Spain but never used, is of particularly breathtaking splendor and brims with treasures. The curiosities include two enormous marble bathtubs in the shape of nautilus shells, Máximo Gómez's death mask, and a cannon made of leather. The museum also features the Salón de las Banderas (Hall of Flags), with magnificent artwork that includes *The Death of Antonio Maceo,* by Menocal; plus exquisite collections illustrating the story of the city's (and Cuba's) development and the 19th-century struggles for independence. Even here you can't escape the ubiquitous anti-Yankee expositions: one top-floor room contains the shattered wings of the eagle that once crested the Monumento del Maine in Vedado, along with other curios suggestive of U.S. voracity and fragility. Old horse-drawn carriages and artillery are among the other exhibits.

The museum is open daily 9:30 A.M.–6:30 P.M. (last entry is at 5 P.M.). Entrance costs US$3 for tourists (US$2 extra for cameras, US$10 for videos, US$1 for a guide).

North Side

The quasi-Moorish, pseudo-baroque, part neoclassical **Palacio del Segundo Cabo** (Palace of the Second Lieutenant), Calle O'Reilly #14, tel. 862-8091, dates from 1770, when it was designed as the Casa de Correos (the city post office, responsible in the early colonial era for all postal communications with Spain). Its facade is somewhat austere, but the inner courtyard is handsome. Its use metamorphosed several times until it became the home of the vice-governor general (Second Lieutenant) and, immediately after independence, the seat of the Senate. Today, it houses the Instituto Cubano del Libro (Cuban Book Institute; open Mon.–Fri. 8 A.M.–4:30 P.M.), which promotes everything to do with literature; and three bookstores (open daily 10 A.M.–5:30 P.M.). Upstairs, the mezzanine is occupied by the **Galería Raúl Martínez** (open Mon.–Fri. 10 A.M.–5 P.M., and Sat. 10 A.M.–3 P.M.) showing works by foremost painters. The Institute hosts readings, seminars, and other public presentations relating to literature (upcoming events are listed on a notice board). It has a small restaurant—Café Literario—tucked down a staircase facing the Castillo de la Real Fuerza.

Immediately east of the palace is a life-size marble **statue of Fernando VII,** holding in one hand a scroll of parchment that from the side appears jauntily cocked (pardon the pun) and is the butt of ribald jokes among locals. In his other hand, he holds a plumed hat.

The **Castillo de la Real Fuerza,** at Calle O'Reilly #2, on the northeast corner of Plaza de Armas, is a pocket-size castle begun in 1558 and completed in 1582. Hence, it's the second oldest fort in the Americas and the oldest of the four forts that guarded the New World's most precious harbor. Built in medieval fashion, it was almost useless from a strategic point of view, being landlocked far from the mouth of the harbor channel and hemmed in by surrounding buildings that would have formed a great impediment to its cannons in any attack. With walls six meters wide and 10 meters tall, the castle forms a square with enormous triangular bulwarks at the corners, their sharp angles slicing the dark waters of the moat like the prows of galleons. The governors of Cuba lived here until 1762.

Visitors enter the fortress via a courtyard full of patinated cannons and mortars. Note the royal coat of arms representing Seville, Spain, carved in stone above the massive gateway as you cross the moat by a drawbridge. The entrance to the vaulted interior features two suits of armor in glass cases. Stairs lead up to the storehouse and battlements, which house an impressive **Museo Nacional de la Cerámica Cubana,** tel. 861-6130, featuring pottery both ancient and new. Works by leading artists such as Roberto Fernández and Teresita Gómez are shown.

You can climb to the top of a cylindrical tower rising from the northwest corner; the tower contains an antique brass bell gone mossy green with age and weather. Originally, the bell was rung to signal the approach of ships, with differing notes for friends and foes. The tower is topped by a bronze weathervane called **La Giraldilla de la Habana**—a reference to the Giralda weathervane in Seville. While rather a pathetic looking thing, much is made of it—it's the symbol of Havana and also graces the label of Havana Club rum bottles. The vane is a copy—the archetype, which was toppled in a hurricane, resides in the city museum. The original was cast in 1631 in honor of Inéz de Bobadilla, the wife of Governor Hernando de Soto, the tireless explorer who fruitlessly searched for the Fountain of Youth in Florida. De Soto named his wife governor in his

THE LITERARY SCENE

Habaneros are avid readers, and not just of home-country writers. The works of many renowned international authors are widely read throughout Cuba: Ernest Hemingway, Tennessee Williams, Gabriel García Márquez, Günter Grass, Isabel Allende, Jorge Amado, Mark Twain, Raymond Chandler, and Dashiell Hammett. Many others, such as George Orwell, are banned, as are the works of many of Cuba's finest homegrown writers.

Cuba's goals and struggles have been a breeding ground for passions and dialectics that have spawned dozens of literary geniuses whose works are clenched fists that cry out against social injustice. Says writer Errol McDonald, "The confluence of the struggle against Spanish and American imperialism, the impact of the cultivation of sugar and tobacco, a high appreciation of the 'low-down' sublimities of Afro-Cuban and Hispanic peasant life, a deep awareness of European 'high' and American popular culture, and the shock of the revolution has resulted in a literature that is staggering for its profundity and breadth—its richness."

Cuban literature was born in exile. The most talented Cuban writers, such as Cirilo Villaverde (whose spellbinding novel *Cecilia Valdés* was written in exile in the 1880s), Virgilio Piñera, Guillermo Cabrera Infante, and Alejo Carpentier, all produced their best works abroad.

During the first years of the Revolution, Castro relished being the "bohemian intellectual." Artists and writers enjoyed relative freedom. As the romantic phase of the Revolution passed into an era of more dogmatic ideology, Castro appointed hard-liners to the Culture Council. In 1961, Castro invited intellectuals to a debate on the meaning of cultural liberty at which he offered his "Words to the Intellectuals," which he summed up with a credo: "Within the Revolution, everything. Against the Revolution, nothing!" The government acquired full control of the mass media. Many talented intellectuals, writers, and artists were intimidated into ideological straitjackets. Thousands chose to leave Cuba or were cast into purgatory as "contagious political bacteria."

The worst years ended when the Ministry of Culture was founded in 1976, ushering in a period of greater leniency.

Many talented individuals stayed, of course, and produced rich and lively works. The past few

absence, and she became the only female governor in Cuba. Every afternoon for four years she climbed the tower and scanned the horizon in vain for his return, and it is said that she died of sorrow. The Giraldilla is a voluptuous albeit small figure with hair braided in thick ropes, bronze robes fluttering in the wind. In her right hand she holds a palm tree and in her left a cross.

The castle is open daily 9 A.M.–7 P.M.; entry costs US$1.

East Side

Immediately east of the castle, at the junction of Avenida del Puerto and O'Reilly, is an obelisk to the 77 Cuban seamen killed during World War II by German submarines (five Cuban vessels were sunk by German U-boats). Cuba formally declared war on Nazi Germany in late 1941. The Nazis placed a spy in Cuba—Heinz August Kenning, alias Enrique Augusto Lunin—to report on the arrival and departure of shipping, which could then be hunted by submarines. Kenning was discovered and executed on November 10, 1942.

A charming copy of a Doric temple—**El Templete**—sits on the square's northeast corner. It was inaugurated on March 19, 1828, on the site where the first mass and town council meeting were held in 1519, beside a massive ceiba tree. The original ceiba was felled by a hurricane in 1828 and replaced by a column fronted by a small bust of Christopher Columbus. A ceiba has since been replanted and today still shades the tiny temple, which wears a great cloak of

years have seen a considerable thaw. Recent Cuban cultural policy has been to salvage many among those writers who, having produced significant works, were never allowed to publish. Many writers previously reduced to "nonpersons" are now being treated with kindness and, often, postmortem canonization. Ironically, the new openness coincided with the onset of the Special Period, which caused a severe paper shortage. By 1993, books were as scarce as food. In Cuba's contemporary economy, where even books are now sold for precious dollars, readers have very little income to spend on reading. Books are now luxuries. Meanwhile, state-employed writers found themselves among the ranks of the unemployed. Many have attempted to go it alone as freelancers.

Alas, Cuba's political climate runs hot and cold. In spring 1996, the government began to cool authors down a bit, and freelancers reported a new tug on the leash. Many authors critical of the regime are forced to smuggle their works out of Cuba in hopes of finding a publisher (Akashic Books, in New York, specializes in publishing the works of Cuban writers). The government continues to harass freelance writers who, since the promulgation of a new law in 1999, must now be cautious against writing anything that can be implied to be "counter-revolutionary," which is interpreted as "supporting the enemy." Contemporary novelists walk a tightrope as they attempt to balance creativity with official sanction. Many figures in novels appear disguised.

UNEAC, the Unión Nacional de Escritores y Artistas de Cuba (National Union of Writers and Artists), Calle 17 #351, Vedado, tel. 832-4551, was created in 1961 as the officially sanctioned body. UNEAC exists to promote the professional interests of its members, who must foremost demonstrate loyalty to "leadership of the Communist Party" (so begins the very first Article of its constitution); no dissident writers are permitted, although the leadership, being composed of artists, tries its best to foster broad-based culture and a climate of tolerance within the straitjacket imposed from above. Political correctness takes precedent over talent in determining who gets published, and much of what gets published is political pabulum of dubious quality. No rigorous forum for unbiased criticism exists and the literary scene is both incestuous and sycophantic. UNEAC has a division—Casa del joven creador—that serves young artists and writers.

bougainvillea. Its interior, with a black-and-white checkerboard marble floor, is dominated by triptych wall-to-ceiling paintings depicting the first Mass, the first town council meeting, and the inauguration of the Templete. In the center of the room sits a bust of the artist, Jean-Baptiste Vermay, whose ashes (along with those of his wife, who died—along with 8,000 other citizens—in the cholera epidemic of 1833) are contained in a marble urn next to the bust. Open 9 A.M.–6 P.M. Entry costs US$1, including interpretive guide.

The building immediately south of El Templete is the former Palacio del Conde de Santovenia, built in the style of the Tuileries Palace in France and today housing the **Hotel Santa Isabel,** Calle Baratillo, e/ Narciso López y Barratillo y Obispo. Its quintessentially Cuban-colonial facade is graced by a becolumned portico and, above, wrought-iron railings on balconies whose windows boast stained-glass *mediopuntos*. The *conde* (Count) in question was famous for hosting elaborate parties, most notoriously a three-day bash in 1833 to celebrate the accession to the throne of Isabel II that climaxed with an ascent of a gaily decorated gas-filled balloon (he was less popular with his immediate neighbors, who detested the reek of oil and fish that wafted over the square from his first-floor warehouses). In the late 19th century, the palace was bought and sanitized by a colonel from New Orleans. He reopened it as a resplendent hotel, a guise it resumed in 1998. President Carter stayed here during his visit to Havana in 2002.

Half a block east of the hotel, on narrow Calle

HEMINGWAY HUNTS THE U-BOATS

In May 1942, Ernest Hemingway showed up at the U.S. embassy in Havana with a proposal to outfit his sportfishing boat, the *Pilar,* as a Q-boat, a vessel disguised as a fishing boat to decoy Nazi submarines within range, but armed with .50-caliber machine guns, other armaments, and a trained crew (with himself at the helm, of course). The boat would navigate the cays off the north coast of Cuba, ostensibly collecting specimens on behalf of the American Museum of Natural History but in fact on the lookout for German U-boats, which Hemingway intended to engage and disable. The writer was "quite prepared to sacrifice his beloved vessel in exchange for the capture or sinking of an enemy submarine."

Hemingway's friend, Col. John W. Thomason Jr., was Chief of Naval Intelligence for Central America and pulled strings to get the plan approved. The vessel was camouflaged and duly set out for the cays. Gregorio Fuentes—who from 1938 until the writer's death was in charge of the *Pilar*—went along (and served as the model for Antonio in *Islands in the Stream,* Hemingway's novel based on his real-life adventures).

They patrolled for two years. Several times they located and reported the presence of Nazi submarines that the U.S. Navy or Air Force were later able to sink. Only once, off Cayo Mégano, did Hemingway come close to his dream: a U-boat suddenly surfaced while the *Pilar* was at anchor. Unfortunately, it dipped back below the surface and disappeared before Hemingway could get close.

Baratillo, is the **Casa del Café,** tel. 33-8061, serving all kinds of Cuban coffees, and, next door, the **Taberna del Galeón,** tel. 33-8476, better known as the House of Rum. Inside it is cool as a well. You can taste various rums at no cost, although it is hoped you will make a purchase from the wide selection (a free *mojito* awaits your arrival). It's open Monday–Saturday 9 A.M.–5 P.M., Sunday 9 A.M.–3 P.M.

The South Side

The **Biblioteca Provincial de la Habana,** on the southeast corner is Havana's provincial library, which houses a meager (and dated) array of books. The building once served as the U.S. Embassy. Next to it is an art gallery and bookstore—**Galería Villena.**

Adjoining it to the west is **Museo Nacional de História Natural,** Calle Obispo #61, e/ Oficios y Baratillo, tel. 862-0353. This well-done museum shows off the rather paltry collection of the Academía de Ciencias and encompasses the Museo de Ciencias Naturales (Museum of Natural Sciences) and the Museo de Ciencias y Técnicas (Museum of Science and Technology), which covers evolution in a well-conceived dis-

play. The museum houses collections of Cuban flora and fauna—many in clever reproductions of their natural environments—plus stuffed tigers, apes, and other beasts from around the world. Children will appreciate the interactive displays. Open Tues.–Sun. 10:30 A.M.–5 P.M. Entrance costs US$3.

For a panorama of the old city, head to the rooftop *mirador* (lookout) of the **Cafetería Mirador de la Bahía** (open 11 A.M.–midnight), betwixt the museum and Galería Villena.

On the plaza's southwest corner, at the junction with Calle Oficios, is **Restaurante Cubano,** housed in a green and ocher 17th-century mansion that was originally the college of San Francisco de Sales for orphan girls. Its central patio, surrounded by galleries of stocky columns and wide arches enclosing slatted doors and *mediopuntos,* is now roamed by peacocks that beg tidbits from diners. The outside patio facing the plaza is occupied by the lively **Café Mina,** where you may sit beneath shady canopies on the sidewalk while dining as Cuban musicians entertain.

Facing the south side of the Palacio de Capitanes Generales, along a 50-meter-long cobbled pedestrian section of Calle Obispo, is a series of gems. Immediately west of Café Mina, the **Casa del Agua la Tinaja,** Calle Obispo #111, sells mineral water (US $0.25 a glass). The source was discovered in 1544, and early explorers made use of the water; in 1831, an aqueduct was built to carry it to the burgeoning town, thereby solving the water shortage. Next door is the wee **Barbería de Plaza de Armas,** tel. 863-0943, a tiny barber's shop where Gilberto Torrente charges US$2 for a trim, and US$1.50 for a shave; open Mon.–Sat. 8 A.M.–noon and 2–5 P.M.

Dulcería Doña Teresa, Obispo #113, is a fine bakery selling custards, ice creams, and other delights behind massive metal-studded doorways that open into what was once a stable. Attached is the **Museo de Plata** (also called Museo de la Orfebrería, or Museum of Silverwork), Calle Obispo # 113, crammed with silver and gold ornaments from the colonial era, including old clocks, coins, medals, and plates. Upstairs you'll find candelabras, a dining set that includes a massive silver *ponchera* (punch bowl), a beautiful replica in silver of Columbus's *Santa María,* walking sticks, and a splendid collection of swords and firearms. Downstairs, a silversmith is occasionally on hand to demonstrate his skills. Open Tues.–Sat. 9 A.M.– 5 P.M., and Sun. 9 A.M.–1 P.M. Entry costs US$1 (plus US$1 for a guide, optional).

Next door is the **Oficina del Historiador de la Ciudad** (Office of the City Historian), Obispo #117-119, with a copper galleon hanging above its door and an old cannon standing upright outside. Appropriately, this is the oldest house in Havana, dating from around 1570. Inside you'll find books on Cuban history and culture for sale and, behind a grilled gate, venerable artifacts including a *quitrín,* a two-wheeled conveyance with a moveable bonnet to protect passengers from the elements, made to be pulled by a single horse (ridden by a *calesero,* a black slave, who dressed in high boots, top hat, and a costume trimmed with colorful ribbons).

Opposite, look closely at the two cannons outside the south side of the Palacio de Capitanes Generales, and you'll note the monogram of King George III. The cannons are relics of the brief English occupation of Cuba in 1762.

At the end of the cobbled pedestrians-only block is a fabric store in a beautiful blue and cream mansion, the former Casa del Marqués de Casa Torre, Obispo #121; and, around the corner, on Mercaderes, the **Casa de las Infusiones,** today a lively bar.

CALLE O'REILLY AND VICINITY

Calle O'Reilly runs from the northwest corner of Plaza de Armas and, although today quite sedate, was before the Revolution a major commercial thoroughfare. "The bells were ringing in Santo Christo, and the doves rose from the roof in the golden evening and circled away over the lottery shops of O'Reilly Street and the banks of Obispo," wrote Graham Greene in *Our Man in Havana.* It is named not, as you may suspect, for an Irishman but rather for a Spaniard, Alejandro

---

RECOMMENDED WALKING TOUR 3

Begin in Plaza de Armas and walk south down Calle Oficios, calling at the **Casa del Árabe** and **Hostal Valencia.** Here, turn left onto Obrapia. Follow it 50 yards to the **Casa de los Esclavos,** and **Jardín Diana de Gales,** then continue east one block into **Plaza de San Francisco.**

After visiting the **Iglesia y Convento de San Francisco de Asís** and **Museo de Arte Religioso,** walk down Oficios to Muralles, and turn left for Avenida del Puerto. At the corner (to the right), visit the **Museo de Ron,** then head south one block to the **Bar Dos Hermanos** to commune with Ernest Hemingway's ghost.

Retrace your steps west up Muralles to **Plaza Vieja,** being sure to visit the **Museo de Naipes,** the **Casa del Conde de Jaruco** (both on the south side) and, on the northeast corner, the **Cámara Oscura,** atop the Edificio Gómez.

Exit the square northbound along Calle Mercaderes, which leads past **La Cruz Verde** to the **Plaza Simón Bolívar** and the **Casa de África,** **Casa de la Obra Pía,** and **Casa de Benito Juárez.**

Mercaderes returns you to Plaza de Armas, calling in at the **Habana 1791** perfumery, the **Museo de Tabaco** and **Museo de Asia,** and the **Maqueta de la Habana Vieja.**

© CHRISTOPHER P. BAKER

Calle San Ignacio

O'Reilly, who arrived to represent the Spanish crown after the British returned the city to Spain in 1763.

Cater-corner to Plaza de Armas, at the corner of O'Reilly and Tacón, a plaque inset in the wall reads, "Two Island Peoples in the Same Seas of Struggle and Hope. Cuba and Ireland." The building is the **Empresa Cubana del Tabaco,** O'Reilly #104, tel. 861-5759, the headquarters of Habanos, S.A., which oversees Cuba's production and sale of cigars. Visitors are welcomed into the lobby to admire its exhibit, including display cases of Cuba's finest cigars.

Walking west, you'll pass **Calle San Ignacio,** a narrow, cobbled thoroughfare that's loaded with atmosphere, leading 50 meters north to Plaza de la Catedral. Half a block west of Calle San Ignacio is **Café O'Reilly,** O'Reilly #205, a charming streetside café with an ornate cast-iron spiral staircase that leads up to a tiny bar. Here you

can sit on a balcony and sip a coffee or beer while watching the tide of people flooding O'Reilly.

Worth a look, too, is the neoclassical **National City Bank of New York,** at O'Reilly and Compostela, where, "passing through great stone portals, which were decorated with four-leaf clovers," Greene's Wormold was reminded of his meager status.

O'Reilly continues westward without buildings of further note.

CALLE OBISPO

Calle Obispo, which links Plaza de Armas with today's Parque Central, has been one of the city's busiest thoroughfares since its inception in the early colonial era. The name means "Bishop's Street," supposedly so named because it was the path favored by ecclesiastics of the 18th century. It became Havana's premier shopping street early on and was given a boost when the city walls went up in the mid-1700s, linking the major colonial plaza with the Monserrate Gate, the main entranceway to the city built into the city wall. Cafés and taverns arose to serve the merchants and mendicants. Its most important structures date from the 1920s, when Obispo became a center for banking—a kind of Cuban Wall Street. The street is in the midst of restoration that has reinvigorated it as Havana's commercial thoroughfare par excellence.

Calle Obispo is still Habana Vieja's most crowded and bustling thoroughfare. Be warned, however, that *jineteros* and *jineteras* concentrate here. Watch your valuables!

The rose-pink **Hotel Ambos Mundos,** tel. 860-9532, Obispo, esq. Mercaderes, was built in the 1920s and recently reopened after a long restoration. Off and on throughout the 1930s, Hemingway laid his head in Room 511, contemplating the plot of *For Whom the Bell Tolls.* After the Revolution, the hotel was turned into a hostelry for employees of the Ministry of Education across the way. However, Hemingway's room—"a gloomy room, 16 square meters, with a double bed made of ordinary wood, two night tables and a writing table with a chair," recalled Colombian author and Nobel laureate Gabriel

HABANA VIEJA

© CHRISTOPHER P. BAKER

Bank of Nova Scotia

García Márquez—has been preserved, down to an old Spanish edition of *Don Quixote* on the night table. His room, which looked out over Plaza de Armas and the Havana's colonial skyline (much of the view has since been blocked), is open to view Monday–Saturday 10 A.M.–5 P.M. (entrance US$1).

A plaque on the exterior wall reads, "The novelist Ernest Hemingway lived in this Hotel Ambos Mundos during the decade of the 1930s," when it formed a perfect base for forays to El Floridita and La Bodeguita, and the novelist could be seen day or night strolling my favorite street. Another plaque tells you that "In this site, on January 3, 1841, George Washington Halsey inaugurated the first photographic studio" in Cuba.

Across the street, on the northwest corner of Obispo and Mercaderes, is the former **Ministerio de Educación,** an ugly modern building that sits atop what was formerly the Convent of Santo Domingo. At last visit it was being gutted and remodeled in period vein and when reopened will feature the **Museo de Automóviles** (Auto Museum). Note the **antique bell** held aloft by modern concrete pillars immediately east of the museum. Its plaque in Spanish commemorates

the fact that this was the original site of the University of Havana, founded in January 1728, and housed in the convent. It was demolished in the mid-19th century; all that remains is the bell, which once tolled to call the students to class.

Havana is replete with dusty old apothecaries, but the **Museo y Farmacia Taquechel,** Obispo #155, tel. 862-9286, is surely the most interesting, with its colorful ceramic jars decorated with floral motifs full of herbs and potions. Dating from 1898, it's named for Dr. Francisco Taquechel y Mirabal. The place is exquisite and sparkles behind modern glass doors. It also sells Cuba's range of Elguea creams and lotions, such as anti-cellulite cream. **Droguería Escolapio,** Calle Obispo #260, esq. Aguiar, tel. 862-0311, two blocks west, also features original mahogany counters and shelves, though these are more meagerly stocked, as it serves as a peso-only pharmacy for Cubans. Open 24 hours.

The most resplendent building is the former Palacio de Joaquín Gómez, now the **Hotel Florida,** Obispo #252, e/ Cuba y Aguiar, with a stunning lobby dating from 1838. Also worth a peek is **La Casa del Consomé La Luz,** Calles Obispo, esq. Havana, another moody apothecary

YOU'VE GOT TO BE JOKING!

After the Revolution, Che Guevara was named Minister of Finance and president of the Banco Nacional de Cuba. According to John Anderson (*Che Guevara: A Revolutionary Life*), Che loved to tell the joke of how he'd gotten the job. Supposedly at a cabinet meeting to decide on a replacement of bank president Felipe Pazos, Castro asks who among them is a "good *economista.*" Guevara raises his hand and is sworn in as Minister of Finance and head of the National Bank. Castro says: "Che, I didn't know you were an economist." Guevara replies, "I'm not!" Castro asks, "Then why did you raise your hand when I said I needed an economist?" to which Guevara replies, "Economist! I thought you asked for a Communist!"

with a white marble floor and old glass cabinets faded with age, filled with chemist's tubes, mixing vases, and mortars and pestles, and lined with bottles of oils, herbs, and powders.

At last visit, **Casa Natal de Félix Varela,** Calle Obispo, e/ Aguacate y Villegas, the birthplace of the Cuban nationalist philosophy-priest, was being restored as a museum.

Félix Varela Morales was born in Havana on November 20, 1788. After his mother's death he lived with his maternal grandfather (a Spanish army colonel and Counselor to the Governor of Florida) in St. Augustine, Florida, which was then a Spanish territory. He returned to Havana and graduated from the Seminario de San Carlos y San Ambrosio, where he later taught philosophy, chemistry, physics, theology and music.

Varela rose to become the leading Cuban intellectual and patriot of the early 19th century. Elected in 1821 to the Spanish legislature, he lobbied for the abolition of slavery and for Cuban independence and in 1823 was forced to flee Cuba for New York with a death sentence over his head. Varela was assigned a New York parish and tended the predominantly Irish diocese throughout the famous cholera epidemic. He eventually became Vicar General of the New York diocese and dedicated the rest of his life to humanitarian causes while continuing to write and lobby on behalf of Cuba's nationalist cause. His *El Habanero* was the first journal dedicated to Cuban independence.

Varela died in St. Augustine, Florida, on February 25, 1853. He is considered the forefather of José Martí, who called Varela "Cuba's Saint." In 2002 his legacy inspired the "Varela Project," in which Cuban dissidents gathered 11,000 signatures demanding reforms.

Havana's Wall Street

The area around Calles Obispo, Cuba, and Aguiar is referred to as "Havana's Wall Street," as the main banks were concentrated here prior to the Revolution. Calle Aguiar was *the* great banking street.

Foremost is the former **Banco Nacional de Cuba,** Calle Obispo #211, esq. Cuba, in a splendid neoclassical building-today occupied by the Ministerio de Finanzas y Precios (Ministry of Finance and Prices)—fronted by fluted Corinthian columns and portals decorated with four-leaf clovers. After the Revolution, Che Guevara was named Minister of Finance. He took over the building and promptly turned it on its head . . . the committed Communist was determined to do away with money altogether! When new banknotes were issued, it was Guevara's job to sign them, which he did dismissively by simply scrawling "Che." Today the old bank houses in its basement vaults the **Museo de las Finanzas,** tel. 867-3000, ext. 2468, dedicated to telling the Cuban government's version of the history of banking in Cuba from the colonial era to the tenure of Guevara's reign as the bank's president in the early 1960s. The museum features the enormous safe within which—when Cuba had such—the nation's gold reserves were held for more than half a century. Open Mon.–Fri. 10 A.M.–3 P.M. Entrance is free.

Another beautiful building is the **Banco del Comercio,** Calle Aguiar #402, esq. Obrapía, a magnificent exemplar of 1920s Mexican baroque, but which began life as the Iglesia y Convento de San Felipe Neri; at last visit it was being converted into a concert hall, and features beautiful interior detail. Today's **Banco Nacional de Cuba,** Calle Aguiar #456, e/ Lamparilla y Amargura, occupies the former Banco de Narciso Gelats, built in resplendent classical style in 1929. The former Banco de la Habana, founded in 1915, today houses a state insurance company: the **Compañia de Seguros Internacionales,** Calle Cuba #314, e/ Obispo y Obrapía. The former Bank of Nova Scotia, Calle Cuba esq. O'Reilly, dating from 1832, has been restored and now houses the **Banco Popular de Ahora.** The former **Royal Bank of Canada,** cater-corner, is now a much-dilapidated parking garage, while the **Bolsa de la Habana** (the former Stock Exchange), Calle Obrapía #257, e/ Cuba y Aguiar, is now a worker's canteen.

CALLE OFICIOS

Calle Oficios leads south from Plaza de Armas three blocks to Plaza de San Francisco. Its newly restored colonial buildings are confections in stone.

On the corner, to the rear of Café Minas, is the **Casa de los Artistas,** Calle Oficios #6, tel. 863-9981, where four prominent Cuban artists have studio-galleries. It operates as part of the *expoventa* scheme run by the City Historian's office. Opening times are: Mon.–Sat. 11 A.M.–5 P.M. (Robert Favelo); Mon.–Sat. 10 A.M.–4 P.M. (Zaida del Río); Mon.–Sat. 11 A.M.–6 P.M. (Ernesto Rancaño Vieites, tel. 862-6521); various times (Pedro Pablo Oliva, tel. 863-6243).

Adjoining it is the **Casa del Árabe** (Arab House), Oficios #12, tel. 861-5868. This mansion (actually, two 17th-century mansions combined) was formerly the Colegio de San Ambriosio, and is an appropriately fine example of Moorish-inspired architecture. It is the only place in Havana where Muslims can practice the Islamic faith. It now houses a museum dedicated to all things Arabic in honor of the many Levantine immigrants who settled Cuba throughout the centuries. You enter into a beautiful place bursting with foliage—a softly dappled courtyard radiating ineffable calm. The

prayer hall is decorated with hardwoods inlaid with mother-of-pearl, tempting you to run your fingers across the floral and geometric motifs to sense the tactile pleasure. The museum displays camel saddles and Oriental carpets, an exact replica of a *souk* (market), models of Arab *dhows* (traditional sailing vessels), and a superb collection of Arab weaponry. Open Tues.–Sat. 9 A.M.–4:30 P.M., and Sun. 9 A.M.–1 P.M. Entrance costs US$1. Cultural activities are hosted in the evenings.

Coin lovers should call in next door at the **Museo Numismático** (the Coin Museum), Oficios #8, tel. 861-5811, in the former 17th-century bishop's residence—Casa del Obispo. This collection dates back to early colonial days and includes "company store" currency printed by the sugar mills. Open Tues.–Sat. 9 A.M.–5 P.M., and Sun. 9 A.M.–1 P.M.

Across the street, Havana's **Museo del Automóvil** (Museum of Automobiles), Calle Oficios #13, no phone, includes an eclectic range of 30 antique automobiles, from a 1905 Cadillac, various Model T and A Fords, a 1924 Packard, 1926 Willys Overland Whippet, and 1930 V-6 Cadillac limousine, to a pre-war Dodge hearse and a 1960s-era Daimler limousine gifted by the British embassy. Several vehicles once belonged to famous figures, such as Che Guevara's 1959 mint-green Chevrolet Bel-Air (used as his government car when he briefly served as Minister of Finance) and Cuban novelist Alejo Carpentier's Volkswagen Beetle. A number of classic Harley-Davidson motorcycles are also exhibited. At last visit, the collection was slated to move to the former Ministerio de Educación building. Open daily 9 A.M.–7 P.M. Entrance costs US$1 (US$2 extra for cameras, US$10 for videos).

Around the corner, in the Casa Garibaldi is **El Caserón del Tango,** Calle Justíz #21, which promotes the melancholic Argentinian dance. There's a theater opposite—**Casa de la Comedia** (also known as Salón Ensayo)—in the headquarters for the Teatro Anaquillé. It hosts children's theater and comedy events on weekends.

Hostal Valencia, Oficios #53, e/ Obrapía y Lamparilla, tel. 867-1037, is a picturesque Spanish-style *posada* that originated in the 17th

CUBAN COLONIAL ARCHITECTURE

Havana, one of the world's great architectural troves, boasts the New World's finest assemblage of colonial buildings. Spanning four centuries, these palaces, mansions, churches, castles, and more simple structures catalog an astonishing progression of styles. The academic classicism of aristocratic 18th-century Spanish homes blends with 19th-century French rococo, while art deco and art nouveau exteriors from the 1920s fuse into the cool, columned arcades of ancient palaces in *mudéjar* (Moorish) style. They were laid out along ruler-straight roads arranged in a grid pattern as decreed by the Laws of the Indies and usually intentionally narrow, conducive to shade.

Havana boasts block after block of intimate streets lined with balconied buildings that are lavish exemplars of their various periods and styles. The finest, most fully-realized examples are in Habana Vieja. But beyond the old city stretch mile after mile of colonial-era houses and belle époque mansions fronted by columns—as impressive in their heyday as those of Paris or London. The economic boom of the 19th century saw a blossoming of civic construction in neoclassical style and imposing dimension.

Many—if not most—are in a woefully sad state of repair. Thousands are teetering wrecks. Tens of thousands of others have already been lost to decay. But at least the Revolution didn't tear them down—to its credit, immediately following the Revolution, the new government canceled an existing plan for a sweeping urban renewal that would have leveled much of Habana Vieja. Thus, the city is covered with a veil of nostalgia of beautiful crumbling decadence.

The Colonial Home

The 17th-century home was made of limestone and modeled on the typical, fairly austere Spanish house, with the only elaboration being a simple portal and balconies with lathe-turned *rejas* (turned wooden rails). Cuba's colonial mansions—with their tall, generously proportioned rooms and shallow-stepped staircases—were usually built on two main floors (the lower floor for shops and warehouses, the upper floors for the family) with a mezzanine between them or an attic above for the house servants. By the 18th century, those houses that faced onto squares had adopted a portico and loggia (supported by arched columns) to provide shelter from sun and rain.

Colonial homes grew larger with ensuing decades and typically featured two small courtyards, with a dining area between the two, parallel to the street and with a central hallway, or *zaguán*, that opened directly from the street and was big enough for carriages. Arrayed around the ground floor courtyard were warehouses, offices, and other rooms devoted to the family business, with stables and servants' quarters to the rear, while the private family quarters were sequestered above around the galleried second story reached by a stately inner stairway. Commercial activity on the ground floor was relegated to those rooms (*dependencias*) facing the street—these were usually rented out to merchants. The arrangement—termed *obra cruzada* (transverse construction)—gave a formal character to the first patio, with laundry and other service functions relegated to the inner, second patio, or *traspatio*. Life centered on this inner courtyard, hidden behind massive wooden doors often flanked by pillars that in time developed ornate multifoil and ogee arches.

The formal layout of rooms on the ground floor was usually repeated on the main, upper story. Another design unique among Cuban cities (borrowed from Jerez and Cádiz) was the *entresuelo*, a kind of mezzanine of half-story proportions tucked between the two stories and used to house servants and slaves (and sometimes rented out).

By the 19th century, the wealthy were building summer homes in the hilly suburbs. These *quintas* were typical of neoclassical style, with extensive front porticos and gardens to the rear. Many, however, were influenced by the Palladian style, fashionable in Europe.

Throughout the colonial period, windows evolved as one of the most decorative elements. Ground floor windows were full-height from ground level and featured shutter doors to permit a free flow of air. The earliest homes were protected by wooden shutter panels. Later windows acquired ornate grilled wooden balusters, which often protruded where streets were sufficiently wide. In the 19th century, glass was introduced, though usually only for decoration in multicolored stained-glass panes inserted between or, more frequently, above the wooden panels, which were louvered to allow free flow of air. Meanwhile, ornate metal grills called *guardavecinos* were adopted for upper stories to divide balconies of contiguous properties and so prevent intrusion.

Religious Buildings

Religious buildings were among the first public buildings and were at first austere. As the 17th-century progressed they became lavishly ornamented with baroque decoration (notably in portals), though less brash and on a smaller scale than their equivalents in Spain. By the 18th century, "Retable-style" reached the full height of church facades, ending with scrolled ogee motifs that would in turn give way to a more restrained neoclassical look in the 19th century, when a triangular pediment typically crowned the portal. Convents were the largest structures and were influential in the adoption of the *mudéjar* style. Neo-gothic was predominant in the early 20th century, giving way to a modernist, even monumentalist, look by the 1940s, as with the Iglesia de San Antonio de Padua, which exemplifies a common feature of church building throughout four centuries: adoption of an austere facade and an adjoining campanile to the side.

A Glossary of Architectural Terms

Cuban structures were heavily influenced by traditional Spanish and *mudéjar* styles, and evolved quintessential Cuban features that included:

Alfarje: Pitched wooden roofs combining parallel and angled beams to create additional definition for interiors, providing a conceptual shift in emphasis to enhance the sense of space. Normally found in churches and smaller homes, they adopted a star pattern.

Antepecho: Ornamented window guards flush with the building facade.

Cenefa: Italianate bands of colored plasterwork used as decorative ornamentation on interior walls.

Entresuelo: Shallow mezzanine levels between ground and upper stories, usually housing slaves' living quarters.

Luceta: Long rectangular windows that run along the edges of doorways and windows. They usually contain stained or marbled glass.

Mampara: Double-swing half doors used in conjunction with a main door and that serve as room dividers or as partial outer doors to protect privacy while allowing ventilation. The *mampara* was described by 20th-century Cuban novelist Alejo Carpentier as "a door truncated to the height of a man, the real interior door of the Creole home for hundreds of years, creating a peculiar concept of family relations and communal living." Typically they contained colored or frosted glass.

Mediopuntos: Stained-glass windows (*vitrales*) in half-moon shape that fan out like peacock's tails, normally used above windows or doorways.

Patio: An open space in the center of Spanish buildings—a Spanish adaptation of the classic Moorish inner court—which permits air to circulate through the house. The patios of more grandiose buildings are surrounded by columned galleries.

(continued on next page)

HABANA VIEJA

CUBAN COLONIAL ARCHITECTURE (cont'd)

Persiana: Slatted shutters in tall, glassless windows, designed to let in the breezes while keeping out the harsh light and rain.

Portal: The main doorway to structures. Early *portales* were fairly simple but soon evolved to monumental proportions and featured elaborate stone molding on the lintel and bas-relief columns to each side.

Portico: Galleried exterior walkways fronting the mansions and protecting pedestrians from sun and rain. The grandest are supported by stone Tuscan columns and have vaulted ceilings and arches. Later, North American influences led to a more sober approach, with square wooden posts (à la the porch).

Postigo: Small doors set at face level into massive wooden doors of Spanish homes.

Reja: Wooden window screens of rippled, lathe-turned rods called *barrotes* that served to keep out burglars (later *rejas* were made of metal).

Vitrales: Windows of stained glass in geometric designs that diffuse the sunlight, saturating a room with shifting color.

century as the home of Governor Count Sotolongo. The hotel looks as if it's been magically transported from a Manchegan village and could have been used as a model by Cervantes for the inn where Don Quixote was dubbed a knight by the bewildered innkeeper. The *hostal* sets out to attract tourists with a liberal coating of green and white paint, various bits and pieces of armor, a handsome bar and courtyard, and a splendid restaurant looking onto Oficios through full-length *rejas* (turned wooden rails).

One block east of Hostal Valencia, is the similarly restored **Hostal El Comendador,** Calle Obrapía #55 e/ Baratillo y Oficios, also serving today as a *posada*-style hostelry. To its rear, and entered by a wrought-iron archway topped by a most-uncommunist fairytale crown, is the **Jardín Diana de Gales,** Calle Baratillo, esq. Carpinetti, unveiled in 2000 as a park to the memory of Diana, Princess of Wales. "A ten-foot, entirely phallic column with, to the side of it and much smaller, a vaginal sun," thought Isadora Tattlin, who attended the dedication and to whom a Latin American journalist whispered breathily in her ear: "the column must be the monument to Dodi Fayed." The column is by acclaimed Cuban artist, Alfredo Sosabravo. There's also an engraved Welsh slate and stone plaque from Althorp, Diana's childhood home, donated by the British Embassy. Cubans admired Princess Diana

for her charitable work—the Cuban government even printed commemorative stamps of Diana. Open daily 9 A.M.–6 P.M.

The garden backs onto the **Casa de los Esclavos,** Calle Obrapía, esq. Avenida del Puerto, where slaves were once landed inside a slave-merchant's home. At last visit it was being restored to house the **Museo de Esclavitud** (Museum of Slavery).

PLAZA DE SAN FRANCISCO

The cobbled Plaza de San Francisco, at Oficios and the foot of Amargura, faces onto Avenida del Puerto and the inner shore of Havana harbor, of which it was once an inlet. During the 16th century, long before the Franciscan convent and church were built here, the area was the great waterfront of the early colonial city. Iberian emigrants disembarked with their dreams, slaves were unloaded, and galleons, their holds groaning with treasure, were replenished with water and victuals for the passage to Spain. A market developed on the plaza, which became the focus of the annual Fiesta de San Francisco each October 3, when a gambling fair was established. In the 17th century, the Customs house and prison were built here, while nobles built their homes on surrounding streets. The plaza has been fully restored, including the cobbles.

© CHRISTOPHER P. BAKER

Fuente de los Leones and Iglesia de San Francisco de Asís

At its heart is a beautiful fountain, **Fuente de los Leones** (Fountain of the Lions), sculpted by Giuseppe Gaggini, erected in 1836, and though moved to different locations at various times, finally ensconced where it began life. The muscular five-story neoclassical building on the north side is the **Lonja del Comercio** (the "Goods Exchange"), Calle Amargura #2, esq. Oficios, tel. 866-9588, dating from 1907, when it was built as a center for trading in food commodities. Duly restored—the shell is original, but the interior is state-of-the-art futuristic (albeit poorly engineered and constructed)—it houses offices of international corporations, news bureaus, and tour companies. Note the beautiful dome, crowned by a bronze figure of the god Mercury. Visitors need to report to security, on the right of the entrance; no cameras or bags are allowed. Open daily 9 A.M.–6 P.M.

Across the way, on the harbor front where Spanish galleons once tethered, the **Terminal Sierra Maestra** cruise terminal faces onto the plaza. It's a fantastic location—imagine arriving by sea. No other cruise terminal in the world opens so immediately onto the heart of such an incredible colonial city. It extends south, where most of the structure is occupied by the headquarters of the **Aduana,** Cuban Customs. Note the rainbow-colored mural of Che Guevara on the wall.

Iglesia y Convento de San Francisco de Asís

Dominating the plaza on the south side is this great church, Calle Oficios e/ Armagura y Brasil, tel. 862-9683, whose construction was launched in 1719. It began humbly but was reconstructed in 1730 in baroque style with a 40-meter bell tower—one of the tallest in all the Americas—crowned by St. Helen holding a sacred Cross of Jerusalem. The church was eventually proclaimed a Minorite Basilica, and it was from its chapel that the processions of the *Vía Crucis* (Procession of the Cross) departed every Lenten Friday, ending at the Iglesia del Santo Cristo del Buen Viaje. The devout passed down Calle Amargura (Street of Bitterness), where Stations of the Cross were set up at street corners and decorated with crucifixes and altars. You can still see the first of the stations—**Casa de la Cruz Verde**—at the corner of Calles Amargura and Mercaderes; it's shaded beneath the eaves, above the *mudéjar*-style balcony.

The Protestant English used the church briefly for worship during their tenure in Havana in 1762; the Catholics refused thereafter to use the Iglesia de San Francisco de Asís again as a church.

The church and adjoining convent were reopened in October 1994 after a complete restoration. The main nave, with its towering roof supported by 12 columns, each topped by an apostle, looks as if it will stand for another 500 years. A marvelous trompe l'oeil extends the perspective of the nave. Alas, the sumptuously adorned altars are gone, replaced by a huge crucifix suspended above a grand piano. Note the Tiffany grandfather clock dating from the 1820s

HABANA VIEJA

EL CABALLERO DE PARIS

Following the Revolution, begging was banned. Most tramps and the mentally retarded who lived on the streets were cared for by the state and, where possible, given new possibilities to be productive members of the community. Yet one man was allowed to continue to roam as a vagabond. He was called El Caballero de Paris (the Gentleman of Paris). The entire city knew and felt affection for the shabby old man with his long white hair and beard and black threadbare cape.

The man, José María Lípez Lledin, was born in 1899 in Vilaseca, into Spanish nobility. Legend says that he was imprisoned for murder and that the experience affected his mind. Throughout the 1950s and '60s he ambled the streets discussing philosophy, delivering eloquent speeches, and handing out colored cards and candy to children. He believed that he lived in a castle and often talked to fellow *habaneros* in medieval lingo befitting Don Quixote. He attained legendary status and even appeared on TV. Eventually, in 1977, he was institutionalized and died in 1985 in a psychiatric ward.

on the far right. On the left side, inset into the walls, are the morbid remains of Teodoro—a Franciscan brother of high regard—pickled in glass jars next to a statue of St. Francis. Members of the most aristocratic families of the times were buried in the crypt, which includes the body of Capitan Don Luís del Velasco, heroic defender of the Castillo de los Tres Reyes de Morro, who fell in battle during the British attack on Havana in 1762. You may peer into the crypts through a glass window in the terra-cotta tile floor, and even climb the 125-foot-tall campanile for a bird's-eye view over Habana Vieja.

The nave opens to the right onto the cloisters of a convent, to which the church belonged (it had 111 cells for members of the religious community). Today it contains the **Museo de Arte Religioso,** featuring fabulous silverwork, porcelain, and other treasures of the Spanish epoch, including a room full of ornately gilded hymnals of silver and even mother-of-pearl displayed in glass cases. Recent additions are the lectern and armchairs used by Fidel and the Pope during the latter's visit in 1998. In the late 1840s, the liberal government expropriated and secularized the property, which became a Customs office, a post office, and, in this century, a warehouse. A music school occupies part of the building.

The church and museum are open daily 9 A.M.–6:30 P.M. Entrance costs US$1, plus US$1

extra for the campanile and US$1 for a guide (cameras cost US$2 extra; videos cost US$10).

The cathedral has metamorphosed into one of Havana's most important concert halls; the music program is posted in the entrance. Performances (usually classical) are given each Saturday at 6 P.M. and Sunday at 11 A.M. (except July and August).

A life-size bronze statue of an erstwhile and once-renowned tramp, **El Caballero de Paris** (see the Special Topic of the same name), by José Villa Soberón, graces the sidewalk in front of the cathedral entrance.

On the east side of the church, on Avenida del Puerto but accessed only through the church is the **Jardín de Madre Teresa de Calcuta,** a small garden dedicated to Mother Theresa, who visited Cuba several times.

South of the Plaza

Calle Oficios runs south from the plaza and is lined with 17th-century colonial buildings that possess a marked *mudéjar* style, exemplified by their wooden balconies. The entire block has been magnificently restored and many of the buildings converted into art galleries. One of the gems is the pink and green **Galería de Carmen Montilla Tinoco,** Calle Oficios #162, tel. 833-8768. Only the front of the house remains, but the architects have made creative use of the empty shell. Through the breezy doorway, you can catch sight of a fabulous 3-D mural by famous Cuban artist Alfredo Sosabravo at the back of an open-air sculpture garden. Art is portrayed in the two-level art gallery. Open Mon.–Sat. 9 A.M.–5 P.M.

Similarly impressive works are displayed next door at the **Estudio Galería Los Oficios,** Calle Oficios #166, tel. 863-0497, offering revolving art exhibitions; open Mon.–Sat. 9:30 A.M.–5 P.M. Entry is free.

About 20 yards south, and around the corner, is the **Aquarium,** Calle Brasil (Teniente Rey) #9, tel. 863-9493, acuavieja@cultural.ohch.cu, displaying tropical freshwater fish in fish tanks. Children's events are hosted each second Wednesday of the month; video screenings each third Wednesday; and lectures each fourth Wednesday. Open Tues.–Sat. 9 A.M.–5 P.M. and Sun. 9 A.M.–1 P.M. Entrance costs US$1 (children free).

The **Coche Presidencial Mambí** railway carriage stands on rails at Oficios and Churruca (a narrow lane connecting Oficios with Avenida San Pedro), on the south side of the convent. It served as the official presidential carriage of five presidents, beginning in 1902 with Tomás Estrada Palma and including Fulgencio Batista. Fidel even used the train shortly after the Revolution. Its polished hardwood interior gleams with brass fittings. Nonetheless, you may be surprised by how simple and confined it is. You enter via the Salón de Protocolo and are given a guided tour of the four bedrooms (including blue and pink "his" and "hers"), five bathrooms, and cramped dining room and kitchen. Entrance costs US$1.

Two blocks south of the plaza de San Francisco is the **Antigua Cámara de Representantes,** Calle Oficios #211, tel. 862-4076, at the corner of Muralla, immediately south of Churruca. This 19th-century building was built to house the Chamber of Representatives during the early Republic, before the Capitolio was built. Later it served as the Ministerio de Educación (1929–60) and following the Revolution it housed the **Asamblea Provincial Poder Popular** (Havana's local government office). The interior lobby is striking for its ornate baroque and neoclassical stucco work, including a magnificent stained-glass skylight. At last visit it was in the final stage of renovation and was preparing to house a concert hall and **Museo de Campaña de Alfabetización** (Museum of the Literacy Campaign). Open Tues.–Sat. 9 A.M.–5 P.M., and Sun. 9 A.M.–noon.

Cater-corner to the Asemblea, on the southeast side of Oficios and Muralla, is **Casa Alejandro Von Humboldt,** Calle Oficios #254, tel. 863-9850, where the famous German explorer (1769–1854) lived and made his botanic and mineral investigations of Cuba during his travels in 1800–01. The restored building is now a museum dedicated to the scientist, and features botanical specimens and prints, navigational instruments such as sextants, exhibits on slavery, and tracts from Humboldt's books. Open Tues.–Sat. 9 A.M.–5 P.M. and Sun. 9 A.M.–noon. Entrance costs US$1.

Muralla extends east beneath an arch to the Museo de Ron (described in the section The Southern Margins later in this chapter).

CALLES MERCADERES

Intimate Calle Mercaderes links Plaza de Armas with Plaza Vieja, four blocks south. Now restored to grandeur, it brims with handsome buildings and museums of interest.

Between Calles Obispo and Obrapía

The block immediately south of Calle Obispo and the Hotel Ambos Mundos includes the **Maqueta de la Habana Vieja,** Calle Mercaderes #114. This model features a 1:500 scale model of Habana Vieja measuring eight by four meters, with buildings color coded by use, and accurate to the ventilator ducts on the roofs. It's housed in a darkened room with floodlights illuminating the model. Guides give a spiel. This is a *must visit.* Don't confuse it with the Maqueta de La Habana, in Miramar. It's open daily 9 A.M.–6 P.M. Entrance costs US$1 (plus US$1 for the guide; US$3 for a camera, and US$10 for videos).

Across the way is the **Museo de Asia,** Calle Mercaderes #111, tel. 863-9740, which downstairs seems unimpressive, holding a few inlaid bowls, rugs, musical instruments, and a marble model of the Taj Mahal. The best rooms are upstairs, containing an astonishing array of carved ivory, silverware, mother-of-pearl furniture,

WHAT'S IN A NAME

Many important street names in Habana Vieja betray a feature of historical note. For example, the ecclesiastics who strolled down Calle Obispo gave it its name: Bishop Street. Similarly, Calle Inquisidor was named for the member of the Spanish Inquisition who lived here; and Calle Mercaderes is named for the merchants who inhabited the street. Calle Empedrado means "cobbled," and is so named because it was the first paved street in the city. Calle Lamparilla means "small lamp," as the first street lamps in the city went up along here. Likewise, Calle Tejadillo is named for the tiles that graced its facades, another first in Havana; and Calle Aguacate (avocado) is named for the avocado tree that grew in the Belén convent.

scimitars, kukris, and other Oriental armaments, plus exquisite kimonos. Most of the collection comprises gifts to Fidel from Asian nations. The foyer features an engraved rock—a gift from the citizens of Hiroshima. The museum also includes a small bonsai garden, and one of the rooms downstairs doubles as a classroom, reminding visitors of the success of Cuba's education program. Open Tues.–Sat. 9 A.M.–5 P.M., Sun. 9 A.M.–1 P.M. Entry costs US$1 (plus US$2 for a camera, US$10 for video).

Next door is **Tienda de las Navegantes,** Mercaderes #117, a beautiful wood- and glass-fronted building featuring a ship's wheel inlaid with a copper galleon above the door. This incongruously positioned store sells maps and nautical charts, including a broad selection of road and city maps.

On the west side, 20 yards further south, are the **Casa de Puerto Rico** and Casa del Tabaco, both at Mercaderes #120. Besides a fine stock of cigars, the latter houses the **Museo del Tabaco** (Cigar Museum), tel. 861-5795, upstairs. The first room, part of which is decorated as a typical middle-class sitting room, with rocking chairs and a cigar displayed on a silver ashtray, contains a collection of lithographs from cigar-box covers. Other exhibits include pipes and lighters from around

the world. Look out for the silver cigar box engraved with the words: "To my godfather Dr. Fidel Castro Ruz from Fidel Charles Getto, August 9, 1959." Open Tues.–Sat. 10 A.M.–5:30 P.M., Sun. 9 A.M.–1 P.M.; no entrance charge.

At the end of the block, at the corner of Obrapía, the pink building with a wraparound wrought-iron balustrade and Mexican flag fluttering above the doorway is the **Casa de Benito Juárez** (also called Casa de México), Calle Mercaderes #116, tel. 861-8166, housing the Sociedad Cubana Mexicana de Relaciones Culturales and displaying artwork and costumes from different Mexican states. A highlight is the collection of priceless Aztec jewelry. Open Tues.–Sat. 10 A.M.–5 P.M., Sun. 9:30 A.M.–12:30 P.M. (Tues.–Sat. 9 A.M.–2 P.M. only in summer). Entrance costs US$1.

Calle Obrapía

The two blocks of Calle Obrapía east and west of Mercaderes, between Oficios and San Ignacio, contain several beautifully restored buildings of historic appeal. The street is named for the *obra pía* (pious act) of Don Martín Calvo de la Puerta, who devoted a portion of his wealth to sponsoring five orphan girls every year.

West of Mercaderes: The most important building is the **Casa de la Obra Pía,** Obrapía #158, tel. 861-3097. This splendid mansion with lemon-meringue-yellow walls on the northwest corner of Obrapía and Mercaderes was built in 1665 by Capitán Martín Calvo de la Puerta y Arrieta, the Cuban solicitor general. The Calvo de la Puerta family—one of the most important families in Cuba in early colonial days—built additions in baroque style, such as voluptuous moldings and dimpled cherubs, as late as 1793. The *casa* comprises two adjacent houses that were later combined and together are one of the finest examples of classical colonial form and layout. Visitors can see the family coat of arms, surrounded by exuberant baroque stonework, emblazoned above the massive, regal *portal* that was brought from Cádiz in 1686. As much as any house in Habana Vieja, Casa de la Obra Pía exemplifies the Spanish adaptation of a Moorish inner courtyard, with a serene, scented coolness illuminated by daylight filtering through *mediop-untos* fanning out like a peacock's tail. It features a permanent exhibition of works by Alejo Carpentier in the foyer (including, rather incongruously, his blue Volkswagen brought back from Paris after his tenure as Cuban ambassador to UNESCO); other rooms contain miscellaneous art. Open Tues.–Sat. 9 A.M.–5 P.M. and Sun. 9 A.M.–1 P.M. (Tues.–Sat. 8:30 A.M.–2:30 P.M. only in summer); entrance US$1.

Across the way is the **Casa de África,** Obrapía #157 e/ Mercaderes y San Ignacio, tel. 861-5798. When flung open wide, its large wooden doors reveal breezy courtyards full of African artwork and artifacts, masks, and cloth. On the third floor, you'll find a collection of paraphernalia used in *santería,* including statues of the leading deities in the Yoruban pantheon, dancing costumes of the Abakuá, and *otanes* (stones) in which the *orishas* (the gods of *santería*) are said to reside. Much of the collection was contributed by various African embassies in Havana. Open Tues.–Sat. 9:30 A.M.–4:30 P.M., Sun. 9:30 A.M.–12:30 P.M. Entrance costs US$2. It was closed for renovation at last visit.

One block farther west, the **Casa de Gaspar Riveros de Vasoncelos,** esq. Calle San Ignacio, is esteemed for its corner balcony with delicately curved balustrades. Though restored in 1985, it is not open to the public. Here, too, is the **Estudio-Galería Yanes,** 862-6195, in the former Casa Quitrín, exhibiting portraits by Orlando Hernández Yanes. Open Tues.–Sat. 10 A.M.–5 P.M. and Sun. 9 A.M.–1 P.M..

East of Mercaderes: Between Mercaderes and Oficios is the **Casa de Oswaldo Guayasamín,** Obrapía #112, tel. 861-3843, housing a museum of plastic arts and photographs from Ecuador, with changing exhibitions of art from other Latin American countries. Guayasamín, a famous Ecuadorian painter called the "Artist of the Americas," lived and worked here for many years; you can see his works—many being portraits of Fidel—on the upper story, where his living quarters are displayed as he left them on his death in 1999. This floor also features 18th-century murals by Cubans José Nicolás de la Escalera and José Andrés Sánchez.

A huge dugout canoe sits in the entrance lobby. Open Tues.–Sat. 9:30 A.M.–4:30 P.M., Sun. 9 A.M.–12:30 P.M. Entrance is free. It was closed for restoration at last visit.

Immediately east is the **Casa de los Abanicos,** where traditional Spanish fans (*abanicos*) are still hand-made and painted. Visitors are welcome. The reception area sells the fans (from US$1.40 to US$144). It's open Monday–Friday 9 A.M.–5 P.M. and Saturday 9 A.M.–2 P.M.

Between Calle Obrapía and Plaza Vieja

Half a block south of Obrapía is **Casa-Museo del Libertador Simón Bolívar,** Mercaderes #160, tel. 861-3988, displaying cultural works and art from Venezuela. The collection includes portraits of the "Great Liberator," ceremonial swords, and coins minted in his honor, plus paintings (unrelated to Bolívar) by contemporary Venezuelan and Cuban artists. The "Great Liberator" stayed here in March 1799; the museum was opened in 1993 to celebrate the 210th year of his birth. Open Tues.–Sat. 9 A.M.–5 P.M. and Sun. 9 A.M.–1 P.M. Entrance costs US$1.

The house faces a tiny landscaped *plazuela* containing a larger-than-life bronze statue of Simón Bolívar atop a marble pedestal. It has a mural by Venezuelan artist Carmen Montilla behind.

Across the street is **Terracota 4,** Calle Mercaderes #156, tel. 866-0417, an *expo-venta* of ceramists Amelia Carballo, Ángel Norniella, and José Ramón González. Open Mon.–Fri. 9 A.M.–5 P.M.

Next door is **Armería 19 de Abril,** Mercaderes #157, tel. 861-8080, no longer a museum (the collection is now incorporated into the Museo de la Revolución) but important in contemporary history. Here four members of Castro's 26th July Movement were killed in an assault on the armory on April 9, 1958. A sign outside reads, "Armaments Company of Cuba, hunting supplies and explosives." The company was a subsidiary of DuPont, the U.S. munitions giant.

Opposite, the building on the northwest corner of the junction of Mercaderes and Lamparilla is recent. The original building was destroyed on May 17, 1890 in a fire that killed 28 volunteer firemen and numerous bystanders

RESTORING OLD HAVANA

Old Havana has been called the "finest urban ensemble in the Americas." The fortress colonial town that burst its walls when Washington, D.C., was still a swamp is a 350-acre repository of antique buildings in an astounding amalgam of styles. More than 900 of Habana Vieja's 3,157 structures are of historic importance. Of these, only 101 were built in the 20th century. Almost 500 are from the 19th; 200 are from the 18th; and 144 are from the 16th and 17th. But only one in six buildings is in good condition. Many are crumbling into ruins around the people who occupy them. Permitting this precious treasure to disintegrate would be more costly to the world's cultural heritage than the phenomenal cost of restoration, like letting Venice sink into its lagoon.

In 1977, the Cuban government named Habana Vieja a National Monument. Cuba formalized a plan to rescue the city from centuries of neglect under the guidance of Eusebio Leal Spengler, the charismatic official city historian, who runs the **Oficina del Historiador de la Ciudad de la Habana,** www.ohch.cu, and has been granted the kind of autonomy reserved only for top-ranking officials. Leal, who grew up in Habana Vieja, is a member of Cuba's National Assembly and both the Central Committee of the Communist Party and all-important Council of State. Thanks to his efforts, in 1982, UNESCO's Inter-Governmental Committee for World Cultural and Natural Protection named Habana Vieja a World Heritage Site worthy of international protection.

The ambitious plan stretches into the future and concentrated initially on five squares: Plaza de Armas, Plaza de la Catedral, Plaza Vieja, Plaza de San Francisco, and Plaza del Cristo. The most important buildings have received major renovations; others have been given facelifts—symbols of triumph over horrendous shortages of materials and money. As more and more buildings have been restored, international support has been garnered, easing the cash burden.

To satisfy a mix of needs, structures are ranked into one of four levels according to historical and physical value. The top level is reserved for museums; the second level for hotels, restaurants, offices, and schools; and the bottom levels for housing. Priority is given to edifices with income-generating tourist value, usually the oldest buildings. Havana contains as many art deco buildings as Miami (perhaps even more), plus countless art nouveau houses.

To its credit, the government granted Leal responsibility for both tourism and conservation. Leal selects sites for renovation, supervises the construction teams, and chooses the hotels and restaurants that will occupy the restored buildings. Hence, wisely and perhaps uniquely, restoration is being run as a self-financing business. A government-run company, **Habaguanex,** Calle Oficios #110, Plaza de San Francisco, tel. 67-1039, fax 60-9761, gerencia.comercial@ habaguanex.ohch.cu, www.habaguanex.cu, has responsibility for opening and operating com-

when explosives that were hidden in the store detonated. The accident was the worst in Havana's firefighting history and the cause of the largest funeral of the 19th century. A mausoleum to the firefighters can be seen in the Cementerio Colón, in Vedado.

The beautifully restored building on the southwest corner is the **Hostal del Conde de Villanueva,** today a hotel in the former colonial mansion of the Count of Villanueva. It faces a small plaza, **Parque Rumiñahui,** with a sculpture

of the Indian Rumiñahui gifted to Fidel by Ecuadorean artist Oswaldo Guayasamin.

One block south, the corner of Mercaderes and Amargura is known as the *Cruz Verde*— green cross—as it was the first stop on the annual *Vía Crucis* pilgrimage.

PLAZA VIEJA AND VICINITY

The last of the four main squares to be laid out in Habana Vieja is Plaza Vieja, the old commercial entities such as hotels, restaurants, cafés, and shops in Habana Vieja. The profits help finance further infrastructural improvements throughout Habana Vieja and elsewhere in the city; 33 percent of revenues are devoted to social projects. Habaguanex, which now employs 4,000 people, earned US$70 million revenue in 2001 and reinvested $21 million in more restoration. Not every palace ends up converted for tourist use, however; some become schools, for example, while others have had their interiors restored as modern, albeit modest, living quarters for the original occupants. One restored 18th-century mansion is now a pediatric rehabilitation center.

Leal—a slight, precise man, who is easily identified by his trademark well-tailored gray cotton suit—was criticized at an early stage for prettifying Habana Vieja with little concern for its inhabitants. He took the criticism to heart and, determined to avoid making the old city merely a quaint stage set for tourists, added a sociologist to the restoration teams to work with those people who have been moved from their homes. Leal wants to avoid gentrification. Explains Nancy Stout: "Leal still wants people to be able to hang out their laundry. He doesn't want to be criticized for gilding rotten lilies." Where do the relocated residents go? Well, for example, Leal has set up a little community—Comunidad Provisoria Plaza Vieja—of plastic houses (imported from Canada) on a *plazuela* on Calle Muralla, half a block southwest of Plaza Vieja, to temporarily house displaced residents. And the community-oriented rehabilitation of San Isidro, in southern Habana Vieja, points to a genuine attempt to save entire neighborhoods. In time, the entirety of Habana Vieja will be restored, although for hundreds of buildings it is already too late. Because of overcrowding, some 30,000 long-time residents will be moved out for good. (Many occupants have already been moved to new apartments in Alamar, the sprawling and monstrous housing project east of the city; alas, the majority of those who've been moved complain about having been transferred from ancient slum quarters to what many consider a modern and soulless slum). Rehabbed buildings that once housed dozens of people in crowded conditions now have roomier apartments for fewer families.

It's an awesome task. In southern Habana Vieja, where there are relatively few structures of touristic interest, far more houses are collapsing than are being restored. As of 2002, the restoration had expanded along the Malecón.

The Bridge for Historic Preservation, 1206 Amberwood Blvd., Kissimmee, FL 34741, 407/847-7892, fax 407/847-2986, www.connect2cuba.org, is a Cuban-American nonprofit organization that exists to assist in Havana's restoration efforts. It offers study tours and requests donations.

mercial square (bounded by Calles Mercaderes, San Ignacio, Brasil, and Muralla), surrounded by mansions and apartment blocks from where residents could look down on processions, executions, bullfights, and wild fiestas. The plaza originally hosted a covered market where peasants and free *negros* sold all manner of produce. At its center sat a stone fountain, with a wide bowl and four dolphins that gushed "intermittent streams of thick, muddy liquid which Negro water vendors eagerly collected in barrels to be sold throughout the city," wrote Cirilo Villaverde in *Cecilia Valdés.*

Lamentably, President Machado built an underground car park here in the 1930s, and the cobbles and fountain fell afoul of the wrecking ball. Time and neglect brought near ruin this century, and many of the square's beautiful buildings sank into a sorry state of disrepair. Fortunately, Eusebio Leal and his maestros have waved a magic wand over the plaza, which at last visit was in the final stages of being restored. Even

© CHRISOPHER P. BAKER

Plaza Vieja

HABANA VIEJA

the white Carrara marble **fountain**—an exact replica of the original by Italian sculptor Giorgio Massari—has reappeared, now gurgling clear water. Renowned for its acoustics, the square is often used for concerts.

The upper stories of many buildings still house tenement apartments.

North Side of Plaza Vieja

The 18th-century Antiguo Colegio Santo Ángel, occupying the northwest side of the square, at San Ignacio and Brasil, was recently restored and is now the **Apartotel Santo Ángel,** with a fine restaurant. An elementary school occupies the newly restored building next door.

Taberna Benny Moré, Calles Mercaderes y Brasil, on the northeast corner, is an upscale and bohemian bar-restaurant, with walls festooned with the personal effects of Cuban's renowned singer-composer, for whom the bar is named.

East Side of Plaza Vieja

The **Edificio Gómez Villa,** on the northeast corner, is the tallest building in the square. Take the elevator to the top floor for views over the plaza and to visit the **Cámara Oscura,** an optical reflection camera (first devised by Aristotle) that revolves through 360 degrees and projects a real-time picture of Havana at 30-times magnification onto a two-meter-wide parabola housed in a completely darkened room. Guides give an intriguing overview of Havana. It's a marvelous intro to the city, with virtually every building of import profiled. *Habaneros* can be seen hanging out laundry and who knows what else. Open daily 9 A.M.–4:45 P.M. Entrance costs US$1.

The **Casa de Juan Rico de Mata,** Calle Mercaderes #307, in the middle of the block, is today the headquarters of **Fototeca,** tel. 862-2530, the state-run agency that promotes the work of Cuban photographers and offers international photo exhibitions in the Salón Nacional de Fotografía. Open Tues.–Sat. 10 A.M.–5 P.M. Note the ceramic wall mural designed by Amelia Peláez.

The old **Palacio Vienna Hotel** (also called the Palacio Cueto), on the southeast corner of Plaza Viejo, is a phenomenal piece of Gaudiesque art nouveau architecture dating from 1906. The frontage is awash in surf-like waves and ballooning balconies. It is scheduled for renovation and will reopen as a deluxe hotel.

South Side of Plaza Vieja

The most important building on the square is the **Casa de los Condes de Jaruco,** Calle Muralla #107, a restored 18th-century mansion highlighted by mammoth doors opening into a cavernous entrance hall. It was built between 1733 and 1737 by the father of the future Count of Jaruco, who gave the building its name. Today it houses several *galerías* and boutiques under the umbrella of the **Fondo Cubano de Bienes Culturales** (BFC, or Cuban Cultural Foundation), tel. 862-3577, the organization responsible for the sale of Cuban art. The BFC headquarters is upstairs, in rooms off the balcony. Whimsical murals are painted on the walls, touched in splashy color by the undulating play of light through *mediopuntos* and by the shifting of shadows through *rejas*. Upstairs, various *expo-venta* galleries sell an eclectic range of creative arts and crafts. The downstairs is occupied by three galleries, including the **Galería Pequeño Formato,** that open to a courtyard surrounded by lofty archways festooned with hanging vines. Open Mon.–Fri. 10 A.M.–5 P.M., Sat. 10 A.M.–2 P.M. Entrance is free.

The **Casa de Marqués de Prado Amero,** on the southeast corner today houses the **Museo de Naipes** (Museum of Playing Cards), Calle Muralla #101, tel. 860-1534. This intriguing museum displays playing cards through the ages. Most are Spanish. The oldest (dating from 1775) is French. My favorite is a collection of cards showing caricatures of famous actors, with Sean Connery as the Ace of Spades, Robin Williams shown in bra and panties, and Woody Allen squeezed between 40DD breasts. Open Tues.–Sat. 9 A.M.–2:30 P.M., and Sun. 9 A.M.–1 P.M. Entrance is free.

West Side of Plaza Vieja

On the northwest corner is the **Casa de las Hermanas Cárdenas,** Calle San Ignacio #352, recently restored with faux brickwork and marble. The building is named for two sisters, María Loreto and María Ignacia Cárdenas, who lived here in the late 18th century. Later it became the site of the Havana philharmonic society. Today it houses the **Centro de Desarollo de Artes Visuales,** tel. 862-3533 or 862-2611.

Through the towering doors, immediately on the left, is a craft workshop where young women can be seen making cloth dolls and naïve animals gaudily painted in the pointillist fashion now common throughout the Caribbean. The inner courtyard is dominated by an intriguing sculpture—a kind of futuristic skyscraper in miniature—crafted by Alfredo Sosabravo. Art education classes are given on the second floor, reached via a wide wooden staircase that leads to the top story, where you'll find an art gallery in a wonderfully airy loft. If the tiny yellow door is locked, ask for the key downstairs. Open Tues.–Sat. 10 A.M.–5 P.M.

Next door is the **Casa del Conde de San Esteban de Cañongo,** at San Ignacio #356. This somewhat forlorn former mansion of a nobleman was awaiting restoration at last visit. Adjoining to the south, the newly restored **Casa del Conde de Casa Lombillo,** San Ignacio #364, is adorned with small frescoes and today is an office of Eusebio Leal, the Official City Historian.

Vicinity of Plaza Vieja

Physicians and scientists inclined to a busman's holiday might walk one block west and one north of the plaza and check out the impressive **Museo Histórico de las Ciencias Naturales Carlos Finlay** (Museum of Natural History), Cuba #460, e/ Amargura y Brasil, tel. 863-4824. The building, which dates from 1868, once served as the headquarters of the Academy of Medical, Physical, and Natural Sciences. Today it contains a pharmaceutical collection and tells the tales of various Cuban scientists' discoveries and innovations. The Cuban scientist Dr. Finlay is honored, of course; it was he who on August 14, 1881 discovered that yellow fever is transmitted by the *Aedes aegipti* mosquito. The museum also contains a medical library of 95,000 volumes and, on the third floor, a reconstructed period pharmacy. Albert Einstein spoke here in 1930. It has a rooftop bar with a good view of the harbor. Open Mon.–Fri. 8:30 A.M.–5 P.M., Sat. 9 A.M.–3 P.M. Entrance is US$2.

Immediately north of the museum is the **Convento y Iglesia de San Francisco el Nuevo,** Calle Cuba, esq. Amargura, tel. 861-8490, completed in

1633 for the Augustine friars. Unlike other churches in Havana, this one bears the influence of the Augustine monks who came to Cuba from Mexico, imbuing their own style with rich Mexican murals. The curves and countercurves of the undulating pinion facade likewise are of Mexican influence. It was consecrated anew in 1842 when it was given to the Franciscans after they lost their tenure at the Iglesia de San Francis de Asís in the eponymous square; hence its name. The church, which has a marvelous domed altar and nave, has been much altered since 1633 and was rebuilt in renaissance style in 1847. It boasts a fine organ and six altars. Open Mon.–Thurs. 9 A.M.–6 P.M. and Sun. 8 A.M.–1 P.M. (Mass is at 10 A.M.). Entrance is free.

One block south is the **Talle de Serigrafía René Portocarrero,** Calle Cuba, a silkscreen workshop where beautiful hand-crafted items are sold.

The Ecclesiastical Core

Southern Habana Vieja is worth visiting for its enclave of important 18th-century ecclesiastical buildings, found throughout the region.

PLAZA DEL CRISTO AND VICINITY

Plaza del Cristo, which still awaits restoration, lies at the west end of Amargura, between Lamparilla and Brasil, two blocks east of Avenida de Bélgica (Monserrate). During the 19th century, the square was named for "the washerwomen," a lively and colorful clique of black women who washed others' clothes for a living and congregated here to seek custom from the wealthy merchants leaving the church after Mass. It was here that Wormold, the vacuum-cleaner salesman turned secret agent, was "swallowed up among the pimps and lottery sellers of the Havana noon" in Graham Greene's *Our Man in Havana.* Wormold and his wayward daughter Millie lived at 37 Lamparilla. Alas, the house was fictional.

The plaza is dominated by the tiny, utterly charming **Iglesia de Santo Cristo Buen Viaje,** Calle Villegas e/ Amargura y Lamparilla, 863-1767. This church is one of Havana's oldest, dating from 1732, but with a Franciscan hermitage—called Humilladero chapel—dating from 1640. Buen Viaje was the final point of the *Vía Crucis* (the Procession of the Cross) held each Lenten Friday and beginning at the Iglesia de San Francisco de Asís. The church is in a splendid state of repair and has an impressive cross-beamed wooden ceiling and stained-glass windows. It was named for its popularity among sailors and travelers, who used to pray in it for safe voyages. It contains several exquisite altars, including one to the Virgen de la Caridad del Cobre showing the three boatsmen being saved from the tempest. Open daily 9 A.M.–noon.

Restaurante Hanoi, Calle Brasil, esq. Bernanza, tel. 867-1029, at the southwest corner of the square, is one of the oldest houses in Havana and is colloquially known as La Casa de la Parre (Grapevine House) for the luxuriant grapevine growing in the patio.

Two blocks east of Plaza del Cristo is the handsome **Iglesia y Convento de Santa Teresa de Jesús,** Calle Brasil, esq. Compostela, the third of Havana's monasteries. Built by the Carmelites in 1705, the separate church and convent each has an outstanding baroque doorway. The church has ever since performed its original function, although the convent ceased to operate as such in 1929, when the nuns were moved out and the building was converted into a series of homes. Call in on Saturday afternoon, when Afro-Cuban music and dance is hosted in the courtyard.

Across the road is the **Drogería Sarrá,** Calle Brasil, e/ Compostela y Habana, tel. 861-0969, a historic pharmacy still doing duty as a Farmacia Roturno Permanente that during the last century had its own laboratory at the rear. Its magnificently carved wooden shelves and patterned ceiling seem more fitting as the altarwork for the church across the way. The paneled shelves bear painted glass murals and are stocked with herbs and pharmaceuticals in colorful old bottles

RECOMMENDED WALKING TOUR 4

From Parque Central, head east one block to Plazuela de Albear and turn south, passing El Floridita (which we'll save for later). Follow Monserrate for six blocks or so (it becomes Egido en route) to the Agropecuario Egido, the farmers market. Continue south to the Estación Central de Ferrocarril (the main railway station), calling in to see the oldest steam train in Cuba (1843) displayed in the lobby; and, facing the station, Casa Natal de José Martí (Martí's birthplace).

Continue down Egido past the Cortina de las Murallas, the remains of the old city walls, and turn left onto Desamparados for the Iglesia de San Francisco de Paula (be careful crossing the street here). Then head west up Leonor Pérez one block to Iglesia y Convento de Nuestra Señora de la Merced, on Cuba.

Continue north on Cuba one block to Iglesia Parroquial del Espíritu Santo, and thence two blocks to the Convento y Iglesia de Santa Clara. Calle Luz then takes you west two blocks to the Iglesia y Convento de Belén, from where you'll turn north along Compostela three blocks to the Iglesia y Convento de Santa Teresa.

From here, follow Brasil (Teniente Rey) west three blocks to the Plaza del Cristo. Return to Monserrate (one block west on Brasil) and turn right.

End your walk at El Floridita with a well-earned daiquirí.

light. The convent was built to house the first nuns who arrived in Havana in 1704. Construction took from 1712 to 1718. The first baroque religious structure erected in Havana, it served as a refuge for poor convalescents under the tenure of Bishop Compostela. In 1842, Spanish authorities ejected the religious order—the Order of Bethlehem—and turned the church briefly into a government office before making it over to the Jesuits. They in turn established a college for the sons of the aristocracy.

The Jesuits were the nation's official weather forecasters and in 1858 erected the Observatorio Real (Royal Observatory) atop the tower. It was in use until 1925.

The church is linked to contiguous buildings across the street by an arched walkway—the Arco de Belén (Arch of Bethlehem)—spanning Acosta. As you enter, note the ornate facade decorated with a nativity scene set in a large niche framed with a shell. The United Nations and the Swiss government are helping pay for its restoration. Two of the six cloisters are slated to become a hotel; a third will host a secondary school; a fourth will host offices of the Academía de Ciencias; a fifth will become a museum of astronomy; and a portion of the building will house a home for the aged (a Spanish order of nuns devoted to elder care has agree to take up residence).

Ask to taste the *caña santa* herbal tea, made in the convent.

Iglesia y Convento de Santa Clara de Asís

Two blocks east of Belén, you'll discover the Convent of Saint Clair of Assisi, Calle Cuba #610, e/ Luz y Sol, tel. 861-5043 or 861-3335, a massive nunnery—the first founded in Havana—begun in 1638 and completed in 1644. It later served as a refuge for girls unfortunate enough to possess an insufficient dowry to attract suitors (only thus could the hapless females preserve their self-respect). The nuns moved out in 1922. It is a remarkable building, with a lobby full of beautiful period pieces. Its inner and outer cloistered courtyard, awash in divine light, is surrounded by columns, one of which is entwined by the roots of a *capulí* tree, whose fruits

and ceramic jars. It has recently been restored to former glory. Open Mon.–Fri. 8 A.M.–5 P.M., Sat. 8 A.M.–noon.

Iglesia y Convento de Nuestra Señora de Belén

Three blocks south is the Church and Convent of Our Lady of Bethlehem, Compostela y Luz, tel. 861-7283, a huge complex (the largest religious complex in Havana) occupying the block between Calles Luz and Acosta, and Compostela and Aguacate. Until recently, it was a derelict shell but was being lovingly restored at last visit, with its original baroque façade a major high-

JEWS IN HAVANA

Havana's Jewish community once thrived. Today it is thought to number only about 1,300, about five percent of its prerevolutionary size, when Havana's Jewish community supported five synagogues, several schools, and a college.

The first Jew, Luis de Torres, arrived with Columbus in 1492 as the explorer's translator. He was followed in the 16th century by Jews escaping persecution at the hands of the Spanish Inquisition (many Jews fled to the Caribbean under assumed Christian identities). Later, Jews coming from Mediterranean countries felt at home in Cuba—for example, Turkish Jews flocked to avoid World War I. They concentrated in southern Habana Vieja, many starting out in Cuba selling ties and cloth based around Bernaza and Muralla Streets and across the bay in Guanabacoa. They were joined at the turn of the 20th century by Ashkenazic Jews from Florida, who founded the United Hebrew Congregation in 1906. Other Jews emigrating from Eastern Europe passed through Cuba en route to the United States in significant numbers until the United States slammed its doors in 1924, after which they settled in Cuba. Arriving during a time of destitution, they were relatively poor compared to the earlier Jewish immigrants and were disparagingly called *polacos.* Many were sustained by the largesse of the United Hebrew Congregation.

Sephardic Jews came later as families and were profoundly religious—the first synagogue opened in 1914. They formed social clubs, opened their own schools, and married their own. By contrast, Ashkenazim most often were single men who went on to marry Cuban (Catholic) women and eventually were assimilated into Cuban society, says Robert M. Levine in his book *Tropical Diaspora: The Jewish Experience in Cuba.* The Ashkenazim were fired with socialist ideals and were prominent in the founding of both the labor and Cuban Communist movements.

Cuba seems to have been relatively free of anti-Semitism (Batista was a friend to Jews fleeing Nazi Europe). Levine, however, records how during the late 1930s the U.S. government bowed to isolationist, labor, and anti-Semitic pressures at home and convinced the Cuban government to turn back European Jews. It is a sordid chapter in U.S. history, best told through the tragic story of the SS *St. Louis* and its 937 passengers trying to escape Nazi Germany in 1939. The ship languished in Havana harbor for a week while U.S. and Cuban officials deliberated on letting passengers disembark; tragically, entry was refused, and the ship and passengers were sent back to Europe and their fate.

By the 1950s, about 20,000 Jews lived in Havana, concentrated around Calle Acosta—still widely known as the capital's "Jewish Street." Back then, Acosta was bustling with kosher bakeries, cafés, and clothes stores. Cuban Jews had prospered in the clothing trade and enjoyed a cosmopolitan life. The Jewish quarter, however, began its decline even before the Revolution, when Jews began migrating to North America. The Revolution itself "had elements of tragedy for the Jewish community," writes Rosshandler, author of the autobiographical novel *Passing*

---

resemble large golden pearls and taste ambrosial. Note the 17th-century fountain of a Samaritan woman, and the beautiful cloister roof carved with geometric designs—a classic *alfarje*—in the the Salón Plenario, a marble-floored hall of imposing stature. Wooden carvings abound. The second cloister contains the so-called Sailor's House, built by a wealthy pirate—he later be-

came a respectable shipowner—for his daughter, whom he failed to dissuade from a life of asceticism. Open Mon.–Fri. 8:30 A.M.–4:30 P.M.; entrance US$2.

The convent has been restored and now houses the **Centro Nacional de Conservación y Museología,** with nine charming rooms for rent. The center offers courses for architects,

Through Havana. Castro gave them "the option of staying and keeping their homes. But they had devoted their energy to business and they could not bear to live in a society that looked down on what they prized." Jews knew the lessons of the totalitarian regimes of Eastern Europe and so became part of the Cuban diaspora. About 95 percent of them fled, and only perhaps as many as 2,000 remained (a few joined the Castro government; two became early cabinet members). Some 500 Cuban Jews were secretly allowed to emigrate to Israel beginning in 1994.

There has been no discrimination against Jews—most of whom are orthodox or conservative—by the Castro government, although practicing the faith was discouraged (as it was for all religious behavior until things eased in 1991). Jewish religious schools were the only parochial schools allowed to remain open after the Revolution and the government even provided school buses. The government has always made matzo available and even authorized a kosher butcher shop on Calle Acosta to supply meat for observant Jews (it's open on Tuesdays; note the Star of David on the gate). And Jews are the only Cubans permitted to buy beef, a nod to restrictions on pork. The Jewish community also has its own cemetery, in Guanabacoa, dating from 1910. However, the community has no rabbi and marriages and circumcisions often must wait for foreign religious officials passing through Havana.

A renaissance in the Jewish faith is occurring, although things are tough. Many new additions come from conversions of non-Jewish Cuban spouses. Synagogues have been refurbished and new ones opened, and the faithful are returning in larger numbers and observing Shabbat. In 1994, the first bar mitzvah took place in over 12 years and the first formal bris in over five years. And the Hebrew Sunday School for children and adults in the Patronato (the Jewish community center on the ground floor of the synagogue in Vedado, Calle I #241, e/ 13 y 15, tel. 832-8953, fax 33-3778) teaches Hebrew and Yiddish. José Miller, President of the Patronato de la Casa de la Communidad Hebrea, Calle I, #261, next door, is head of the Cuban Jewish community.

To learn more, look for screenings of the documentary films *Havana Nagila: The Jews of Cuba,* by Laura Paull, and *Next Year in Havana,* by Lori Beraha.

The following Jewish organizations send medicines, humanitarian aid, and religious articles to Cuba (donations are needed), and/or offer organized trips: the **B'nai B'rith Cuban Jewish Relief Project,** 1831 Murray Ave. #208, Pittsburgh, PA 15217, 412/521-2390, bbaov@aol.com; the **Cuba-America Jewish Mission,** 1442A Walnut St. #224, Berkeley, CA 94709, CAJM13@aol.com, www.thecajm.org; the **Cuba Jewish Connection,** P.O. Box 10205, Marina Del Rey, CA 90295, cubatrips@jewban.org; **Cuban-Jewish Aid Society,** P.O. Box 4145, Highland Park, NJ 08904, fax 908/846-6884; **Jewish Solidarity,** 4714 SW 74th Ave., Miami, FL 33155, 305/262-9994, fax 305/260-9998, xael@bellsouth.net, www.jewish cuba.org; and **Sephardic Friendship Committee,** 800/243-7227, fax 714/508-8474, info@sephardicfriends.com, www.sephardicfriends.com.

HABANA VIEJA

planners, conservationists, and the like. A café serves basic refreshments.

Iglesia Parroquial del Espíritu Santo

Havana's oldest church, the Parish Church of the Holy Ghost, Calle Acosta #161, esq. Cuba, tel. 862-3410, lies two blocks south of Santa Clara de Asís. The church, which dates from 1638, was originally a hermitage "for the devotions of free Negroes" (the circa 1674 central nave and facade, and circa 1720 Gothic vault are later additions). Later, continuing in liberal tradition, King Charles III issued a royal decree giving the right of asylum here to anyone hunted by the authorities, a privilege no longer bestowed today.

The church reveals many surprises, including a

gilded, carved wooden pelican in a niche in the baptistery. The sacristy, where parish archives dating back through the 17th century are preserved, boasts an enormous cupboard full of baroque silver staffs and incense holders. Catacombs to each side of the nave are held up by subterranean tree trunks. Explore the eerie vault that runs under the chapel and peeking between the niches (still containing the odd bone) you will see, almost erased by time and damp, a series of paintings of skeletons crowned with tiaras and holding miters. They represent the dance of death. The body of Bishop Gerónimo Valdés had been laid to rest in the church. He remained in a kind of limbo, his whereabouts unknown, until he turned up, buried under the floor, during a restoration in 1936. Today, he rests in a tomb beside the nave, which boasts a carved wooden altar. The sturdy tower holds four bells. Steps lead up to the gallery, where you may turn the handle of a carillon. Open daily 8 A.M.–noon, and 3–6 P.M. Mass is Mondays and Wednesday–Sunday at 6 P.M.

Iglesia y Convento de Nuestra Señora de la Merced

Two blocks south brings you to this small, handsome church and convent—Our Lady of Mercy—at Calle Cuba #806, esq. Calle Merced, tel. 863-8873. Trompe l'oeil frescoes add color to the ornate interior containing romantic dome paintings (added during a remodeling in 1904) and an alcove lined with fake stalactites in honor of Nuestra Señora de Lourdes. It is one of the most resplendent of the city's church interiors and features the Capilla de Lourdes (Lourdes Chapel), containing early 20th-century religious frescoes by acclaimed Cuban artists. The church, begun in 1755, has strong Afro-Cuban connections (the Virgin of Mercy is also Obatalá, goddess of earth and purity), and it is not unusual to see devotees of *santería* kneeling in prayer.

Notwithstanding, it was the favored church for weddings of the aristocracy. Try to time your visit for September 24, when scores of gaily colored worshippers cram in for the Virgen de la Merced's feast day. More modest celebrations are held on the 24th of every other month. Open daily 8 A.M.–noon, and 3–5 P.M. Mass is Monday–Saturday at 9 A.M. and Sundays at 9 A.M. and noon.

Jewish Heritage Sites

The area around Calle Belén was also the site of the first community of Sephardic Jews in Cuba following their expulsion from Castile and Aragon in 1492. Over ensuing centuries, a Jewish community became well established, centered along Calle Acosta.

The Cuban government proposes to reconstruct the Jewish settlement, having made a start by rehabilitating the **Sinagoga Adath Israel,** Calle Picota #52, esq. Acosta, tel. 861-3495, which now sports a new wooden altar carved with scenes from Jerusalem and historic Havana. Salim Tache Jalak, the Administrator of Adath Israel, welcomes visitors to services. This being an Orthodox synagogue, men in yarmulkes and women chant prayers in Hebrew, separated by an opaque glass wall, before crossing over to mingle after the passing of the Torah. The service is followed by a feast. Open daily 8 A.M.–noon, and 5–8 P.M. Services are Monday–Friday 8 A.M. and 6 P.M., Saturday at 9 A.M. and 6 P.M., and Sunday at 9 A.M.

Chevet Achim, Inquisidor, e/ Luz y Santa Clara, tel. 832-6623, was built in 1914 and is the oldest still extant synagogue in Cuba. The building is owned and maintained by the Centro Sefardi, but is closed and not used for ritual or community purposes. It can be viewed by appointment. A Jewish museum is supposedly to be opened at Chevet Achim.

The Southern Margins

ALONG THE HARBOR FRONT

South of the Plaza de San Francisco, Havana's waterfront boulevard, Avenida del Puerto, swings along the harbor front, changing names as it curves: Avenida San Pedro, Avenida Leonor Pérez, Avenida Desamparados. It is overshadowed by portside warehouses and sailors' bars where Hemingway and prostitutes once hung out.

Much of the area is derelict, but Calle San Isidro is at the forefront of a remarkable remake. Earnings from tourism in the showier parts of Habana Vieja are underwriting a community-oriented rehabilitation under the aegis of Habaguanex. Residents have been given loans, skills training, and technical assistance to enable them to repair their own homes. New water, sewer, and power lines were being laid at last visit.

Museo de Ron

The Fundación Destilera Havana Club, or Museum of Rum, on Avenida San Pedro #262, e/ Muralla y Sol, tel. 861-8051, fax 62-1825, opened in 2000 in the former harbor front colonial mansion of the Conde de la Mortera. It's a *must see* and provides a solid and intriguing introduction to the mystery and manufacture of Cuban rum. Your tour begins with an audiovisual presentation on the history and production of rum. Exhibits include a mini-cooperage; and *salas* (rooms) dedicated to an exposition on sugarcane and to the colonial sugar mills and factories where the cane was pressed and the liquid processed. Exhibits include *pailes* (sugar boiling pots) and original wooden *trapiches* (sugarcane presses). An operating mini-production unit replete with bubbling vats and copper stills demonstrates the process, from the growing of sugarcane and fermentation to the distillation and aging process that results in some of the world's finest rums.

The museum's highlight is a model of an early 20th-century sugar plantation at 1:22.5 scale,

CLEANING UP HAVANA BAY

Havana Bay has been named by the United Nations as one of the world's 10 most polluted. When the tides ebb sufficient to draw out the harbor waters, petroleum scums the ocean fronting the Malecón, and the stench hangs over the port city like Banquo's ghost. This is nothing new—the plight dates back to prerevolutionary days, when, Hemingway wrote, "the smoke blew straight across the sky from the tall chimneys of the Havana Electric Company and . . . the water was as black and greasy as the pumpings from the bottom of the tanks of an oil tanker . . . and the scum of the harbor lay along the sides blacker than the creosote of the pilings and foul as an unclean sewer."

Oil spills from freighters and cruise ships have added to the foul sludge disgorged by the city's aging sewer system and the detritus delivered by the three rivers that flow like the gutters of an abattoir into the bay. Add to that pollution from industrial factories and an oil refinery on the banks of the bay, belching out vaporous plumes in a bouquet of bilious colors.

The Havana Bay Task Force was created in the mid-1990s to clean up the mess. The concerted clean-up effort began several years ago, and efforts have been made to reduce pollutants, including construction of a water treatment plant on the Luyano River, and installation of container booms and oil skimmers to scoop up spills from passing vessels.

The waters are slowly coming back to life. Increasing numbers of seabirds and even pelicans have returned to Havana Bay, although the water is still not safe for swimming; when navigating the low road of Havana's fouled shore it is best not to notice the children splashing about in the black-as-night soupy water.

complete with milling machines and plantation grounds with workers' dwellings, a church, and a hotel—all transporting you back in time. A railroad runs through the plantation, with two steam locomotives pulling sugarcane carriers, water tanks, and passenger carriages.

Your tour ends in the Bar Havana Club (intended as a smaller replica of Sloppy Joe's), where you can tipple the wares before buying in the adjoining store, which has a well-stocked humidor. Among the various Havana Club rums for sale is a 12-year-aged Ron Añejo Solera, sold nowhere else and raffled monthly to a lucky visitor.

Open Mon.–Sat. 9 A.M.–5 P.M. (the bar is open 11 A.M.–2 A.M.); the US$5 entrance includes a guide and drink.

Plazuela de la Luz and Vicinity

This triangular plaza is a tiny expanse of greenery at the junction of Oficios, Luz, and Avenida San

© CHRISTOPHER P. BAKER

Columna O'Donnell, Alameda de Paula

Pedro. On the northeast corner is the **Casa del Conde de Casa Barreto,** built in 1732 and today housing the **Centro Provincial de Artes Plásticas y Diseño,** Calle Oficios #362, esq. Luz, tel. 862-3295, open Mon.–Sat. 9 A.M.–5 P.M. On the north side is the **Hotel Armadores de Santander,** opened in 2002.

Be sure to call at **Dos Hermanos,** Avenida San Pedro #304 at Sol, tel. 861-3436, two blocks north of the plaza. This simple bar was once favored by Hemingway who liked to get tight here before kicking someone's ass into the dusty street; and, in earlier days, by Spanish poet Frederick García Lorca. A strong *mojito* will provide a pick-me-up and steel you for a close look at the polluted harbor.

Further south, at the junction with Calle Oficios, San Pedro takes a name change: Avenida Leonor Pérez, which runs alongside the **Alameda de Paula.** The Alameda, a 100-meter-long raised promenade, was the first such boulevard within the ancient city walls. It is lined with marble and iron street lamps. Midway along the Alameda stands a carved column with a fountain at its base, erected in 1847 to pay homage to the Spanish navy. It bears an unlikely Irish name: **Columna O'Donnell,** named for the Capitán General of Cuba, Leopoldo O'Donnell, who dedicated the monument. It is covered in relief work on a military theme and crowned by a lion with the arms of Spain in its claws.

Plazuela de Paula and Vicinity

At the southern end of the Alameda sits **Plazuela de Paula,** a small circular plaza with the **Iglesia de San Francisco de Paula** in the middle of the road at the junction with Calles San Ignacio and Leonor Pérez. This wee church was abandoned ages ago and today, duly restored, features a panoply of marvelous artworks, including stained-glass pieces by Nelson Domínguez and Rosa María de la Targa, plus an astonishing triptych panel by Cosme Proenza. It is also used for concerts of chamber music. Note the national hymn, "La Bayamesa," inscribed in metal on the interior wall to the left.

The Plazuela housed the old P&O docks, where the ships from Miami and Key West used

HAVANA'S CITY WALLS

Construction of Havana's fortified city walls began on February 3, 1674. They ran along the western edge of the bay and, on the landward side, stood between today's Calle Egido, Monserrate, and Zulueta according to a plan by Spanish engineer Cristóbal de Rodas. To pay for construction, the Court of Spain voted an annual budget from the Royal Chests of Mexico and even decreed a tax on wine sold in Havana's taverns.

Under the direction of engineer Juan de Siscaras, African slaves labored for 23 years to build the 1.4-meter-thick, 10-meter-tall city wall that was intended to ring the entire city using rocks hauled in from the coast. The 4,892-meter-long wall was completed in 1697, with a small opening for the mooring of ships, and a perimeter of five kilometers. The damage inflicted by the British artillery in 1762 was repaired in 1797, when the thick wall attained its final shape. It formed an irregular polygon with nine defensive bastions with sections of wall in-between, and moats and steep drops to delay assault by enemy troops. It was protected by 180 cannons and garrisoned with 3,400 troops. In its first stage, it had just two entrances (nine more were added later), opened each morning upon the sound of a single cannon and closed at night the same way.

As time went on, the *intramuros* (the city within the walls) burst its confines. In 1841, Havana authorities petitioned the Spanish Crown for permission to demolish the walls. Just 123 years after the walls went up, they came down again. The demolition began in 1863, when African slave-convicts were put to work to destroy what their forefathers had built under hard labor. The demolition wasn't completed until well into the 20th century.

Regrettably, only fragments remain, most notably at the junction of Calle Egido and Avenida del Puerto, near the railway station at Avenida del Puerto and Egido, and at Monserrate and Teniente Rey streets. Sentry boxes still stand in front of the Presidential Palace, between Calles Monserrate and Zulueta, and at the west end of Calle Tacón.

to dock and where Pan American World Airways had its terminal when it was still flying the old clipper flying-boats. Before World War II, when the U.S. Navy took over the docks, San Isidro had been the great whorehouse street of the waterfront. According to Hemingway, many of the women were Europeans. After the war, the Navy closed the brothels and "shipped all the whores back to Europe. Many people were sad after the ships had gone and San Isidro had never recovered. . . . There were gay streets in Havana and there were some very tough streets and tough quarters, such as Jesús y María, which was just a short distance away. But this part of town was just sad as it had been ever since the whores had gone," wrote Hemingway.

South of the plazuela, the harbor front boulevard becomes Desamparados, which runs south to the junction with Avenida de Bélgica (Egido), where there's a traffic circle; and the **Cortina de la Habana,** a remnant section of the old fortress

wall enclosing Habana Vieja in colonial days. On the north side of Desamparados, immediately east of the junction, is the **Archivo Nacional,** Compostela #906 esq. San Isidro, archnac@ceniai.inf.cu, the National Archives, taking up an entire block between Desamparados and San Isidro and Compostela and Picota. Entering this once-impressive establishment comes as a shock . . . as if you've been transported back to the Dickensian era. The tumbledown file drawers and filing system (dog-eared, thumb-stained file cards) pre-date the Revolution. Tragically the archives are crumbling to dust. Time apparently stopped on December 31, 1958.

One hundred meters south of the Cortina, you'll see the **Monumento Mártires del Vapor La Coubre** made of twisted metal fragments of *La Coubre,* the French cargo ship that exploded in Havana harbor on March 4, 1960. The vessel was carrying armaments for the Castro government, and it is generally assumed that the CIA or other counterrevolutionaries blew it up. The monument honors the seamen who died in the explosion.

AVENIDA DE BÉLGICA (EGIDO)

Avenida de Bélgica, colloquially called Egido, follows the hollow once occupied by Habana Vieja's ancient walls. It is a continuation of Monserrate (see the Avenida de los Misiones section earlier in this chapter) and flows downhill from two blocks east of Parque de la Fraternidad to the harbor. It is lined with once-beautiful buildings constructed during the urbanization that followed demolition of the walls. Though built during the mid-19th century, the buildings have the appearance of being much older, as with the **Palacio de la Condesa de Villalba,** esq. Calle Muralla, a Renaissance-style edifice facing onto the **Plazuela de los Ursulinos.** Similarly, the **Palacio de los Marqueses de Balboa,** one block south, speaks of erstwhile beauty through a layer of grime and decay.

The street's masterpiece is the **Estación Central de Ferrocarril,** esq. Calle Arsenal, Havana's impressive Venetian-style railway station. The station was designed in 1910 by a North American architect, blending Spanish Revival and Italian Renaissance styles and featuring twin towers displaying the shields of Havana and Cuba. It is built atop the former Arsenal, or Spanish naval shipyard. Sitting on rails in its lobby is an 1843-model steam locomotive (Cuba's first) called *La Junta.*

On the station's north side is a small shady plaza—**Parque de los Agrimensores** (Park of the Surveyors)—pinned by a large remnant of the old city wall.

Egido slopes south to the Cortina de la Habana at the junction with Desamparados, and is lined with remnants of the **Murallas de Habana,** the original city walls. Just north of Desamparados is the **Puerta de la Tenaza,** the only ancient city gate still standing. Here a plaque inset within a still extant remnant of the old wall shows a map of the old city and the extent of the original walls and fortifications.

Museo Casa Natal de José Martí

The birthplace of the nation's preeminent national hero is at Leonor Pérez #314, esq. Avenida de Bélgica, tel. 862-3778, one block south of the railway station (the street is named after José Martí's mother). This simple house, painted ocher with blue-green window and door frames and terra-cotta tile floors, is a shrine for Cubans who flock to pay homage. Martí was born on January 28, 1853 and spent the first four years of his life here. The house and museum are splendidly kept, in fairly humble style. The entrance lobby displays letters from Martí. Many of his personal effects are here, too, including a beautiful lacquered *escritorio* (writing desk) and a broad-brimmed Panama hat given to him by Ecuadorean President Eloy Alfaro. (Panama hats don't come from the country of Panamá—they're made in Ecuador.) Many of Martí's original texts, poems, and sketches are on display. There's even a lock of the hero's hair from when he was a child. Guides follow you around, at a discreet distance. Open Tues.–Sat. 9 A.M.–5 P.M., Sun. 9 A.M.–1 P.M. Entrance US$1 (US$1 extra for guides, US$2 for cameras, US$10 for videos). The building across the street houses a *Salón de Expociones,* where piano recitals and other cultural activities are hosted.

ATARÉS

Habana Vieja extends southwest from Egido to encircle Havana bay. Avenida del Puerto (Desamparados) continues south from the junction with Egido and curls around the bayshore, lined by warehouses and docks: "A panorama of torpor," wrote Martin Cruz Smith. Throughout much of this century, the Atarés shorefront was a staging area for the arrival of American automobiles and goods and, later, for Soviet oil and produce. "One decrepit warehouse dragged down its neighbor, which destabilized a third and spewed steel and timbers into the street until they looked like a city that had undergone a siege . . . Ofelia had done invasion training in Atarés and remembered how convincing it was to carry make-believe wounded across a landscape of collapse," wrote Smith, in *Havana Bay,* speaking of the 1990s, following the collapse of the Soviet Union and, with it, the maritime trade.

Trade has improved significantly in recent years. The only site of interest is the **Castillo de Santo Domingo de Atarés,** built in 1767 atop a rise called Loma Soto and intended to forestall any invasion from the south. It's not open to public viewing.

Parque Histórico Militar Morro-Cabaña

Looming over Habana Vieja, on the north side of the harbor channel, is the rugged cliff face of the Cabaña, dominated by two great fortresses that constitute Morro-Cabaña Historical Military Park, Carretera de la Cabaña, Habana del Este, tel. 862-7653. Together, the castles comprise the largest and most powerful defensive complex built by the Spanish in the Americas. Maintained in a superb state, the two castles are must sees on any visitor's itinerary (you should visit by both day and night), and offer fabulous views over Habana Vieja and toward Vedado, especially at dawn and dusk.

The first military structure dated back to 1563, when Governor Diego de Mazariegos ordered a tower built on the *morro* (headland) to extend the vision from the heights and to serve as a reference for galleons. To aid in navigation, the tower was whitewashed. Cannons and a sentry post were later added. However, Havana's treasures were never safe from marauding pirates, against which the feeble tower (and the Castillo de la Real Fuerza, below on the harbor channel) proved inconsequential. Thus, in 1589 King Philip II approved construction of a fortress: the Castillo de los Tres Reyes del Morro.

Open daily, 8 A.M.–8 P.M.

Getting There

Visitors arriving by car reach the complex via the tunnel (no pedestrians or motorcycles without sidecars are allowed) that descends beneath the Máximo Gómez Monument off Avenida de Céspedes. The well-signed exit for the Morro and Fortaleza de San Carlos is immediately on your right after exiting the tunnel on the north side of the harbor. Buses from Parque de la Fraternidad pass through the tunnel and will drop you by the fortress access road—the *ciclobus* permits bicycles.

You can also get there by day by taking the little ferry that bobs its way across Havana harbor

to Casablanca. From here you can walk uphill (it's a steep 10-minute climb) to an easterly entrance gate to the Foso de los Laureles in the Cabaña. However, the easterly access gate closes at dusk, so don't take this route if you plan on seeing the *cañonazo*, described later in this chapter.

CASTILLO DE LOS TRES REYES DEL MORRO

This handsome, ghost-white castle, Carretera de la Cabaña, tel. 863-7941 or 861-3635 (lighthouse), is built into the rocky palisades of Punta Barlovento, crowning a rise that drops straight to the sea at the entrance to Havana's narrow harbor channel. Canted in its articulation, the fort—designed by

moat of Castillo de los Tres Reyes del Morro

HABANA VIEJA

Italian engineer Juan Bautista Antonelli and initiated in 1589—follows a tradition of military architecture established by the Milanese at the end of the Middle Ages. It forms an irregular polygon that follow the contours of the rocky headland on which it was built, with a sharp-angled bastion at the apex, stone walls 10 feet thick, and a series of batteries stepping down to the shore. Hundreds of slaves toiled under the lash of whip and heat of the sun to cut the stone *in situ,* extracted from the void that forms the moats. El Morro took 40 years to complete and served its job well, repelling countless pirate attacks and withstanding for 44 days a siege by British cannon in 1762.

The castle has been restored to former glory and has lost none of its commanding composure, with plentiful cannons on trolleys in their embrasures.

Originally the castle connected with the outside world principally by sea, to which it was linked via the **Plataforma de la Estrella,** the wharf at the southern foot of the cliff. Today you enter via a drawbridge across the deep moat that leads through a long tunnel—the **Túnel de Aspillerado** (Tunnel of Loopholes)—to the vast wooden gates. The gates open to the **Camino de Rondas,** a small parade ground (Plaza de Armas) with, to the right, a narrow entrance to the **Baluarte de Austria** (Austrian Bastion), a covered area with cannon embrasures for firing down on the moat—it is named for the period when the Austrian House of Hapsburgs ruled Spain. A cobbled ramp—also to the right—leads up from the plaza to the **Baluarte de Tejeda,** a wide, windswept platform with further embrasures and a splendid view east past the **Batería de Velasco** (with cannons added in the 19th century) and along the coast. On the seaward side of the Tejeda bastion— named for the governor and military leader who began work on the castle—you can look down into the crevasse caused by the explosion that breached the Caballero del Mar wall in the 1762 siege by the British. Various plaques inset in the bastion commemorate heroic figures of the siege—even the Royal Navy is honored on a plaque placed by the British Embassy. From here you can walk the curtain wall where rusting can-

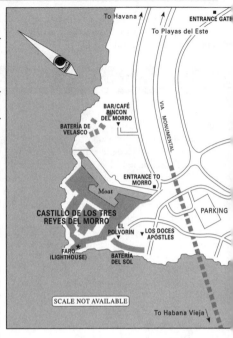

nons of the **Morrillo** (High Battery) are in place, with the Low Battery on the level below. Do not be tempted to walk the wind-battered battlements, which are canted seaward and have no guardrails. One false step, and you could easily tumble onto the wave-swept rocks below.

The Camino de Rondas surrounds a central building built in 1763 atop the cisterns that supplied the garrison of 1,000 men with water. The galleries of this two-story structure are now exhibition rooms, including the **Museo de Navegación** (also called Sala de Cristóbal Colón) with expositions on the colonial sea voyages of Columbus and later Portuguese and Spanish explorers; and the **Sala de Historia del Faro y Castillo,** which profiles the various lighthouses in Cuba, including a scale model.

To the left of the Plaza de Armas is the **Surtida de los Tinajones,** where giant earthenware vases are inset in stone. They once contained rapeseed oil as fuel for the 15-meter-tall lighthouse—**Faro del Morro**—reached by a small ramp over the *surtida.* The lighthouse was constructed beside the

**PARQUE HISTÓRICO
MILITAR MORRO – CABAÑA**

FORTALEZA DE SAN
CARLOS DE LA CABAÑA

PARKING

LUNETO DE
SAN LEOPOLDO

BALUARTE
DE SAN
AMBROSIO

El Foso de los
Laureles

To El Cristo de Casablanca

ENTRANCE TO LA
CABAÑA

BAR EL
ARTILLERO

LA TRIADA

CENOTAPH TO JUAN
CLEMENTE-ZENEA

TELEPHONES

TOILETS

MUSEO DE
LA CABAÑA

MOAT
GATE

PLAQUE COMMEMORATING
EXECUTED CUBAN
NATIONALISTS

SHOPS

RESTAURANTE
SAN FRANCISCO

TOILETS

CAPILLA DE
SAN CARLOS

MUSEO DE
MAQUETAS

MUSEO DE
FORTIFICACIONES Y ARMAS

RESTAURANTE LA
FORTALEZA

MOAT
GATE

MUSEO CHE
GUEVARA

Plaza de Armas

BODEGÓN DE
LOS VINOS

SEMI-BALUARTE DE
SAN LORENZO

PARKING

LA DIVINA
PASTORA

LA CORTINA

SITE OF EL
CAÑONAZO
CEREMONY

BATERÍA DE LA
DIVINA PASTORA

BAR EL MIRADOR

To Estación Casablanca
and Muelle de Casablanca

B a h í a   d e   l a   H a b a n a

M

HABANA VIEJA

fortress in 1844, replacing a defensive tower whose role had long ago become obsolete. The original wood-fired lantern was eventually replaced by one fueled by rapeseed; then, in 1928, by an acetylene lantern; and, finally in 1945, an electric lantern that still flashes its light every 15 seconds, sending a beam 18 miles long. You can climb to the top for a bird's eye view of the castle—the last leg of the climb is tight, and not for claustrophobics.

All maritime traffic in and out of Havana harbor is controlled from the **Estación Semafórica,** the semaphore station atop the castle, accessed via the Baluarte de Tejeda. With luck, the station master may invite you in to scan the city using 20 x 120-power Nikon binoculars. The flagpole outside was used to signal information to the city fortresses and harbormasters about approaching traffic. It was here, too, that the English raised the Union Jack to proclaim their capture of Cuba—and where the Spanish flag was raised again one year later. The flagpole came to take on political significance, so it was here

that the Stars and Stripes replaced the flag of Spain when the latter came down for the last time in 1898. Today, the tradition of adorning the flagpole with multicolored signal flags is continued on public holidays.

Below the castle, facing the city on the landward side and reached by a cobbled ramp, is the **Batería de los Doce Apóstoles** (Battery of the Twelve Apostles). It boasts massive cannons and a little bar—El Polvorín (The Powderhouse).

The Morro is open daily 8 A.M.–8 P.M. (entrance US$3, plus US$1 for a guide, US$2 for cameras, US$5 for videos). The lighthouse is open 10 A.M.–8 P.M. (US$2 extra).

FORTALEZA DE SAN CARLOS DE LA CABAÑA

This massive fortress, Carretera de la Cabaña, tel. 862-0671, lining Loma Cabaña half a kilometer east of the Morro, enjoys a fantastic strategic position, with a clifftop balcony over the city and harbor. It is the largest fort in the Americas,

© CHRISTOPHER P. BAKER

Capilla de San Carlos, Fortaleza de San Carlos de la Cabaña

covering 10 hectares and stretching 700 meters in length. It was built 1764–74 following the English invasion, and cost the staggering sum of 14 million pesos (when told the cost, the king after whom it is named reached for a telescope; surely, he said, it must be large enough to see from Madrid). From the very beginning, the castle was powerfully armed and could count in the mid-19th century some 120 bronze cannons and mortars, plus a permanent garrison of 1,300 men (the castle was designed to hold 6,000 troops in times of need). While never actually used in battle, it has been claimed that its dissuasive presence won all potential battles—a tribute to the French designer and engineer entrusted with its conception and construction. The castle has been splendidly restored.

The fortress is reached from the north. You pass through two defensive structures before reaching the monumental baroque portal—flanked by great columns and a pediment etched with the escutcheon of Kings Charles III and plaques dedicated to various colonial governors—and a massive drawbridge over a 12-meter-deep moat, one of several moats carved from solid rock and separating individual fortress components.

Beyond the entrance gate, a paved alley leads to the **Plaza de Armas,** centered on a grassy, tree-shaded park fronted by a 400-meter-long curtain wall. Immediately ahead upon entering the plaza is the **Museo de la Comandancia de Che,** where Che Guevara had his headquarters in the months following the Triunfo del Revolución. Guevara's guerrilla army occupied the fortress on January 3, 1959 and here he set up his revolutionary tribunals for "crimes against the security of the state." The small museum is dedicated to saluting the Argentinian doctor-turned-revolutionary who played such a key part in the Cuban Revolution. His M-1 rifle, sub-machine gun, radio, and rucksack are among the exhibits.

Calle Marina leads east to a large cannon-filled courtyard, from where steps lead down to **La Divina Pastora** restaurant, beside the wharf where supply ships once berthed.

To the west, the cobbled street leads past a small **chapel** with a charming vaulted interior containing a beautifully carved wooden altar, plus a spired belltower and an even more impressive baroque facade surrounding blood-red walls. Venerated here were three saints: San Carlos, patron saint of the fortress; Santa Barbara, patron saint of artillerymen; and Nuestra Señora del Pilar, patron saint of sailors.

Immediately west, on the north face of the plaza, is a building that contains the **Museo Monográfico de la Fortaleza,** tracing the castle's development. The museum features a room containing various torture instruments and dedicated to the period when political executions took place; and another containing uniforms and weaponry from the colonial epoch, including a representation of the *cañonazo* ceremony. A portal here leads into a garden—**Patio de Los Jagüeyes**—that while today a place of repose, once served as a *cortadura,* a defensive element packed with explosives that could be ignited to foil the enemy's attempts to gain entry.

A long building runs west from here, following the slope of the plaza. The **Museo de las Maquetas** features 3-D models of each of Cuba's castles, including a detailed model of the Cabaña that helps in understanding the concepts that made this fortress so formidable; plus a *maqueta* (model) showing Havana's early defenses. Next door, the **Museo de Fortificaciones y Armas** contains an impressive collection of suits of armor and weaponry that spans the ancient Arab and Asian worlds and stretches back through medieval times to the Roman era. Never seen a battering ram or ballistic catapult? Check 'em out here.

On the north side of the block is the **Calle Marina,** a cobbled street lined with former barracks, armaments stores, and prisoners' cells. Converted, they now contain the **Restaurante La Fortaleza,** the more upscale **Bodegón de los Vinos** (serving Spanish cuisine with traditional entertainment), and **Casa del Tabaco y Ron,** displaying the world's longest cigar (11 meters long).

Midway down Calle Marina, a gate leads down to the **El Foso de los Laureles.** The massive Moat of the Laurels contains the execution wall where hundreds of nationalist sympathizers were shot during the wars of independence, when the fortress dungeons were used as a prison for Cuban patriots—a role that Generals Machado and Batista continued. A plaque commemorates Cuban nationalists and leftists executed prior to the Revolution, and a cenotaph is dedicated to

one in particular: Juan Clemente Zenea, executed in 1871. Following the Revolution, scores of Batista supporters and "counter-revolutionaries" met a similar fate here.

On the north side of the moat is a separate fortress unit, the **San Juliá Revellín.** It contains examples of the missiles installed during the Cuban Missile Crisis (called the October 1962 Crisis by Cubans), among them a Soviet nuclear-tipped R-12 rocket.

At the north end of the Plaza de Armas, a covered path leads to the **Semibaluarte de San Lorenzo,** an expansive and maze-like fortification offering vast views over the harbor from the cannon embrasures. Note the sentry box of San Lorenzo at the far end—it makes a great foreground for a picture-perfect photo over Habana Vieja.

The curtain wall—**La Cortina**—runs the length of the castle on its south side and formed the main gun position overlooking Havana. It is lined with ceremonial cannons engraved with lyrical names such as *La Hermosa* (The Beautiful). By night the mood changes, looming deeper into the shadows of Havana's past. Here, nightly at 9 P.M., a small unit assembles in military fashion, dressed in scarlet 18th-century garb and led by fife and drum. Soon enough, you'll hear the reverberating crack of the *cañonazo*—the nightly firing of a cannon, which used to signal the closing of the city gates and the raising of the chain to seal the harbor mouth. Today, it causes unsuspecting visitors to drop their drinks and keeps open the sea lane of memory between the present and the colonial past.

The castle is open daily 10 A.M.–10 P.M. Entry costs US$3, children US$1.50 (plus extra US$1 for guide, US$2 for cameras, US$10 for videos) and includes the *cañonazo* (you can visit the castle by day and return at night on the same ticket; entry after 6 P.M. costs US$5). The rest of the fortress grounds is still used as a military base, making most of the surrounding area off-limits.

Excursions are available to witness the *cañonazo,* usually followed by dinner at La Divina Pastora. You can make reservations through any of the tour agencies listed in the Getting Around section of the Transportation chapter.

HABANA VIEJA

CASABLANCA

The Cabaña looms over the village of Casablanca, which clings to the shore on the northeast side of Havana harbor, in the easterly lee of the Fortaleza de San Carlos de la Cabaña ("Casablanca looked as if it had started at the top of the hill at Christ's feet and then rolled down to the water's edge," wrote Martin Cruz Smith). The village was named for a prominent white-painted warehouse commanding the waterfront. Casablanca's narrow main street is overhung with balconies, and from here tiers of houses rise up the hillside. Today, a few rusting freighters sit in dry dock, and fishing boats bob along the waterfront. Casablanca is also the departure point for the Hershey Train, a three-car passenger train once belonging to the Hershey-Cuban Railroad (see the Special Topic "A Sugar of a Journey" in the Transportation chapter for more information).

The domed **Observatorio Nacional** (National Observatory) sits atop the *cabaña*. However, this is part of the sprawling military complex that occupies the rocky palisade and it is not open to tourists.

Estatua Cristo de la Habana

A great statue of Jesus Christ, on Carretera del Asilo, looms over Casablanca, dominating the cliff face immediately east of the Fortaleza. The 15-meter-tall statue stands atop a three-meter-tall pedestal and was hewn from Italian Carrara marble by female Cuban sculptor Jilma Madera. The figure stands with one hand on his chest and the other raised in a blessing.

From the *mirador* (viewing platform) surrounding the statue, you have a bird's-eye view of the deep, flask-shaped harbor. The views are especially good at dawn and dusk, and it is possible, with the sun gilding the waters, to imagine great galleons slipping in and out of the harbor, laden with treasure en route to Spain.

The statue, which was unveiled on December 25, 1958 ("just seven days before the triumph of the Antichrist in Cuba," said Fulgencio Batista), is accessible by a 10-minute uphill walk from the Muelle de Casablanca dock. Either climb the staircase beginning in the plazuela 100 meters north of the ferry terminal or take the winding roadway that leads west from the plazuela.

Getting There

A small ferry runs to Casablanca every 20 minutes or so from the Muelle la Luz (10 centavos) on the south side of the Terminal Sierra Maestra, at the foot of Calle Santa Clara, in Habana Vieja. Bicycles can be taken.

Casablanca is also reached by car from the Vía Monumental; the exit is marked about one kilometer east of the tunnel.

Centro Habana and Cerro

Centro Habana

Centro Habana (Central Havana—pop. 175,000) lies west of the Paseo del Prado and Habana Vieja. Laid out in a near-perfect grid, Centro is mostly residential, with few sights of note. The region is a 19th-century extension of Habana Vieja and evolved following demolition of the city walls in 1863. Prior, it had served as a buffer zone. The first streets to lead from the walled city were Calles Reina (today's Avenida Salvador Allende) and Monte, and Calzada de San Lázaro, which led to the leper's hospital. Today, Centro comprises block upon block of residential streets with dimensions not dissimilar to those of Habana Vieja. The buildings have a similar look, but are deeper and taller, of four or five stories, built mostly as apartment units, with air shafts instead of interior patios. Hence, the population and street life are denser (a "Dickensian space in the tropics," thought Claudia Lightfoot, "you feel that every doorway . . . hides a Fagin or a Mrs. Gamp").

In prerevolutionary days, east-central Centro was the retail heart of the city, and still is, albeit a bit faded from the days when there were more goods to sell. In recent years, the main shopping streets of San Rafael, Neptuno, and Galiano have sprung back to life, and the famous department stores of prerevolutionary days have reopened, stocked now, as then, with mostly imported goods sold for dollars only. Centro was also the heart of Havana's red-light district, and scores of prostitutes roamed such streets as the ill-named Calle Virtudes (Virtues).

Believe it or not, there's also a small Chinatown— Barrio Chino—delineated by Calles Zanja, Dragones, Salud, Rayo, San Nicolás, and Manrique.

Many houses along and inland of the Malecón, having been battered by waves and salt air over decades, are in a tumbledown state—

Quinta las Delicias

about one in three houses have collapsed. Parts of Centro are so dilapidated that they conjure up images of what Dresden, Germany, must have looked like after it was bombed in World War II.

Orientation

The two major west-east thoroughfares are the Malecón to the north, and the Zanja and Avenida Salvador Allende through the center; plus two important shopping streets—Calles Neptuno and San Rafael—between the Malecón and Zanja. Three major thoroughfares run perpendicular, north–south: Calzada de Infanta, forming the western boundary; Padre Varela, down the center; and Avenida de Italia (Galiano), farther east.

MALECÓN AND VICINITY

When questioned by an immigration official as to why he had come to Cuba and stayed for 10 years, Costa Rican composer Ray Tico replied: "I fell in love with Havana's seafront drive." The **Malecón** (officially known as Avenida Antonio Maceo, and more properly the Muro de Malecón, literally "embankment," or "seawall") winds sinuously and dramatically along the Atlantic shoreline between the Castillo de San Salvador de la Punta and the Río Almendares. The six-lane seafront boulevard was designed as a jetty wall in 1857 by Cuban engineer General Francisco de Albear but not laid out until 1902, by U.S. governor General Woods. It took 50 years to reach the Río Almendares, almost five miles to the west.

"Silver lamé" was what composer Orlando de la Rosa called the boulevard. The metaphor has stuck, although it is today only a ghostly reminder of its former brilliance—what Martha Gellhorn called a "19th century jewel and a joke." The Malecón is lined with once-glorious houses, each exuberantly distinct from the next. Unprotected by seaworthy paint, they have proven incapable of withstanding the salt spray that crashes over the seawall in great airy clouds and then floats off in rainbows. Their facades—green trimmed with purple, pink with blue, yellow with orange—many of the seaside homes belonged to millionaires and were painted red, blue, or yellow according to the owner's political

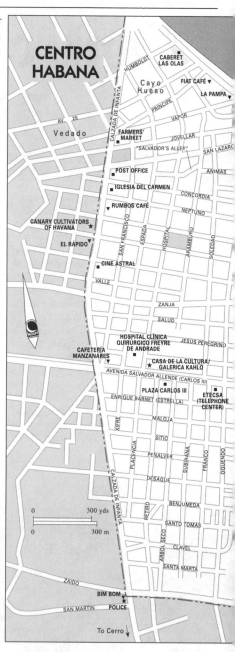

© AVALON TRAVEL PUBLISHING, INC.

STRAITS OF FLORIDA

CASTILLO DE SAN SALVADOR DE LA PUNTA
CASA PARTICULAR RENE PÉREZ
CENTRO CULTURAL DE ESPAÑA
PALADAR TORRESÓN

Habana Vieja

RREÓN DE N LÁZARO
CONVENTO DE LA IMACULADO CONCEPCIÓN
MONUMENTO ANTONIO MACEO
RUMBOS CAFE
CLÍNICA INTERNACIONAL
HOSPITAL CLÍNICO QUIRÚRGICO HERMANOS ALMEIJEIRAS
CASA DE LA CULTURA

AVENIDA MACEO (MALECÓN)
HOTEL DEAUVILLE
SAN LÁZARO
TROCADEO
BLANCO
AGUILA
CRESPO
INDUSTRIA
COLÓN
REFUGIO
MORRO
PASEO DE MARTÍ (PRADO)
AVENIDA DE LAS MISIONES
(ZULUETA)

LAGUNAS
ANIMAS
LA CASONA COLONIAL
VIRTUDES
LA GUARIDA
CONCORDIA
PADRE VARELA (BELASCOAÍN)
LUCENA
MARQUES GONZÁLEZ
GERVASIO
ESCOBAR
LEALTAD
PERSEVERANCIA
CAMPANARIO
MANRIQUE
SAN NICOLÁS

CADECA

CENTRO

HOTEL LINCOLN
MUSEO LEZAMA LIMA
CASA PARTICULAR ELSA Y JULIO ROQUE
HOTEL LIDO
HOSTAL EL PARADOR NUMANTICO
EL RÁPIDO
IGLESIA DE NUESTRA SEÑORA DE MONSERRATE
CINE AMÉRICA
CASA DE VICTORIA RIVERO NUÑEZ
CASA DE LA MÚSICA
ÓPTICAS MIRAMAR
CASA DEL TANGO
CADECA
RESTAURANTE FORNOS CHA
LA ÉPOCA
CASA DE LA CULTURA
TELEPHONE
BAR NAUTILUS
SODERÍA BOULEVARD
LA CALESA CAFETERÍA
HOTEL INGLATERRA
BANCO DE CRÉDITO Y COMERCIO
SAN MARTÍN (SAN JOSÉ)
BAR PEKIN
CABARET PALERMO
CABARET NACIONAL
PERIÓDICO KWONG WAH PO
RESTAURANTE PACÍFICO
CASA PARTICULAR NORMA PINEDA
CASA PARTICULAR DE BIENVENIDOS
HABANA
RESTAURANTE BAVARIA
CUCHILLO
CASA ABUELO LUNG KONG
CASA PARTICULAR AMÉRICA FERNÁNDEZ
RESTAURANTE TIEN-TAN
RESTAURANTE BARCELONA
BRASIL
GRAN TEMPLO IONAL MASONICO
IGLESIA DE LA CARIDAD DEL COBRE
DISCO CHANG
HOTEL NUEVA YORK
RESTAURANTE CHUNG SAN
CAPITOLIO
CORREO ELECTRÓNICO
RESTAURANTE CHI TACK TONG
RESTAURANTE TAI PI (REINA)
DRAGON GATE
DRAGONES
IGLESIA DEL SAGRADO CORAZÓN DE JESÚS
AVENIDA SIMÓN BOLÍVAR
FÁBRICA DE TABACO H. UPMANN
Parque de la Fraternidad
PALACIO DE ALDAMA

SAN MIGUEL
SAN RAFAEL
NEPTUNO
VIRTUDES
PRESERVANCIA
MAESTRANZA
MONSERRATE
BERNAZA
VILLEGAS
AGRAMONTE
CONSULADO
AMISTAD
BARCELONA
AVENIDA DE ITALIA (GALIANO)
RAYO
SAN NICOLÁS
MANRIQUE
CAMPANARIO
LEALTAD
ESCOBAR

Parque Central
XYLUACATE
AVENIDA DE BÉLGICA (MONSERRATE)
(TENIENTE REY)

BRICA DE TABACO OMEO Y JULIETA
PENALVER
CONDESA
CONCEPCIÓN DE LA VALLA
IGLESIA DE SAN NICOLÁS
APODACA
APONTE SOMERUELOS
CIENFUEGOS
CÁRDENAS
ECONOMÍA
CONSERVATORIO MUNICIPAL DE HABANA
FIGURAS
SITIO
LAVANDERÍA EL GUERRILLERO
MISIÓN
ESPERANZA
ESTACIÓN CENTRAL DE FERROCARRIL
EGIDO

NUEVA DEL PILAR
LINDERO
MÁXIMO GOMEZ (MONTE)
SAN NICOLÁS
CORRALES
GLORIA
FLORIDA
ALAMBIQUE
AGUILA
REVILLAGIGEDO
SUÁREZ
FACTORÍA
ARROYO (AVENIDA MANGLAR)
AVENIDA DE ESPAÑA (VIVES)
PUERTO GERRADA
DESAMPARADOS
TERMINAL LA COUBRE
CUATRO CAMINOS (FARMER'S MARKET)
ESTACIÓN CRISTINA

allegiance—are now decrepit, supported by wooden scaffolding, while the broad limestone walkway is now pitted and broken.

At long last, the restoration of the Malecón is well underway. Underwritten with aid from several regional governments in Spain, 14 blocks of the Malecón are in various stages of redevelopment, while new wrought-iron street lamps in classical style are going up, adding much-needed beauty. The renovation includes the structures' interiors, too. Families have been moved out temporarily while the plumbing and electrical cables are relaid. The area behind the seafront boulevard, however, is virtually beyond the pale. Many of the buildings were constructed of concrete-slab and I-beam that for lack of paint and maintenance has deteriorated to the point where salt from sea spray has corroded the steel beams.

Alas, much of the renovation betrays typically Communist shoddy workmanship and at last visit, much of the newly restored seawall and sidewalk was already crumbling, and the newly-painted houses already peeling—most were painted in haste without prep for the Pope's visit in 1998.

All along the shore are the worn remains of square baths—known as the "Elysian Fields"—hewn from the rocks below the seawall, originally with separate areas for men, women, and *negros*. Since the Revolution, they are more democratic. These **Baños de Mar** precede construction of the Malecón and were cut into the steps of rock alongside the Calzada de San Lázaro. Each is about 12 feet square and six to eight feet deep, with rock steps for access and a couple of portholes through which the waves of this tideless shore wash in and out.

The Malecón is the city's undisputed social gathering spot. It offers a microcosm of Havana life: the elderly walking their dogs; the shiftless selling cigars and cheap sex to tourists; the young passing rum among friends; fishermen (called *neumáticos* since they sit in giant inner tubes) tending their lines and casting off; and always, scores of couples courting and necking—the Malecón is known as "Havana's sofa" and acts, wrote Claudia Lightfoot, as "the city's drawing room, office, study, and often bedroom." All

through the night, lovers' murmurings mingle with the crash and hiss of the waves.

The Malecón—the setting for spontaneous riots in the early 1990s—is also a barometer of the political state of Havana. During times of tension, the police presence is abnormally strong and the Malecón becomes eerily empty. *Jineteros* and *jineteras* disappear. Even law-abiding citizens stay away. At other times, keep one hand on your purse and gold chain!

Every October 26, schoolchildren are bussed here to throw flowers over the seawall in memory of revolutionary leader Camilo Cienfuegos, killed in a mysterious air crash on that day in 1959.

Parque Maceo

Dominating the Malecón to the west is the massive bronze **Monumento Antonio Maceo,** atop a marble base in a newly laid out plaza with fountain. The classical monument was erected in 1916 in honor of the mulatto general and hero of the Wars of Independence who was known as the "Bronze Titan." He is perhaps the only soldier of any war to have survived 24 bullet wounds, but died in battle near Havana in 1896.

The motley tower that stands at the west end of the plaza is the 17th-century **Torreón de San Lázaro,** with loopholes for snipers aiming along the Malecón. Although it looks fairly modern, it was built in 1665 to guard the former cove of San Lázaro, reportedly a favored landing site for pirates.

Facing the park is the **Hospital Hermanos Almeijeiras** at the foot of Avenida Padre Varela (Belascoain). The hospital was built atop what was intended to be the Banco Nacional de Cuba, but Guevara, as the revolutionary Minister of Finance, nixed the plans, despite which local rumor has it that the vaults still contain Cuba's meager gold reserves.

The **Convento y Capilla de la Inmaculada Concepción,** Calle San Lázaro #805, e/ Oquendo y Marqués González (Lucena), tel. 878-8404, is immediately west of the hospital. This beautiful church and convent was built in gothic style in 1874. It later became a private girl's school. The chapel, with its stained-glass windows and painted altar, is again occupied by nuns and at last visit was being restored. Services are held Monday, Wednesday, and Friday 7 A.M. and 5 P.M.; Thursday and Saturday 5 P.M.; and Sunday 9 A.M.

Barrio Cayo Hueso

Immediately west of the Plaza Antonio Maceo is a triangular area bordered by the Malecón, Calle San Lázaro, and Calzada de Infanta, forming the northwest corner of Centro Habana. Known as Barrio Cayo Hueso, the region dates from the early 20th century, when tenement homes were erected atop what had been the Espada cemetery (hence the name, Cay of Bones). Some 12,000 homes are squashed into the compact and deteriorated region, accessed by a warren of irregular alleyways comprised of sagging walls and peeling paint.

© CHRISTOPHER P. BAKER

Salvador González Escalona and his sculptures, Callejón de Hamel

In 1995, because of its deteriorated state, Cayo Hueso became the first area of Havana earmarked for an experimental program to halt its decline. A new microbrigade effort was launched to renovate existing buildings, providing experts to guide inhabitants in the rehabilitation of their own units and utilizing supplies that are placed in their hands. Supposedly, almost 20 government agencies have involved in the restoration—each agency has adopted a street—and an effort has been made to educate the local community as to its own history and culture, although at last visit there seemed little to show for their efforts.

On Calle Hornos, the first cultural center dedicated to tango was formed. Today it still hosts tango dancing. Other cultural events are hosted on **Callejón de Hamel,** e/ Aramburu y Hospital, an alley one block south of San Lázaro, where local artist Salvador González Escalona has adorned walls with evocative murals in sun-drenched yellow, burnt orange, and blazing reds, inspired by *santería,* reflecting his religious beliefs and ties to Afro-Cuban culture. The authorities tried to close down González's project when it was nascent, but locals came into the streets to protect the now-precious heritage, which includes a *santería* shrine and fantastical totemic sculptures, such as a silver bathtub on wheels suspended on rails above head height. González, a bearded artist with an eye for self-promotion, has an eclectic art gallery, **Estudio-Galería Fambá,** tel. 878-1661, where he sells his works for US$500 and up. Open Mon.–Sat. 10 A.M.–6 P.M.; Sun. 9 A.M.–3 P.M. On Sundays González hosts Afro-Cuban *rumbas.*

The government isn't comfortable with Callejón de Hamel, and police keep a close eye on things.

The **Edificio Solemar,** Calle Soledad #205 e/ San Lázaro y Ánimas, was a novel architectural inspiration when built in 1944 as an apartment complex with sinuous balconies, "like stacks of curved ribbons," thought Eduardo Luis Rodríguez. In counterpoint, two blocks west, at San Lázaro #1016, e/ Espada y Hospital, is **Edificio de Ildefonsa Someillán,** another dynamic apartment complex but this one with balconies that angle in every direction.

Museo Fragua Martiana, Calle Príncipe #108,

esq. Hospital, tel. 870-7338, is a small museum dedicated to the life and works of José Martí. Open Mon.–Fri. 10 A.M.–4 P.M. To its rear is an exposed wall of coral rock encaged by wrought iron marking the spot where Martí was forced to break rocks as a prisoner at the San Lázaro quarry.

BETWEEN PASEO DEL PRADO AND GALIANO

Literature buffs may be intrigued by the **Museo Lezama Lima,** Calle Trocadero #162 e/ Crespo y Industria, tel. 863-4161, three blocks inland from the Malecón and two blocks west of the Prado. The museum, which opened in 1995, is in the former home of prodigious writer José Lezama Lima, author of *Paradiso,* an autobiographical, sexually explicit, homoerotic baroque novel that viewed Cuba as a "paradise lost" and was eventually made into a renowned movie. Lima was the leading literary figure of his time and his house served as a rendezvous; the literary review *Orígenes* was founded here. The building evokes the rich and varied universe of the writer, variously described by Guillermo Cabrera Infante as a "fat man with a perennial cigar" and a "deeply mystical influence." Lima fell afoul of

Fidel Castro and became a virtual home-bound recluse until his death in hospital in 1975. It was closed for renovation at last visit.

The Hotel Lincoln, Galiano, e/ Animas y Virtudes, two blocks north, was where Argentina's world champion race-car driver Fangio was kidnapped by Castro's revolutionaries in 1958 during the Cuban Grand Prix. Room #810 is today the **Museo de Juan Manuel Fangio,** with photos, magazines, and other relics from the period presenting a predictably one-sided version of the affair.

The **Cine América,** Galiano #253, tel. 862-5416, at the junction of Concordia, dates from 1941 and boasts an interior that is a model of art deco grace. The foyer features a terrazzo floor with zodiac motifs and an inlaid map of the world, with Cuba, which lies at the very center, picked out in polished brass. Its tiers of ballooning balconies and curvilinear box seats melt into the walls of the vaulted auditorium, which boasts a moon-and-stars ceiling. Albeit severely deteriorated and crying out for restoration, it remains one of the world's great modern-style theaters.

Cater-corner, the **Iglesia de Nuestra Señora de Monserrate,** Galiano, esq. Concordia, dates from 1843.

HEADLINE! FANGIO KIDNAPPED!

In February 1957 Cuba had initiated the Cuban Gran Premio, and 30 of the world's leading auto racers, including England's Stirling Moss and the four-time world champion Argentinian driver, Juan Manual Fangio, roared down the Malecón in their Ferraris and Maseratis. The Batista government spent $150,000 to promote the race and enacted strict press censorship to ensure that the more than 20 bombs that exploded on the streets of Havana in the three weeks preceding the race went unreported.

Fidel Castro's 26th of July Movement had tried to cripple the race. "They had circulated bulletins for three days, warning Cubans to stay off the streets and away from public spectacles," reports Rosalie Schwartz. "To reinforce their point, they had hurled phosphorus bombs into seats and aisles of Radio Centro Theater in the heart of Havana."

On February 23, 1958, on the eve of the second Cuban Gran Premio, Fangio was kidnapped at gunpoint by Castro's revolutionaries in the lobby of the Hotel Lincoln. The news was trumpeted around the world.

After the race, Fangio showed up safe and sound, and proclaimed that the rebels might have saved his life: the world champion was referring to a terrible accident during the race that had killed four people and injured more than 50, but his appreciative words were taken out of context and provided a major public relations coup for Castro's rebels.

Calle San Rafael, linking Parque Central with Avenida de Italia (Galiano), is a pedestrian precinct lined with department stores, many of which still bear prerevolutionary neon signs promoting U.S. brand names from yesteryear, such as Hotpoint and Singer. Paralleling San Rafael to the south is **Calle Neptuno,** a secondary shopping street. The city's first department store, El Encanto, was erected on the corner of Galiano in the 1930s. It was destroyed by arson in 1961 and the site has ever since been a memorial park to the staff member who died.

Fans of tango might check out the **Caserón del Tango,** Neptuno #303, e/ Águila y Italia, tel. 863-0097, a tiny cultural center-cum-museum run by tango lover Edmundo Daubal in honor of the dance. Here, you'll learn (questionably) that Cuba, not Argentina, invented the tango. Even Jorge Luis Borges (1899–1986), the great Argentinian writer, called Havana "the mother of tango." The displays feature magazine covers, record covers, and other mementos. Open 10 A.M.–8 P.M.

The flamboyant multi-tiered **Edificio Etecsa,** Calle Águila #5665, tel. 860-5711, at the junction of Dragones and Acosta, was built in 1927 in eclectic-cum-Spanish Renaissance style to house the headquarters of the American-owned Cuban Telephone Company.

Fábrica de Tabaco H. Upmann

This cigar factory, Calle Amistad #407, e/ Barcelona y Dragones, tel. 862-0081, two blocks west of the Capitolio, is officially known as the Fábrica de Tabaco José Martí. It was begun by the German brothers Herman and Agustín Hupmann in 1844 (the brothers dropped the "H," as it was silent in Spanish, and adopted it as an initial, for *hermanos,* or "brothers"). In its heyday at the turn of the century, the factory was by far the largest producer of cigars in the country. The Upmann name remains synonymous with the highest quality Havana cigars—mild to medium-flavored, very smooth and subtle, and available in more than 30 sizes (not to be confused with H. Upmanns made in the Dominican Republic). Cigar connoisseurs consider that the best Montecristos come from this factory, including the

mammoth Montecristo A, Cohiba Robusto, and Espléndido. The factory's almost 50 rollers are all rated "grade seven," the highest ranking a cigar roller can possess in Cuba, although only three rollers possess the skills and strength to roll the whopping Montecristo A, of which only about 15,000 are made annually. Many Habano cognoscenti, says *Cigar Aficionado,* "scour cigar shops around the world for boxes with the coveted 'JM' initials printed on the bottom." It's open Monday–Friday 8 A.M.–4 P.M. for call-by visitors. Tours are offered at 10:30 A.M. and 1:30 P.M. (US$10).

BARRIO CHINO

The first Chinese immigrants arrived in Cuba in 1847 as indentured laborers—only 206 of the 300 laborers who set sail on January 2 survived the journey. Over ensuing decades, as many as 150,000 Chinese "yellow slaves" may have arrived to work the fields. They were contracted to labor for eight years for miserable wages insufficient to buy their return. Most stayed, and many intermarried with blacks. The Sino-Cuban descendants of those who worked off their indenture gravitated to Centro Habana, where they settled in the zones bordering the Zanza Real, the aqueduct that channeled water to the city. Here they worked as domestics or opened vegetable shops, laundries, and restaurants. They were later joined by other Chinese fleeing persecution in California, including a wealthy group of California Chinese who arrived with investment opportunities in mind. In time Havana's Chinese quarter, Barrio Chino, became the largest in Latin America—a mini-Beijing in the tropics. The Chinatown flourished and became wealthy—many Chinese profited immensely during the "Dance of the Millions" sugar boom of the 1920s—and rich merchants sponsored masquerades and other exotic Chinese festivities.

Barrio Chino became known for the strength of its theater, and traditional operas were a cultural staple. During the "sordid era," however, Barrio Chino evolved as a center of opium dens and brothels; many of the traditional theaters became peep shows and sex clubs. At the infamous Shanghai theater, for US$1.25 one could see a "nude cabaret of extreme obscenity with the bluest of blue films in the intervals," wrote Graham Greene, who "watched without much interest Superman's performance with a mulatto girl (as uninspiring as a dutiful husband's)," then "smoked marijuana, and [saw] a lesbian performance at the Blue Moon," before snorting a little cocaine. Superman—also known as El Toro (The Bull)—had a 14-inch penis and earned US$25 nightly. He became so famous that he was immortalized in *The Godfather II,* in the scene in which the mobsters are in Cuba watching a live sex show. Greene made the Shanghai—Havana's paramount *exhibición*—a setting in *Our Man in Havana,* when Wormold wisely opts to take Beatrice to the Tropicana instead.

Today, Barrio Chino is a mere shadow of its former self, with about 400 native-born Chinese and perhaps 2,000 descendants still resident in the area. The vast majority of Chinese left Cuba in the years immediately following the Revolution. Barrio Chino has since lost most of its personality along with its colorful characters, who were encouraged to become "less Chinese and more Cuban." Nonetheless, there's enough to remind you of how things once were. Chinese lanterns still hang outside the doorways, alongside signs written in Chinese. You'll recognize Chinese features, too, in the lively free market held daily (except Wednesday) on tiny Calle Cuchillo. The community's Chinese-language newspaper (*Periódico Kwong Wah Po*) is typeset by hand and printed on ancient presses for a readership of a few hundred; the office is at Calle San Nicolás #520, e/ Zanja y Dragones, tel. 863-3286. And many Cuban Chinese still worship Cuan Cung, a red-faced, long-bearded deity synchronistically akin to Changó, the African warrior god in *santería.*

The **Casa de Artes y Tradiciones Chinas,** Calle Salud #313, e/ Gervasio y Escobar, tel. 863-9632, works to promote Chinese culture and features a small gallery. Tai chi and dance classes are offered. Open Mon.–Fri. 8:30 A.M.–5:30 P.M., Sat. 8:30 A.M.–noon.

In 1995, the government of China agreed to help rebuild Havana's Chinatown and funded a

Pórtico Chino (Dragon Gate) across Calle Dragones, announcing visitors' entry from the east. Supposedly, it's the largest Dragon Gate in the world. No restoration had taken place at last visit.

If you can, time your visit to coincide with Chinese New Year at the end of January into early February, when the streets are charged with the staccato pop of firecrackers meant to scare away evil spirits and the lion comes out to leap and dance through the streets of Barrio Chino.

The most overtly Chinese street is diminutive, pedestrian-only **Calle Cuchillo,** which runs less than 100 meters and is lined with a dozen genuine Chinese restaurants. It's best visited at night, when the Chinese lanterns are aglow. Ernest Hemingway used to eat at **Restaurante Pacífico,** Calle San Nicolás, esq. Cuchillo, tel. 863-3243, on the top floor of the five-story building to which Castro is still an occasional visitor. "To get there," recalls Hemingway's son, Gregory, "you had to go up in an old elevator with a sliding iron grille for a door. It stopped at every floor, whether you wanted it to or not. On the second floor there was a five-piece Chinese orchestra blaring crazy atonal music. . . . Then you reached the third floor, where there was a whorehouse. . . . The fourth floor was an opium den with pitifully wasted little figures curled up around their pipes."

The **Casa Abuelo Lung Kong Cun Sol,** Calle Dragones #364, e/ Manrique y San Nicolás, tel. 862-5388 or 863-2061, is a social club—one of 13 associations—that exists to support elders in the Chinese community. It offers a genuine Chinese ambience. Oldsters sit in their rockers, gossiping and reading newspapers, while others gobble down free meals with their *palillos* (chopsticks). You could be in Hong Kong. It has a more elegant restaurant upstairs and, on the third floor, the **Templo San Fan Kong,** with an exquisitely carved, centenary gold-plated altar imported from Canton. Visitors are usually made welcome, but it's a common courtesy to ask permission before sticking your nose inside. Open daily noon–midnight.

The **Sociedad Chung Shan,** Dragones #311, e/ San Nicolás y Rayo, tel. 862-0909, is another Chinese cultural society where you can witness classes in Mandarin Chinese and tai chi, plus games of mah-jongg. You can also see worshipers paying homage—often in secret rituals—at a shrine of Cuan Cung in the **Farmacia Chung Wah,** Calle Zanja, which still dispenses homeopathic medicines.

The **Iglesia Nuestra Señora Caridad del Cobre,** Calle Manrique #570, esq. Salud, tel. 861-0945, was erected in 1802 and features exquisite statuary, stained-glass windows, and gold-leaf altar. Open Tues.–Fri. 7:30 A.M.–6 P.M.; Sat. 7:30 A.M.–noon; Sun. 7:30 A.M.–noon and 4–6 P.M.

AVENIDAS SIMÓN BOLÍVAR AND SALVADOR ALLENDE (CARLOS III)

Avenida Simón Bolívar (formerly Avenida Reina) runs west from Parque de la Fraternidad. Beyond Avenida Padre Varela (Belascoain) it broadens into a wide boulevard called Avenida Salvador Allende laid out in the early 19th century by Governor Tacón, when it was known officially as Carlos III.

Simón Bolívar is lined with once-impressive colonial-era structures gone to ruin. One of the few structures not seemingly on its last legs is the **Iglesia del Sagrado Corazón de Jesús,** Avenida Simón Bolívar e/ Padre Varela y Gervasio, tel. 862-4979, a gothic inspiration in stone that could have been transported from medieval England. It was built in 1922 with beamed ceiling held aloft by great marbled columns. Gargoyles and Christian allegories adorn the exterior, featuring a 77-meter-tall spire topped by a bronze cross. Its stained-glass windows rival the best in Europe. The church, one of the most active in Cuba, also boasts a fabulous soaring altar of carved wood. Open daily 8 A.M.–noon, and 4–7 P.M. Services are offered Monday–Saturday 8 A.M. and 4:30 P.M.; Sunday 8 A.M., 9:30 A.M., and 4:30 P.M.

The **Gran Templo Nacional Masónico,** Avenida Salvador Allende e/ Padre Varela y Lucena, was established in 1951 as Havana's Grand Masonic Temple. Though no longer a Freemason's lodge, it retains a fading mural in the lobby depicting the history of masonry in Cuba.

Farther west, at Salvador Allende y Árbol Seco is the **Casa de la Cultura Centro Habana,** hosting cultural activities for the local community and containing the **Galería Kahlo** in a colonial mansion of note (Salvador Allende #720, e/ Soledad y Castillejo, tel. 878-4727, open Mon.–Sat. 11 A.M.–6 P.M. except Friday).

Avenida Salvador Allende continues westward of Calzada de Infanta towards the Nuevo Vedado district. The summer house of the Capitanes Generales (the Spanish governors) was built here in 1837, setting a trend for many of Havana's nobility.

CALLE INFANTA

This broad boulevard, lined with arcaded *porticos* its entire length, runs south from the Malecón to Avenida Salvador Allende and forms the border of Centro Habana and Vedado.

© CHRISTOPHER P. BAKER

Iglesia del Sagrado Corázon de Jesús

VISITING HAVANA'S CIGAR FACTORIES

You'll forever remember the pungent aroma of a cigar factory, a visit to which is de rigueur. The factories, housed in fine old colonial buildings, remain much as they were in the mid-19th century. Though now officially known by ideologically sound names, they're still commonly referred to by their pre-Revolutionary names, which are displayed on old signs outside. Each specializes in a number of cigar brands of a particular flavor—the government assigns to certain factories the job of producing particular brands. And revolutionary slogans exhort workers to maintain strict quality—"Quality is respect for people."

© CHRISTOPHER P. BAKER

The five major cigar factories in Havana—altogether, there are 42 throughout Cuba—all now welcome visitors. Unfortunately, the tours are not well organized and often crowded with tour groups, few of whom have any genuine appreciation for cigars. Explanations of tobacco processes and manufacturing procedures are also sparse. Tours usually bypass the tobacco preparations and instead begin in the *galeras* (rolling rooms), then pass to the quality-control methods. Visitors therefore miss out on seeing the stripping, selecting, and dozens of other processes that contribute to producing a handmade cigar.

Although the government has con-

Parque de los Mártires Universitarios, Infanta, e/ Calles Jovellar y San Lázaro, honors students of the University of Havana who were murdered or otherwise lost their lives during the fights against the Machado and Batista regimes. The junction was an important scene of battles between students and police. A memorial plaque in the plazuela recalls that it was from Calle Jovellar #107 that Castro set out for Santiago de Cuba on July 25, 1953 in a blue Buick sedan, initiating the attack on the Moncada barracks that would launch his revolution.

The **Convento y Iglesia del Carmen,** Calle Infanta, e/ Neptuno y Concordia, tel. 878-5168,

is one of Havana's largest and most impressive churches. Built in baroque fashion, it features a 60.5-meter-tall tower atop which soars a 7.5-meter-tall sculpture of Our Lady of Carmen. Inside, the church features beautiful stained glass and statuary. Open Mon.–Sat. 8–10 A.M. and 4–7 P.M.; Sun. 7:30 A.M.–12:30 P.M. and 4:30–7:30 P.M. Mass is held Monday–Saturday 8 A.M. and 6:30 P.M., and Sundays at 8:30 A.M., 11:30 A.M., and 6:30 P.M.

At the junction of San Rafael you'll discover a tiny enclosed plaza where members of the Asociación Nacional Ornithológica de Cuba (National Ornithological Association of Cuba),

sidered banning tours (it did so briefly in 1997 at the Partagás and La Corona factories), the income comes in handy. A portion is given to the factories and ostensibly is used to improve workers' conditions.

You can book tours through tour desks in major hotels or call the factories direct. Be sure to book ahead, for every entrance is guarded by an ever-present, stern-faced female concierge determined to stop you from entering. Writes Nancy Stout: "These women are tougher than the civil guard nearby, in his green khakis with a tie-on red armband and pistol around his waist."

Habanos, S.A. has its headquarters at **Empresa Cubana del Tabaco,** O'Reilly #104 e/ Tacón y Mercaderes, Habana Vieja, tel. 861-5775, fax 33-8214. **Tabacuba,** Calle 19, esq. M, tel. 53-5871, is in charge of exports.

The Factories

See the appropriate regional sightseeing chapter for details.

Fábrica La Corona, Calle Agramonte #106, e/ Refugio y Colón, Habana Vieja, tel./fax 862-6173, is open to the public Monday–Saturday 7 A.M.–5 P.M.

Fábrica Partagás, Calle Industria #502, e/ Dragones y Barcelona, Habana Vieja, tel. 862-0086 or 878-4368, offers guided tours daily at 10 A.M. and 2 P.M. (US$10).

Fábrica H. Upmann, Calle Amistad #407, e/ Dragones y Barcelona, Centro Habana, tel. 862-0081, is open Monday–Friday 8 A.M.–4 P.M. for call-by visitors. Tours are offered at 10:30 A.M. and 1:30 P.M. (US$10).

Fábrica Romeo y Julieta, on Padre Varela e/ Desague y Peñal Verno, Centro Habana, tel. 878-1058 or 879-3927, is open for 30-minute tours. Mon.–Fri. 8:30–11 A.M. and noon–3 P.M.

Fábrica El Laguito, Avenida 146 #2302, e/ 21 y 21A, Cubanacán, tel. 208-4654, allows visits by appointment only. Permission must be requested from the Empresa Cubana del Tabaco.

Fábrica Héroes del Moncada, Avenida 57 #13402, e/ 134 y 136, Marianao, tel. 260-9058. *Cigar Aficionado* considers this one of the top three cigar factories in Cuba. Leaf processing takes place on the ground floor, and the rolling upstairs. Tours are offered Monday–Friday at 10 A.M. and 11 A.M.; US$10. The factory receives very few visitors, and you must arrange in advance through CATEC, Calle 148 #905, e/ 9 y 9A, Cubanacán, tel. 208-6071.

colloquially termed the **Canary Cultivators of Havana,** gather to make bird-talk and buy cages and seed. Their headquarters is half-a-block away, at Infanta #402, tel. 33-5749. Here, ANOC members display and buy and sell their rainbow-hued birds, and the place is full of the shrilling of finches and parakeets. The members breed birds, which the association exports. It's open Monday–Friday 8:30 A.M.–5:30 P.M.

SOUTHERN CENTRO HABANA

South of Avenidas Simón Bolívar and Salvador Allende, Centro is traversed down its center by Calle Padre Varela and bounded by Infanta (west) and Máximo Gómez (east). The area is sadly diminished since being laid out last century. Many edifices are ready for the wrecking ball, and this is one of Havana's most down-at-heels neighborhoods.

Fábrica de Tabaco Romeo y Julieta, Padre Varela, e/ Desague y Peñal Verno, tel. 878-1058 or 879-3927, was founded in 1875 by Inocencia Álvarez and is known officially today as the Antonio Briones Montoto cigar factory. The exquisite three-story building has ironwork balconies. Green glazed tiles cover the interior walls of the lobby, and an iron staircase twirls

Iglesia de San Nicolás

gracefully toward the ceiling, decorated with classical moldings with pink and green laurel wreaths. The factory specializes in medium-flavored brands including, since 1875, the fine Romeo y Julieta. It also makes the heavyweight, high-quality, and limited-quantity Saint Luís Rey cigars favored by actor James Coburn and Frank Sinatra. Like most Havana cigar factories, duties vary by floor, with leaf handling on the ground floor, and stemming, sorting, rolling, box decorating, and ringing on the upper two floors.

In 2001, the factory gained a well-stocked La Casa del Tabaco store, plus a cocktail bar (which includes coffee-tasting), a walk-in humidor (and a second reserved for VIPs). The factory is open for 30-minute tours offered every 30 minutes, Mon.–Fri. 8:30–11 A.M. and noon–3 P.M. (US$10, children free). No cameras.

Another cigar factory—**Fábrica El Rey del Mundo**—hides behind the Romeo y Julieta factory at Calle San Carlos 816, tel. 870-9336. Currently known as the Carlos Balino factory, and formerly as the Díaz Brothers, Cuesta Rey & Co., this small factory produces cigars under the El Rey del Mundo label.

One block south of Fábrica de Tabaco Romeo y Julieta, is the **Conservatorio Municipal de Habana,** Padre Varela, esq. Carmen, a music conservatory boasting a well-preserved classical facade.

Padre Varela continues south four blocks to Cuatro Caminos, an all-important junction where six major thoroughfares meet.

The **Iglesia de San Nicolás,** one block west of Avenida Máximo Gómez, on Calle San Nicolás, is a splendidly restored yet tiny church with ocher walls and a circular bell tower.

Cerro

South of Centro, the land rises gently to Cerro (pop. 130,000), a separate administrative district. During the last century, Cerro developed as the place to retire during the torrid midsummer months; many wealthy families maintained two homes in Havana—one in town, another on the cooler hill (*cerro* means "hill"). The area is replete with once-glorious *casas quintas* (summer homes) in neoclassical, beaux arts, and art nouveau styles. Alas, the region is terribly deteriorated, and the majority of buildings transcend sordid. Cerro spreads out expansively and is renowned for some of the more disreputable areas of the city, including centers of drug trading. Avoid the Barrio Canal and Sucel districts.

The district is anchored by Avenida Máximo Gómez (popularly called Monte or Calzada de Cerro), which snakes southwest from Parque de la Fraternidad and is surely one of the saddest streets in all Havana.

AVENIDA MÁXIMO GÓMEZ AND CALZADO DE CERRO

This sinuous avenue connects Habana Vieja with Cerro. During the 19th century, scores of summer homes in classical style were erected here, each more extravagantly Italianate than the next. Many of the luxurious houses went up along Avenida Máximo Gómez, or Monte as locals prefer to call it (it changes its name to Calzada de Cerro west of the junction with Calzada de Infanta), described by writer Paul Goldberger as "one of the most remarkable streets in the world: three unbroken kilometers of nineteenth-century neoclassical villas, with colonnaded arcades making an urban vista of heartbreaking beauty." Heartbreaking is correct. The avenue ascends gradually, marching backward into the past like a classical ruin, looking as Herculaneum must have looked during its decline. Monte's once-stunning arcades are now in desperate condition, and houses are decaying behind lovely facades.

Novelist James Michener, exploring Cerro while looking for a house in which to set the Cuban portion of a novel on the Caribbean, was told "in elegiac tones" by his guide: "The steps went down by decades. 1920s the mansions are in full flower. 1930s the rich families begin to move out. 1940s people grab them who can't afford to maintain them, ruin begins. 1950s ten big families move into each mansion, pay no rent, and begin to tear it apart. 1960s during the first years of the Revolution, no housing elsewhere, so even more crowd in, ruin accelerates. 1970s some of the weakest begin to fall down. 1980s many gone beyond salvation."

A drive along Monte will provide a lasting memory. The government has talked grandly about assisting residents to restore their homes, but at last visit there was no sign that local residents had received any assistance. Heartrending . . . as the same lack of money that saved these once-glorious edifices from the wrecking ball is today insufficient to save them from their own extinction.

Of interest is the **Cuatro Caminos,** tel. 870-5934, the nation's largest farmers market, taking up the entire block between Máximo Gómez and Cristina (also called Avenida de México), and Manglar Arroyo and Matadero. This much-dilapidated 19th-century market hall still functions as such and is worth a visit for its bustling color and ambience. Here you can buy live goats, geese, pig's heads, and all manner of fruits and veggies. Open Tues.–Sat. 7 A.M.–6:30 P.M. and Sun. 7 A.M.–2 P.M.

At the other end of Calzada de Cerro, one of the most splendid mansions still extant is the **Quinta del Conde de Santovenia,** Calzada de Cerro #1424, e/ Patria y Auditor, tel. 870-6449, erected in 1845 in subdued neo-classical style, with a 1929 neo-gothic chapel addition. It has served as an old people's home (*Hogar de Ancianos*) for more than a century.

Further west, one block south of Calzada de Cerro, is the tiny **Plaza de Galicia,** Calle Peñón, esq. Santo Tomás. Shaded by venerable ceiba trees and bougainvillea bowers, the square features the diminutive **Iglesia de Peñón** at its heart.

The church bears a Corinthian frontage and is topped by a round spire. It is open most afternoons and for mass on Sunday. The plaza was dedicated in 1991 to the Pueblo Gallego (the Galician people).

Estadio Latinoamericano, Cuba's main baseball stadium, rises over Cerro five blocks north of Máximo Gómez, on Calle Consejero Aranjo.

Fábrica de Ron Bocoy

The most intriguing site in Cerro is this venerable former home-turned rum factory, on Máximo Gómez #1417, e/ Patrio y Auditor, tel. 877-5781, bocoy@tuhv.cha.cyt.cu, facing Quinta del Conde de Santovenia, immediately east of Hospital Salvador Allende. You can't miss the two-tone pink facade and the legend "BOCOY" above the wide, handsome door: its facade is decorated with four dozen cast-iron swans painted blue-and-white and marching wing to wing, "each standing tall and slim, its long neck bent straight down in mortal combat with an evil serpent climbing up its legs to sink its fangs," wrote James Michener. Hence the building's colloquial nickname: *Casa de Culebras* (House of Snakes). It was formerly owned by the Condes de la Villanueva (the swans were a symbol of wealth that the snakes were meant to guard). Michener chose this building to be the model for the house in which lived "once-intimate liberal relatives" of a conservative Cuban exile family in his book *Caribbean.*

Beyond the swan-filled portico, the mansion is one of Havana's most important distilleries, making Cuba's famous Legendario rums and liquors, although a comparative taste test betrays the fact that Legendario is one of Cuba's least prestigious rums. The vaults contain great oak casks up to seven meters tall stacked in dark recesses— "something out of Piranesi, a ghostly affair with a single unshaded lightbulb." The distillery manufactures five types of rum, three brandies, sweet wine (*vinos dulces*), and liqueurs made of plantain, anis, cacao, mint, and coffee.

Bocoy also manufactures one of the choicest rums in Cuba, intended solely for Fidel Castro to give as gifts to notable personalities. The special libation is packaged in a bulbous earthenware bottle inside a miniature pirate's treasure chest labeled La Isla del Tesoro (Treasure Island), on display in the small upstairs museum that boasts an original 19th-century copper distillery.

Fábrica de Ron Bocoy

Free tours of the distillery are offered. It has a showroom and a bar, plus a Casa del Tabaco. Open Mon.–Sat. 9 A.M.–5 P.M., Sun. 9 A.M.–3 P.M.

CALZADA PALATINO

This westerly extension of Calzada de Cerro crosses the Vía Blanca and dead-ends at Avenida de Santa Catalina, on the edge of the Víbora district. The junction is dominated by the **Quinta las Delicias,** Avenida Santa Catalina, esq. Palatino, tel. 867-0205 or 841-1526, a sumptuous French art nouveau mansion built in 1905 by Charles Brun for Rosalia Abreu, a socialite who populated the extensive grounds with almost 200 monkeys . . . hence the popular name, Finca de los Monos (Villa of Monkeys). Beyond the castellated entrance, the vestibule is graced by a mural by Cuban artist Arturo Mendocal, and by a gloriously decorated ceiling and stained-glass

ventrales. The woodsy gardens feature fountains and pergolas, plus a neo-gothic family chapel. It functions today as a youth center. Visits by appointment. Open Mon.–Fri. 8 A.M.–5 P.M.

Two blocks away stands the **Pabellón de los Depósitos del Acueducto de Albear,** Calle Fomento, e/ Chaple (pronounce "chap-lay") y Recreo, two blocks east of Calzada Palatino. This lavishly adorned neo-classical aqueduct and reservoir (with giant frogs to each corner) was designed in 1856 by Francisco de Albear and Francisco Ruizen to supply gravity-fed water to the ever-expanding city by tapping the Vento springs. It is considered a masterful piece of engineering and garnered awards at the International Expositions in Philadelphia (1876) and Paris (1878). It still functions as the modern, albeit much dilapidated waterworks, and supplies one-fifth of Havana's water. However, tourists are not allowed in without special permission.

Vedado and Plaza de la Revolución

The *municipio* of Plaza de la Revolución (pop. 165,000), west of Centro Habana, comprises Vedado and, to the southwest, the modern enclave of Nuevo Vedado. The leafy residential streets of northern Vedado are a joy to walk in serendipitous pursuit.

The sprawling region is hemmed to the north by the Malecón, to the east by Calzada de Infanta, to the west by the Río Almendares, running in a deep canyon, and to the southeast by the Calzada de Ayestaran and Avenida de la Independencia.

Vedado

The conclusion of the brief Spanish-American-Cuban War, in 1898, brought U.S. money rushing into Havana. A new age of elegance evolved in Cuba's capital, concentrated in hilly Vedado ("forest reserve" or "forbidden"), formerly a vast open space between Centro Habana and the Río Almendares; until the early 19th century, construction in Vedado was prohibited and the area served as a buffer zone in case of attack

Alma Mater, University of Havana

from the west. In 1859, however, plans were drawn up for urban expansion using a grid system and firm mathematical proportions that graced Vedado with a lovely, organic ambience. Strict building regulations, for example, defined that there should be 15 feet of gardens between building and street, and more in wider *avenidas*. Regularly spaced parks were mandated. Fine parks and monuments to generals were added, along with an extension of the Malecón, the wide promenade anchoring the waterfront. In time, civic structures, large hotels, casinos, department stores, and lavish restaurants sprouted alongside nightclubs displaying fleshly attractions.

Vedado—the commercial heart of "modern" Havana—has been described as "Havana at its middle-class best." The University of Havana is here. So are the fabulous Cementerio Colón, many of the city's prime hotels and restaurants, virtually all its main commercial buildings, and block after block of handsome mansions and apartment houses in art deco, eclectic, beaux arts, and neoclassical styles . . . luxurious and humble alike, lining streets shaded by stately jagüeys dropping their aerial roots to the ground like muscular tendrils. Nowhere are they more lavishly displayed than along Calle 17. While exploring, watch for stone lions flanking the gates of large mansions. These revered symbols denote the home of a nobleman. Some time late last century, a commoner who had amassed a fortune bought himself a title and erected lions. The proper grandees of Spain were so outraged that they tore theirs down in a protest known as La Muerte de los Leones—The Death of the Lions.

The government ministries are here, too, centered on the Plaza de la Revolución and including the Palacio de la Revolución (the seat of government) and the towering José Martí monument.

For a bird's-eye view of Vedado, head to the top of the Hotel Habana Libre or the Focsa building.

ORIENTATION

Vedado follows a grid pattern aligned NNW by SSE and laid out in quadrants. Odd-numbered streets (calles) run east–west, parallel to the shore.

Even-numbered calles run perpendicular. To confuse things, some "calles" are "avenidas," although there seems to be no logic as to which these are. West of Paseo, calles are even-numbered; east of Paseo, calles run from A to P. The basic grid is overlain by a larger grid of broad boulevards averaging six blocks apart.

Dividing the quadrants east–west is Calle 23, which rises (colloquially) as La Rampa from the Malecón at its junction with Calzada de Infanta. La Rampa runs uphill to Calle L and continues on the flat as Calle 23. Paralleling it to the north is a second major east–west thoroughfare, Calle 9 (Línea), five blocks inland of the Malecón, which it also intersects to the northeast.

Four major roadways divide the quadrants north–south: Calle L to the east, and Avenida de los Presidentes, Paseo, and Avenida 12 further west. Vedado slopes gently upward from the shore to Calle 23 and thence gently downward toward the Cerro district. Almost every major avenue in Vedado debouches onto the Malecón.

Nuevo Vedado, southwest of Vedado, has an irregular pattern. Avenida de los Presidentes, Paseo, and, to the west, Avenida 26, connect Vedado to Nuevo Vedado. Most roadways converge on the Plaza de la Revolución, which divides Avenida Carlos M. de Céspedes on its north side and Avenida de Rancho Boyeros on its south side. The two meet westward to form Avenida de la Independencia, which runs to the international airport.

THE MALECÓN

The Malecón runs along the bulging, wave-battered shorefront of northern Vedado, curling east–west from La Rampa in the east to the Río Almendras in the west, a distance of three miles, where the seafront boulevard meets Calzada (7ma) and dips under the tunnel that links it with Miramar. This portion of the Malecón is less dramatic than that along the shoreline of Centro Habana. However, there are several important sights.

Many of the 1950s skyscrapers that line the shore are decrepit, though they still have their luxury penthouses with swimming pools on the

STRAITS OF FLORIDA

SEE "VEDADO: THE CORE" MAP

© AVALON TRAVEL PUBLISHING, INC.

"SEÑORES IMPERIALISTAS..." BILLBOARD

MALECÓN

POLICE

PALADAR EL BISTROT

U.S. INTERESTS SECTION

ANTI-IMPERIALIST PLATFORM (PROTESTODROMO)

ESTADIO JOSÉ MARTÍ

MINREX

HOSPEDAJE/CASA PARTICULAR MARPOLY

PALADAR CHANSONNIER

TEATRO BRECHT

MUSEO DE LA DANZA

EL PATRONATO

CASA PARTICULAR MARTA VITONTE

JARDÍN JOHANN STRAUSS

IGLESIA DE SAN JUAN DE LETRAN

Parque Coppelia

UNEAC

STATUE OF VICTOR HUGO

COPPELIA

MERCADO AGROPECUARIO

ALIANZA FRANCESA

MONUMENT TO LEONOR PÉREZ

CENTRO SEFARDÍ

INSTITUTO INTERNATIONAL DE PERIODISMO

PALADAR DOÑA LAURA

LAS ESCALERAS

MUSEO DE ARTES DECORATIVAS

EL COSTILLAR DE ROCINANTE

CASA DE LOS INFUSIONES

CASA PARTICULAR FRANCISCO RODRÍGUEZ

PALADAR EL GRINGO VIEJO

PALADAR LOS HELECHOS

PHYSICS FACULTY

FALCULTY OF MANAGEMENT

MARTINAIR

HOSPITAL CALIXTO GARCÍA

ESTADIO JUAN ABRAHANTES

MONUMENTO Á JOSÉ GÓMEZ

POST OFFICE

FALCULTY OF CHEMISTRY

HOSPITAL ORTOPEDICO

LA MADRIGUERA

AGENCIA VEDADO

REFECTORY

FALCULTY OF ARTS & LECTURES

QUINTA DE LOS MOLINOS

JARDÍN BOTÁNICO

FALCULTY OF FOREIGN LANGUAGES

AV. SALVADOR ALLENDE

Revolución

CASTILLO DEL PRINCIPE

POLICE

ZAPATA

ROSENBERG MONUMENT

BRUZÓN

HOTEL BRUZÓN

SALA POLIVALENTE RAMON FONST/MUSEO DEPORTIVOS

TERMINAL DE ÓMNIBUSES INTERPROVINCIALES

To José Martí Int'l Airport

VEDADO: THE CORE

STRAITS OF FLORIDA

Plaza de la Dignidad
STATUE JOSÉ MARTÍ

MALECÓN

0   10 mi
0   10 km

REX RENT-A-LIMOUSINE
MONUMENTO DEL MAINE
SERVI-CUPET GAS STATION
PANAUTOS RENT-A-CAR
CLÍNICA CAMILO CIENFUEGOS/FARMACIA INTERNACIONAL
BANCO FINANCIERO INTERNATIONAL
CUBALINDA
ETECSA TELEPHONES
RUMBOS (HQ)
VILLA NIDIA
GATO TUERTO
CABARET PARISIENNE
HOTEL NACIONAL
EL RÁPIDO
MONUMENTO A SINO-CUBANOS
SUPERMARKET
TRANSTUR/ HAVANAUTOS
AIRLINE OFFICES
BIM BOM/ MICAR RENT-A-CAR
EL EMPERADOR
FOCSA BUILDING
PALADAR GRILL
TEATRO GUIÑOL
BURO DE CONVENCIONES
TRANSAUTO RENT-A-CAR
EL CONEJITO
HOTEL UNIVERSARIO
SALA ROJA
CLUB SCHERAZADA
RESTAURANTE MONSEIGNEUR
ETECSA BOOTH
FARMERS' MARKET
CASA DE TABACO
HOTEL CAPRI
CLUB 21
INTERNATIONAL PRESS CENTER/TELECORREO/ PHOTOSERVICE
CASA DEL TABACO
ARTEX
PIZZERÍA MILANO
HOTEL VICTORIA
HORIZONTES (HQ)
CINE LA RAMPA
PALADAR NEREI
TV STUDIOS
CAFÉ SOFIA
WAKAMBA
LA ROCA/MICAR RENT-A-CAR
CLUB 23
LA ZORRA Y EL CUERVO
PALADAR HURÓN AZUL
CLUB COCTEL HABANA
PABELLÓN CUBA
CLUB TIKORA
HOTEL ST. JOHN
CAFÉ LA ARCADA
TRATORRIA MARAKAS
CASA PARTICULAR MAGALIS SÁNCHEZ LÓPEZ
TRANSTUR HQ
TRANSTUR RENT-A-CAR
RESTAURANTE MANDARIN
CRAFTS MARKET
EL RÁPIDO
LIBRERIA CENTENARIO DEL APOSTOL
PAIN DE PARIS
IGLESIA DE SAN JUAN DE LETRAN
INDIAN EMBASSY
DINO'S PIZZA
CINE YARA
TOUR AND TRAVEL/FINCIMEX
HOTEL VEDADO
CABARET LAS VEGAS
Parque Coppelia
CAFÉ LA RAMPA
RESTAURANTE EL POLINEESIO/ AIR FRANCE/CUBATUR
CASA MUSEO ABEL SANTAMARÍA
CASA PARTICULAR FAMILIA MARTÍNEZ
CASA PARTICULAR FAMILIA VILLALÓN
COPPELIA
HOTEL HABANA LIBRE TRYP
ARTEX
RESTAURANTE VEGETARIANO LA TERRAZA
Parque Victor Hugo
COPPELIA (DOLLARS)
LAS BULERIAS
BANCO FINANCIERO INTERNACIONAL/ GALERÍA COMERCIAL HABANA LIBRE
AGENCIA DE INFORMACIÓN NACIONAL
ETECSA BOOTH
EDIFICIO L Y 25
RESTAURANTE BIKI
CASA PARTICULAR DE JORGE COLLA POTTS
RESTAURANTE SIETE MARES
CASA PARTICULAR BASILIA PÉREZ
LIBRERIA FERNANDO ORTIZ
CASA DE LA PRENSA
TEATRO EL SÓTANO
HOTEL COLINA
LAS ESCALIRETA
TABERNA DON PEPE
CONCORDIA
FEDERACIÓN DE ESTUDIANTES UNIVERSITARIOS
FALCULTY OF BIOLOGY
STUDENT'S UNION
CASA PARTICULAR KARLITA
NEPTUNO
CASA DE LA PRENSA
EL COCHINITO
UNION DE JÓVENES COMUNISTAS
MONUMENTO A JULIO MELLA
ALMA MATER
PARKING/ MICAR RENT-A-CAR
CASA PARTICULAR DANIA BORREGO
FACULTY OF LAW
PALADAR ARIES
PHARMACY FACULTY
SAN MIGUEL
CINE RIVIERA
FACULTY OF PHILOSOPHY AND HISTORY
LIBRARY
RECTORY
MUSEO NAPOLEÓNICO
UNIVERSIDAD DE LA HABANA
SARACÉN ARMORED CAR
FACULTY OF PSYCHOLOGY
AULA MAGNA
FACULTY OF MATHEMATICS AND COMPUTAION

VEDADO

© AVALON TRAVEL PUBLISHING, INC.

CHRISTOPHER P. BAKER

fishermen on the Malecón

top floors. Many have been turned into bars and *paladares,* not all of them legal.

Hotel Nacional and Vicinity

The landmark **Hotel Nacional,** Calle O y 21, tel. 33-3564, is dramatically perched atop a small cliff at the junction of La Rampa and the Malecón. Now a national monument, this grande dame hotel was designed by the same architects (McKim, Mead & White) who designed The Breakers in Palm Beach, which it closely resembles. It opened on December 30, 1930, in the midst of the Great Depression. The elaborately detailed, Spanish-style neoclassical hotel suffered from bad management and was badly in need of refurbishment when mobster Meyer Lansky persuaded General Batista to let him build a grand casino and convert some of the rooms to luxurious suites for wealthy gamblers. The hotel's mob associates run deep; in 1946 Lucky Luciano called a summit here to discuss carving up Havana. In 1955, the casino and nightclub opened, drawing society figures from far and wide. Luminaries from Winston Churchill and the Prince of Wales to Marlon Brando have laid their heads here, as attested by the photos in the lobby bar. It

is still favored as the hotel *par excellence* for visiting big-wigs . . . "Gosh! Is that Naomi Campbell swanning through the lobby?"

You approach via a palm-lined drive that delivers you at a Palladian porch, which opens to a vestibule lavishly adorned with *mudéjar* (Moorish) patterned tiles. The sweeping palm-shaded lawns to the rear slope toward the Malecón, above which sits a battery of cannons from the Wars of Independence. The cliff is riddled with defensive tunnels built since the 1970s.

Fronting the hotel by the shore is the **Monumento a las Víctimas del Maine** (Maine Monument), dedicated by the republican Cuban government to the memory of the 260 sailors who died when the U.S. warship exploded in Havana harbor in 1898, creating a prelude for U.S. intervention in the Wars of Independence. Two rusting cannons tethered by chains from the ship's anchor are laid out beneath 40-foot-tall Corinthian columns dedicated in 1925 and originally topped by an eagle with wings spread wide. Back then, relations between the two nations were warm, and when a hurricane toppled the eagle, it was replaced by a more aerodynamic sibling—the original now resides in the former residency of the U.S. Ambassador, still occupied by the head of the U.S. Interests Section. Following the Revolution, the monument was a point for anti-Yankee rallies. Immediately after the failed Bay of Pigs invasion in 1960, it was desecrated by an angry mob that toppled the eagle from its roost and broke its wings—its body is now in the Museum of the City of Havana, while the head hangs on the wall of the cafeteria in the U.S. Interests Section. The Castro government later dedicated a plaque that reads, "To the victims of the *Maine,* who were sacrificed by imperialist voracity in its eagerness to seize the island of Cuba." Recent evidence, however, suggests that the explosion was an accident.

Betwixt the monument and the Hotel Nacional is **El Gato Tuerto,** Calle O e/ 17 y 19, a popular nightclub housed in an eclectic centenary house that in 1960 architect Evelio Pina fitted out in modernist style within a revivalist space graced by Corinthian columns. Note the pond out front, spanned by a bridge guarded by a one-eyed cat (*el gato tuerto*).

Plaza de la Dignidad

This plaza is immediately west of the Maine Monument. At the height of the Elián González fiasco in 1999–2000, bulldozers appeared overnight and began tearing up what was then just a grassy knoll in front of the U.S. Interests Section. In short order there appeared a new plaza—Plaza of Dignity. Round-the-clock work crews gave surface makeovers to the crumbling façades of apartment blocks in view of the TV cameras; the neighbors got no such treatment. A **statue of José Martí** went up at the plaza's eastern end, bearing in one arm a bronze likeness of young Elián while with the other he points an accusatory finger at the Interests Section.

The Cuban government also pumped US$2 million into constructing the **Tribuna Abierta Anti-Imperialista** (José Martí Anti-Imperialist Platform)—called jokingly by locals the *"protestadromo"*—at the west end of the plaza to accommodate the masses bussed in to taunt Uncle Sam.

At the western end of the plaza is the unmarked **U.S. Interests Section** (formerly the U.S. Embassy), Malecón y Calle L, where low-profile U.S. diplomats and CIA agents serve Uncle Sam's whims behind a veil of mirrored-glass windows. It was designed and built in 1953 by a North American company, which failed to factor in Cuba's tropical climate: they exposed too much unshaded glass . . . hence the mirrored glass fitted during a recent renovation. The building is well guarded by Cuban police and security personnel—by coincidence there's a police headquarters adjoining—who will shoo you away if you attempt to sit on the seawall within 100 meters or so of the U.S. Interests Section. Nor are you permitted to walk past the U.S. Interests Section on the inland side of the road.

About 100 meters further east, beyond the police station that is a vision of Beaux Geste, is a huge, brightly painted billboard showing a fanatical Uncle Sam growling menacingly at a Cuban soldier, who is shouting, *"Señores Imperialistas: ¡No les tenemos absolutamente ningún miedo!"* ("Imperialists: We have absolutely no fear of you!").

Further West

Westward, the Malecón curls in much denuded state past an open-air sports stadium, the **CVD José Martí,** of a Bauhaus design in concrete. Immediately to the west, at the foot of Avenida de los Presidentes, is the **Monumento Calixto García,** with a tall bronze figure of the 19th-century rebel general on horseback atop a black marble pedestal. The statue is surrounded by cannons and a wall with verdigris-coated bronze plaques showing battle scenes from the Wars of Independence.

Immediately to the west is a massive apartment tower dating from 1967, interesting as one of the most sophisticated built since the Revolution, although its dangerously deteriorated state makes evident Communist Cuba's atrocious construction standards. Continuing on, you'll reach the **Hotel Cohiba,** at the base of Paseo, a late-1990s edifice whose contemporary face launched Havana toward the millennium; and the **Hotel Riviera,** the Mafia's last and most ambitious attempt to eclipse Las Vegas. Mobster Meyer Lansky owned the hotel but was registered as the kitchen manager to evade taxes. When opened in 1958, it was considered a marvel of modern design using an array of kitsch forms and cantilevered eaves that seemed to draw inspiration from the fins of Cadillac Eldorados. It boasted an egg-shaped, gold-leafed casino topped by a ceramic-clad dome, and a nightclub whose opening was headlined by Ginger Rogers. Recently restored, it still functions as one of Havana's leading hotels. Nonetheless, walking into the Riviera's swank lobby is like stepping into a time machine, with its curving walls and low-slung couches, sunburst clocks behind the check-in desk, and a floating stairway to nowhere—an homage to Miami Beach's Fontainebleau hotel.

The last bend of the Malecón brings you to the mouth of the Río Almendares, guarded by a small fortress, the **Torreón de Santa Dorotea de la Luna de la Chorrera,** colloquially known as La Chorrera. It was built to guard the western approaches to Havana following the English invasion in 1762. Today, it houses a restaurant.

Immediately beyond, overhanging the river mouth, is the **Restaurant 1830,** Malecón, esq. 20, tel. 33-4521, built in the 1920s as a private mansion by Carlos Miguel de Céspedes, son of Carlos Manuel de Céspedes and Secretary of Public Works under General Machado. Today it is a restaurant and cabaret. However, you should visit by day for the remarkable garden . . . a Gaudiesque inspiration that includes a dramatic cupola and a tiny island—**Isla Japonesa**—in Japanese style, with bridges and bird cages.

LA RAMPA (CALLE 23) AND VICINITY

Millionaires, *mafiosi*, presidents, paupers, and pimps all once walked the five blocks of Calle 23, which rises steeply from the Malecón to Calle L. La Rampa was the setting of *Three Trapped Tigers,* Guillermo Cabrera Infante's famous novel about swinging 1950s Havana, for it was here that the ritziest hotels, casinos, and nightclubs were concentrated in the days before the Revolution.

La Rampa's flavor is that of a tree-lined boulevard in Buenos Aires or even Spain, with its candy-stripe awnings shading faded restaurants and nightclubs from the heyday of sin. Not until the 1950s did La Rampa begin to acquire its present look, however—prior to that, it was a shantytown. In 1963, multicolored granite tiles created by Cuba's leading artists—Wilfredo Lam, René Portocarrero, and others—were laid at intervals in the sidewalks. It is art to be walked on—or respectfully skirted.

Modern, vital, and busy, La Rampa climbs steadily past the major airline offices, major nightclubs, cinemas, travel agencies, TV studios, and art-deco apartment buildings mingling with highrise office buildings. It crests at Calle L, pinned by Parque Coppelia, Cine Yara (Havana's premier cinema and a hang-out at night for the city's gay and transvestite community), and the 416-foot-tall modernist Hotel Habana Libre, the city's landmark highrise hotel.

Midway up La Rampa is the **Seguro Médico** apartment and office tower, e/ M and O, unmistakable for its faded multicolored sea-view balconies. It was built in 1958 with a slender rectangular tower turned 90 degrees from its base (the narrow end faces the street). The ugly structure across the way, on the north side of La Rampa, is the **Pabellón Cuba,** an exhibition hall with a statue of Sancho Panza on his mule.

The **Hotel Habana Libre,** occupying the block between L y M and 23 y 25, tel. 33-4011, was once *the* place to be after opening as the Havana Hilton in April 1958 on the eve of the Revolution. Castro even had his headquarters here briefly in 1959. "A bazooka . . . was under the bed, sticking out," wrote Marita Lorenza, who at the age of 19 was briefly one of Fidel's lovers (she was forced to abort his child) and was hired by the CIA to kill Castro but refused to do the deed. For years the hotel teemed with shady foreigners—many of them, reported *National Geographic,* "not strictly tourists" and all "watched by secret police agents from the 'ministry,' meaning MININT, the Ministry of the Interior." The lobby contains many fine contemporary art pieces, including a mosaic mural by René Portocarro. The hotel is fronted by a spectacular contemporary mural—*Carro de la Revolución* (the Revolutionary Car)—by ceramist Amelia Peláez made of 525 pieces in the style of Picasso. The mural was originally created in 1958, but falling tiles killed a hotel guest and injured several

I SCREAM FOR ICE CREAM

Coppelia is the name of a park in Havana, the flying saucer-like structure at its heart, and the brand of excellent ice cream served there.

In the bad old good old days, the trendy area at the top of La Rampa was full of ice cream parlors. But, as Tom Miller claims in *Trading with the Enemy,* the lower classes and blacks weren't welcome, so in 1966 the government built a big, lush park with a parlor in the middle as the ultimate democratic ice cream emporium—surely the biggest ice creamery in the world, serving an estimated 30,000 customers a day. Cuba's rich diversity is to be found standing in line at Coppelia on a sultry Havana afternoon.

Before the Revolution, Cuba relied on its northern neighbor for much of its ice cream supply, and Howard Johnson's (on the corner of Calles 23 y G) 28 flavors were the ice cream of choice. Castro, however, promised to outdo the Yanks with 29 flavors—a boast Cuba failed to achieve. Before the Special Period, you used to be able to choose anything from a one-scoop cone to complex sundaes as well as more than two dozen flavors, including exotic tropical fruits that Ben and Jerry have never heard of. In 1996, after five years of the Special Period, Coppelia could manage only one flavor a day. It was doing a bit better at last visit, but everyone swears the quality is not what it once was.

The strange concrete structure—the "cathedral of ice-cream"—that looms over the park, suspended on spidery legs, shelters a marble-topped diner-bar where Cubans sit atop tall bar stools and slurp ice cream from stainless steel bowls. A series of circular rooms is arranged overhead like a four-leaf clover, offering views out over three open-air sections where *helados* (ice cream) can be enjoyed beneath the dappled shade of fulsome yagüey trees. Each section has its own *cola* (line) proportional in length to the strength of the sun. Even on temperate days, the *colas* snake out of the park and onto nearby streets like lethargic serpents. The *colas* move forward at a pace barely distinguishable from rigor mortis—fortunately, since the Cine Yara is nearby, there's time to pop across the road to watch a movie while you wait. Just when you are about to give up all hope, the line will surge briskly forward. Trying to make sense of the lines is a puzzle, and determining the last person in line—*el último*—is never easy. Cuban lines are never static. *Habaneros* wander off willy-nilly to sit in the shade while others disappear from view completely, lending the impression of having given up. But they always reappear at the critical moment, and your *cola* will coalesce in perfect order, thanks to some unfathomable and puissant osmosis. Young waitresses in red tartan miniskirts seat you at communal tables made of local marble. Coppelia is a family diner.

Coppelia featured in Tomás Gutiérrez Alea's trenchant classic movie, *Fresa y Chocolate,* which was based on Senel Paz's short story, *The Woods, the Wolf, and the New Man.* The movie is named for a scene at Coppelia where Diego, a homosexual, had ordered strawberry ice cream, much to the consternation of David, a loyal *fidelista:* "Although there was chocolate that day, he had ordered strawberry. Perverse." After the success of the movie, Cuban males, concerned with their macho image, had taken a cue from the movie and avoided ordering *fresa.*

others, so it was removed. It was refabricated and remounted more securely (we hope) by Mexican experts and reinaugurated in January 1997 during the Pope's visit.

Cater-corner to the Hotel Habana Libre, at the top of the hill, is **Parque Coppelia,** esq. Calle L, an entire block devoted to the consumption of ice cream, of which Cubans are consummate lovers. The ice cream is excellent and worth the long wait in line.

Anyone interested in Cuba's revolutionary history should step south one block to the **Casa Museo Abel Santamaría,** Calle 25 #164 e/ Infanta y O, tel. 870-0417, where the martyr—

brutally tortured and murdered following the attack on the Moncada barracks in 1953—once lived. Prior to the attack, the simple two-room, sixth-floor apartment (no. 603) was used as the headquarters of Fidel Castro's revolutionary movement, the MR-26-7. The original furnishings are still in place: a roped-off sofa bed, a small bookcase, Fidel's work desk with a statue of José Martí, and a kerosene fridge. You'd have to be a serious leftist or student of history to thrill to this place, but it's of interest in passing. The adjoining room (no. 604) has a small exhibition—mostly photos—of Abel's sister Haydee Santamaría, Fidel, and other revolutionaries (curiously, the only photo of Abel is as a two-year-old). Open Tues.–Sat. 10 A.M.–6 P.M., Sun. 10 A.M.–5 P.M. Entry is free. The guide gives an enthusiastic spiel.

UNIVERSITY OF HAVANA AND VICINITY

Follow Calle L south from La Rampa three blocks, and you arrive at the junction with San Lázaro and an immense stone staircase at Colina Universitaria. The famous 88-step *escalinata* (staircase) leads up to the **Universidad de la Habana,** tel. 878-3231, www.uh.cu, although the main entrance is on Calle 37 (Avenida la Universidad), at Calle J. You'll need to get authorization to take photos; tel. 832-9844. Visitors are allowed to stroll the grounds, although peeking into the classes requires advance permission. The campus is off-limits on weekends, and access is restricted by conscientious *custodios* Monday–Friday 8 A.M.–6 P.M. The campus and museums are also closed July–August.

The university was founded by Dominican friars in 1728 and was originally situated on Calle Obispo in Habana Vieja. Admission back then was based on "purity" of bloodline: Jews, Moors, other non-Christians, and, of course, blacks and mulattoes were barred. The university was secularized in 1842, although admission remained the privilege of the privileged classes.

During the 20th century, when things had eased up, and blacks and women were freely admitted, the university was composed of 13

© CHRISTOPHER P. BAKER

University of Havana

schools, each with its own president. The presidents elected the president of the University Students' Federation, the pillar of student political activity and an extremely influential group amid the jungle of Cuban politics. The university was an autonomous "sacred hill" that neither the police nor the army could enter—although gangsters and renegade politicians roamed the campus. Its most notable of many notable students was Castro, who enrolled in the law school in October 1945 and was involved in the gangsterism.

A patinated bronze **statue of the Alma Mater,** cast by Czech sculptor Mario Korbel in 1919, sits on a pedestal at the top of the 50-meter-wide staircase. The twice life-size statue of a woman is seated in a bronze chair with six bas-reliefs representing various disciplines taught at the university and shown in classical motif. She is dressed in a long-sleeve tunic and extends her bare arms, beckoning all those who desire knowledge. The Alma

Mater looks down upon the *escalinata,* which in Batista days was famous as a setting for political rallies and riots, and the Alma Mater was adopted as a symbol by the young revolutionaries.

The staircase is topped by a porticoed, columned facade beyond which lies a peaceful square—**Plaza Ignacio Agramonte**—surrounded by more columned arcades supporting classical buildings—the tree-shaded campus was loosely modeled after New York's Columbia University. A **Saracen armored car** sits in the quadrant—it was captured in 1958 by students in the fight against Batista.

The **Aula Magna** (Great Hall) features a marble urn containing the ashes of Félix Varela plus a magnificent mural by Armando Menocal. It is usually only opened for special events.

The university contains two museums, foremost the **Museo Antropológico Montane** (Montane Anthropology Museum), Escuela de Ciencias, tel. 879-3488, on the second floor of the Felipe Poey Science Building, to the left (south side) of the quadrant beyond the portico at the top of the *escalinata.* The museum contains a valuable collection of pre-Columbian artifacts, including carved idols and turtle shells. Open Mon.–Fri. 9 A.M.–noon and 1–4 P.M. Closed during summer recess. Entry costs US$1. Entrance is from Calle 39 (Avenida la Universidad), on the north side.

The **Museo de Ciencias Naturales Felipe Poey** (Felipe Poey Museum of Natural Sciences), tel. 832-9000, fax 832-1321, downstairs in the same building, displays an excellent array of pre-Columbian artifacts and the inert remains of dozens of endemic species, stuffed or pickled for posterity within glass cases. There's even a pilot whale suspended from the ceiling, while snakes, alligators, and sharks hang in suspended animation on the walls. The museum—the oldest in Cuba—dates from 1842 and is named for its French-Cuban founder. Poey (1799–1891) was versed in every field of the sciences and founded the Academy of Medical Sciences, the Anthropological Society of Cuba, and a half-dozen other societies. Open Mon.–Fri. 9 A.M.–noon and 1–4 P.M. Closed August. Entry costs US$1.

The **Monumento a Julio Antonio Mella,**

across Calle L at the base of the *escalinita,* is a dour modernist monument of concrete containing the ashes of Mella, founder of the Federación de Estudiantes Universitarios (University Student's Federation) and, later, founder of the Cuban Communist Party. Mella was assassinated in Mexico in 1929. Ironically, the contemporary university structures date from the Machado era, when the dictator-president signed bills to fund construction of the Acropolis-like buildings and staircase.

The **Federación de Estudiantes Universitarios** is in a beautiful beaux arts mansion at the corner of Calles 27 and K.

Museo Napoleónico

Who would imagine that so much of Napoleon Bonaparte's personal memorabilia would end up in Cuba? But it is, housed in the Napoleonic Museum, Calle San Miguel #1159, e/ Ronda y Masón, 879-1460, in a splendid Florentine renaissance mansion on the south side of the university. The 7,000-piece collection was the private work of a politician, Orestes Ferrara, one-time Cuban ambassador to France. Ferrara brought back from Europe such precious items as the French emperor's death mask, toothbrush, and the pistols Napoleon used at the Battle of Borodino. Other items were seized from Julio Lobo, the former National Bank president, when he left Cuba for exile. The museum—housed in Ferrara's former three-story home, built entirely from materials filched from the Capitolio construction (Ferrara was also forced out by the Revolution)—is replete with portraits of the military genius. A library is organized chronologically to trace the life of the "Great Corsican." Open Mon.–Sat. 10 A.M.–5:30 P.M. Entrance costs US$3. A guide costs US$2.

The large antenna next door is supposedly used to block the signals of TV Martí, beamed from the United States.

EAST OF AVENIDA DE LOS PRESIDENTES

The 35-story **Focsa,** between 17 y 15 and M y N, is a controversial Havana landmark. This prerev-

Focsa building

olutionary V-shaped apartment building was built 1954–56 as one of the largest reinforced concrete structures in the world, with 28 floors (plus five penthouse floors in a rooftop tower) and 375 apartments. Following the Revolution it was used to house East European and Soviet personnel. Today most of its apartments are eerily empty (reportedly, old copies of *Pravda* still flutter around amid the detritus). The building looks a bit decrepit and the lifts are death-traps (in 2000, one of the elevators fell 21 floors, killing four Cubans). You can take a more trustworthy (fingers crossed!) elevator to the top where La Torre restaurant offers a panoramic view of the city.

Nearby is the **Hotel Capri,** Calle 21 y N, tel. 33-3747, built in 1958 by the American gangster Santo Trafficante. The hotel was a setting in the movie, *The Godfather.* It was here that actor George Raft, who ran the casino, famously told the revolutionary mob to get lost when they came to trash the casino. Although the hotel design is uninspired, an interior decorator might kill for the lavish '50s chandeliers hanging in the lobby. The rooftop bar, with a swimming pool used as the opening setting for the movie *Soy Cuba,* offers a magnificent bird's-eye view of Havana.

The gothic **Iglesia San Juan de Letran,** Calle 19 e/7 I y J, in the residential district south of Coppelia, dates from the 1880s and is one of Havana's most impressive ecclesiastical edifices, with some of the finest stained-glass windows in Cuba. It is actively used, but rarely open to view.

One block west of the church is **Parque Victor Hugo,** e/ 21 y 19, and I y H, centered on a pergola. A monument to the 19th century French novelist (author of *Les Miserables*) stands on the northeast corner of the park. To the northwest corner is a memorial to Leonor Pérez Cabrera, mother of José Martí, with a letter from Martí to his dearly beloved *mamá* inscribed in metal. The southeast corner bears a monument to Bobby Sands and nine other IRA nationalists ("martyrs" says the plaque) who died on hunger strike in Crumlin Road jail, Northern Ireland, in 1981.

One block northwest is **UNEAC** (Unión Nacional de Escritores y Artistas de Cuba, or National Union of Writers and Artists), Calle 17 #351, esq. H, tel. 832-4551, fax 33-3158, uneac @cubarte.cul.cu. It's usually crowded with writers and artists. It is housed in the Casa de Juan Gelats, a spectacular exemplar of the beaux arts style, built in 1920 and one of the "row of

A TROVE OF ARCHITECTURAL TREASURES

Complementing Havana's astonishing trove of colonial structures are modernist designs with a tropical twist . . . from streamlined art deco apartment blocks to modernist villas whose "glassy severity," thought writer Jonathan Lerner, "is a perfect foil for Cuba's lush intensity."

Independence for Cuba from Spain and establishment of the Republic at the turn of the 20th century spawned a desire for modernity. A nation seeking to free itself of a parochial past adopted North American and Europe influences with remarkable fervor as Havana entered a period of profound innovation. Modern architecture brought about an artistic and cultural renaissance that went so far as to create an unmistakable look . . . undeniably striking and original, defined by a sinuous, sensual, exhibitionist nonchalance.

Although no uniquely Cuban architecture evolved, a subtle "Cubanization" transformed styles introduced to the island. In particular, Cuba underwent rapid Americanization spearheaded by the arrival of several firms of U.S. architects, while Cuba developed its own world-class Cuban School of Architecture whose graduates showed occasional displays of genuine brilliance. The period 1925–65 was uniquely inventive, notes Eduardo Luis Rodríguez: "it was then that Cuba accomplished its most unprecedented achievements in building. For the first time in its history, Cuba's national architecture was viewed in terms of richness and quality as good as or better to that being practiced in other, more developed countries."

Art Nouveau and Beaux Arts

The city's explosive 20th-century growth was wed to an influx of exuberant architectural styles from around the world. First came art nouveau, which arrived from Europe around 1905. Franco-Belgian, Viennese, and Catalan versions of art nouveau appeared in overlapping succession. Havana gained hundreds of highly decorative, even whimsical, confections in stone. A notable example is the Palacio Cueto, on the southeast corner of Plaza Vieja, built in 1906 in a style influenced by Barcelona's Gaudiesque *modernismo.* The Centro Gallego (1915) and Centro Asturiano (1927), erected by Spanish communities in Havana, are other fine examples.

American architect Thomas M. Newton and Cuban architect Emilio Heredia were instrumental in bringing the classicism of the 1920s beaux arts style to Havana, influenced by the École de Beaux Arts in Paris. Cuban architects returning from Paris were inspired by the baroque, classical, renaissance, and neoclassical architecture (fused to define the beaux arts style), then all the rage in Europe. Corinthian columns. Pompeiian fresoes. Lavish use of stained glass. These all defined the movement, as did the adoption of symbolic statues, such as those adorning the staircase to the Capitolio, designed to convey a message of power and grandeur. The ornate interior of the Capitolio is Cuba's grandest tribute to beaux arts, defying the classical sobriety of the building's exterior. Purely neo-renaissance edifices—such as the legendary Hotel Nacional (1930)—also went up in quintessentially Cuban versions of Italian, French, and Spanish style. Nonetheless, domestic architecture set the trend. Vedado is replete with homes in beaux arts style. The finest examples are the Casa de José Gómez Mena (Calle 17 #502), today housing the Museo de Artes Decorativas; and the Casa de Juan Gelats (Calle 17 #351), today the seat of the National Union of Writers and Artists of Cuba (UNEAC).

Eclecticism and Art Deco

During the same period, Havana adopted the so-called Eclectic style, which incorporated revivalist trends melded to elements of neoclassicism, renaissance, and beaux arts forms. The most prominent Eclectic structures were public edifices. Notable exemplars of eclecticism are the

Cuban Telephone Building (at the corner of Dragones and Águila), designed by Leonardo Morales and built in 1927; and the Presidential Palace, completed in 1919 with interior decorations by Tiffany's yet giving an impression of tentativeness appropriate to the new republic. Soon, art deco followed and coincided with the heyday of Hollywood movies. Public edifices were adorned with lavish ornamentation inside and out. Perhaps the finest exemplar of early art deco is the Edificio Bacardi (1930), Esteban Rodríguez's masterful granite structure fringed and highlighted by multi-hued terracotta motifs. The Cine-Teatro Fausto (1938), on the Prado, and the Cine América (1940), on Galiano, are fine exemplars of the splendid movie houses that graced Havana. Art deco even found its way into church styling, as with the Iglesia de Santa Rita de Casia, bringing the Catholic Church into the 20th century.

Cuban art deco designs often anticipated forms that would soon take hold in Miami, such as stilts, partially open floor plans, and angularity that presaged the arrival by the end of the 1930s of the "streamlined" modern look. This was the great age of transport and Cuban architects were inspired to infuse their art deco buildings with slick streamlined forms. Decorative panels and geometric motifs were relegated to the interiors of buildings, while exteriors were graced by gradually rounded curves and horizontally banded parapets and verandas representing bodies streaking through air. Centro Habana, in particular, boasts many apartment buildings in this streamlined style, such as the Edificio Solimar, at Soledad e/ San Lázaro y Ánimas.

Modernismo

By the 1940s, patios, *porticos,* and other traditional elements were back in vogue but tailored to suit the Cuban environment. Wed to a contemporary avant-garde style led by architects Eugenio Batista, Mario Romanach, and Max Borges Recio, this "modernism" came into its glory in the 1950s. Cuba was at the frontier of the modernist movement, which continued into the early years of the Revolution. Thousands of magnificent homes in experimental contemporary fashion blossomed throughout Havana, especially in Miramar, Cubanacán, and other suburbs. Back came stained glass, tile detailing, jalousies, and the inner patio, fused with asymmetrical cubist elements, cantilevered stairs, parabolic structures, and cast shell roofs popularized by architect Max Borges Recio. The best of Borges' work is exemplified by his magnificent Tropicana nightclub, combining complexity with a tropical sensuality defined by graceful curves.

Modernismo reached for the sky. Cuba's pioneering architects changed the Vedado skyline with towering hotels and apartment buildings funded, often, by Mafia money. The 22-story Habana Libre (1958) soared 416 feet over the city, while the Hotel Capri and Hotel Riviera (1957) made their own marks. So, too, did the Edificio Focsa (1956), a vast apartment complex today considered a ghastly blight on the city.

Ecclesiastical architecture also took a turn, marked in 1940 by the completion of the Iglesia de San Agustín with its solid, stepped silhouette and a central arch enclosed by glass, with concrete arches forming a single nave. Meanwhile, the influence of monumentalist edifices associated with European fascist regimes was assimilated into new public structures, such as the Palace of Justices (now the Palace of the Revolution), typified by the use of massive, smooth columns lined up across the front porticos of buildings.

Following the Revolution, many leading architects fled the country and the closure of the school of architecture in 1965 spelled the end of a glorious era.

magnificent mansions" described by Alejo Carpentier. Beyond the sinuously curved entrance you enter a vestibule with a spiral white marble staircase lit by colored light filtering subaqueously through six art deco stained-glass windows. It features a recently opened art gallery plus bookstore, and hosts Afro-Cuban, literary, and other cultural events.

Among the other palatial villas along the "row of magnificent mansions" is that now housing the **Instituto Cubano de Amistad con los Pueblos** (Cuban Institute for People's Friendship), Calle #301, e/ H y I.

Cuba's Jewish heritage is maintained with a passion, as demonstrated by the dedication of José Miller—the doyenne—and his staff at **Bet Shalon Sinagoga** (El Patronato), and the adjoining **Casa de la Comunidad Hebrea de Cuba,** Calle I #241, e/ 13 y 15, tel. 832-8953, which works to preserve Hebrew traditions and pride. The synagogue is quite beautiful; you can witness services with permission. It contains an active community center and a large library on Judaica, Israel, and related themes. Open Mon.–Sat. 9:30 A.M.–5 P.M. Services are Friday at 7 P.M. (May–Sept.) and 6 P.M. (Oct.–April); and Saturday at 10 A.M. (year-round).

The eight-meter-tall black marble column at the corner of Línea and L was erected in 1931 to commemorate Havana's *chinos* (Chinese) who fought for Cuban independence.

BETWEEN AVENIDA DE LOS PRESIDENTES AND PASEO

Avenida de los Presidentes (Calle G) is a wide boulevard that might be considered Vedado's backbone. It runs perpendicular to Calle 23 and flows downhill to the Malecón. A wide, grassy, tree-lined median runs down its spine, dividing separate roadways running uphill and downhill. The avenue is named for the statues of various Cuban presidents that grace its length, along with statues of such notables in American history as Mexican Benito Juárez, Venezuelan Simón Bolívar, and Chilean president Salvador Allende, erected since the Revolution. The busts of Tomás Estrada Palma and José Miguel Gómez, the first

and second presidents of the Cuban republic, were toppled following the Revolution, as they were accused of being "puppets" of the U.S. government. All that is left of the monument to Estrada, at Calzada, are his bronze shoes! As is the strange way of Cuba, the bust of Gómez was recently replaced. Note the handsome bronze statue of Alejandro Rodríguez y Velasco (a brigadier general in the Cuban wars of independence)—on a granite pedestal guarded by a bronze figure of Perseus—at Línea and Avenida de los Presidentes.

To each side of the avenue are grand colonial homes in various states of repair and disrepair. Many now function as schools or government departments.

Casa de las Américas, 3ra Calle, esq. Avenida de los Presidentes, tel. 55-2707, fax 33-4554, casa@artsoft.cult.cu, www.casa.cult.cu, is a cultural center formed in 1959 by revolutionary heroine Haydee Santamaría to study and promote the cultures of Latin America and the Caribbean. It has a large library and exhibits in two nearby galleries—the **Galería Haydee Santamaría,** 5ta Avenida and G, and the **Galería Mariano,** Calle 15 #607, e/ B y C, tel. 55-2702—containing the Art Collection of New America. This collection comprises more than 6,000 pieces of sculpture, engravings, paintings, photographs, and popular art representing artists throughout the Americas and the Caribbean. The center contains a silkscreening shop and hosts concerts, film screenings, and theater and dance programs. It also has a small bookstore with a focus on the arts. Museum: open Mon.–Fri. 8 A.M.–4:45 P.M. Galleries: open Tues.–Fri. 10 A.M.–5 P.M., Sat. 10 A.M.–3 P.M.

Midway between Avenidas de los Presidentes and Paseo is the recently restored **Parque Villalón,** between 5ra y Calzada (7ma) and C y D. While there's nothing noteworthy about the park, it's surrounded by some important edifices, including, on its southeast side, the grandiose Romanesque **Teatro Amadeo Roldán,** recently restored to haughty grandeur as a concert hall and headquarters for the National Symphony Orchestra. Next door is the headquarters of the **Ballet Nacional de Cuba,** Calzada #510 e/ D y E, Vedado, Ciudad Habana, C.P. 10400, tel.

832-4625, www.balletcuba.cu, founded and run by Alicia Alonso, a national icon. The ballet school is closed to visitors (who might disturb the dancers' concentration), but sometimes you can spot the dancers practicing their pirouettes if you peek through the gate. The school was scheduled to move to new headquarters at Paseo de Martí #207, Habana Vieja, tel. 862-7053.

Galería Habana, Calle Línea #460, e/ E y F, tel. 832-7101, exhibits and sells works by leading Cuban artists, as well as upcoming newbies. Open Mon.–Fri. 10 A.M.–4 P.M. and Sat. 10 A.M.–1 P.M.

The 19th-century **Iglesia del Sagrado Corazón de Jesús** (colloquially called Parroquia del Vedado), on Línea, e/ C y D, tel. 832-6807, the parish church, is two blocks west. Mass is Monday–Friday at 8:30 A.M., Saturday at 8:30 A.M. and 5 P.M., and Sunday at 9:30 A.M. and 6 P.M.

The **Museo de la Danza,** Calle Línea #365, esq. Avenida de los Presidentes, tel. 831-2198, in a restored mansion, opened on the 50th anniversary of the Ballet of Cuba. Its four well-presented salons are dedicated to Russian ballet, modern dance, the National Ballet of Cuba, and other themes. Exhibits include wardrobes, recordings, manuscripts, and photographs relating to the history of dance. Such oddities as Nijinsky's wedding certificate are displayed. Alicia Alonso, founder and *prima ballerina absoluta* of the Ballet of Cuba, contributed her valuable personal collection, including her first ballet shoes and the costume she wore in *Carmen.* The museum contains a library and video archives. Open Tues.–Sat. 11 A.M.–6:30 P.M. Entrance costs US$2.

On the west side of Avenida de los Presidentes and Línea is a small triangular park: **Jardín Vienés Johann Strauss,** dedicated by the Austrian government in March 2002, with a lifesize gold-painted statue of the composer playing a violin.

The **Museo de Artes Decorativas** (Museum of Decorative Arts), Calle 17 #502, e/ D y E, tel. 832-0924, is housed in one of the more extravagant mansions, two blocks west of Avenida de los Presidentes. The villa, which formerly belonged to a Cuban countess, brims with a lavish collection of furniture, paintings, textiles, and chinoiserie from the 18th and 19th centuries.

Most of the furniture, however, is European, not Cuban. No matter, it's staggering in its sumptuous quality. Upstairs, where the landing is festooned with ivory figures, you'll find a boudoir decorated Oriental style, its furniture inlaid with mother-of-pearl. Highly recommended. Open Tues.–Sat. 11 A.M.–6 P.M. Entrance costs US$2 (US$5 extra for cameras, US$10 for videos).

Nearby is the **Centro Sefardi,** at Calle 17 #462, esq. E, tel. 832-6623, a Conservative Jewish synagogue built as a Hebrew Center between 1957 and 1960 in the form of a rectangular prism.

South of Calle 23

South of Calle 23, Avenida de los Presidentes climbs to the **Monumento a José Miguel Gómez,** designed by Italian sculptor Giovanni Nicolini and erected in 1936 in classical style to honor the former Republican president (1909–13). It is topped by nubile figures and features bas-reliefs depicting scenes from Gómez's life.

The road then drops down through a canyon lined with ancient and giant jagüey trees, which form a fantastical glade over the road. Hidden from sight on the bluff—Loma Aróstegui—above (to the west) is the **Castillo del Príncipe,** built in a pentagon between 1767 and 1779 following the English invasion. The castle is off-limits and rarely mentioned in Cuban tourist literature because it is a military zone and houses a prison. The hill is riddled with vaulted tunnels that permit protected troop movements; some of the entrances can be seen from the road. They were built in the 1980s and run for miles beneath Vedado . . . occasionally collapsing.

Warning: This section of Avenida de los Presidentes is known for exhibitionists exposing themselves to passersby.

Avenida de los Presidentes drops down to a major junction with Avenida Salvador Allende, Zapata, and Avenida Rancho Boyeros.

Immediately west, on the north side of Salvador Allende, is the once-graceful **Quinta de los Molinos,** e/ Infanta y Luaces, reached via a decrepit cobbled, gladed drive. The mansion, built between 1837 and 1840, is named for the royal snuff mills that were built here in 1791 to take advantage of the waters of Zanja Real; you can still see part of the original aqueduct inaugurated in 1592 to the rear of the time-worn *quinta*. The mansion originated as a summer palace for the captains-general and in 1899 was granted as the private residence of General Máximo Gómez, the Dominican-born commander-in-chief of the liberation army. It now houses the **Museo de Máximo Gómez,** tel. 879-8850, in honor of the hero of the Cuban Wars of Independence. His sword and a few other personal effects are on display, and maps show his progress during the wars. The collection is motley and poorly presented. Lectures, art classes, and other activities are hosted here for community members. Open Tues.–Sun. 10 A.M.–6 P.M. (US$1). The museum was closed for renovation at last visit.

The grounds of the Quinta form the unkempt **Jardín Botánico** (Botanical Gardens), stretching east to Infanta. This was a popular recreation spot in colonial days, when it was the site of the pleasure gardens of the governor's summer palace. Slaves newly arrived from Africa were kept here in barracoons, where they could be displayed to passersby. Following the Revolution, the once exquisite gardens were later transferred to the University of Havana and are now an overgrown mess littered with tumbledown statues, fountains, and grottoes with giant jagüeys and other trees twining around them, many with voodoo dolls and other strange *santería* offerings stuffed in their interstices. For all its eeriness, it draws plenty of *habaneros*: musicians practicing their clarinets or saxophones, for example, and lovers seeking out shady places of coital convenience. One semi-tumbledown building, **La Madriguera,** is a hang-out for Havana's alternative culture. Rock and rap concerts are even held here. The gardens are open Tuesday–Sunday 7 A.M.–7 P.M.

PASEO TO CALLE 12

Paseo parallels Avenida de los Presidentes seven blocks to the west of the latter. Like the Avenida de los Presidentes, the Paseo is a broad linear park flanked by two avenues considered as one, being

one way in either direction. Although itself a pleasant stroll, Paseo offers little of touristic interest.

An exception is the **Casa de Juan Pedro Baró,** Paseo #406, e/ 17 y 19. This old mansion of generous proportions was built in 1926 in Italian Renaissance style (with an art deco interior), with a surfeit of Carrara marble. Don Pedro Baró had it built for Catalina Laza, a stunningly beautiful woman who was married to the vice-president's son. She and Baró were lovers. Alas, divorce was illegal in Cuba, so the couple eloped to Paris. When Cuba legalized divorce in 1917, the couple returned and Laza became the first Cuban woman to divorce under the laws. Today the house is run by the Cuban state as the **Casa de la Amistad,** tel. 830-3114, a "friendship house" (it was formerly the Cuban–Soviet friendship headquarters) with rooms for entertaining, plus a Casa del Tabaco and a meager snack bar out back overlooking the unkempt gardens. It's a popular trysting spot for Cubans and makes a good place to break your perambulations with a cool drink. Open Mon.–Fri. noon–midnight; Sat. noon–2 P.M.; Sun. noon–6 P.M.

On the southern end of Paseo, at the junction of Paseo and Zapata, is the **Memorial a Ethel y Julius Rosenberg,** a curiosity in passing. Here a small park is pinned by a tree shading an inconspicuous red-brick wall designed by Cuban artist José Delarra, bearing cement doves and an inset sculpture of the U.S. couple executed in Sing Sing Prison, New York, in 1953 for passing nuclear secrets to the Soviet Union—later evidence suggests they may have been innocent. An inscription reads, "Assassinated June 19, 1953." Julius's final words are engraved, too: "For Peace, Bread, and Roses, We Face the Executioners." The Cuban government holds a memorial service here each June 19.

"Parque Lennon"

Following John Lennon's death in 1980, a gathering of Havana bohemia took place at a small quiet park between Calles 6 and 8 and 15 and 17. In 2000, on the 20th anniversary of his death, a lifesize bronze statue was unveiled in the presence of Fidel Castro and Minister of Culture, Abel Prieto, much to local astonishment. Lennon, who is dressed in open-neck shirt, sits on a bench, his head slightly tilted, right leg resting on his left knee, with his arm draped casually over the back of the dark-green cast-iron bench, and plenty of room for anyone who wants to join him. The sculpture was rendered by Cuban artist José Villa, who inscribed the words "People say I'm a dreamer, but I'm not the only one," at the foot of the statue. The Cuban Lennon has gradually been turned into a saint. *Habaneros* heap bunches of fresh flowers, light votive candles, and leave notes and poems and a motley miscellany that includes *milagros* asking that a wish might be granted. By night, a spotlight shines on Lennon, denying him sleep. A *custodio* is always there, 24/7.

It's all a bit surreal considering that in the 1960s and '70s, Lennon & Co. were anathema to Cuban authorities, who banned possession of Beatles records. Castro has denied any knowledge of official persecution. Whatever! All's now forgiven, and the statue is living acknowledgment of a catharsis, suggesting that Fidel is now a Lennonist as well as a Leninist. Havana's youth culture has also caught Beatlemania. A devoted, almost institutional following of the group's music exists. There's even a book titled *Los Bea-*

tles en Cuba, which chronicles a series of lectures given during an international symposium on The Beatles held in Havana in 1997. The degree of knowledge about the Beatles, even the most obtuse aspects, will astound.

CALLE 12 TO THE RÍO ALMENDARES

Paralleling Paseo six blocks to the west is Calle 12. **Galería 23 y 12,** on the northwest corner of Calles 23 and 12, marks the spot where on April 16, 1961, Castro announced—on the eve of the Bay of Pigs invasion—that Cuba was henceforth socialist. The anniversary of the declaration of socialism is marked each April 16th, when Castro speaks here. The facade bears a patinated bronze bas-relief showing the heroes who were killed in the U.S.-sponsored strike on the airfield at Marianao that was a prelude to the invasion. The plaque, of course, most prominently features Castro, shown in his usual defiant pose. Today the building houses an art *salón.*

Here, too, is a former Woolworth's (you can still pick out the faded mosaic on the threshold), today known as **Té-sé.**

Cementerio Colón

CEMENTERIO COLÓN

CALLE 14

CALLE 12

CALZADA DE ZAPATA

CALLE A

★ RAFAEL MARIA DE MENDIVE

JOSÉ RAÚL ★CAPABLANCA

INFORMATION ■   MAIN GATE

MARTA ABREU Y ESTÉVEZ ★

CÁRDENAS CASTAÑER FAMI

CALLE B

CALLE 4

GENERAL MÁXIMO GÓMEZ BÁEZ ★

CUBAN EMIGRÉS

★ CALIXTO GARCÍA

RITA LONGA SCULPTURE ★

CALLE C

Plaza Nordoeste

CALLE D

NÚÑES GÁLVEZ ★

FRANCHI-ALFARO ★

REPLICA OF MICHAELANGELO STATUE ★

Plaza Cristóbal Colón

CALLE E

GENERAL QUINTÍ BANDERAS BETANCOURT

CALLE 18

CALLE 16

CALLE 14

CALLE 12

CALLE 8

EDUARDO CHIBAS ★

CALLE 6

★ JOSÉ F. MATTA

AVENIDA CRISTÓBAL COLON

CALLE F

CALLE 10

MAUSOLEUM OF THE VICTIMS OF THE 1890 FIRE ★

PANTHEON OF ★ THE BARÓ FAMILY

★ FALLA-BONET

LA MILAGROS

COUNT OF RIVERO ★

CALLE G

RELATIVES OF THE SPANISH ROYAL FAMILY

DOMINGO LEÓN ★

ANTONIO GUITERAS HOLMES ★

★ HUBERT DE BLANCK

AVENIDA OBISPO FRAY JACINTO

CAPILLA CENTRAL (1886)

CUBAN VICTIMS OF THE SECOND WORLD WAR ★

VETERANS OF THE ★ WARS OF INDEPENDENCE

CALLE H

CALLE 18

CALLE 16

CALLE 14

CALLE 12

CALLE 10

CALLE 8

CALLE 6

FRENCH COLONY OF CUBA ★

AVENIDA OBISPO ESPADA

FRANCISCO D ALBEAR Y LAI

CALLE I

★ MARTYRS OF THE MACHADO TYRANNY

CALLE 2

CALLE 4

MÁRTIRES DEL GRANMA ★

RITA MONTANER ★

CALLE J

JAPANESE COLONY OF CUBA ★

ASSOCIATION OF ★ HAVANA REPORTERS

GENERAL JOSÉ LACRET Y MORLOT

PANTHEON OF THE PRELATES ★

CALLE K

CALLE L

ASSOCIATION OF MERCHANT MARINE ★ ★ CAPTAINS

ASSOCIATION OF NAVAL ENGINEERS ★

REVOLUTIONARY ★ ARMED FORCES

ROBAINA FAMILY ★

CALLE M

JOE WESTBROOKE ROSALES & OTHER MARTYRS OF THE REVOLUTION ★

ABUKUA SECRET SOCIETY ★

CALLE N

SAN ANTONIO CHIQUITO

CALLE 8

CALLE 10

CALZADA DE ZAPATA

CALLE A

★ ALEJO CARPENTIER

★ TOBÍAS GALLERY

CALLE B

★ JOSÉ DE LA LUZ Y ★ CABALLERO

CARLOS J. FINLAY BARRES ★

MEDICAL STUDENTS 1871

★ JOSÉ ANTONIO CORTINA

JULIO DE QUESADA AND FAMILY

MARQUES DE BELLA ★ VISTA Y DE LOS CONDES DE PEÑALVER

CALLE C

★ JOSE GENER Y BATET ★

Plaza Nordeste

★ CUBAN ASSOCIATION OF THEATRICAL, CINEMATOGRAPHIC AND RADIO ARTISTS

MANUEL FERNÁNDEZ SUPERVIELLE ★

CALLE D

CALLE E

MEDICAL STUDENTS ★ 1871

CALLE 3
CALLE 5
CALLE 7
CALLE 9
CALLE 11
CALLE 13
CALLE 15
CALLE 17

CALLE F

★ VASCO-NAVARRA ASSOCIATION OF CHARITY

★ CONILL FAMILY

COL. JUAN DE MUSSET ★

CECILIA VALDES ★

★ CIRILO VILLAVERDE

COLONEL JUAN ALVAREZ & HIS SONS ★

CALLE G

★ SOCIETY OF GALICIANS

EDUARDO FESSER ★ Y DIAGO

CALLE 35

AVENIDA OBISPO FRAY JACINTO

RAÚL DE ZARRAGA FAMILY CRYPT ★

CALLE H

CALLE 13

CALLE I

CALLE 37

CALLE 3
CALLE 5
CALLE 7
CALLE 9
CALLE 11

★ CHRISTIAN ASSOCIATION OF BASEBALL PLAYERS, UMPIRES & MANAGERS

CALLE 15
CALLE 17

CALLE LOMA

CALLE J

★ MARTYRS OF THE ASSAULT ON THE PRESIDENTIAL PALACE 1957

GENERAL OSSUARY ★

CALLE K

CALLE L

ABUKUA SECRET ★ SOCIETY

MOON

CALLE M

0   300 yds

0   300 m

CALLE 39

CALLE N

AVENIDA DE COLON

VEDADO

While walking down Calle 12, you'll pass a Castro "safe house" between Línea and 13, where the road is cordoned off as a "Zona Militar." Note the cameras watching your every move from the rooftops.

At the end of Calle 23, beside the bridge over the Río Almendares, once stood the infamous interrogation center where Batista's police tortured many hundreds to death. It was torn down immediately after the Revolution.

Cementerio Colón

Described as "an exercise in pious excesses," Havana's Necrópolis Cristóbal Colón is renowned for its flamboyant mausoleums, vaults, and tombs embellished with angels, griffins, cherubs, and other ornamentation. The cemetery, covering 56 hectares on land once owned by the Catholic Church, contains more than 500 major mausoleums, chapels, family vaults, and galleries (in addition to countless gravestones) containing the remains, supposedly, of about one million persons! The cemetery represents Havana's major architectonic expression of the era and has been declared a national monument. It was laid out between 1871 and 1886 in 16 rectangular blocks, or *insulae*, like a Roman military camp. The designer, a Spaniard named Calixto de Loira, divided the cemetery by social status, with separate areas for non-Catholics and for victims of epidemics—appropriately, Loira was among the first to be buried here. It was originally open only to nobles, who competed to build the most elaborate tombs, with social standing dictating the size and location of plots. Here the wealthy vied for immortality on a grand scale.

The cemetery is a petrified version of society of the times, combining, says the *Guía Turística* (available at the entrance gate), a "grandeur and meanness, good taste and triviality, popular and cosmopolitan, drama and even an unusual black humor, as in the gravestone carved as a double-three, devoted to an emotional elderly lady who died with that domino in her hand, thus losing both game and life at one time." The *doble tres* was that of Juana Martín, a domino fanatic who indeed died as described.

Famous *criollo* patricians, colonial aristocrats, and war heroes such as Máximo Gómez are buried here alongside noted intellectuals, merchants, and corrupt politicians (as well, of course, as the rare honest one, such as Eduardo Chibás). The list goes on and on: José Raúl Capablanca, the world chess champion 1921–27 (his tomb is guarded by a marble bishop); Alejo Carpentier, Cuba's most revered contemporary novelist; Hubert de Blanck, the noted composer; and Celia Sánchez, Haydee Santamaría, a plethora of revolutionaries killed for the cause, and even some of the Revolution's enemies. The Bacardí family mausoleum is surrounded by railings topped by cast iron bats—the family motif. The cemetery's many collective vaults reflect Cuba's heterogeneous roots. You'll even find Greco-Roman temples in miniature, an Egyptian pyramid, and medieval castles, plus baroque, Romantic, renaissance, art deco, and art nouveau art, allegories, and metaphors of human life by a pantheon of Cuba's leading sculptors and artists. Says Nancy Stout: "Eclecticism is the key to cosmetics here."

The most visited grave is the flower-bedecked tomb of Amelia Goyri de Hoz, revered as **La Milagrosa** (The Miraculous One), at the corner of Calles 3 and F, and to whom miraculous healings are attributed as a protector of sick children. According to legend, she died during childbirth in 1901 and was buried with her stillborn child at her feet. When her sarcophagus was later opened, the baby was supposedly cradled in her arms. Ever since, superstitious Cubans have paid homage by knocking three times on the tombstone with one of its brass rings, before touching the tomb and requesting a favor. One must not turn one's back on the tomb when departing. Many are the childless women who pray here in hopes of a pregnancy. It is always strewn with flowers and scraps of paper pleading for intercession in personal tragedies.

Many of Cuba's top architects of the time were commissioned to design individual tombs and chapels, such as the **Nuñez-Gálvez Tomb,** Calle 10, esq. D, by Max Borges Recio and Enrique Borges. Many of the funerary monuments belong to such communities as the Abakuá Secret Society, the Asturians, and the Galicians, and to groups such as film and radio stars. There is even a monument of sorts to the victims of the USS *Maine,* which exploded in Havana harbor in 1898. The plot, now empty and untended, rubble-filled and penned by a rusted fence, marks the spot where the marines who died were buried temporarily before being returned to the United States.

The **Tobias Gallery** is one of several underground galleries; this one is 100 meters long and contains 256 niches containing human remains that include those of Calixto de Loira.

The impressive Romanesque-Byzantine entrance gate of locally quarried coral stone is at the top of Calle 12 and Calle Zapata, which runs along its north face. The triple-arched gate was inspired by the Triumphal Arch in Rome with relieves in Carrara marble that depict the crucifixion and Lazarus rising from the grave. It is embellished with a marble sculpture of the coronation stone representing *The Theological Virtues:* Faith, Hope, and Charity . . . the work of José Vilalta de Saavedra. The major tombs line the main avenue that leads south from the gate to an ocher-colored, octagonal neo-Byzantine church, the **Capilla Central,** containing a fresco of the Last Judgement.

You could take all day to discover all the gems. Fortunately, benches are provided beneath shade trees. Still, wear your sunglasses against the glare of the incandescent sun bouncing off a surfeit of Carrara marble.

To the right of the entrance is an information office, tel. 833-4196 or 832-1050; you must pay an entrance fee here (US$1). Guided tours are available free of charge, but tips would be welcome. Consider buying a guidebook containing a map (US$5). Open 8 A.M.–5 P.M.

Cementerio Chino

The Chinese built their own cemetery immediately southwest of Cementerio Colón, on the west side of Avenida 26, e/ 28 y 33, with graves that appeal to an Asian culture. The circular gateway derives from the *pai lou,* the monumental Chinese arches erected by custom at the entrance to processional ways, palaces, and tombs. Traditional lions stand guard over hundreds of graves beneath highly pitched burial chapels with upward-curving roofs of red and green tile in the traditional *xuan-shan* (hanging mountain) gabled style. Entry is free, but the gates are usually locked. To arrange a visit, call the Periódico Kwong Wah Po, tel. 52-0522.

Plaza de la Revolución

A visit to Havana's largest and most important plaza is de rigueur, although the plaza itself is an ugly tarred square accurately described by P.J. O'Rourke as "a vast open space resembling the Mall in D.C., but dropped into the middle of a massive empty parking lot in a tropical Newark." You can't blame the Revolution. The trapezoidal complex measuring one kilometer in length and spanning 11 acres was laid out during the Batista era, when it was known as the Plaza Cívica. All the major edifices date back to the 1950s and were erected with Jaimanitas stone façades to create a unified look. The plaza occupies the Loma de los Catalanes (Hill of the Catalans) and today forms the administrative center for Cuba. A huge rally is held here each May 1 . . . a great occasion to visit.

It's a 30-minute walk from the Habana Libre Hotel, but you can take bus no. 84 from the bottom of La Rampa, at Calle 0 and Humboldt. The plaza is under close surveillance and loitering is discouraged. Parking is strictly controlled; the designated parking zone is on the east side of the plaza. If you park on the plaza or along the road, soldiers will quickly move you along.

Monumento y Museo José Martí

This spectacular monument, on the south side of the square, sits atop a 30-meter-tall base that spans the entire square and is shaped as a five-pointed star. It is made entirely of gray granite and marble and was designed by architect Enrique Luis Varela. It predates the Revolution, having been completed in 1958. Today the plinth is used as a reviewing

JOSÉ MARTÍ

A knowledge of José Martí—"Pepe," as he became affectionately known—is an absolute prerequisite to understanding contemporary Cuba. He is the most revered figure in Cuban history . . . the avatar of Cuba's independence spirit and the "ideological architect" of the Cuban Revolution. His name has been appropriated by the Castro government *and* the fiercely anticommunist exiles in Florida.

"Cubans take José Martí into their consciousness with their first breath and their mother's milk," writes Claudia Lightfoot. Cubans of every stripe quote their saintly hero by heart. So important is Martí within the Cuban psyche that foreigners who admit to never having heard of him are usually met with a wide-mouthed, uncomprehending stare. There is hardly a quadrant in Havana that does not have a street, square, or major building named in his honor. Every year on January 28 the entire country honors Martí's birth with a national celebration.

Martí was born in 1853 in a small house on Calle Paula (also known as Leonor Pérez, to honor his mother) in Habana Vieja. Martí came from peninsular stock. His father was from Valencia, Spain and became a policeman in Cuba; his mother came from the Canary Islands. He spent much of his youth in Spain before his parents returned to Cuba. When the War of Independence erupted in 1868, Martí was 15 years old. Already he sympathized with "the cause."

At the age of 16, he published his first newspaper, *La Patria Libre* (Free Fatherland). He also wrote a letter denouncing a school friend for attending a pro-Spanish rally. The letter was judged to be treasonous, and Martí was sentenced to six years' imprisonment, including six months' hard labor at the San Lázaro stone quarry in Havana (Martí suffered a hernia, and gained permanent scars—*los anillos de hierro*—from his shackles). In 1871, his sentence was commuted to exile on the Isla de Pinos, and briefly thereafter he was exiled to Spain, where he earned a degree in law and philosophy and gravitated to the revolutionary circles then active in Madrid.

He traveled through Mexico and Guatemala, where he worked as both reporter and teacher, but was expelled for incendiary activities by the respective governments. In 1878, as part of a general amnesty, he was allowed to return to Cuba but was then deported again. He traveled through France and Venezuela and, in 1881, to the United States, where he settled in New York for the next 14 years with his wife and son. Here he worked as a reporter and acted as a consul for Argentina, Paraguay, and Uruguay.

The Pen and the Sword

Dressed in his trademark black frock coat (*al saco negro*) and bow tie, with his thick moustache waxed into pointy tips, Martí devoted more and more of his time to winning independence for Cuba. He wrote poetry heralding the liberation of his homeland during a "time of fervent repose," the years following the Ten Years' War. His writing wedded the rhetoric of nationalism to calls for social justice, fashioning a vision of a free Cuba that broke through class and racial

stand and podium, from which Castro tutors, harangues, and encourages the masses. To each side, great arching stairways lead to a 18-meter-tall (59-foot) gray-white marble statue of National Hero José Martí sitting in a contemplative pose, like Rodin's *The Thinker*. Author Claudia Lightfoot, however, claims it was based on a 1940s design for a Schenley's whisky advertisement.

Behind looms a slender, 109-meter-tall Babylonian edifice stepped like a soaring ziggurat from a sci-fi movie. The tower—its tip is the highest point in Havana—is made entirely of gray marble quarried from Cuba's Isla de la Juventud. The top bristles with antennas. Vultures soar overhead and roost on the narrow ledges, lending an added eerie quality to the scene. Its

barriers. He was one of the most prolific and accomplished Latin American writers of his day, wholly original and unsurpassed in the inspiration he fired.

Martí is revered as much for the genius of his writing, which helped define the school of modern Latin American poetry. He admired the liberty of America but became an arch-anticolonialist and his voluminous writings are littered with astute critiques of U.S. culture and politics. He despised the expansionist nature of the United States, arguing that U.S. ambitions toward Cuba were as dangerous as the rule of Spain. "It is my duty . . . to prevent, through the independence of Cuba, the USA from spreading over the West Indies and falling with added weight upon other lands of Our America. All I have done up to now and shall do hereafter is to that end."

His works have been seized upon by Cubans on both sides of the Straits of Florida, being "full of the lament of exile and the passion for the lost homeland," thought Lightfoot.

Prophetically, Martí's writings, which collectively comprise 27 volumes, are full of invocations to death. It was he who coined the phrase *La Victoria o el Sepulcro* (Victory or the Tomb), which Fidel Castro has turned with great success into a call for *"Patria o Muerte"* (Patriotism or Death), and more recently, *"Socialismo o Muerte."*

Theory into Action

In 1892, Martí met with leading Cuban exiles and presented his "Fundamentals and Secret Guidelines of the Cuban Revolutionary Party," outlining the goals of the nationalists: independence for Cuba, equality of all Cubans, and establishment of democratic processes. That year, Martí began publishing *Patria*. Through dint of passion and idealism, he had established himself as the acknowledged political leader of the independence cause. He melded the various exile factions together, formulated a common program, and managed to integrate the cause of Cuban exile workers into the crusade—they contributed 10 percent of their earnings to his cause. He also founded a revolutionary center, Cuba Libre (Free Cuba), and La Liga de Instrucción, which trained revolutionary fighters.

In 1895, Martí presented the *Manifesto de Montecristi*, outlining the policy for the war of independence that was to be initiated later that year. Martí was named major general of the Armies of Liberation, while General Máximo Gómez was named supreme commander of the revolutionary forces.

On April 11, 1895, Martí, Gómez, and four followers landed at Cojababo, in a remote part of eastern Cuba. Moving secretly through the mountains, they gathered supporters and finally linked up with Antonio Maceo and his army of 6,000. The first skirmish with the Spanish occurred at Dos Rios on May 19, 1895. Martí was the first casualty. He had determined on martyrdom and committed sacrificial suicide by riding headlong into the enemy line. Thus, Martí—the "Apostle of the Nation"—brought the republic to birth, says Guillermo Cabrera Infante, "carrying a cadaver around its neck."

construction is said to have cost every citizen in Cuba one centavo.

Until early 1996, soldiers barred the way up to the monument, from where sentries surveyed passersby—and often icily shooed them away. The guards have since departed, and the edifice has been opened as the **Museo José Martí,** tel. 882-0906, within the base of the tower. The state-of-the-art museum depicts everything you could wish to know about Martí. Among the exhibits are many first-edition works, engravings, drawings, and maps, as well as reproductions of significant artifacts in Martí's life. Of course, the largest photograph of all depicts Castro, shown in saintly homage on the beach at Cojababo, the site in Guantánamo province where

Martí put ashore in 1896 after a 16-year exile. The museum also displays the original plans for the design of the monument and plaza, including a Parthenon-like scheme that seems a copycat version of Washington's Lincoln Memorial. Planning, construction, and urbanization of the area around the plaza are traced with large black-and-white photos that display key moments that have occurred here since the Revolution. New Age music plays in the background, drawing you to a multiscreen broadcast on the wars of independence and the Revolution. One of the four exhibition rooms is dedicated to traveling exhibits, which change every three months. To one side is a small art gallery featuring portraits of Martí by numerous leading artists.

The museum is open Monday–Saturday 9:30 A.M.–5:30 P.M., Sunday 10 A.M.–2 P.M. Entrance costs US$5 (US$5 extra for cameras, US$10 for videos). For an additional US$5, you can take the elevator to a viewing gallery at the top of the tower (open Mon.–Sat. 9 A.M.–4 P.M., Sun. 2–4 P.M.). From above, you can see that the entire structure is designed as a five-pointed star. Each star in the *mirador* contains windows on each side, providing a 360-degree view over Havana. On a clear day, you can see 50 miles. Inset in the floor of each point is a compass showing the direction and distance of national and international cities (New York, for example, is 2,100 km away, and the North Pole is 7,441 km away).

Other Sights

The center of government is the **Palacio de la Revolución,** tel. 879-6551, immediately behind the José Martí monument. This vast, monumentalist structure was inspired by the architecture then popular in Fascist Europe and was built 1954–57 as, ironically, the Palace of Justice. Today, it is where Castro and the Council of Ministers work out their policies of state. The labyrinthine, ocher-colored palace adjoins the buildings of the Central Committee of the Communist Party and is fronted by a broad staircase built by Batista for the Cuban Supreme Court and national police headquarters. It boasts fine marble floors. An enormous ceramic tile mosaic of birds, animals, and flowers dominates the re-

ception hall. The artist apparently cast the intricately etched tiles while the architect was still designing the interior, and, through a misunderstanding, the ceiling was built too low. The top two rows wouldn't fit, robbing the mosaic of its crown. Castro's study is a simple room with a desk lined with telephones, a sofa, lounge chairs, and a small conference table. An entire wall is fronted by a bookcase with bound books gifted by the president of Mexico. No visitors are allowed in the palace.

To the north and east of the square are government ministries apparently of soulless post-Stalinist style but actually dating from the late 1950s in monumentalist style. These include, on the northwest side, the tall **Ministerio del Interior** (the ministry in charge of national security), built in 1953 to be the Office of the Comptroller with a windowless horizontal elevator block that today bears a soaring bronze "mural" of Che Guevara—the image is drawn from Alberto "Korda" Gutiérrez's world-renowned photo—and the words "Hasta la Victoria Siempre" (Until Victory Forever), erected in 1995.

To the east of the Ministry of the Interior is the **Ministerio de Comunicaciones,** bearing the word *Venceremos* ("We will overcome") on its roof. It contains the **Museo Postal Cubano,** Avenida Rancho Boyeros, esq. 19 de Mayo, tel. 870-5581, on the ground floor. Serious philatelists will find it fascinating. The well-cataloged collection is kept in vertical pull-out glass file drawers. A complete range of Cuban postage stamps (including the first, dating from 1855) is on display, plus a large collection of stamps from almost 100 other countries, including numerous "penny blacks" from 1850 and other valuable stamps from England and elsewhere. Check out the little solid-propellant rocket that was launched in 1936 by a group of enthusiastic philatelists eager to promote rocket propulsion to speed up mail delivery. The museum has a well-stocked *filatélica* (stamp shop) selling stamps. Open Mon.–Sat. 9 A.M.–5 P.M.; entrance US$1.

Across Avenida Rancho Boyeros, on the east side of the plaza, is Cuba's largest library, the **Biblioteca Nacional,** tel. 55-5442, built 1955–57 in a similar monumental style as the

Palace of Justice. Visitors are not allowed beyond the lofty-ceilinged entrance hall, generously clad in marble and boasting two stained-glass panels cast in Paris: one in the ceiling represents the universality of knowledge; a second depicts Minerva, goddess of wisdom surrounded by the signs of the Zodiac.

On the plaza's southeast side, is the 21-story **Ministerio de Defensa** (originally built as the municipal seat of government, with the top floor as the mayor's residence); and, behind, the headquarters of *Granma*, the national daily newspaper of the Cuban Communist Party.

One block to the northwest of the plaza, across Avenida de Céspedes, is the modern but rundown and poorly constructed **Teatro Nacional**, tel. 879-6011, with a convex glazed facade. Built 1954–60 in a trapezoidal form, with two theaters, much of the advanced technology intended for installation was never put in place, and it wasn't until 1979 that the theater was opened to the public. It has not withstood the test of time and remained in tatterdemalion condition at last visit. The theater is underutilized—"waiting," wrote novelist Donald Westlake, "for a theatrical season that had never quite arrived."

One block northeast of the plaza, in the **Sala Polivatente Ramón Fonst** sports stadium—a gross architectural obscenity—on Rancho Boyeros between 19 de Mayo and Bruzón, you'll find the **Museo de Historia del Deportivo,** tel. 881-4696, which tells the history of Cuban sports. Open Tues.–Sun. 10 A.M.–5 P.M.; entrance US$1. It's worth popping into the stadium to watch youngsters training to be future Olympians . . . astounding!

The stadium faces the **Terminal de Omnibus,** built between 1948 and 1951 with highly dynamic curves and angles to express the notion of speed. Note the sculpture by Florencio Gelabert on the southwest corner, representing velocity; and, inside, a mural—*Alboradas de la Revolución* (Dawn of the Revolution)—by Orlando Suárez, in the style of Diego Rivera.

The large park south of the terminal once formed the foundations of a building that burned down in the 1980s, causing a mad evacuation of the basement . . . which was being used as a secret arms depot!

Nuevo Vedado

Nuevo Vedado, which stretches south from Cementerio Colón and southwest of Plaza de la Revolución, is a sprawling complex of mid-20th-century housing, including high-rise, postrevolutionary apartment blocks arrayed in irregular grids interlinked (unusual for Havana) by serpentine thoroughfares. There are also some magnificent modern edifices, notably private homes built in modernist style in the 1950s; for example, the **Casa de Paulio Ingelmo,** Calle 47 #807, e/ Conill y Santa Ana; the **Casa de Lilia Muñoz,** Calle 38 #125, e/ Zoológico y Edison; and the **Casa de Timoth James Ennis,** Calle Bosque #7, e/ Nueva y 38.

The main site of interest is the **Jardín Zoológico de la Habana,** Avenida 26 y Zoológico, tel. 881-8915 or 881-5724, Havana's provincial zoo (not to be confused with the national Parque Zoológico on the city's outskirts). The zoo, which opened in 1939 to international acclaim, is today a sad affair that suffers from poor management and lack of both resources and attention. The hippopotamus, crocodiles, caimans, flamingoes, and other water-loving species wade and wallow in polluted lagoons. It has many monkeys and chimpanzees—six generations in lineage and thereby apparently the oldest chimp collection of any zoo in the world—but, tragically, they are kept apart, and though their cages abut each other they are separated by walls so that no monkey or ape has a view of its neighbors. Other species on view include Andean condors, water buffalo, jaguars, leopards, lions, and a gorilla, which suffered a stoning from a child while I was there. The animals and visitors alike are further tormented by modern music piped over loudspeakers at deafening levels. A children's playground offers pony rides, and there's a basic snack bar. Open Tues.–Sun. 9:30 A.M.–5:30 P.M. (US$2).

On the southern edge of Nuevo Vedado is the **Palacio de Deportes** (Sports Palace), on the southeast side of the traffic circle at Avenida 26, Avenida de la Independencia (Rancho Boyeros), and Vía Blanca. Colloquially called "El Coliseo," it was built 1955–57 to house 15,000 spectators and boasts an unsupported cupola roof spanning 289 feet. The ground level is decorated with sporting theme murals. The "Coliseum" is the center of **Ciudad Deportiva** (Sports City), finalized following the Revolution.

Parque Almendares and Bosque de la Habana

From the city zoo, you can follow Avenida Zoológica west to the bridge over the Río Almendares, and by turning right at the end, enter the **Bosque de la Habana** (Havana Forest). This wild woodland stretches along the canyon and plain of the river, forming a ribbon of vine-draped virgin forest in a virtually untouched state, for which it is popular with lovers seeking a private spot—a veritable Garden of Eden. There is no path—you must walk along Calle 49C, which parallels the river.

Bosque de la Habana merges northward with **Parque Almendares,** a landscaped park laid out in the 1950s on the west bank of the river and spanned by the Puente Almendares bridge bearing Calle 23 and linking Vedado with the Kohly district.

To the south, the woods extend to **Los Jardines de la Tropical,** Calle Rizo, tel. 881-8767, a landscaped park built 1904–10 on the grounds of a former brewery and designed by the Tropical beer company for promotional purposes— a free round of drinks was offered to picnickers. The park was paid for by Catalonians resident in Cuba and, appropriately, found its inspiration in Antoni Gaudí's Parque Güell in Barcelona, with winding paths shaded by almond trees and ficus snaking like castaway ropes through the 12.5-acre site. It features gazebos, watchtowers, pergolas, a castle with a Moorish interior inspired by the Alhambra in Granada, a pigeon house, and other attractions along the way, including

THE GREEN LUNG

The Río Almendares is Havana's green lung. During the 16th century, a covered aqueduct called the Zanja Real (the "royal ditch") was built to carry water from the river to supply Habana Vieja. At the time, the river was called the Río Casigüaguas; it was renamed the following century when Bishop Almendáriz claimed that its healing waters had cured his rheumatism. No such luck today. Beginning in the 18th century, settlements went up along its banks. Its banks were deforested. Sewers opened into the river. Industrial pollution in ensuring centuries added more noxious stews.

In 1989, the idea to create an ecological park along the river took hold. The 30-year environmental plan (which is partly funded by international nongovernmental organizations including, foremost, the Canadian International Development Agency) calls for the creation of **Parque Metropolitano de la Habana** (PMH), to span 700 hectares (2.7 square miles), beginning at the river mouth and stretching along 9.5 kilometers. Efforts to date include closure of some of the worst offending factories, while others are said to now recycle waste products. Alternative technologies for sewage treatment were to be introduced, and trees are to be planted. As of last visit, however, there had been little visual progress.

For information, contact Oneida Meulener Pérez, Parque Metropolitano de la Habana (PMH), Calle 19 #1466, e/ 28 y 30, Plaza, La Habana, tel. 831-2154, fax 66-2131, pmh@ceniai .inf.cu, www.interlog.com/~cui/homepmh.htm (in Spanish).

Gaudiesque concrete columns shaped as tree trunks and railings resembling logs. Alas, it is today in near derelict status—the result of four decades of neglect—and looks like an abandoned set from *Lord of the Rings*. Open Tues.–Sun. 9 A.M.–6 P.M.

The Polar brewing company competed by opening the smaller **Jardines de La Polar,** a short distance further south on the north side of Calzada de Puentes Grandes, between the confluence of the Río Almendares and Río Mordazo.

A bicycle trail (*ciclovía*) leads east from the Río Mordazo through Parque Forestal, today the grounds of a hospital—Clínico Quirúrgico Joaquín Albarrán—south of Calzada de Puentes Grandes.

The entire complex is in a neglected state. Supposedly, the park system is being restored using volunteer labor, including school brigades, as part of the ambitious Proyecto Parque Metropolitano de la Habana (see the Sidebar "The Green Lung"); there was no sign of any progress at last visit. The headquarters is at **Aula Ecológica,** Ciclovía, tel. 881-9979, near Calzada de Puentes Grandes, which features a meager **visitors center** with 1:2,000 scale model of the project. Open Mon.–Fri. 9 A.M.–5 P.M.

It's wise not to explore the forest and parklands alone, as robberies have been reported. Its entire length borders a Zona Militar, so be careful where you point your camera.

Playa (Miramar and Beyond)

West of Vedado and the Río Almendares stretches an expansive region where, prior to the Revolution, the wealthy and middle classes lived in lowrise apartments and columned and balustraded mansions. The *municipio*—called Playa—extends to the western boundary of Havana, beginning in the east, with the seaside district of Miramar extending west about four miles as far as the Río Quibu. The further west you go, the more sumptuous the residences are.

The rich and foreign who were forced to depart left their grandiose homes and classy apartments as valuable "gifts" to the Revolutionary government—in reality, of course, the

properties were seized—which turned many into clinics, kindergartens, and clubs. A few mansions for which no public use could be found were divided up into private apartments and communal dwellings for multiple families flooding in from the countryside; unfortunately, their new occupants have lacked the resources to maintain them, and many of the mansions have degenerated into slums. The population is much "whiter" than more easterly districts, reflecting prerevolutionary demographics. Many mansions have since fallen into ruin, reminding novelist James Michener of "an Arthur Rackham painting of a country

Iglesia Jesús de Miramar

© CHRISTOPHER P. BAKER

in which a cruel king has laid waste the mansions of his enemies."

Many of the finest houses, of course, were discreetly handed over to Communist bigwigs; this is still where most top party functionaries live in style, divorced from the less-fortunate masses. Others became protocol houses for visiting dignitaries, while many have become embassies or serve as homes for foreign commercial representatives and their families (even the U.S. Marines have a house), preserving a sense of the privileged past. The top private dollar hospitals are here; so, too, the best-stocked dollars-only stores; as well as the international schools. The areas themselves were renamed, however. Gone are Country Club and Biltmore, replaced with politically acceptable names such as Atabey, Cubanacán, and Siboney, in honor of Cuba's indigenous past.

West of Miramar, Playa boasts the city's *balnearios* (bathing areas), which line the shore of the Náutico and Flores districts, cut through by 5ta

BUSES TO PLAYA

Bus no. 264 runs to Playa from Habana Vieja, departing from Desamparados e/ Picota y Compostela. Buses no. 132 and 232 run to Playa from Dragones at Industria, on the south side of the Capitolio. Bus no. 34 leaves from here for Mariano.

Buses no. 9 and 420 run along 5ta Avenida in Miramar and travel to Flores and Marina Hemingway.

Avenida. Playa also boasts Havana's most luxurious residences, concentrated along the leafy boulevards of the hilly Cubanacán district, on the slopes inland of the shore. Adjacent Siboney is now a center for biogenetic research.

You'll need a detailed map for navigating Siboney and Cubanacán, whose convoluted roads follow no logical order.

Miramar

Leafy Miramar is Havana's upscale residential district, laid out in an expansive grid of tree-shaded streets lined by fine mansions and homes. It makes for delightful walking. Other than its incredible mansions, dedicated sites of interest are few, although you'll find two museums, a few churches, the national aquarium, and a fistful of miscellaneous attractions.

Miramar is at the forefront of Cuba's quasi-capitalist remake. Even upscale condominiums have gone up, with ritzy apartments for sale to foreigners—Cubans, ironically, are not permitted to buy or sell property. Cuba's future can be seen here, with dozens of cranes and construction crews at work erecting new hotels and offices for Cuban and foreign-owned corporations. In spring 1999, the government launched the Miramar Trade Center, a 27,000-square-meter complex with adjoining offices—many of them complete and ready to rent—opposite gleaming new hotels (including the Meliá Habana, Novotel Miramar, and Hotel Panorama).

Orientation

Access to Miramar from Vedado is via two tunnels under the Río Almendares. The first, at the west end of the Malecón, leads west of the river to 5ta Avenida. The second, at the west end of Línea (Calle 9) leads west of the river to 7ma Avenida and Avenida 31, which leads to Marianao. In addition, Calle 23 crosses the river via the Puente Almendares bridge to become Avenida 47, linking Vedado with the Kohly district and Marianao.

You can also cross via a steel footbridge (the Puente de Hierro) at the west end of Calle 11.

Miramar comprises four broad east-west avenues, beginning with 1ra Avenida, which runs along the shore. Inland, running parallel at intervals of about 100 meters, are 3ra Avenida, 5ta Avenida, and 7ma Avenida.

5ta Avenida is a broad boulevard and Miramar's most important thoroughfare. Inland of 5ta Avenida Miramar slopes south, uphill to the suburban Marianao district. In between, and considered part of Miramar, are the residential

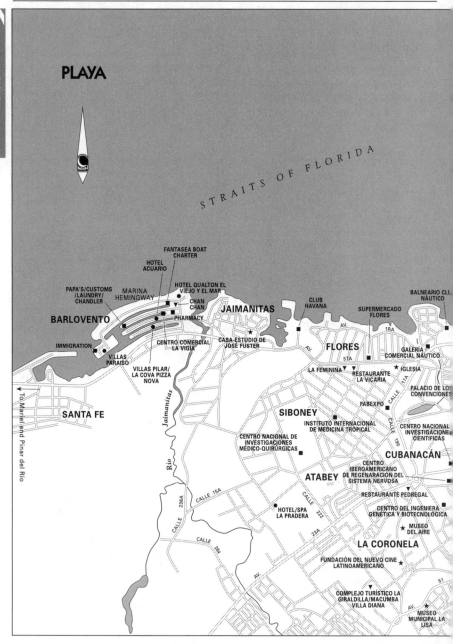

PLAYA

STRAITS OF FLORIDA

FANTASEA BOAT CHARTER

HOTEL ACUARIO

PAPA'S/CUSTOMS /LAUNDRY/ CHANDLER

MARINA HEMINGWAY

HOTEL QUALTON EL VIEJO Y EL MAR

CHAN CHAN

JAIMANITAS

CLUB HAVANA

BALNEARIO CLU NÁUTICO

SUPERMERCADO FLORES

BARLOVENTO

PHARMACY

IMMIGRATION

CENTRO COMERCIAL LA VIGÍA

CASA-ESTUDIO DE JOSÉ FUSTER

FLORES

AV. 1RA

GALERÍA COMERCIAL NÁUTICO

VILLAS PARAISO

VILLAS PILAR/ LA COVA PIZZA NOVA

5TA

IGLESIA

LA FEMININA

RESTAURANTE LA VICARIA

SANTA FE

Río Jaimanitas

SIBONEY

PABEXPO

PALACIO DE LOS CONVENCIONES

INSTITUTO INTERNACIONAL DE MEDICINA TROPICAL

CENTRO NACIONAL INVESTIGACIONE CIENTIFICAS

CENTRO NACIONAL DE INVESTIGACIONES MÉDICO-QUIRÚRGICAS

CUBANACÁN

CALLE 15A

ATABEY

CENTRO IBEROAMERICANO DE REGENARACIÓN DEL SISTEMA NERVOSA

RESTAURANTE PEDREGAL

To Mariel and Pinar del Río

CALLE 236A

HOTEL/SPA LA PRADERA

CALLE 222

CENTRO DEL INGENIERA GENÉTICA Y BIOTECNOLÓGICA

MUSEO DEL AIRE

CALLE 23A

LA CORONELA

CALLE 264

FUNDACIÓN DEL NUEVO CINE LATINOAMERICANO

51

COMPLEJO TURÍSTICO LA GIRALDILLA/MACUMBA VILLA DIANA

AV.

MUSEO MUNICIPAL LA LISA

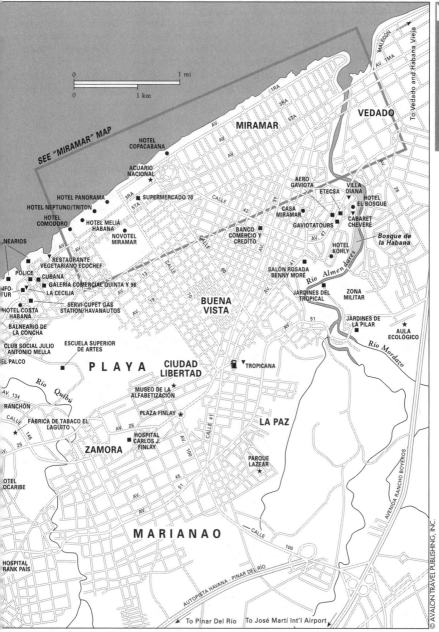

PLAYA

areas of La Sierra and Almendares in the east, and Buenavista further west.

1RA (PRIMERA) AVENIDA

1ra Avenida (First Avenue) runs along the Miramar seafront. It's a lively spot, popular with Havana's youth, and Havana's answer to South Beach or Santa Monica without the sand and the pier, although you *are* likely to see an occasional svelte girl in hot pants being pulled along on roller blades by a dog.

The shoreline is comprised of raised coral outcrops and lacks beaches, except to the extreme west. *Balnearios* (bathing areas) are found all along Miramar's waterfront, cut into the coral shore. Most are concentrated west of the Hotel Comodoro, beginning at Calle 84. They're time-worn, battered by one too many Caribbean storms, and of limited appeal to tourists, although they draw Cubans in huge numbers on hot summer days. More appealing beaches—the Playas del Oeste—begin half a kilometer farther west in the Náutico district

and extend west to Flores and Jaiminitas. Even surfing has come to Cuba; the surfing crowd finds its waves in the coastal section fronting the Hotel Neptuno/Tritón on 1ra Avenida between 70 and 84.

1ra Avenida is witnessing a boom, with many embassies, restaurants, and commercial entities opting for a locale by the sea.

A stroll along the avenue is pleasant—don't underestimate its length, about two miles—but there are only two sites of interest.

Maqueta de la Habana

The must-see *maqueta* (model) is a 1:1,000 scale replica of the city. It is housed in a lofty, hangar-sized, air-conditioned building called the Pabellón, Calle 28 #113, e/ Avenida 1 y 3, tel. 204-2661 or 202-7303. The 144-square-meter model represents 144 square km of Havana and its environs. The *maqueta*—one of the largest city models in the world—took nine experts more than 10 years to complete and shows Havana in the most intimate detail. Every contour is included, every building, every bump on every

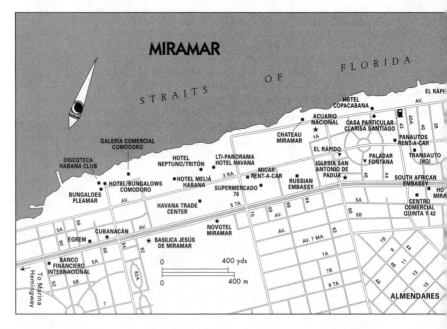

PLAYA

TOURIST INFORMATION OFFICE

Infotur, tel. 33-3333, oficturi@ofitur.mit.tur.cu, www.infotur.cu, the government tourist information bureau, has offices at Calle 28 #303, e/ 3ra y 5ta, tel. 204-0624, fax 204-8164, oficturi@ofitur.mitcma.net; and at 5ta Avenida, esq. Calle 112, tel. 204-7036, fax 204-3977, infomira@teleda.get.cma.net. Open 8:30 A.M.–8:30 P.M.

hill, even the balconies on buildings are there. It is color-coded by age: colonial-era buildings are painted crimson; buildings from 1900 to 1959 are ocher; postrevolutionary buildings are ivory; and projected buildings are white. The color-coding shows how urbanization began at the harbor and spread systematically westwards.

The model is made of sections that can be moved on rails to allow access to make changes. There's a balcony with telescopes for viewing the model from on high. It's impressive—but, more

important, a visit here puts the entire city in accessible 3-D perspective, allowing you to understand Havana's layout.

It's open Tuesday–Saturday 9:30 A.M.–5:30 P.M.; entrance costs US$3 (US$1 for students, seniors, and children). A guided spiel costs US$20.

The Pabellón also contains the offices of the **Grupo para el Desarrollo Integral de la Capital,** tel./fax 202-7925, gdic@ceniai.inf.cu, the government institution responsible for overseeing the integrated development of Havana.

Acuario Nacional

On weekends, Cuban families flock to the National Aquarium, 3ra Avenida, esq. Calle 62, tel. 203-6401 or 202-5872, fax 204-1442, acuario@ama.cu, www.acuarionacional.cu, which reopened in 2001 in new facilities after a complete and much-needed restoration that has graced the aquarium with fine theater areas. Alas, most of the tanks got no treatment and remain woefully inadequate by international standards. It exhibits 450 species of sea life, including anemones, corals, exotic

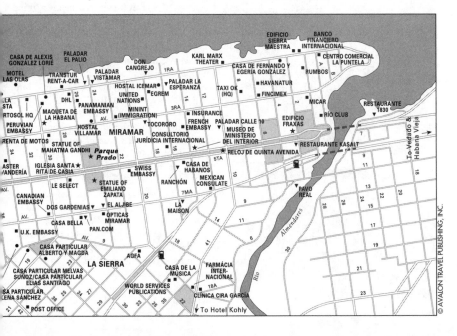

tropical fish, sharks, hawksbill turtles, sea lions, and dolphins.

Daily activities are offered. The highlight is the **sea lion show,** held Tuesday–Friday 11:30 A.M., 1 P.M., 4 P.M., and 8:30 P.M., and Saturday–Sunday at 11 A.M., 1 P.M., 3 P.M., and 5 P.M. The sea lions perform enthralling tricks while a commentator offers an educational program in Spanish. A **dolphin show** was scheduled to be reintroduced—the previous dolphins died of a disease, and new dolphins were being retrained at last visit. Take the kids, who have an opportunity to participate.

A theater show for kids is held every hour on the half hour, and an aquatic ballet is held nightly at 7:30 P.M.

Facilities include a small library, public toilets, and a basic snack bar.

The aquarium is open Tuesday–Friday 10 A.M.–10 P.M. and Saturday–Sunday 10 A.M.–6 P.M. Entrance costs US$5; children US$3.

© CHRISTOPHER P. BAKER

Acuario Nacional

5TA (QUINTA) AVENIDA AND VICINITY

Miramar's main thoroughfare and Havana's busiest boulevard is the wide fig-tree-lined boulevard called 5ta Avenida (Fifth Avenue). "Quinta" is flanked by mansions, many of which have been restored to an earlier grandeur and are now occupied by various Cuban commercial agencies or leased (or sold) to foreign corporations. 5ta Avenida is also "Embassy Row" and also offers several fine restaurants. The broad central median runs virtually ruler-straight for five miles, drawing gymnasts and joggers . . . many inured to the heat in their impossibly heavy sweats, while others wear much less. On the sidelines, predominantly at night, stands an array of young ladies dressed in equally minimalist attire . . . but beware, no small number are transvestite hookers.

A curiosity is the **Edificio Fraxas,** 5ta Avenida, esq. Calle 2, a near-derelict, green-roofed mansion immediately west of the tunnel under the Río Almendares. The roof is full of holes and the place looks like something out of the old *Munsters* TV show. An old lady lives here, defiantly refusing to move out or sell. Inside, supposedly, is "surreal to the point of wooziness," wrote Isadora Tattlin.

One block north of 5ta Avenida is an ornate Chinese-style mansion, built in the 1950s by Li Kim, a wealthy merchant. He fled Cuba after the Revolution, when his home was converted into the **Restaurante Pavo Real** (Peacock), 7ta Avenida #205, e/ Calle 2 y 4, tel. 204-2315. It features beautiful stained-glass screens, mother-of-pearl furnishings, and a magnificent second-floor cupola. Immediately east is an iron bridge—**Puente de Hierro** (pedestrians only; open 7 A.M.–7 P.M.)—over the bank of the Río Almendares. Beneath it is the **Parque de los Paticos** (Park of the Little Ducks), named for ducklings that used to splash about in the river here.

Back on 5ta Avenida, the **Reloj de Quinta Avenida,** Calle 10, is a large clock erected in 1924 in the central median. Today it's the official symbol of Miramar.

Another oddity is the monstrously ugly **Confederation of Independent States' Embassy,** a peculiar Cubist tower—formerly the Soviet Em-

The **Parque de los Ahogados** (Park of the Drowned), spanning 5ta Avenida between Calles 24 and 26, is shaded by massive jagüey trees, seemingly supported by their aerial roots dangling like cascades of water. On the south side of the road is **Plaza Emiliano Zapata,** with a life-size stone statue of Zapata, Mexico's revolutionary hero, appropriately surrounded by cacti; on the north side is **Parque Prado,** with a Romanesque temple and behind it a bronze bust to Mahatma Gandhi.

Rising over the west side of the plaza is **Iglesia de Santa Rita de Casia,** 5ta Avenida, esq. Calle 26, tel. 204-2001. This exemplar of modernist church architecture dates from 1942 and mixes neocolonial and modern features. Vast parabolic arches support a wooden roof. Its main feature is a modernist statue of Santa Rita by Rita Longa. Mass is Tuesday, Thursday, and Saturday at 5:30 A.M.; Wednesday and Friday at 10:30 A.M.; and Sunday at 8 A.M.

Two blocks south, on 9a Avenida between 24 and 28, is a fortified cash depository in the most unlikely of places. A sturdy steel wall has been built around the entire block, with electric gates and plenty of security. Havana's dollar assets are stored here. It's best to refrain from taking photos.

The massive Byzantine-style church to the west is the **Iglesia Jesús de Miramar,** 5ta Avenida #8003, e/ 80 y 82, tel. 203-5301, built in 1953 with a magnificent organ with 5,000 pipes—alas, termites have caused irreparable damage. The church features 14 oversize paintings of the Stations of the Cross by Spanish artist César Hombrados Oñativa featuring portraits of real people; some are considered blasphemous, such as the artist's wife as the Virgin Mary. Open daily 8 A.M.–noon and 4–6 P.M. Mass is Tuesday–Friday 8:30 A.M., Saturday 5 P.M., and Sunday 9 A.M. and 5 P.M.

Monte Barreto, the vast expanse of heretofore undeveloped land covering 35 city blocks that rises behind the church is now being developed in part with high-tech hotels and offices; the southern portion is occupied by a nursery (open 7 A.M.–7 P.M.), 9a Avenida y Calle 78, and is touted to become an ecological park. On the north side of 5ta Avenida is the still-in-evolution **Miramar Trade Center,** which will eventually cover 18 city blocks.

Russian Embassy

bassy, now the Russian Embassy (Embajada Rusa)—in the middle of 5ta Avenida, e/ Calles 62 y 66. Construction began in 1978 and was ongoing at the time of the Soviet collapse.

The modernist-style Romanesque church one block east is **Iglesia San Antonio de Padua,** Calle 60 #316, esq. 5ta Avenida, tel. 203-5045, dating from 1951 and quite simple yet peaceful within. It boasts a magnificent, albeit non-functional, organ. If the main door is locked, try entering via the sacristy. Mass is Monday, Tuesday, Thursday, Saturday and Sunday at 5 P.M.; Wednesday at 8:30 A.M.; and Friday at 10 P.M.

The **Casa de la Habana,** 5ta Avenida, esq. 16, is one of Havana's premier cigar outlets and features a beautiful stained-glass window.

One block west is **Che Guevara's former home,** Calle 18, e/ 5ta y 7ma, where the revolutionary icon narrowly escaped assassination on February 24, 1961, when a gun battle erupted outside his home a few moments after he had set out for work.

Museo del Ministerio del Interior

The Museum of the Ministry of the Interior, 5ta Avenida, esq. Calle 14, tel. 203-4432, is dedicated to the CIA's decades of inept villainy and efforts to dethrone Fidel. The seal of the CIA looms over a room full of photos and gadgets—oddities straight from a spy movie. It displays small arms, bazookas, and the like. It also features exhibits honoring MININT's good work in solving homicides—there's even a stuffed German shepherd that was used by police in their sleuthing. As always, Fidel is there in black and white. Among the many gleeful finger-in-your-eye accounts told in the museum is that 151 U.S.-financed agents were caught in Cuba. Almost all were of Cuban ancestry and, apparently, had been recruited by the U.S. Interests Section in Havana but were detected because 27 of the spies were Cuban double-agents. To make things easier for the CIA should it ever take another stab at Fidel, the museum shows a video giving details of Castro's security plans, including tunnels that lead from his residence (one of many) in Jaimanitas—adjacent to Marina Hemingway—to the nearby Ciudad Libertad military airstrip and to an underground bunker designed to protect him against an aerial bombardment.

The building, apparently, is also the headquarters of the First Chief of Operations of State Security . . . Cuba's top spy position.

Open Tues.–Fri. 9 A.M.–5 P.M., Sat. 9 A.M.– 4 P.M. Entry costs US$2 (plus US$1 for a guide).

A COMEDY OF ERRORS

The CIA's attempts (now defunct) to oust Castro were set in motion by President Eisenhower as early as March 1959. The bitter taste left by the CIA's botched Bay of Pigs invasion led to an all-out secret war against Castro, an effort code-named Operation Mongoose and headed by Bobby Kennedy. Mongoose eventually involved 500 case workers handling 3,000 anti-Castro Cubans at an expense of more than $100 million a year. The CIA's plans read like a James Bond novel—or a comedy of errors. In true James Bond fashion, the agency even recruited Cuban embassy staff by "dangling stunning beauties . . . exceptionally active in amorous adventures." James Bond's creator, Ian Fleming, even volunteered a few ideas. Some plots were straightforward, such as the attempt to kill Castro with a bazooka. The CIA's Technical Services Division (TSD) was more imaginative. It impregnated a box of cigars with botulism (they were tested on monkeys and "did the job expected of them") and hoped—in vain—to dupe Castro into smoking one. No one knows whether they reached Castro or whether some innocent victim smoked them. The spooks also tried to damage Castro's image by sprinkling his shoes with thallium salts (a strong depilatory), hoping that his beard would fall out, apparently in the belief that his beard was the source of his strength. Another box of Castro's favorite cigars was contaminated with a chemical that produced "temporary disorientation."

Eventually, the CIA turned to the Mob. It hired assassins handpicked by Johnny Rosselli, who had run the syndicate's Sans Souci casino in Havana. The killers were on both the FBI's 10 most wanted criminals list and Bobby Kennedy's target list of organized crime figures. The marksmen disguised as Marxmen didn't fool Castro, who correctly assumed the CIA would hire assassins. He considered them inefficient, claiming that an assassin "does not want to die. He's waiting for money, so he takes care of himself." Several assassins were caught and executed.

Meanwhile, Cuban-American terrorist organizations such as Operation 40 were funded and armed. (They were responsible for bombing Havana's Encanto department store and a Cubana plane, killing all 82 passengers.) All this, of course, backfired miserably. The secret war to oust Castro caused the Russians to increase their military commitment to Cuba. In the end, it helped provoke the missile crisis, bringing the world to the brink of nuclear disaster.

Náutico, Flores, and Jaimanitas

Beyond Miramar, 5ta Avenida curls around the half-moon Playa Marianao, and passes through the Náutico and Flores districts, the setting for Havana's most elite social clubs in days of yore.

PLAYAS DEL OESTE

This shorefront region is lined with *balnearios* (bathing areas). The beaches—collectively known as **Playas del Oeste**—are small, and most are nothing to write home about, but they're extremely popular with Cubans on weekends, when they get crowded. Most of the aging *balnearios* date from prerevolutionary days, when most of them served the social elite. Many went up in the 1920s and '30s, during the early years of Havana's tourist heyday, when there was even an eponymous mini-version of New York's famous Coney Island theme park. Following the Revolution they were reopened to the hoi polloi and rechristened—the Miramar Yacht Club, for example, became the Club Social Patrice Lumumba.

Commanding the scene is the palatial, *mudéjar*-style former **Balneario de la Concha,** between 112 and 146, which had no racial exclusionist policy; and immediately west, the former **Havana Yacht Club,** at the junction with 146. The "Yacht," as the latter was colloquially called, was founded in 1886 and became the snootiest place in Havana until the Revolution wrote a new chapter. Following the Revolution, the Havana Yacht Club became the Club Social Julio Antonio Mella, for workers. It was here that mulatto President Fulgencio Batista was famously refused entry for being too "black"—the voting followed the ancient, secret Roman style using white and black marbles. Both the Balneario de la Concha and Havana Yacht Club have since deteriorated dramatically and at last visit were still in an ignoble state, though slated for restoration.

Note the sensual entrance gate to the former **Club Náutico** (Nautical Club), 5ta Avenida y 152, another erstwhile prestigious private *balneario* designed by Max Borges Recio in 1953 in a series of enormous arched porticos. It primarily served high-income white-collar workers. It still functions as a *balneario . . .* for the masses.

Beyond the Río Quibu, 5ta Avenida passes into the Flores district. Here was the **Havana-Biltmore Yacht and Country Club,** dating from 1928, with a grandiose Moorish tower topping archways separated by ornate columns, and a veranda from which a broad stairway swept down to a beautiful expanse of white sand. In its heyday it was billed as the world's grandest resort. It was *the* place to see and be seen in Havana and boasted among its membership a Vanderbilt, an Astor, candy man Hershey, and an entire coterie of international notables. The Biltmore commanded (and owned) the beach called La Playa, which stretches east, with a bathing pavilion with 1,000 *cabañas*. After the Revolution the beach was opened to all Cubans, black and white, for a peso while the former casino went for the use of a worker's union, and the hotel became the Casa Cultural de Trabajadores de Construcción. Today, as the **Club Habana,** 5ta Avenida, e/ 188 y 192, Playa, tel. 204-5700, fax 204-5705, it has reverted to its former role as a private club for the social elite . . . annual membership costs US$1,500! This palatial private "nautical and social club" is operated by Palco (the Conference Center agency) and managed by Sol Meliá. It covers 10 hectares and boasts a fine beach of white sand, plus a handsome pool and sundeck. The main clubhouse is regally appointed and features a business center with Internet service, an elegant restaurant, a plush bar with marble floors, a separate piano bar, and a Casa del Tabaco and cigar lounge. A fitness center offers sauna and massage, and a nursery takes care of the kids. Sports facilities include yacht, surfboard, Aqua bike, and sea kayak rental; scuba diving; a golf range; and beach volleyball. It offers shows and cabarets on Saturday nights. Club membership is made up mostly of foreign diplomats and businesspeople, but nonmembers are welcome (entrance costs US$10 Mon.–Fri., US$15 Sat.–Sun.).

JAIMANITAS

You can also swim at **Marina Hemingway,** 5ta Avenida y Calle 248, tel. 204-1150, fax 204-1149, comercial@comermh.cha.cyt.cu, one kilometer west of Club Habana in the Jaimanitas district, 15 kilometers west of downtown. This huge yachting marina has several swimming pools. The best pool is that of the Hotel Acuario, while Papa's has a kiddie pool, waterslide, aqua-trampoline, and pedal-boat rentals. Take your pick of numerous restaurants and bars, including Papa's, which get lively with Cubans on weekends, drawing flirty *cubanas* eager to find positions as captains' mates. Deafening music is played constantly, and the cabaret hosts shows at night.

Additional beaches lie west of the marina along the Santa Fe waterfront.

The complex amid shade trees opposite the entrance to Marina Hemingway is **Escuela Superior del Partido Nico López** . . . for imparting Communist doctrines to government functionaries.

Fidel Castro's main domicile is nearby, but you can't see it. The large yet simply appointed home, complete with tennis and basketball courts, is set in an expansive compound surrounded by pine trees, electrified fences, and heavy security. All streets surrounding it are marked as one-way, heading away from the house.

Artist José R. Fuster, a noted painter and ceramist nicknamed the "Picasso of the Caribbean," has an open-air workshop-gallery at **Casa-Estudio de José Fuster,** Calle 226, esq. Avenida 3A, tel. 271-2932, fuster@cubarte.cult.cu, www.geocities.com/jfuster99. You step through a giant doorway—La Puerta de Fuster—to discover a surreal world made of ceramics. Many of the naïve, childlike works are inspired by farmyard scenes, such as *El Torre del Gallo* (Rooster's Tower), a 12-feet-tall statement on male chauvinism that also doubles as an oven. Other allegorical, often baroque, creations—puppet-like forms, buses bulging with people—pay tribute to Compay Segundo (of *Buena Vista Social Club* fame) and other provincial figures. The pool has a ceramic mermaid. Pop upstairs to view the ceramics studio and, above that, the painting studio; and then the rooftop *mirador* (lookout) with ceramic cow and surreal image of Changó. Open Mon.–Fri. 10 A.M.–6 P.M. Call ahead to arrange a visit. Several neighbors have adopted equally decorative themes for their houses.

Cubanacán and Vicinity

Cubanacán is—or was—Havana's Beverly Hills, a rolling area on either side of the Río Quibu. It was developed in the 1920s in a "garden-city" style, with winding tree-lined streets and enormous lots on which the most grandiose of Havana's mansions arose. An 18-hole golf course at the Havana Country Club served Havana's middle and wealthy classes, lending the name Country Club Park to what is now called Cubanacán, then as now the most exclusive address in town.

Following the Revolution, most of the area's homeowners decamped and fled Cuba. After the Revolution, other mansions were dispensed to party officials, many of whom still live in glorious isolation. Castro himself maintains several homes here, and security is strict. Others have been splendidly maintained amid neatly trimmed lawns and serve either as "protocol" houses—villas where foreign dignitaries and VIPs are housed during visits to Cuba—or as foreign embassies and ambassadors' homes—Frank Sinatra's former residence in Cubanacán is now a protocol house. Among them is the U.S. Residency, heavily guarded for obvious reasons, on immaculate and spacious grounds where, at the end of a long promenade, the eagle that once stood atop the Monumento del Maine on the Malecón spreads its magnificent wings.

Cuba's admirable biotechnology industry is also centered here and extends beyond Cubanacán, westward, into the flatter districts of Atabey and Siboney respectively. About 30 structures are dedicated to scientific research, earning the area the moniker Scientific City.

CIUDAD CIENTÍFICA

Cuba is a biotech minipower. Under Fidel Castro's personal patronage, Cuba has evolved one of the world's most advanced genetic engineering and biotechnology industries, with large-scale investment coming from public sources such as the Pan American Health Organization and the World Food Program. Together the various institutions, centered on the Cubanacán, Siboney, and Atabey districts, supply state-of-the-art health products to the world, bringing in more than US$100 million annually.

Cuba has developed nearly 200 products, both innovative and derivative. It invented and manufactures vaccines for cerebral meningitis, cholera, hepatitis B, interferon for the treatment of AIDS and cancer, and a skin growth factor to speed the healing of burns. For years, Cuba has touted a cure for the skin disease vitiligo. Recently it developed PPG, a "wonder drug" that reputedly washes cholesterol out of blood and, incidentally, is said to increase sexual potency (the source of a brisk black market for peddlers selling the drug to tourists). In 1996, CIGB scientists even began testing a vaccine to prevent HIV infection. Other advances have been made in agriculture and industrial bioengineering. Unfortunately, U.S. law prevents these lifesaving wonders from being sold in the United States.

The **Centro de Ingeneria Genética y Biotecnología** (Center for Genetic Engineering and Biotechnology), Avenida 31, e/ 158 y 190, tel. 271-6413 or 271-5149, www.cigb.edu.cu, is Cuba's main research facility, with many impressive accomplishments in creating new vaccines and treatments. The center, perhaps the most sophisticated research facility in the Third World, opened in 1986 at a cost of US$140 million.

The **Centro Nacional de Investigaciones Científicas,** Avenida 25 y 158, tel. 271-8066, is most famous for having developed PPG, or Ateromixol, Cuba's homespun anticholesterol wonder drug. PPG is considered a precursor to Viagra and many *jineteros* sell pills—or fakes?—illegally on the streets.

You can arrange visits to these and neighboring institutions.

The area is also replete with military camps and security personnel.

Bus no. 32 operates between La Rampa in Vedado and Cubanacán (five pesos).

CUBANACÁN

The **Palacio de las Convenciones**—Havana's impressive convention center—is on Calle 146, e/ 11 y 13, tel. 202-6011, fax 271-9496, palco@palco.get.cma.net, www.cubaweb.cu/palco. It was built in 1979 for the Non-Aligned Conference, and the main hall (one of 15 halls), seating 2,200 delegates, hosts meetings of the Cuban National Assembly. To its rear is **Pabexpo,** Avenida 17 y 180, tel. 271-6775, with four exhibition halls for hosting trade shows.

The area has many outstanding houses, particularly of modernist styles of the 1950s. Good examples include the **Casa de Ana Carolina Font,** Calle 216A #703, e/ 7A y 9, designed in 1956 by Mario Romanach; the **Casa de Antonio Barquet,** 5ta Avenida #16407, e/ 164 y 17, designed by Manuel Gutiérrez and unique for being the only house in Cuba entirely designed of circular forms; and **Casa de José Noval Cueto,** Calle 17A #17409, e/ 174 y 190, also by Romañach a stunning, sharp-angled masterpiece currently used as a protocol house. A recommended guide to the houses is *The Havana Guide: Modern Architecture 1925–65,* by Eduardo Luis Rodríguez (see Suggested Reading).

Instituto Superior de Arte

Following the Revolution, Fidel Castro and Che Guevara famously played a few rounds of golf at the exclusive Havana Country Club before tearing it up and converting the grounds to house

© CHRISTOPHER P. BAKER

Instituto Superior de Arte

Cuba's leading art academy, the National Art School, Calle 120 #1110, esq. 9a Avenida, tel. 208-0288, isa@cubarte.cult.cu. "The most beautiful academy of arts in the whole world," touted Fidel, even before ground was broken, in 1961. The school was designed by three young "rebel" architects: Italians Roberto Gottardi and Vittorio Garatti, and Cuban Ricardo Porro, who between them had little experience. Their sensual, experimental "garden complex" design was at first considered an architectural and metaphorical wonder. Gradually, as the five main buildings emerged, however, they were thought too sensual, too avant garde, for grim Communist tastes. Porro's art school was a deliberate evocation of the female form, complete with fountain shaped as a *mamey*, or papaya, also the Cuban slang term for vagina; "the open *mamey* with its perspiration and color—what does it suggest?" asked Porro. The project fell out of favor and was brought to a halt before completion, though the school did open. The two Italians, who had settled in Cuba, were eventually driven to leave—Sr. Gottardi was even jailed on trumped up espionage charges—while loyal Castroites strewed decapitated chickens on Sr. Porro's lawn to express

their disgust. Amazingly, in 2001 the Cuban government approached the three architects and asked them to complete the project.

The former club building became the Faculty of Music. Additional buildings made up the Escuela de Música (School of Music), Escuela de Ballet (Ballet School), Escuela de Baile Moderno (School of Modern Dance), and Escuela de Bellas Artes (School of Fine Arts). Lacking steel beams, the trio supported their structures with domed Catalan vaults. The dance school boasts a roof resembling shattered glass, symbolizing the Revolutionary overthrow of the old order. The snake-like music school is filled with light and shadow. The brick and concrete buildings "deliquesce," says Nancy Stout, "into the surrounding topography without need of camouflage; their vaulted roofs are a most fitting metaphor for nature's own mounds and hills. No other buildings in Havana are so forcefully driven to the tellurian." I find little aesthetic appeal however, and apply here Stout's words: "Disrespectful building has, unfortunately, not forsaken Havana," though she speaks of somewhere else in the city.

The ghostly complex is made more so by four decades of pitiful ruin scattered across acres of

rough lawn and overgrown forest, with long ten-
tacles of branches and roots creeping into the
buildings. "Abandoned in the middle of the jungle, a Tikal of the 1960s," thought Cuban art
critic Gerardo Mosquera.

For the best views, drive along Calles 15 and
134. In the summer the facility is closed.

Fábrica El Laguito

This cigar factory, at Avenida 146 #2302, e/ 21 y
21A, tel. 208-4654, about 600 meters south of
the Palacio de las Convenciones, opened in 1966
as a training school in the former home of the
Marques de Pinar del Río. The fabulous mansion,
which took its name from this part of the city,
was built in 1910 and later adorned with 1930s
art deco glass and chrome, a spiral staircase, and
abstract floral designs in the stucco detailing.
Because of its origins as a mansion, the factory
components are dispersed eccentrically, with
some store and selection rooms located at the
end of long palm-lined paths.

El Laguito makes Montecristos and the majority of Cohibas—*the* premium Havana cigar—
rich, rather spicy, and in 11 sizes. It is claimed that
Che Guevara initiated production while in charge
of the Cuban tobacco industry; his objective was
to make a cigar that surpassed every other prerevolutionary cigar. However, Nancy Stout in
her book, *Habanos,* says that it was started by
revolutionary heroine Celia Sánchez as a place of
employment for women (men have been employed as rollers here only since 1994), while
Guevara had his own little offshoot factory in
the Cabaña fortress.

Since Cohibas are made from only the finest
leaves, El Laguito is given first choice from the
harvest—"the best selection of the best selection," says factory head Emilia Tamayo). The
Cohiba was initially made solely for distribution
to foreign diplomats and dignitaries. Since
1982, it has been available for general consumption—bodybuilder-turned-actor Arnold
Schwarzenegger prefers Cohibas, as did Castro before he stopped smoking. Today, 3.4 million Cohibas are produced annually—about
one percent of Cuban production. El Laguito
also makes the best cigar in the world—the

Trinidad, a cigar you'll not find in any store.
The seven-and-a-half-inch-long cigar is made
exclusively for Castro, who presents them to
diplomats and dignitaries. The 2,000 Trinidads
produced monthly are, says Tamayo, "the selection of the selection of the selection."

Visits by appointment only.

LA CORONELA

La Coronela, south of Cubanacán and Atabey
and separated from them by Avenida 23, offers
the **Museo del Aire** (Air Museum), Avenida
212, e/ Calles 29 y 31, tel. 271-7753. The 50 or
so civilian and military aircraft displayed includes helicopters, missiles, bombers, and fighter
planes. It features Soviet MiGs, Che Guevara's
personal Cessna 310, a P-51 Mustang fighter, a
World War II-era AT6, and a turn-of-the-century
biplane hanging from the ceiling, plus three
main rooms replete with aviation mementos. A
section dedicated to the Bay of Pigs battle evokes
poignant memories; remnants of planes destroyed in the fighting and black-and-white photos speak with mute eloquence of the Cuban
pilots who died defending the island. There's
also a collection of model aircraft, and a space
section honoring Yury Gagarin and Col. Arnaldo Tamayo Méndez, the first Cuban cosmo-
naut. The museum also has a restoration
program. An artisans' shop and restaurant are
planned. Open Tues.–Sun. 10 A.M.–5 P.M. Entrance US$2; a guided tour costs US$1; photos cost US$2. The museum is hard to find:
from 5ta Avenida, take 17-A south to the round-
about; take the first exit to the right, heading
west on Avenida 23; then the first left, onto
198; then the first right onto 212, disregarding
the sign that reads 27; the museum is 100 yards
further on your left.

The **Fundación del Nuevo Cine Latinamericano,** Avenida 212, esq. 31, La Coronela, tel. 271-8967, www.fncl.cult.cu, about 100
yards further along 212, on the right, is the Havana branch of the film institute presided over by
Gabriel García Márquez. Housed on the former
estate of the Loynaz family, the *centro* features a
bookstore, a patio bar, and an air-conditioned

movie theater with glass sidewalls (and curtains) where movies are shown daily at 3 P.M. (two pesos); a movie for children is shown on Saturdays at 10 A.M. It gets very few visitors.

For a swim and refreshments, call in at **Complejo Turístico La Giradilla,** Calle 272 e/ 37 y 51, tel. 33-0568, gerencia@giralda.cha.cyt.cu, in the La Coronela district. Popular with the Cuban elite, this restaurant and entertainment complex occupies a huge 1920s mansion on expansive grounds. The restored gardens in mock-Versailles style feature a huge swimming pool and sundeck, and there's a covered stage for floor shows adjoining Havana's hippest disco.

Marianao

This untouristed *municipio,* on the heights south of Miramar, began life as an old village. By the mid-19th century, wealthy Spaniards began to build fine summer homes along newly laid streets on its breeze-swept slopes. Sections still bear the stamp of the colonial past. Access from Miramar is principally via Avenida 31 and Avenida 51, which continues west to the districts of La Lisa and La Coronela. Much of the region is extremely run-down, however, and draws few tourists. South of Avenida 51, the land slopes downhill; shanties—homes thrown together from scrap—mar the hillsides.

During the 1920s, Cuban developers promoted the area and established the Mariano Country Club, the Oriental Park racetrack, and the Grand Nacional Casino. Marianao became a center of tourism and was given a boost on New Year's Eve 1939 when the Tropicana nightclub opened as the ritziest establishment Havana had ever seen. Marianao remained a pleasure center until the Revolution, when Las Fritas, Marianao's erstwhile three-block-long strip of restaurants, beer parlors, shooting galleries, peep shows, and cabarets, was shut down.

CAMP COLUMBIA AND VICINITY

Following the U.S. occupation of Cuba in 1898, the U.S. military governor, General Fitzhugh Lee, established his headquarters in Marianao and called it Camp Columbia. Campamento Columbia later became headquarters for Batista's army; it was from here that the sergeant effected his *golpes* (coups d'états) in 1933 and 1952. Camp Columbia—renamed Ciudad Libertad following the Revolution—continued to operate as a military airstrip. It is still a *zona militar*), although Castro, true to his promise, had turned Batista's barracks into a school complex—**Ciudad Escolar Libertad** for 12,000 students.

In an attempt to destroy Castro's air force, Camp Columbia airstrip was bombed on April 15, 1960 by B-26 light bombers falsely painted in Cuban colors during the prelude to the CIA-run Bay of Pigs invasion. The attack failed, although five of Castro's planes were destroyed. The bombers struck houses in the densely packed neighborhood of Ciudad Libertad, killing seven people and wounding 52, giving Castro a grand political victory in his calls for solidarity against U.S. aggression—one of the dying men wrote Castro's name in blood on a wall. The following day he announced for the first time that Cuba was undergoing a "socialist revolution."

In 1961, Ciudad Escolar Libertad became the headquarters for Castro's national literacy campaign. Today, it features the **Museo de la Campaña de Alfabetización,** Avenida 29E, esq. 76, tel. 260-8054, dedicated to the amazing campaign, when 120,632 uniformed *brigadistas,* mostly comprising students—the youngest teacher was eleven-year-old Elan Manuel Menendez Menocal—spread out across the country to teach illiterate peasantry to read and write. The brigadistas were armed with lamps and two manuals, displayed along with photographs, maps, and various artifacts relating to the campaign, including reading glasses distributed to peasants with optical problems. The museum is a fascinating memorial to a splendid achievement, initiated on January 1, 1960 and completed on December 22, 1961. Fidel commands the lobby with a larger-than-life photo and quote. Open Mon.–Fri. 8 A.M.–5 P.M., and Sat. 8 A.M.–noon. Entrance is free.

Most of the former military complex comprises collapsing schoolrooms, rutted roads, and weeds. Fortunately, at last visit, a partial restoration was under way.

A tower in the center of the traffic circle—**Plaza Finlay**—outside the main entrance, at Avenida 31 and Avenida 100, was erected in 1944 as a beacon for the military airfield. In 1948 a needle was added so that today it is shaped like a syringe in honor of Carlos Finlay, the Cuban who in 1881 discovered the cause of yellow fever.

The scientist is also honored at **Plaza Lazear,** Calle 90, e/ 61 y 61A, in a slum section of the Pogolotti district—from Avenida 51 turn south on Calle 92; go six blocks to 59A; turn left; after one block cross 61. Here, Walter Reed, head of the U.S. Army Yellow Fever Commission, irrefutably validated Finlay's discovery at Camp Lazear, a quarantined experimental station. Casita #1, one of the two original quarantine huts, still stands at the memorial park atop a plinth that bears plaques to Finlay, Reed, et al. For a detailed and fascinating history, including great photos, of Camp Lazear and the battle to eradicate Yellow Fever, visit the website: http://yellowfever.lib.virginia.edu.

Iglesia de San Francisco Javier de Los Quemados, Avenida 51 y Calle 108, tel. 260-7598, is a simple church built in 1747 with an exquisite interior highlighted by its wooden altar and baroque carved pulpit and pews. Mass is Tuesday and Thursday at 6 P.M.; Wednesday at 9 A.M.; and Saturday–Sunday at 9 A.M. and 6 P.M.

The **Museo Municipal de Marianao,** Calle 128B #5704, esq. 57, tel. 260-9706, is housed in the former Casa de José Morada, a beautiful home erected in 1880 as a country *quinta* (villa) and boasting beautiful stained-glass windows and wrought-iron railings. The house teems with period pieces, plus armaments, documents, and a kitchen preserved in its original state. A gallery offers rotating art exhibits. Open Mon.–Sat. 8:30 A.M.–noon and 1–4 P.M.

The **Fábrica Héroes del Moncada,** Avenida 57 #13402, e/ 134 y 136, tel. 260-9058, is a

modest-scale cigar factory established in 1952, when it was moved by its owner from Las Villas Province (today's Villa Clara). All the major brands of export cigars are manufactured here, including Cohibas. *Cigar Aficionado* considers this one of the top three cigar factories in Cuba. Leaf processing takes place on the ground floor, and the rolling upstairs. Tours are offered Monday–Friday at 10 A.M. and 11 A.M.; US$10. The factory receives very few visitors, and you must arrange in advance through CATEC, Calle 148 #905, e/ 9 y 9A, Cubanacán, tel. 208-6071.

Turn south on Calle 114 from Avenida 51 and after about two kilometers you arrive at **Central Manuel Martínez Prieto,** a sugar mill—yes, a *sugar mill* in Havana!—built in 1875 and still supplying much of the city's sugar. Alas, no visitors are allowed. The nearby community of **Toledo,** comprising 1920s wooden bungalows, hosts the **Fiesta Toledana** each May to celebrate the end of the *zafra* (sugarcane harvest).

The Tropicana

A nocturnal visit to the Tropicana nightclub, off Calle 72 between 41 and 45, tel. 207-0110, fax 207-0109, Cuba's premier cabaret, is a *must.* The whirlwind show began in 1939 in an open-air theater in the gardens of a mansion that once housed the U.S. ambassador. The Tropicana quickly eclipsed Havana's other nightclubs in grandeur and extravagance, and featured the world's top performers. Most of the structures date from 1951, when the club was restored in modernist style with a new showroom—the **Salon Arcos de Cristal** (Crystal Bows)—designed by Max Borges Recio with a stupendous roof of five arcing concrete vaults up to 30 meters in span and curving bands of glass to fill the intervening space. Built in decreasing order of height, they produce a telescopic effect that channels the perspective toward the orchestra platform. Borges also added the famous sculpture—representing a mathematical formula in three dimensions—that still forms the backdrop to the main stage, in the outdoor *Salon Bajo las Estrellas.* A stone statue of a ballet dancer shown pirouetting on the tips of her toes by the renowned Cuban sculptor Rita Longa was added to the lush foliage in front of the entrance. The statue, which has become Tropicana's motif, is joined by a fittingly sensuous statue of the Greek maenads by Longa (the maidens first floated on a pond of the Gran Casino Nacional), with the bacchants performing a wild ritual dance to honor Dionysius at night amid the woods, as in the original myth.

Visitors are not welcome by day, when the dancers practice. You must visit at night, when the lavishly costumed, statuesque showgirls perform beneath the stars.

Western Suburbs

BARACOA

This down-at-heels coastal community, about 15 kilometers west of Marina Hemingway, still exists partly from fishing—although out on a limb, it lies within the municipality of Havana. Its beach offers no appeal. The sole interest is the **Casa de Petrona,** a simple family home with an exterior entirely covered with shells.

En route, you'll pass a former Naval Academy that in 1999 became the **Escuela Latinoamericana de Ciencias Médicas** (Latin American School of Medical Sciences) to teach medicine to students from throughout the Americas, Caribbean, and Africa.

EL CANO

This small village, on the southwestern outskirts, was founded in 1723 and has retained elements of its historic charm. Immigrants from the Canary Islands and Majorca brought a tradition of pottery making. Their descendants are still known as skilled potters (*alfareros*), who use local red clays shaped on foot-operated wheels and fired in traditional wood-fired kilns. The village is centered on a quaint church.

A **Museo Popular de Alfarería** (Pottery Museum) is planned. And the community comes alive each September when it hosts the three-day **Fiesta de los Alfareros.**

For information contact Rigoberto Gómez Sulimán, Avenida 81, esq. 286, tel. 208-8163.

To get there, take Avenida 51 to La Lisa and turn south on 81.

Accommodations

RESERVATIONS

Officially, it's de rigueur to book at least two nights' accommodation prior to arrival. Cuba immigration officials are assiduous in ensuring that arriving visitors have prebooked rooms. If you're lucky, the immigration official won't ask to see a hotel voucher. If he or she does and you can't produce a voucher, you'll be marched to the tour desk to make a booking . . . and to pay for it. For this reason, do not leave the address line on your tourist visa blank. Even if you don't have *any* reservation, it's best to fill in the name of a mid-price hotel. You can give a private address if you have reservations at a *casa particular* (private room rental).

Tourist visas state that tourists must receive express permission from immigration authorities if wishing to stay at any place other than a hotel or "authorized accommodation," which includes *casas particulares*. Some immigration officials don't seem clear about this or, being loyal revolutionaries, attempt to force tourists to book a hotel room regardless. If this happens to

bedroom, Casa de Jorge Coalla Potts

you, point out that registered *casas particulares* pay taxes and are legal; stick to your guns!

Havana is in the midst of a tourism boom, and many hotels are often fully booked . . . another reason to secure accommodation in advance. The Christmas and New Year's season is particularly busy. Make reservations well ahead of time as it might be days, or even weeks, before you get a reply . . . even when communicating by email. Normally, a deposit will not be required.

Don't rely on mail to make reservations. Call direct, send a fax or email, or have a Cuban state tour agency or a tour operator abroad make your reservation. Most of the tour agencies listed in the Transportation chapter can make bookings for you. Alternately, you can book direct with the various hotel entities: see the Special Topic "Hotel Chains."

Insist on receiving written confirmation, and be sure to take copies of such with you to Cuba, as Cuban hotels are notorious for not honoring reservations.

WHICH DISTRICT?

Location is important in choosing your hotel.

Habana Vieja puts you in the heart of the old city, within walking distance of Havana's main touristic sights. Choose from several Spanish-style *posadas* and exquisite colonial palaces-turned-hotels, plus a fistful of turn-of-the-century hotels that have all been, or are being, upgraded.

Centro Habana, although offering few sites of interest, has several budget-oriented hotels that lie close to the Prado and Habana Vieja. This predominantly run-down residential district also has a large number of reasonably-priced *casas particulares.*

Vedado's mid-20th-century offerings are well-situated for sightseeing and include several first-class hotels. Havana's reenergized night life is here. Farther out, in western Vedado, are the renovated Riviera and the deluxe Cohiba. Vedado also has some of the best *casas particulares.*

Playa and Marianao has a number of moderate hotels popular with tour groups, such as the Comodoro, Copacabana, and Kohly, plus an increasing number of modern deluxe hotels,

such as the Novotel Miramar and the Panorama. All are far away from the main tourist sights and you'll need wheels to get around.

The Suburbs are represented by the hotels of Ciudad Panamericano and Playas del Este. Avoid these at all costs unless you're determined to have a second-rate beach holiday—in Ciudad Panamericano, you'll find yourself out on a limb, without even a beach to amuse you.

PRICES

Don't expect major bargains! The Cuban government has a monopoly and like most monopolies often charges outrageous prices. Prices shot up in recent years until Havana was no longer a bargain; however, in 2002 rates began to fall as tourism plummeted, and at last visit many hotels were offering over-the-counter discounts on publicized rates.

Each price category in this chapter is divided by district: **Habana Vieja, Centro Habana, Vedado,** and **Playa and Marianao.**

Prices at many hotels vary for low and high season. Usually low season is May–June and September–November, high season is December–April and July–August. However, this varies. Some hotels have four rates, adding peak high season and low low season. Usually, single rooms cost about 20 percent less than double rooms. Cuba imposes no room tax or service charge to guests' bills. It pays to book through a travel agent or tour operator (or any of Cubatour's or Havanatur's international representatives) since Cuban hotels offer discounts as much as 50 percent to wholesalers. Canadians and Europeans can keep costs down by buying a charter package tour with airfare and hotel included, although standards vary widely and often the less notable hotels are used. If you book your hotels from abroad, you'll be issued hotel vouchers that you present upon arrival in Cuba (usually through the Cubatur representative at the airport).

Budget hotels are few and far between and exist to serve a Cuban clientele. They usually have two prices: a peso price for Cubans and a dollar price for foreigners. The best way to keep

FAWLTY TOWERS?

Cuba's hotel foibles conjure up déjà vu for viewers of *Fawlty Towers,* the BBC's hilarious sitcom. Most hotels have a few petty annoyances. For example, after a hot, sticky day, you return to your room to find no hot water—a plight for which you're supposed to get 10 percent off your bill. No running water at all? Twenty percent off. Ah! The water is running—but, alas, there's no plug. In theory, you're entitled to a well-defined refund for each such contingency. A sorry mattress is worth a 10 percent discount, according to the State Prices Commission.

In Havana, things have dramatically improved of late, and newly refurbished and more expensive hotels come close to Western standards. However, things remain far from perfect, with the number of faults in inverse proportion to price—away from Havana, things deteriorate quickly. At the cheapest places, you'll find gurgling pipes, no toilet seat (quite likely), no bathplugs (virtually guaranteed), and sunken mattresses (guaranteed). "Staying in less-than-two-star hotels . . . means passing below the rock bottom of comfort, to the point where involuntary abuse of guests begins," wrote Isadora Tattlin. In barebones hotels, even hot water may only be tepid—and available at certain times of day. Shower units are often powered by electric heater elements, which you switch on for the duration of your shower. Beware! It's easy to give yourself a shock from any metal objects nearby.

Hotels also supply towels and soap, but only the most deluxe ones provide shampoo, conditioner, and body lotion. Lower-priced hotels are often missing towels; insist that your maid supply one or you may be charged.

Though many of the staff are mustard-keen, far too many hotels have abysmal service. Castro agreed: "Cubans are the most hospitable, friendly, and attentive people in the world. But as soon as you put a waiter's uniform on them, they become terrible." Sometimes the opposite is true. Chambermaids, for example, often rearrange your belongings until you can no longer find them—which may be the whole point.

To be fair, things are improving. Cuba is aggressively addressing the deficiencies and has set up hotel management training schools run by Austrians—world leaders in the hospitality industry. However, hotel management still leaves much to be desired. Very few Cubans seem to care about their clients or their jobs, and there rarely seems to be a manager on-site. It's enough to make you wonder if Basil Fawlty is running the show.

costs down is to rent a *casa particular,* a private room in a family home.

WHAT TYPE OF ACCOMMODATION?

Havana is blessed with accommodations of every stripe. The motley and dowdy hostelries of a few years ago have been upstaged by a blossoming of deluxe and boutique hotels, and skyrocketing demand has fostered the arrival of foreign name-brand hotels run as joint ventures with Cuban state-owned tourism agencies. Hotels built in recent years reflect standards necessary to attract a foreign clientele—most would be rated three- or four-star, though few would be considered deluxe by international standards, and all suffer from poor design, shoddy construction, cheap materials, and inadequate upkeep.

Cuban hotels are graded by the conventional star system, but the ratings are far too generous—in lower-grade properties, for example, rooms are generally small by North American standards, and lighting tends to be subdued, usually because the wattage is low. Most hotels in reality fall one or two categories below their international equivalents.

Especially noteworthy are the splendidly restored colonial-era hotels of Habana Vieja, and those deluxe hotels under foreign management. Havana also has some appallingly dreary options. Upkeep and lousy management are the main problems, so that hotels rapidly deteriorate and a newly constructed or renovated hotel today might appear rundown a year or two later. Even the more upscale hotels are not entirely free of Cuban quirks, all of which makes the unduly high prices doubly annoying. No one thinks to clean the fixtures, for example, so that hotels only one or two years old become grimy. Says *Cigar Aficionado:* "A number of hotels in Havana still look like low-income housing or urban crack houses." You can go horribly wrong in your choice of hotel.

Several hotels were closed following the September 11, 2001, terrorist attacks and were being upgraded.

Camping

The Cuban term *campismo* refers to basic huts at established sites. There are no campsites in or around Havana.

Peso Hotels

About half a dozen hotels cater to Cubans and are extremely cheap—usually the equivalent of less than US$1 for Cubans, who pay in pesos. A few still ostensibly accept tourists, who must pay in dollar equivalent (usually about US$10–25). Although a few are quite attractive, most are dour by Western standards.

You cannot book peso hotels through any state tourism organization; you will have to do this face-to-face in Cuba. Don't believe it if you're told that a pesos-only hotel is full. That's a standard answer given to foreigners. Be persistent . . . and be nice. If the receptionist warms to you, a room can magically be found. But don't count on it, as things have tightened up in recent years. An exception is the Islazul properties, which cater to both Cubans and foreigners.

Tourist Hotels

All tourist hotels in Cuba are owned by state enterprises. Six Cuban hotel entities compete for business, operating in cooperative management agreements with foreign hotel groups.

Though Cubans are barred from staying at tourist hotels, many such hotels open their swimming pools to Cubans, who flock in summer, when pool areas are often raucous venues. Also avoid rooms near hotel discos, which are also open to Cubans.

Aparthotels

Aparthotels offer rooms with kitchens or kitchenettes (pots and pans and cutlery are provided), and sometimes small suites furnished with sofas, tables, and chairs. One- or two-bedroom units are the norm. Aparthotels are particularly economical for families. Most are characterless: it's all a matter of taste. Many are linked to regular hotels, giving you access to broader facilities.

Villas, Apartments, and Protocolos

Self-catering apartments are available for rent, as are fully staffed villas, including *protocolos*—special houses reserved for foreign dignitaries. Most of the *protocolos* are splendid mansions in the Cubanacán region, and they include Frank Sinatra's former home.

Casas Particulares

My favorite way to go is to seek out a *casa particular* (literally, private house)—a room in a family home. This can be anything from a single room with a live-in family, to a self-sufficient apartment. Some families are willing to vacate their entire home on a moment's notice. Invariably, the homeowner and his or her family are gracious and friendly folks. The going rate is US$20–50, often with breakfast included. Most often, however, any meals are extra (US$3 for breakfast is typical), as is laundry. If you're guided to a particular *casa particular* by a tout, his or her commission—usually US$5—will be added to your rent.

Legally licensed houses post a blue tent-like *Arrendador Inscripto* triangle on the front door—those with a red triangle are licensed to rent only to Cubans, in pesos. There are also many illegal, unlicensed *casas particulares,* which should be avoided, not least because the legal houses have a tough time of things, and get nothing back in return for the excessive taxation charged by the government.

Competition is fierce and touts do a brisk business trying to steer tourists to specific *casas.* You'll not be five minutes in the city before being approached by touts working on commission.

BEARING A BURDEN

Since the triumph of the Revolution, the Urban Reform Law explicitly prohibited the rental of housing, despite which *casas particulares* began to blossom in the mid-1990s following the restrictions on having Cuban guests in hotel rooms—foreign guests turned to renting private rooms for their liaisons. With tourism booming, the government faced a room shortage. Hence, in 1996 the law was begrudgingly reformed: Cubans are now permitted to rent out up to two rooms, albeit under rigid state observation. A stiff tax code was also introduced, intended to sting *casas particulares* as stiffly as possible. The tax varies according to district—US$100 monthly in a nontourist zone, and US$250 in a tourist zone, plus a yearly percentage of their earnings—and is payable whether the home-owner receives guests or not. The government has its own undisclosed minimum that it is prepared to accept as monthly declared income; if the *casa particular* owner declares less, he or she is presumed to be lying and is fined.

An ever-increasingly burdensome lot of regulations attempts to make life difficult for private renters. For example, additional fees are levied if houses provide off-street parking or meals, and for any advertising. And the owner of a *casa particular* may not operate any other business, including car rental or guide services.

Your host must record your passport details, which must be presented to the Ministry of the Interior within 24 hours, so MININT is always abreast of every foreigner's whereabouts.

You're permitted to have Cuban guests, including overnight—although there were hints at last visit that this might change—but your host must record your partner's name and other pertinent details for presentation to MININT within 24 hours (MININT, which keeps a close watch on any intimate relations with Cubans, runs the Cubans' names through a computer database; if the name of a *chica* appears three times with a different man, she is arrested as a *jinetera* and gets a mandatory jail term. Your Cuban partner must be at least 18 years of age—if you are discovered with anyone underage, the owner of the *casa particular* can lose their home along with their license. Ostensibly, your partner should be your steady *novio* or *novia* (boyfriend or girlfriend), not a *jinetera*.

Until recently, few hosts insisted on this. In 2002 police, however, began raiding *casas particulares* in the pre-dawn hours and disturbing tourists in their beds! Woe betide any *casa particular* owner whose guest has an unrecorded Cuban in his or her bed.

Inspectors visit regularly to check the books and property. The slightest infractions are dealt with harshly: a US$1,500 fine is standard!

They may try to guide you to specific houses, and are not above telling tourists lies, such as telling you that a particular house you might be seeking has closed.

Since conditions vary remarkably, it's important not to agree to rent until you've checked a place out and compared it with several others. Often, especially in Habana Vieja, you might arrive at a narrow doorway with a staircase of grime-stained, broken tiles and perhaps even a scent of urine. Don't let this put you off, as usually such places are in communal structures and often the *casa particular* itself is clean and gracious. In most, the owners have fixed things up—

even rejigged so that your room may be a self-contained apartment with its own separate entrance—with standards and facilities that far exceed those of your host. Neighborhood noise is often a factor.

If you have a car, you'll need private parking—alternately, the owner may recommend a secure place nearby, or even hire someone to guard the car for about US$2 a night.

Heavy taxation and ever-more burdensome restrictions have recently forced many *casas particulares* to close. And at last visit, no new applications for private room rentals were being considered by the government. The situation

HOTEL CHAINS

Cubanacán, Avenida 7ma #6624, e/ 66 y 70, Miramar, tel. 204-7649, fax 208-9080, comercial@hoteles.cyt.cu, www.cubanacan.cu, has about 12 hotels in Havana, from modest to luxury.

Gaviota, Edificio La Marina, Avenida del Puerto y Justíz, Habana Vieja, tel. 866-6777 or 866-6765, fax 33-2780, gaviota@gaviota.gav.tur.cu, www.gaviota-grupo.com, (a branch of the Cuban military!), owns three three-star hotels in Havana.

Gran Caribe, 7ma Avenida #4210, e/ 42 y 44, Miramar, tel. 204-0575, fax 204-0565, armando@grancaribe.gca.cma.net, www.grancaribe.cu, has mostly top-end establishments, including the landmark Hotel Nacional.

Horizontes, Calle 23 #156, e/ N y O, Vedado, tel. 33-4042, fax 33-3161, crh@horizontes.ht.cma.net, www.horizontes.cu, has nine hotels in Havana, in the two- and three-star categories.

Hoteles Habaguanex, Calle Oficios #110, e/ Lamparilla y Amargura, Habana Vieja, tel. 867-1039, fax 60-9761, gerencia.comercial@habaguanex.ohch.cu, www.habaguanex.cu, operated nine historic hotels in Habana Vieja at last visit, with several more slated for coming years. Most are recently restored historic charmers. Some are termed *"hostales"* (hostels) but they are in fact full-fledged and gracious hotels.

Islazul, 3ra Calle y Avenida de los Presidentes, Vedado, tel. 832-0570, fax 33-3458, comazul@teleda.get.cma.net, www.islazul.cubaweb.cu, operates basic hotels primarily for Cubans (who pay in pesos), but they also accept tourists. Islazul hotels can be noisy, and facilities are usually sub-par.

is fluid. Many *casa particular* owners support one another by offering recommendations for other rentals.

No Cuban agencies may make reservations for private room rentals.

A good resource is www.casaparticular.com, a well-organized site that displays details (except contact information) and photos of individual *casas particulares* and acts as a booking agent. Similar websites include www.contactcuba.com/casaparticular, www.havana-rentals.com, and www.cuba-rentals.com.

STAYING WITH CUBAN FRIENDS

Big Brother keeps tabs on the whereabouts of every foreigner nightly. Hence, if you're staying with friends, you must ostensibly present yourself to the Ministry of Interior (MININT) within 24 hours and request an A-2 visa (US$25 to make the change). The Cuban embassy in Canada posts the following advisory: "With tourist cards you are supposed to stay at hotels in Cuba, but if you are using it to stay at a private residence, you must go to the nearest immigration office, once in Cuba, with the person you wish to stay and request a change of your visa category, so that you may stay there without any problem with Cuban authorities."

SECURITY

Most hotel lobbies have MININT security agents in dark suits with microphones tucked in their ears. They were posted following the spate of bombs planted in Havana's hotels in 1997 and serve to prevent a repeat performance, but also do double duty to keep Cubans from slipping upstairs with foreign guests. Unfortunately, they don't seem entirely to trust foreigners—a surreal situation!—and are not above bothering hotel guests and their legitimate friends.

Theft is an issue, especially in budget hotels. Most tourist hotels have safe-deposit boxes at the front desk or in individual guest rooms. Be sure to use it for any valuables, especially your passport, camera, and money. Clothing is often stolen. Consider locking *all* your items in your suitcase each time you leave your room. Before accepting a room, ensure that the door is secure and that your room can't be entered by someone climbing in through the window. *Always* lock your door.

Keep your suitcase locked when you're not

SEEKING A CUBAN PIED-À-TERRE?

So you want to make a life in Havana, if only for a year or two. First the bad news . . . The Cuban government doesn't want you! Not unless you offer unique skills that the country needs—for example, teaching English to Cuban teachers and adults is possible if you have a recognized qualification in teaching English as a foreign language. Students are permitted to study here for periods of one year or longer. Otherwise most foreigners are employees of NGOs (nongovernmental organizations) or international corporations doing joint business with the Cuban government; or embassy staff; or news correspondents; or folks on the lam from the law (Cuba harbors some 19 former Black Panthers on the FBI's "most wanted" list, alongside terrorists of the ETA Basque separatist movement, and who knows what other kind of no-goods). You can count the number of other foreigners on one hand.

Your best bet, if you're not going to be employed by a corporation or NGO, is to visit Cuba on a tourist visa and present yourself to the Ministerio de Imigración (Calle 22 y Avenida 3, Miramar) and present a rationale for wanting to stay . . . along with proof of financial solvency. With only rare exceptions are foreigners permitted to open any kind of business.

And forget that old mansion you've been coveting. Buying a home is out of the question, at least in your own name. The exception is condominiums that the Cuban government offers for sale to foreigners—the program was briefly ended when foreigners, understandably, began re-selling their properties to higher bidders. These include developments in the Miramar and Siboney districts, plus a separate development at Santa María del Mar . . . for a not-so-socialist US$1,450 per square meter. At the upper end of the market are the condominiums at Monte Carlo Palacio, a ritzy, spanking new block of apartments on 5ta Avenida, e/ 44 y 46, selling for more than US$200,000 apiece.

For information, contact **Real Inmobiliaria,** 5ta Avenida #2007, Miramar, tel. 204-9874, fax 204-9875, realin@colombus.cu, based in Monaco.

A handy resource is *Living and Investing in the New Cuba,* by Christopher Howard, Costa Rica Books, Suite #1 SJO 981, P.O. Box 025216, Miami, FL 33102-5216, crbooks@racsa.co.cr, www.costaricabooks.com

in your room, as maids (who are paid a pittance) have been known to make off with clothing and other items.

GUEST CARDS

Upon registering at a hotel, you'll be issued a *tarjeta de huésped* (guest card), identifying you as a hotel guest. The card may have to be presented when ordering and signing for meals and drinks, when changing money, and often when entering the elevator to your room.

CUBAN GUESTS

There are strictures against Cuban women (and men) entering hotel lobbies alone, and no Cubans are permitted in guest rooms in tourist hotels. A tourist apartheid is in force. Even Cubans with pockets full of *fula* (dollars) can't register in hotels (Islazul excepted), under the pretext that this protects tourists. Unless you can prove that a Cuban companion is your spouse, rest assured that hotel staff will turn your partner away.

Cubans and foreigners are allowed to share hotels run by Islazul, where the clientele is *primarily* Cuban; foreigners and Cubans generally come and go and interact without restriction. However, the policy is in flux as the government finesses its handling of *jineteras* (prostitutes) and *jineteros* (illicit marketeers) in hotels. At press time even Islazul hotels did not permit their Cuban guests to enter the rooms of foreign hotel guests, and vice versa—the hotel staff go to ridiculous lengths to prevent such occurrences.

It is still legal to have a Cuban as your guest if you're staying in a *casa particular*.

The government is sensitive to the needs of every man and woman, and has created state-run, 24-hour love hotels—*posadas,* but also known as "motels"—which exist to provide relief for the large percentage of Cubans who live together with aunts, uncles, parents, and even grandparents along with the children, often in conditions in which rooms are subdivided by curtains. At these hotels, couples can enjoy an intimate moment together, although conditions are often dour. Most couples are married, sometimes to each other. Conditions are modest, to say the least, although some more congenial facilities have air-conditioning and music in the rooms, such as El Monumental—12 kilometers west of Havana—which is favored by government officials. Rooms are usually rented for three hours, typically for five pesos (US$.25), for which the state sometimes provides a bottle of rum by the bed.

GAY COUPLES

Technically, it is illegal for two men to share the same bed, although hotels and most *casa particulares* do not apply the law. There seems to be no such proscription on two women.

Habana Vieja

Habana Vieja is in the midst of a hotel boom, with many colonial-era mansions and erstwhile grande dame hotels having come online after splendid makeovers. They have the advantage of superb locations to add to their considerable charms.

Habaguanex, the state corporation that administers tourist commercial enterprises in Habana Vieja, is slated to open additional historic hotels in Habana Vieja in the next few years, including a residential complex with villas and a hotel planned for the Parque Histórico Militar Morro-Cabaña; the Hostal Raquel (San Ignacio, esq. Amargura) with a grand becolumned lobby; the Hotel Casa del Marqués de Arcos (Calle Mercaderes, e/ Empedrado y O'Reilly); and a 250-room deluxe hotel, the Miramar-Malecón, to be built at the foot of the Prado in a joint venture with the Chinese government.

CASAS PARTICULARES

Although much of the housing is in decrepit condition, off-putting exteriors belie some surprisingly clean and modern interiors.

Casa de Daniel Carrasco Guillén, Calle Cristo #16, 2ndo piso, e/ Teniente Rey y Muralla, tel. 862-7362, is recommended. The owner and his friendly family rent five rooms, including three lofty-ceilinged rooms (one with a private bathroom) with modest furnishings in the colonial home, and two modern rooms (sharing a bathroom) upstairs atop the roof. The latter can get hot during midday, but are cross-ventilated. All rooms have air-conditioning and hot water and are clean. Breakfasts cost US$3. Rates are US$25.

Casa de María Elena Hernández, Calle Refugio #108, e/ Prado y Moro, tel. 863-9177, cubarent@yahoo.com, www.cubanasol.com, is a simply furnished upstairs apartment one block from the Prado. The single air-conditioned bedroom with two single beds has a separate entrance and a private bathroom with hot water, but no windows. Guests get use of the family TV lounge. María speaks English. Complimentary dinner is provided on the first night (and thereafter for US$5–15). Room rates are US$35 including breakfast.

Casa de Miriam Soto Delgado, Calle Cuba #611, Apto. 4, e/ Santa Clara y Luz, tel. 862-7144, a stone's throw from the Convento de Santa Clara, rents one simply furnished air-conditioned room with TV and adjoining bathroom for US$20. There's a TV lounge. Meals are provided on request.

Casa de Alfonso Rodríguez, Calle Cuarteles #10, e/ Cuba y Aguiar, tel. 861-0457, is a colonial home with three air-conditioned rooms, each with fans, lofty ceilings, and simple but adequate furnishings that include a double and single bed. A shared bathroom has hot water. Guests can use the family TV lounge. Rates are US$30.

Casa de Migdalia Caraballe Martín, Calle Santa Clara #164, Apto. F, e/ Cuba y San Ignacio, tel./fax 61-7352, has three air-conditioned double rooms with fans. There's a safe, plus a TV lounge, and the hostess is a delight.

Casa de Eugenio Barral García, Calle San Ignacio #656, e/ Jesús María y Merced, tel. 862-9877, is one of the best private room rentals in southern Habana Vieja. The owner offers three air-conditioned bedrooms with fans and refrigerator in an old home graciously and eclectically appointed with antiques and precious ornaments. Rooms share two modern bathrooms with hot water. Rates are US$25 including breakfast.

Casa de Margarita López, Calle Obispo #522, Apto. 8, e/ Bernaza y Villegas, tel. 867-9592, larin@infomed.sld.cu, has a fourth-floor two-bedroom apartment with a sitting room with color TV, telephone, and ceiling fan, plus a small kitchen. It sleeps up to six people, and has a private entrance. The larger bedroom has a balcony overlooking Obispo and gets lots of light. The owner Juan speaks English. Rates are US$40 one room, US$50–60 both rooms.

UNDER US$50

Residencia Académica Convento de Santa Clara, Calle Cuba #610, e/ Luz y Sol, tel. 861-3335, fax 33-5696, reaca@cencrem.cult.cu, in the former 17th-century convent, represents a bargain. The restored building is beautiful and today houses the National Center for Conservation and Museology (Centro Nacional de Conservación y Museología), which offers residential courses to foreign and Cuban academics. It has nine charming, modestly furnished but well-kept dorm rooms plus some private rooms for US$25 per person, including breakfast. The rooms lack air-conditioning and can be stifling, especially in mid-summer. A café serves refreshments. (Habaguanex.)

Hotel Isla de Cuba, Máximo Gómez #169, e/ Cienfuegos y Aponte, tel. 867-1128, on the south side of Parque de la Fraternidad, is used almost entirely by Cubans. The building is aged

and gloomy but has antique charm. Beyond the massive 10-meter-tall mahogany doors, its narrow, soaring atrium is surrounded by 64 rooms. The hotel was closed for renovation at last visit. (Islazul.)

Hotel Caribbean, Paseo de Martí #164, esq. Colón, tel. 860-8233, fax 860-9479, relpub@caribean.hor.tur.cu, is a favorite of budget travelers, and rightly so after a splendid renovation. It has 38 small air-conditioned rooms, meagerly yet adequately furnished in lively Caribbean colors, with tiny cable TVs, telephones, in-room safe-boxes, and small yet pleasant bathrooms with plumbing. There's a small, simple bar, and the Café del Prado (open 7 A.M.–3 A.M.) serves the hotel and passersby with pizza, sandwiches, and spaghetti. Rates are US$33 s, US$48 d low season, US$36 s, US$54 d high season. (Horizontes.)

US$50–100

Hostal Valencia, Oficios #53, e/ Obrapía y Lamparilla, tel. 867-1037, fax 860-5628, hostales@hvhc.ohch.cu, www.hostalvalencia.cu, might induce a flashback to the romantic *posadas* of Spain. Appropriately, this quaint 12-room hotel is managed by a Spanish firm. The recently restored 18th-century mansion exudes charm, with its lobby—entered through a tall doorway—of hefty oak beams, Spanish tiles, wrought-iron chandeliers, hardwood colonial seats, and statuettes. The inner courtyard, surrounded by a lofty balcony, is a setting for live music and has a cigar store. The 12 spacious rooms have cool marble floors but are furnished in dilapidated modern utility style. All have private bathrooms—hot water is said to be unreliable—TVs, telephones, refrigerators, and walls decorated with ceramic plaques. Some have French doors that open onto the street. The lobby opens to the atmospheric La Paella restaurant and charming Bar Entresuelo. Rates are US$40 s, US$60 d, US$75 suite low season; US$49/78/93 high season. (Habaguanex.)

Hotel El Comendador, Calle Obrapía #55 e/ Baratillo y Oficios, c/o 867-1037, fax 860-5628, hostales@hvhc.ohch.cu, behind the Hostal

ACCOMMODATIONS

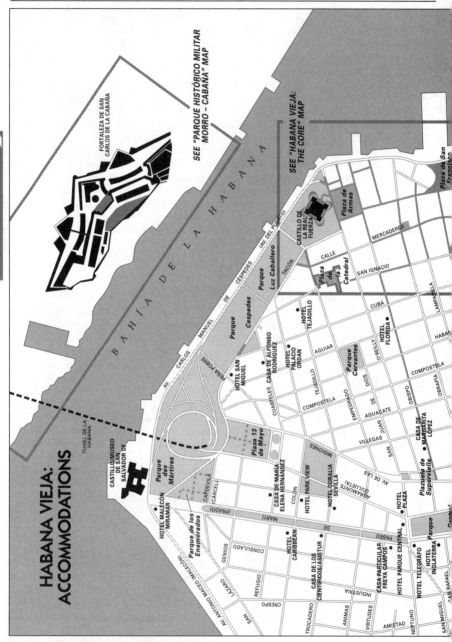

HABANA VIEJA:
ACCOMMODATIONS

BAHÍA DE LA HABANA

FORTALEZA DE SAN
CARLOS DE LA CABAÑA

SEE "PARQUE HISTÓRICO MILITAR
MORRO - CABAÑA" MAP

SEE "HABANA VIEJA:
THE CORE" MAP

Plaza de San
Francisco

Plaza de
Armas

MERCADERES

Plaza
de la
Catedral

SAN IGNACIO

CUBA

HOTEL
FLORIDA

HABAN

LAMPARILLA

O'REILLY

COMPOSTELA

OBRAPIA

OBISPO

CASA DE
MARGARITA
LÓPEZ

Plazuela de
Supervielle

Parque

HOTEL
PLAZA

HOTEL
TELÉGRAFO

HOTEL
INGLATERRA

SAN RAFAEL

SAN MIGUEL

CASTILLO DE
LA REAL
FUERZA

CALLE

TACÓN

Parque
Luz Caballero

Parque
Céspedes

CÉSPEDES

MANUEL DE

CARLOS

AV.

PEÑA POBRE

(AV. DEL PUERTO)

HOTEL
TEJADILLO

AGUIAR

HOTEL
PALACIO
ORDAN

TEJADILLO

Parque
Cervantes

DIOS

DE

EMPEDRADO

AGUACATE

SAN JUAN

VILLEGAS

CASA DE ALFONSO
RODRÍGUEZ

HOTEL SAN
MIGUEL

CUARTELES

COMPOSTELA

MISIONES

AV. DE LAS

ARRAMONTE
(IZULETA)

Plaza 13
de Mayo

CASA DE MARÍA
ELENA HERNÁNDEZ

COLÓN

HOTEL PARK VIEW

HOTEL CORALIA
SEVILLA

CÁRCEL

MARTÍ

DE

(PRADO)

PASEO

HOTEL
CARIBBEAN

CASA DE LOS
CIENTÍFICOS/ASSISTUR

CONSULADO

GENIOS

CAPDEVILA

CÁRCEL

CASA PARTICULAR
FREYA CAMPOS

HOTEL PARQUE CENTRAL

INDUSTRIA

AMISTAD

ANIMAS

VIRTUDES

NEPTUNO

TUNEL DE LA
HABANA

CASTILLO/MUSEO
DE SAN
SALVADOR DE

Parque
des
Mártires

Parque de los
Enamorados

HOTEL MALECÓN
MIRAMAR

AV. ANTONIO MACEO MALECONI

SAN

LÁZARO

REFUGIO

CRESPO

TROCADERO

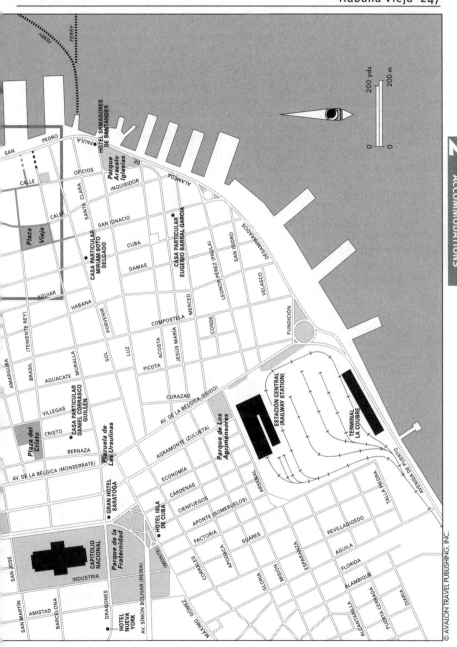

ACCOMMODATIONS

Valencia, is another endearingly restored colonial home. Its 14 exquisite rooms feature marble floors, iron-frame beds, antique reproduction furnishings, security boxes, local TVs, old-style phones, and mini-fridges. The thoroughly modern bathrooms have claw-foot bathtubs, hairdryers, and toiletries. Rooms on the mezzanine are cramped; take an upper story room with a lofty ceiling. To the rear of the lobby is an *Exposición Arqueológica* containing pre-Columbian graves and skeletons discovered during restoration work. Rates are US$50 s, US$60 d low season; US$65/75 high season. (Habaguanex).

Casa de Científicos, Prado #212, e/ Calles Trocadero y Colón, tel. 862-4511, fax 33-0167, is a lofty-ceilinged, four-story colonial mansion—the old Casa José Miguel Gómez-adorned with faded rococo ceilings and marble floors. A rickety elevator and a marble staircase with a magnificent stained-glass atrium ceiling lead upstairs to 12 air-conditioned rooms modestly furnished with a medley of antiques and unappealing utility furniture, plus satellite TVs, and large, well-lit bathrooms with white tilework. The vast suite boasts a bathroom in black marble. A rooftop bar sometimes hosts entertainment. Downstairs, the elegant Restaurant Los Vitrales is replete with exquisite antiques. Rates are US$25 s, US$31 d, US$37 t with shared bathroom with cold water only, US$45 s, US$55 d, US$64 t with private bathroom.

El Mesón de la Flota, Calle Mercaderes #257, e/ Amargura y Brasil, tel. 863-3838, haba guanexhmflota@ip.etecsa.cu, is a classic Spanish *bodega* with five intimate rooms above the bar, with private bathrooms and hot water. Each features antique reproductions, and one has a magnificent *vitral* (stained-glass window). Rates are US$50 s/d low season, US$60 s/d high season. (Habaguanex.)

Hotel Park View, Calle Colón, esq. Morro, tel. 861-3293, fax 863-6036, habaguanex@park view.co.cu, first opened as a hotel in 1928 but fell into disrepair and eventual closure after the Revolution. It reopened in 2002 after a complete restoration in a sober green and ocher color scheme. This small facility has 55 lofty-ceilinged rooms, nicely furnished with green marble highlights. Some bathrooms have stand-up showers; others have tubs. Take a third floor room for the balcony. It has minimal facilities, but there are plenty of restaurants at hand, and the Hotel Sevilla is around the corner. Rates are US$50 s, US$66 d low season, US$57 s, US$72 d high season. (Habaguanex.)

US$100–150

Hotel Ambos Mundos, Calle Obispo #153, e/ San Ignacio y Mercaderes, tel. 860-9530, fax 860-9532, gerencia.comercial@habaguanex.ohch.cu, www.hotelambosmundos.com, splendidly situated one block west of Plaza de Armas, lets you rest your head where Ernest Hemingway found inspiration. The recently restored hotel originally opened in 1920. The compact lobby is airy and breezy, with tall French doors running the length of its walls. A pianist plays in the mahogany lobby bar. The hotel offers 49 air-conditioned rooms and three junior suites arranged atrium style, each with cable TV and direct-dial telephone. Most rooms are small and dark, but feature modern albeit undistinguished furnishings. Some face the interior courtyard, which are quieter in early morning when the street cacophony can intrude. Facilities include a modest rooftop restaurant and solarium. Hemingway's room—511—is preserved in suspended animation; avoid the fifth floor, which is a thoroughfare for sightseeing gawkers, who fill the single, rickety old elevator (the wait is interminable) and amble up and down the narrow marble stairs. Rates are US$70/100 s/d low season, US$80/115 s/d high season; minisuites were US$130/1/40 low/high season. (Habaguanex.)

Hotel Conde de Villanueva, Calle Mercaderes #202, esq. Lamparilla, tel. 862-9293, fax 862-9682, hconde@villanueva.ohch.cu, www.hostal condevillanueva.cu, is an intimate *bodega*-style hotel in the beautifully restored mansion of the Conde de Villanueva, the man responsible for the first railway in Cuba. Breezes waft through lofty doors, cooling the spacious lobby-lounge, with its bottle-green sofas and blood-red cushions, terracotta floor, and beamed ceiling with chandeliers. Beyond is an intimate courtyard, with caged birds, tropical foliage, and rockers beneath *porticos*. The eight large, airy, and simply appointed rooms and one suite (with whirlpool tub) are arranged on two levels, with *ventrales* on the upper balcony diffusing sunlight in rainbow hues. There's a small restaurant and bar. The hotel aims at cigar smokers, with a Casa de Habanos outlet and a sumptuous smokers' lounge. Rates are US$95 to US$120 d, US$175 suite. (Habaguanex.)

Hotel San Miguel, Calle Cuba #52, esq. Peña Pobre, tel. 862-7656, fax 863-4088, reservas@sanmiguel.ohch.cu, www.hostalsanmiguel.com, is a recently restored three-story waterfront mansion featuring stained-glass windows, ironwork, and genuine antique furniture. It features 10 spacious air-conditioned rooms with gracious antique and antique reproduction furnishings, marble floors, plus exquisite bathrooms, safety boxes, minibars, satellite TVs, and direct-dial telephones. Facilities include a third-floor bar and restaurant with a terrace where champagne is served at 9 P.M. for the nightly *cañonazo* ceremony. It has an elevator. Rates are US$70/90 s/d. (Habaguanex.)

Hotel del Tejadillo, Calle Tejadillo, esq. San Ignacio, tel. 863-7283, fax 863-8830, comercial@tejadillo.ohch.cu, www.hostaldeltejadillo.cu, is another recently converted colonial mansion. Beyond the huge doors is an airy marble-clad lobby with a quaint dining area to one side. It offers 32 air-conditioned rooms around two courtyards with fountains and plants. The cool, high-ceilinged rooms are graced by *mediopuntos* and modern furniture, and feature a safety box, minibar, and simple bathrooms. Rates are US$65/85 s/d low season, US$70/95 high season; US$85/125 s/d suites low season, US$90/135 high season. Prices include breakfast. (Habaguanex.)

Hotel Armadores de Santander, Calle Luz #4, esq. San Pedro, tel. 862-8000, fax 862-8080, comercial@santander.co.cu, opened in 2002 after a complete restoration that returned this formerly derelict building to its former glory as a hotel. It comprises three adjoining buildings named for the Spanish shipping companies and shipbuilders—*armadores*—who had offices here in the 19th century, and has 39 capacious rooms, including three duplexes, a junior suite, and a

thoroughly contemporary suite—perhaps the finest room in Havana!—with a whirlpool tub in the center of the mezzanine bedroom featuring a four-poster bed. All rooms feature lush hardwoods, colonial tile floors, and handsome furnishings and gold and blue color schemes, including state-of-the-art bathrooms. One room is handicap accessible. A rooftop terrace offers views over the harbor, plus there's a bar, billiards room, and a restaurant serving Cuban and international fare. Rates are US$70/100 s/d, US$110/140 s/d junior suite, US$200 suite low season; US$80/120 s/d, US$120/160 s/d junior suite, US$200 suite high season. (Habaguanex.)

Hostal Las Frailes, Calle Teniente Rey, e/ Oficios y Mercaderes, tel. 862-9383, fax 862-9718, comercial@habaguanexhfrailes.co.cu, www.hostalosfrailes.cu, is another restored historic property, this one half a block from the Convento de San Francisco de Asís. The hotel plays on an ecclesiastical theme, with staff dressed in *hábitos de frailes* (monks' habits). There are even lifesize copper figures of friars standing in the doorway and sitting on leather sofas in the lounge. The decor is suitably monastic: lots of heavy timbers, stained glass, wrought-iron, murals, and earth tone brown decor. It has 23 air-conditioned rooms set around a patio with an *aljibe* (well) and fountain. The rooms have patterned terra-cotta tile floors, sponge-washed walls, religious prints, plus TVs, period telephones, minibar, safety box, and spacious bathrooms. Doors even have *postales* (peepholes). It has a bar, but no restaurant. Rates are US$60/80 s/d low season; suites cost US$78/106 s/d low season. Rates are 25 percent more in high season. (Habaguanex.)

Hotel Telégrafo, Paseo del Prado #408, esq. Neptuno, tel. 861-1010, fax 861-4741, subgerente@telegrafo.co.cu, served as a famous hotel in the late 19th century, but fell foul of the Revolution. In 2002 it reopened after a complete restoration that melds its classical elements into an exciting contemporary vogue. Track lighting. Silver sofas! However, as always in Cuba, construction standards are wanting, and I noted signs of water leaks. It has 63 rooms with beautiful furnishings and trendy color schemes, including sponge-washed walls and bare stone, plus marble floors and classy bathrooms. The hip lobby bar is skylit within an atrium framed by colonial ruins. It has a cyber café, plus one of Havana's best restaurants. Rates (single/double) were US$60/100 standard, US$80/140 suite low season; US$75/120 standard, US$100/170 suite high season. (Habaguanex.)

Apartotel Santo Ángel, Calle Brasil, esq. San Ignacio, tel. 861-1626, on the northwest corner of Plaza Vieja, opened in 2001 as a very elegant apartment option for long-term rentals (US$950–1,600 monthly). Rooms are graced by antique reproductions. The highlight is the acclaimed restaurant—one of the best in Habana Vieja—serving Spanish and continental cuisine.

US$150–250

Hotel Plaza, Calle Agramonte #267, esq. Neptuno, tel. 860-8583, fax 860-8869, reserva@plaza.gca.cma.net, built in 1909 in the grand old style, occupies the northeast corner of Parque Central. The lobby is supported by Corinthian columns. A marble stairway leads upstairs to the 186 lofty-ceilinged, air-conditioned rooms and suites, furnished with dark hardwood antiques and reproductions, cable TVs, radios, safe-deposit boxes (US$5 extra), and heaps of closet space. Some rooms are gloomy, and those facing the street can be noisy. A reader reported in 2002 that "the spartan guest rooms were edging into disrepair—dangling shower heads, an absent light bulb, etc." The gracious lobby bar is lit by stained-glass skylights by day, and by gilt chandeliers at night, when a pianist hits the ivories. The Restaurant Real Plaza offers a chic setting. The top (fifth) floor has a terrace restaurant, plus a gift store, pharmacy, and solarium. Rates are overpriced at US$75 s, US$105 d, suites US$110/120 s/d low season; US$90 s, US$130 d, suites US$130/140 s/d high season. (Gran Caribe.)

Hotel Inglaterra, Paseo del Prado #416, esq. San Rafael, tel. 860-8593, fax 860-8254, reserva@gcingla.gca.cma.net, on the west side of Parque Central, was a favorite of visitors in the 19th century, although travelers' accounts—such as those of Winston Churchill, who laid

Hotel Santa Isabel, Plaza de Armas

© CHRISTOPHER P. BAKER

his head here in 1895—"reverberate with wails about the hard mattresses and the offhand service." The recently renovated hotel has been named a National Monument. The extravagantly decorated lobby features a lobby bar and restaurant that whisk you off to Morocco with their arabesque archways and mosaics of green, blue, and gold. Of the 83 air-conditioned rooms, three offer panoramic views. Noise from the square can be a problem, especially in the early morning. All rooms have a telephone, satellite TV, safe-deposit box, hair dryer, and minibar, but they remain dark and musty. The patio bar is popular, and the rooftop bar hosts cabaret. Rates are over-priced at US$75 s, US$100 d low season, US$80 s, US$120 d high season. (Gran Caribe.)

Hotel Florida, Calle Obispo #252 esq. Cuba, tel. 862-4127, fax 862-4117, reservas@florida .ohch.cu, www.hotelflorida.cu, in a stunning colonial building—the Casa de Joaquín Gómez, built in 1835 for a wealthy merchant—is a compact hotel with a soaring atrium with stained-glass skylight. This charmer aims primarily at businesspeople and is sumptuously furnished. Its 25 rooms feature marble floors, wrought-iron beds, a tasteful contemporary interpretation of colonial decor, plus satellite TV, phone, minibar, and security box. There are even telephones (and bidets) in the bathrooms. The downstairs restaurant is elegant. Rates are US$85/130 s/d low season, US$106/162 high season; US$125/170 s/d suites low season, US$155/210 high season. (Habaguanex.)

Hotel Coralia Sevilla, Calle Trocadero #55, e/ Prado y Zulueta, tel. 860-8560, fax 860-8582, reserva@sevilla.gca.tur.cu, is famous as the setting for Graham Greene's *Our Man in Havana*—Wormold stayed in room 501. You enter via a lofty arched doorway of Gaudiesque proportions to a lobby straight out of *1,001 Arabian Nights*. The hotel was built in 1924 and despite a recent remake, its 178 rooms remain uninspired. They're small, low on light, and furnished with tacky outdated furniture, although each has a safe, minibar, telephone, and satellite TV. The top-floor restaurant is a sumptuous gem, although the food quality has slipped again since the French Accor group, which recently took

over management, has again departed. There's a tour and car-rental desk, an outdoor swimming pool, four bars, a beauty parlor, and assorted shops. Rates are US$84 s, US$128 d low season, US$105 s, US$135 d high season.

Hotel Golden Tulip Parque Central, Neptuno, e/ Prado y Agramonte (Zulueta), tel. 866-6627, fax 866-6630, reservation@gtpc.cha.cuy.cu, www.goldentuliphotels.nl; in the Netherlands, Golden Tulip, Stationsstraat 2, P.O. Box 619, 1200 AP Hilversum, tel. 35-284588, fax 35-284681; in Canada, 800/344-1212; in the UK, tel. 020/8770-0333, a joint venture with the Dutch Golden Tulip hotel chain, occupies the north side of Parque Central. This modern, well-managed hotel is one of the best in town. The exterior is hardly inspirational, but the gracious lobby offers a surfeit of marble and lively decor in ocher and bottle green, blending a contempo style with colonial hints. Its 281 air-conditioned rooms are done up contemporary style in soft greens and creams and feature cable TV, antique reproduction furnishings, and king-size beds, plus marble bathrooms with separate tub and shower, vanity mirrors, ceilings inset with halogen bulbs, and heaps of fluffy towels. Avoid the second- and third-floor rooms on the southwest corner, which have tiny windows at waist level. Many rooms have no views whatsoever, so be sure to ask for an exterior room. The suites are vast. A mezzanine has an upscale cigar lounge-bar, executive meeting rooms, a business center, and art gallery. There are upscale boutiques, plus a rooftop swimming pool and whirlpool tub, and fitness room and rooftop grill. Rates are US$150/190 s/d US$315 suite low season. (Cubanacán.)

Hotel Santa Isabel, Calle Baratillo #9 e/ Obispo y Narciso López, tel. 860-8201 or 866-9619, fax 860-8391, reservas@santaisabel .ohch.cu, a small and intimate hostelry, enjoys a fabulous setting overlooking Plaza de Armas—some rooms face eastward toward the harbor, however. The splendid building began life as a lodging at the end of the 17th century, later became a palace of the Countess of Santovenia, and, in the 19th century, the Hotel Santa Isabel. Recently restored, it recaptures the elite colonial ambience. Decor includes plush velvet sofas, antiques, and modern art in the marble-floored lobby. The hotel has 27 lofty-ceilinged, air-conditioned rooms (refurbished in 2002) arrayed around an airy atrium with fountain. Standard rooms occupy the third floor; 10 suites occupy the second floor. Rooms are furnished in pinks and blues, with marble or stone and ceramic floors, poster beds, reproduction antique furniture, cable TV, direct-dial telephone, Internet access, and safety box, plus leather recliners on wide balconies. Choose from twin or king-size beds. Suites have whirlpool tubs. There's an elegant restaurant, a small lobby bar, a patio bar, and a rooftop *mirador* where live musicians perform. Readers have complained about management, and about reservations not being honored. President Carter and his entourage stayed here in May 2002, which perhaps explains the inflated rates. Rates are US$160/200 s/d standard, US$180/300 s/d junior suite, and US$315/400 suites, including breakfast, low season (25 percent more in high season).

Centro Habana and Cerro

CASAS PARTICULARES

Casa de Rene Pérez, Malecón #51, e/ Tenios y Carcel, tel. 861-8108, rmichelpd@yahoo.com, is an unusually lavish option with two spacious and romantic air-conditioned rooms decorated with fantastic antiques. They share a mediocre bathroom with hot water, and neither has windows. The vast lounge is sumptuously appointed—it has genuine Tiffany lamps—and has a TV/VCR and fabulous views along the Malecón and toward El Morro. René is a successful go-getter (his pride and joy are his fighting cocks). Entry is to the rear, via the car park; secure parking is offered (US$1). Rates are US$40.

Hostal el Parador Numantino, Consulado #223, e/ Animas y Trocadero, tel. 862-7629, is a surprisingly contemporary conversion. Downstairs the spacious air-conditioned lounge has a gleaming ceramic floor and comfy leather sofas. The four air-conditioned bedrooms upstairs are somewhat small and feature fans, TV, and minifridge, plus private bathrooms with hot water for US$30. Meals are offered 24 hours.

Casa de Victoria Rivero Núñez, Consulado #304, Apto. 2-D, e/ Neptuno y Virtudes, tel. 863-7750, has one room in a third-floor apartment in a high-rise block for US$30. The bedroom receives plentiful light, and has two single beds, a fridge, TV, and small balcony, plus a pleasant bathroom. A second air-conditioned room with two single beds, fridge, and ceiling fan, is offered upstairs with Victoria's parents at

Casa de Georgina Núñez, tel. 863-0440, also for US$30; here guests get use of a somewhat cramped but cozy TV lounge.

Casa de Elsa y Julio Roque, Calle Consulado #162, Apto. 2, e/ Colón y Trocadero, tel. 861-8027, julioroq@yahoo.com, has a pleasant lounge with leather sofas, a small library, and works of art. The couple (he a doctor, she an engineer) offers two rooms with air-conditioning, fans, wicker furniture, and modern private bathrooms with hot water. Each room has an independent entrance. Rates are US$20 or US$25 with fridge and TV.

Casa de Freya Campos, Prado #360, Apto. 5, e/ Neptuno y Virtudes, tel. 861-1473, freyacu @yahoo.com, one block from Parque Central, has a spacious air-conditioned apartment with marble floor, small window, fridge, fans, and modern bed, plus a small modern bathroom with hot water. It has its own entrance. Rates are US$30.

Casa de América Hernández, Dragones #355, e/ Manrique y San Nicolás, tel. 867-3002, is for budget hounds. This *casa* in the heart of Barrio Chino, has two small, basic rooms with fans and shared bathroom with hot water, plus a small, dim-lit air-conditioned apartment with a kitchenette, TV, and telephone. The rooms cost US$15 low season, US$20 high season; the apartment costs US$25, or US$30 for up to five people.

Casa de Norma Pineda, Calle Barcelona #62, Aguila y Amistad, tel. 863-8236, has two air-conditioned rooms open to a pleasant courtyard.

Though they're a bit dark, each is clean and simply but adequately furnished, and share a modest bathroom with hot water. Rates are US$25.

Casa Bienvenidos, San Martín #116, e/ Industria y Consulado, tel. 861-6372, is another good option for those preferring good company above cozy decor. The chatty owner, Bienvenido Pérez Proenza, a former engineer in the Cuban navy, offers three meagerly furnished, lofty-ceilinged rooms with fans for US$20–25. A simple TV lounge overlooks the Capitolio. Bienvenido runs the "Cadena Capitolio," a mutual recommendation chain for owners of *casas particulares* nationwide.

La Casona Colonial, Gervasio #209, e/ Concordia y Virtudes, tel. 870-0489, cubarooms@mixmail.com, www.cubanasol.com, is a gracious place with four bedrooms, each with private bathroom, fans and/or air-conditioning. Guests get use of the kitchen. It has a nice courtyard plus security, including two dogs. Jorge Díaz, the owner, speaks English, French, Italian, and Russian. Rooms cost US$25.

UNDER US$50

Hotel New York, Dragones #156, e/ Amistad y Águila, tel. 862-5260, one block west of Parque de la Fraternidad, is a dour Islazul property that serves a mostly Cuban clientele. It has 75 basic rooms with ceiling fans, private bathrooms, and cold water. Mattresses are said to be well-worn and uncomfortable. It has a small bar and restaurant in the lobby and a popular patio bar and restaurant on the corner outside the hotel. Rates are US$18 s/d year-round. (Islazul.)

Hotel Lido, Consulado, esq. Animas, tel. 867-1102, fax 33-8814, is a budget hotel that awaits a thorough renovation, although some rooms had been refurbished at last visit. The modest air-conditioned rooms feature utility furniture, telephones, radios, and tiny balconies. Safety boxes are available (use them— the Lido has a reputation for theft), and a bar serves snacks in the dreary, overly air-conditioned lobby, which now offers Internet service. The rooftop restaurant is open 24 hours. Rates (including breakfast) are US$25 s, US$35

d low season; US$36 s, US$46 d high season. (Horizontes.)

Hotel Lincoln, Avenida de Italia (Galiano) #164, esq. Virtudes, tel. 861-0702 or 33-8209, is a better option. This modest hotel dates from 1926 and features graceful public arenas, including a lobby boasting chandeliers and Louis XVI-style furnishings. The 139 air-conditioned rooms are clean and pleasant, with radio, telephone, satellite TV, and mini-fridge in 16 suites. Facilities include a reasonable restaurant, a rooftop terrace bar with Chinese restaurant, and nightly entertainment that runs from Afro-Cuban cabarets to dance classes. An attendant is imprisoned in the tiny elevator to prevent Cubans getting off on tourist floors, and vice versa. Rates (including breakfast) are US$28 s, US$37 d low season; US$35 s, US$46 d high season. (Islazul.)

Hotel Deauville swimming pool

© CHRISTOPHER P. BAKER

ACCOMMODATIONS

US$50–100

Hotel Deauville, Avenida Italia (Galiano), e/ Malecón y San Lázaro, tel. 33-8812, fax 33-8148, is a gloomy cement tower that journalist Martha Gellhorn called "a postwar, prerevolutionary blight on the Malecón." True enough. It lies midway between Habana Vieja and Vedado, and is as ugly within as without. The 148 air-conditioned rooms with TV, radio, and telephone, remain dreary despite a recent refurbishment. Facilities include a rooftop swimming pool and a disco, with a cabaret on Saturday. Service is terrible and everyone who stays here has a complaint (it has been described as a "roach hotel with no hot water and disgusting food"). At least the views over the city are splendid from upper-level rooms. Rates are overpriced at US$40 s, US$61 d, US$80 t low season; US$55 s, US$85 d, US$114 t high season. (Horizontes.)

Vedado and Plaza de la Revolución

El Costillar de Rocinante, Avenida de los Presidentes #503, e/ 21 y 23, tel. 832-0566, docencia @prensaip.co.cu is a centenary mansion being prepared at last visit as a residence for journalists, including foreigners. It's run by the Instituto Internacional de Periodismo José Martí, which offers residential courses (surreal! . . . what on earth Cuba can teach in journalism is beyond anyone's guess).

CASAS PARTICULARES

Casa de Jorge Coalla Potts is always my first choice. Great family. Great location. Great room.

There are dozens of other possibilities. The following alternatives only scratch at the surface. **Casa Particular Magalis Sánchez López,** Calle 25 #156, e/ Infanta y O, tel. 870-7613, has two air-conditioned rooms to the rear of a patio with arbor. Both have a TV, fridge, and radio-cassette. Guests get use of the centenary home with lofty ceilings, a kitchen, and TV lounge with Mexican decor. The place is always busy with family members shooing in and out. There's secure parking. Rates are US$30.

Casa Karlita, Calle San Lázaro #1207, Apto. E, e/ Mazon y Basarrate, tel. 878-3182, offers two clean, lofty-ceilinged, well-lit and well-ventilated, simply furnished rooms on the second floor—one room has a TV. They share a modern bathroom with hot water. The family lounge has limestone walls, colonial tile floor, soft-cushioned sofas, and a balcony with views over San Lázaro. Rates are US$20–25.

Casa de Ibis Galvez, Calle L #454 bajos, Apto. 13, e/ 25 y 27, tel. 832-4015, is recommended by a reader, who raves about the hospitality. I found the place a bit gloomy. Ibis has one modestly furnished air-conditioned room with ceiling fan, fridge, and clean private bath with hot water and bidet for US$25. There are three other *casas particulares* in the same building, including **Casa de Selene,** Apto. 18, tel. 832-4214, offering one modestly furnished and well-ventilated air-conditioned room with fridge, telephone, and small but modern private bathroom for US$25 or US$30 (choose your room). The family members are all artists; modern art festoons the walls.

Casa de Brasilia Pérez, Calle 25 #361, Apto. 7, e/ K y L, tel. 832-3953, bpcdt@hotmail.com, has two air-conditioned rooms, each with fridge, fan, and TV, telephone, and private bathroom with hot water for US$25. They're in a pleasant home secluded behind an apartment block, and each has an independent entrance.

Casa de Dania Borrego, Calle J #564B, e/ 25 y 27, no tel., has two upstairs air-conditioned rooms in the home of this pleasant family. Each has fans, modern furnishings, and private modern bathroom with hot water. Guests get use of a well-lit lounge, plus secure parking. Rates are US$30.

Casa de Marta Vitorte, Avenida de los Presidentes #301, e/ 17 y 19, tel. 832-6475, martavitorte@hotmail.com, is a splendid three-room, two-bath apartment that takes up the entire 14th floor and boasts wraparound glass windows on a balcony that offers fabulous views over the city. Her lounge has plump leather sofas, lounge chairs,

CASA DE JORGE COALLA POTTS

I've rented four or five *casas particulares* and inspected scores of others, and always return to a pleasing ground-floor unit in a modern apartment block superbly situated close to Calle 23 in the heart of Vedado, only two blocks from Coppelia and the Hotel Habana Libre. **Casa de Jorge Coalla Potts** is run by Jorge and his wife Marisel and offers a large, well-lit and well-furnished bedroom to the rear of their spotless apartment home. It has a telephone and refrigerator, plus a cool tile floor underfoot and a lofty ceiling with a large, silent fan. There's also air-conditioning, but you shouldn't need it. It has a beautifully tiled bathroom with plentiful hot water.

The airy living room has a sofa, four *mecedoras* (rocking chairs), an antique mahogany dining table, and a profusion of potted plants. There's a TV and VCR. A large window faces the street

© CHRISTOPHER P. BAKER

at ground level, so that you can take pleasure on leaning at the windowsill, sipping a demitasse of Marisel's thick, sweet Cuban coffee while watching Cuban life pass by.

The couple are an absolute delight and go out of their way to make you feel right at home. Jorge speaks broken English. The couple has a young daughter, Jessica.

There's a gas stove if you wish to cook for yourself, and a garage can be arranged; there's also a secure parking lot one block away.

An old man often sits outside and tells arriving guests that it's full. He's poaching for his own illegal *casa particular* nearby. Don't believe him.

Contact Jorge Coalla Potts, Calle I #456, Apto. 11, e/ 21 y 23, Vedado, tel. 832-9032, jorgepotts@web.correosdecuba.cu.

and antiques. The three rooms, which are rented separately, are clean and beautifully kept and feature antique beds and private bathrooms with hot water. Marta formerly worked in Havana's International Press Center and is an engaging conversationalist who speaks fluent English. She has an answering machine. Rates are US$35 per room. The only drawback is the rickety elevator.

Casa de Familia Martínez, Calle J #411, e/ 19 y 21, tel. 832-9008, is a centenary home with tile floor and a long hallway with eight rooms (four upstairs, four downstairs) to the side. One has air-conditioning, the others have fans. Two have private bathrooms with hot water; six rooms

share two bathrooms. All have modest furnishings and are a bit musty. Guests get to use the family TV lounge. Rates are US$20–30.

Casa Familia Villazón, Calle 21 #203, e/ J y K, tel. 832-1066, is in a timeworn house of palatial proportions and full of antiques, but with walls screaming for a fresh pot of paint. The owners offer one room in the house with a firm mattress and a shared bathroom with hot water and a bidet. Two other rooms are in a more modern addition upstairs and reached by an outside stairway. They're not particularly attractive and have tiny bathrooms, but all have air-conditioning and telephone. Rates are US$25.

Hospedaje Marpoly, Calle K #154, e/ 11 y 13, tel. 832-2471, is an antique filled colonial home with two lofty-ceilinged air-conditioned rooms (without fans), with 1950s furnishings, and modern tiled bathrooms for US$35, including breakfast. It has secure parking. It also functions as a *paladar.*

Villa Nidia, Línea #59, e/ M y N, tel. 832-7748, almacona@yahoo.com, is a colonial home with tile floors and plentiful antiques. It has two modern air-conditioned rooms in a sun-drenched patio, with fans, antique beds, and modern private bathrooms with hot water for US$30. Meals are prepared in a large, modern kitchen.

Hospedaje Gisela Ibarra, Calle F #104 (altos), e/ 5ta y Calzada, tel. 832-3238, is a beautiful colonial-era home decorated with antiques and modern art. The delightful elderly owners, Gisela and Daniel, have three air-conditioned rooms with antiques (including antique double beds), safety boxes, and refrigerators. One room has its own modern tiled bathroom; two rooms share a bathroom. There's a roof terrace, plus parking, and a TV lounge gets the breezes. Meals are served in a gracious dining room. Rates are US$30 including large breakfasts.

Casa de Antonio Llibre Artigas, Calle 24 #260, e/ 17 y 19, tel. 833-7156, offers two rooms in a well-kept, cross-ventilated house with lofty ceilings in western Vedado. There's also a two-bedroom air-conditioned apartment with a small kitchen and TV. It has secure parking. Sr. Llibre is a fascinating character. He was formerly aide-de-camp to Fidel in the Sierra Maestra, as photographs and diplomas in his office attest. Today, he's a lawyer and historian with a much-faded library. Rates are US$25–30.

Casa de Francisco Rodríguez, Calle 17 #558, e/ C y D, tel. 832-5003, is another well-kept centenary home with floral tile floors, lofty ceilings, and antiques. The ample lounge looks like my grandma's! It has two rooms with private bathrooms with hot water; one room has air-conditioning; the other is well-ventilated and has fans. A patio to the rear has shade trees, and there's secure parking. Rates are US$25.

Casa Blanca, Calle 13 #917, e/ 6 y 8, tel. 833-5697, cbl917@hotmail.com, www.caspar.net /casa, in the heart of western Vedado, is a gracious colonial home that is kept spick-and-span and boasts exquisite antiques. It has an air-conditioned room with two double beds, stereo, safety box, and a clean, modern private bathroom with hot water for US$25 (plus US$3 for breakfast). It also has email service for guests.

Nuevo Vedado: Although a bit out of the way, here you're a few blocks from the Víazul bus station.

Casa de Enrique, Avenida Zoológico #103, e/ 36 y 38, tel. 881-4518, is a spacious modern home with seven rooms for rent (three with air-conditioning), all with private bathrooms and reached by a spiral marble staircase with dramatic stained-glass window. Furnishings are modest. Guests get use of a TV lounge. Rates are US$30–35.

Casa Mayra Sardaín Piña, Avenida Zoológico #160, e/ 38 y 40, tel. 881-3792, is a better option. This graciously decorated house has a sun-kissed lounge with wicker furnishings and modern art. Three pleasingly furnished air-conditioned rooms reached by a spiral staircase have TVs and fridges. One has a private bathroom; two share a bathroom. There's a small swimming pool in the rear courtyard. Rates are US$40 low season, US$50 high season, including breakfast.

Casa Grande, Avenida 26 #1002, esq. 32, Nuevo Vedado, tel. 881-0101, gisela@fox-hiker.cjb.net, is a superb option in a quiet residential neighborhood. This 1950s gem offers four air-conditioned rooms with TV, mini-bar, and audio-cassette player, plus telephone and safety box, plus thoroughly modern private bathrooms. The home is beautifully furnished and kept spick-and-span by Gisela Martínez. The spacious dining room has a fabulous modern bas-relief mural, and exquisite stained glass. Outside there's a peaceful patio with arbor and a plunge pool. The owners speak English and Italian. Rates are US$50–60.

Casa de Ileana Pérez Valera, Calle 30 #768, e/ 41 y Kohly, tel. 881-1904, www.cubanasol.com, nearby, has three beautiful air-conditioned double rooms. Two have clean, modern private bathrooms. The friendly owners (both university professors) permit use of the kitchen.

There's secure parking plus a tree-shaded garden and patio. Room rates are US$40.

UNDER US$50

Hotel Bruzón, Calle Bruzón, e/ Avenida Rancho Boyeros y Pozos Dulces, tel. 867-5684, just north of the Plaza de la Revolución, is a modest property with a disadvantageous position. The 46 air-conditioned rooms have barebones utility furniture, small TVs, and radios, plus basic bathrooms with cold water only. Still, it will do in a pinch for hardy budget travelers. It has a small bar and a disco. Rates are US$13 s, US$15 d low season, US$18 s, US$21 d high season. (Islazul.)

Villa Residencial Estudiantil del MINSAP, Calle 2, e/ 15 y 17, tel. 832-9830 or 832-8411, run by the Ministry of Public Health, is in a converted mansion with simple rooms for about US$20 s, US$25 d. It has a small restaurant and a broad, breeze-swept veranda with rockers.

Hotel Universitario, Calle L y 17, tel. 33-3403, fax 33-3022, hoteluni@enet.cu, run by the Ministry of Education, is a basic, wood-paneled affair with a gloomy student-union-style bar and a pleasant restaurant downstairs behind the glum lobby. Its 21 rooms offer the essentials but lack noteworthy ambience. Rates are US$25 s, US$34 d, US$45 t, US$40 suite year-round.

US$50–100

Hotel St. John's, Calle O #206, e/ 23 y 25, tel. 33-3740, fax 33-3561, reservas@stjohns2 .hor.tur.cu, is a popular bargain in the thick of Vedado. Beyond the chill lounge, this 14-story property has 96 recently renovated air-conditioned rooms, each with radio, telephone, and TV. A cabaret is offered in the rooftop nightclub (Tues.–Sun.), plus there's a rooftop swimming pool. Other facilities include a tourism bureau, and the Steak House Toro (known for quality steaks). Rates are US$50 s, US$63 d low season; US$63 s, US$80 d high season. (Horizontes.)

Hotel Vedado, Calle O #244, e/ 23 y 25, tel. 33-4062, fax 33-4186, recep@vedado.hor.tur.cu, is of similar standard to its neighbor, Hotel St. John's. It has a tiny, uninspired lounge. Its 194 air-conditioned rooms are small but done up in pastel colors, with satellite TV, telephone, tile floors, and small bathroom. The basement El Cortijo Restaurant specializes in Spanish cuisine, and there's a disco and cabaret, plus a swimming pool and tour desk. Free guided tours of Havana are offered. Rates are US$50 s, US$67 d low season, US$63 s, US$80 d high season, including breakfast. (Horizontes.)

Hotel Colinas, Calle L, e/ 27 y 29, tel. 33-4071, fax 33-4104, is an uninspired option. The 79 depressingly hokey air-conditioned rooms feature satellite TVs and telephones. The facilities include a tour desk, modest restaurant, and a patio snack bar good for watching the world go by. Rates (including breakfast) are US$40 s, US$50 d low season; US$44 s, US$54 d high season. (Horizontes.)

Hotel Capri, Calle 21 #8, esq. N, tel. 33-3747, fax 33-3750, is a charmless Miami-era hotel (it was built by mobster Santo Traficante Jr) that was closed for renovation at last visit. The airy lobby is flooded with light from plate-glass windows, as are the 215 air-conditioned rooms, which were previously dowdily furnished but feature TV, telephone, and safety box. The rooftop swimming pool and restaurant both offer spectacular views. The former casino is now a drab dining room, and the hotel features the Salon Rojo cabaret. It has a tour booth. Rates are US$52 s, US$64 d low season, US$63 s, US$75 d high season. (Horizontes.)

US$100–150

Hotel Presidente, Calzada #110, esq. Avenida de los Presidentes, tel. 55-1801, fax 33-5753, reserva@gcpresi.gca.cma.net, is a high-rise art deco–style property inaugurated in 1927 and gleaming afresh from a complete renovation—however, there were hints of shoddy workmanship and water leaks at last visit. It retains its maroon exterior and a carnal-red and pink interior lent elegance by its sumptuous Louis XIV-style furnishings and Grecian urns and busts that rise from a beige marble floor. It has 160 spacious rooms with modern tile floors and tasteful contemporary furnishings on a pink and gold theme. Bathrooms are graced by marble. One suite is appointed in Louis XIV style. The elegant restaurant specializes in Italian and nouvelle Cuban fare. There's a peaceful outdoor swimming pool, plus gym and sauna. It is managed by Spain's Hoteles C group. Rates are US$92 s, US$142 d; suites US$220 s, US$300 d year-round. (Gran Caribe.)

Hotel Victoria, Calle 19 #101, esq. M, tel. 33-3510, fax 33-3109, reserva@victoria.gca.cma.net, is a charming Victorian-style, neoclassical hotel that began life in the 1920s as a guesthouse. It retains its personal feel and today focuses on a business clientele. It has 31 elegant, albeit somewhat small air-conditioned rooms refurbished with 1970s decor, with hardwoods and antique reproduction furnishings. There's a small swimming pool, an intimate lobby bar, and the elegant restaurant is one of Havana's finest. Rates are US$80 s, US$100 d low season, US$90 s, US$120 d high season. (Gran Caribe.)

Hotel Habana Riviera, Malecón y Paseo, tel. 33-4051, fax 33-3739, reserva@gcrivie.gca.cma.net, is a legacy from the heyday of sin. Mobster Meyer Lansky's old hotel recently underwent restoration to recapture its 1950s luxe, *sans* casino (Lansky's 20th-floor suite, stripped of memorabilia, is available for US$200 a night). The idiosyncratic '50s lobby now boasts graceful contemporary furnishings and a pleasant cocktail lounge, while retaining its acres of marble and glass. The 332 spacious air-conditioned rooms come up to international standards and have soothing pastel decor, conservative contemporary furniture, satellite TV, safety box, and minibar. The hotel boasts a large seawater pool, plus tour desk, boutique, restaurant, gym with sauna and massage service, coffee shop, cigar store, and the swank Salón Internacional nightclub with cabaret. Rates are US$72 s, US$96 d low season; US$98 s, US$120 d high season, including breakfast. (Gran Caribe.)

US$150–250

Hotel Nacional, Calle O y 21, tel. 55-0294, fax 33-5171, reserva@gcnacio.gca.cma.net, is Havana's flagship hotel. Luminaries from Winston Churchill and the Prince of Wales to Marlon Brando have laid their heads here. This 1930s icon still dominates important events, when

Hotel Nacional

© CHRISTOPHER P. BAKER

celebrities flock. The property recently emerged from a thorough restoration that revived much of the majesty of the neoclassical gem, perched on a cliff overlooking the Malecón. It is entered via a palm-lined driveway, while a greenswathe to the rear is studded with slender Royal palms and ceibas. The 457 large air-conditioned rooms each have cable TV, telephone, safe, and self-service bar. The Executive Floor has 63 specially appointed rooms and suites (for which a US$30 premium applies). The Comedor de Aguiar restaurant is noteworthy. The hotel's Cabaret Parisien is one of the hottest cabarets in town. The top-floor cocktail lounge offers a magical view; and the lobby-level bar offers a yellowing collage of luminaries, including Mob titans Lansky, Santo Trafficante, and others. There are two swimming pools, plus upscale boutiques, beauty salon, spa, tennis courts, and tour desk. Rates are US$120 s, US$170 d standard, US$215 s/d one-bedroom suite, US$390 two-bedroom suite, US$400 to US$1,000 special suites. (Gran Caribe.)

Hotel Habana Libre Tryp, Calle L, e/ 23 y 25, tel. 55-4011, fax 33-3141, reserva@rlibre .tryp.cma.net, is Havana's landmark high-rise hotel. It was built in the 1950s by the Hilton chain and soon became a favorite of mobsters and high rollers. After the Revolution, Castro set up his headquarters here, and you used to hear that the whole place was bugged. The Habana Libre is still popular with foreigners and Cuban VIPs. Since 2000 it has been managed by the Spanish Grupo Sol Meliá group. A recent renovation included replacing the formerly capricious plumbing. The atrium lobby with glass dome features a fountain and bar with a '50s retro feel. The 533 rooms feature satellite TV, direct-dial telephone, minibar, safety box, and hair dryers in the bathrooms. It also offers 36 junior suites and three suites, plus 24-hour room service. The hotel is loaded with facilities—all-important tour desks, a bank, airline offices, boutiques, post office, and international telephone exchange, as well as a snack bar–style café, two full-service restaurants, an open-air swimming pool, plus cabaret-lounge on the 25th floor, and an underground parking lot. Rates are US$140 s, US$160 d, US$250 suite, including breakfast. (Gran Caribe.)

Melía Cohiba, Paseo, e/ 1ra y 3ra, tel. 204-3636, fax 33-4555, melia.cohiba@cohiba1 .solmelia.cma.net, is a deluxe hotel run by the Spanish Grupo Sol Meliá in a handsome post-modern minimalist design. The 22-story hotel has first-rate executive services and is popular with foreign businesspeople. The spacious lobby boasts plentiful marble, artwork, and magnesium-bright lighting. Its 462 spacious and elegant air-conditioned rooms feature brass lamps; marble floors; Romanesque chairs with contemporary fabrics; a mellow color scheme of beige, gold, and rust; and mirrored walls behind the bed. The bathrooms are dazzling, with bright halogen lights and huge mirrors, bidets, hair dryers, and fluffy towels. There are three standards of suites. Facilities include two swimming pools, gym, solarium, shopping center, business center, four restaurants, five bars, and the Habana Café nightclub. Rates are US$175 s, US$225 d, US$250 junior suite, US$300 suite year-round.

Playa (Miramar and Beyond)

You're a long way from the sights, so expect to fork out big bucks for taxi fares into town. Miramar is slated to receive many new upscale hotels over the next few years, including **Hotel Casa Habana,** 5ta Avenida, esq. Calle 96; the **LTI-Panorama Hotel Havana,** 3ra Avenida, esq. 70; and a five-star, 650-room hotel to be built by a Chinese company at Marina Hemingway.

CASAS PARTICULARES

Casa de Fernando y Egeria González, 1ra Avenida #205, e/ 2 y 4, Miramar, tel. 203-3866, is a superb property. This gracious family home offers two spacious and airy air-conditioned rooms with huge and exquisite tiled bathrooms. The family is a delight. There's secure parking, and a patio to the rear. Rates are US$35.

Casa de Clarisa Santiago, 1ra Avenida #4407, e/ 44 y 46, tel. 209-1739, opposite the Hotel Copacabana, is another excellent option. Clarisa offers an independent air-conditioned apartment in the rear patio. It's modern throughout and has nicely decorated bedroom with TV and fan, plus a modern bathroom has a small shower and hot water. A separate, well-stocked kitchen (by Cuban standards) has a tall refrigerator. There's secure parking and daily maid service. Rates are US$30.

Casa de Alexis González Lorié, 1ra Avenida #2803, 5ta piso, e/ 28 y 30, tel. 209-3955, is a splendid, tastefully decorated fifth-floor air-conditioned apartment with one double room with marble floors, rattan furniture, and a whirlpool tub. The lounge has a smoked-glass solarium offering ocean views. It has secure parking.

Casa de Alberto y Magda, Calle 34 #1911, e/ 19 y 21, tel. 203-8748, magdatrujillodelpino@yahoo.es, is another excellent choice, granting almost complete independence. The delightful couple have a third-floor, self-contained apartment with a comfy lounge with telephone and fridge, a spacious air-conditioned bedroom with TV and radio and ceiling fan, and a private bathroom with hot water. Magda speaks English. The couple doesn't prepare meals, but there are

plenty of good breakfast and dining options nearby on 7ma, and secure parking nearby outside the British embassy.

Casa de Elena Sánchez, Calle 34 #714, e/ 7ma y 17, tel. 202-8969, nearby, is a handsome, well-kept, two-story home. It has two modestly furnished air-conditioned rooms, each with TV, fridge, and private bathrooms with hot water. A large lounge has leather sofas plus rockers, and there's secure parking. Rates are US$30–35.

Casa de Melvas Suñoz, Calle 34 #1704, e/ 17 y 19, tel. 202-4721, is a nicely maintained one-story home with one air-conditioned room with fridge and private bathroom with hot water for US$25–30. It has rockers on a shaded terrace, plus secure parking.

Casa de Elia Santiago, Calle 34 #1708, e/17 y 19, tel. 203-4642, fax 203-4642, is another well-kept house with three spacious air-conditioned rooms with modern utility furniture, TV, telephone, fridge, and private bathroom with hot water for each room, which vary in size. Rates are US$35–40.

Casa Miramar, Calle 30 # 3502, between 35 and 37, Miramar, tel. 209-5679, in Canada 604/874-4143, mail@casamiramar.com, www.casamiramar.com, is an exquisite 1926 home with original marble floors and vaulted ceilings. It has three air-conditioned rooms with one shared bathroom. Each room has its own character and is appointed with early 1900s art nouveau furnishings, a queen-size box spring and goose down pillows. The master suite has its own mission-style library. Bedding and towels are changed daily. Breakfast is served on the terrace, and dinner is available by request. There's a safety deposit box that you can program with your own PIN, plus secure parking. Rates are US$30–40.

Casa de Adriana y Miriam, Calle 28 #4312 e/ 43 y 45, Reparto Kohly, tel. 203-5528, is recommended by a reader. This colonial style home has three rooms: one with two double beds, an armoire, and a private bathroom (US$40); two smaller rooms share a second bathroom. A hearty

American breakfast costs US$4. The couple speaks minimal English and some Italian.

UNDER US$50

Motel Las Olas, Calle 32, esq. 1ra Avenida, tel. 209-4531, serves Cubans and foreigners. The meagerly appointed rooms—slated for refurbishment at last visit—overlook the shore. It has an air-conditioned restaurant, pool with poolside grill, video games, and a bar. The pool fills with Cuban families on weekends and hot summer days. Despite its "motel" status, it's not a love hotel: it's a workers' hotel. Rates are US$21 s, US$36 d, US$45 t, US$48 q.

US$50–100

Hostal Icemar, Calle 16, e/ 1 y 3, tel. 203-7735 or 203-6130, fax 202-1244, operated by the Ministerio de Educación (MINED), is mostly utilized by foreign students. However, anyone can check into this 1950s Miami-style hotel with 54 large air-conditioned rooms with TV and hot water. Rooms facing the sea have more light. Rates are US$27 s, US$44 d, US$60 t high season. You can also select any of six apartments across the road (same rates as rooms). They're huge (some sleep up to eight people), but some are rather gloomy and minimally furnished.

Hotel Universitaria Ispaje, 1ra Avenida, esq. Calle 22, tel. 203-5370, likewise a MINED option, offers eight rooms with private baths for US$25 s, US$35 d, including breakfast. It has a swimming pool and bar, plus secure parking. MINED's **Villa Universitaria Miramar,** Calle 62 #508, e/ 5ta-A y 5ta-B Avenida, tel. 832-1034, offers 25 rooms with private baths for US$18 s, US$20 d. There's a bar with pool table, popular with Cuban students and expats. MINED's **Hostal Costa Sol,** 3ra Avenida y Calle 60, tel. 209-0828, also takes tourists as well as student guests. It has 11 air-conditioned rooms, plus a restaurant. Rates are U$25 s, US$48 d.

Hostal Villamar, Calle 24 #2402, esq. 3ra, tel. 203-3778, in a colonial mansion, offers five spacious air-conditioned rooms nicely furnished with modern accoutrements, plus TV (local stations only), radio, and mammoth tiled bathrooms. It has a rustic bar and restaurant with wood-beamed ceilings and a fireplace, serving *criollo* food and open 24 hours. Rates are US$29 s, US$48 d, US$66 t. It also rents houses.

Villa Costa 1ra Avenida, e/ 34 y 36, tel. 209-2250, fax 204-4041, a very handsome seafront villa just east of the Hotel Copacabana, was previously used as a protocol house for visiting dignitaries. At last visit it had been knocked down and appeared to be being rebuilt.

Hotel Kohly, Avenida 49 y 36A, Reparto Kohly, Playa, tel. 204-0240, fax 204-1733, reserva@kohly.gav.cma.net, run by Gaviota, is a modest 1970s-style property popular with tour groups. Its out-of-the-way location offers no advantages. The 136 air-conditioned rooms were recently refurbished in lively fabrics and tasteful albeit simple furniture, and have satellite TV, radio, telephone, minibar, safety box, and spacious showers in handsome bathrooms. Most have a balcony. Facilities include two modest restaurants, a tour desk, car rental, bar, pool tables, and 10-pin bowling alley. Rates are US$50 s, US$62 d low season, US$54 s, US$68 d high season. (Gaviota.) Hotel Kohly also has five mansions (from two to six bedrooms) for rent.

Hotel el Bosque, Calle 28A, esq. Avenida 47, tel. 204-9232, fax 204-5637, reservas@bosque.gav.cma.net, is an attractive Gaviota property. The breezy lobby has a bar with pool tables and opens to the rear onto a hillside patio where snacks are served. Its 61 air-conditioned rooms are modestly furnished with bamboo, and include satellite TV, telephone, safety box, and French windows opening to balconies (some rooms only). The Villa Diana restaurant plus the restaurants of the Club Almendares are close-by. There are taxis and car rentals, a laundry, and a tour desk. Rates are US$49 s, US$61 d year-round. (Gaviota.)

Hotel Mirazúl, 5ta Avenida #3603, e/ Calle 36 y 40, tel. 204-0088, fax 204-0045, a Wedgwood blue mansion run by the Ministry of Higher Education, offers 10 rooms of varying sizes for tourists as well as educators and students. Rooms vary, but most are spacious and have modest bamboo furnishings, satellite TV, air-conditioned, telephone, and bathroom with hot water. Facilities include a restaurant, pool table, and rooftop sauna and sundeck. Rates are US$40 s, US$50 d, including breakfast. Lower rates are offered to students and teachers.

Hotel Neptuno/Tritón, 3ra Avenida y Calle 72, tel. 204-1606, fax 204-0042, was recently renovated. The facelift, however, has done little to assuage the dreary nature of this twin-tower high-rise complex. It has 524 air-conditioned rooms and suites, each with modest furnishings, satellite TV, telephone, radio, safe-deposit box, and refrigerator. The tennis courts, large pool, and sun terrace with funky plastic furniture lack appeal, as does the rocky shoreline. At least the hotel has shops, a pleasant bar, and three restaurants. Rates are US$55 s, US$70 d, US$90 t low season, US$70 s, US$90 d, US$110 t high season. (Gran Caribe.)

Hotel y Villas Marina Hemingway, 5ta Avenida y Calle 248, Santa Fe, tel. 204-7628, fax 204-4379, comercial@comermh.cha.cyt.cu, in the Marina Hemingway complex, includes the **Hotel Qualton El Viejo y el Mar,** tel. 204-6336, fax 204-6823, reservas@oldman.cha.cyt.cu, with 186 rooms boasting modern furnishings, satellite TV, telephone, radio, minibar, security box, and balcony. Its attractive lobby features a piano bar, shop, tour desk, business center, and restaurant. **Hotel Acuario,** tel. 204-7628, fax 204-4379, on Intercanal B, has 314 air-conditioned rooms including eight suites and 12 junior suites, all with satellite TV, telephone, radio, minibar, safety box, and balcony. Facilities include a buffet restaurant, café, two bars, splendid swimming pool, shop, games room, bicycle rental, and tour bureau. Rates for both hotels are US$62/82 s/d standard, US$68/88 s/d junior suite, US$100 single or double suite low season; US$72/92 s/d standard, US$78/98 s/d junior suite, US$110 single or double suite high season. Also see Villas Pilar and Villas Paraíso. (Cubanacán.)

Hotel Carrusel Bellocaribe, Calle 158, esq. 31, tel. 33-9906, fax 33-6838, reservas@bellocaribe.colombus.cu, serves the nearby Convention Center and biotech facilities, and is too far out to offer any appeal for the general traveler. This faceless modern property has 120 modestly furnished air-conditioned rooms (including 15 suites) featuring satellite TV, radio, telephone, safe-deposit box, and minibar. Facilities include car rental, tour desk, tennis court, shops, Casa del Tabaco, Cybercafé, beauty salon, swimming pool with separate kiddie pool, plus the appealing La Estancia restaurant. A free shuttle bus for guests runs to the Hotel Comodoro and Habana Vieja five times daily. Rates are US$45 s, US$64 d, US$77 suite low season, US$57 s, US$81 d, US$93 suite high season. (Cubanacán.)

Hotel Carrusel Mariposa, Autopista Novia del Mediodía Km 6, Arroyo Arenas, La Lisa, tel. 204-9137, fax 204-6131, comercio@maripos .cha.cyt.cutel, is a modest hotel west of the Cubanacán district. It has 48 air-conditioned rooms with satellite TV, safety box, and minibar. Facilities include a restaurant, bar, swimming pool, car rental, and nightly entertainment. Rates are US$23/30 s/d standard, US$28/37 s/d suite low season; US$26/35 s/d standard, US$32/42 s/d suite high season. (Cubanacán.)

US$100–150

Hotel Copacabana, 1ra Avenida, e/ Calles 34 y 36, tel. 204-1037, fax 204-2846, reserva@ copa.gca.tur.net, is an oceanfront hotel first opened in 1955 by a fervent admirer of Brazil. The atmosphere still has a Brazilian flavor and uses names from that country—the Itapoa steak house, the Do Port pizza and snack bar, the Caipirinha bar and grill. Not surprisingly, the place does a healthy trade with package groups from Brazil and Argentina, as well as from Europe. The 170 rooms boast hardwood furnishings, floral bedspreads, small TV, telephone, and safety box. The Restaurant Tucano looks out over the huge swimming pool, popular with Cuban day-visitors. A separate bar serves the pool, and there's a pizzeria. Facilities include a discotheque, tourism bureau, car-rental office, and boutique, and scuba diving is offered. Rates are US$75 s, US$110 d low season, US$80 s, US$120 d high season. (Gran Caribe.)

Chateau Miramar 1ra Avenida, e/ 60 y 70, tel. 204-1951, fax 204-0224, reservas@chateau .cha.cyt.cu, on the lonesome shorefront, aims at business clientele. The handsome five-story hotel has 50 rather sterile rooms, albeit neat furnishings. They feature satellite TV, minibar, radio, and safety box. Nine of the rooms are one-bedroom suites with whirlpool tub. Facilities include a pool and children's pool, elegant restaurant, two bars, executive office, small shop, Casa del Tabaco, massage, plus entertainment. Year-round rates are US$95 s, US$120 d standard; US$150 single or double junior suites; US$170 single or double suites. (Cubanacán.)

Hotel Comodoro, 1ra Avenida y Calle 84, tel. 204-5551, fax 204-2028, reserva@comodor .cha.cyt.cu, was originally built for the Cuban armed forces, but revamped as a training school for apprentice Cuban hotel staff. It has 134 spacious air-conditioned rooms, including 15 suites, with modern furnishings plus satellite TV and telephone. Some rooms have a balcony. Safety boxes cost US$2 per day. It has a full range of facilities, which include a selection of bars, the Havana Club disco, plus a bathing area in a natural ocean pool protected by a pier. The adjacent shopping complex has boutiques, a clinic, and beauty salon. At last visit, the lobby has received a spiffy remake in contemporary vogue, plus enhancements to the four restaurants, but the rooms continue to look a bit rundown. A free shuttle bus for guests runs to Habana Vieja five times daily. Rates are US$65 s, US$90 d, US$135 suite low season, US$80s, US$110 d, US$155 suite high season. (Cubanacán.) Far better are the Comodoro's bungalows, which are recommended and described later in this chapter.

Hotel y Villas Marina Hemingway also offers attractive two-story waterfront bungalows and villas in the **Villas Pilar** and **Villa Paraíso** complex, featuring about 100 houses and bungalows with one, two or three bedrooms. All have terraces, TV and video, safe-deposit box, and kitchen. Rates are US$94 bungalows low season, US$100 high season; US$102 one-bedroom villas low season, US$120 high season; US$170/210/340/450 two-/three-/five-/six-bedroom villas year-round. (Cubanacán.)

Hotel Palco, Avenida 146, e/ 11 y 13, tel. 204-7235, fax 204-7236, admon@hotel.palco.cu, adjoining—and run by—the Palacio de Convenciones (Convention Center), aims at business traffic. This five-story hotel has an expansive lobby and stylish modern decor, albeit hints of second-rate construction. The 144 rooms and 36 junior suites are arrayed around an atrium with a skylit, stained-glass roof. The spacious, recently refurbished air-conditioned rooms have modern decor in lively colors, plus satellite TV, telephone, minibar, safety box, tile floors, and large, bathrooms with hair dryers. Facilities include a business center, elegant restaurant, outdoor snack bar, split-level pool, and small sauna and gym. Rates are US$74 s, US$94 d low season, US$91 s, US$111 d high season, US$130–150 junior suites year-round.

Spa La Pradera, Calle 230, e/ 15 y 17, Reparto Siboney, tel. 204-7473, fax 204-7198, comercia@pradera.cha.cyt.cu, offers an advantageous position for conventioneers and scientists visiting the local biotech facilities but is otherwise out of the way. The modern, 164-room low-rise hotel is gracious and peaceful and looks out over a large pool and nicely landscaped gardens. All rooms feature air-conditioning, satellite TV, telephone, minibar, and security box. The resort hosts entertainment and features squash, basketball, and volleyball courts plus a tiny gym with sauna. The hotel specializes in medical and spa treatments focusing on "life enhancement" and holistic treatments, and most guests arrive for treatments. Rates (single/double) are US$66 s, US$92 d, US$132 single or double suite low season; US$82 s, US$105 d, US$143 single or double suite high season. (Cubanacán.)

US$150–250

Comodoro Bungalow Apartments (see Hotel Comodoro), is an aesthetically striking Spanish-style village with 320 beautiful posada-style, two-story, one-, two-, and three-bedroom villas facing onto two massive amoeba-shaped swimming pools. Rooms have a balcony or patio, plus kitchen, living room, and minibar. Facilities include a 24-hour coffee shop, business center, Photo Service outlet, upscale boutiques, travel agency, pharmacy, and restaurant. A cabaret *espectáculo* and other entertainment are offered. Rates are US$89 s, US$118 d low season,

US$98 s, US$137 d high season for one bedroom; US$153–184 single or double low season, US$180–216 high season for two bedrooms; and US$188–204 single or double low season, US$220–248 high season for three bedrooms. (Cubanacán.)

US$250 AND UP

Hotel Meliá Habana, 3ra Avenida, e/ 76 y 80, tel. 204-8500, fax 204-8505, centros@habana .solmelia.cma.net, is a luxury hotel that aims at a business clientele. Although its concrete and plate-glass exterior jars, the expansive lobby is beautiful, with a surfeit of gray and green marble and ponds, and a sumptuous lobby bar plus the elegant Bosque Habana restaurant. The 405 air-conditioned rooms and four suites fronting the shore come up to international standards and feature balconies, satellite TV, telephone with fax and modem lines, and safety boxes. The executive floor offers more personalized service plus data ports and safes. Facilities include four restaurants, five bars, swimming pool, tennis courts, hairdresser, gym, and business center, plus meeting facilities. Rates are US$175 s, US$225 d standard floors, US$265 s/d junior suite.

Novotel Miramar, 5ta Avenida, e/ 72 y 76, tel. 204-3584, fax 204-3583, reserva@miramar .gav.tur.cu, in North America, 800/221-4542, is a joint project with the French Accor group that can justifiably claim to be Havana's only truly deluxe hotel. This sublimely decorated property features a surfeit of limestone, marble, and gracious neoclassical wrought-iron furniture in the vast lobby where Escher-style murals abound. It has 427 cavernous rooms, including eight suites, and five rooms fully rigged for handicapped travelers. All are done up on regal dark blue and gold decor, with artwork. Glorious! The master suite has a rooftop terraza. To the rear is a huge swimming pool and terrace where cabaret are held. A commercial gallery features a beauty salon, plus there's a squash court and full health center, a business center, noteworthy restaurants, bars. Rates (single/double) are US$128/171 standard, US$153/201 deluxe, US$173/226 junior suite, US$303/311 suite. (Gaviota.)

Food

Cuba's weakest link is undoubtedly its food. You *can* eat well in Havana, which is improving all the time, but in general all the horror stories about Cuban dining are true. Rationing has become a permanent fixture of Castro's Cuba—Cubans tell jokes such as, "What are the three biggest failures of the Revolution? Breakfast, lunch, and dinner;" or, "My wife thinks she's going blind. Whenever she opens the refrigerator, she doesn't see anything!" American Isadora Tattlin, who lived in Havana during the late 1990s, records how one elderly man to whom she offered a homemade chocolate-chip cookie began to cry: "I remember this taste," he said.

Imported chocolate-chip cookies and other goodies *are* readily available in Havana, but for dollars at inflated prices.

The Cuban government likes to blame the U.S. embargo, but, in fact, the inefficient Communist system is almost entirely to blame. Even tourist hotels are subject to the shortages imposed by a mismanaged economy. After a while, you'll get bored of fried chicken, ham sandwiches (*bocaditos*), and vegetables either overcooked or from a can. Bite the bullet. As a tourist, you're privileged to get the best that's available.

Today, all but a handful of Cuba's restaurants are state owned—state-run restaurants come in

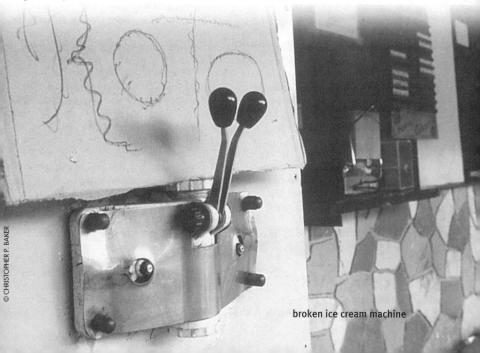

broken ice cream machine

grades one to seven, one being the best—and the blasé socialist attitude toward dining and general inefficiencies of the system are reflected in boring menus, low standards—for example, tablecloths rarely get washed—and excessive prices and gouging. Some restaurants are great values, but many others would give even the Japanese a nasty case of sticker shock. Don't be fooled by extensive menus, as many items will probably not be available. Add to that "tedious lackadaisical service . . . accompanied by instant headache music," complains one reader.

You have to search hard for cuisine of international standard, and most "Chinese" and "Italian" dishes are really Cuban dishes with a twist. Cuba's ethnic restaurants make do as best they can with limited items. Salads are dismal and all look the same: usually lettuce, cucumber, tomatoes, and sometimes beets and overcooked green beans. And pizzas everywhere are dismal by North American standards—usually with a bland base covered with a thin layer of tomato paste and a smattering of cheese and ham, although they usually provide filling meals nonetheless.

Now the Good News

The country has begun to invest in culinary and management training in order to resolve the deplorable inadequacy of restaurant food. Today, Havana *does* have some fine restaurants—it was renowned for its excellent restaurants *before* the Revolution—with more coming all the time. Many of the best restaurants are in the top-class hotels, with specialty restaurants offering *à la carte* menus. In recent years foreign—primarily French—chefs have arrived to show the way.

Fortunately, wherever you eat you're likely to be serenaded by troubadours to add cheer to even the dreariest meal. Tip the musicians, as their salaries are usually about US$10 . . . monthly! Most have a CD or cassette of their music that they try to flog to patrons for US$10–15.

A FEW PRACTICALITIES

Be relaxed about dining; expect service to take much longer than you may be used to. Some-

times the service is swift and friendly, sometimes protracted and surly. At times, you can wait 10 minutes for a waiter, another half-hour for your meal to arrive, 15 minutes for the bill, and another 10 for the change.

Many restaurants serve until midnight, some 24 hours. However, Cuban restaurants—particularly *paladares*—open and close on a whim; it often pays to call ahead, but don't expect any promise of late-night opening to be honored.

As a rule of thumb, avoid the more sophisticated dishes, particularly with "international" menus, because few chefs have the ingredients or know-how to make them. Unbelievably, in past years state bureaucrats provided the menus—many date from the 1960s—with explicit instructions on how particular dishes should be prepared, and chefs have been barred from experimentation. Don't trust your hotel concierge—he's been instructed to point you to the high-priced government restaurants.

Take a sweater—many restaurants have the air-conditioning cranked up to freezing. In general, avoid wines. And bring your own cigars—few restaurants sell them.

In the better restaurants, waiters expect to be tipped 10 percent, even where a service charge (now the norm in tourist restaurants) has been added to your bill; this is because the waiters and staff see only a small fraction of the service charge, which the government pockets. Many Cuban waiters haven't yet figured out that a tip is meant to reward good service—instead they perform poorly and rely on good will—but others provide excellent service and deserve to be tipped. Don't be stingy! Remember . . . your waiter dressed in a tux probably lives in a slum and is being paid less than US$1 a day.

Cajitas (boxed lunches) sold at little restaurants offer bargain-priced meals, usually for US$1–1.50.

Virtually all restaurants charge tourists in dollars, even though at some restaurants Cubans may pay in pesos. The price in pesos is usually converted one-to-one into dollars, which translates into vast overcharging of tourists without any commensurate preference in quality of food or service. Don't assume that you get what you pay for. It doesn't work that way in Cuba. Some of the lousiest service and dishes can be had for the most outrageous prices.

RESTAURANT SCAMS

Check your bill carefully. The creativity that Cubans apply to wheedle dollars from tourists has been turned into an art form in restaurants. Below are a few tricks to watch out for.

Added Items: Bread and butter is often served without your asking, but you may be charged extra for it. Mineral water, coffee, and even beer often appear on your bill, even though you didn't ask for them . . . or they never arrived.

À la carte . . . be damned!: The restaurant has a fixed price for a set menu but your bill might charge separately for itemized dishes, which add up to considerably more. When you challenge it, you might be told that you were given the "lunch menu," say. Don't accept such lame explanations.

Bait and Switch: You ask for a cola and are brought an imported Coca-Cola (US$2) instead of Tropicola (US$.50), its perfectly adequate Cuban equivalent.

Commissions: The *jinetero* who leads you to a recommended *paladar* gets his commission added to your bill . . . even if he's merely picked you up outside the *paladar* you've already chosen and "guided" you to the door.

Dollars or Pesos?: The "$" sign is used for both dollars and pesos. If you eat in a peso restaurant, you may be told that the "$" prices are in dollars. Sometimes this is legitimate. Even so, change may be given in pesos.

¡No Hay!: You're dying for a Hatuey beer but are told *¡no hay!* (there are none). The waiter brings you a Heineken. Then you notice that the *habaneros* are drinking Hatuey. When you question this, you're told that the Hatueys aren't cold . . . or that Heineken (which is more expensive) is better.

Overpricing: Compare the prices on your bill against those on the menu. One or two items on your bill may be inflated.

Short Change: Count your change carefully. Cubans are normally pretty good mathematicians . . . except when it comes to giving change.

Variable Pricing: Always ask for a printed menu with prices. Some places charge according to how much they think you are worth. If you're dressed in Gucci, expect to pay more than your neighbor who's wearing faded jeans.

What to Eat and Drink

CUBAN DISHES

Cuban *criollo* food is mostly peasant fare, usually lacking in sauces and spices (you'll be hard-pressed to find spicy food in Cuba). Pork (*cerdo*) and chicken (*pollo*) are the two main protein staples, most commonly served with rice and black beans (*moros y cristianos,* or "Moors and Christians") or rice with red beans (*arroz congrí*) and fried banana or plantain (*plátanos*).

Cerdo asado (succulent roast pork) might be considered the national dish. Another national dish is *ajiaco,* (hotchpotch), a stew of meats and vegetables, although rarely available. By far the most common dish is fried chicken (*pollo frito*) and grilled chicken (*pollo asado*). Grilled pork chops are also common. Beef is rare out-side the tourist restaurants, where filet mignons and prime rib tend to be far below Western standards—often overcooked and fatty. Only state restaurants are permitted to sell beef, and stiff prison terms are mandatory for any infractions. Ham and cheese, the two most ubiquitous foods, find their way into fish and stuffed inside steaks as *bistec uruguayo.* Occasionally, you'll find rabbit (*conejo*).

Meat finds its way into snacks sold at roadside snack stalls, such as *empanadas de carne,* pies or flat pancakes enclosing meat morsels; *ayacas,* a kind of tamale made of a corn tortilla filled with meat and spices; and *picadillo,* a "meatsome mass" of spiced beef or soy, onion, and tomato. Crumbled pork rinds are often added to *fufu,* mixed with cooked plantain.

Fish had never been a major part of the traditional diet and has made its way onto the national menu only in recent years. Sea bass (*corvina*), swordfish (*filet de emperador*), and red snapper (*pargo*) are the most commonly eaten species. You can find some splendid fish dishes in tourist restaurants in Havana and beach resorts, but in the provinces and restaurants serving Cubans, chefs typically zealously overcook your fish steak until it resembles a boot sole.

Lobster and jumbo shrimps are readily available, although legally only permissible in state-run restaurants, which usually charge exorbitant prices. Most *paladares*—private restaurants—sell lobster under the table at bargain prices; you can enjoy an entire lobster with trimmings and beer for US$10.

VEGETABLES

Cubans consider vegetables "rabbit food." Fresh vegetables rarely find their way onto menus other than in salads, which usually come in only one form in Cuba: mixed salads (*ensalada mixta*), usually consisting of a plate of lettuce or cucumbers (*pepinos*) and tomatoes (often served green, yet sweet) with oil and vinaigrette dressing. *Palmito*, the succulent heart of palm, is sometimes used. Often, you'll receive shredded cabbage (*col*), beetroot, and/or overboiled string beans.

Yucca, which closely resembles a stringy potato in look, taste, and texture, is prepared and served like a potato in any number of ways. A popular side dish is *boniato* (sweet potato), and other root vegetables such as *malanga,* a bland root crop rich in starch grown by the native Indian population and a rural staple.

Vegetables are most often used in soups and stews, such as *ajiaco* and garbanzo.

Beans (*frijoles*) are the most common vegetable and are used in many dishes. *Congrí oriental* is rice and red beans cooked together (the term refers to the Congo). *Frijoles negros dormidos* are black beans cooked and allowed to stand till the next day.

FRUITS

Cuba's rich soils and amicable climate nourish a panoply of fruits, although shortages are a constant reminder of the failures of the *acopio,* or state distribution system. Virtually the entire fruit harvest goes to produce fruit juice. To buy fruits, head to the *mercado agropecuario* (private farmers market).

The most common fruit is the *plátano,* a relative of the banana but used as a vegetable in a variety of ways, including as *tostones,* fried green plantains eaten as a snack, much like thick chips or English crisps.

In addition to well-known fruits such as papayas (called the *fruta bomba* in Havana, where "papaya" is a slang term for vagina), look for such lesser-known types as the furry *mamey colorado,* an oval, chocolate-brown fruit with a custardy texture and taste; the cylindrical, orange-colored *marañón,* the cashew-apple, whose seed grows *outside* the fruit; the oval, coarse-skinned *zapote,* a sweet granular fruit; and the large, irregular-shaped *guanábana,* whose pulp is sweet and "soupy," with a hint of vanilla. *Canitel* (familiar to travelers to Jamaica as ackee) is also grown, through rarely found. Surprisingly, coconuts are rare.

Count yourself lucky to get your hands on mangoes, whose larger versions are referred to in the feminine gender, *mangas,* because of their size.

BREAD AND DESSERTS

Cuba's infamously horrible bread is most often served as buns or twisted rolls, which Maurice Halperin found, whether toasted or not, "formed a sticky mass difficult to dislodge from between cheek and gum." I disagree—usually it's dry as a bone. Cuba's reputation for lousy bread predates the Revolution. "Why can't the Cubans make decent bread?" Che Guevara is reported to have asked. Of course, Cubans eat rice, not bread, as they have since the early 19th century, when it became the staple food of black slaves; only well-to-do Cubans ate bread. To be fair, the situation has improved markedly since the signing of a contract with a French company that now supplies breads to tourist hotels and sweet and tasty confections through outlets under the Pain de Paris banner.

Cubans make great desserts, often available for a few centavos at bakeries (*panaderías*). Hotel confections tend toward biscuits and sponge cakes (usually rather dry) topped with jam and canned cream. *Flan,* a caramel custard, is also popular—a variant is a delicious pudding called *natilla.* Marmalade and cheese is also a popular dessert.

Also try *tatianoff,* chocolate cake smothered with cream; *chu,* bite-size puff pastries stuffed with an almost bitter cheesy meringue; and *churrizo,* deep-fried doughnut rings sold at every bakery and many streetside stalls, where you can also buy *galletas,* ubiquitous sweet biscuits sold loose. The many coconut-based desserts include *coco quemado* (coconut pudding) and *coco rallado y queso* (grated coconut with cheese in syrup).

The best dessert of all is ice cream *(helado),* most notably that made by Coppelia. Cubans use specific terms for different kinds of scoops.

NONALCOHOLIC DRINKS

Coca-Cola and Pepsi (or their Cuban-made equivalent, Tropicola), plus Sprite, Fanta (or Cuban-made Najita), and other soft drinks are readily available at hotels, restaurants, and dollar stores. *Malta* is a popular nonalcoholic drink that resembles a dark English stout but tastes like root beer.

Roadside snack stalls sell *refrescos,* chilled fruit juices (usually 20-50 centavos a glass), and *batidos,* delicious and refreshing fruit drinks blended with milk and ice. More thirst quenching and energy giving is *guarapo,* fresh-squeezed sugarcane juice, sold cold at a fistful of roadside *guaraperías* (they're hard to find in Havana; ask around).

Cubans take frequent coffee breaks, and no home visit is complete without being offered a *cafecito,* thick and strong, like espresso, served black in tiny cups and heavily sweetened. Unfortunately, much Cuban domestic coffee has been adulterated with other products, usually chicory, into *café mezclado.* The best export brand is Cubita, sold vacuum-packed. *Café con leche* (coffee with milk) is served in tourist restaurants, usually at a ratio of 50:50, with hot milk. Don't confuse this with *Café americano,* which is usually diluted Cuban coffee.

ALCOHOLIC DRINKS

Cuba makes several excellent German-style beers (US$.75–3, depending on where you drink). Hatuey and Bucanero are full-flavored lagers. Cristal, the most widely available beer, and Lagarto are lighter. The inexpensive (typically one peso) and duller *clara* is brewed for domestic consumption. You'll also find Heineken, Labatts, Ice, some U.S. brands, and Tecate at most bars and in dollar stores (US$1.50-4).

Cuba's specialty is rum and rum-based cocktails. Cuban rums resemble Bacardí rums—which is not surprising, since several key rum factories in Cuba were originally owned by the Bacardí family—and come in three classes: light and dry (*ligero y seco*) Carta Blanca, aged for three years and also known as *tres años;* golden and dry (*dorado y seco*) Carta de Oro, aged for five years (*cinco años*); and dark seven-year-old *añejo* (*siete años*). There are several brands, most notably the Habana Club label.

Golden and aged rums are best drunk straight, although many Cubans drink *tragos*—shots—of overproof *aguardiente,* cheap white rum. White rum is ideal for cocktails, such as a *piña colada,* daiquirí, or *mojito.* Dark rums are also used in cocktails such as the appropriately named *mulata,* with lime and cocoa liqueur.

Most upscale restaurants serve Chilean, French, Spanish, and even California wines, although generally at twice the price or more of the United States or Europe—expect to pay US$5 and upward for a tiny glass, from US$15 for a bottle. Most are poorly kept and prove disappointing: Cuba's hot climate is hell on fresh wines, and few restaurants know how to store them. Stick to steadfast staples such as Torres and Concha y Toro. Avoid the deplorable Cuban wines. The most memorable thing about it is the hangover. Occasionally wine is served diluted with water!

Forget hard liquors, which are readily available in touristy bars but usually very expensive. You can buy bottles of your favorite imported liquor at most dollar supermarkets.

FOOD

CUBA'S COCKTAILS

Cuba's cocktails are legendary. Refreshing and simple to make, the "big three" are the hit of any party.

Cuba Libre

Who can resist the killer kick of a rum and Coke? Supposedly, the simple concoction was named more than a century ago after the war cry of the independence army: "Free Cuba!" *(Cuba libre)*. It's the official drink today of the Cuban-American community in Miami.

The Perfect *Cuba Libre:* Place ice cubes in a tall glass, then pour in 2 oz. of seven-year-old Havana Club *añejo* rum. Fill with Coca-Cola, topped off with 1 oz. of lemon juice. Decorate the rim with a slice of lemon. Serve with a stirrer.

Daiquirí

The daiquirí is named for a Cuban hamlet 16 miles east of Santiago de Cuba, near a copper mine where the mining firm's chief engineer, Jennings S. Cox, first created the now world-famous cocktail that Hemingway immortalized in his novels. Cox had arrived in 1898, shortly after the Spanish-American War, to find workers at the mines anxious about putatively malarial drinking water. Cox added a heartening tot of local Bacardí rum to boiled water, then decided to give his mixture added snap and smoothness by introducing lime juice and sugar.

The concoction was soon duplicated, and within no time had moved on to conquer every high-life watering hole in Havana. It is still most notably associated with El Floridita, and Hemingway's immortal words: *"Mi mojito en La Bodeguita, mi daiquirí en El Floridita."*

Shaved—frappéd—ice, which gave the drink its final touch of enchantment, was added by Constante Ribailagua, El Floridita's bartender, in the 1920s. The frozen daiquirís, "the great ones that Constante made," wrote Hemingway, "had no taste of alcohol and felt, as you drank them, the way downhill glacier skiing feels running through powder snow and, after the sixth and eighth, felt like downhill glacier skiing feels when you are running unroped."

A daiquirí should include all of Cox's original ingredients (minus the water, of course). It may be shaken and strained, or frappéd to a loose sherbet in a blender and served in a cocktail glass or poured over the rocks in an old-fashioned glass. The "Papa Special," which Constante made for Hemingway, contained a double dose of rum, no sugar, and a half ounce of grapefruit juice.

The Perfect Daiquirí: In an electric blender, pour half a tablespoon of sugar, the juice of half a lemon, and 1.5 ounces of white rum. Serve semi-frozen blended with ice (or on the rocks) in a tall martini glass with a maraschino cherry.

Mojito

The *mojito* is the classic drink of Cuba, favored by tourists today as it has been since the 1940s, when Ángel Martínez, then owner of La Bodeguita del Medio, hit upon the idea of giving credit to writers, who popped in to sup, establishing a bohemian scene that promoted the bar and its drink. The *mojito* supposedly originated as a lowly drink favored by slaves.

Comparatively few bars make up daiquirís, but almost every bar concocts the *mojito*. Alas, today La Bodeguita del Medio serves the worst *mojitos* in town.

The Perfect *Mojito:* With a stirrer, mix half a tablespoon of sugar and the juice of half a lime in an eight-inch highball glass. Add a sprig of *yerba Buena* (mint), crushing the stalk to release the juice; two ice cubes; and 1.5 oz. of Havana Club Light Dry Cuban rum. Fill with soda water, add a small splash of angostura, then dress with a mint sprig. *¡Salud!*

MERCADOS AGROPECUARIOS (FARMERS MARKETS)

Habana Vieja

Calles Compostela y Sol
Calles Egido y Zulueta

Centro Habana and Cerro

Avenidas Máximo Gómez (Monte) y Manglar
    Arroyo (Mercado Único de Cuatro Caminos)
Calzada de Cerro y Calzada de Palatino, Cerro
Calles San Nicolás y Trocadero
Zanja y Dragones

Vedado and Plaza de la Revolución

Calles 17 y F
Vía Blanca y Colina, Nuevo Vedado

Miramar and Vicinity

51 y 88, Marianao
51 y 124, Marianao
51 y 190, La Lisa

Suburban Havana

10 de Octubre y Colina, Santos Suárez
Calle 8 y Tejar, Lawton

SELF-CATERING

You can purchase Western goods at dollars-only stores, open to foreigners and Cubans alike and stocked with packaged and canned goods from all over the world (including from the good ol' USA) and sold at inflated prices. Havana even has supermarkets stocked with everything you'd expect to find in a Safeway or Sainsbury's.

For the average Cuban, however, shopping for food is a dismal activity. The state-run groceries, called *puestos,* where fresh produce—often of questionable quality—is sold, can make Westerners cringe.

Fortunately, since 1994, when free trading was legalized for farmers, Havana has sprouted produce or farmers markets —*mercados agropecuarios*

or *agros* for short—which sell meats, fruits, and, vegetables. Carrots, cucumbers, chard, and pole beans are about the only vegetables available year-round; tomatoes disappear about May and reappear around November, when beets, eggplants, cabbages, and onions are in season. Every district has at least one *agro,* selling in both dollars and pesos. Bring your own plastic bags. Hygiene is always questionable (think flies!). See the Special Topic "Mercados Agropecuarios" for locations.

Don't expect to find potatoes, the sale of which is restricted to the *libreta* (ration book), nor the many exotic fruits that may be familiar to you from other Caribbean islands. And cheese, which Cuba made in many varieties prior to the Revolution, is a precious scarcity. Chicken and pork are sold at *agros,* but not beef. Meat is very scarce, as is fish. The government-run Pescaderías Especiales sell fish and other seafood; each municipality has one.

As a result, most Cubans are forced to rely on the black market. For more insights into the food problem, read *Mi Moto Fidel: Motorcycling Through Castro's Cuba* and *Cuba Diaries*; see Suggested Reading.

HEALTH CONCERNS

Eating in Cuba doesn't present the health problems associated with many other destinations in Latin America. However, hygiene at streetside stalls is often questionable, as is shellfish. So, too, is the state of Havana's plumbing. Tap water is best avoided. Stick to bottled mineral water, which is widely available and comes carbonated (*con gas*) or non-carbonated (*sin gas*).

VEGETARIANS

If you're on an extended stay in Havana, maintaining a well-balanced intake takes attention. Few Cubans understand the concept of vegetarianism . . . protein, especially meat, is a valued scarcity. Moreover, since colonial days meat has been at the very center of Cuban cooking. Cubans adore meat and, in general, disdain greens, preferring an unhealthy sugar- and starch-heavy diet. Only a few restaurants serve vegetarian dishes—

servers in restaurants may tell you that a particular dish is vegetarian, even though it may contain chunks of meat. Most beans are cooked in pork fat, and most *congrí* dishes contain meat.

That said, at last visit, the opening of a chain of vegetarian restaurants in Havana had blessed the city with about half a dozen vegetarian restaurants. *Proteína vegetal* translates as "soy product."

Vegans who plan to fend for themselves shouldn't expect *agropecuarios* (farmers markets) to have many leafy greens or anywhere near the range of vegetables you may be used to abroad.

BREAKFAST

Few places serve breakfast. For pastries, try the **Pain de Paris** bakeries (see the Cafés, Bakeries, and Ice Cream sections for each area later in this chapter). A new chain of 24-hour restaurants called **Pan.Com** (pronounced "Pan-punto-com") is opening branches that serve omelets, croissants, yogurt, and the like.

Most hotel restaurants serve variations on the same dreary buffets (*mesa sueca,* or Swiss table): ham, cheese, boiled eggs, and an array of fruits and unappetizing cakes and biscuits. The variety is usually limited by Western standards, and presentation often leaves much to be desired. Top-class hotels do a bit better. Nonguests are usually welcome. Some hotels offer an *oferta especial* (special offer) that grants guests a discount up to 25 percent on buffet meals.

Hotel room rates rarely include breakfast, although members of tour groups usually have breakfasts (and most dinners) included in the cost of their tour. Refunds are not made for meals not taken.

PESO EATERIES

Foreigners can buy basic *criollo* dishes at state-run *merenderos* (lunch counters), and at a small number of pesos-only restaurants—most such restaurants, however, will not accept foreigners. Usually only one or two dishes are available and the cuisine is usually undistinguished at best.

The way to go is to follow the Cuban route to survival by eating at private roadside snack stalls (*cafeterías*) that usually display their offerings in glass cases. A signboard indicates what's available, with items noted on strips that can be removed as particular items sell out. These accept pesos from foreigners and are an incredibly cheap way of appeasing your stomach—you can eat for an entire day on US$3 or less . . . but note that the "$" sign at peso eateries refers to Cuban pesos, not US dollars. Many private *cafeterías* are run out of the most unlikely, hard-to-find places.

The staples at these places are fatty pork *boca-ditos* (sandwiches in a bun), basic *pizzetas* (pizza), *pan con queso (basic but tasty cheese sandwich in a bun), pay de coco* (coco flan), *refrescos* ("refreshments," usually fresh-squeezed orange juice), and *batidos* (refreshing iced milkshakes).

A few *guaraperías* sell fresh-squeezed sugarcane juice.

PALADARES

A good bet is to eat at private restaurants—*paladares.* The word means "palate," and comes from the name of the restaurant of the character Raquel, a poor woman who makes her fortune cooking, in a popular Brazilian TV soap opera, *Vale Todo.* Here you can fill up for US$5–15, usually with simple, albeit bloat-inducing, meals. Often, the price includes a salad and dessert, as well as beer. The owners put great energy into their enterprises, often displaying an inventiveness in preparing good food and service that Castro himself noted lacking in state restaurants. However, Castro also says that the *paladares* are "enriching" their owners and has refused to dine at them.

Paladares were legalized in September 1994 to help resolve the food crisis but have always been fettered by onerous taxation and rigorous restrictions that are usually honored in the breach. For example, *paladares* are not allowed to sell shrimp or lobster, a state monopoly. Nonetheless, most do, so ask: it's easy enough to find a huge lobster meal for US$10, including beer or soft drink. Beef is also illegal: the state maintains a monopoly and anyone found selling beef can face a lengthy spell in jail. Hence, you're not likely to find steaks in *paladares.* Though rela-

TOP PLACES TO EAT

Nowhere in Havana can rival the better restaurants outside the country, and you'll be hard-pressed to rank highly any additional restaurants beyond the following, which represents my recommended top 15 places to eat in Havana. See the regional sections for details.

Habana Vieja

La Bodeguita del Medio. This well-aged *bodega* serves some of the best traditional Cuban food in Havana.

El Floridita. The *other* Hemingway haunt, and the yin to the Bodeguita's yang. Specializes in seafood—notably lobster—served in opulent rococo surrounds.

Restaurante Santo Ángel. Excellent nouvelle Cuban cuisine. Conscientious service. And a splendid breeze-swept patio setting on Plaza Vieja.

Restaurante Telégrafo. Combines spirited contemporary decor, conscientious service, and quality nouvelle Cuban cuisine.

La Paella. This charmer boasts provincial Spanish decor and tasty paellas.

Centro Habana

La Guarida. Havana's most famous and popular *paladar* serves creative French-inspired cuisine in a dramatic bistro-style setting in the midst of a slum.

Plaza de la Revolución

Restaurante Biki. Clean, bargain-priced, and offering an unusually varied vegetarian buffet.

Coppelia. Tremendous setting, tremendous ice cream, and a chance to commune with *habaneros*.

El Gringo Viejo. Well executed cuisine in a clean, contemporary *paladar* setting.

Le Chansonnier. A fine *paladar* in a colonial mansion, serving quality creative fare.

Paladar Hurón Azul. Cuba's entrepreneurial spirit at its best. Quality food at fair prices. And a marvelous ambience.

Playa (Miramar and Beyond)

Cocina de Lilliam. Well-above-average *criollo* fare in this favored *paladar* with secluded patio dining.

Complejo Turístico La Giraldilla. Quality nouvelle Cuban cuisine in pleasing surrounds, with an optional disco-cabaret to follow.

El Aljibe. The best *criollo* fare and bargain in town. Havana's chic in-crowd dines here, as well as any visiting Hollywood mavens.

La Esperanza. A delightful *paladar* in a venerable home. Creative cuisine comes well-prepared at fair prices.

tives can assist, the owners cannot hire salaried workers—domestic squabbles in the kitchen are common, providing comic entertainment while you dine. And restaurant owners are also allowed only to serve up to 12 people at one seating, although several are politically favored and brazenly cram far more guests in that are legally allowed.

At press time, no new licenses for *paladares* were being issued, and the crippling monthly licensing fee and taxes—which have risen from US$150 a month on average, to up to US$1,500 a month . . . a phenomenal sum by Cuban standards—had put many *paladares* out of business, as intended. You should not balk at tipping in private restaurants, as the little extra can make all the difference to the hard-pressed family. Many *paladares* may seem overpriced, but now you know why. Unofficial figures suggest the number of private restaurants in Havana has fallen from 600 to only about 200 at last visit, and many establishments mentioned in this book may be closed by the time you arrive.

Taxi drivers may offer recommendations for *paladares,* as will touts on the street, who may approach you *sotto voce.* Normally they're getting a commission from the owner (who may be family), so their recommendations should be taken with a grain of salt. The commission will be added to your bill. If the tout seems hasty, it's usually because they want to move the transaction along before the police swoop. If you choose to take the recommendation, the tout will go with you . . . or no commission. Feel free to check out the kitchen (often a stomach-churning experience) before choosing to dine.

Many are open 24 hours; some are closed or operate at restricted hours during the summer off-season.

FAST FOOD

There are as yet no McDonald's or KFCs in Havana. However, the Cuban government has established a chain of tacky equivalents, including KFC-style fried-chicken joints called **El Rápido.** No surprise . . . food often runs out or is severely limited, and the quality is ho-hum at best. Cuba's answer to McDonald's is **Burgui,** open 24 hours. Are you sure that's *meat?*

CAFÉS, BAKERIES, AND ICE CREAM

Havana has plenty of sidewalk cafés, although most of the prerevolutionary *cafeterías* (coffee stands) that used to make coffee on every corner have vanished, as have most of the former tea shops (*Casas de Té* or *Casas de Infusiones*). Most cafés are really snack bars-cum-restaurants; there are few in the purist Parisian tradition, and as of yet, no Starbucks-style coffee shops.

In the past few years, Havana has been blessed with French-run bakeries called **Pain de Paris: Croissants de France,** 1ra Avenida y 182, Flores, tel. 33-7670. Some are open 24 hours and are good for croissants, sandwiches, and baked goods. Mondays and Tuesdays are usually best; after that the selection diminishes.

Cubans have a sweet tooth, as befits the land of sugar. They are especially fond of sickly sweet sponge cakes (*kek* or *ke*) covered in soft "shaving-foam" icing. Look for them being delivered by hand—usually by bicycle with the huge flat cake perched precariously atop a board held waiter-like over the passenger's shoulder. Usually they're on their way to a special event, such as a wedding or a *quince años* celebration.

Cubans are also renowned lovers of ice cream, and there are plenty of *heladerías* to appease them. You can buy ice creams for dollars in most tourist hotels and restaurants, or you can do as Cubans do and buy from *heladerías* on the street for a few pesos. **Coppelia** (see the Vedado section of this chapter) is the best show in town.

Habana Vieja

BREAKFAST

La Monserrate, Avenida de Bélgica (Monserrate), esq. Obrapía, tel. 860-9751, offers bacon and eggs (US$1.50), toast (US$1), and American-style coffee (US$.75). **Pastelería Francesca,** Prado #410, e/ Neptuno y San Rafael, tel. 862-0739, opens for breakfast at 8 A.M.

PESO EATERIES

Peso pickings are slim. The dingy and austere **Casa de los Vinos,** Esperanza #1, esq. Factoria, tel. 862-1319, near the main railway station, is a basic restaurant that began life as a workers' canteen in 1912. With luck, you'll find sausage and bean soup—two of its specialties—although it has fallen on hard times of late and offered a meager menu at last visit. The decor is highlighted by walls inlaid with tiles inscribed with love poems and proverbs, such as "The wind and women change by the minute."

Cafetería la Primera de Aguacate, Calle Aguacate #12, e/ Tejadillo y Chacón, is a great place for cheap *cajitas* (boxed lunches). Open noon–10 P.M.

The **Casa del Pru,** Calle Luz #321, e/ Habana y Compostela, sells *pru* (a nonalcoholic infusion of rice water) for one peso. For a refreshing glass of fresh-squeezed sugarcane juice (50 centavos), try the *guarapería* on Bernaza, esq. Obrapía.

PALADARES

The pocket-size **La Moneda Cubana,** San Ignacio #77, e/ O'Reilly y Plaza de la Catedral, tel. 861-0401 or 867-3852, is a tiny, well run place with speedy service and serving huge portions. The menu offers the usual Cuban staples such as grilled chicken or fried fish (US$9) and even pork chops (US$10) served with rice and beans, mixed salad, and bread. Open daily noon–11 P.M. Take your business card or a foreign banknote (*moneda*) to add to the wall.

Doña Eutimia, La Callejón de Chorro, tel.

860-2223, is around the corner off Plaza de la Catedral. The building is dilapidated, but the staircase pops you into a small rooftop dining room with a marvelous view. Try the *mariscada* (mixed seafood) house plate for US$15. Open noon–midnight.

El Rincón de Eleguá, Calle Aguacate #257, e/ Obispo y Obrapía, tel. 867-2367, serves complete meals for US$10, but it also has à la carte offerings for US$8–15. I recommend the excellent enchilada de pescado (fish chunks in spicy tomato sauce, US$6), although some of the dishes aren't memorable, and the salads are meager. Downstairs can get hot; upstairs is overly chilled. Open noon–11 P.M.

La Julia, Calle O'Reilly #506A, e/ Bernaza y Villegas, tel. 862-7438, is a tiny and simple place recommended for its traditional cooking. The ambience is kitschy, the family service is friendly and efficient, and the prices are right (US$4–9) for set plates that include pork, chicken, or lamb. Open noon–midnight.

Paladar Don Lorenzo, Calle Acosta #260A, e/ Habana y Compostela, tel. 861-6733, is one of the most intriguing options. This rooftop restaurant has a thatched bar and large, creative menu (US$5–18) that includes stuffed tomatoes (US$2.50), crocodile soup (US$4.50), and octopus vinaigrette (US$5) appetizers, and main dishes such as squid in ink (US$14), crocodile in mustard sauce (US$18), and roast chicken in cider (US$15). *Don't buy the marine turtle . . .* a protected and endangered species! Open noon–midnight.

Nearby, **Paladar El Sobrino,** Calle Obrapía #458, e/ Villegas y Aguacate, tel. 862-9107, is a small and intimate place serving filling albeit overpriced chicken and fish plates (US$12–15). Open noon–midnight.

CRIOLLO (CUBAN)

La Bodeguita del Medio, Calle Empedrado #207, e/ San Ignacio y Cuba, tel. 862-1374 or 33-8857, one block west of Plaza de la Catedral,

HABANA VIEJA: FOOD

FORTALEZA DE SAN CARLOS DE LA CABAÑA

SEE "PARQUE HISTÓRICO MILITAR MORRO - CABAÑA" MAP

SEE "HABANA VIEJA: THE CORE" MAP

BAHIA DE LA HABANA

TUNEL DE LA HABANA

CASTILLO/MUSEO DE SAN SALVADOR DE LA PUNTA

AV. ANTONIO MACEO (MALECON)

Parque des Enamorados

Parque des Mártires

Plaza 13 de Mayo

Parque Cespedes

Parque Luz Caballero

CARLOS MANUEL DE CESPEDES

PEÑA POBRE

AV. CARLOS

AGUIAR

CUARTELES

TEJADILLO

COMPOSTELA

AGUACATE

VILLEGAS

MISIONES

AGRAMONTE (ZULUETA)

AV. DE LAS

SAN JUAN DE DIOS

EMPEDRADO

Parque Cervantes

CASTILLO DE LA REAL FUERZA

Plaza de Armas

MERCADERES

CALLE

SAN IGNACIO

Plaza de la Catedral

CUBA

O'REILLY

OBISPO

OBRAPIA

HABA

LAMPARILLA

LA LLUVIA DE ORO

CAFÉ RESTAURANTE VIÑALES

PALADAR EL RINCÓN DE ELEGUA

DULCERIA EL SEGUNDO COMERCIO

LA CASA DE ESCABECHE

PALADAR LA JULIA

GENTILVOMO

Plazuela de Supervielle

EL FLORIDITA

Parque

A PRADO Y NEPTUNO

PANADERÍA FRANCESCA

Plaza de San

Plaza de San

SLOPPY JOE'S

CAPDEVILA

CÁRCEL

COLÓN

MARTÍ

PASEO DE

REFUGIO

GENIOS

CONSULADO

PALADAR DOÑA BLANQUITO

CAFÉ DEL PRADO

PRADO 264

CAFETERIA PRADO Y ANIMAS

MARTÍ (PRADO)

TROCADERO

ANIMAS

VIRTUDES

AMISTAD

NEPTUNO

SAN MIGUEL

INDUSTRIA

CRESPO

SAN LAZARO

TACON

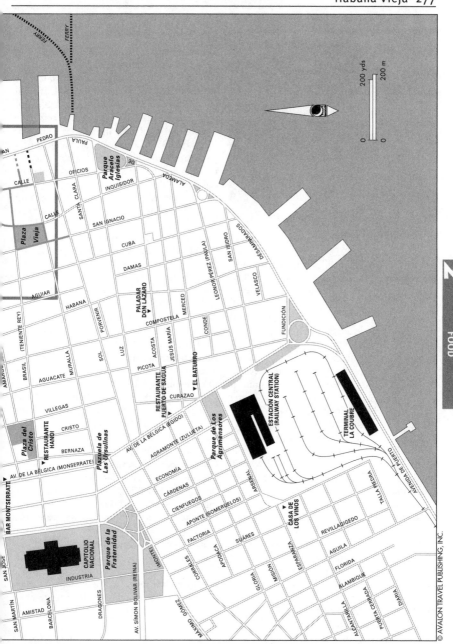

FERRY

FERRY

200 yds

200 m

0

0

PEDRO

PAULA

CALLE

OFICIOS

INQUISIDOR

Parque
Aracelo
Iglesias

ALAMEDA DE

SANTA CLARA

CALLE

SAN IGNACIO

Plaza
Vieja

CUBA

DAMAS

SAN ISIDRO

AGUIAR

LEONOR PEREZ (PAULA)

DESAMPARADOS

HABANA

PORVENIR

PALADAR
DON LÁZARO

COMPOSTELA

MERCED

VELASCO

BRASIL (TENIENTE REY)

LUZ

SOL

MURALLA

AGUACATE

ACOSTA

JESÚS MARÍA

CONDE

FUNDICIÓN

PICOTA

RESTAURANTE
PUERTO DE SAGUA

EL BATURRO

CURAZAO

VILLEGAS

AMARG

CRISTO

Plaza del
Cristo

RESTAURANTE
HANOI

BERNAZA

Plazuela de
Las Ursulinas

AV. DE LA BÉLGICA (EGIDO)

AGRAMONTE (ZULUETA)

Parque de Los
Agrimensores

ESTACIÓN CENTRAL
(RAILWAY STATION)

TERMINAL
LA COUBRE

AV. DE LA BÉLGICA (MONSERRATE)

BAR MONTSERRATE

ECONOMÍA

CÁRDENAS

CIENFUEGOS

APONTE (SOMERUELOS)

ARSENAL

TALLA PIEDRA

SAN JOSÉ

CAPITOLIO
NACIONAL

Parque de la
Fraternidad

FACTORÍA

SUÁRES

CASA DE
LOS VINOS

REVILLAGIGEDO

AVENIDA DE PUERTO

INDUSTRIA

APODACA

ESPERANZA

AGUILA

SAN MARTÍN

AMISTAD

BARCELONA

DRAGONES

AV. SIMÓN BOLÍVAR (REINA)

CORRALES

GLORIA

MISIÓN

FLORIDA

ALAMBIQUE

SAN MARTÍN

MÁXIMO GÓMEZ

(MONTE)

PUERTA CERRADA

ALCANTARILLA

DIARIA

FOOD

© AVALON TRAVEL PUBLISHING, INC.

© CHRISTOPHER P. BAKER

La Bodeguita del Medio

FOOD

specializes in traditional Cuban dishes—most famously its roast pork, steeped black beans, flat-fried bananas, garlicky yucca, and sweet guava pudding "overflowing," thought Nicolás Guillén (Cuba's national poet) "with surges of aged rum." You may luck out and get a great dish, but many readers report ho-hum fare. And though Ernest Hemingway did like to drink *mojitos* here, the drinks here are today the worst in Havana. You may have to wait for an hour or more to be seated, but a tip or friendly banter with Tito or Caesar, the "house captains," should get you a good table. The service is relaxed to a fault, and the atmosphere bohemian and lively. Troubadours entertain. The food is generally fresher at lunch than at dinner, for which you'll pay US$10–20 (a US$10 minimum applies). Reservations are advised. Open daily noon–midnight (bar open 10:30 A.M.–1 A.M.).

Restaurante Hanoi, Calle Teniente Rey, esq. Bernaza, tel. 867-1029, also known as La Casa de la Parre (Grapevine House) for the luxuriant grapevine growing in the patio, offers bargain meals. The restaurant is in one of the oldest houses in Havana. Although it promotes its Vietnamese cuisine, the menu is Cuban (Vietnamese is limited to one rice dish). However, no single dish costs more than US$3.50, and it offers "combination specials" for below US$3. And the *mojitos* cost a mere US$1. It

gets packed, so expect a long wait. Open noon–11 P.M.

Restaurante El Patio, tel. 867-1034, on Plaza de la Catedral, features the 24-hour El Portal patio bar, where jazz trios rotate shifts. It serves snacks such as an El Patio sandwich (US$3.50), hamburger (US$3), and *gazpacho* (US$4.50), plus main dishes such as *pierna de cerdo asado* (roasted pork leg; US$9) and steak palomilla with fries (US$2.75). The mansion also features a main restaurant with courtyard dining plus three air-conditioned dining rooms, one purportedly specializing in Mexican cuisine. It has set menus and serves overpriced dishes such as shrimp *al ajillo* (in garlic) and even T-bone steak (US$16–28) . . . all consistently mediocre. Patio bar open 24 hours; main restaurant open noon–midnight.

Café/Restaurante La Mina, Calle Obispo #109, esq. Oficios, tel. 862-0216, facing onto Plaza de Armas, offers shaded patio dining out front, where snacks and salads (US$3–5), *tamales,* and Cuban dishes (US$4–12) are served. It's very much on the tourist track, but the waiters are efficient, the setting is wonderful, and there's always live music. To the rear, you'll find the **Restaurante Cubano,** where you dine in a courtyard with an arbor and free-roaming peacocks. Open noon–midnight (bar open 24 hours).

Restaurant Viñales, O'Reilly, esq. Compostela, is an airy place with open-sided walls with *rejas* granting views onto the streets. The menu spans pizzas (US$4), pastas (US$2–3), and the usual Cuban fare.

Restaurante Colonial, Paseo del Prado #416, esq. San Rafael, tel. 860-8593, on the ground floor of the Hotel Inglaterra, has a wide-ranging menu of Cuban dishes, such as shrimp *en salsa roja* (US$12), *pollo asado* (US$5), and fried beef in creole sauce (US$5.50).

Restaurant Los Vitrales, Prado #212, e/ Calles Trocadero y Colón, tel. 862-4511, in the Casa de Científicos, is impressive for its exquisite rococo decor, colorful *vitrales,* and fine antiques, though the menu is less distinguished, with the usual Cuban fare running to chicken, fish, and steaks (US$6–26).

One of the best bargains in town is the hidden restaurant in the **Asociación Canaria de Cuba,**

Avenida de las Misiones #258, e/ Neptuno y Animas, tel. 862-5284. It serves fruit cocktails (US$.50), shredded beef stew (US$2), shrimp enchilada (US$5) and the like at rates less than half the price of most restaurants. Even lobster *con queso*—with cheese—costs only (US$7). Service is efficient and friendly. It's tucked into the rear at the top of the stairs. Open Wed.–Sun. noon–8:30 P.M.

The **Centro Andaluz,** Prado #104, e/ Genios y Refugio, tel. 863-6745, is another colonial Spanish social club with a bargain-priced *criollo* restaurant. Flamenco dancing is hosted on Saturday at 9 P.M. and Sunday at 6 P.M.

Taberna Benny Moré, Calle Mercaderes #531, esq. Brasil, tel. 861-1637, on the northeast side of Plaza Vieja, is a lively and modestly elegant place serving creative *criollo* fare (US$5–12). A nine-piece band usually performs traditional numbers. The waiters are renowned for scamming tourists. Inspect your bill carefully.

Another restaurant to beware is **Restaurante Bar Cabaña,** Calle Cuba #12, esq. Peña Pobre, tel. 860-5670, popular with passing tourists unawares that they're about to be ripped off. The staff are renowned for their scams.

El Mirador de la Bahía, on the rooftop above the Museo Nacional de Historia Natural, Calle Obispo #61, e/ Oficios y Baratillo, in Plaza de Armas (the unmarked entrance is immediately east of the museum; take the elevator), offers views over the old city. The glass-enclosed restaurant also has an open patio. It serves breakfasts and the usual range of Cuban dishes.

Los Doce Apóstoles, tel. 863-8295, at the base of Morro Castle, serves some unusual dishes, such as "African puree" soup (US$2). Creole chicken costs US$5.50. It offers a recommended meat plate with—shock! horror!—real *beef* (US$12). Locals flock for late night dancing. Open noon–2 A.M.

NOUVELLE CUBAN

Restaurante Santo Ángel, Brasil, esq. San Ignacio, tel. 861-1626, on the northwest corner of Plaza Vieja, is one of the best restaurants in Havana. The menu features gazpacho (US$2), garlic mushrooms (US$3.75), curried shrimp (US$15), and pork chops in mustard (US$10). Fresh-baked breads come with a superb *comport de champiñones* (mushroom paté) in olive oil; note that the bread is charged extra on your bill, which includes a 10 percent service charge. The tiramisu is first rate. A large wine list includes California labels (US$14–25); let Andrés del Río, the Spanish-trained sommelier, guide you. It has troubadours by day, and live jazz in the evenings. It's open 11 A.M.–11 P.M.

Restaurante Telégrafo, Paseo del Prado #408, esq. Neptuno, tel. 861-1010, is equally impressive, not least for its classy contempo decor. It has a creative, bargain-priced menu that includes such starters as an excellent onion soup, plus cold fettuccine with prawns, basil, and olives (US$4), and main dishes such as lobster, chicken, and squid in red wine (US$14), or filet mignon with rum and onions (US$9). Portions are generous. It has a large wine list; avoid the awful Cuban wine. Service is professional.

Restaurante Cantabria, Calle Luz #4, esq. San Pedro, tel. 862-8000, in the Hotel Armadores de Santander, is another splendid and elegant option that serves nouvelle Cuban international cuisine. It specializes in seafood, including salmon with green peas (US$10–23).

The **Roof Garden Restaurant,** Calle Trocadero #55, e/ Prado y Agramonte, tel. 860-8560, atop the Hotel Sofitel Sevilla, offers sublime decor that includes an effusive Renaissance paneled ceiling and marble floors, and tall French doors open to balconies overlooking the city. The food—a fusion of Cuban and French—remains mediocre, however (US$5–30), as did service at last visit. Happy-hour cocktails are served 6:30–8:30 P.M. Open 6:30–10 P.M.

The elegant **Restaurante El Paseo,** Neptuno, e/ Prado y Agramonte (Zulueta), tel. 866-6627, in the Hotel Golden Tulip Parque Central, has a creative menu that includes such starters as monkfish ravioli with sweet pepper sauce (US$14.50), and blackened scallops with anise veloute (US$20) for a main course. An alternative is the hotel's **Restaurante Mediterráneo,** serving the likes of shellfish bisque (US$7.50), Mediterranean salad (US$8.75), and confit legs of duck with gratin potatoes and mushrooms (US$18.50). Desserts include tiramisu (US$6.50). The cuisine is well-executed, if overpriced, and the service unpolished.

ARABIC

Restaurante al Medina, Calle Oficios e/ Obispo y Obrapía, tel. 867-1041, in the Casa de los Árabes, one block south of Plaza de Armas, offers predominantly *criollo* items such as fish and rice (US$3), salsa chicken (US$2.50), and vegetarian specialties for US$3. But you'll also find couscous and lamb dishes (US$6), as well as kebabs (US$5), kibbe (minced meatballs, US$4), and hummus (US$2.20). The best bargain is the *Gran Plato* (US$15). An all-female band plays traditional numbers. Open daily noon–11 P.M.

CONTINENTAL

The **Restaurante Real Plaza,** Calle Agramonte #267, esq. Neptuno, tel. 860-8583, on the ground floor of the Hotel Plaza, is elegant, with gilt fittings and marvelous high-backed modern chairs.

Café Mercurio, Calle Oficios, e/ Lamparilla y Amargura, tel. 860-6188, facing onto Plaza de San Francisco, is an elegant restaurant and bar offering a wide-ranging menu of continental and Cuban fare, including lobster (US$25) and grilled fish (US$8), plus sandwiches and simple salads. It offers air-conditioned seating inside or shaded dining alfresco on the cobbled plaza. Cappuccinos and espressos are served. The *mojitos* cost only US$2; beers cost US$2.50. Open 24 hours.

Restaurant El Condado, Calle Baratillo #9 e/ Obispo y Narciso López, tel. 860-8201, in the Hotel Santa Isabel on Plaza de Armas, is a regal option serving creative fare such as shrimp in mango sauce (US$19) and pork loin fried with orange and garlic (US$12). Open 11 A.M.–11 P.M.

Italian

A Prado y Neptuno, tel. 860-9636, named for its location, is a modern, air-conditioned place serving a range of pizzas and pastas (US$3.50-7),

plus steaks, fish, and chicken dishes (US$4–25). Open noon–midnight.

Cantiluomo, Obispo, e/ Monserrate y Bernaza, shares the kitchen with El Floridita (described later in this chapter) and offers a simple Italianate ambience and unambitious pasta dishes from US$4. It has a good wine list.

Dominica, O'Reilly #108, esq. Mercaderes, tel. 860-2918, serves pastas (US$7–11), good pizzas, plus meat dishes and seafood (US$6–24) in elegant surroundings. Live musicians perform. The place is foreign-managed and the food and service above average. Open noon–midnight.

Don Giovanni, Calle Tacón #4, e/ O'Reilly y Empedrado, tel. 867-1036, is a café-restaurant in a beautiful colonial mansion with good views from the balcony. You can dine on the lower courtyard, or upstairs in more elegant surroundings and look down over Calle Tacón and the harbor. It has a choice of mediocre pizzas and seafood (US$4–15), but the kebabs are recommended. You'll be charged extra for side salad, sometimes delivered without request. Open noon to midnight.

Spanish

El Mesón de la Flota, Calle Mercaderes #257, e/ Amargura y Brasil, tel. 863-3888, is a classic Spanish *bodega* with Iberian decor and a menu featuring *tapas,* tortillas, *criollo* entrees (US$4–18), and Spanish wines (US$1.50 a glass). Open 11 A.M.–11 P.M. (bar open 24 hours).

La Paella, Calle Oficios #53, esq. Obrapía, tel. 867-1037, in the Hostal Valencia, serves various paellas (for two people, although one person could ostensibly eat a double serving) for US$7–15. The *caldo* (soup) and bread is a meal in itself (US$3). You can also choose steak, grilled fish, and chicken dishes (US$4–10), washing them down with steeply priced Spanish wines (US$6–13). Try the excellent vegetable house soup. You'll dine beneath colonial chandeliers surrounded by antique dark-wood furnishings in a genuine Spanish *bodega*. Open noon–11 P.M.

Bodegón Ouda, Calle Obrapía, esq. Baratillo, tel. 867-1037, around the corner in the Hotel Comendador, is a quaint tapas bar with plenty of atmosphere. It serves *empanadas, tortillas* (US$1–2), *piquillos* (fried green peppers, US$1.50), pizza slices, and the like, washed down with sangría. Open noon–4 P.M. and 7–10 P.M.

Castillo de Farnés, Monserrate #361, esq. Obrapía, tel. 867-1030, is a Havana landmark famous since its founding as a Spanish restaurant in 1896. Castro used to frequent it while a student; he ate here again with Che Guevara on January 9, 1959, following his triumphal entry into Havana. Its menu includes excellent appetizers, such as garbanzo (US$3.50) and shrimp cocktail (US$3), plus omelets (US$4), garlic shrimp (US$9), and lobster and steak (US$15–20). It also serves sandwiches and reasonably priced *mojitos* and other cocktails (US$1.50). Take a sweater. A live band sometimes kicks up. It has a patio snack bar out front that draws *jineteros.* Open noon–midnight (bar open 24 hours).

La Zaragoza, Calle Monserrate #352, e/ Obispo y Obrapía, tel. 867-1033, is a dark and moody Spanish-style *bodega* that maintains its Spanish ties with regional flags and soccer memorabilia. It serves mostly *criollo* fare, however, but offers seafood such as squid rings (US$6), garlic shrimp (US$12), and *ceviche peruano* (US$2.50), plus lamb stew (US$9), tortillas (US$3), and pizza (from US$2). It's usually fairly empty except on Thursday and Saturday nights, which include cabaret. Open 7 A.M.–3 A.M.

El Baturro, Avenida de Bélgica (Ejido), esq. Merced, tel. 860-9078, offers *tapas* (US$.25) and *escabeche* shrimp (US$3.50) as well as other Spanish and Cuban dishes amid Spanish surroundings: barrels, a bull's head, bullfight posters, ceramic murals, and brass lamps. The long bar serves a full range of liquors.

Bodegón de los Vinos, in the Fortaleza de San Carlos de la Cabaña, offers a genuinely Spanish experience. It's built into the vaults of the castle and has traditional *manchego* (from La Mancha) decor. It serves *tapas,* sausages, and other Spanish dishes (US$2–17), washed down by sangría (US$3). Flamenco dancers entertain.

The new **Bar Restaurante San Francisco,** tel. 862-0617, ext. 502, also in the Fortaleza de San Carlos de la Cabaña, is a modern take on a Spanish theme. This air-conditioned restaurant serves Spanish and *criollo* dishes.

La Tasca, Prado, esq. Trocadero, on the ground floor arcade of the Hotel Coralia Sevilla, replicates a Spanish *bodega.*

ASIAN

Torre de Márfil, Mercaderes #121, e/ Oficios y Obrapía, tel. 867-1038, has all the trappings: the Chinese lanterns, screens, and even a banquet table beneath a pagoda. It's staffed by Chinese waiters, but the service is disorganized and excruciatingly slow. The menu includes authentic spring rolls and reasonable chop suey, chow mein, fried wontons (US$1.50), and shrimp and lobster dishes (US$14). Entrées range US$5–15. It serves set dinners from US$6. Open Mon.–Thurs. noon–10 P.M., Fri.–Sun. noon–midnight.

SURF AND TURF

El Floridita, Monserrate, Habana Vieja, tel. 867-1299 or 867-1300, immortalized in Ernest Hemingway's *Islands in the Stream,* has a circular restaurant that wears a Romanesque livery of red and gold—plus an original mural of the old port—and still has a *fin de siècle* ambience. Today, however, it is overly air-conditioned and rather sterile, cleansed of the heady atmosphere of the days when Papa drank here—it has been called a "glitzy huckster joint" in *Travel & Leisure.* Many of the dishes (mostly seafood) are disappointing and ridiculously overpriced. The house special is *langosta mariposa* (lobster grilled with almonds, pineapple, and butter; US$42) but it is best to stick with simple dishes such as prawns flambéed in rum. A shrimp cocktail costs US$15; oyster cocktails cost US$5. You can even have frog's leg soufflé (US$19). The wine list is impressive, and choice cigars are offered. A string trio serenades. The service is surly. Open noon–11 P.M. (bar open noon–1 A.M.).

La Casa del Escabeche, Calle Obispo, esq. Villegas, tel. 863-2660, a simple bar with flagstone floor and *rejas* open to the street, serves

M

FOOD

delicious *escabeche* (cube chunks of fish marinated with lime and salsa) for pennies. It has live music.

Café del Oriente, Calle Oficios, esq. Amargura, tel. 860-6686, on the west side of Plaza de San Francisco, is a ritzy place with marbletop bar, tux-clad waiters, and a jazz pianist downstairs in the Bar Café (heck, you could be in New York or San Francisco). The upstairs restaurant is yet more elegant, with sparkling marble and antiques, French drapes, and a magnificent stained-glass ceiling. It offers mostly steaks and seafood dishes (US$12–30). Open noon–midnight (bar open 24 hours).

Puerto de Sagua, Avenida de Bélgica (Egido) #603, e/ Jesús María y Acosta, tel. 867-1026 or 863-6186, is a pleasant seafood restaurant designed on a nautical theme. Its eclectic menu ranges from paella (US$10 minimum two people) and pizza (US$1.50 to US$4) to garlic shrimp (US$8) and lobster enchiladas (US$6.50). It has an atmospheric bar with fish tanks in the porthole windows. Open noon–midnight.

La Divina Pastora, Parque Histórico Militar Morro-Cabaña, tel. 860-8341, 200 meters east of and below the Morro castle, is housed in a handsome hacienda-style structure fronted by a battery of cannons. The atmosphere is splendid, especially on the patio in late afternoon. The menu includes such appetizers as Peruvian ceviche (US$5) and lobster cocktail (US$7), and such entrées as lobster creole (US$20) and grilled shellfish (US$25), usually prepared to perfection. Live entertainment is offered. Parking costs US$1. Open noon–11 P.M.

Behind the restaurant, on the harbor front, is the wonderful little *bodega*-type **Bar la Tasca,** with a breezy terrace offering fabulous views over the harbor. It features lances and medieval armor on the walls. The simple menu includes lobster and seafood dishes from US$8.

SNACK BARS

Doña Isabel Cafetería, on Calle Tacón #4, esq. Empedrado, tel. 863-3560, one block north of Plaza de Armas, serves sandwiches, pizzas, and other snacks alfresco.

Café O'Reilly, O'Reilly #203, e/ Cuba y San Ignacio, one block south of Plaza de la Catedral, is a good place to relax over Cuban coffee and simple snacks—mostly sandwiches and pizza these days—on the upstairs balcony, reached via a metal spiral staircase. Open 24 hours.

The **Café París,** Calle Obispo, esq. San Ignacio, is a very lively social scene for both Cubans and tourists. You'll sit at rustic wooden furniture and look out through open trellised windows on life flowing down Obispo. Lively Latin music is usually playing from a jukebox. Ho-hum fare includes fried chicken (US$2.50), hamburger (US$2), Spanish sausage with potato (US$2.50), and various sandwiches. Open 24 hours.

Café del Louvre, Prado, e/ Neptuno y San Rafael, the patio bar of the Hotel Inglaterra, is a popular spot for gazing over Parque Central. It serves sandwiches, tortillas, tapas, and burgers (US$3–8), plus desserts and coffees.

For a special treat, head to the small bar—an art deco stunner—just inside the **Edificio Bacardí,** Monserrate #261, which also serves tuna, cheese, and ham sandwiches, plus grilled chicken. You go for the ambience, not the food. Open 10 A.M.–8 P.M. Mon.–Sat. It was closed for repair at last visit.

CAFÉS, BAKERIES, AND ICE CREAM

Restaurant La Luz, Calle Obispo, e/ San Ignacio y Mercaderes, sells cappuccinos, espressos, and various coffees. About 20 yards east is **Al Cappuccino,** Calle Obispo #109, esq. Oficios, next to Café Mina, a tiny coffee house serving homemade pastries and custard for US$1.

The **Casa del Café,** Baratillo, e/ Obispo y Justíz, tel. 860-8061, on the southeast corner of Plaza de Armas, also sells cappuccinos (US$2), plus various grades of Cuban coffees. It's open Monday–Saturday 10 A.M.–6 P.M., Sunday 9 A.M.–3 P.M.

Café Prado y Ánimas, Prado, esq. Ánimas, is a pleasant modern café in period decor, serving sandwiches, snacks, and coffees, including cappuccinos. It's open 7 A.M.–7 P.M.

The **Pastelería Francesca,** Prado #410, e/ Neptuno y San Rafael, tel. 862-0739, betwixt the

Hotel Inglaterra and Hotel Telégrafo, on the west side of Parque Central, is part of the Pain de Paris chain, which also has an outlet on Calle Obispo, just off Plaza de Armas. It has a clean, pleasant decor and sells scrumptious croissants, cakes, cookies, and sandwiches for US$.10 upwards. It also has ice creams, including the *tres gracias* banana sundae (US$1.75). Open 8 A.M.–11 P.M.

Panadería San José, Calle Obispo #161, e/ Mercaderes y San Ignacio, tel. 860-9326, also sells a tempting array of confections from US$.10. Open 24 hours.

Dulcería el Segundo Comercio, Calle O'Reilly #468, esq. Villegas, is a local bakery selling birthday cakes for 10 pesos, and slices for 3.65 pesos.

Ice Cream: Small streetside outlets scattered throughout Habana Vieja sell ice cream cones for one peso. **Cremería el Naranjal,** Calle Obispo, esq. Cuba, for example, sells various ice cream sundaes, including a banana split (US$1.50 to US$3), but they're overpriced. Instead, walk two blocks west to **Variedades Obispo,** Obispo, esq. Habana, where you can buy a cone for one peso.

SELF-CATERING

For Havana's largest—and most colorful—*agropecuario* (farmers market), go to Cuatro Caminos, Máximo Gómez (Monte), esq. Arroyo (Avenida Manglar), tel. 870-5934. You may not want to buy a pig's head, or live ducks and chickens trussed up on a pole, but if these or herbs, vegetables, and fresh fruit or fish catch your fancy, you're sure to find it here.

Another large open-air market can be found on Avenida de Bélgica (Egido), e/ Apodada y Corrales.

Imported salamis and meats are sold at **La Monserrate,** Monserrate, e/ Brasil y Murallas, an air-conditioned butcher shop; and at **Harris Brothers** Avenida de Bélgica #305, e/ O'Reilly y Progreso, Habana Vieja, tel. 861-1644, a department store with various foodstuffs sections.

Supermercado Isla de Cuba, Máximo Gómez #213, esq. Factoria, tel. 33-8793, on the south side of Parque de la Fraternidad, is reasonably well-stocked by Cuban standards. Open Mon.–Sat. 10 A.M.–6 P.M., and Sun. 9 A.M.–1 P.M.

Centro Habana and Cerro

PESO EATERIES

Pickings are slim. Your best bet is **Cuatro Caminos,** Máximo Gómez (Monte), esq. Arroyo (Avenida Manglar), tel. 870-5934, the huge farmers market where a section is devoted to stalls selling tacos and other snacks, plus coconut meat, *batidos* (fruit milkshakes), and fresh fruit juices for pesos.

The **Cafetería Manzanares,** Salvador Allende, esq. Infanta, serves tacos (2 pesos) and tortillas, washed down with local beer (6 pesos).

PALADARES

Private restaurants are few and far between in residential Centro, but ironically, the area boasts the best *paladar* in town: **La Guarida** (see the Special Topic "*Un Paladar Especial*").

Paladar Torresón, Malecón #27, tel. 861-7476, e/ Prado y Industria, has a balcony dining room offering views along the seafront boulevard and good for viewing the sunset. Its *criollo* menu includes vegetarian meals. Typical meals cost US$10–15, but watch for bread and side dishes sneaking onto the bill as extras. Open noon–midnight.

Paladar Doña Blanquita, Prado #158, e/ Colón y Refugio, tel. 867-4958, is extremely popular and offers a choice of dining in the elegant *sala* or on a balcony overlooking the Prado. Its *criollo* menu features large portions for US$5–10. However, you really go for the kitsch. The place overflows with whimsical Woolworth's art such as cheap *muñequitas* (dolls), plastic flowers, animals, and cuckoo clocks. Open noon–3 A.M.

Paladar Bellomar, Calle Virtudes #169, esq.

UN PALADAR ESPECIAL

The most famous of Cuban *paladares* is **La Guarida,** Calle Concordia #418, e/ Gervasio y Escobar, Centro Habana tel. 862-4940, a unique gem on the third floor of a once glamorous, now dilapidated, 18th-century townhouse-turned-crowded *ciudadela* in an equally run-down section of Centro Habana. Don't be put off by the funky staircase, lent an operatic stage set air by laundry. It's one of the hippest joints in Havana, reminding diners perhaps of a cozy bistro in New York's SoHo. You may recognize it as a setting for scenes in the Oscar-nominated 1995 movie, *Fresa y Chocolate.*

La Guarida (the name means "hideaway") is usually jam-packed with Havana's cognoscenti . . . usually a mix of diplomats, foreign businessmen with glamorous Cuban models, and perhaps even a sprinkling of royalty or Hollywood figures. The walls are festooned with period Cuban pieces, giant prints showing famous personages who've dined here, plus fashion shoots on the crumbling stairway.

You dine at tables lit by dripping red candles. Owners Enrique and Odeysis Nuñez serve up creatively conceived dishes. The menu changes frequently and features such mouth-watering treats as gazpacho (US$4) and tartar de *atún* (tuna) (US$6) for starters; for entrées, there's atún with sugarcane and coconut (US$12) and chicken breast with pepper sauce (US$12). The couple knows how to make their food dance, although quality is far from consistent and there are some duds (the Caesar salad needs work). The restaurant has a large wine list, but only one white and two reds by the glass (US$3). A lunch menu emphasizes salads and pastas.

Open 7 P.M.–midnight. Closed June–July. Reservations are essential.

Amistad, tel. 861-0023, is a down-to-earth family restaurant serving no-frills chicken and fish dishes for about US$2. Open noon–midnight.

Paladar Las Delicias de Consulado, Consulado #309, e/ Neptuno y Virtudes, has a simple dining room with balcony over the street. It serves simple *criollo* fare for about US$46. Open 9 A.M.–1 A.M.

CRIOLLO

The **Restaurant Colonial,** Galiano esq. Virtudes, tel. 861-0702, in the Hotel Lincoln, is one of the better restaurants in Centro and has soups, fish, shrimp, and chicken dishes for less than US$4. The service is swift and conscientious, and a piano player tickles the ivories. Open 11 A.M.–midnight.

Restaurante Fornos Cha, Neptuno #251, esq. San Miguel, tel. 862-8964, is a pleasant, albeit overly air-conditioned modern option serving set four-course meals for US$5 to US$10. Open Thurs.–Mon. noon–3 A.M. A live female band plays in the evening.

ASIAN

The Barrio Chino boasts a score of Chinese restaurants, many staffed by wait-staff in traditional costumes. Most are concentrated along Calle Cuchillo's 50-meter-length. However, this isn't Beijing or Hong Kong. If you're looking for the "best food in Chinatown," as the waiters who try to drag you into their restaurants proclaim, you're better off taking a flight to San Francisco. Most restaurants on Cuchillo (knife) offer both indoor and patio dining, where all manner of *jineteros* and *jineteras* tout their wares while you dine. Annoying! But the color is marvelous . . . from flower-sellers to acrobats to not-so-subtle prostitutes.

Restaurante Tien-Tan, Calle Cuchillo #17, tel. 861-5478, is the best of a dozen options on Cuchillo. The extensive menu—probably the longest list in Cuba—includes such tantalizing offerings as sweet-and-sour fried fish balls with vinegar and soy (US$7), and pot-stewed liver with seasoning (US$7). The budget-minded will find many dishes for around US$2 but dishes run to US$18. This is the most genuinely

Chinese cuisine in Cuba, and the only place that I've ever had highly spiced food on the island, though it still falls short of Chinese cuisine in New York or San Francisco. Chef Tao Qi hails from Shanghai and speaks English. If he befriends you, he might offer a rice wine, but it is rough stuff. Stick to beer. A 20 percent service fee is charged. Open 11 A.M.–midnight.

Restaurante Pacífico, Calle San Nicolás, esq. Cuchillo, tel. 863-3243, boasts genuine albeit jaded (no pun intended) Chinese furniture and Cantonese favorites such as lobster or shrimp chow mein (US$7) and lobster chop suey (US$7). There are restaurants on all five floors, though the main restaurant is on the third. More exclusive guests gather on the fifth, where Hemingway used to eat—Castro is an occasional visitor.

Casa Abuelo Lung Kong Cun Sol, Calle Dragones #364, e/ Manrique y San Nicolás, tel. 862-5388, has a restaurant upstairs open to Cubans (pesos) and tourists (dollars). *Maripositas chinas* (fried wontons) cost 10 pesos; chop suey and other entreés range 10-75 pesos. This is the real McCoy: Chinese staff, Chinese ambience, Chinese patrons. Open noon–midnight. **Chi Tack Tong,** tel. 861-8095, immediately east, competes.

Restaurant Tai Pi, Dragones #313, e/ San Nicolás y Rayo, tel. 862-2757, with an authentic Chinese atmosphere in its upstairs restaurant. Balconies offer views along Dragones. Its simple Chinese menu offers *maripositas chinas* for 10 pesos and chow mein for 43 pesos.

Restaurant Bavaria, Dragones #414, esq. Cam-panario, tel. 863-2068, also offers a quasi-genuine Chinese ambience and the usual Cuban-Chinese fare like wonton soup (US$1.50), chop suey, and chow meins (US$1.20). Open Tues.–Thurs. noon–11 P.M. and Fri.–Sun. noon–1 A.M.

OTHER

La Cailesa Cafetería, Calle San Rafael, e/ Prado y Concordia, is a taquería offering tacos (US$2–4), refried beans, corn tortillas, and other Mexican fare. Here you can sit in the open air beneath a shady canopy and watch the tide of shoppers flooding down San Rafael.

El Rápido, Calzada de Infanta, esq. San Rafael, serves fast-food junkies with fried chicken.

SELF-CATERING

Almacenes Ultra, Avenida Simón Bolívar #109, esq. Rayo, is a reasonably well-stocked grocery, open Mon.–Sat. 9 A.M.–6 P.M. and Sun. 9 A.M.–1 P.M. Similarly, try the basement supermarket in **La Época,** Avenida de Italia, esq. Neptuno; open Mon.–Sat. 9:30 A.M.–9:30 P.M., and Sun. 9 A.M.–1 P.M.

ICE CREAM

Sodería Boulevard, Calle San Rafael, esq. Aguiar, is a clean, air-conditioned ice creamery selling cones and sundaes for dollars, as does **Sodería Alondra,** Neptuno, esq. Manrique, tel. 862-7236.

Vedado and Plaza de la Revolución

BREAKFAST

Café la Rampa, Calle L, outside the Hotel Habana Libre Tryp, is open 24 hours and is a good bet if you don't care for quality. It serves meager American-style breakfasts (US$2–6), plus tortillas (US$2.50–4), and has a breakfast special of coffee and toast for US$2, with eggs, bacon, coffee, and juice for US$7. The food is ho-hum.

The **Hotel Habana Libre,** Calle L, e/ 23 y 25, also offers a breakfast buffet (US$9) in its mezzanine restaurant, 7–10 A.M. Better yet, head to the 24-hour **Cafetería El Rincón del Cine,** Calle O, esq. 21, tel. 33-3564, in the Hotel Nacional, where a full American breakfast costs US$9.50.

PESO EATERIES

There's no shortage of little in-house *cafeterías* around the University of Havana.

Penny-pinching or otherwise, you should head to **Pizza Celina,** Infanta y San Rafael, alias "Pie-in-the-Sky." Reports student Bridget Murphy: "Celina the capitalist genius hasn't let the fact that she lives on the third floor stop her from running a successful pizza business. Scream up your order from across the street, and then in a few minutes pick up your pizzas from, and drop your *pesos* into, the plastic basket (complete with red bows) that comes crashing down." Welcome to Cuba! It's pretty good pizza, too.

A little in-house spot at the corner of Calle 19 y K sells high-quality pizzas; the *super-vegetal* is recommended.

For *cajitas,* try **Cajitas,** Calle L, esq. 25 (go down the stairs into the home). It's closed Sundays.

Doña Laura's, Calle H, e/ 21 y 23, is a great bargain. This roadside cafetería serves good food, including sandwiches for five pesos. A *cajita* costs 23 pesos. Open 11 A.M.–4 P.M. At last visit, however, it was closed for the summer and it was unsure if it would reopen. Also try **Casa Sarasua,** Calle 25 #510, Apto. 1, e/ H y I, tel. 832-2114, a *peso paladar* that specializes in meat dishes. However, the best reason to dine here is the fabulous

weapon collection and the loquacious owner, happy to regale you with his family history.

PALADARES

Le Chansonnier, Calle J #259, e/ 15 y Línea, tel. 832-1576, in a venerable home with soaring ceilings, is among the best *paladares* in Vedado and is recommended for creative fare inspired by France. Well-prepared trademark sauces highlight simple yet tasty and hearty fare such as roasted rabbit in mustard sauce; lamb in tomato sauce, olives, and wine; calamari enchilada; or duck with *salsa guayabera*. Most main dishes cost US$10. Foie gras was to be introduced. The restaurant delivers huge portions, and the service is efficient and courteous. It's gay-friendly and draws local gays, not least for its rich, warm ambience that includes an antique clock collection. Open 1 P.M.–1 A.M.

Paladar Hurón Azul (Blue Ferret), Humbolt #153, esq. P, tel. 879-1691, dehuronzaul@hotmail.com, is favored by Cuban intelligentsia, reflected in the original works of art by Cuba's leading painters, floodlit by halogens. This superb *paladar* offers inexpensive but excellent nouvelle Cuban food, including bargain-priced *cajitas* (boxed lunches). Presentation would do Wolfgang Puck proud. The escabeche (US$4.50), garbanzo (US$3.50), and octopus vinaigrette (US$5.50) starters are superb. Main dishes include oven-roasted chicken with provençal herbs and honey sauce (US$9). Its house combo, *La Guajira* (US$9), comprises a seasoned pork steak, stuffed corn tamale, fried plantains, *congrí,* and salad. Rice is served in eight different styles. And desserts include trifle (US$5) and cheesecake (US$3.50). For most dishes, expect to pay US$5–10. A six-course "Menu Gourmet" costs US$20–25, by reservation only. Service is polite and professional. And the waiting room boasts a huge wine (141 labels) and liquor collection (Arctic Whale vodka?) any oenophile or booze-hound would be proud of. Champagne? At least five types are served, including Don Perignon (US$150).

Only insipid Cuban wine is served by the glass, however. Open noon to midnight.

Restaurante Gringo Viejo, Calle 21 #454, e/ E y F, Vedado, tel. 832-6150, is a classy eatery favored by Cuban celebrities. There's a kind of speakeasy feel to this quirky place crawling with plastic vines, stained glass, and colored lights. It offers inventive cuisine served in large portions. For a starter try the seasoned garbanzos with chorizo, tomatoes, green peppers, and onions (US$5), with perhaps the fricasseed chicken steeped in red wine (US$12) to follow. It has a fully-stocked bar and attentive service. The *gringo viejo* ("old gringo") refers to Gregory Peck, who mugs on a large movie poster. Open Mon.–Sat. noon–11 P.M.

Paladar Restaurant Monguito, Calle L, e/ 23 y 25, directly opposite the Hotel Habana Libre Tryp, is a bargain and for that reason almost always full. *"China,"* your host, serves simple but filling Cuban dishes such as *pollo asado,* grilled fish, and pork dishes (US$3–6).

Paladar Aries, Avenida Universidad #456, e/ J y K, is a small but popular *paladar* serving meals in a colonial room full of antique clocks. The menu includes a crab cocktail starter (US$6) and such creative entrees as liver with onions, pepper, and wine (US$7).

Paladar Marpoly, Calle K #154, e/ 11 y 13, tel. 832-2471, is in a colonial home full of religious icons and intriguing antiques. You can dine in the parlor, or to the rear, where a makeshift *bohío* is roofed in thatch. The creative menu includes a house special of seafood with pineapple and melted cheese served in a pineapple (US$11, with salad and side dishes). *Do not order the* cagüama—*turtle—as it's a protected species.* Marpoly offers a five-course house plate (US$17). Watching you eat are monkeys, a dozen or so exotic dogs, and a score of parrots and other birds. Tragic! And hygiene is questionable. Look for a house with rust-red pillars and a mural of Santa Barbara on the wall, illumined at night. Open noon to midnight.

Paladar Nerei, Calle 19, esq. L, tel. 832-7860, serves filling soups, tuna salad (US$3.50), spaghettis, grilled fish (US$7.50), calamari (US$8), and *criollo* dishes on a shaded veranda of a colonial home. The wide-ranging menu includes creative dishes such as duck with onions (US$7.50) and lamb in tomato sauce (US$7.50). Open Mon.–Fri. noon–midnight, and Sat.–Sun. 6 P.M.–midnight.

Paladar Familia Fernández, Calle Línea #10, Apto. 602, e/ N y O, is recommended for superb cooking—"magnificent," said one reader of Olga's *criollo* cooking and salads, with tomatoes from her own garden (US$15 full meal).

El Bistro, Calle K #12, esq. Malecón, tel. 832-2708, has terrace dining overlooking the ocean. For long it was known for its Cuban cuisine with a quasi-French twist, but today it serves hearty portions of traditional *criollo* fare served in skillets that add flavor. Main dishes include chicken or fish, each served a dozen ways (US$8–10). Open noon–midnight.

Paladar Las Tres Bs, Calle 21, e/ K y L, tel. 832-9276, is a sparse and kitsch-filled option run by the Alfonso family, who tout their simple but filling meals as *"bueno, bonito y barato"* (good, pretty, and cheap). Dishes typically cost about US$10. Open 11 A.M.–11 P.M. Nearby, and in similar vein is **Paladar Los Amigos** Calle M #253, e/ 19 y 21, adjacent to the Focsa building. It offers a simple menu that includes Uruguayo (pork or chicken stuffed with ham and cheese), plus fish filet. Open noon–midnight.

El Recanto, Calle 17 #957, e/ 8 y 10, tel. 832-4396, is tucked away behind a battered door of a decaying mansion in western Vedado. Persevere, for the daunting approach is deceiving. After ascending a crumbling staircase, a gloomy passage leads to an iron-grilled door and through living quarters before expelling you onto the roof. Here, in a thatched eating area, you are served large portions of *criollo* dishes at unbelievably low prices (US$1–2). Open noon–6 A.M.; closed Wednesday.

Restaurante Capitolio, Calle 13 #1159, e/ 16 y 18, tel. 832-4947; open noon–midnight, in a handsome 1920s Southern California-style home, serves simple yet tasty fare that includes seafood in tomato, red pepper and onion sauce; crispy smoky pork chops; and barbecued lamb on occasion.

Paladar Las Mercedes, Calle 18 #204, e/ 15 y 17, tel. 833-7512 (c/o neighbor), is a charming option where excellent quality *criollo* dishes with an imaginative twist are served. I recommend the *Pescado a la Mercedes* (two types of fish with cheese sauce). The kebab (*brocheta*) is also good. It includes a set menu (US$15). It's close to Villa Eulalia (used by students at the University of Havana). It has a student deal for US$3 before 7 P.M. Open noon–midnight.

La Casa, Calle 30 #865, e/ 26 y 41 in Nuevo Vedado, tel. 881-7000, open noon–midnight, is worth the drive, according to *Cigar Aficionado,* which offers this description: "Located in a 1950s-style house with a modish decor, La Casa serves such delicious dishes as fresh prawns sautéed in butter with garlic, and juicy roasted pork with beans and rice." It serves no-frills Cuban food such as grilled fish and rice and black beans. The place is lush with tropical plantings. An indoor-outdoor patio features waterfalls and pools full of drowsy terrapins.

El Decamerón, Línea #753, e/ 2 y Paseo, tel. 832-2444, has been recommended for high quality *criollo* cuisine and its pleasant ambience enhanced by heaps of tropical plants and antique clocks. It has a full bar in the waiting room. And **Escorpión,** Calle 17 #105, e/ L y M, near the Focsa building, has been recommended for its good food and "extremely friendly and fast" service. Open 24 hours.

CRIOLLO

Restaurante El Barracón, Calle L, e/ 23 y 25, in the Hotel Habana Libre Tryp, serves *criollo* dishes, especially pork dishes, such as roast pork for US$12, and more adventurous fare such as "jerked horsemeat stew" for US$10, in atmospheric surroundings, with entrées US$7–15; open noon–midnight.

El Conejito (The Little Rabbit), Calle M #206, esq. Avenida 17, tel. 832-4671, is another splendid option, not least for its Old English or Teutonic ambience. A pianist plays while you dine on *conejo* served any of a dozen ways. It also serves beef, chicken, and pasta dishes, plus a decent grilled fish. Your mixed salad—lettuce and carrots—may truly be termed "rabbit food." Entrées average US$7. It has inexpensive "student

nights" on Wednesday and weekends. Open noon–midnight.

Casona del 17, Calle 17, e/ Calle K y L, tel. 33-4529, is in an old mansion that once belonged to Fidel's godparents. The reasonably priced menu presents a tasty paella (US$7), lobster enchilada (US$10), and such staples as grilled fish and pork, plus beef dishes to be enjoyed on a breezy outdoor patio or within the air-conditioned neoclassical building showing off contemporary art on the walls. It also has an outdoor, thatched barbecue grill. Open noon–midnight.

Taberna Don Pepe, Calle San Lázaro, esq. Infanta, is a rustic *bodega*-style bar and restaurant where simple fare such as *pollo frito* averages US$2 a plate. **La Carreta,** Calle K #402, esq. 21, tel. 832-4485, offers similarly rustic ambience and simple Cuban fare, mostly to Cubans (in pesos; you'll pay dollars).

Wakamba, Calle O #155, e/ La Rampa y Humboldt, tel. 878-4526, once a famous prerevolutionary nightclub, has been turned into an ascetic restaurant-bar. It serves pork steaks (US$3.50), chicken *uruguayo* (stuffed with ham and cheese) for US$7.50, and the like. Side salads are charged extra, and may be delivered without you ordering. Open Sun.–Wed. noon–midnight, and Thurs.–Sat. 24 hours.

Ditú MiConuco, Malecón, esq. E, is a thatched enclave with an open, often salt-sprayed patio. It offers inexpensive and basic *criollo* fare that draws locals, including pizzas (US$1.50) and forgettable burgers (US$1.35), plus three main dishes with side orders (US$2–5).

CONTINENTAL

Café Concerto Gato Tuerto, Calle O, e/ 17 y 19, tel. 55-2696 or 66-2224, is especially good for late-night dining. You can dine indoors, or on the breeze-swept balcony with a view over the Malecón. It serves sandwiches and *criollo-cum-continental* dishes, plus a consistently excellent grilled fish (US$12.50). The sweet-and-sour lobster (US$19) has been recommended. Open 8 P.M.–2 A.M.

Restaurante Monseigneur, Calle O, esq. 21, tel. 832-9884, opposite the entrance to the

Hotel Nacional, is a bit gauche for some tastes but soups, salads, and tortillas are a real bargain at US$2–3, and entrées are reasonably priced. The large menu leans to seafood, highlighted by *mar y tierra* (surf and turf) for US$20; but also includes filet mignon (US$9) and simpler dishes. Desserts include baked Alaska. Bring a sweater.

Comedor de Aguiar, Calle O, esq. 21, tel. 33-3564, in the Hotel Nacional, will burn a hole in your pocket. This super-elite restaurant fairly glitters with chandeliers and silverware. The waiters are liveried to the T and trained to provide top-notch service. And the creative and well-executed menu featuring creative international cuisine is highlighted by shrimp with rum flambé, and smoked salmon with capers and onion for starters (US$6–12). Main courses are priced US$12–36. Open 7 A.M.–midnight. You'll save money by heading downstairs to the hotel's **Buffet Veranda,** with a well done all-you-can-eat self-service continental buffet. Open 7–10 A.M., 11:30 A.M.–3 P.M., and 7–10 P.M.

Restaurante Hotel Victoria, Calle 19 #101, esq. M, tel. 33-3510, is conducive to romance, with lots of hardwoods, brass lamps, and gilt place settings. The menu—with an extensive wine list—offers grilled lobster (US$22), roasted snapper (US$12), filet mignon (US$11), and spaghetti with seafood (US$4). Open noon–midnight.

El Emperador, Calle 17, e/ M y N, tel. 832-4998, on the ground floor of the Focsa building, is favored by Cuban VIPs, but its Vincent Price decor—blood-red curtains and Louis XIV-style furnishings, and off-tune pianist—are a bit over the top. It serves soups and tortillas (US$2–4), plus Cuban staples and continental dishes such as *filet uruguayo* (US$8–25), but has lackluster service. Open 7–11 P.M.

La Torre, Calle 17 #155, e/ M y N, tel. 832-2451, atop the Focsa building, offers splendid all-around views over the city and some of the best cuisine in the city, although standards have slipped a bit since French chef Frank Picol has departed. His influence is still there, however, in the menu, which offers such tempting treats as roasted leg of lamb (all meats are imported) with garlic and

rosemary (US$16), and filet of beef in pastry with onion confilore and red wine (US$27), backed by a large selection of wines. The bar offers reasonable priced cocktails. Open noon–midnight—the bar is open 11:30 A.M.–12:30 A.M.

Don't be fooled by the pretensions to French cuisine advertised by the **Bar/Restaurante Potín,** Paseo, esq. Línea. It serves Cuban fare.

Restaurante 1830, Malecón #1252 y 20, tel. 55-3090, in a 1920s mansion just east of the Almendares tunnel, offers a choice of plush dining rooms. Service is now up to par, and the food has improved under recent, albeit departed, French management (although the chefs are now Cuban). One room serves continental cuisine, including a smoked Chilean salmon starter (US$6.75), and breast of duck in orange sauce (US$14.25). A second room serves sandwiches and snacks. Open noon–11:45 P.M.

The **Unión Francesa,** Calle 17 y 6, facing Parque Lennon, is a quasi-*paladar* in that it's the private restaurant of the French immigrants' association. Your dollars are sufficient to grant you "temporary membership."

Italian

The best place is **La Piazza Ristorante,** Paseo, e/ 1ra y 3ra, tel. 33-4501, on the first floor of the Hotel Cohiba. It offers 17 types of pizza (US$7–20), but also has minestrone (US$7.50), gnocchi (US$9.50), and seafood (from US$11). It has a baseball motif, incongruous with the Mediterranean decor. Bring a sweater against the air-conditioning. Service can be terribly slow, and the place can get smelly with smoke from the oven.

Restaurante Chez Menito, Avenida de los Presidentes, e/ Calzada y 5ta, in the Hotel Presidente, is old-world elegant and offers well-prepared Italian dishes for US$4–23.

Also recommended are **Dino's Pizza,** Calle 23, esq. L, a 24-hour fast-food joint serving basic pizzas for US$.40 a slice; **Pizza Nova,** Calle 17 y 12, tel. 204-6969, which delivers pizza with a US$2 delivery charge including 10 percent tip; and **Trattoria Marakas,** Calle O e/ 23 y 25, next to the Hotel Vedado, with reasonably priced Italian fare using real parmesan cheese.

Spanish

First and foremost, head to **Centro Vasco,** 3ra Avenida, esq. 4, tel. 833-9354. It was opened by a Basque in 1954 and retains its original modestly elegant decor, including a wall-to-wall mural showing Basque mountain scenes. It claims Basque cuisine, such as pickled octopus (US$6), paella (US$8.50), and seafood (US$5–20), but the preparation varies little from the usual Cuban fare. Bring a sweater, as the air-conditioning is usually cranked up full bore. Open noon–midnight.

Mesón La Chorrera, Malecón, esq. 20, tel. 862-0215, in the old fortress at the mouth of the Río Almendares, also specializes in Spanish cuisine and features ancient weaponry on the walls. And the **El Cortijo Restaurant,** Calle O, esq. 25, in the Hotel Vedado offers paella and sangría (US$8) and a few other Spanish dishes on its mostly *criollo* menu.

CHINESE

Restaurante Mandarín, Calle 23 #314, e/ L y M, below Cine Yara, tel. 832-0677, offers ho-hum Chinese dishes in a modestly Chinese ambience. It has a vegetarian fried rice special for US$4.25. Its chop sueys (US$6.50 to US$9) include shrimp or lobster options. Open noon–4 A.M.

The **Polinesio,** Calle 23, e/ L y M, tel. 55-4011, ext. 131, opposite the Mandarín and part of the Hotel Habana Libre Tryp, exudes Tahitian-style ambience, despite its quasi-Chinese cuisine. Hints of the South Seas find their way subtly into the menu—it used to be a Trader Vic's back in the 50s. Your overpriced meal might run upward of US$20, but it offers a lunch special for US$15 with *maripositas chinas* (fried wontons), cheese balls with sweet-and-sour sauce, mediocre barbecued chicken (prepared in a wood-fired stone oven to view), plus cocktail, dessert, and coffee. Open noon–3:30 P.M. and 7:30–11 P.M.

SURF AND TURF

Steak House Mirador Habana, Prado, esq. Malecón, on the 20th floor of the Hotel Habana Riviera offers all kinds of meat dishes, from steaks to sausage, pork, and ham. Open 6 P.M.–6 A.M.

Steak House Toro, Calle O #206, e/ 23 y 25, tel. 33-3740, in the Hotel St. John's, is a better bet. The menu ranges from pricey burgers (US$5) to 12-oz rib-eye (US$18), and T-bone steak (US$25), all served with rice or baked potatoes plus veggies. The meats are all imported from Canada. An all-you-can-eat roast beef special with beer or wine costs US$9.90. Open noon–midnight.

VEGETARIAN

Restaurante Biki, Infanta, esq. San Lázaro, tel. 879-6406, is a tremendous vegetarian outlet with an unusually varied buffet with stuffed eggplant (aubergine) and the like, plus salads (4.50 to 7 pesos, rice with veggies (7 pesos), and a wide range of natural juices (3 pesos). At last visit, foreigners could pay in pesos, but don't expect this to last. Open 10 A.M.–10 P.M.

Restaurante Naturista, Línea, esq. C, tel. 832-3453, is another reasonable bargain, and the setting in an old mansion is pleasant. Foreigners can pay in pesos. It offers tacos (2–4 pesos) in an open-air patio, and a larger vegetarian menu in the indoor restaurant, including salads (from 3.50 pesos), soups (5 pesos), tortillas, and paella (12 pesos), which proves to be rice and mixed veggies. Service is conscientious.

Restaurante El Carmelo de Calzada, Calzada, esq. D, tel. 832-4495, is another modern, clean vegetarian restaurant along the lines of Restaurante Biki; open 10 A.M.–10 P.M. Likewise, **La Terraza Vegetariana,** Calle M, e/ 23 y 25. Bring a sweater!

SNACK BARS

The 24-hour **Café La Rampa,** Calle L, esq. 23, outside the Habana Libre, is popular with Cubans and tourists alike. It has a special offer: sandwich, pizza, or burger with soft drink for US$5. The shaded patio of **Las Bulerias,** Calle L #414, e/ 23 y 25, tel. 832-3283, facing the Hotel Habana Libre Tryp on Calle L, serves *bocaditos, papas fritas,* and other simple fare for US$2–5. Open 24 hours.

Café 21, Calle 21, esq. N, opposite the Hotel

Capri, has a shaded patio and serves sandwiches, tortillas, and other items for a few dollars. The dark, air-conditioned restaurant next door—**Club 21**—has a dress code (no shorts) and serves soups, salads, and *criollo* dishes. Open 24 hours.

OTHER

Habana Café, Paseo e/ 1ra y 3ra, tel. 33-3636, next to the Hotel Meliá Cohiba, at the foot of Paseo, is Havana's version of the Hard Rock Café. It serves reasonable quality but overpriced burgers (from US$5) delivered American style with ketchup and mustard, plus sandwiches (US$6.50), Caesar salad (US$7.50), filet mignon (US$17), and such desserts as a "banana split" (US$5). Check your bill carefully, as scams are frequent.

CAFÉS, BAKERIES, AND ICE CREAM

There are no coffee shops along European or North American lines except for **Pain de Paris** Línea, e/ Paseo y A; and at Calle 25 #164 esq. O, tel. 33-3347. They sell excellent croissants and other pastries for less than US$1, plus sandwiches and coffees. Open 24 hours.

Coppelia, Calle 23, esq. Calle L, tel. 832-6149, serves ice cream of excellent quality in stainless steel bowls—Cubans complain that the quality has deteriorated in recent years. Tourists are normally steered toward a separate dollars-only section offering immediate service. *No way!* If you stick to your guns, foreigners are permitted to pay in pesos in any of half a dozen communal peso sections—choose from indoor or outdoor dining. Although the small dollar section offers the advantage of immediate service, an *ensalada* (three scoops) here costs US$2.60 while the peso sections offer larger *ensaladas* (five scoops) for only five pesos. A *jimagua* (two scoops) costs two pesos, and a *marquesita* (two scoops plus a sponge cage) costs 2.50 pesos. Want more? Ask for *adicional.* Forsake the dollar section and join the *cola* (line) to savor your ice cream with the Cubans—a far more rewarding experience—but be prepared for a *long* wait, especially on hot summer days. Note that some lines are for inferior (lower fat) Veradero ice cream. Open daily 11 A.M.–11 P.M. (closed Mon.).

Bim Bom, Calle 23, esq. Infanta, tel. 879-2892, at the bottom of La Rampa, is run along the lines of Baskin-Robbins and offers all kinds of sundaes for dollars. Unlike Coppelia, which normally has only one or two flavors, Bim Bom has several dozen. You even get fudge sauce.

Street stalls sell ice cream cones for about 2.50 pesos. However, the milk may not be pasteurized and hygiene is always a question.

SELF-CATERING

There's an *agropecuario* selling fruits and vegetables at Calle 19 between F and Avenida de los Presidentes, and a much smaller one at the corner of Calles 21 and J.

There is a grocery stocking Western goods, plus a bakery, on the north side of the Focsa building on Calle 17, between M and N. Open Mon.–Sat. 9 A.M.–6 P.M., and Sun. 9 A.M.–1 P.M.. Also try **Supermercado Meridiano,** 1ra, esq. Paseo, in the Galería del Paseo; open Mon.–Sat. 10 A.M.–5 P.M. and Sun. 10 A.M.–2 P.M..

The **Pescadería Especial,** Calle 25 between N and O, was selling shrimp for 22 pesos per pound, snapper (*pargo*) at 35 pesos per pound, and squid for 25 pesos per pound at last visit.

Playa (Miramar and Beyond)

PALADARES

Miramar is blessed with some of the best *paladares* in Havana.

La Esperanza, Calle 16 #105, e/ 1ra y 3ra, tel. 202-4361, is an exceptional *paladar* inside a 1930s middle-class home with a *sala* (lounge) full of art nouveau furnishings, antiques, books, historic photos and prints, and glass cabinets stuffed with intriguing knick-knacks. Tasteful jazz or classical music is normally playing. Most folks opt to eat in the gracious dining room (Delft platters line the walls), but you can opt for a tiny little plant-filled patio to the rear. Your waiter will read off the day's mouth-watering dishes . . . always unique French inspirations served with lively sauces. On my last visit, I enjoyed a superb eggplant *de ochún* (in honey) stuffed with chicken. The service is friendly and professional. And prices are fair (budget US$20 for a meal). A reservation is essential. Open 8 A.M.–4 P.M. and 7–11:30 P.M. Closed Thursday.

Cocina de Lilliam, Calle 48 #1311, e/ 13y and 15, Miramar, tel. 209-6514, is in the lush grounds of a 1939s era mansion romantically lit at night. It seats about 40 diners—three times the legal limit!—on a brick-lined patio shaded by arbors, with colonial lanterns and wrought-iron tables and chairs. Lilliam Domínguez, who is super attentive, conjures up tasty Cuban fare with a creative twist—call it nouvelle Cuban. Her appetizers include tartlets of tuna-and-onion, garbanzo-and-onion with three types of ham, and a savory dish of garbanzo beans and ham with onion and red and green peppers. Entrées include such Cuban classics as *ropa vieja* ("old clothes") of simmered lamb with onions and peppers; chicken breast with pineapple; plus fresh fish dishes and oven-roasted meats served with creamy mashed potatoes. You can opt for an air-conditioned dining room. Budget US$15–20 apiece. A reservation is essential, and it's a good idea to dine fairly early, as the house often runs out of more popular dishes by 9 P.M. Open noon–3 P.M., and 7–10 P.M. Closed Sunday, and August 1–15 plus December.

Paladar Doña Maricela, Calle 48 #310, e/ 13 y 15, tel. 832-1342, is set in a beautiful, old, high-ceilinged home with granite floors and more lavish furnishings than is the norm in contemporary Cuba. The menu offers some creative dishes such as red snapper in a sauce of tomatoes, onions and green peppers, though mostly it's a lively take on *criollo* fare, as with its fried *chicharrones* (pork rinds) and tender, oven-baked chicken *asado,* which is recommended. Lamb also features on the menu. Leave room for caramel-flavored flan. It's pricey however; budget US$15–20 for main plates. There's a full bar. Open noon to midnight.

Paladar Calle 10, Calle 10 #314, e/ 3ra y 5ta, tel. 209-6702, is to the rear of a mansion and features a dramatic recreation of a country theme, including thatched roofing and an outdoor *parillada* (grill). Very attractive! The limited menu features 10 house dishes, all creatively prepared and presented. I enjoyed a splendid *filete de salmon al ajillo* (garlic salmon). A reader described the *chivo* (young goat) stew as "succulent." The portions are huge, and the food tasty and filling. Live music is offered. Open 11 A.M.–midnight.

Paladar Vistamar, 1ra Avenida #2206, e/ 22 y 24, tel. 203-8328, in a modern house on the seafront, is popular for its high-quality cuisine and has the advantage of views over a pool and out to sea from the terrace through plate-glass windows. It serves continental fare as well as Cuban staples for US$10–18. Starters include fish cocktail (US$3) and mushroom soup (US$3.50), while main dishes include *pescado milanés* (US$12), and grilled fish with garlic (US$11.50). Set meals cost US$12. Open 11 A.M.–midnight.

Paladar Ristorante El Palio, 1ra Avenida #2402, esq. 24, one block west, serves Italian-*criollo* cuisine and is one of the most popular *paladares* in town for elite Cubans. Pastas, fettuccines, and seafood dishes average US$5. You dine on a shaded patio to the rear, with suitably Italian decor. No telephone. It's open noon–midnight.

La Fontana, 3ra Avenida #305, esq. 46, tel. 202-8337, specializes in barbecued meats from an outdoor grill serving T-bone steak! Starters include salads (US$1–3), *escabeche* (US$5), and onion soup (US$2.50); main dishes include a greasy fillet *grillé* with garlic (US$8). Rice and extras cost additional. Review your bill closely. Choose cellar or garden seating in a traditional country *bohío* setting, including seating beneath an arbor. It has caged birds and animals, including Pablo the friendly pelican. Service is hit or miss. Open noon–midnight.

Paladar Los Cactus de 33, Avenida 33 #3405, e/ 34 y 36, tel. 203-5139, in a fine mansion with overhead fans, plus photos of and letters from Che Guevara and rifles on the walls, is favored by European businessfolk and diplomats and has even been used as a setting for a TV shoot. The menu isn't anything special, however, and includes the usual *criollo* fare at inflated prices (US$7.50 to US$15). Open noon–midnight.

Sailors berthed at Marina Hemingway should head to **El Canal VB & SA,** 5ta Avenida #26402, e/ 264 y 266, tel. 209-8247, or **El Laurel,** 5ta Avenida #26002, e/ 260 y 262, tel. 209-7767, both overlooking the harbor channel and with patio dining with thatched *palapas.* The service at both is excellent, the food good, and prices for *criollo* dishes below US$10. El Laurel (open noon–11 P.M.) serves a usually fresh catch-of-the-day (US$8).

El Buganvíl, Calle 190 #1501, e/ 15 y 17, Siboney, tel. 271-4082, in the far west neighborhood of Siboney, is tucked down a tree-shaded street. It offers a *criollo* menu (US$8–15) but for a special treat the owners will prepare a *lechón asado* (roast suckling pig) for a minimum of six persons; you have to order at least 24 hours in advance.

CRIOLLO

I find myself returning time and again to **El Aljibe,** 7ma Avenida, e/ 24 y 26, tel. 204-1583, my favorite state-run restaurant in Havana, serving the best Cuban fare in town and popular with the Havana elite and foreign businessmen showing off their trophy Cuban girlfriends. You dine beneath a soaring bamboo roof. The superb house dish, the *pollo asado el aljibe,* is standard but far from ordinary—glazed with a sweet orange sauce whose ingredients are closely guarded, then baked and served with fried plantain chips, rice, French fries, and black beans served liberally (and literally) until you can eat no more. Feel free to take away what may be left over. It's a tremendous bargain at US$12—desserts and beverages cost extra. Other *criollo* dishes are served (US$10–20), but you really should order the house chicken. For dessert, try the flan, coconut pie, or chocolate cake. The bread and salad side dish delivered to your table will be charged to your bill even if you didn't order it, and a 10 percent service charge is automatically billed. The service is prompt and ultra-efficient even when the tour groups are in, so tip extra, as the service charge goes to the government, not the staff. Open noon–midnight.

Restaurante Criollo, Calle 26, esq. 7ma Avenida, tel. 204-2353 or 204-9662, in the Dos Gardenias complex next to El Aljibe, serves a whole meal for US$4, including bread, salad, beer (or soft drink) and main course of chicken, *aporreodo de ternera,* or *picadillo a la criolla.* It also has a roast beef special for US$9.90. Soups and salads—a plate of cucumber—cost US$1. Choose from chilly air-conditioned interior or outdoor patio dining. Open noon–midnight.

El Ranchón, 5ta Avenida, esq. 16, tel. 204-1185, is acclaimed as one of Havana's best restaurants, although it serves traditional Cuban cooking, notably grilled fish and meats (the grilled pork chops are particularly good). More creative dishes include a delicious appetizer of stuffed red peppers with tuna. Chef Juan Luís Rosalas prepares a daily special, from roast beef to lamb chops. The restaurant has good mixed salads. The food is well prepared and the portions are huge. Budget US$10–20. Open noon–midnight.

El Rancho Palco, Avenida 19, esq. Calle 140, tel. 208-9346, in jungly surroundings in the heart of Cubanacán, is a handsome, open-sided *bohío* with a terra-cotta floor, Tiffany-style lamps, and decor featuring saddles, wooden toucans, and parrots on swings. You can opt to dine on a patio or beneath thatch, or in an air-conditioned dining room. It serves meat dishes (US$10–30), seafood (US$12–26), and the usual *criollo* fare. Quality is hit or miss, ranging from undistinguished to near sublime, depending on your timing; on a good night it serves the best filet mignon (US$11) in Cuba. It offers floor shows at night. It is popular among the government elite. Scan your bill carefully! Open noon–11 P.M.

La Estancia Restaurant, Calle 158, e/ 29 y 31, tel. 33-7835, adjoins the Hotel Bellocaribe and offers a variety of air-conditioned rooms in an elegant colonial mansion. The tables arrayed around the intimate courtyard are preferable. It serves *criollo* fare, plus boneless chicken (US$8), filet mignon (US$12), and such rarities as blood sausage (US$2) and tuna salad (US$4). It offers a lunch and dinner special (US$14 and US$20, respectively). Bring a sweater!

SEAFOOD

Don Cangrejo, 1ra Avenida, e/ 16 y 18, tel. 204-4169, offers some of the finest seafood in town—it should; it's overseen by the Ministry of Fisheries—served in a converted colonial mansion with glass windows offering views over the flagstone patio—good on calm days for alfresco dining. The menu features such appetizers as crab cocktail (US$6), crab-filled wontons (US$3), house specialties such as crab claws (US$15), and garlic shrimp (US$12.50), plus paella, lobster, and fish dishes. The wine list runs to more than 150 labels. It's popular with the dollar-bearing Cuban elite and has been described as a "take on Joe's Stone Crab in Miami." Open noon–midnight.

CONTINENTAL

Paleta Bar y Amelia Restaurante, 3ra Avenida, e/ 70 y 82, tel. 204-7311, on the ground floor of the Miramar Trade Center, is an elegant contemporary restaurant decorated with modern art. The hip marble-topped bar is a fine place to bend your elbow. The fairly simple menu includes sandwiches, burgers (US$3), steaks, and the likes of shrimp enchiladas (US$7). Open 8 A.M.–midnight.

Restaurante Comodoro, 1ra Avenida y Calle 84, tel. 204-5551, in the Hotel Comodoro, is an elegant and romantic place with banquet seating and a creative menu that includes char-grilled filet mignon (US$8) and crocodile with onion and white wine (US$15). Open noon–midnight.

El Patio, 5ta Avenida, e/ 72 y 76, tel. 204-3584, in the Novotel Miramar, does a good job of presenting nouvelle cuisine, such as rabbit terrine with roasted horseradish (US$7) for a starter, and baked sea bream with basil cream sauce (US$15), and roasted pork loin (US$15).

Villa Diana, Calle 28A, Reparto Kohly, tel. 204-9232, ext. 621, offers an all-you-can-eat buffet for US$12. The fare, which claims to be continental, is really *criollo* with a hint of Europe. It has live music. Open noon–6 A.M.

Tocororo, Calle 18 #302, esq. 3ra Avenida, tel. 204-2209, housed in a neoclassical mansion, is a vastly overpriced and elitist restaurant where ordinary Cubans can't even think of setting foot. Supposedly, it's Gabriel García Márquez's favorite eatery; the Colombian novelist is known for his fondness for fine food, but here he seems to have missed the beat. The antique-filled lobby extends out into a garden patio with rattan furniture, Tiffany lamps, and heaps of potted plants, wooden toucans and parrots hanging from gilt perches, and real *cotorros* (parrots) in cages. A pianist and jazz ensemble entertain. The food is typical Cuban fare with an international twist. Or is it international with a *criollo* twist? Try the grilled lamb chops and mixed seafood brochette or local favorites such as *frijoles*. Expect to pay from US$25 for a run-of-the-mill grilled steak; and watch for the 10 percent service charge. The wines, reputedly, are "normally in bad condition." Open noon–midnight.

La Cecilia, 5ta Avenida #11010, e/ 110 y 112, tel. 204-1562 or 202-6700, is another elegant option in the middle of a large garden. Most of the tables are outdoors and lit by Tiffany lamps surrounded by bamboo. It serves typical Cuban dishes such as *ajiaco* (a stew), *tasajo* (jerked beef), *churrasco* (broiled steak), and *pollo con mojo* (chicken with onion and garlic), as well as grilled lobster. Entrées cost US$12–25. It has a lengthy wine list at reasonable prices. It hosts a *cabaret espectáculo* Thurs.–Sun. 9 P.M.–2 A.M. Open noon–midnight.

La Ferminia, 5ta Avenida #18207, e/ 182 y 184, tel. 271-0360, competes, though less competently. This antique-filled restaurant, in a colonial mansion, is a training restaurant for newbie service staff. It has six private rooms, each in a separate color scheme—the pink room is full of Meissen porcelain—and you can also dine on an outside patio beneath a timbered roof. The menu includes onion soup (US$4), filet mignon with port (US$10), and salmon with red wine (US$14); the house specialty is a mixed grill (US$28) with shrimp, lobster, fish, chicken, and scallops. Food often comes to your table cold; and the staff have a habit of charging for items you never ordered . . . so check your bill! The large wine list includes California, Australia, and South Africa labels. Open noon–midnight.

Complejo Turístico La Giraldilla, Calle 222 e/ 37 y 51, tel. 33-0568, fax 33-6390, gerencia @giralda.cha.cyt.cu, in La Coronela, is well-worth the long journey. It serves recherché nouvelle dishes under the baton of foreign management (Argentinian at last visit). Choose from a selection of dining rooms, including the Bistro Gourmet, with a stunning beamed ceiling and National Heritage furnishings; and El Patio Los Naranjos, serving *criollo* dishes alfresco (it has a US$12 six-course special). I enjoyed a superb creamed vegetable soup (US$4), sautéed prawns in garlic (US$17), and sautéed salmon (US$19). The gazpacho (US$4.50) and lobster in Ricard sauce are also recommended. On Saturdays it hosts a US$18 "La Noche del Búfalo" special for steak lovers. La Bodega del Vino basement tapa bar serves everything from tacos to chicken mole, washed down with sangría. With more than 200 labels, it has Havana's largest wine list. Open 10 A.M.–5 A.M. A well-stocked cigar store guarantees postprandial pleasures. Diners who spend US$25 get free entrance to the Macumba disco and cabaret.

Restaurante Pedregal, Avenida 25, esq. 198, La Lisa, tel. 33-7832, is an elegant modern restaurant and dramatic architectural statement in Frank Lloyd Wright style, with natural stone walls, marble floors, lofty wooden ceilings, and a lush jungle-like ambience. The ambitious menu features cream of asparagus soup (US$2), filet mignon (US$12), grilled diced tenderloin with gravy and mustard (US$14), and lobster tail with pineapple (US$24).

Italian

The **Ristorante Italiano,** 7ma Avenida, esq. 26, in the Dos Gardenias complex, offers undistinguished pizzas, spaghettis, and raviolis for less than US$5. Take your sweater. Open noon–midnight. Nearby, the Quinta and 42 commercial complex houses the flashy looking **Ristorante Italiano Rossini,** 5ta-A Avenida, esq. 40, tel. 204-2072.

La Terraza di Roma, 3ra Avenida y Calle 84, tel. 204-5551, in the Hotel Comodoro, is an excellent option. The menu features calamari (US$4.25), antipasti (US$2), risotto (US$4–7), and main dishes for US$8 to US$18. Open noon–midnight.

La Cova Pizza Nova, 5ta Avenida, esq. 248, tel. 204-1150, in Marina Hemingway, has good pizza. Unlike most places in Cuba, you can design your own topping combinations. It offers takeaway service (11:30 A.M.–midnight), but you have to pick up yourself. Open 11 A.M.–1 A.M. Also here is **La Fiesta,** tel. 204-1150, serving paella and calamari house specials, as well as *brocheta* (kebab) and tuna salads. It has a resident band. Open Tues.–Sun. 1–9 P.M.

ASIAN

Pavo Real, 7ma Avenida #205, e/ Calle 2 y 4, tel. 204-2315, has quintessential Chinese decor but serves undistinguished Chinese classics such as chow mein dishes for US$7 and up, plus Japanese tempura (US$9 and up), and Thai chicken (US$6.50). Open noon–midnight. It was recently renovated.

Shanghai, 7ma Avenida, esq. Calle 26, in the Los Gardenias complex, has soups (US$1.50), chow mein (US$6.50), and set plates (US$4–5) and combination plates (US$7–10).

El Morambón, 5ta Avenida, esq. 32, tel. 203-3336, may satisfy a hankering for grilled eels, *kim ch'i, chu'sok,* and other Korean specialties. The cuisine is lackluster and overpriced, but you can eat it until 2 A.M.

Sakura, Calle 18, esq. 3ra, tel. 204-2209, in

the Tocororo, is Cuba's first Japanese restaurant. Small and quaint, it serves sushi and traditional Japanese dishes, plus sake and Japanese beers. The sushi menu is understandably restricted, but the quality is surprisingly good. Miso soup (US$3), tempura (US$12), and sashimi (US$12) are served. It's open noon–midnight.

OTHER

La Pampa, 3ra Avenida, esq. Calle 84, tel. 33-2028, fax 33-1168, in the Hotel Comodoro, specializes in Argentinian dishes such as *morcillas* (blood sausage) and *chinchulines* (grilled tripe stuffed with garlic).

Mi Jardín, Calle 66 #517, esq. 5ta Avenida B, tel. 203-4627, is a private restaurant (*paladar*) run by an affable and conscientious Mexican from Michoacán and his Italian wife. They serve genuine Mexican fare . . . well, as much as the government prohibition on beef allows. The chicken *mole cubano* is recommended. You'll also find enchiladas, nachos *(topopas),* and *papas fritas con mojo* (chips with garlic with salsa), plus Italian and *criollo* dishes. Save room for the spiced ice cream! Open noon–midnight.

SNACK BARS

Pan.Com (pronounced "Pan-punto-com"), Calle 26, esq. 7ma, makes every kind of sandwich (including club and turkey) for US$1.50 to US$3.85. It also has omelets, burgers (US$2.50), tortillas (US$1), yogurts, fruit juices, *batidos* (milk shakes), and cappuccinos. Open 6 A.M.–3 A.M.

CAFÉS, BAKERIES, AND ICE CREAM

Pain de Paris, Calle 26 e/ 5ta y 7ma, in the Dos Gardenias complex, is good for cappuccinos and an excellent range of croissants; open 6 A.M.–midnight. There's another at Avenida 26, esq. Kohly, tel. 55-5125. You can also buy delicious pastries, loaves, and iced cakes at **Nonaneli Panadería Dulcería,** 5ta Avenida, esq. Calle 42, in the Quinta y 42 shopping complex. And **La Francesa del Pan,** Calle 42, esq. 19, tel. 204-2211, sells a variety of quality breads and baked goods.

Bosque de la Habana, 3ra Avenida, e/ 78 y 80, tel. 204-8500, in the Hotel Meliá Habana, is an ice-cream store with an excellent choice of baked desserts. Open 24 hours.

"Rum Hut," 7ma Avenida, e/ 2 y 4, opposite Pavo Real, is recommended by student Bridget Murphy for sundry groceries, large bowls of ice cream, and chocolate ice cream cakes (US$1.50).

SELF-CATERING

Supermercado 70, 3ra Avenida, e/ 62 y 70, Miramar, is Cuba's largest supermarket, with all manner of imported foodstuffs. Prices are exorbitant. It's popular with diplomats from Africa, Vietnam, and North Korea, who get a 33 percent discount and load up their shopping carts to overflowing . . . then brazenly sell the produce outside their diplomatic residences to Cubans by undercutting the *diplo* prices.

There are lesser supermarkets in the **Miramar Trade Center,** 3ra Avenida, e/ 70 y 82; at **Comercio Náutico,** 5ta Avenida y 152, tel. 208-6812; and **Centro Comercial La Vigía,** 5ta Avenida, esq. 248, tel. 204-1151, at Marina Hemingway (open Mon.–Sat 10 A.M.–7 P.M., Sun. 10 A.M.–2 P.M.).

You can buy peso wine and sangría at various street outlets, but you'll need to bring your own bottle. Try the corner of Avenida 31 and Calle 36 (recommended as the best place for sangría by student Bridget Murphy); or 7ma Avenida, e/ 4 y 6; and Calle 6, e/ 3ra y 5ta Avenidas, where you can get beet wine, and other creative concoctions. You may need to ask on the street.

Entertainment and Recreation

Entertainment

OK, so the bar scene is dismal. But don't believe anything you've read about Communism having killed the capital city's zest. *Habaneros* love to paint the town red (so to speak). You can still find as much partying as party line in Havana, especially in the realm of music—the pulsing undercurrent of Cuban life. Author Norman Mailer scolded President Kennedy for the Bay of Pigs defeat by asking, "Wasn't there anyone around to give you the lecture on Cuba? Don't you sense the enormity of your mistake—you invade a country without understanding its music."

Legendary jazz names such as Chucho Valdés (perhaps the world's greatest jazz pianist) and his band Irakere play

venues throughout the city, including such hole-in-the-wall spots as La Zorra y el Cuervo, while big-name salsa bands such as Los Van Van and NG La Banda play glitzy function rooms such as at the Hotel Riviera, where the local girls and guys grind against each other to the smoldering music. *Son* ballads popularized by the Buena Vista Social Club are heard all over town . . . often performed by the maestros themselves. Meanwhile, younger musicians such as the Orishas experiment with rap music. Cubans even enjoy the anguished, melancholy verses of the tango, which sprang from Buenos Aires's brothels almost a century ago but perfectly fits Cuba's mood today.

Above all, Havana pulsates with the Afro-Latin spirit, be it energy-charged musical sessions or

May Day Parade, Plaza de la Revolución

THE BUENA VISTA SOCIAL CLUB

In 1996, eclectic U.S. slide guitarist Ry Cooder made a musical pilgrimage to Cuba in search of a clique of legendary but largely forgotten veteran musicians to make a comeback album, the *Buena Vista Social Club*, named for a Havana venue where many of the artists performed in the fifties. German film director Wim Wenders tagged along with his Beta steadicam to chronicle how Cooder rounded up the half-forgotten relics of prerevolutionary Cuba, ushered them into recording studios, and in a rare perfect mixture of studio chemistry cut an album of sepia-toned tunes and dispatched them on a wildly successful world tour. The documentary celebrates the elderly musicians' performance on the world stage and offers a portrait of their life back in an impoverished Cuba.

The tender heart of the movie is crooner Ibrahim Ferrer, a soft-spoken septuagenarian who had been a singer with the legendary Benny Moré band in the 1950s, but who was shining shoes at the time Cooder's team rediscovered him for the "Buena Vista" album. His weathered yet still nimble voice is supported by the arthritic fingers of 76-year-old pianist Rubén González, creator in the early 1940s of the modern Cuban piano sound, flying into action after long retirement—his piano had been reduced to dust by termites when Cooder brought him back from obscurity; the slick guitar work of 90-odd-year-old Francisco Repalido, known as "Compay Segundo," the grandfather of *son* music, who plays in his trademark Panama hat; guitarist Eliades Ochoa, a maestro of the *guajira* (country lament), easily recognized in his trademark cowboy hat; and the dulcet voice of Omara Portuono, who was once one of the leading *bolero* singers in Cuba.

This suave old bunch of codgers wowed the world when the documentary movie, produced by Cooder, was released in 1999, swept the United States, and introduced it to the richness of *son, danzón,* and bolero in a style untouched by contemporary trends. The result was a runaway success. The CD (by the London-based World Circuit label) won the Grammy for Tropical Music and topped the charts among Latin albums, taking Cuban music international for the first time, selling more than a million copies worldwide, and creating international nostalgia for the old Havana whose charmingly dilapidated streets are the setting for Wenders' wonderful movie.

You can buy the CD at a discount at www.cubabooks.com.

---

the sacred chantings of *santería*. If it's a *santería* saint's day, you might get whisked in off the street to attend someone's home-based celebration, where drummers beat out thumping rhythms and you are pulled bodily and irresistibly to dance overtly sexual *changüí* numbers. Dance, from the earliest *guaguancó* to the mambo craze, has always been a potent expression of an enshrined national tradition—Cuban sensualism. *Guaguancó* is an erotic rumba—"a vertical suggestion of a horizontal intention," it has been called—in which the man tries to make contact with the woman's groin with whatever part of his body he can, and the woman dances defensively, like a female *matador* with a bull. Girls are whisked onto the dance floor and whirled through

a flurry of complicated steps and sensuous undulations, the intensity of which makes their North American counterparts look like butlers practicing the waltz. Young or elderly, every Cuban undulates with coquetry, swaying to the rhythm just a little closer than cheek to cheek. It's a wonder Havana's birth rate isn't higher.

Sure, the city has lost the Barbary Coast spirit of prerevolutionary days, when, according to Graham Greene, "three pornographic films were shown nightly between nude dances" in the Shanghai Theater. But at night, the pace still quickens. Nowhere else in the Caribbean has as many discotheques, cinemas, and cabarets to choose from, even if many venues are slightly rundown—many of the famous clubs from the "sordid era," which ended in the 1950s, remain in name, their neon signs reminders of what was. Many—those still used by Cubans—are seedier than they were three decades ago, albeit without the strippers, and often somewhat surreal, too, because in many the decor hasn't changed.

Nonetheless, Havana is catching on to modern times. Hip cigar lounges, trendy bistro-bars, and takeoffs on the internationally renowned Hard Rock Café have even begun to appear. Almost all boast live music, everything from salsa bands to folkloric trios. Romantic crooners are a staple, wooing local crowds with dead-on deliveries of Benny Moré classics while sensual all-female bands entice tourists with the ubiquitous *"bésame, bésame mucho . . ."* The best musicians tend to move from bar to bar like Latino lovers as "in" places get discovered, up their prices, and lose favor.

Havana also offers earthy discos (called cabarets) and *centros nocturnos* (open-air discotheques) serving the locals, who with few exceptions are deprived of access to tourist spots by high dollar prices—many venues to which entrance was once free now have a cover charge.

More cultured entertainment is present aplenty. Since the Revolution, the government's sponsorship of the arts has yielded a rich harvest in every field. The Centro Nacional de Escuelas de Arte (National Center of Schools of Art), created in 1960, has 41 schools in Havana under its umbrella, including the national Escuela de la Música, a national folkloric school, two ballet schools, two fine arts schools, and a school of modern dance. The graduates are superbly trained, despite great shortages of instruments, sheet music, leotards, dance shoes, paints, brushes, and other materials. And each *municipio* has a *Casa de la Trova* where you can hear traditional ballad-style *trova* (love songs rendered with the aid of guitar and drum), often blended with revolutionary themes; and a *Casa de la Cultura*, which hosts movies, art exhibitions, and other cultural events for the locals. Havana also has ongoing music concerts, choral recitals, and art and sculpture exhibits. The only fault to be found is the quality of Cuban theater.

The scene is fluid. Sudden restrictions imposed by the government occasionally put a damper on Havana's nightlife. All of which means that *habaneros* mostly socialize impromptu, on the street. *Peñas* (private soirées on an artistic and literary theme) are a staple, usually hosted at someone's home; many have become a permanent fixture of the weekly or monthly calendar thanks to the *apagones* (electricity blackouts that often close down nightclubs) and tourism-inspired commercialization that keeps such nightclubs beyond the means of most Cubans.

Caution!: Several clubs apply a *consumo mínimo* (minimum charge) policy, which sometimes applies to the entire evening and sometimes to the first purchase. The system is rife with *trampas* (frauds) and *estafas* (swindles). For example, if a US$5 *consumo mínimo* applies to your first purchase and you order several beverages during the evening, be sure that the first drink you order is a more expensive drink—you'll be charged US$5 even for a mineral water—and that any inexpensive item you might order later in the evening doesn't appear as the first drink on your bill.

Resources

Havana lacks a reliable, widely-circulated forum for announcements of upcoming events. Word of mouth is the best resource—there are no posters or flyers. Ask around, and keep your ears open, otherwise important events and major *artiste* appearances will have come and gone before you get wind. Note that *none* of the publications below is entirely trustworthy. If you read about an event, call ahead to double-check dates, times, and venue.

The weekly newspaper *Cartelera* publishes information on exhibitions, galleries, performances, and TV programming. It's available in many hotel lobbies, and at the editorial office, Calle 15 #602, e/ B y C, Vedado, tel. 33-3732. Another reasonable source is the monthly *Guía Cultural de la Habana*, Calle 4 #205 e/ Línea y 11, Vedado, tel. 832-9691. It provides up-to-date information on what's on in town, as does the monthly *La Isla: Catálogo Cultural*, Calle 21 #459, e/ E y F, Vedado, tel. 55-3840, juglar @juglar.get.tur.cu. Free copies are distributed at tour desks in leading hotels. *Granma*, the daily Communist Party newspaper, also lists the forthcoming week's events.

Radio Taíno (FM 93.3), serving tourists, offers information on cultural happenings, as does **Hurón Azul,** the tourist TV program that airs Thursdays at 10 P.M.

Paradiso: Promotora de Viajes Culturales, Calle 19 #560 esq. C, Vedado, tel. 832-6928, fax 33-3921, paradis@turcult.get.cma.net, www.ceniai.inf.cu/paradiso, promotes artistic and cultural events, festivals, courses, seminars, workshops, and conferences in the arts, sciences, and technology. It also arranges participatory courses for foreigners in cultural courses.

The leading cultural website is that of **Centro de Informática y Sistemas Aplicados a la Cultura** (CEISIC), tel. 55-2270, fax 55-1804, www.cult.cu, which provides a thorough listing on events . . . although, alas, only in Spanish at press time.

FESTIVALS AND EVENTS

During the mid-1980s, Cuba was a rest-and-relaxation capital for the Latin Left—Havana is still popular with South Americans, who flock to the Latin American Film Festival, Havana Jazz Festival, and other annual world-class cultural extravaganzas. The annual calendar is filled with cultural events, including *cumbanchas,* the Cuban equivalent of street parties, also called *rumbas,* or sprees that might go on all night and that almost always involve traditional Afro-Cuban music and dance.

For a list of forthcoming festivals, conferences, and events, contact **Paradiso,** Calle 19 #560 esq. C, Vedado, tel. 832-6928, fax 33-3921, paradis@turcult.get.cma.net, www.ceniai.inf.cu/paradiso, or the **Buró de Convenciones,** Calle 146 e/ 11 y 13, Playa, tel. 202-6011, fax 271-9496, buroconv@buroconv.mit.tur.cu.

Religious Events

Religious parades were suppressed following the Revolution and are still few. The noted exception is the **Procesión de los Milagros** (Procession of the Miracles) each December 17, when hundreds of pilgrims—many of them dragging stones or crawling on their knees—make their way to the Santuario de San Lázaro, the "leper of the miracles," to beseech a miracle or give thanks for miracles they imagine he has granted.

Daily Events

Be sure to attend the **Ceremonia del Cañonazo** (Cannon Ceremony), tel. 862-0671, held nightly at 9 P.M. at the Fortaleza de San Carlos de la Cabaña, where troops dressed in 18th-century military garb light the fuse of a cannon to announce the closing of the city gates, maintaining a tradition going back centuries. You are greeted at the castle gates by soldiers in traditional uniform, and the place is lit by flaming lanterns. About 8:50 P.M., a cry rings out, announcing the procession of soldiers marching across the plaza bearing muskets, while a torch-bearer lights flaming barrels. The soldiers ascend to the cannon, which they prepare with ramrod. Latter-day soldiers have pre-prepared the explosives and are on hand to guard the show. When the soldier puts the torch to the cannon, you have about three seconds before the thunderous boom. Your heart skips a beat. But it's all over in a millisecond, and the troops march away.

Your US$3 entrance (US$5 after 6 P.M.) to the castles includes the ceremony and museums. Be sure to get there no later than 8:30 P.M. if you wish to secure a place close to the cannon. The ceremony is popular with Cuban families, and the place gets jam-packed.

Hotel tour desks offer excursion tours. Some agencies combine the ceremony with a cabaret.

Weekly Events

The place to be on Sunday at noon is "Salvador's Alley" for **Rumba del "Salvador's Alley,"** Callejón de Hamel, e/ Aramburo y Hospital, a narrow pedestrian alley linking Calzada de Infanta and San Lazaro in Cerro. Here, Salvador González Escalona, tel. 878-1661, callejondehamel@hotmail.com, hosts a weekend *rumba* with Afro-Cuban music and dance in an alley painted from pavement to sky in gaudy tropical murals. The house band, Clave y Guaguancó, is one of the best *rumba* groups in Cuba. Sunday 11 A.M.–3 P.M.

González also hosts a traditional music night every last Friday of the month at 8:30 P.M.

Habaguanex hosts the **Noches en la Plaza**

Rumba del "Salvador's Alley"

(Nights in the Plaza), supposedly every Saturday at 9 P.M., although in actuality the calendar is fickle. Take your pick of Plaza de la Catedral or Plaza de San Francisco. It's a glorious evening in either plaza, when a *criollo* dinner is served and a folkloric *espectáculo* takes place on the steps of the cathedral. The wide-ranging entertainment includes the Conjunto Folklórico JJ, ballet, and *boleros* (ballads). Tickets cost US$14 with appetizers and drinks, or US$22 with dinner. Reservations can be made at tour agencies or through Habaguanex, Calle Oficios #110, e/ Lamparilla y Amargura, tel. 867-1034 or 860-6686, www.habaguanex.cu.

Annual Events

Each *municipio* has its own cultural festival, featuring live music. In addition, the following annual events are held:

January: The **Cabildos** festival is held on January 6, when Habana Vieja resounds with festivities recalling the days when Afro-Cuban *cabildos* danced through the streets in vivid costumes and painted faces. Contact Habaguanex (Calle Oficios #110, e/ Lamparilla y Amargura, tel. 867-1034 or 860-6686, www.habaguanex.cu).

February: Literati and bookworms should time their visit to coincide with the **Feria Internacional del Libro Habana** (Havana Book Fair), organized by the Instituto Cubano del Libro (Cuban Book Institute), Calle O'Reilly #14, Habana Vieja, tel. 862-8091, in Plaza de Armas.

March: The **Festival de Música Electroacústica** (Electroacoustic Music Festival), is a biennial held every even-numbered year, with various cafés and cultural centers as venues. Contact the Instituto Cubano de la Música (ICM), Calle 15, esq. F, Vedado, tel. 832-8298, icm@cubarte.cult.cu.

April: April 4 is the **Día de los Niños** (Day of Children), when venues throughout the city host special entertainment for kids.

The **Festival Internacional de Percusión** (International Percussion Festival), tel. 203-8808, percuba@mail.com, is also held each April.

May: When May 1 rolls around, head to the Plaza de la Revolución for the **Primero de Mayo** (May Day Parade). The day is meant to honor workers and is intended to appear as a spontaneous demonstration of revolutionary loyalty. In reality it is a carefully choreographed affair—hundreds of buses bring workers and children from surrounding regions. While loyalists display genuine enthusiasm, the majority of attendees

CARNAVAL!

Havana's Carnaval, which was initiated in the city to promote tourism in the early 1930s, was revived in 1996 after a five-year hiatus. Tourists throw inhibitions to the wind and join local residents in colorful pre-Lenten revelry as traditional *comparsas* (music and dance troupes originally tied to slaves' tribe of origin) parade through the streets. The party mood is highlighted by outdoor concerts, street fairs, conga lines, and colorful parades. While many performers go lavishly gowned, others ecstatically flaunt their freedom, having cast off customary controls along with most of their clothing.

Carnaval in Cuba has been performed since the 19th century, when it was an Easter celebration. Originally it was called the Fiesta de las Mamarrachos (Festival of the Nincompoops), when slaves were given time off and the opportunity to release their pent-up energies and frustrations in a celebration full of sinister and sexual content. The celebration was bound irrevocably to the secret societies of ancient Africa, transformed in Cuba into neighborhood societies called *carabalí* that vied with one another to produce the most colorful and elaborate processions (*comparsas*) led by a frenzied melée of fife, drum, and maracas. There are representations of the *orishas* (gods) in the *comparsas* and characters representing the various gods lead the way. Since each *comparsa* comes from a different neighborhood, each dance and tune varies.

Most prominent in Havana's Carnaval history were the parades of the Los Marquesas de Atares. The *comparsas* were brought together by the *rumberos, santeros,* and *abakuas* of the Atares district. It was they who infused the traditional Afro-Cuban folkloric with the pantomime mockery of aristocratic society by introducing ceremonial dances and fabulous gowns. The celebrants dressed in period costume, such as dress coats and wigs worn beneath three-cornered hats, and danced minuets to the rhythms of drums, pans, maracas, and the shrill melodies of trombones. The Los Marquesas *comparsa* is still a traditional component of Havana Carnaval, as is La Jardinera *comparsa*, which recreates a garden theme and derives from the Jesús del Monte district; and El Alacrán *comparsa*, representing the Cerro district and showing by stages the killing of a grass snake and scorpion.

Havana builds gradually towards Carnaval, which is usually not announced, and lasts one to two weeks. The hour-glass drums of the ancestors begin to pound out their *tun q'tu q'tu q'-tun* rhythm (the most common drum is the tall, cone-shaped *bocué*). The wail of Chinese cornets (*corneta china*) and clatter of bells adds to the racket as troupes of dancers in gay costumes shake themselves into an erotic frenzy. The conga lines full of clowns and celebrants in colonial period dress are followed by floats (sponsored by various Cuban agencies) graced by girls (*luceros*—morning stars) in riotous feathers and sequined bikinis or outrageous dresses. Huge papier-mâché heads supported by dancing Cubans bash into each other. Young and old alike find a release from the melancholy of everyday life, culminating in a beer-infused, sexually charged orgy of dance.

The main procession takes place on the Malecón, where viewing stands are erected for spectators. Every year there's a different theme, and contestants are judged on originality and popularity.

attend for fear of being black-marked by CDRs and party officials at work. The disaffected scoff and stay home. Cuban stooges use the tannoys to work up the crowd with chants of *"Viva Fidel!"* Gone are the days when Soviet tanks and missiles were paraded. Today, the overriding theme reflects the anti-U.S. flavor of the day; thus, the 2002 parade was heavily imbued with denunci-ations of U.S. bombing in Afghanistan and calls for release of five Cuban spies—"political prisoners," says Fidel—jailed in 2001 in Miami. You'll be surrounded by as many as 500,000 people waving colorful banners and placards and wearing T-shirts painted with revolutionary slogans. Castro applauds from the viewing stand in saintly fashion.

The **Feria Internacional del Disco "Cubadisco"** (International Record Show), hosted by ICM (see March events), is a week-long music festival in which the best album of the year is decided. The various musicians perform at venues throughout Havana.

The **Havana Cup Yacht Race** is an annual boat race from Florida to Havana. Typically, 100 to 250 yachts compete in the race to Havana's Marina Hemingway, 5ta Avenida y Calle 248, tel. 204-1150, fax 204-1149, comercial @comermh.cha.cyt.cu.

The **Festival Internacional de Guitarra** (International Guitar Festival & Contest), hosted by ICM (see March events), is a biennial usually held at the Teatro Roldán in even-numbered years.

June: The **Festival Internacional Boleros de Oro** (International Boleros Festival), sponsored by the National Union of Writers and Artists of Cuba (UNEAC), Calle 17 #351, e/ G y H, Vedado, tel. 832-4551, fax: 33-3158, uneac@ cubarte.cul.cu, features traditional folk music, with artists from Cuba, Spain, and Latin America.

The **Encuentro International de Bandas de Conciertos** (International Concert Band Festival) is held in odd-numbered years and features big-bands playing sounds from the Glenn Miller era.

July: The **Carnaval de La Habana** (Carnaval in Havana), tel. 832-3742, atic@cubarte.cult.cu, is held the last two weekends of July and the first two weekends of August, when thousands of *habaneros* take to the streets and for an entire week, the Malecón becomes a stage for the island's hottest folkloric, salsa, and jazz groups. It's an amateurish affair compared to the more lavish festivals of Rio de Janeiro and Trinidad, but its fun nonetheless . . . and free. Beware pickpockets; don't take valuables!

The **Coloquio Internacional Hemingway** (International Hemingway Colloquium), takes place in early July every odd-numbered year, with international experts in attendance. It draws literary figures to the somewhat solemn debates and study sessions. The venue changes each year.

The **Festival Nacional de Humor** (National Comedy Festival), tel. 832-3914, cph@cubarte .cult.cu, takes place at the Teatro Mella and other venues. You'll need to be fluent in Spanish.

August: Every odd year sees the **Festival Internacional de Música Popular Benny Moré**, named for the popular Cuban composer-singer referred to as *lo más bárbaro del ritmo* (the guy with the most terrific rhythm). The festival features a panorama of popular Cuban music. The festival takes place in Havana concurrently with events in Cienfuegos.

The **Festival de Rap de Alamar** (Alamar Rap Festival), in late August, brings U.S. hip-hop groups to perform alongside Cuba's best rap groups in a most unlikely venue: the Anfiteatro de Alamar and the Casa de la Cultura de Alamar, Calle 164, esq. 5taB, Zona 7, Alamar, tel. 65-0624. For information, contact the Asociación Hermanos Saíz, La Magriguera, Quinta de los Molinos, Avenida Salvador Allende, e/ Infanta y Luaces, Vedado, tel. 879-8175.

Cuba Danza (Dance Cuba), tel. 879-6410, cnae@min.cult.cu, featuring modern dance performances and workshops, is hosted every even-numbered year by the Danza Contemporáneo de Cuba.

September: The 10-day biennial **Festival Internacional de Teatro** (International Theater Festival of Havana), sponsored by the Consejo Nacional de Artes Escénicas (National Council of Scenic Arts), Calle 4 #257, Miramar, tel. 832-4126, is held in odd-numbered years and features international theater companies covering drama, street theater, musicals, and contemporary and traditional dance.

Los Días de la Música (Days of Music), sponsored by the Asociación Hermanos Saíz (see August), features performances by lesser-known musicians, including rock, rap, and *nueva trova*.

October: The annual **Festival de La Habana de Música Contemporáneo** (Havana Festival of Contemporary Music) spans a week in early October. Venues include the Teatro Nacional, Gran Teatro, La Casa de las Américas, and the Basílica de San Francisco de Asís, with performances ranging from choral to electro-acoustic. Contact UNEAC (see June).

The **Festival Internacional de Ballet** (International Ballet Festival) features dancers and choreographers from around the world—the Bolshoi, New York City Ballet, and Opera de

Paris have performed in past years— as well as the acclaimed Ballet Nacional de Cuba (BNC). Contact the BNC, Calzada #510 e/ D y E, Vedado, Ciudad Habana, C.P. 10400, tel. 832-4625, www.balletcuba.cu; or Paseo de Martí (Prado) #207, Habana Vieja, tel. 862-7053.

November: The annual **Festival de San Cristóbal de la Habana** celebrates the anniversary of the founding of the city with a wide range of musical, theatrical, and other performances.

The prestigious **Bienal de la Habana** (Havana Biennial), hosted in even-numbered years by the Centro Wilfredo Lam, Calle San Ignacio #22, tel. 861-2096 and 861-3419, wlam@art soft.cult.cu, www.cnap.cult.cu, features artists from more than 50 countries around the world. It features workshops in printmaking and other disciplines, as well as soirées and other activities held in venues throughout Habana Vieja.

The **Festival de Raíces Africanas "El Wemilere"** (Festival of African Roots), tel. 97-0202, paradis@turcult.get.cma.net, which honors African folkloric traditions, takes place at venues throughout Guanabacoa.

December: The **Festival del Nuevo Cine Latinoamericano** (International Festival of New Latin-American Cinema, also known as the Latin American Film Festival) is one of Cuba's most glittering events. Castro is usually on hand, schmoozing with Hollywood actors and directors in the lobbies of the Hotel Nacional and Habana Libre. The menu of movies—shown at more than 20 cinemas and theaters across the city—includes films from throughout the Americas and Europe and culminates with Cuba's own version of the Oscar: the Coral prizes. This being Cuba, you buy your tickets for particular cinemas well before the programming is announced; or you can buy a pass (US$25) good for the duration of the festival. For further information, contact the Instituto de Cinematografía, Calle 23 #1155, Vedado, tel. 831-3145, 833-4634, or 55-2418, cinemateca@icaic.inf.cu, www.havana filmfestival.com.

The biennial star-studded **Festival Internacional de Jazz** (International Havana Jazz Festival) is held mid-month in even-numbered years, highlighted by the greats of Cuban jazz, such as Chucho Valdés and Irakere, Los Van Van, Juan Formell, and Grupo Perspectiva. Concerts are held at various venues, including the Hotel Riviera's Salón Internacional and Teatro Nacional. For information, contact ICM (see March). Prearranged group tours to the festival are offered through **Plaza Cuba**, P.O. Box 318135, San Francisco, CA 94131, 510/848-0911, plaza cuba@yahoo.com, www.plazacuba.com, in the US. In Canada, **Vacation Culture Cuba,** 5059 Saint-Denis, Montreal H2J 2L9, 514/982-3330 or 888/691-0101, fax 514/982-2438, info@ culturecuba.com, www.culturecuba.com, offers a Jazz Fest package.

New Year's Eve celebrations are comparatively muted. Most Cubans celebrate at home. Beware while walking the streets, as Cubans dump buckets of water from their balconies, regardless of pedestrians below. Even bottles go sailing through the air to smash on the pavement.

FOLK MUSIC AND DANCE

In Cuba, folkloric music (*música folklórica*) usually refers to Afro-Cuban music. The capital city fairly vibrates to the pounding of the bongo drum and the strumming of guitars. Each district also has its own Casa de la Trova and Casa de la Cultura, where *sones* and *boleros* and other forms of traditional music and dance can be heard.

Watch for performances by the Conjunto Folklórico Nacional, Calle 4 #103, e/ Calzada y 5ta, Vedado, tel. 833-4560, which often performs at the Noches en la Plaza (see the Festivals and Events section).

An absolute *must* experience is Dulce María Baralt's **Encounter with Cuban Music** soirée (see the Special Topic "Sweet María's").

Habana Vieja

Several groups perform throughout the day at cafés such as **Café Mina,** at Obispo and Oficios; and **Bar y Restaurante El Patio,** on Plaza de la Catedral.

The **Casa de la Cultura**, Aguiar #509, esq. Brasil, tel. 863-4860, hosts traditional music and dance *peñas* featuring *bolero, son, boleros y poesia,*

"SWEET MARÍA'S"

Each Monday night, Dulce María Baralt, an intoxicatingly warmhearted singer and songwriter, hosts a soirée called **Encounter with Cuban Music,** at Calle San Ignacio #78, e/O'Reilly y Callejón del Chorro, tel. 861-0412, in Habana Vieja.

Climbing a rickety staircase to the top of the dilapidated three-story building, you emerge on her apartment *azotea* (rooftop) overlooking the Plaza de la Catedral. Hands are extended. You are hugged warmly by Cubans you do not know. Dulce's band, Son de Cuba, gears up with a rumba. The rhythms of the marimbas, bongos, and a guitar called a *tres* pulse across the rooftops of Habana Vieja. Rum and beer are passed around, and soon you are clapping and laughing while Dulce (Sweet) María belts out traditional Cuban compositions, her hips swaying to the narcotic beat that washes over the rooftops of Habana Vieja. The ice is broken. The infectious beat lures you to dance. It is like the plague—you can only flee or succumb.

Each song is introduced, with the history and meaning behind the song explained. You're invited to bring your own instrument. Says Dulce: "If we don't know it, we'll invent it."

Entry costs US$5, including a drink. Feel free to donate a bottle of rum.

comedy, and even karaoke. Afternoon and evening performances are given. Every Saturday at 3 P.M. the Compañía "JJ" Túrarte performs Afro-Cuban rumba in the courtyard of the Iglesia adjacent San Agustín. *Jineteros* (hustlers) and *jineteras* (hookers) prowl for good pickings; watch out for "false friends." Entrance costs US$2–3.

An all-female *son* group plays at the **Casa de las Infusiones,** Calle Mercaderes, e/ Obispo y Obrapía, tel. 862-0216, noon–5 P.M. and Tues.–Sat. at 7 P.M., where other traditional music groups also perform.

The **Palacio de las Artesanías,** Calle Tacón, e/ Cuba y Peña Pobre, offers a Noche Afrocubana Friday–Monday at 9:30 P.M. (US$3), plus what it calls *salsa espectáculos* (US$4). And the **Hotel Santa Isabel,** on Plaza de Armas, hosts a Noche

Cubana each Friday at 8 P.M. (US$15 including five-course dinner).

Yola en Familia, Calle Cuba, e/ Brasil y Muralla, is a similar—and very popular—informal street *peña* named after founder Yolanda Torres and held at 4 P.M., each third Saturday of the month. Yolando also hosts **Yola en la Comunidad,** Calle Muralla, esq. Compostela, another *peña* held on Thursdays 3–5 P.M. And **Peña de la Rumba,** Calle Empredado #258, e/ Cuba y Aguiar, takes place each Sunday 2–6 P.M.

Las Mulatas del Caribe, an all-female group of drummers and singers, play rumba and *guaguancó* at their base at Calle Obispo #213A.

Centro Habana and Cerro

The **Casa de la Trova,** San Lazaro #661, e/ Padre Varela y Gervasio, tel. 879-3373, is the real McCoy and has live music—everything from *filin* (romantic music) to *son* and *nueva trova*—Thursday–Sunday at 7 P.M. There's no bar, so BYOB. Locals flock most nights, but Friday evening is best. Entrance costs US$5.

The **Casa de la Cultura,** Salvador Allende #720, e/ Soledad y Castillejo, tel. 878-4727, hosts *peñas,* open Mon.–Sat. 11 A.M.–6 P.M. (except Fri.). Also try the **Casa de la Cultura,** Calzada del Cerro #1461, Cerro, tel. 870-4872.

Folkloric groups practice at the **Salón de Ensayo Benny Moré,** Neptuno #960, tel. 878-8827, Tues.–Sat. 9:30 A.M.–noon and 2–5 P.M. Visitors are welcome.

La Peña de Joya, San Lázaro #667, Apto. 9, e/ Padre Varela y Gervasio, has been going for two decades, transcending the recent death of Joya, a Josephine Baker type who one reader described as "a bit of a character" and a "mix between Marilyn Monroe and Muhammad Ali." Adherents of romantic *filin* music still flock on Friday 10 P.M.–1 A.M.

Vedado and Plaza de la Revolución

The group Son de Ahora plays daily except Saturdays, 5–7 P.M., in the outdoor courtyard of the **Hotel Nacional.**

My favorite nightspot is **Café Concerto Gato Tuerto,** Calle O #14, e/ 17 y 19, tel. 55-2696 or 66-2224, which hosts *música filin, trova* and

CUBAN MUSIC

The development of Cuban music styles since 1800—from *contradanza, danzón, habanera,* mambo, and *son* to *nueva trova*—is the story, writes Erroll McDonald, "of a swinging dialectic between West African choral and percussive genius and European melodic and harmonic sophistication." Here's a historical rundown to help you appreciate the sounds and moves of Havana.

Folkloric Music and Dance

The earliest influence was Spanish. The colonists brought the melodies such as the *bolero,* guitars, and violins from which evolved early *criollo* folk music. Most of Cuba's folk music, or *guajira,* is European music that has been influenced through contact with black culture. Examples include the all-important *danzón* (the first dance in Cuba in which couples actually touched each other), the *punto,* and the *zapateo,* all popular in past centuries among white country people and accompanied by small accordions, kettledrums, gourds, and calabashes. The fusion gave rise to *punto campesino* (peasant dances), still performed in country towns, including the slow and sensual *yambú* and the *columbia,* a solo men's dance performed blindfolded with machetes. The melancholic love song *Guantanamera* is undoubtedly the most famous of Cuban *guajiras,* recorded by everyone from Pete Seeger to Julio Iglesias (who is barred from Cuba, as are his recordings, for offending Castro's sensibilities with comments he made years ago).

From Europe, too, came the *trovas,* poetic songs (*canciones*) concerned with great historical events and, above all, with love. Emphasis was given to the lyrics, accompanied by exquisite guitar melodies. *Trovas,* which were descended from the medieval ballad, were sung in Cuba throughout the colonial period. *Trovadores* performed for free, as they still do at *casas de la trova* islandwide. The Matamoros Trio is perhaps the best known in the genre. This century has seen the evolution of *nueva trova,* songs about contemporary life. The movement has ties to the American folk protest-song movement of the 1960s and often includes outspoken criticism of current situations. The contemporary works of Pablo Milanés and Silvio Rodríguez, for example, echo the revolutionary dreams and restlessness of the current generation.

The African Influence

Almost from the beginning, the Spanish guitar—from the tiny *requinto* to the *tres,* a small guitar with three sets of double strings—joined the hourglass-shaped African *bata* and bongo drum, claves (two short hardwood sticks clapped together), and *chequerí* (seed-filled gourds) to give Cuban music its distinctive form. Slaves played at speakeasies in huts in the slaves' quarters. Their jam sessions gave birth to the *guaguancó,* a mix of flamenco guitar and African rhythm that is the mother of Cuban dance music. Later, slaves would take the *guaguancó* a few steps farther to create the sensuous *rumba,* a sinuous dance from the hips—the rumba has African roots, but the melody is very Spanish—and from which tumbled most other forms of Cuban music. The distinctly African *rumba* evolved around the turn of the century in Havana. Typically playing on makeshift instruments (such as the rumba box) and bottles hit with spoons, performers sang of everyday life using African phrases while dancers mimed an overtly sexual act. Rumba remains deliriously popular among Cuba's blacks. The *tumba francesa,* a dance of French-African fusion, also derived from the *guaguancó.*

From the rumba came *son,* traditionally performed by *sextetos* . . . six-person groups using the bongo, clave, double bass, *güiro* (or scraper), plus guitar, and the *tres* as its defining instrument. *Son,* which originated in the eastern provinces of Oriente, derived as a campesino (peasant)-based form combining African call-and-response verse to Spanish folk tunes. In turn, *son* birthed *danzón* and was eventually adopted in the cities where it became massively popular and was actually banned by authorities. By the 1920s, artists such as Rita Montaner and Ignacio Piñero's Septeto Nacional orchestra had made *son* the national music form.

By the 1930s, *son* was adopted by large band orchestras with percussion and horn sections, epitomized by the roaring success of Benny Moré (1919–63), the flamboyant *lo más bárbaro del ritmo* (guy with the most terrific rhythm) who became a national idol and had his own big band—the Banda Gigante. Such contemporary groups as Los Van Van have incorporated the *son,* which has its own variants, such as the fast, infectious, overtly sexual *son changüí* from Guantánamo province, typified by the music of Orquestra Revé. Meanwhile, the runaway success of the *Buena Vista Social Club* has helped revive an appreciation of traditional *son* abroad.

The mambo, like the cha-cha, which evolved from *son,* is a derivative of the *danzón,* jazzed up with rhythmic innovations. Mambo is a passé but still revered dance, like the jitterbug in the United States, danced usually only by older people. Created in Cuba by Orestes López in 1938, mambo stormed the United States in the 1950s, when Cuban performers were the hottest ticket in town. Though the craze died, mambo left its mark on everything from American jazz to the old Walt Disney cartoons where the salt and pepper shakers get up and dance. People were titillated by the aggressive sexual overtures required of women in the elegant but provocative dance. Captivated by the earthy break from the more modest swing, Americans created a simpler but equally risqué spin-off—"dirty dancing."

The mix of Cuban and North American sounds created blends such as *filin* ("feeling") music, as sung by Rita Montaner and Nat "King" Cole, who performed regularly in Havana; and *Cu-bop,* which fused bebop with Afro-Cuban rhythms, epitomized by Moré, who was considered the top artist of Cuban popular music.

Modern Sounds

The Revolution put a crimp in the music scene. Foreign performers stayed away, while many top performers left Cuba, such as Celia Cruz, the "queen of salsa." Salsa, a sensual, fast-paced derivative of *son,* has flourished since the 1980s, when the government began to lighten up. It is the heartbeat of most Cuban nightlife and a musical form so hot it can cook the pork. Los Van Van—one of Cuba's hottest big, brassy salsa-style bands—and Irakere have come up with innovative and explosive mixtures of jazz, classical, rock, and traditional Cuban music that have caused a commotion in the music and entertainment circles. They regularly tour Europe and Latin America, earning the country scarce hard currency.

For a long time, the playing of jazz in Cuba was completely discouraged (it was seen as "representative of Yankee imperialism, the music of the enemy"). Cuban musicians missed out on the Latin Jazz effervescence of the 1960s. Paquito D'Rivera, for example, was discouraged from playing jazz when he became director of the Orquestra Cubana de Música Moderna in 1970. Today, Cuba boasts wonderful jazz players of every stripe, and there is a growing stable of places where jazz can be heard.

Cuban jazz zigzags from bebop to fusion and European classical to Afro-Caribbean rhythms. It is "a bravura, macho form of jazz; trumpeters playing the highest notes and pianists going as fast as they can go." Cuban jazz musicians are admired the world over for their unique creativity and spirit. "When this is over and the musicians start coming out of Cuba, we'll all have to go back to school to catch up," said North American jazz maestro Tito Puente. Many leading international stars are Cuban. Celebrated trumpeter Arturo Sandoval left Irakere and Cuba in 1990, and D'Rivera left Cuba for New York in 1980. Like many artists, however, his departure had nothing to do with politics. "I fell in love with being a jazz musician in New York since first listening to a Benny Goodman record," he says. Nonetheless, both groups' music was pulled from the shelves in Cuba; those who leave Cuba take their *cubanidad* with them and become nonpersons at home.

The undisputed king of contemporary jazz is Chucho Valdés, winner of four Grammy awards for his scorching hot compositions.

bolero nightly until 4 A.M. Gato Tuerto (one-eyed cat) is popular with a monied Cuban crowd; foreigners and their Cuban consorts fill the empty seats. It gets packed, so get there by 10 P.M. for a good seat. There's no cover charge. The restaurant upstairs serves until 2 A.M.

In a similar vein, try **Club Imágenes,** Calzada #602, esq. C, tel. 33-3606, a stylish piano bar hosting *boleros* and other traditional music for the late-night crowd. Open noon–3 A.M. And **Cabaret Pico Blanco,** Calle O #206, 3/ 23 y 25, tel. 33-3740, in the Hotel St. John, is known colloquially as *El rincón de filin* (*filin* corner) and features traditional Cuban *boleros* and *trova* nightly, 10 P.M.–4 A.M. (US$5). A disco follows.

The **Bar Hurón Azul,** Calle 17 #351, esq. H, tel. 832-4551, in the Unión Nacional de Escritores y Artistes de Cuba (UNEAC), hosts a *peña* with Afro-Cuban music and dance on Wednesdays at 5 P.M., plus *boleros* and *trovas* on Saturday night (US$5). A listing of upcoming events is posted on the gate. It's a great place to meet Cuban intellectuals. Tucked in the rear is a *cinemateca/salón de video* where first-rate movies are shown (two pesos . . . that's US$.10). Open 5 P.M.–2 A.M.

The Conjunto Folklórico Nacional (National Folklore Dance Group) performs Sábado de Rumba, held each Saturday at 2 P.M. in the courtyard of **El Gran Palenque,** Calle 4 #103, e/ Calzada y 5ta, tel. 33-9075. The group is acclaimed for its Afro-Cuban renditions. Open 10 A.M.–10 P.M. (US$5).

Casa de la Amistad, Paseo #406, e/ 17 y 19, tel. 30-2468, offers live music nightly, plus on Tuesdays at 9 P.M. you can sway your hips to rumba and boleros played by Compay "Chan Chan" Segundo's band, Compay y Los Amigos, though you are hardly likely to catch the man himself. The US$5 cover includes one drink. *Son* is also featured on Saturdays. At any other time it's a relaxing place to enjoy a *mojito.* Open Mon.–Fri. 11 A.M.–midnight, Sat. 11 A.M.–2 A.M., Sun. 11 A.M.–6 P.M. (Sun.–Mon. free; US$5 Tues. and Sat.)

Likewise, the **Casa de las Américas,** 3ra Calle, esq. Avenida de los Presidentes, tel. 55-2706, fax 33-4554, casa@artsoft.cult.cu, www.casa.cult.cu,

hosts an eclectic range of traditional and contemporary concerts, typically Monday–Friday 8 A.M.–4:30 P.M. (five pesos). And the **Casa de la Cultura de Plaza,** Calzada #909, e/ 6 y 12, tel. 831-2023, hosts various concerts, including *bolero, son,* and jazz on Saturday nights. Open Mon.–Sat. 9 A.M.–10 P.M. (US$3–5).

Club Scherazada Calle M, e/ 19 y 17, tel. 832-3042, is a small, dingy, and smoky basement bar on the southwest side of the Focsa building. It has a *peña yoruba* with rumba and other Afro sounds Saturday 3–8:30 P.M., plus *trovas* and *boleros* on other days.

Elda, the owner of Paladar Amor, hosts a free rooftop Peña Coordinación con Elda, Calle 23 #759, e/ B y C, 3ra piso, tel. 833-8150, on the first Sunday afternoon (2–6 P.M.) of each month. It draws scores of people, who pack in to get their groove on to an eclectic mix of sounds. It sometimes features comedy acts, and even break dancing. The *peña* is a benefit for a children's cancer hospital. Complimentary drinks are served, but you should contribute a bottle of rum or similar. At last visit, the event seemed to have fallen afoul of authorities. Call ahead.

Playa (Miramar and Beyond)

For *boleros,* head to **Boleros,** 7ma Avenida, esq. Calle 26, tel. 204-2353, in the Dos Gardenias complex. Open 10:30 P.M.–3 A.M. (US$10). The **Salón La Tarde,** in the same complex, offers nightly entertainment from 7:30 P.M. (US$5).

CABARETS (ESPECTÁCULOS)

One of the first acts of the revolutionary government was to kick out the Mafia and close down the casinos and brothels. "It was as if the Amish had taken over Las Vegas," wrote Kenneth Tynan in a 1961 edition of *Holiday.* Not quite! Cabarets (called *shows,* pronounced with a "ch"), remain a staple of Cuban entertainment. Cuban couples delight in these razzmatazz spectacles with their sensual displays of flesh, and shake their heads at any puritan's concept that these shows are sexist. Cuban cabarets are no longer topless, but they may as well be!

Although the term "cabaret" sometimes refers to a disco, more frequently, it refers to *cabarets espectáculos,* Las Vegas-style song-and-dance routines highlighted by long-legged mulattas wearing high heels and skimpy costumes with lots of sequins, feathers, and frills. Usually, they're accompanied by smaller dance troupes of barechested male performers. Singers, magicians, acrobats, and comedians are often featured. The most flamboyant parts of the shows usually come towards the end. *Espectáculos* are usually followed by discos.

The larger hotels have their own *espectáculos,* as do several restaurants. You can book excursions to the cabarets through hotel tour desks. Reservations are advised.

One of the best ways to enjoy the cabarets is to go with a group and to reserve a table. A bottle of Havana Club rum, cans of Coke, and ice bucket and glasses will be delivered to your table when you arrive.

Habana Vieja

The rooftop bar of the **Hotel Inglaterra** features a small *cabaret espectáculo* (US$5) on weekends.

Club Oasis, Prado #256, e/ Animas y Trocadero, tel. 863-3829, is a simple place popular with Cuban youth. A small *cabaret espectáculo* is offered nightly at 11 P.M., followed by dancing. Open 9 P.M.–3 A.M. (US$3).

Centro Habana and Cerro

Cabaret Nacional, San Rafael, esq. Prado, tel. 863-2361, in the dingy basement of the Gran Teatro, has a modest *espectáculo* nightly at 11:15 P.M.. (US$5). The bar opens at 9 A.M. and the show is followed by a disco. It's primarily patronized by Cuban youth, with plenty of *jineteras.* A dress code applies.

Disco Ribera Azul, Avenida de Italia, e/ Malecón y San Lázaro, tel. 33-8813, in the basement of the Hotel Deauville, has a small *cabaret espectáculo* Fri.–Sun. at 11 P.M. (US$5).

Habaneros without dollars to throw around get their cabaret kicks at **El Colmao,** Calle Aramburu #366, e/ San José y San Rafael, tel. 870-1113. Open 8 P.M.–2 A.M. Cubans pay in pesos, but you may be required to pay in dollars.

Vedado and Plaza de la Revolución

The most lavish show is the **Cabaret Parisien,** Calle O, esq. 21, tel. 33-3564, in the Hotel Nacional, second only to the Tropicana. The *Ajiaco Cubano* show is offered Fri.–Wed. at 10 P.M., with a smaller show at 12:30 A.M. Entrance costs US$30 (US$50 with dinner). The place is cramped, however, and gets smoke-filled.

Salón Turquino, atop the Hotel Habana Libre (see Discotheques and Dancing later in this chapter), offers a medley of entertainment varying nightly, with a *cabaret espectáculo* Wednesday and Thursday (US$15) followed by a disco.

The small-scale cabaret at **Salón Rojo,** Calle 21, e/ N y O, tel. 33-3747, beside the Hotel Capri, is cheaper and appeals mostly to Cubans (the carpet is thoroughly stained and the seating is tattered). The doors open at 10 P.M., but the show is much later and is followed by dancing. Open Tues.–Sun. at 11:30 P.M. (US$10 including two drinks).

The **Habana Café,** Paseo, e/ 1ra y 3ra, tel. 202-7712, adjoining the Hotel Meliá Cohiba, offers cabaret nightly. Havana's homespun version of the Hard Rock Café attempts to rekindle the spirit of the 1950s. A classic Harley-Davidson, an old Pontiac, and a 1957 open-top canary-yellow Chevy add a dramatic effect, as do period gas pumps and a small airplane with Cubana motif suspended from the ceiling. Suddenly the car horns beep and the headlamps flash, you hear the roar of an airplane taking off, then the curtains open and—voilá—the show begins. The cabaret-bar lures everyone from tour groups to cigar-chomping bigwigs and a parade of discreetly permitted Cuban hookers working the single guys for US$100 a pop. Entertainment is offered nightly, 8 P.M.–3 A.M., including a small cabaret, a juggling act, and a Benny Goodman-style band. A group plays traditional music noon–4 P.M., and a pianist playing *bolero* music keeps patrons amused 4–8 P.M. At last visit, entrance was free (US$15 on Sundays), but in past years a *consumo mínimo* policy has applied. Watch for rip offs.

The **Cabaret Copa Room,** Paseo y Malecón, tel. 33-4051, in the Hotel Riviera, hosts a cabaret Wednesday–Monday at 10:30 P.M. (US$15, or US$29 with dinner and cocktail).

Club 1830, Malecón #1252 y 20, tel. 55-3091, hosts a limited cabaret outdoors Thursday–Saturday at 11 P.M. It's a small affair and draws many Cubans for the brief disco that follows. Entrance costs US$5, including the show.

Also serving mostly impecunious Cubans is the **Cabaret Las Vegas,** Infanta #104, e/ Calles 25 y 27, tel. 870-7939, with a show at 11 P.M. followed by a disco. The *espectáculo* is a feeble, short-lived affair with a five-member dance troupe, and not worth the billing—"The *chicas,*" wrote Tom Miller, "danced in earnest but seldom in sync, their tattered fishnet stockings running before our eyes" while the solo singer "singing off-key into her cordless mike . . . would have been better served had she carried a mikeless cord." The gloomy bar—the hangout for the protagonist in Guillermo Cabrera Infante's bawdy *Three Trapped Tigers,* has a pool table. Go for the seedy charm. Open 10 P.M.–5 A.M. (US$5 per couple).

The equally seedy **Centro Nocturno La Red,** Calle 19 #151, esq. Calle L, tel. 832-5415, has a small *espectáculo* at midnight, followed by a disco; open 10 P.M.–4 A.M. (Mon.–Thurs. US$1, Fri.–Sun. US$2). Similar, and nearby, is **Karachi**

Club, Calles 17 y K, open nightly 10 P.M.–5 P.M.; US$5.

Playa (Miramar and Beyond)

The shining star in Havana's cabaret constellation is the **Tropicana,** Calle 72 #4504 y Línea del Ferrocarril, Marianao, tel. 267-1717, fax 267-0109, reserva@tropicana.gca.tur.net. Cuba's premier Las Vegas–style nightclub, boasting more than 200 performers, has been described as "like looking at a Salvador Dali painting come to life" and is a de rigueur treat. The show, enhanced by a fabulous orchestra, takes place in the open-air Salón Bajo Las Estrellas Tuesday–Sunday at 9 P.M. Entrance costs US$60, including a *cuba libre,* but you can sit at the bar for US$25; you'll need to bring your passport. Sometimes discounts are offered when tourism to the island hits troughs. You can purchase tickets at the reservation booth, open 10 A.M.–6 P.M., or directly at the entrance from 8:30 P.M. (call ahead to check availability), but it's virtually essential to book in advance through your hotel tour desk, as the show is often sold out to tour groups. Whole or partial refunds are offered if the show is rained out—if the rains

dancers at the Tropicana

© CHRISTOPHER P. BAKER

ENTERTAINMENT

are intermittent, the show merely takes a break, then resumes. You're charged US$5 for cameras, US$15 for videos. Cocktails cost US$3, but it's usually best to buy a bottle of rum and a can of Coke to last you all night. A second, smaller show is offered during peak tourist season in the Arco Cristal cabaret room featuring dancers in 1950s costumes; performances are at midnight, after which a disco gets in the groove until 5 A.M. The Tropicana features two eateries: the elegant sky-lit Los Jardines, serving tasty continental fare (open 6 P.M.–1 A.M.); and the 1950s diner–style Rodney Café, serving salads, soups, burgers, and tortillas to a mostly Cuban crowd (open noon–2 A.M.).

Macumba Habana, Calle 222, e/ 37 y 51, tel. 33-0568, fax 33-6390, gerencia@giralda.cha .cyt.cu, in the La Giraldilla complex in the La Coronela district, offers a top-class, albeit small *espectáculo* at 10:30 P.M. with a different theme nightly, followed by one of Havana's top discos. Entry costs US$10; US$15 on Fridays and Saturdays. A dinner special costs US$30. The club is open 9 P.M.–5 A.M.

The **Hotel Comodoro,** 1ra Avenida y Calle 84, tel. 204-5551, features an *espectáculo* as part of its entertainment for guests. **Discoteca Habana Club,** tel. 832-9375, behind the Hotel Comodoro, also has a cabaret (see the Discotheques and Dancing section later in this chapter). **Club Ipanema,** 1ra Avenida, e/ 44 y 46, tel. 204-1037, adjacent to the Hotel Copacabana, has a Noches Azules *espectáculo* followed by a disco. Open 10 P.M.–4 A.M. (US$5). And **La Cecilia,** 5ta Avenida #11010, e/ 1110 y 112, tel. 204-1562, has an *espectáculo* Thursday–Sunday 9:30 P.M., with a disco afterward.

Cabaret Chévere, Avenida 49C, esq. Calle 28A, tel. 204-4990, in Reparto Kohly, at Club Almendares, has an open-air cabaret with a band and fashion parade—but no *espectáculo*—Friday–Sunday 10 P.M.–6 A.M. (US$5). The bar is open 24 hours, and there's a pool hall (US$1 per game).

DISCOTHEQUES AND DANCING

There's no shortage of discos in dance-crazy Havana. The "best" (i.e., glitzy Western-style, air-conditioned discos playing a mix of pop, R&B, and Latin sounds) are money-milking machines serving well-heeled foreigners and dollar-rich Cubans. Males can expect to be solicited outside the entrance to these dollars-only discos: Cuban women take a stranger's arm and beg to be escorted in ("*¡por favor!*"), because the cover charge is beyond their means and/or because the venue only permits access to couples—many Havana nightclubs do not let in single females. Drink prices in the touristy discos can give you sticker shock. The best bet is usually to buy a bottle of rum—but expect to fork out at least US$20 for a bottle—and Coca-Cola.

Discos catering to the Cuban masses are cheap, usually run-down, unpretentious affairs, usually with kitschy prerevolutionary decor. Most are preceded by a basic *cabaret espectáculo*. But hey! Be prepared for dancing hot enough to cook the pork! *Merengue,* salsa, and the even sexier *timba.* If you, a foreigner, can't dance—it is said *baila como un Sueco*—"you dance like a Swede"—you may be told the answer lies in learning to "dance" in bed. "If a man did not learn how to move his hips and get his butt gyrating [when making love], he would never be able to dance the music of the Caribbean," thought Alicia, the protagonist in Daniel Chavarría's *Adios Muchachos.* "Alicia usually started the learning process by having a dressage on a broad mat on the floor [and] maintained that with this technique she . . . had succeeded in getting a German, a Swede, and even a Cossack to swing their hips without looking like a walrus."

Many discos are open until dawn. There's little point in arriving early; few discos get in the groove before the clock strikes 12.

Taxis are available outside the entrances of the best discos in the wee hours, and freelancers are on hand to run you home for a negotiable fare.

Also see the Cabarets section for *espectáculo* venues that have discos after the show.

Habana Vieja

The *Havana Princess* sails from the small wharf by the Fuente de Neptuno (Neptune Fountain), Avenida Carlos M. de Céspedes, at the foot of

PARADISE UNDER THE STARS

Showtime! Señoras y señores. *Ladies and gentlemen.* Muy buenas noches . . . Bienvenidos, *as we say in our beautiful language . . . Tropicana, the most fabulous nightclub in the world . . .* presenta . . . *presents . . .* su nueva espectáculo . . . *its new show . . .* El Trópico en Tropicana . . . . *It's time to get warm and that will be with our coming show. In fact to many of you it will mean heat! And I mean, with my apologies to the very, very old-fashioned ladies in the audience, I mean Heat. And when, ladies and gentlemen, I mean heat, is HEAT!*

Guillermo Cabrera Infante, Tres Tristes Tigres (Three Trapped Tigers)

The prerevolutionary extravaganza now in its sixth decade of Vegas paganism—girls! girls! girls!—has been in continuous operation since New Year's Eve 1939, when it opened (in the gardens of a mansion—Villa Mina—that once housed the U.S. ambassador) as the most flamboyant nightclub in the world. The casino has gone, but otherwise neither the Revolution nor the recent economic crisis has ruffled the feathers of Cuba's most spectacular show.

Tropicana, the club to which Wormold took Millie on her seventeenth birthday in *Our Man in Havana,* quickly won the favor of the elite of society and soon eclipsed all other clubs in the grandeur and imagination of its productions. The Congo Pantera revue, which simulated a panther's nocturnal hunt in lush jungle, established the Tropicana's trademark, with dancers in the thick vegetation illuminated by colored spotlights and the panther, performed by Tania Leskoya, coming down from a majestic tree—the name Tropicana melds the world *trópico*—tropics—with *palma cana,* for the fan palm.

In its heyday, the Tropicana spent more than US$12,000 nightly on its flamboyant shows, which ranged from the "Asian Paradise," portraying the exotic Orient, to choreographed Haitian voodoo rituals. International celebrities such as Nat "King" Cole, Josephine Baker, and Carmen Miranda headlined the show, which was so popular that a 50-passenger "Tropicana Special" flew nightly from Miami for an evening of entertainment that ended in the nightclub's casino, where a daily US$10,000-bingo jackpot was offered and a new automobile was raffled for free every Sunday.

Empedrado; the two-hour cruises depart at 7 P.M., with disco to follow until 5 A.M. (Mon.–Thurs. US$10, Fri.–Sat. US$15). Alas, no Cubans are allowed on board . . . ostensibly so that the boat isn't hijacked.

Disco Karaoke, in the Hotel Plaza, packs Cubans in thick as sardines nightly 11 P.M.–5 A.M. (US$4).

Also see **Club Oasis,** in the Cabaret section earlier in this chapter.

Centro Habana and Cerro

One of the new hot spots in town is the **Casa de la Música,** Galiano, e/ Concordia y Neptuno, tel. 862-4165, a modern a/c theater that packs in a younger crowd for daily concerts and *espectácu-*los. Open 4–7 P.M. and 10 P.M.–3 A.M. Entrance costs US$10.

The **Los Tres Chinitos,** Dragones, e/ Campanario y Manrique, in Barrio Chino, has a no-frills disco drawing serious dancers, nightly 11 P.M.–6 A.M. (US$3). *Jineteras* also flock.

Nearby **Disco Chang,** Calle San Nicolás #517, e/ Dragones y Zanja, tel. 862-1490, is an earthy private disco above the Chang Weng Chung Tong association. It, too, packs in the locals and foreigners for dancing, Friday–Sunday 10:30 P.M.–3 A.M. (US$5 men, US$1 women). This is where the girls are at!

Disco Ribera Azul (see the Cabaret section earlier in this chapter), caters to a mix of locals and tourists. It has disco nightly; open 10 P.M.–

In the 1950s, the club was owned by Martín Fox, who held a legal monopoly on the installation and maintenance of slot machines in Cuba (*máquinas traganickeles*). Managing the casino was Mob associate Lefty Clark. Fox was a friend of mobster boss Santo Trafficante, whose lawyer, Frank Ragano, visited Havana in 1958 and was treated to a tour of the sex scene. Fox gave him a choice seat for a special performance at Tropicana. The night's theme was "Miss Universe." Fox offered Ragano any girl he desired. "Take your pick," he told Ragano. "You want two girls? Three girls? Anything you want!" Figuring that "Miss Cuba" would be the obvious winner and therefore the most beautiful, Ragano chose her sight unseen. Sure enough, after the show Miss Cuba was shown to his table.

Now, as then, the key attraction is the sensual mulatta parade. Talent scouts scoured Cuba for the most beautiful models and dancers. That is still the case and the more than 200 performers are still hand-picked from the crème-de-la-crème of Cuba's singers and dancers—although they are no longer topless. And famous international entertainers still occasionally perform, enhancing the superbly choreographed skits of *danzón, son,* salsa, Brazilian *yatratá,* Latin jazz, Afro-Cuban legends, and romantic ballads, interspersed with astonishing acrobatic feats.

The "paradise under the stars," which takes place in the open air, begins with the "Dance of the Chandeliers," when a troupe of near-naked showgirls parades down the aisles wearing glowing chandeliers atop their heads. Then a troupe of besequined males and long-legged showgirls rush onto the stage in a high-kicking flurry of flesh and feathers. The sexually charged show consists of creative song and dance routines and a never-ending parade of stupendous mulattas gyrating their glistening copper-colored bodies into an erotic frenzy. Patrons watch mesmerized as rainbow-hued searchlights sweep over the hordes of showgirls, and mocha-skinned mulattas, gaudily feathered, parade twenty feet up among the floodlit palm trees, quivering beseechingly like the most exotic of tropical birds. Between numbers they rush offstage and reappear in sexy outfits from a Frederick of Hollywood's catalog: tassled thongs with ruffled tails, sequined bikinis with bras of coiled foil tipped by fake rubies, skin-tight bustiers with pull-ring zippers, bejeweled chokers, elbow-length gloves, and sensational headdresses more ostentatious than peacocks.

3 A.M. (US$3). And the simple rooftop **La Terraza,** Avenida de Italia #164, esq. Virtudes, tel. 33-8209, atop the Hotel Lincoln, draws locals for a mixed music package, Mon.–Thurs. 9 P.M.–midnight, and Fri.–Sat. 9 P.M.–2 A.M.

La Pampa, Calle Marina, esq. Vapor, features dancing nightly except Monday; US$1, including cabaret, but also hip-hop, drawing a hip albeit impecunious crowd. Leave your jewelry at home.

Vedado and Plaza de la Revolución

The **Salón Internacional** Malecón y Paseo, tel. 33-4051, in the Hotel Havana Riviera, specializes in the Latin beat and often features the top names in live Cuban music, such as Los Van Van. It's Havana's top spot for serious salsa fans, but relies heavily on the tourist trade and there's no shortage of *jineteras.* Open daily 10 P.M.–3 A.M. (US$15–25, depending on who's performing).

Salón Turquino, Calle L, e/ 23 y 25, tel. 55-4011, atop the Hotel Habana Libre, draws tourists and Cubans with dollars to spend. Ataché Havana, a popular 12-piece band, perform Monday–Tuesday nights; Lady Salsa, another house band, performs Thursday–Saturday nights. Comedy is offered on Wednesdays and Sundays. There's sometimes a small cabaret, but mostly this is salsa heaven. Entrance costs US$15 (US$5 for hotel guests). No single women allowed. Open 10:30 P.M.–3 A.M. The hotel's **Salón de los Embajadores** also features live performers.

Also try the **Pico Blanco,** Calle O e/ 23 y 25, tel.

THE GAY SCENE

G ay life in Havana has expanded noticeably in recent years—lesbianism has not become quite so accepted—although homosexual venues remain subject to police crack-downs as political whims change without warning. There are no established gay bars or clubs, which are banned, and the gay "scene" typically is relegated to "hang-out" street locales.

Cruising

The main cruising section is the **Malecón** opposite the Fiat Café, two blocks east of La Rampa, where the party spreads along the seafront boulevard in the wee hours (there are *jineteros*—male hookers—in the crowd). The corner of La Rampa and L, outside the **Cine Yara,** is another cruising spot, and draws a strong contingent of transvestites. Also in Vedado, **Avenida de los Presidentes** is a secondary cruising scene. And in Habana Vieja, the **Parque de la Fraternidad** has a lesser late-night cruising scene.

Ballet performances (think men in tights!) always draw a strong gay crowd, particularly to the **Gran Teatro.**

For gay beaches, head to the **Playa Boca Ciega** section of Playas del Este, east of town. In town, try **Playita de 16,** the rocky *balneario* at Calle 16 in Miramar; and **Playa Tritón,** in front of the Hotel Neptuno/Tritón. **Playa El Chivo,** immediately east of the tunnel under Havana harbor channel, is also said to draw a gay crowd, but you should use caution here.

Cafés and Clubs

El Café Mercurio, in the Lonja del Comercio, on Plaza de San Francisco, attracts gay clientele.

The **Castropol,** Malecón #107, esq. Genios, Centro Habana, tel. 861-4864, draws Cuba's intelligensia to its drag cabaret, Mon.–Thurs. at 11:30 P.M. (US$1). The **Fiat Café,** Malecón, e/ Marina y Principe, Centro Habana, tel. 873-5827, is favored as a wee-hour hang-out; open 24 hours. Nearby, **La Pampa,** Marina #102, esq. Vapor, tel. 878-3426, is a smoky, down-to-earth disco that draws a mixed bag, including a large gay contingent; open 24 hours.

In Vedado, the **Café Monseigneur,** Calle O, e/ La Rampa y 21, tel. 832-9884, is a gay hangout, and **Club Tropical,** Línea, esq. F, tel. 832-7361, occasionally acts as a gay venue, drawing a younger, fashion-hip crowd that includes a fair share of *jineteros*. It's a cramped, humid venue. Call ahead to ascertain the night's theme. Open 10 P.M.–4 A.M. **Club Saturno,** Línea, e/ 10 y 12, tel. 833-7942, is a steamy cellar bar drawing a similar crowd to Club Tropical.

In Miramar, *transvesti* hookers trawl for clients by night along 5ta Avenida. Straight males be warned . . . that gorgeous brunette in mini-skirt and high heels could be a man.

Parties

Most nights there are one or more gay parties, often at private venues, where entrance typically costs US$2. Havana society is non-exclusionary, however; everyone is welcome, and the mix usually includes a sprinkling of straight, lesbian, and even *transvestis*. There are also private parties known as *fiestas de diez pesos,* which charge a 10 peso cover, predominantly serve the lesbian community, and often feature drag shows. The "floating party" venues change nightly as they try to stay one step ahead of the police.

The best way to find out that night's happening spot is to ask the gay crowd that congregates at night outside the Cine Yara.

33-4187, in the glass-enclosed top floor of the Hotel St. John's (US$5–10). It has salsa on Monday and *rumba* on weekend afternoons. Famous artists occasionally put in an impromptu appearance.

Tiny **Las Bulerias,** Calle L, e/ 23 y 25, tel. 832-3283, opposite the Hotel Habana Libre, is a smoky, moody place that plays mostly salsa. It doesn't get going until about 11 P.M. Entrance costs US$3; beers are US$1.

UjoteCa (Union of Young Communists) runs the **Pabellón,** La Rampa, esq. Calle N, tel. 832-4921, which features a gamut of activities Wednesday–Sunday, including salsa on Wednesday, disco and rap Thursday–Saturday, and disco with rock music on Sunday. Open 9 A.M.–5 P.M. (US$1–5).

Nearby, **Club Sofia,** Calle 23 (La Rampa) #202, esq. Calle O, tel. 832-0740, is a modest café with live music daily each afternoon and 8 P.M.–2 A.M., plus an *espectáculo* and disco Saturday and Sunday at midnight (US$2). Open 24 hours. On the same block, **Club Tikoa,** Calle 23 #177, e/ N y O, tel. 832-9773, also draws a youngish Cuban crowd for *merengue* and salsa. Open 10 P.M.–4 A.M. (US$2).

Cubans also flock to **Café Cantante,** Paseo, esq. 39, tel. 873-5713, in the Teatro Nacional, one block west of the Plaza de la Revolución. Sometimes recorded disco music is played. There's a dress code for guys—no hats, T-shirts, or shorts. The *jineteras* are like fleas . . . dressed (barely) to kill in show-it-all clothing, and eager to part you from your dollars. Open Tues.–Sat. 9 P.M.–5 A.M. Entry costs US$3, or US$10–20 when top groups perform. Also, go on Fridays, 4–6 P.M. for live salsa; only Cubans go and with luck you'll be charged in pesos.

Piano Bar Delirio, on the third floor of the Teatro Nacional, also has live music and a variety show, Thursday–Saturday noon–4 P.M. A US$5 *consumo mínimo* applies.

Club Scherazada, Calle M, e/ 19 y 17, tel. 832-3042, offers a medley of musical offerings each night from 6 P.M.; a disco cranks up at 10:30 P.M. It has a US$2.50 per-person cover (the sign outside says *"US$5 por pareja,"* but the doorman sometimes tries to con solo guests who don't know that this means "per pair").

Farther west, the **Turf Club,** Calzada #452, esq. F, tel. 66-2261, is a popular nightclub among the locals; open Tues.–Fri. 4 P.M.–2 A.M., and Sat. 4 P.M.–4 A.M. (US$3). And the **Club 1830** has a modest open-air disco (US$5). It's open nightly, 10 P.M.–4 A.M. Nearby **Club Atelier,** Calle 17, esq. 6, tel. 832-6808, is a basement club with a small *cabaret* followed by dancing, 10 P.M.–4 A.M. (US$5).

If you think you can pass for a Cuban, try the **Casa de FEU,** an outdoor dance spot in the University of Havana, supposedly for students only. It has recorded salsa and disco music Thursdays 6–10 P.M. and Fridays and Saturdays 9 P.M.–2 A.M.

Playa (Miramar and Beyond)

The hippest spot in Havana is **Macumba Habana,** Calle 222, e/ 37 y 51, tel. 33-0568, fax 33-6390, in the La Giraldilla complex, in the La Coronela district. This open-air disco boasts great music and draws the chic crowd—mostly well-heeled foreign males and beautiful *habaneras.* It has a dress code. Only couples (*parejas*) are allowed entry, though this can include two women. Entry costs US$10; US$15 on Fridays and Saturdays. Open 10 P.M.–5 A.M.

Discoteca Habana Club, 1ra Avenida, esq. 84, tel. 202-7712, behind the Hotel Comodoro, also attracts a chic in-crowd—a blend of Cuban females and tourists or resident expats (mostly male)—who bop to yester-decade's Abba tunes, pop hits, techno, and salsa played at top volume between cabaret floor shows. Many of the females are *jineteras* who hit up the males for a going rate of US$100! Drinks are also outrageously priced. To disguise this outright theft, patrons are given a card upon entry; your drink purchases are punched onto the card and you get your bill as you exit (don't lose it or you'll be charged US$50). You'll need a stiff drink for the shock! An afternoon matinee disco is offered Sundays 2–7 P.M. for 16–30 year-olds (US$3). Open Mon.–Sat. 10 P.M.–5 A.M. Entrance costs US$10.

Club Río (colloquially called Johnny's), Calle A #314, e/ 3ra y 5ta, is one of the hippest spots in town. DJs spin the most up-to-date

LEARNING THE MOVES

The first time you see Cubans dancing you'll wish you'd taken some lessons to at least learn the basics. There's no shortage of Cubans willing to offer private lessons.

For one-on-one instruction in rumba, cha-cha-cha, and other traditional popular and Afro-Cuban dance forms, I recommend **Dulce María Baralt,** Calle San Ignacio #78, e/ O'Reilly y Plaza de la Catedral, Habana Vieja, tel. 861-0412; or **Danzamor,** offered by two colorful characters, Adelaida Borges and Wilki Arencibia, Calle Aguiar #361 e/ Obispo y Obrapía, 4to piso, Habana Vieja, tel. 862-7706.

Gilberto Capote, Calle O'Reilly #362, Apto. 6, 3er piso, e/ Habana y Compostela, Habana Vieja, tel. 861-7080, has been recommended, as has **Mayra Varona,** Calle Concordia #151, Apto. 9, e/ San Nicólas y Manrique, Centro Habana, tel. 863-1075, a choreographer well known throughout Cuba.

For modern dance, try American **Lorna Burdsall,** c/o Teatro Nacional, Avenida Carlos M. de Céspedes, esq. Paseo, Vedado, tel. 879-6011, lorna@cubarte.cult.cu, founder of the Danza Contemporánea de Cuba; or **Hilda Rosa Barrera,** Calle Habana Park #114, e/ Sánchez y Manila, Cerro, tel. 870-9273, or **Luz María Collazo,** Calle 40 #157, Apto. 25, e/ 36 y Zoológico, Nuevo Vedado, tel. 881-0729, both of whom also teach sensual rumba and other dances.

Dance classes for the casual tourist are offered at the Hotel Lincoln Tuesday 4–6 P.M.

See the Special Topic "Studying In Cuba" in the Planning Your Trip chapter for information on formal dance classes.

---

tunes. It also has a cabaret on the sunken dance floor. Couples only are permitted, and lone females outside get harassed by the police. Watch those drink prices! It has a reputation for pickpockets and occasional fights. Open 10 P.M.–4 A.M. US$10.

The **Club Ipanema,** 1ra Avenida, e/ 44 y 46, tel. 204-1037, at the Hotel Copacabana plays plenty of techno in its eclectic mix. The clientele is mostly Cuban, and the atmosphere subdued. There's no entry charge, but a *consumo mínimo* of US$6 applies. It's open 10 P.M.–4 A.M.

Farther out, **Salón Rosado Benny Moré,** Avenida 41, esq. 48, tel. 209-0985 or 203-5322, an open-air concert arena, is popular for serious dancing on weekends, when top-billed Cuban salsa bands such as Los Van Van perform. The place gets jam-packed . . . and rum-induced fights often break out. For better or worse, foreigners are usually kept apart from *habaneros.* It's open Friday–Monday 7 P.M.–2 A.M. with live groups; and Tuesday and Wednesday for cabaret (US$3–10).

Papa's, 5ta Avenida, esq. Calle 248, tel. 209-7920, at Marina Hemingway, has a live floor show and disco popular with young *habaneras*

seeking positions as captain's mates. Open Tues.–Sun. 10 P.M.–4 A.M. (US$10 cover includes all-you-can-drink)

Cabaret Chévere, Avenida 49C, esq. Calle 28A, tel. 204-4990, in Reparto Kohly, has an open-air disco and hosts live bands. Open 5 P.M.–midnight (US$3–20).

Cubans without dollars find their fun at such spots as **Juventud 2000 Discoclub,** 1ra Avenida, e/ 8 y 10, tel. 203-0801, in the Teatro Karl Marx, Havana's largest concert theater. Big names—the Buena Vista Social Club, Los Van Van, Isaac Delgado—play here. Open Fri.–Sun. 9 P.M.–2 A.M. (cover charge varies).

Los Jardines de la Tropical, Calle 51 y Puente Grande, tel. 881-8767, is a terribly run-down open-air facility and is all-Cuban—you'll likely be the only tourist. It offers live salsa bands on Sundays, noon–7 P.M. Entrance costs five pesos.

JAZZ AND SALSA VENUES

Following the Revolution, jazz was discouraged as a bourgeois form of music. But things have changed, and the city is picking up more and more dedicated jazz joints. (Also see the Discotheques and Dancing section earlier in this chapter for salsa venues.)

Habana Vieja

A jazz trio performs in the **Café del Oriente,** Oficios #112, esq. Amargura, tel. 860-6686, on the west side of Plaza de San Francisco, where you can enjoy cocktails at the ritzy marbletop bar.

Centro Habana and Cerro

Cine América, Galiano #253, esq. Neptuno, tel. 862-5416, hosts jazz.

Vedado and Plaza de la Revolución

The **Jazz Café,** Paseo, esq. 1ra, tel. 55-3475, on the third floor of the Galería del Paseo, at the base of Paseo, is a classy joint with plate-glass windows, contemporary decor, and some of the best live jazz in town, including from resident maestro Chucho Valdés and Irakere. The music doesn't get going until about 11:30 P.M., though the seats usually fill up well before then. There's no cover; instead a US$10 *consumo mínimo* applies. Open 11 A.M.–3 A.M.

The basement **La Zorra y el Cuervo** (the Fox and the Crow), Calle 23, e/ N y O, tel. 66-2402, zorra@cbcan.cyt.cu, offers jazz in a dreary basement setting. Occasional foreign bands perform here, as do the Cuban greats such as Chucho Valdés and up-and-coming star Roberto Fonseca. There's "blues" on Thursdays. The first set normally kicks off at 10:30 P.M. Get there early to guarantee a seat. The crowd is mainly foreign. Open 9 P.M.–3 A.M. (US$10 admission includes drinks).

Jazz and salsa are staples at the **Jazz Cafetería,** Calzada #909, e/ 6 y 8, tel. 831-2023, in the Casa de Cultura de Plaza, especially on Saturday nights. The Casa de Cultura is one of the venues for the annual International Havana Jazz Festival. Open Mon.–Sat. 9 A.M.–10 P.M. (US$3–5).

Jazz can also be heard at the **Salón Internacional** in the Hotel Riviera, and **Salón Turquino,** atop the Habana Libre Hotel.

Playa (Miramar and Beyond)

The **Casa de la Música,** Avenida 25 y 20, tel. 204-0447, sometimes has free jazz jam sessions during the day as well as performances by such legends as Chucho Valdés, who lives close by (US$10–20). The forum has different performances—but mostly salsa—in the *sala de espectáculos,* nightly at 10 P.M. except Monday (US$15–20 cover). It draws Havana's hippest, plus plenty of *jineteras.* You can attend sizzling hot afternoon sessions, however, for a fabulously cheap 10 pesos.

A jazz group performs at the **Tocororo,** Calle 18 y 3ra Avenida, tel. 202-4530.

RAP, HIP-HOP, AND REGGAE VENUES

Yes, rap has come to Cuba. An international hip-hop festival has been held in Havana every year since 1991. There's even a hip-hop radio show, *La Esquina de Rap* (Rap Corner). Although the message is different, the rhythms, gestures, and posturing take their cues from U.S. urban ghettoes. Cuban hip-hop is gentler, less dependent on guttural, driving aggression and more based on melodic fusion.

The most prominent Cuban rap groups are the Orishas (who now live in Paris and were fêted by Fidel during a Cuba tour in 1999), Obsesión (duo Magia López and Alexey Rodríguez), and the all-female rap trio Instinto. Look for Anónimo Consejo, another favorite with the hip-hop crowd.

Alamar, in Habana del Este, is the acknowledged center of rap, and its "godfather" is composer-producer Edesio Alejandro. The **Festival de Rap de Alamar** is held here in August.

Rap concerts are also held at **La Madriguera,** Avenida Salvador Allende, e/ Infanta y Luaces, Centro Habana, an unlikely spot in the overgrown former botanical gardens of the Quinta de los Molinos; contact the **Asociación Hermano Saíz,** tel. 879-8175. The association is a youth wing of UNEAC and represents younger musicians and artists, including those "on the fringe." La Madriguera is open Monday–Wednesday and Friday 9 A.M.–7 P.M., and Thursday 9 A.M.–midnight (five pesos), when a disco is hosted.

The **Teatro América,** Avenida de Italia #253, e/ Concordia y Neptuno, tel. 862-5416, hosts rap and reggae concerts Tues.–Sun. 10 P.M.–4 P.M.

(US$5). An earthier favorite is the run-down **Cabaret Palermo,** Calle San Miguel y Amistad, tel. 861-9745, drawing mostly Afro-Cuban youth for rap. It sometimes has live music and is open Monday–Sunday 9 P.M.–2 A.M. (US$2). And the **Pabellón,** Calle 23 (La Rampa), esq. Calle N, tel. 832-4921, features rap most Thursdays–Saturdays (US$5).

Reggae, too, has a following, attested by Cubans with their hair in dreads. A key reggae band is Mañana Reggae. You'll find many reggae fans sporting dreadlocks, such as Carlos Alfonso Valdés, the leader of a popular Cuban funk band, Síntesis, with dreadlocks nearly down to his waist.

ROCK VENUES

Rock and roll was once officially banned. Cuba's *roqueros* (rockers) and *friquis* (freaks, known for their torn clothes and punkish scruffy hair) faced a hard time of things for many years, as the government considered them social deviants and, hence, harassed and suppressed them. In recent years, the Young Communists have lassoed the popularity of modern music to corral disaffected youth. These days, the government tolerates domestic rock groups, whose fans wear the same stereotypical uniforms—long hair, tattered Led Zeppelin and Metallica T-shirts (heavy metal fans are known as *metálicos,* while "hippies" are called *friquis*)—as do those beyond Cuban shores. Foremost groups include Combat Noise, Zeus, and Garage Hall.

However, the government keeps its rock musicians on short leashes. Playing unofficial venues can get *roqueros* arrested. To a large degree, the state decides what music can be played. Electricity rationing also sometimes pulls the plug on rehearsals and concerts, which are advertised through the grapevine.

Roqueros gravitate to **Patio de María** (formally Casa de la Cultura Roberto Branly), Calle 37 #262, e/ Paseo y 2, Vedado, tel. 881-0722, where María Gattorno has overcome years of official opposition to her providing a venue for rock fans—the persuading argument was her hosting of AIDS benefits and the foreign support that this garnered. Groups such as Zeus per-

form live concerts, and there's also disco Friday and Sunday 9 P.M.–midnight. Open 7:30 A.M.–11 P.M. (five pesos).

The **Pabellón,** La Rampa, esq. Calle N, tel. 832-4921, features rock music on Sunday (US$7).

TANGO AND FLAMENCO

Flamenco is hosted at **Centro Andaluz en Cuba,** Prado #104, e/ Genios y Refugio, tel. 863-6745, a Spanish cultural center with live music and dancing Fridays and Saturday at 10 P.M. Entrance is free. Lessons are offered Tuesday–Thursday 9–11 A.M. (US$15 per hour). The center is open Tuesday–Thursday noon–8 P.M., Friday–Sunday noon–midnight.

El Colmao, Calle Aramburu #366, e/ San José y San Rafael, tel. 870-1113, has a traditional floor show highlighted by flamenco. **El Mesón de la Flota,** Calle Mercaderes #257, e/ Amargura y Brasil, tel. 863-3888, is a classic Spanish *bodega* that also hosts flamenco (open 11 A.M.–11 P.M.), as does the **Bodegón de los Vinos,** in the Fortaleza de San Carlos de la Cabaña.

Into tango? The **Caserón de Tango** Calle Justíz #21, e/ Baratillo y Oficios, tel. 861-0822, one block south of Plaza de Armas in Habana Vieja, highlights the Argentinian music and dance form with tango *peñas* on Wednesday and Friday at 5 P.M., and shows on Saturdays at 10 P.M. and Sunday at 9:30 P.M. Here, the Asociación Nacional Promotora del Tango offers tango lessons (US$5) Thursday at 4–6 P.M. and Saturday 2–4 P.M., and other days by arrangement.

Fans of tango might also check out the **Caserón del Tango,** Neptuno #303, e/ Águila y Italia, tel. 863-0097, a tiny cultural center that hosts tango *peñas* and has live music and dance—*"siempre con tango"*—on Mondays, 5–8 P.M.

BARS

Havana has scores of bars. Take your pick between dollars-only haunts, where a beer might set you back US$3 a pop, to grim local bars where one peso will buy a beer.

A fistful of bars recall the heyday of the 1950s, including Dos Hermanos, La Bodeguita del

Medio, and El Floridita, all haunted by Hemingway's ghost. But you can count the classic bars on your fingers—the city is relatively devoid of the kind of lively sidewalk bars that make Rio de Janeiro buzz and South Beach hum. Long gone are the days when places like Sloppy Joe's packed 'em in like sardines and Havana's bar scene buzzed like a beehive. Most touristy bars are pretty dead, despite the de rigueur live bands. No cigars are sold—bring your own.

Most bars serving locals for pesos are, well . . . rather sad, being run down often to the point of dilapidation. Typically, they serve shots of *aguardiente* (cheap rum; your glass will likely be a sawn-off beer bottle) or beer served in 1.5 liter bottles (50 pesos). Many of their habitués are drunkards. And one visit to their toilets will turn you off them forever.

Habana Vieja

No visit to Havana is complete without sipping a *mojito* at **La Bodeguita del Medio,** Calle Empredado #207, e/ Cuba y Tacón, tel. 33-8276, as Ernest Hemingway did almost daily. However, the *mojitos* are weak, the mint usually wilted, and the servings far too small for the US$4 tab. Hemingway would throw a fit if he tasted the consistently insipid concoctions served to tourists today by consistently surly bar staff. Go for the ambience. Open noon–midnight.

Another Hemingway favorite—and one offering far better (and cheaper; US$2.50) *mojitos*—is the **Dos Hermanos,** Avenida San Pedro #304, esq. Sol, tel. 861-3436, a down-to-earth wharf-front saloon where Hemingway bent elbows with sailors and prostitutes at the long wooden bar, open to the street through wooden *rejas.* Spanish poet García Lorca also drank here. The *mojitos* are good, served by friendly staff, and there's often live music by a great house band comprising a family of musicians. Open 24 hours.

Nearby, the bar in the **Museo de Ron,** Avenida San Pedro #262, e/ Sol y Muralla, tel. 861-8051, is usually empty, except when the cruise ships are in. Visit in the evening, when most tourists are absent. Here you can take your time to savor the full selection of Havana Club rums. A singer performs.

The lobby bar in the **Hotel Ambos Mundos,** Calle Obispo, esq. Mercaderes, tel. 860-9529, is a quiet and pleasant spot. A pianist entertains, and you can watch the flood of pedestrians down Calle Obispo through the lofty French windows. The hotel also has a peaceful rooftop bar where you can sip while looking out over the rooftops of Habana Vieja. Musicians perform Thursday–Sunday and Tuesday 11 A.M.–6 P.M. Open 7 A.M.–11 P.M.

Hemingway enjoyed his daily daiquirí at **El Floridita,** Calle Obispo, esq. Monserrate, tel. 867-1300. The frosty daiquirí for which the bar is famous is a perfect pick-me-up after a hot stroll through town, but be sure to ask for the *Daiquirí Nature,* a hand-shaken version (the regular daiquirís are today made in an electric blender). It may not quite live up to its 1950s aura, when *Esquire* magazine named it one of the great bars of the world, but to visit Havana without sipping a daiquirí here would be like visiting France without tasting the wine.

The atmospheric wood-paneled **Bar Monserrate,** Avenida de Bélgica (Monserrate), esq. Obrapía, tel. 860-9751, just south of El Floridita, is popular with Cubans and is noted for its *Coctel Monserrate* (one teaspoon of sugar, two ounces of grapefruit juice, five drops of grenadine, two ounces of white rum, ice, and a sprig of mint; US$2.50). It's a good spot to while away the afternoon listening to live music that sometimes lasts through the night, drawing Cubans for sizzling salsa. It also draws *jineteros* and *jineteras* eager to sponge a drink or form a more binding union. The staff is no more trustworthy . . . count your change! Open 11 A.M.–3 A.M.

An undiscovered gem is the small bar just inside the **Edificio Bacardí,** Monserrate #261, e/ Progreso y Empredado, tel. 862-9271. Formerly the private bar of the Bacardí family, it is run by Miguel and his mom Doña Rebeca, who speaks English and was taught how to mix cocktails before the Revolution, when a good cocktail really mattered. Her mojitos are strong. The bar is an astonishing exemplar of art deco that casts you right back to the 1920s. Settle into a leather seat and admire your reflection in the mirrored walls. Snacks are served. Open Mon.–Sat. 8 A.M.–8 P.M. It was closed for restoration at last visit.

The **Café Louvre,** Prado, esq. San Rafael, tel. 860-8595, the patio bar of the Hotel Inglaterra, is a good spot to sip a beer or *cuba libre* and watch the comings and goings around Parque Central. Better yet is to nip up to the somewhat secretive little rooftop bar offering great views and live music and dancing.

La Lluvia de Oro, Calle Obispo #316, esq. Habana, tel. 862-9870, is a lively, down-to-earth bar popular with foreigners come to sample the live music and pick up wayward *cubanas* and *cubanos.* It serves cheap but strong *mojitos* (US$2.50), and features live *son* music throughout the day. Open Mon.–Thurs. 8 A.M.–1 A.M., Sat.–Sun. 8 A.M.–3 A.M. Its likeness is the more intimate and always buzzing **Café París,** Calle San Ignacio #202, esq. Obispo, which packs in a mix of Cubans and visitors and is open 24 hours.

Nearby, **La Casa del Escabeche,** Calle Obispo, esq. Villegas, tel. 863-2660, is a simple bar serving delicious *escabeche* fish, *mojitos,* and other cocktails for US$2.50. It has live music.

Taberna Benny Moré, Calle Mercaderes #531, esq. Brasil, tel. 861-1937, on the northeast side of Plaza Vieja, is an upscale bohemian restaurant with walls festooned with the personal effects of Cuban's renowned singer-composer, for whom the place is named. There's live music, and the long bar is a handsome place to bend an elbow. It's mostly frequented by tourists and lacks the soulfulness of places to which Cubans are welcome. Watch your bill . . . I've been scammed by the waiters *every* visit! Open 11 A.M.–midnight.

The **Club Los Marinos,** Avenida Carlos M. Céspedes, tel. 867-1402, overhanging the harbor one block east of Plaza de Armas, is popular with a younger Cuban crowd. It offers music on the jukebox. Open noon–midnight.

The **Bar La Marina,** Avenida San Pedro, esq. Luz, in the Hotel Armadores de Santandar, tel. 862-8000, is an upscale contemporary bar with a nautical motif, including staff in mariners' uniforms. It has live music and is a good spot to enjoy a cocktail and cigar. **Puerto de Sagua,** Avenida de Bélgica (Egido) #603, e/ Jesús María y Acosta, tel. 867-1026 or 863-6186, also has an atmospheric bar with nautical theme, including fishtanks in the porthole windows. Open noon–midnight.

The chicest bar in Habana Vieja is that in the restaurant of the **Hotel Telégrafo,** Paseo del Prado #408, esq. Neptuno, tel. 861-1010, a small yet handsome bar that would look right at home in New York, Los Angeles, or London.

The roof terrace bar in the **Castillo de la Real Fuerza,** on Plaza de Armas, tel. 861-2876, serves snacks and is a peaceful place to sip a cocktail or beer while enjoying the excellent view. Open 9 A.M.–midnight.

For a truly down-to-earth experience, check out **Bar Actualidades,** Monserrate #264, tel. 861-1083, behind the Hotel Plaza. This compact and dingy little bar is favored by Cubans and offers an insight into the nocturnal pleasures of impecunious Cubans. Its red light and raffish Afro-Cuban quality might have appealed to Sammy Davis Jr. and the Rat Pack.

Parque Histórico Militar Morro-Cabaña

Across the harbor channel, the atmospheric **Bar La Tasca,** on the harborfront facing Havana between the Morro and La Cabaña fortresses, is an intimate oak-beamed place full of Spanish weaponry, with a terrace where you can sip your *mojito* while enjoying the views. **El Polvorín,** at the foot of the Morro castle, has a patio with a view past the cannons and across the harbor mouth toward Havana.

Centro Habana and Cerro

This area has few bars of note. To commune with locals, try **Bar Nautilus,** Calle San Rafael, e/ Prado y Consulado, a moody and gloomy place, yet quite lively, with fish tanks in the wall; or **Bar Pekín,** Manrique, esq. Zanja, tel. 860-5085, a clean air-conditioned place popular with Cuban youth.

The **Bar Los Tres Monitos,** Avenida de Italia (Galiano) #164, esq. Virtudes, tel. 33-8209, in the Hotel Lincoln, is a 24-hour bar with karaoke.

Vedado and Plaza de la Revolución

Many bars are associated with the leading hotels. The **El Relicario Bar,** Paseo, e/ 1ra y 3ra, tel. 204-3636, in the Hotel Meliá Cohiba, is popular with a monied, cigar-loving crowd and offers an elegant Edwardian ambience and relative serenity. It has a pool table. The unassuming lobby bar of the **Hotel Habana Libre Tryp,** Calle L, e/ 23 y 25, tel. 55-4011, is a pleasant place for a quick tipple, as is that of the **Hotel Habana Riviera,** Malecón y Paseo, tel. 33-4051.

The **Bar Vista del Golfo,** Calle O, esq. 21, tel. 33-3564, in the Hotel Nacional, has a jukebox, and walls festooned with photos of such famous visitors as Errol Flynn, Johnny Weismuller, and assorted mobsters. Better yet is the hotel's back-garden patio **Bar La Terraza,** where a sea breeze caresses the palms, calming music is offered, and you can sit snug in a sofa chair with a cigar and cocktail in hand. Open 24 hours.

For superb views of the city, try the rooftop bar at the Hotel Nacional, as well as the **Turquino,** on the 25th floor of the Hotel Habana Libre, plus **La Torre,** Calle 17 #55, e/ M y N, tel. 832-2451, atop the Focsa Building (entrance US$1).

For US$1 *mojitos* and US$.50 rum shots head to the **Casa de los Infusiones,** Calle 23, esq. Avenida de los Presidentes, tel. 832-9375, also called Casa del Coctel. Open 24 hours. It was closed for renovation at last visit. Also on the same junction is **La Fuente,** tel. 66-2514, where you can tipple cocktails for US$2, straight rum shots for US$.30, and beers for US$.85 in a reclusive garden.

Playa (Miramar and Beyond)

All the hotels in this area have bars. In addition, two piano bars to consider are at **Dos Gardenias** 7ma Avenida at 26, tel. 204-2353, and **Piano Bar Piel Canela,** at La Maison (Calle 16 #701, esq. 7ma Avenida, Miramar, tel. 204-1543), which sometimes hosts *bolero* and even comedy. Open 10 P.M.–4 A.M. (US$5).

The elegant sky-lit **Los Jardines** Calle 72 e/ 41 y 45, Marianao, tel. 207-0110, in the Tropicana nightclub, is a good place to tipple before or after the show, although it gets few patrons.

CINEMA

Cubans are passionate moviegoers and Havana is blessed with cinemas (by one account more than

170). Hollywood culture saturated the Havana of the 1930s, and the bloom of movie houses coincided with the heyday of art deco and modern styles. Overnight, Havana was graced with a crop of streamlined, futuristic facades suggestive of fantasy. Since then, most cinemas have been allowed to deteriorate to the point of near-dilapidation. And the old film-roll projectors still in use are no less in need of repair . . . remember the days when the celluloid would stick and burn? Nonetheless, *habaneros* have lost none of the prerevolutionary enthusiasm for *el cine,* notably during the annual Latin American Film Festival, when hundreds of movies are shown citywide. Cuba's cinema-going audiences are extremely cultured and will applaud in critical appreciation of good directing.

All movies in Cuba—their making, importation/exportation, and distribution—are under the control of the **Instituto Cubano de Cinematografía** (ICAIC, the Cuban Film Institute), Calle 23 #1155, Vedado, tel. 831-3145 or 833-4634 or 55-2418, cinemateca@icaic.inf.cu, next to the Charlie Chaplin movie house (described later in this chapter). It often has preview screenings of new Cuban releases in its studios.

Movie houses on La Rampa, in Vedado, tend to be less run-down than those in Habana Vieja and Centro Habana. Usually each cinema has only one theater, and thereby one movie at a time; multiplexes have yet to reach Havana.

The menu is surprisingly varied, albeit a bit campy. Leading Hollywood productions are shown (normally within a year or two of release), as are kung fu flicks and other foreign productions, particularly those of socially redeeming quality, alongside movies from Cuba's gifted directors. Adult XXX films are banned, as are certain politically "offensive" movies—*The Wonderful Country,* starring Robert Mitchum, was banned because the villains were called the Castro brothers. Movies are often subtitled in Spanish; others are dubbed, so to enjoy these you'll need to be fluent in Spanish.

The latest issue of *Granma* and *Cartelera,* available for 50 centavos at street kiosks, and sometimes free in hotel lobbies, will list what's currently showing. Children under 16 years of age

CUBA'S MOVIE GREAT

The most respected of Cuba's filmmakers is Tomás Gutiérrez Alea (1928–96), one of the great masters of international cinema, whose work is part of a general questioning of things—part of the New Latin American Cinema. The Film Institute has granted a relative laxity to Gutiérrez, whose populist works are of an irreverent picaresque genre. For example, his 1966 *La muerte de un burócrata (Death of a Bureaucrat)* was a satire on the stifling bureaucracy imposed after the Revolution; and *Memorias del subdesarrollo (Memories of Underdevelopment),* made in 1968, traced the life of a bourgeois intellectual adrift in the new Cuba. He followed it with *La última cena (The Last Supper),* which dealt with a member of the upper class confronting the emerging social phenomenon that was about to topple them.

Gutiérrez started filming in 1947 while an undergraduate law student. Upon graduation, he attended the Centro Sperimentale film school in Rome, where he was heavily influenced by Rosselli and other Italian exponents of the neo-realism movement. He made his first serious work in 1955, filming a documentary on the plight of charcoal workers, earning him black marks with the Batista regime. He contributed to the Revolution at an early stage at the fore of the cinematic section of the Revolutionary army and, following Castro's triumph, the first post-victory documentary, *Esta tierra nuestra (This Land of Ours).* Gutiérrez was instrumental in the formation of ICAIC, the Cuban Film Institute.

His later films are criticisms of the Revolution, in the sense that they are "part of the public dialog as to how the Revolution should proceed." Gutiérrez's work was frequently misinterpreted outside Cuba, and the critical, parodying nature of his films led to the producer being regarded incorrectly as an arch anti-Castroite, much to his own dismay. The extraordinary subtleties of films such as the masterly *Memories of Underdevelopment* proved too sophisticated for Cold War mentalities to the north and had been seized upon by U.S. propagandists in ways that may never have been intended.

Gutiérrez's finest film, a true classic of modern cinema, is *Fresa y chocolate (Strawberries and Chocolate),* which when released in 1994 caused near-riots at cinemas in Havana because the crush for entry was so great. The poignant and provocative movie, set in Havana during the repressive heyday of 1979, explores the nettlesome friendship between a flagrant homosexual and a macho Party member, reflecting the producer's abiding questioning of the Revolution to which he was nonetheless always loyal. It portrays the marginalization of intellectuals, the implementation of prejudices, the idealization of "norms" of behavior, the struggles to be different in a rigid revolutionary context. It is less an indictment than a social analysis of the purge against homosexuals that climaxed in the 1970s, profoundly affecting Cuba's cultural movement.

Fresa y chocolate and the subsequent movie, *Guantanamera,* the producer's last, starred his wife, Mirta Ibarra, in a leading role.

Gutiérrez's faith in the Revolution never faltered. Like Castro, he clung to the thread of his dream as the health of his country deteriorated alongside that of his own.

are not allowed in, regardless of movie content. See the Sidebar "Where To Take The Kids" for information on children's cinema.

Entrance usually costs two pesos—foreigners are rarely charged in dollars.

Habana Vieja

Cine Actualidades, Avenida de Bélgica (Monserrate) #362, e/ Animas y Neptuno, tel. 861-

5193, is a small and rather dingy place known for showing international genre movies. **Cine Cervantes,** Calle Lamparilla #312, e/ Aguacate y Compostela, tel. 863-0026, is a terribly run-down place. **Cine Payret,** Prado #503, esq. San José, tel. 863-3163, opposite the Capitolio, is Havana's largest (albeit much-jaded) cinema and has as many as six showings daily, beginning at 12:30 P.M. It has midnight shows Friday–Sunday.

Centro Habana and Cerro

Cine Águila de Oro, Calle Rayo #108, e/ Dragones y Zanja, tel. 863-3386, is a cramped, grungy, noisy cinema specializing in kung-fu and Japanese movies. The recently renovated **Cine Astral,** Calzada de Infanta #501, esq. San Martín, Centro Habana, tel. 878-1001, is now the comfiest *cine* in Havana. **Cine El Mégano,** Calle Industria #416, esq. San Martín, tel. 863-8023, is rundown and shows all types of films. **Cine América,** Galiano, esq. Neptuno, tel. 862-5416, was once a spectacular art deco cinema, but is sadly rundown. It rarely shows films, however, being dedicated mostly to theater and concerts.

The **Alliance Française,** Avenida de los Presidentes #407, e/ 17 y 19, tel. 33-3370, shows French films in the library on Mondays (11 A.M.), Wednesdays (3 P.M.), and Fridays (5 P.M.). Entrance is free.

Vedado and Plaza de la Revolución

Cine 23 y 12, Calle 23 #1212, e/ 12 y 14, tel. 833-6906, is a small cinema that screens at 8 P.M. **Cine Acapulco,** Avenida 26, e/ 35 y 37, tel. 833-9573, has movies starting at 4:30 P.M. **Cine Charles Chaplin,** Calle 23 #1155, e/ 10 y 12, tel. 831-1101, shows daily except Tuesday at 5 and 8 P.M. (box office opens 30 minutes prior). The Chaplin has been called the largest theater in the world. Also here is the **Centro Cultural Cinematográfico ICAIC,** a *sala de video* specializing in cult movies. **Cine La Rampa,** Calle 23 #111, e/ O y P, tel. 878-6146, shows daily except Wednesday from 4:40 P.M.; it mostly shows Cuban and Latin American films (plus the occasional obscure foreign movie) and is one of Havana's more comfy cinemas. The usually hot (due to fickle air-conditioning) **Cine Riviera,** Calles 23 y H, tel. 832-9564, has predominantly action or other Hollywood movies daily from 4:40 P.M. **Teatro Cine Trianón,** Línea #706, e/ Paseo y A, tel. 832-9648, tends towards classic oldies, although its movie schedule is irregular. And **Cine Yara,** Calle 23 y Calle L, tel. 832-9430, opens at 12:30 P.M. and is Havana's "main" theater.

Playa (Miramar and Beyond)

The **Sala Glauber Rocha,** Avenida 212, esq. 31, La Coronela, tel. 271-8967, in the Fundación

Cine Riviera

del Nuevo Cine Latinoamericano, shows movies (mostly Latin American), Tues.–Fri. at 3 P.M. and 5:30 P.M. (US$2).

Salas de Video

Havana also has plenty of *salas de video,* tiny screening rooms (often illegal) where usually recent-release foreign movies are shown on TVs. Often the movies have been pirated from satellite TV and are sometimes of dubious quality. Many cinemas have *salas de videos* attached . . . often in the bar. These include the Cine Águila de Oro, Cine Alhambra, Cine Yara, and the **Sala de Video Charlot,** at ICAIC, which has seasons focusing on the works of single directors.

THEATER, CLASSICAL MUSIC, AND DANCE

Havana has seven major theaters, although they are used mostly for operatic, symphonic, and

ENTERTAINMENT

FARÁNDULAS

Just like any cosmopolitan capital, Havana has its bohemian social scene that revolves around current events. Havana's culture vultures are collectively known as *los farándulas,* literally "troupe of strolling players," but colloquially meaning the "in-the-artistic-swing scene." Each cultural bent has its own *farándula,* such as the *nueva trova* adherents, with their long hair and hippyish duds; and the ballet-buffs, which are largely gay and dress to the nines. More than other cities, however, Havana's *farándulas* are fluid and move between scenes, demonstrating an appreciation for the cross-section of arts.

other concerts. Theater is the least developed of Cuba's cultural media and has been usurped by the Revolution as a medium for mass consciousness raising. As such, it became heavily politicized. In recent years, an avant-garde theater offering veiled political criticism has begun to evolve.

Although legitimate or live theater has yet to take off, Cubans are enthusiastic lovers of ballet and classical music. "In the realm of classical music Cuba has been an inspirational locale rather than a breeding ground for great composers and instrumentalists," says noted pianist Daniel Fenmore. Nonetheless, it is astounding how many contemporary Cubans are accomplished classical musicians. Everywhere you go, you will come across violinists, pianists, and cellists serenading you for tips while you eat.

Ballet appeared in Cuba as early as 1842, and throughout the 19th century, foreign ballet companies performed, notably at the Teatro Tacón. Finally, in 1931, Havana got its own ballet company: the Sociedad Pro-Arte Música, with a conservatory that produced many outstanding ballet dancers, including the most famous, Alicia Alonso.

Alonso studied with the American Ballet following its inception in the 1940s and became a prima ballerina with the company. In 1948, she returned to Cuba and, sponsored by Batista—who hated ballet but considered her star status a propaganda bonus—that year founded the Ballet Alicia Alonso, which in 1955 became the Ballet

de Cuba. Alonso was outspoken in her criticism of the "Sordid Era," and she went into exile in 1956 when Batista withdrew his patronage. The Revolution later adopted her—Alonso is a favorite of Fidel—and her ballet company was reformed and renamed the Ballet Nacional de Cuba, which became a showpiece for the Cuban Revolution, making regular forays abroad, including to the United States in 1978. After many notable performances around the world, she gave her last public performance in 1995 at age 75.

Alonso is revered as a national icon and an exemplar of the cultural achievements of the postrevolutionary years. There is no doubting her technical excellence and her inspirational character, and her company is renowned worldwide for its original choreography and talent. However, many critics consider her a *prima donna* (a "legendary figure" with an "overweening personal ambition," wrote Claudia Lightfoot), and she has been accused of maintaining a lilywhite dance corps.

Cuba boasts several classical orchestras, notably the National Symphony Orchestra, known for the occasional pings of dropped bows and triangles. It first performed in November 1960 and has a repertoire ranging from 17th-century works to contemporary creations, with a special emphasis on popularizing works by Latin American and Cuban composers, such as Amadeo Roldán (1900–39) and Alejandro García Caturla (1906–40), who fought the "musical colonialism" of the era to imbue their compositions with Afro-Cuban elements. Watch, too, for performances by Frank Fernández, Cuba's finest classical pianist.

Audiences are known to rise to their feet and yell with delight at the end of concerts.

It's often difficult to make a reservation by telephone—few box office operators speak English in any event. Instead, you should go ahead to the venue and buy a ticket in advance or just before the performance. You'll generally be charged in U.S. dollars; Cubans will pay the equivalent in pesos.

Avant-Garde Troupes: Look for performances by **Así Somos,** Calle A #310, Apto. 7B, e/ 3ra y 3raA, Miramar, tel. 203-4276, lorna@cubarte .cult.cu, an avant-garde dance company under the tutelage of Lorna Burdsall, an American who trained at the Julliard, in New York; **Argos Teatro,** Calzada de Ayestarán #507A, esq. 20 de Mayo, Nuevo Vedado, tel. 878-5551, a foremost experimental theater company formed by graduates of the equally exciting and innovative Teatro Buendía; **DanzaAbierta,** Calle 4 #103, e/ Calzada y 5ta, Vedado, tel. 833-4560, a socially and politically conscientious dance troupe that has performed abroad to critical acclaim; **Danza Combinatorio,** Calzada de Infanta, esq. Arroyo, Edif. 20 plantas, piso 6, Apto. 65, Centro Habana, alhm@artsoft.cult.cu, a nine-member troupe known for its surrealistic sensualism; and **Danza Contemporánea de Cuba,** (see Teatro Nacional), an internationally acclaimed contemporary dance troupe at the spearhead of the Cuban movement.

Venues

The most important theater is the baroque **Gran Teatro de la Habana,** Paseo de Martí #458, e/ San Rafael y San Martín, Habana Vieja, tel. 861-3078 or 33-1526, on the west side of Parque Central. It's the main stage for the acclaimed Ballet Nacional de Cuba (Calzada #510 e/ D y E, Vedado, Ciudad Habana, C.P. 10400, tel. 832-4625, www.balletcuba.cu; or Paseo de Martí (Prado) #207, Habana Vieja, tel. 862-7053) as well as the Ballet Español de la Habana, and the national opera company. The national ballet corps is world-class. However, anyone used to a live orchestra may be disappointed, as mostly the ballet is performed to taped music. Why? Well, suggests Claudia Lightfoot: "The Ballet Orchestra is the only example of truly awful music I have ever heard in Havana." Jazz and other performances are often given, and most weeks throughout the year, you can even see Spanish dance here. The building has three theaters—the Teatro García Lorca, where ballet and concerts are held, and the smaller Sala Alejo Carpentier and Sala Antonin Artaud, for less-commercial, experimental performances, such as those the Centro Pro Arte Lírico, which produces opera, including traditional comic operettas called *zarzuelas.* Don't be surprised if the audience gets into the act by singing along! Performances are generally Thursday–Saturday at 8:30 P.M. and

Sunday at 5 P.M. (US$3, or US$10 for best orchestra seats). A dress code (no shorts or hats) applies for performances.

The **Basílica de San Francisco de Asís,** Calle Oficios, e/ Amargura y Brasil, Habana Vieja, tel. 862-9683, in Habana Vieja, also hosts classical concerts in the former cathedral nave. Performances are daily at 6 P.M. (US$2–10). Nearby, **Gaia,** Brasil, e/ Cuba y Aguiar, tel. 862-0401, offers predominantly British works, with sponsorship by the British Council. Classical and ecclesiastical concerts are featured in the diminutive **Iglesia de San Francisco de Paula,** Avenida del Puerto, esq. Leonor Pérez, Habana Vieja. The **Museo de la Música,** Calle Capdevilla #1, Habana Vieja, tel. 861-9846, offers classical concerts and *peñas* Saturday and Sunday at 4 P.M. (US$2).

Look for performances of the National Symphony at the modern **Teatro Nacional,** Avenida Carlos M. de Céspedes, esq. Paseo, Vedado, tel. 879-6011, tnc@cubarte.cult.cu, one block west of the Plaza de la Revolución. It has two main performance halls—the Sala Avellaneda, for concerts and opera, and the Sala Covarrubias—and three small spaces. Avant-garde works are showcased on the Noveno Piso (ninth floor) theater . . . a "death trap" thought writer Claudia Lightfoot, reached by "unlit dilapidated stairs." It also hosts important Communist Party functions and revolutionary celebrations. The Danza Contemporánea de Cuba is based here. Concerts are held Friday–Saturday at 8:30 P.M. and Sunday at 5 P.M. (US$2–10). The ticket office is open Tuesday–Thursday 10 A.M.–6 P.M., and Friday–Sunday 3–9 P.M.

The **Teatro Mella,** Línea #657, e/ A y B, Vedado, tel. 833-5651, is noted for its contemporary dance and theater, including contemporary and avant-garde performances by the Danza Contemporánea de Cuba and Conjunto Folklórico Nacional (US$5–10). **Teatro Cine Trianón,** Línea #706, e/ Paseo y A, tel. 832-9648, often features avant-garde foreign classics, such as the works of Arthur Miller and Tennessee Williams, performed by the Teatro el Público company (five pesos).

The 150-seat **Teatro Buendía,** Calle Loma y

HAVANA'S MUSEUMS

You can purchase a one-day ticket for US$9 good for all the museums in Habana Vieja; it's available from the Museo de la Ciudad, in the Palacio de los Capitanes Generales.

Museum opening times are fickle and change frequently. Most official resources regarding opening times give conflicting information. Different hours often apply for July and August. Call ahead.

Most labels in museums are in Spanish only. Some museums have guided tours, usually with English-speaking guides. At others, a US$1 tip will usually get you a guided tour. However, not all the guides are particularly versed in the subject matter.

Most museums charge extra for the privilege of taking photographs—usually US$2 to US$5 for cameras, and US$10 to US$15 for videos. A few museums charge per photograph.

Churches: Most churches are closed except during church services. However, there is usually a *sacristán* or church worker with a key living nearby. They're usually happy to open up for visitors (don't forget to tip).

Habana Vieja

Casa-Museo del Libertador Simón Bolívar (House and Museum of Liberator Simón Bolívar): Calle Mercaderes #160, e/ Lamparilla y Obrapia, tel. 861-3988.

Museo Casa Natal de José Martí (Birthplace Museum of José Martí): Calle León Pérez, Habana Vieja, tel. 862-3778.

Museo de Arte Colonial (Museum of Colonial Art): Calle San Ignacio #61, Plaza de la Catedral, tel. 862-6440.

Museo de Arte Religioso (Museum of Religious Art): Iglesia y Convento de San Francisco de Asís, Calle Oficios, e/ Armagura y Brasil, tel. 862-9683. A must see!

Museo de Ásia (Asia Museum): Calle Mercaderes #111, e/ Obispo y Obrapia, tel. 863-9740.

Museo de Automóviles (Automobile Museum): Calle Obispo, e/ Mercaderes y San Ignacio (in preparation at press time).

Museo de Bomberos (Museum of Firemen): Calle Agramonte #257, e/ Neptuno y Animas, tel. 862-7762.

Museo de Campaña de Alfabetización (Museum of the Literacy Campaign): Antigua Cámara de Representantes, Calle Oficios #211, tel. 862-4076.

Museo de la Ciudad de La Habana (City of Havana Museum): Calle Tacón #1, e/ Obispo y O'Reilly, tel. 861-2876. A must see!

Museo de Esclavitud (Museum of Slavery): Calle Obrapía, esq. Avenida del Puerto (in preparation at press time).

Museo de las Finanzas (Finance Museum): Banco Nacional de Cuba, Calle Obispo #211, esq. Cuba, tel. 867-3000, ext. 2468.

Museo y Archivo de la Música (Music Archives and Museum): Calle Capdevila #1, tel. 861-9846 and 863-0052.

Museo y Farmacia Taquechel (Taquechel Museum and Pharmacy): Obispo #155, e/ Mercaderes y San Ignacio, tel. 862-9286.

Museo Histórico de las Ciencias Naturales Carlos Finlay (Historic Museum of Natural Sciences): Cuba #460, e/ Amargura y Brasil, tel. 863-4824.

Museo Nacional de Bellas Artes (National Fine Arts Museum): Calle Trocadero, e/ Zulueta y Monserrate, tel. 863-9042 or 861-2332 (Cuban section); Calle San Rafael, e/ Zulueta y Monserrate, tel. 861-3858 or 862-0140 (International section). A must see!

Museo Nacional de Cerámica (National Ceramic Museum): Castillo de la Real Fuerza, Plaza de Armas, tel. 861-6130.

Museo Nacional de História Natural (National Natural History Museum): Calle Obispo #61, e/ Oficios y Baratillo, tel. 862-0353.

Museo de Naipes (Museum of Playing Cards): Calle Muralla #101, Plaza Vieja, tel. 860-1534.

Museo Numismático (Numismatic Museum): Calle Oficios #8 e/ Obispo y Obrapía, Habana Vieja, tel. 861-5811.

Museo de los Orishas (Museum of the Orishas): Prado #615, e/ Dragones y Monte tel. 863-5953 (*santería* exhibition).

Museo de Plata (Museum of Silverwork): Calle Obispo # 113, e/ Obispo y Mercaderes.

Museo de la Revolución (Museum of the Revolution): Calle Refugio #1 e/ Agramonte y Monserrate, tel. 862-4091. A must see!

Museo de Ron (Museum of Rum): Avenida del Puerto #262, e/ Churruca y Sol, tel. 861-8051, fax 862-1825. A must see!

Museo de San Salvador de la Punta: Castillo De San Salvador De La Punta, Avenida Carlos M. de Céspedes, esq. Prado y Malecón (salvaged colonial treasures).

Museo del Tabaco (Cigar Museum): Calle Mercaderes #120, e/ Obispo y Obrapia, tel. 861-5795.

Parque Histórico Militar Morro-Cabaña (Morro-Cabaña Historical Military Park): Carratera de la Cabaña, Habana del Este, tel. 862-7653. A must see!

Centro Habana

Museo Fragua Martiana (Museum of Martí's Hard Labor): Calle Principe #108, esq. Hospital, tel. 870-7338.

Museo de Juan Manuel Fangio: Hotel Lincoln, Galiano, e/ Animas y Virtudes (tells of world-race car driver Fangio's kidnapping).

Museo Lezama Lima: Calle Trocadero #162 e/ Crespo y Industria, tel. 863-4161 (dedicated to novelist Lezama Lima).

Vedado

Casa Museo Abel Santamaría (House of Abel Santamaría): Calle 25 #154, tel. 870-0417 (dedicated to the martyred revolutionary hero).

Museo Antropológico Montane (Montane Anthropological Museum): Escuela de Ciencias, Universidad de La Habana, Calle L y San Lázaro, tel. 879-3488.

Museo de Artes Decorativas (Museum of the Decorative Arts): Calle 17 #502, e/ D y E, Vedado, tel. 832-0924.

Museo de la Danza (Dance Museum): Calle Línea #365, esq. Avenida de los Presidentes, tel. 831-2198.

Museo de História del Deportivo (Museum of Sports History): Sala Polivatente Ramón Fonst, Avenida Rancho Boyeros, e/ 19 de Mayo and Bruzón, tel. 881-4696.

Museo de História Naturales Felipe Poey (Felipe Poey Natural History Museum): Escuela de Ciencias, Universidad de La Habana, Calle L y San Lázaro, tel. 832-9000.

Museo José Martí: Plaza de la Revolución, tel. 882-0906 (dedicated to the national hero). A must see!

(continued on next page)

HAVANA'S MUSEUMS (cont'd)

Museo de Máximo Gómez: Quinta de los Molinos, Avenida Salvador Allende, e/ Infanta y Luaces tel. 879-8850 (dedicated to the hero of the Wars of Independence).

Museo Napoleónico (Napoleonic Museum): Calle San Miguel #1159, e/ Ronda y Masón, 879-1460.

Museo Postal Cubano (Philately Museum): Avenida Rancho Boyeros, esq. 19 de Mayo, Plaza de la Revolución, tel. 870-5581.

Playa (Miramar and Beyond)

Museo de la Campaña de Alfabetización (Museum of the Literacy Campaign): Avenida 29E, esq. 76, tel. 260-8054. A must see!

Museo del Ministerio del Interior (Museum of the Ministry of Interior): 5ta Avenida, esq. Calle 14, tel. 203-4432.

Museo Nacional del Aire (National Air Museum): Avenida 212, e/ Calles 29 y 31, tel. 271-7753.

Suburban Havana

Museo Ernesto Hemingway: Calle Vigía, San Francisco de Paula, tel. 91-0809.

Museo de Municipal de Habana del Este (Municipal Museum of Habana del Este): Calle 504 #5B12, esq. 5C, Guanabo, tel. 96-4184.

Museo Municipal de Guanabacoa (Municipal Museum of Guanabacoa): Calle Martí #108, e/ Valenzuela (Versallse) y Quintín Bandera, tel. 97-9117.

Museo Municipal de Regla (Municipal Museum of Regla): Calle Martí #158 e/ Facciolo y La Piedra, Regla, tel. 94-6989.

38, Nuevo Vedado, tel. 881-6689, in a converted Greek Orthodox church, hosts performances by the eponymous theater company, considered to be Cuba's most innovative and accomplished. It is frequently on world tours, but when in Cuba usually performs here Friday–Sunday at 8:30 P.M. (five pesos).

The **Teatro Amadeo Roldán** Avenida 7ma, esq. D, Vedado, tel. 832-1168, on the east side of Parque Villalon, was recently restored to grandeur and features classical concerts year-round (US$5–10). Nearby is the **Teatro Hubert de Blanck,** Calzada #657, e/ Calles A y B, tel. 833-5762, known for both modern and classical plays. It hosts the Teatro Estudio theater company . . . said to be Cuba's finest. Shows (in Spanish) are usually Friday–Saturday at 8:30 P.M. and Sunday at 5 P.M. (US$5). And the **Teatro Bertolt Brecht,** Calle 13, esq. I, tel. 832-9359, hosts three theater companies producing a wide range of works.

Sala Teatro El Sótano, Calle K #514, e/ 25 y 27, Vedado, tel. 832-0630, hosts contemporary theater Friday–Saturday at 8:30 P.M. and Sundays at 5 P.M.

Casa de la Música, Calle 20 #3308, e/ Avenida 33 y 35, Miramar, tel. 204-0447, offers concerts by soloists and chamber ensembles.

Comedy

Comic theater is popular with Cubans. It is considered part of the national culture and was an important element in 19th-century life. Most cabaret shows also feature stand-up comedy. However, you'll need to be fluent in Spanish to get many giggles out of the shows, which although heavy on easy-to-understand burlesque are also full of subtly hidden references to politically sensitive third-rail issues. They're also, by Western standards, definitely *not* politically correct. Women, blacks, and homosexuals are the constant butt of crude jokes based on well-known stereotypes.

In Habana Vieja, head to **Casa de la Comedia** (also called Salón Ensayo), Calle Justíz #18, esq. Baratillo, tel. 863-9282, one block southeast of Plaza de Armas. It hosts comic theater on weekends at 7 P.M. (US$2).

Teatro Fausto, Prado #201, esq. Colón, Habana Vieja, tel. 862-5416, also has comedy Friday–Saturday at 8:30 P.M. and Sundays at 5 P.M.

Bar Monserrate, Avenida de Bélgica (Monserrate), esq. Obrapía, tel. 860-9751, has a "Noche del humor" (comedy night) each Saturday at 10 P.M. (US$6 *consumo mínimo*).

Comedy is also featured as part of the vaudeville routines at **Teatro América,** Avenida de Italia, e/ Concordia y Neptuno, tel. 862-5416, held Saturday at 8:30 P.M. and Sundays at 5 P.M.

In Vedado, the **Teatro Bertolt Brecht,** Calle 13, esq. I, tel. 832-9359, specializes in comedy, offered Tuesdays at 8:30 P.M. The **Teatro Guiñol,** Calle M, e/ 17 y 19, tel. 832-6262, on the west side of the Focsa building, is Cuba's leading children's theater with comedy and puppet shows on Fridays at 3 P.M., Saturdays at 5 P.M., and Sundays at 10:30 A.M. and 5 P.M. (US$2). **La Torre,** Calle 17, e/ M y N, the top-floor restaurant in the Focsa, hosts an evening of comedy, karaoke, and *animación* Friday–Sunday 11 P.M. (US$15 including a bottle of rum).

The **Sala Teatro El Sótano,** Calle K #514, e/ 25 y 27, Vedado, tel. 832-0630, has comedy every Thursday evening, at 5–8:30 P.M.; the **Club Scherazade,** Calle M, e/ 19 y 17, has comedy on Tuesdays at 8 P.M.; and **El Cortijo,** Calle 25, esq. O, adjoining the Hotel Vedado, has comedy and magic show Friday–Saturday 11 P.M.–2 A.M.

Comedy is also sometimes performed at the **Café Cantante,** Paseo, esq. 39, tel. 873-5713, in the Teatro Nacional; and at **Humor Club Cocodrilo,** Avenida 3ra and 10, Vedado.

MUSEUMS AND GALLERIES

Few cities in Latin America can match Havana's showcase museums and galleries. Havana has about 40 major museums and several dozen art galleries, many of which host revolving exhibitions.

The bimonthly *Galerías de Arte Programación,* available from the **Centro de Desarrollo de las Artes Visuales,** at San Ignacio #352, in Plaza Vieja, lists openings.

See the Sightseeing chapters for details on museums.

Art Galleries

The **Museo Nacional de Bellas Artes,** tel. 861-3858 or 862-0140, musna@cubarte.cult.cu, www.museonacional.cult.cu, in Habana Vieja, is Cuba's leading gallery. It has separate Cuban (Calle Trocadero, e/ Zulueta y Monserrate) and international (Calle San Rafael, e/ Zulueta y Monserrate) sections. See the Habana Vieja chapter for details.

Havana's revolving art, sculpture, and photo exhibitions often draw top international artists as well as Cubans of stature. Cuba makes great efforts to display art from other countries, notably the Caribbean and Latin America, as for example the "Art of Our Americas" collection, housed in the **Galería Haydee Santamaría,** Avenida de los Presidentes, e/ 3ra y 5ta, Vedado, tel. 832-3537. The collection comprises more than 6,000 pieces encompassing sculpture, engravings, paintings, photographs, and popular art. The gallery is part of the **Casa de las Américas,** 3ra Calle, esq. Avenida de los Presidentes, tel. 55-2707, fax 33-4554, casa@artsoft.cult.cu, www.casa.cult.cu, a nongovernmental institution that has studied and promoted every aspect of Latin American and Caribbean culture since 1959. Parts of the collection are housed in the **Galería Marianao,** Calle 15 #607, tel. 55-2702.

The **Centro Wilfredo Lam,** Calle San Ignacio #22, tel. 861-2096 and 861-3419, wlam@artsoft.cult.cu, has a collection of 1,250 contemporary art pieces from Cuba and around the world. Open Mon.–Fri. and alternate Sat. 8:30 A.M.–4:30 P.M. Entrance costs US$2. It sponsors the prestigious **Bienal de la Habana**.

OTHER ENTERTAINMENT

Aqua Espectáculos

Swimming pool *espectáculos* (also called *ballets acuáticos*) are choreographed water ballets with sound and light and are offered at the **Hotel**

Meliá Cohiba Wednesday at 8 P.M.; and the **Hotel Nacional,** Sundays at 8 P.M. The **Aquario Nacional,** 3ra Avenida, esq. Calle 62, tel. 203-6401 or 202-5872, offers a *ballet acuático* Tuesday–Sunday at 10:30 A.M., noon, 5 P.M., 7 P.M., and 9 P.M.

The **Hotel El Viejo y el Mar,** 5ta Avenida, esq. Calle 248, Santa Fe, tel. 204-1909, in the Marina Hemingway complex, also offers a *ballet acuático* Tuesday at 9 P.M.

Fashion Shows

La Maison, Calle 16 #701, esq. 7ma Avenida, Miramar, tel. 204-1543, is renowned for its *desfiles de modas* (fashion shows) held beneath the stars in the terrace garden of an elegant old mansion, on a stage lit by a sound and light show. Reservations are recommended. Entrance costs US$10 (US$15 including transportation and a bottle of rum). A 4 P.M. matinee show is offered on weekends; and an *espectáculo* (cabaret show) is hosted along with the fashion show on Friday and Saturday. It offers a dinner and show package for US$30; the dinner is nothing to write home about . . . the usual *criollo* mix. The **La Maison en Verano** café, to the rear, serves snacks, plus grilled fish and chicken dishes (US$2.50 to US$6); it has a pool that draws families with kids. A disco follows the show, and there's a piano bar in a separate air-conditioned building. Open 9:30 P.M.–1 A.M.

The **Hotel Nacional** hosts a fashion show in the garden each Sunday at 2 P.M.

Poetry Readings and Literary Events

La Moderna Poesía, Calle Obispo #525, esq. Bernaza, Habana Vieja, tel. 861-5600, hosts literary events; as does the **Unión Nacional de Escritores y Artistas de Cuba** (UNEAC), Calle 17, esq. H, Vedado, tel. 832-4551, and UNEAC's **Casa de la Poesia,** Calle Muralla #63, e/ Oficios y Inquisidor, Habana Vieja, tel. 861-

8251; the **Casa de las Américas,** 3ra Calle, esq. Avenida de los Presidentes, tel. 55-2706, fax 33-4554, casa@artsoft.cult.cu, www.casa.cult.cu; the **Fundación Alejo Carpentier,** Empedrado # 215, Habana Vieja, tel. 861-3667; and **La Madriguera,** a popular hangout for university students at Avenida Salvador Allende, e/ Infanta y Luaces, Centro Habana.

The **Museo Nacional de Bellas Artes,** tel. 861-3858 or 862-0140, musna@cubarte.cult.cu, www.museonacional.cult.cu, also hosts literary events, as well as film screenings and musical presentations.

The *azotea* (rooftop) has been a traditional meeting ground for literary groups. Ask around at UNEAC for upcoming *azotea* events.

Transvestite Shows

Cubans have a tremendous sense of satire, and transvestite humor is a staple of any comedy show. Transvestite shows are sometimes hosted upstairs in the **Centro Cultural del Árabe** Prado #256, e/ Refugio y Trocadero, tel. 861-0582, Fri.–Sun. 9 A.M.–midnight (US$15).

Castropol, Malecón #107, esq. Genios, Centro Habana, tel. 861-4864, is also popular for its drag cabaret, Mon.–Thurs. at 11:30 P.M. (US$1). Another *tranvestis* show is hosted at the **Sociedad Cultural Rosalía de Castro,** Avenida de Bélgica #504 (altos), e/ Máximo Gómez y Dragones, tel. 862-3193, facing the Plazuela de las Ursulinas.

Bar de las Estrellas, Calle A #507, e/ 15 y 16, in the Lawton district, south of Cerro, is a *paladar* (private restaurant) with a transvestite cabaret at 10 P.M.

Cigar Lounges

There are a number of cigar shops with lounges attached. For details, see the Where To Buy section, under Cigars, in the Shopping chapter.

Sports and Recreation

Havana has many *centros deportivos* (sports centers). The largest is the **Complejo Panamericano,** Vía Monumental Km 1.5, Ciudad Panamericano, Habana del Este, tel. 95-4140. It includes an Olympic athletic stadium, tennis courts, a swimming pool, and even a velodrome for cycling.

Cubadeportes, Calle 20 #710, e/ 7 y 9, Miramar, manages Cuban sports and access to them for foreigners. For sports events in Cuba call tel. 204-7230.

Most outdoor recreational activities are under the bailiwick of two state entities: **Cubamar,** Calle 15 #752, esq. Paseo, Vedado, tel. 66-2423 or 95-2309, fax 33-3111, cubamar@cubamar .mit.cma.net, and **Rumbos,** Línea #60, Vedado, tel. 66-2113 or 33-4171, fax 33-3110, director @rumvia.rumb.cma.net.

Organized Tours

Agencia de Viajes Cubadeportes, tel. 204-1914, specializes in sports tourism and arranges visits to international sporting events, training facilities, and related locations.

Last Frontier Expeditions, 4823 White Rock Circle, Suite H, Boulder, CO 80301-3260, 303/530-9275, Bob@cubatravelexperts.com, www.cubatravelexperts.com, specializes in trips to Cuba for sporting enthusiasts.

In Canada, **Eleggua Project,** 7171 Torbram Rd., Suite 51, Mississauga, ON L4T 3W4, 905/678-0426 or 800/8181-8840, fax 905/678-1421, cancuba@pathcom.com, www.pathcom .com/~cancuba, specializes in athletic and sports study programs to Cuba.

PARTICIPATORY ACTIVITIES

Bicycling

See By Bicycle, in the Transportation chapter, for general details on bicycling in Cuba, including renting bicycles.

A good resource is Ignacio Villaverde Rivero, president of the **Club Nacional de Cicloturismo Gran Caribe,** Lonja del Comercio #6D, Calle Oficios, Habana Vieja, tel. 96-9193, fax 66-9908, trans@ip.etecsa.cu, which offers weekend and week-long cycle trips.

Cuba's **Confederación Panamericana de Ciclismo,** Vía Monumental Km 4, Ciudad Panamericano, tel. 95-1286, oversees Cuba's competitive race team, which trains at the **Velodromo Reynaldo Passiero,** tel. 97-3776. The confederation also welcomes cyclists of all levels to the **Escuela de Ciclismo de las Américas** (Cycling School of the Americas).

Another good resource is Colin Hearth, tel./fax 31-46252, former director of the Canadian Cycling Association and who now lives in the city of Las Tunas. Also read *Cuba is Not Only Varadero,* by Jarzy Adamuszek, a personal account of a bicycle journey in 1994, available through www.cubabooks.com.

Organized Tours: In North America, **Global Exchange,** 2017 Mission St. #303, San Francisco, CA 94110, 415/255-7296, fax 415/255-7498, info@globalexchange.org, www.global exchange.org, offers bicycle adventures in Cuba (US$1,600, including airfare from Cancún), as do **Active Journeys,** 4891 Dundas St. W, Suite 4, Toronto, ON M9A 1B2, Canada, 416/236-5011 or 800/597-5594, fax 416/236-4790, info@activejourneys.com, www.activejourneys .com; and **Niagara Safaris,** 38 Nickerson Ave., St. Catharines, ON L2N 3M4, Canada, 905/646-7505, fax 905/646-8010, biketours @niagarasafari.com, www.niagarasafari.com.

Citizen Diplomats, P.O. Box 7293, Philadelphia, PA 19101, 215/222-1253, tourdecana@aol .com, offers bicycle tours in association with the International Bicycling Fund and Tour de Caña.

The largest selection of bicycle tours is offered by **MacQueen's Adventures Tours,** 430 Queen St., Charlottestown, Prince Edward Island, Canada CIA 4E8, 902/368-2453 or 800/969-2822, fax 902/894-4547; biketour@macqueens .com, www.macqueens.com.

Lucie Levine, 15543 Maplewood Dr., Sonoma, CA 95476, tel./fax 707/996-1731, also arranges bike trips.

In Germany **Kubareisen,** Lindwurmstr. 207, D-80337 Munich, tel./fax 89/7479-1064, info@

cycle-cuba.com, www.ccc-tours.de, offers bicycle tours of Cuba.

Bowling

You can practice your 10-pin bowling at an alley in the **Hotel Kohly,** at Avenida 49 esq. 36A, Reparto Kohly, Vedado, tel. 204-0240 (US$5 per hour); or at **La Bolera,** at the Club de Golf Habana. The club has a fully mechanized two-lane bowling alley and full-size pool tables (US$2.50 for 10 innings, US$5 per hour; open noon–midnight).

Golf

Club de Golf Habana, Carretera de Vento Km 8, Capdevila, Boyeros, tel. 55-8746 or 33-8919, fax 33-8820, is hidden east of Avenida de la Independencia in the industrial-residential area called Capdevilla, about 20 km south of Havana. The "Diplo Golf Course" was opened as the Rover's Athletic Club in 1948 by the British community and maintained by the British Embassy until given to the Cuban government in 1980. Of four courses in Havana in 1959, this is the only one remaining. The nine-hole course—with 18 tees and 22.5 hectares of fairway—is no Palm Springs. The two sets of tees, positioned for play to both sides of the fairway, make the holes play quite differently. The course, a "woodland parkland-style layout" that is compared to Pinehurst in North Carolina, starts off badly, but the fifth and sixth holes are described as "well-designed holes that could hold their own on almost any course of the world." The place is popular on weekends with Cuban families, who flock to the swimming pool, not the golf course. Plans to expand to 18 holes had not materialized at press time.

"*Golfito*" (as the locals know it) has a minimally stocked pro shop, plus five tennis courts, a swimming pool, and two restaurants. The Bar Hoy 19 (19th Hole) overlooks the greens. The club hosts golf competitions. Membership costs US$70 plus US$45 monthly (US$15 for additional family members). A round costs nonmembers US$20 for nine holes (US$30 for 18). You can rent clubs for US$10. Caddies cost US$6. A US$3.50 fee is charged to use the pool, US$2 for the tennis facilities. Jorge Duque is the affable resident golf pro; he charges US$5 per 30 minutes of instruction.

The **Club Habana** 5ta Avenida, e/ 188 y 192, Reparto Flores, Playa, tel. 204-5700, fax 204-5705, has a practice range. The club serves its members, but nonmembers are welcome (entrance costs US$10 Mon.–Fri., and US$15 Sat.–Sun.).

Wings of the World, 237 McRae Drive, Toronto, ON Canada M4G 1T7, 416/482-1223, fax 416/486-4001, info@wow.on.ca, www.wow.on.ca, and **Last Frontier Expeditions** (4823 White Rock Circle, Suite H, Boulder, CO 80301-3260, 303/530-9275, Bob@cubatravelexperts.com, www.cubatravelexperts.com) both offer golf tours from North America.

Gyms and Spas

Most upscale tourist hotels have gyms or spas. One of the best facilities is at **Club Habana,** 5ta Avenida, e/ 188 y 192, Reparto Flores, Playa, tel. 204-5700, fax 204-5705; open 7 A.M.–1 A.M. The **Hotel Golden Tulip Parque Central** has a splendid rooftop gym with a whirlpool tub; open 8 A.M.–8 P.M. The **Hotel Kohly** has a sauna and massage services, plus gym; open 8 A.M.–8 P.M. The **Hotel Meliá Cohiba, Hotel Riviera,** and **Hotel Meliá Habana** have gyms with sauna, massage, and aerobics. Otherwise, don't expect equipment and facilities to be up to Western standards.

Two of the better gymnasiums are **Gimnasio Integral Bioamérica,** Calle 17, esq. E, Vedado, tel. 832-9087; open Mon.–Sat. 8 A.M.–8 P.M.; and **Gimnasio Monte,** Calle Monte, e/ Suárez y Revillagigedo, Centro Habana, tel. 861-7748; open 8 A.M.–8 P.M.

Several residential clinics offer full-service spa treatments. Notable is **Centro Internacional de Salud la Pradera,** Calle 230, e/ 15A y 17, Siboney, tel. 33-7473, fax 33-7198, offering everything from anti-cellulite treatments and massage to specialist care for orthopedic and other conditions (this is where Argentinian soccer prima donna Diego Maradona "detoxed" in 2000 to cure his drug addiction).

Horseback Riding

Three outlets in **Parque Lenin,** Calle 100 y Carretera de la Presa, tel. 44-2721 or 44-3026, in Arroyo Naranjo, offer horseback riding.

Horseback riding is also offered near Playas

del Este at **Finca de Recreo Guanabito** and nearby at **Rancho Mi Hacienda** (see Minas, in the Exploring Suburban Havana chapter).

Running

The Malecón is a good place to jog, although you need to beware the uneven surface and massive potholes. For wide-open spaces, head to Parque Lenin, where the road circuit provides a perfect running track. Runners in search of a track might head to the **Estadio Panamericano,** Vía Monumental Km 4, Ciudad Panamericano, tel. 97-4140; the **Estadio Juan Abrahantes,** Zapata, south of the university; or **Ciudad Deportiva,** Vía Blanca, esq. Avenida de Rancho Boyeros, tel. 54-5022, in Nuevo Vedado.

Annual **road races** include the 5K International Terry Fox Race (February), the 98K Ultra Marabana (April), the 5K Día del Madre (Mother's Day Race; May), the 10K Clásico Internacional Hemingway (May), and the Habana Marabana (Havana Marathon; November). Contact the **Comisión Marabana,** at the Ciudad Deportiva, for information.

Sailing

Yachts and motor vessels can be rented at **Fantasea Boat Charters,** Marina Hemingway, 5ta Avenida, esq. Calle 248, Santa Fe, tel. 204-1150, fax 204-1149, comercial@comermh.cha.cyt.cu; and **Marina Puertosol Tarará,** Vía Blanca Km19, Playa Tarará, tel. 97-1510 or 97-1462, fax 97-1499, marina@mit.tur.cu, www.puertosol.net (in Havana: Marinas Puertosol, 1ra Avenida #3001 esq. 30, Miramar, tel. 204-5923, fax 204-5928).

Club Habana, 5ta Avenida, e/ 188 y 192, Reparto Flores, Playa, tel. 204-5700, fax 204-5705, also offers yacht rental.

Scuba Diving

There's excellent diving offshore of Havana. The Gulf Stream and Atlantic Ocean currents meet west of the city, where many ships have been sunk through the centuries, among them the wreck of the *Santísimo Trinidad;* a merchant ship called the *Coral Island;* and the *Sánchez Barcastegui,* an armored Spanish man-o'-war that foundered in 1895. Their wooden and iron hulls

make for fascinating exploration. This western shore, known as Barlovento, also has plenty of corals, gorgonians, sponges, and caves, as does the so-called "Blue Circuit," a series of dive sites extending east from Bacuranao, about 10 kilometers east of Havana, to the Playas del Este.

Visibility ranges from 15 to 35 meters. Water temperatures average 80°F to 85°F.

Cuban divemasters are all trained by internationally recognized organizations and are highly skilled. The standard of equipment is good. Nonetheless, it's a good idea to bring your own equipment (leave tanks and weight belts at home, as all scuba diving centers have steel 12- or 15-liter tanks). If you need to replace O-rings, batteries, or straps, most supplies are available.

Cuba: Recreational Diving Guide, by Gustavo G. Gotera, is an in-depth guide that provides detailed accounts of major dive sites.

There's a **decompression chamber** at Hospital Luís Díaz Soto, Vía Monumental y Carretera Habanas del Este, tel. 95-4251.

Dive Centers: Marina Hemingway offers scuba diving from **Centro de Buceo La Aguja,** 5ta Avenida y 248, Santa Fe, tel. 204-5088 or 271-5277, fax 204-6848 or 204-1149, which charges US$28 for one dive, US$50 for two dives, US$60 for a "resort course," and US$360 for an open-water certification. It also rents equipment.

The **Centro de Buceo Cocosub** Carretera Panamericana Km 23.5, Caimito, tel./fax 880-5089, at the Hotel Cocomar, 23 kilometers west of Havana, also has a scuba facility, and charges US$25/50 one/two dives.

Centro de Buceo Caribbean, Marina Puertosol, 7ma Calle, e/ 3ra y Cobre, Tarará, tel. 97-1462, fax 97-1499, marina@mit.tur.cu, charges US$30/45 one/two dives; offers certification program (US$300) and three-hour initiation dives (US$45). It rents equipment.

Club Habana, 5ta Avenida, e/ 188 y 192, Reparto Flores, Playa, tel. 204-5700, fax 204-5705, also has scuba facilities. Entrance costs US$10 for nonmembers Monday–Friday, US$15 Saturday–Sunday.

In North America, **Scubacan International,** 1365 Yonge St., Suite 208, Toronto, Ontario M4T 2P7, 416/927-1257 or 888/799-2822, fax

WHERE TO TAKE THE KIDS

The Cuban government likes to look after its children and has outfitted Havana with plenty of venues to keep kids amused, especially each April 4—the **Día de los Niños** (Children's Day)—when the city resounds to children's laughter, with clowns and other entertainment throughout the city.

The **Tren Turística Bella Época,** tel. 66-2476, a motorized "train" with shaded open-air carriages, provides a sightseeing tour of Havana. It departs from the Terminal Sierra Maestra, on the east side of Plaza de San Francisco, daily 10 A.M.–1 P.M. (US$1).

SIGHTS NOT TO MISS
Habana Vieja

Aquarium, Calle Brasil (Teniente Rey) #9, tel. 863-9493, displays tropical freshwater fish. Open Tues.–Sat. 9 A.M.–5 P.M. and Sun. 9 A.M.–1 P.M.. Entrance costs US$1 (children free). It shows films (in Spanish) relating to the exhibits on Tuesdays at 3 P.M.

Museo de la Revolución (Museum of the Revolution), Calle Refugio #1 e/ Agramonte y Monserrate, tel. 862-4091. Teenage boys may get a thrill from the armaments.

Museo Nacional de Historia Natural, Calle Obispo #61, e/ Oficios y Baratillo, tel. 862-0353, on Plaza de Armas, has interactive children's exhibits on wildlife, plus children's video games.

Museo de Ron (Museum of Rum), Avenida San Pedro #262, e/ Muralla y Sol, tel. 861-8051, features interesting exhibits plus a scale-model of a rum factory with steam train.

Parque Histórico Militar Morro-Cabaña (Morro-Cabaña Historical Military Park), Carretera de la Cabaña, Habana del Este, tel. 862-7653, on the north side of the harbor channel, comprises a castle and massive fortress with cannons, soldiers in period military garb, and some intriguing museums. Be sure to stay for the *Ceremonia del Cañonazo,* the nightly firing of the cannon, at 9 P.M.

Vedado

Coppelia, Calle 23, esq. L, Vedado, tel. 832-6149, is a *must visit* for a delicious ice-cream treat . . . but you'll need patience for the long lines.

Jardín Zoológico de la Habana, Avenida 26 y Zoológico, tel. 881-8915 or 881-5724, Havana's provincial zoo sure can't rival the San Diego Zoo, but has enough wildlife to keep kids amused.

Museo de Ciencias Naturales Felipe Poey (Felipe Poey Museum of Natural Sciences), tel. 832-9000, fax 832-1321, in the University of Havana campus, features natural history exhibits.

Playa (Miramar and Beyond)

Acuario Nacional (National Aquarium), 3ra Avenida, esq. Calle 62, tel. 203-6401 or 202-5872, displays aquatic species, including sharks and sea lions. It also has dolphin and sea lion shows.

Museo Nacional del Aire (National Air Museum), Avenida 212, e/ Calles 29 y 31, tel. 271-7753, displays about 50 civilian and military aircraft.

Suburban Havana

Parque Zoológico (the national zoo), Avenida Zoo-Lenin (Avenida 8), esq. Avenida Soto, tel. 44-7613, in the Arroyo Naranjo suburb, has an African wildlife park plus hundreds of other species.

Parque Lenin, Calle 100 y Carretera de la Presa, tel. 44-2721 or 44-3026, in Arroyo Naranjo, has all manner of attractions for children.

ENTERTAINMENT

Children's Cinema

Children and youth can attend screenings at the **Cinemateca Infantíl y Juveníl,** at Cinema 23 y 12, Calle 23 #1212, e/ 12 y 14, Vedado, tel. 833-6906, every Saturday at 2:30 P.M.; at **Cinecito,** Calle San Rafael #68, esq. Consulado, Centro Habana, tel. 863-8051, Saturday and Sunday at 2:30 P.M.; and the **Fundación del Nuevo Cine Latinoamericano,** Avenida 212, esq. 31, La Coronela, tel. 271-8967, every Saturday at 10 A.M.

Children's Theater and Puppet Shows

Casa de la Comedia, Calle Justíz, Habana Vieja, tel. 863-9282, hosts children's theater and comedy events on weekend afternoons.

Clowns, magicians, and ventriloquists perform at the **Iglesia y Convento de San Francisco de Asís,** Calle Oficios e/ Armagura y Brasil, tel. 862-9683, on Tuesday afternoons.

Salvador González Escalona, tel. 878-1661, callejondehamel@hotmail.com, hosts a **children's program** the third Saturday of each month at 10 A.M. at Callejón de Hamel, e/ Aramburo y Hospital, Centro Habana.

Teatro Guiñol, Calle M, e/ 17 y 19, Vedado, tel. 832-6262, has puppet shows for kids on Friday at 3 P.M., Saturdays at 5 P.M., and Sundays at 10:30 A.M. and 5 P.M. The **Teatro Fausto,** Prado #201, esq. Colón, Habana Vieja, tel. 863-1173, has children's shows Friday and Saturday at 10 A.M.; and **Teatro Mella** Línea #657, e/ Ay B, Vedado, tel. 833-5651, has children's, circus, and variety shows on Sundays at 11 A.M.

All these shows are in Spanish, so much of the performance might be over the heads of non-Spanish-speaking children.

La Colmenita is a troupe of stilt-legged clowns that performs on the streets of Habana Vieja.

Parques de Diversiones (Amusement Parks)

There's no Disneyland in Cuba and only two or three video arcades. However, numerous children's amusement parks cater to kids. Most of those that have bumper cars *(carros locos),* carousels, and other rides do not come up to Western safety standards.

Parque Infantil la Maestranza, in Parque Anfiteatro, Calle Tacón, Habana Vieja, offers electric train rides plus all the fun of the fair.

In Vedado, try **Jalisco Parque,** Calle 23 at 18. **Club Almendares,** on Avenida 49C in Reparto Kohly, tel. 204-4990, offers miniature golf and a kiddie pool.

Parque Lenin has a *parque de diversiones* with a miniature big dipper and other rides. A highlight of a visit to **Parque Lenin** is a ride on an old steam train. Both the **Jardín Zoológico de la Habana** (Havana Zoo) and the **Parque Zoológico** (the national zoo) also have *parques de diversiones.*

Pony Rides

Pony rides are offered in **Parque Luz Caballero,** between Avenida Carlos M. Céspedes and Tacón, in Habana Vieja; three pesos buys a ride, offered Saturday and Sunday 11 A.M.–6 P.M. and daily during public and school holidays.

El Rodeo, tel. 57-8893, in Parque Lenin, offers pony rides on weekends, plus a *rodeo cubano* every other Sunday 9 A.M.–5 P.M. The **Jardín Zoológico de la Habana** and the **Parque Zoológico** also offer pony rides for kids. No helmets are provided.

LOCO POR BÉISBOL

Béisbol (or *pelota*) is as much an obsession in Cuba as it is in the United States—more so, in fact. Baseball was introduced to Cuba in the 1860s, the island's first professional team—the Habana Baseball Club—was formed in 1872, and the first league was formed six years later. In 1909, Ralph Estep, a salesman for Packard, journeyed through Cuba and found the country to be "baseball crazy." Baseball terminology found its way into the Cuban lexicon, while many aspiring young Cubans—black and white alike—fulfilled their dreams of making it to the big leagues; prior to the Revolution, many Cubans found positions in the U.S. leagues, prompting sports columnist W.O. McGeehan to joke that: "The rush of Cubans to the big leagues may cause an appeal for an amendment to the immigration laws." The flow went both ways. Babe Ruth and Willy Mays played for Cuban clubs, for example, as did Tommy Lasorda, who played five seasons in Cuba and—in 1959—pitched the national team into the Caribbean world series.

Just watch Cuban kids playing, writes author Randy Wayne White, "without spikes, hitting without helmets, sharing their cheap Batos gloves, but playing like I have never seen kids play before. It wasn't so much the skill—though they certainly had skill—as it was the passion with which they played, a kind of controlled frenzy." No wonder Cuba traditionally beats the pants off the U.S. team in the Olympic Games.

Needless to say, the U.S. professional leagues are still well aware of this enormous talent pool. Players who make the Cuban national team and barnstorm the Olympics earn about 400 pesos a month—about the same as the average laborer—and it's not surprising that many are still tempted by the prospect of riches in the United States. More than 30 Cuban baseball stars have fled Cuba since 1991, when Rene Arocha, now a star pitcher for the St. Louis Cardinals, split from the Cuban national team during a stopover in Miami. In September 1995, Cuban pitcher and national team member Osvaldo Ferná left Cuba and signed a $3.3 million deal with the San Francisco Giants. Cuban pitcher Rolando Arrojo defected during the 1996 Olympics, and that year, Livan Hernández left and was snatched up for $4.5 million by the Florida Marlins—he went on the win the World Series MVP.

The defection of Hernández so rankled Castro that in a fit of pique, Livan's half-brother, Orlando "El Duque" Hernández, one of the world's greatest pitchers, was barred from playing for life. Castro—who, as a youth, used to storm off the field if his team was losing—even forbade

416/927-8595, specializes in scuba vacations in Cuba. Likewise, Mexican-based **Scuba Cuba,** cuba@another-world.com, www.diving-cuba .com, offers scuba packages.

Sportfishing

So many gamefish run offshore, streaming through the Gulf Stream that Hemingway called his "great blue river," that deep-sea fishing here has been compared to "hunting elk in the suburbs." Hardly a season goes by without some IGFA record being broken. The big marlin run begins in May, when they swim against the Gulf Stream current close to the Cuban shore. In places, the stream begins only a quarter-mile offshore, with the depth sounder reading 1,000 feet; another quarter-mile and the bottom plummets another 5,000 feet. Unfortunately, in this Cuba of food shortages, the Cubans aren't yet into tag-and-release, preferring to let you sautée the trophy for a cut of the steak.

Marlin, S.A., on Canal B at Marina Hemingway, tel. 204-1150, ext. 735, charges from US$285 for four hours; from US$395 for eight hours, depending on the craft, and including skipper and tackle. **Puertosol,** in Tarará, Vía Blanca Km19, Playa Tarará, tel. 97-1510 or 97-1462, fax 97-1499, marina@mit.tur.cu, www .puertosol.net, and in Havana, 1ra Avenida #3001 esq. 30, Miramar, tel. 204-5923, fax 204-5928, also offers sportfishing excursions.

Fishing Tournaments: Cuba hosts several

the Cubans to watch the 1997 World Series that year. Hernández was relegated to work in the Havana Psychiatric Hospital. Understandably, in January 1998 he fled Cuba on a homemade raft and was signed by the Yankees for US$6.6 million. Imagine the fury of Castro, who, says Andrei Codrescu, "has railed against Yankee imperialism for years."

Still, not every player is eager to leave. In 1995, Omar Linares, slugging third baseman for the Pinar del Río team and considered to be one of the best amateur baseball players in the world, rejected a $1.5 million offer to play for the New York Yankees. "My family and country come first," said Linares. "I'm aware of what a million-and-a-half dollars means, but I'm faithful to Fidel." In 2002, however, Linares and third baseman Omar Kindelan signed to play with Japanese teams for $4,000 monthly, with the Cuban government taking a slice of the salary.

Ah, yes, Fidel. Cuba is led by a sports fanatic. In the early years of power, Castro would often drop in at Havana's Gran Stadium (in 1971 it was renamed Estadio Latinoamericano and holds 55,000 people; it was state-of-the-art when opened in 1946 with 35,000 seats) in the evening to pitch a few balls at the Sugar Kings' batters. And everyone knows the story of how Castro once tried out as a pitcher for the old Washington Senators. Who knows? If his curveball had curved a little better, Fidel might have become a Senator and not a dictator.

Cuba's stars play more than 100 games a season on regional teams under the supervision of the best coaches, sports doctors, and competition psychologists outside the U.S. big leagues. Each province has a team on the national league (*Liga Nacional*), and two provinces and the city of Havana have two teams each, making 18 teams in all. The last game of every three-game series is played in a *pueblo* away from the provincial capital so that fans in the country can see their favorite team play live. The season runs December–June. The teams play a 39-game season, with the top seven teams going on to compete in the 54-game National Series.

Stadiums are oases of relaxation and amusement. There are no exploding scoreboards or dancing mascots, and beer and souvenir hawkers are replaced by old men wandering among the seats with thermoses, selling thimble-size cups of sweet Cuban espresso. Spam sandwiches replace hot dogs in the stands, where the spectators, being good socialists, also cheer for the opposition base-stealers and home-run hitters. Balls—knocked out of the field by aluminum Batos bats made in Cuba—are even returned from the stands, because everyone understands they're too valuable to keep as souvenirs.

sportfishing tournaments. The big three competitions are based in Marina Hemingway; contact the public relations department: rpublicas @prto.mh.cyt.cu. The Ernest Hemingway International Billfishing Tournament, is held each June and may well be the world's most sought-after fishing trophy; the International Blue Marlin Fishing Tournament is held each September; and the International Wahoo Fishing Tournament is held each November.

Wings of the World, 237 McRae Drive, Toronto, ON Canada M4G 1T7, 416/482-1223, fax 416/486-4001, info@wow.on.ca, www.wow.on.ca, and **Last Frontier Expeditions,** 4823 White Rock Circle, Suite H, Boulder, CO 80301-3260, 303/530-9275, Bob@cuba

travelexperts.com, www.cubatravelexperts.com, offer sportfishing trips from North America.

Swimming

Most large tourist hotels have pools that permit use by nonguests. Most pools are popular with Cuban families on hot days and can be noisy and crowded. Nonswimmers need to beware the sudden step that plunges you into the deep end (a common fault in the design of Cuban swimming pools).

In Habana Vieja, head to the small rooftop pool of the **Hotel Parque Central,** or to **Piscina Hotel Sevilla,** Prado, esq. Animas, to the rear of the Hotel Sevilla; entrance US$8, deductible from the price of your drinks and food (entry is free to guests of the Hotel Sevilla; US$2.50 for children and guests of the Hotel Plaza).

In Vedado, the **Hotel Nacional** has a mediocre pool (US$5 per nonguest). Also try the small rooftop pool of the **Hotel Capri** and the attractive outdoor mezzanine pool in the **Hotel Habana Libre Tryp.** In Miramar, the **Hotel Novotel Miramar** and **Hotel Meliá Habana** have excellent pools. The pools at the **Hotel Copacabana** and **Hotel Co-modoro** are popular with Cuban families. **Club Almendares,** Avenida 49C, esq. Calle 28A, tel. 204-4990, in Reparto Kohly, has a large pool (US$3 adults, US$1 children).

Club Habana, 5ta Avenida, e/ 188 y 192, Reparto Flores, Playa, tel. 204-5700, fax 204-5705, has a large swimming pool, plus splendid beach that shelves gently into calm waters. The **Complejo Turístico La Giraldilla,** Calle 222 e/ 37 y 51, tel. 33-0568, gerencia@giralda.cha.cyt.cu, in La Coronela, has a splendid swimming pool. And the pools at the Hotel Acuario and at Papa's, both in **Marina Hemingway,** are very popular with Cubans.

Farther afield, there are public swimming pools in **Parque Lenin,** tel. 57-8154, and also an Olympic pool, **Piscina Olímpica,** Avenida 99 #3804, Lotería, tel. (06820) 4807, southeast of Havana in the *municipio* of Cotorro. In Habana del Este, try the **Hotel Panamericano** pool.

SPECTATOR SPORTS

Cuba is a world superstar in sports and athletics—out of all proportion to its diminutive size—as it was even before the Revolution, especially in baseball and boxing. In 1971, the Cuban government formed the **Instituto Nacional del Deportivo y Recreo** (National Institute for Sport, Physical Education, and Recreation, INDER), tel. 57-7084. The state invested huge sums in bringing sports to the Cuban people. Sports training is incorporated into every school curriculum and many adult education programs.

Most facilities are basic by Western standards, but, hey, it's the results that count—and in that, Cuba is David to the U.S.'s Goliath.

Curiously, the game of jai alai, popular prior to the Revolution, has since disappeared.

Baseball

Cubans are baseball *(béisbol)* fanatics. The baseball season runs December–June.

Havana has two teams: the Industriales (colloquially called "Los Azules," or "The Blues"), considered the best team in the National League; and the Metropolitanos (known as "Los Metros"). Both teams play at the 60,000-seat **Estadio Latinoamericano,** Consejero Aranjo y Pedro Pérez, Cerro, tel. 870-6526, the main baseball stadium. Games are played Tuesday–Thursday at 7:30 P.M., Saturday at 1:30 and 7:30 P.M., Sunday at 1:30 P.M. (three pesos). Tickets are sold on a first come, first serve basis, although a few seats are reserved for foreigners. When one team is touring, the other plays at the stadium. No reservations are accepted.

You can also watch games being played at the **Estadio Juan Abrahantes** (also called Estadio Universitario), Zapata, Vedado.

For further information, contact the **Federación Cubana de Béisbol,** tel. 79-7980.

Also see the Special Topic "Loco Por Béisbol."

Basketball

While many young *habaneros* play hoop on the street, basketball does not inspire anywhere near the same passions as *béisbol.* The Liga Superior de Baloncesto (National Basketball League) comprises four teams—Havana's team is the Capitalinos—and runs September–November. Games are played at the **Coliseo de Deportes,** Vía Blanca, esq. Avenida de Rancho Boyeros, tel. 40-5933 or 54-5000, at Ciudad Deportiva, in Nuevo Vedado (Mon.–Fri. 8 A.M.–5 P.M.); and at the **Sala Polivalente Ramón Fonst,** Avenida de la Independencia, esq. Bruzón, Plaza de la Revolución, tel. 882-0000 (Mon.–Sat. 8:30 P.M., and Sun. 3 P.M.).

For further information, contact the **Federación Cubana de Baloncesto,** tel. 57-7156.

Boxing and Martial Arts

Little Cuba has always punched above its weight in the world of boxing—it has won the overall Olympic standings at *every* competition since 1972—and as of 2000 held 77 Olympic gold medals and dozens of world titles. The names of boxing heroes such as Eligio "Kid Chocolate" Sardiñas, Teófilo Stevenson, and Félix Savon are regarded with national awe.

Cuba's boxing elite compete each April in the Torneo Girardo Córdova Cardín championships, held at a different city each year. In Havana, championship matches are hosted at the **Coliseo de Deportes,** Vía Blanca, esq. Avenida de Rancho Boyeros, tel. 40-5933 or 54-5000, base for the **Federación Cubana de Boxeo,** tel. 57-7047.

The main boxing training center is the **Centro de Entrenamiento de Boxeo** Carretera Torrens in Wajay, tel. 202-0538, in Boyeros.

You can watch boxing and martial arts at the **Gimnasio de Boxeo Rafael Trejo,** Calle Cuba #815, Habana Vieja, tel. 862-0266 (Mon.–Fri. 8 A.M.–5 P.M.), and at **Sala Polivalente Kid Chocolate,** Prado, e/ San Martín y Brasil, Habana Vieja, tel. 862-8634, opposite the Capitolio.

Likewise, Cuba kicks ass in martial arts: it brought home 13 medals from the 2000 Olympics in Sydney. Martial arts are hosted at the **Sala Polivalente Ramón Fonst,** Avenida de la Independencia, esq. Bruzón, Plaza de la Revolución, tel. 882-0000; and at **Sala San Isidro,** Calle San Isidro, Habana Vieja, tel. 867-6069 (Mon.–Fri. 8 A.M.–6 P.M.).

OTHER SPORTS
Volleyball

Voleibol is a major sport in Cuba; the national women's team—Las Morenas del Caribe (the Caribbean Brown Sugars)—is the best in the world, and took gold at the 2000 Olympics for the fourth time. Volleyball games are hosted at the **Sala Polivalente Kid Chocolate** and **Sala Polivalente Ramón Fonst,** Avenida de la Independencia, esq. Bruzón, Plaza de la Revolución, tel. 882-0000. Major tournament games are held at the **Coliseo de Deportes,** Vía Blanca, esq. Avenida de Rancho Boyeros, tel. 40-5933 or 54-5000, which hosts the Liga Mundial de Voleibol (World Volleyball League) each spring. In 2001, six members of the national volleyball team defected while touring in Belgium, since which volleyball has

virtually disappeared from the Cuban press! For further information, contact the **Federación Cubana de Voleibol,** tel. 41-3557.

Fencing

No surprise, Cuba sticks it to the rest of the world in fencing. Head to **ExpoCuba,** Carretera del Rocío Km 3.5, Calabazar, tel. 54-9111, in Arroyo Naranjo.

Hockey

Hockey is played at the **Terreno Sintético de Hockey,** Calle 17, esq. 2, Santiago de las Vegas.

Skating

Sorry . . . no ice! The **Complejo de Pelota Vasca y Patinodromo,** at Ciudad Deportiva, Vía Blanca, esq. Avenida de Rancho Boyeros, in Nuevo Vedado, has a roller-skating track.

Soccer

Futbol has a seasonal following and is adopted as the sport of choice by Cubans when baseball season ends. However, Cuba's soccer league is not well developed, although there *is* a national league. Havana's team is Ciudad Havana (nicknamed "Los Rojos"—The Reds). Games are played at the **Estadio Pedro Marrero,** Avenida 41 #4409, e/ 44 y 50, Reparto Kohly, tel. 203-4698.

Squash and Tennis

The national tennis *equipo* (team) trains at **Complejo Panamericano,** Vía Monumental Km 1.5, Ciudad Panamericano, Habana del Este, tel. 95-4140, where six tennis courts (*canchas de tenis*) can be rented. **Club Habana,** 5ta Avenida, e/ 188 y 192, Reparto Flores, Playa, tel. 204-5700, fax 204-5705, has squash and tennis courts for rent. The **Club de Golf de Habana,** Carretera de Vento Km 8, Capdevila, Boyeros, tel. 55-8746 or 33-8919, fax 33-8820, also rents courts, as do the **Hotel Copacabana** (squash and tennis), **Hotel Meliá Habana** (tennis), **Hotel Nacional** (tennis), and **Hotel Novotel Miramar** (squash and tennis).

For information, contact the **Federación Cubano de Ténis,** tel. 97-2121.

Shopping

You don't come here for factory outlets or designer boutiques. But for high-quality arts and crafts, Havana is unrivaled in the Caribbean. The two big-ticket items are cigars and rum, with the world's best cigars selling for one-third or less of their sale price in North America. And silver jewelry belies Cuba's images as a stodgy vacuum of creativity. You're not going to find anything of interest in peso stores, which are meagerly stocked with shoddy Cuban-made plastic and tin wares.

Shopping requires searching in Havana. There are no concentrated shopping areas, as in most of the world's capital cities. Exceptions include Calle Obispo in Habaja Vieja, and Calles San Rafael and Neptuno around Avenida de Italia (Galiano) in Centro Habana.

Shoppers are not permitted to take any bags into stores. You must leave your handbags and other belongings at the *guardabolsas*. Be sure to take your wallet and important items with you, however. A security guard will check your receipt upon exit to ensure any items you carry have been paid for.

A good rule for buying in Cuba . . . if you see something you want, *buy it!* If you dally, it most likely will disappear.

Most stores selling dollar goods now accept

rum and cigars

EXPORTING ARTS AND ANTIQUES

The security staff at Havana's international airport checks all artwork and antiques. Anything deemed of antique value or high value will either be confiscated or taxed. An export permit is required for quality works of art not purchased from state galleries and shops where official receipts are given. You'll be required to show this receipt to Customs on leaving Cuba. The permit is usually good enough for you to export your item without further requirement. It generally doesn't apply to kitschy art bought at street markets, but the Cuban government sure doesn't want you walking off with that rare Wilfredo Lam some old biddy sold you in desperation. You should always be sure to obtain an official receipt/export permit. Without it, you run the risk of Cuban Customs taking any affected items, which include artwork, antiquarian books, stamp collections, furniture, and porcelain and other ornamental antiques.

Authorized sellers such as state-run commercial galleries and *expo-ventas* (galleries representing freelance artists) will issue an export permit or arrange authorization for any items you buy. Export permits for items for which you have not received an official receipt must be obtained from the **Registro Nacional de Bienes Culturales** (National Registry of Cultural Goods), Calle 17 #1009, e/ 10 y 12, Vedado, te. 831-3362; open Mon.–Fri. 8:30–11:30 A.M.. The permit is good for up to five works of art and costs US$10–30. You must bring the object for inspection (or a photo if the object is too large). Allow several hours for the visit and up to two days for processing.

---

foreign credit cards, except those issued by U.S. banks. However, processing can take forever, and frequently the credit card machines aren't working. Take sufficient cash.

ANTIQUES

Havana's museums and private homes overflow with colonial-era antiques—to the degree that armed robbers have been known to raid houses and make off with the family jewels. Cubans complain that the biggest thief of all is the government, which has been buying up antiques and gold from its own populace for a fraction of their market value. There are few antique stores, however, as the government is keen to prevent a wholesale exodus of the country's treasures. Perhaps the best place is **Casa de Antigüedades,** Calle 36 #4704, esq. Avenida 47, Kohly, tel. 204-2776, selling everything from crystal chandeliers to art deco lamps. Items come with an export license. The place operates like a pawn shop, except the Cuban owners aren't allowed to buy back their items, sold to the state for a pittance. Prices are negotiable. Open Mon.–Fri. 10 A.M.–3:30 P.M.

La Vajilla, Avenida de Italia, esq. Zanja, tel. 862-4751, has an eclectic range of antiques. You

might occasionally come across a gem certified for export. Open Mon.–Sat. 10 A.M.–5 P.M.

Eurl Trium, Zona Franca, Wajay Nave 11, Boyeros, tel. 54-0120, sells Cuban and French antiques. Open Mon.–Fri. 8 A.M.–5 P.M.

Colección Habana, Calle Mercaderes #13, e/ Empedrado y O'Reilly, Habana Vieja, tel. 861-3388, sells antique reproductions and decorative items, plus personal fashion wear such as silk scarves made in Spain. Open 9 A.M.–6 P.M.

ARTS AND CRAFTS

Cuba's strong suit is arts and crafts, sold by artisans at street stalls and also in stores by state agencies such as the Fondo de Bienes Culturales and ARTEX. The best stuff is sold in the gift stores of the upscale hotels, which mark up accordingly; often you can find identical items on the street at half the price.

The shortest walk through Havana can be a magical mystery tour of homegrown art. In recent years, art has been patronized by the tourist dollar, so the city is overflowing with whimsical Woolworth's art: cheap canvas scenes (popular works include old cars, old mulattas smoking cigars, and the facades of La Bodeguita del

CONTEMPORARY ARTISTS IN CUBA

In recent years, Cuban artists have taken the Western art world by storm. Says *Newsweek*, "Like the German and Italian neoexpressionists who took over the scene in the 1970s and '80s, the Cuban artists may be on the brink of changing the face of contemporary art." Cuban artists express an intense Afro-Latin Americanism in their passionate, visceral, colorful, socially engaged art. Painters and other artists imaginatively stretch their limited resources to produce widely interpretive modern and postmodern works. The work is eclectic, but there is energy in it all.

In the late 1960s, the government tried to compel Cuban artists to shun then-prevalent decadent abstract art and adopt the realistic style of the party's Mexican sympathizers such as Diego Rivera and David Alfaro Siqueiros, who turned from easel painting to wall murals because, in the words of Siqueiros: "While it is technically possible to play a revolutionary hymn on a church organ, it is not the instrument one would prefer." The artists who grew up *after* the 1959 revolution—the "generation of the '80s"—have been given artistic encouragement.

Cuba has 21 art schools, organized regionally with at least one per province. The **Instituto Superior de Arte,** Calle 120 #1110, esq. 9a Avenida, tel. 208-0288, isa@cubarte.cult.cu., Cuba's premier art school, remains key as an educational center and gateway to the world of Cuban art.

The art educational system is both traditional and modern, with fundamental classical drawing and painting techniques at its core. The Cuban state has always fostered academic training in still life, landscape, and figure form. As a result, says critic Tina Spiro, "most Cuban artwork, regardless of its style, is informed by a precision of line and a beautiful technical finish." On attaining mastery of these skills, artists are encouraged to depart on experiments in expression to the extent of their imaginations—and without overstepping Castro's 1961 dictum to think more of the message than the aesthetic.

Upon matriculation from art school, artists receive the support of the **Fondo Cubano de Bienes Culturales,** Muralla #107, esq. San Ignacio, Habana Vieja, tel. 862-3577, in marketing and presenting their work to the public. The Cuban Cultural Fund offers gallery exhibitions,

Medio or Havana cathedral), busty cigar-chomping ceramic mulattas, kitschy erotic carvings, papier-mâché masks and vintage Yankee cars, and animal figurines painted in pointillist dots. There is also plenty of true-quality art, ranging from paintings and tapestries to handworked leather goods and precious wood carvings representing a solid investment. Ceramics range from small rough-clay ashtrays with a clay cigar attached, to creative vases and ceramicware. You'll also see *muñequitas* (dolls) representing the goddess of the *santería* religion—Cuban women are great doll collectors and often keep their childhood dolls into late adulthood.

Avoid the appalling *ceniceros* (ashtrays) made of stuffed frogs doing various acrobatic maneuvers. *Don't buy these*—doing so contributes to the devastation of Cuba's endemic wildlife. Likewise, turtle shell products and black coral.

Souvenir Stores

You'll find **ARTEX,** 5ta Avenida #8010, Miramar, tel. 204-5846, shops throughout the city. All of them stock postcards, books, music cassettes and CDs, T-shirts, arts and crafts, rum, cigars, and other souvenirs.

Manzana de Gómez, a shopping complex on the northeast side of Parque Central, contains several souvenir stores.

Open-Air Markets

Artists sell their works on the streets. A limited amount of bargaining is normal at street markets. However, most prices are very low to begin with, and Cubans are scratching to earn a few dollars. Be reasonable. Don't bargain simply to win a battle. If the quoted price seems fair—and it usually is—then pay up and feel blessed that you already have a bargain.

SHOPPING

cataloging services, shipping, and transportation, and is currently trying to transform itself into a more marketing-oriented entity. Many artists show their works through *expo-ventas,* small galleries in private homes licensed to act as such by the Fondo Cubano de Bienes Culturales. The gallery owner gets a small commission on any sales and arranges for any requisite export license. Habaguanex, the commercial division of the Oficina del Historiador de la Ciudad, also runs galleries and receives 20 percent commission on any sales.

Until recent years, artists were employed by various Cuban state institutions and received a small portion of receipts from the sale of their work. In 1991, the government finally recognized that copyright belongs with the artist. It has created independent profit-making, self-financing agencies, such as ARTEX, to represent individual artists on a contractual basis whereby the agency retains 15 percent of sales receipts. Regulations provide that artists (including performers) can, ostensibly, retain up to 85 percent of earnings from the sale or licensing of copyrights abroad. A portion of the retained earnings goes to provides resources for arts training and public arts programs.

The artists themselves are increasingly shaking off their clichés and conservatism. In 1980, when the Cuban government began to loosen up, it even sponsored a show of avant-garde work influenced by international formats. Artists began holding unofficial exhibitions in their homes. Much of current art subtly criticizes the folly of its sociopolitical environment, but usually in a politically safe, universal statement about the irony in human existence, often expressing the hardships of daily life in a darkly surreal way. Not surprisingly, contemporary Cuban art is heavily influenced by Salvador Dalí. Within limits, this artistic dissent is not censored.

By the late 1980s, many artists were overstepping their bounds—*The Orgasm on the Bay,* by Tomás Esson, for example, depicted an ejaculating cigar in Castro's mouth. Armando Hart, Minister of Culture, decided that the Cuban artists' enthusiasm should be promoted from afar. Mexico City was selected, and a community of deported artists has evolved—quixotically, with official Cuban sponsorship.

The largest market is the **Feria de Artesanía,** Calle Tacón, Habana Vieja, selling everything from little ceramic figurines, miniature bongo drums, and papier-mâché 1950s autos, to banana-leaf hats, crocheted bikinis, straw hats, and paintings. Open 8:30 A.M.–7 P.M.

An out-of-the-way flea market called the **Area de Vendedores por Cuenta Propia,** Máximo Gómez #259, esq. Suárez, inside La Nueva Isla Ropa y Sedería store on the south side of Parque de la Fraternidad, sells leather belts and sandals, antiquarian books, *santería* items, and a motley miscellany good for the attic.

In Vedado, a small open-air market on La Rampa, e/ Calle M y N, sells woodcarvings, jewelry, shoes, and leather goods. Open daily 8 A.M.–6 P.M. A better bet is the larger **Feria del Malecón,** Malecón, e/ Calles D y E, where about 300 artisans sell handicrafts, including silver bracelets, beaten copper pieces, leather sandals, woodcarvings, paintings, and ceramics. Open Tues.–Sun. 8:30 A.M.–6 P.M.

Art Galleries

Havana is home to a dizzying galaxy of galleries, most with both permanent and revolving exhibitions as well as art for sale. Most galleries with art for sale are concentrated in Habana Vieja.

Formal Galleries: These galleries are run by state organizations and tend to sell top quality work at high prices. In addition to paintings, most sell ceramics, silver and coral jewelry, Cuban Tiffany-style lamps, wooden carvings, and papier-mâché creations

For information on workshops and galleries, contact the **Fondo Cubano de Bienes Culturales,** Muralla #107, Habana Vieja, tel. 862-3577, in Plaza Vieja, which sells quality work in its **Galerías de la Casona.** The most creative treasures are in the upstairs galleries, one of which displays some of the strongest statements in Cuban art. Open Mon.–Fri. 10 A.M.–5 P.M., Sat. 10 A.M.–2 P.M. Nearby, experimental art is for sale at the **Centro de Desarrollo de los Artes Visuales,** Casa de las Hermanas Cárdenas, Plaza Vieja, tel. 862-3533.

One of the best places is **Galería del Centro Gallego,** Prado #458, Habana Vieja, tel. 861-6494, next to the Gran Teatro on Parque Central.

Of a similar standard is the **Galería Victor Manuel,** Calle San Ignacio #46, e/ Callejón del Chorro y Empedrado, tel. 861-2955, on the west side of Plaza de la Catedral; open 9:30 A.M.–9 P.M. Around the corner is the **Taller Experimental de la Gráfica,** Callejón del Chorro, tel. 862-0979, which has exclusive lithographic prints for sale upstairs in the **Galería del Grabado** (US$20–US$1,000). If you visit on the last Wednesday of every month, you may be able to purchase in pesos, but don't count on it. Open Mon.–Fri. 9 A.M.–4 P.M.

The **Galería Forma,** Calle Obispo #255, tel. 862-0123, sells artwork of international standard, including intriguing sculptures, ceramics, and copper pieces. The **Palacio de Artesanía,** Calle Cuba #64, esq. Tacón, tel. 867-1118, also sells arts and crafts; open daily 9 A.M.–6 P.M.

The **Centro Wilfredo Lam,** on San Ignacio, tel. 861-2096, fax 33-8477, wlam@artsoft.cult.cu, offers works by leading Caribbean and Latin American artists during the Havana Arts Biennial, in May.

In Vedado, the **Casa de las Américas,** on Calle 15 e/ B y C, tel. 55-2707, casa@artsoft.cult.cu, also hosts exhibitions with works for sale. The small gallery in the lobby of the **Hotel Nacional** also exhibits and sells paintings by the Cuban masters. The Hotel Meliá Cohiba's **Galería Cohiba,** tel. 33-3636, is another good source.

Private Galleries: Artists' studios and *expoventas* (commercial galleries representing freelance artists) have mushroomed of late, notably along Calle Obispo, in Habana Vieja. However, in 2001 the government initiated a crack-down on what it considers "illegal" privately-owned galleries, which clearly were doing good—perhaps too good—

business (the government claimed that the art was "not representative of the country"). Several artists are represented on the Internet; for example **Cuba Fine Art,** www.artecubano.com, displays the works of five artists on the web, complete with online purchase at rather astronomical rates.

The various galleries along Obispo include that of experimental ceramist Roberto Fernández Martinez, Obispo #515, who explores the influences of African and Indo-Cuban mythology. His eclectic paintings range through a variety of styles from Klee to Monet.

The **Asociación Cubana de Artesana Artistas,** Obispo #411, tel. 66-6345, has a store where individual artists have small booths selling jewelry and arts and crafts. Check out the fantastical, museum-scale wall hangings and fabulous statuettes in the gallery at the rear. Open Tues.–Fri. 1–6 P.M., Saturday 10 A.M.–4 P.M.

Jewelry

Most open-air markets offer silver-plated jewelry at bargain prices—a favorite form is old cutlery shaped into bracelets—while most upscale hotels have *joyerías* (jewelry stores) selling international-quality silver jewelry, much of it inlaid with black coral (to be avoided) and in a distinctly contemporary style.

In Habana Vieja, try the **Palacio de las Artesanías,** and **Galería del Centro Gallego** and **Galería Victor Manuel,** Calle San Ignacio #46, e/ Callejón del Chorro y Empedrado, tel. 861-2955, as well as the *joyería* in the **Hotel Parque Central.**

Joyería La Habanera, Calle 12 #505, e/ 5ta y 7ma Avenidas, Vedado, tel. 204-2546, has an exquisite array of gold and silver jewelry. Open Mon.–Fri. 10 A.M.–6 P.M., Sat. 10 A.M.–2 P.M.

In Miramar, most upscale hotels have quality jewelry stores, as do **La Maison,** Calle 16, esq. 7ma Avenida, tel. 204-1543, and **Le Select,** 5ta Avenida y 30, Miramar, tel. 204-7410, plus the **Joyería Balla Cantando,** in the Club Habana, 5ta Avenida y 188, tel. 204-5700.

Miscellany

You can buy hand-made Spanish fans (*abanicos*) for US$2 to US$150 at the **Casa de Abanicos,**

Calle Obrapía #107 e/ Mercaderes y Oficios, tel. 863-4453. Open Mon.–Sat. 10 A.M.–5 P.M.

Miniaturists and military buffs will find tiny soldiers, pirates, and other figurines in the store in **Museo de San Salvador de la Punta,** Avenida Carlos M. de Céspedes, esq. Prado y Malecón.

BOOKS, PERIODICALS, AND STATIONERY

For a city of two million literate and cultured people, Havana is appallingly short of books. Books are severely restricted by the Cuban government, which controls access to all information and maintains an iron fist over what may be read. Alas, this is especially true of periodicals. There are *no* newsstands or newsagents! Foreign periodicals are not for sale except in the lobbies of upscale tourist hotels (the range is meager).

Most tourist outlets sell a limited range of English-language coffee-table books, travel-related books, and political treatises, all of a pro-*fidelista* perspective, that have been approved by the censors. Otherwise only a few bookstores stand out, but don't get your hopes up—Havana is desperately in need of a Barnes & Noble. The few bookstores that exist stock mostly Spanish-language texts, including the classics of international literature—at least those on the right side of politics. Most works are socialist texts glorifying the Revolution. Castro's own writings are the most ubiquitous works, alongside those of Che Guevara and José Martí. Most gift stores sell coffee-table books on Cuba.

Warning: Cuba's antiquarian books are considered part of the national heritage and may require an export license (see the Special Topic "Exporting Arts and Antiques").

The **Instituto Cubano de Libro** (Cuban Book Institute), Calle O'Reilly #4, esq. Tacón, tel. 861-8585, in the Palacio del Segundo Cabo on Plaza de Armas, has three small bookshops, though only a fistful of books are in languages other than Spanish. Open Mon.–Sat. 9 A.M.–4:30 P.M.

Plaza de Armas is also the setting for the **Mercado de Libros,** a secondhand book fair where you can rummage through the dreary collection of faded texts. You'll find all kinds of tattered tomes, including atlases of Cuba, books on and by Ernest Hemingway, and a panoply of works by and about Che Guevara and Fidel Castro. Occasionally there are some true gems. But you'll be amazed at how expensive even the most mundane and dog-eared text costs. Open Mon.–Sat. 9 A.M.–7 P.M.

Librería Anticuaria El Navío, Calle Obispo #119, e/ Oficios y Mercaderes, also specializes in antiquarian books, but also has more modern fare, including stamp collections and photos. Open 9 A.M.–7 P.M. Nearby, **Librería Cervantes,** Calle Bernaza #9, esq. Obispo, tel. 862-2580, also sells secondhand books. Open Mon.–Sat. 10 A.M.–5 P.M. And in Vedado, **Librería Centenario del Apóstol,** Calle 25 #164, e/ Infanta y O, tel. 870-7220, has a broad selection of used texts; open 9 A.M.–9 P.M.

Librería La Internacional, Calle Obispo #528, Habana Vieja, tel. 861-3238, stocks a limited selection of historical, sociological, and political texts in English, plus a small selection of English-language novels. Open Mon.–Sat. 9 A.M.–4:30 P.M. **La Moderna Poesía,** Calle Obispo #527, esq. Bernaza, tel. 861-5600, is Cuba's largest bookstore, although virtually the entire (albeit limited) stock is in Spanish. Open 10 A.M.–8 P.M.

Librería Fernando Ortiz, Calle L esq. 27, Vedado, tel. 832-9653, is perhaps your best bet for English-language books. Its collection is meager but spans a wide range of subjects, and includes some arcane titles. Open Mon.–Fri. 10 A.M.–5 P.M., Sat. 9 A.M.–3 P.M.

Other small outlets include **Librería Casa de las Américas,** Calle 15 e/ B y C, tel. 55-2707, casa@artsoft.cult.cu, selling art books and contemporary literature, open Mon.–Fri. 9 A.M.–5 P.M.; **Librería de la UNEAC,** Calle 17, esq. H, Vedado, tel. 832-4551, open Mon.–Fri. 8:30 A.M.–4:30 P.M., selling books from the organization's own publishing house; and **Librería Internacional José Martí,** Calzada #1259 e/ J y I, Vedado, tel. 832-9838, open Mon.–Fri. 9 A.M.–4 P.M.

Tienda Chaplin, Calle 23, e/ 10 y 12, tel. 55-2845, specializes in works related to the cinema

CUBAN CIGARS

There is no substitute for our tobacco anywhere in the world. It's easier to make good cognac than to achieve the quality of Cuban tobacco.

Fidel Castro

It seems ironic that Cuba—scourge of the capitalist world—should have been compelled by history and geography to produce one of the most blatant symbols of capitalist wealth and power. Yet it does so with pride. The unrivaled reputation of Cuban cigars as the best in the world transcends politics, transubstantiating a weed into an object capable of evoking rapture. Cubans guard the unique reputation scrupulously.

Cuban cigars—*Habanos* (Havanas)—are not only a source of hard currency; they're part and parcel of the national culture. Although Castro gave up smoking in 1985 (after what he called a "heroic struggle"), Cubans still smoke 250 million cigars domestically every year. Another 160 million or so are exported annually. Although some 20 percent of Cuban cigars are machine-made, the best are still hand-rolled.

How Cigars Got Their Start

The cigar tradition was first documented among the indigenous tribes by Christopher Columbus. The Taíno Indians made monster cigars—at the very least, they probably kept the mosquitoes away—called *cohiba*. The word "cigar" originated from *sikar*, the Mayan word for smoking, which in Spanish became *cigarro.*

The popular habit of smoking cigars—as opposed to tobacco in pipes, first introduced to Europe by Columbus—began in Spain, where cigars made from Cuban tobacco were first made in Seville in 1717. Demand for higher-quality cigars grew, and *Sevillas* (as Spanish cigars were called) were superseded by Cuban-made cigars. Soon, tobacco was Cuba's main export and received a boost after the Peninsula Campaign (1806–12) of the Napoleonic wars, when British and French veterans returned home with the cigar habit, creating a fashion in their home countries. By the mid-19th century, there were almost 1,300 cigar factories throughout Cuba.

The demand fostered a full-fledged cigar-making industry in the United States. By 1905, there were 80,000 cigar-manufacturing businesses in the United States, most of them mom-and-pop operations run by Cuban émigrés. But it was to Cuba that the cognoscenti looked for the finest cigars of all. "No lover of cigars can imagine the voluptuous pleasure of sitting in a café sipping slowly a strong magnificent coffee and smoking rhythmically those divine leaves of Cuba," wrote American pianist Arthur Rubinstein.

but also has books on art and music, as well as posters and videos. Open Mon.–Sat. 2–9 P.M.

Most bookshops sell a modicum of stationery items. For dedicated stationery stores, try **La Papelería,** O'Reilly #102, esq. Tacón, Habana Vieja, tel. 863-4263, cater-corner to the Plaza de las Armas. It sells pens, paper stock, and other basic office supplies, plus briefcases and office equipment. Open 9 A.M.–7 P.M. **Papelería San Francisco,** Calle Oficios #52, e/ Amargura y Brasil, Habana Vieja, is a smaller but similar outlet. Open Mon.–Fri. 9 A.M.–5 P.M., Sat. 9 A.M.–1 P.M.

CIGARS

The quality of Cuban cigars declined significantly in the mid-1990s as the government set to boost production, and quality and consistency have only moderately improved in recent years. Nonetheless, prices have increased dramatically. Accordingly, reported *Cigar Aficionado:* "Whereas not too long ago one could find a box of 25 Partagas Serie D No. 4s for US$68 or a box of Punch Double Coronas for US$86, cigar lovers can now expect to pay about

Bundled, Boxed, and Boycotted

Cuban cigars were sold originally in bundles covered with pigs' bladders and, later, in huge cedar chests. The banking firm of H. Upmann initiated export in cedar boxes in 1830, when it imported cigars for its directors in London. Later, the bank decided to enter the cigar business, and the embossed cedar box complete with colorful lithographic label became the standard form of packaging. Each specific brand evolved its own elaborate lithograph, while different sizes (and certain brands) even evolved their own box styles.

The Montecristo was the fashionable cigar of choice. In the 1930s, any tycoon or film director worth the name was seen with a whopping Montecristo A in his mouth. Half of all the Havanas sold in the world in the 1930s were Montecristos, by which time much of Cuba's tobacco industry had passed into U.S. ownership. Among the devotees of Cuban cigars was President Kennedy, who smoked Petit Upmans. In 1962, at the height of the Cuban Missile Crisis, Kennedy asked his press secretary, Pierre Salinger, to obtain as many Upmans as he could. Next day, reported Salinger, Kennedy asked him how many he had found. Twelve hundred, replied his aide. Kennedy then pulled out and signed the decree establishing a trade embargo with Cuba. Ex-British premier Winston Churchill also stopped smoking Havanas and started smoking Jamaican cigars, but after a time he forgot about politics and went back to Havanas. His brand was Romeo y Julieta.

The embargo dealt a crushing blow to Cuba's cigar industry. Castro nationalized the cigar industry and founded a state monopoly, Cubatabaco. Many dispossessed cigar factory owners immigrated to the Dominican Republic, Mexico, Venezuela, and Honduras, where they started up again, often using the same brand names they had owned in Cuba—today, the Dominican Republic produces 47 percent of the handmade cigars imported into the United States. Experts agree, however, that these foreign "Cuban" brands are inferior to their Havana counterparts.

At the time of the Revolution, about 1,000 brands and sizes of Havanas existed. There are now about 35 brands and 500 cigar varieties. Only eight factories make handmade export-quality cigars in Cuba today, compared with 120 at the beginning of the century. All cigar factories produce various brands. Some factories specialize in particular flavors, others in particular sizes—of which there are no fewer than 60 standard variations, with minor variations from brand to brand.

Holy Smoke, by Guillermo Cabrera Infante, and *Cuban Counterpoint,* by Fernando Ortíz, are particularly good tomes about Cuban cigars and tobacco.

US$100 to US$150, respectively, for such cigars. On the bright side, cigars purchased in Havana are anywhere from one fourth to one half the price of similar cigars in London or Geneva and about 15 percent less than prices in Spain."

If you're buying for speculation, buy the best. The only serious collectors' market in cigars is in prerevolutionary cigars, according to Anwer Bati in *The Cigar Companion.* Older cigars produced before the 1959 Revolution are commonly described as "pre-Castro." Those made before President Kennedy declared the U.S. trade embargo against Cuba in February 1962 are "pre-embargo." Pre-Castro or pre-embargo cigars are printed with MADE IN HAVANA-CUBA on the bottom of the box instead of the standard HECHO EN CUBA used today. Since 1985, handmade Cuban cigars have carried the Cubatabaco stamp plus a factory mark and, since 1989, the legend "Hecho en Cuba. Totalmente a Mano" (Made in Cuba. Completely by Hand). If it reads "Hecho a Mano," the cigars are most likely hand-*finished* (i.e., the wrapper was put on by hand) rather than hand*made.*

MAKING HAVANA CIGARS

From Leaf to Cigar

The tobacco leaves, which arrive from the fields in dry sheets, are first moistened and stripped. The leaves are then graded by color and strength—each type of cigar has a recipe. A blender mixes the various grades of leaves, which then go to the production room, where each *tabaquero* or *tabaquera* receives enough tobacco to roll approximately 100 cigars for the day.

The rollers work in large rooms, where they sit at rows of *galeras* (workbenches) resembling old-fashioned school desks. Two workers sit at each desk, with piles of loose tobacco leaves at their sides. The rollers take great pride in their work, and it's a treat to marvel at their manual artistry and dexterity. The rollers' indispensable tool is a *chaveta*, a rounded, all-purpose knife for smoothing and cutting leaves, tamping loose tobacco, "circumcising the tips," and sometimes banging a welcome to factory visitors on their desks in rhythmic chorus like a percussion orchestra. Most workers are born to their tasks, following in the footsteps of other family members, carrying on their traditional skills from one generation to the next.

While they work, a *lector* (reader) reads aloud from a strategically positioned platform or high chair. Morning excerpts—beginning promptly at 8 A.M.—are read from the *Granma* newspaper; in the afternoon, the *lector* reads from historical or political books, or short stories and novels. Alexandre Dumas, Agatha Christie, and Ernest Hemingway are favorites; Dumas' novel *The Count of Monte Cristo* was such a hit in the 19th century that it lent its name to the famous Montecristo cigar. The practice dates back to 1864, when the unique institution was set up to alleviate boredom and help the cause of worker education. Says city architect Mario Coyula: "In Cuba before the Revolution, men who were completely illiterate knew the classics, the plays of Shakespeare, and most modern novels. And even though they could not read or write, they were well versed in current political issues."

© CHRISTOPHER P. BAKER

Rolling the Cigar

The *torcedor* (cigar roller) fingers his or her leaves and, according to texture and color, chooses two to four filler leaves, which are laid end to end and gently yet firmly rolled into a tube, then enveloped by the binder leaves to make a "bunch."

The rough-looking "bunch" is then placed with nine others in a small wooden mold that is screwed down to press each cigar into a solid cylinder. Next, the *tabaquero* selects a wrapper leaf, which he or she trims to size. The "bunch" is then laid at an angle across the wrapper, which is stretched and rolled around the "bunch," overlapping with each turn. A tiny quantity of flavorless tragapanth gum (made from Swiss pine trees) is used to glue the *copa* down. Now the *torcedor* rolls the cigar, applying pressure with the flat of the *chaveta*. Finally, a piece of wrapper leaf the size and shape of a quarter is cut to form the cap; it is glued and twirled into place, and the excess is trimmed.

The whole process takes about five minutes. Hence, a good cigar maker can roll about 100 medium-sized cigars a day (the average for the largest cigars is far less).

Cigar rollers serve a nine-month apprenticeship—each factory has its own school. Many fail. Those who succeed graduate slowly from making petit corona cigars to the larger and specialized sizes. Rollers are paid piece rates based on the number of cigars they produce. They receive on average 350–400 pesos for a six-day workweek. In addition, they can puff as much as they wish on the fruits of their labor while working.

Today, the majority of rollers are women. Prior to the Revolution, only men rolled cigars; the leaves were selected by women, who often sorted them on their thighs, giving rise to the famous myth about cigars being "rolled on the dusky thighs of Cuban maidens."

And So to Market

The roller ties cigars of the same size and brand into bundles—*media ruedas* (half-wheels)—of 50 using a colored ribbon. These are then fumigated in a vacuum chamber. Quality is determined by a *revisador* (inspector) according to eight criteria, such as length, weight, firmness, smoothness of wrappers, and whether the ends are cleanly cut. *Catadores* (professional smokers) then blind test the cigars for aroma, draw, and burn, the relative importance of each varying according to whether the cigar is a slim panatela (draw is paramount) or a fat robusto (flavor being more important). The *catadores* taste only in the morning and rejuvenate their taste buds with sugarless tea.

Once fumigated, cigars are placed in cool cabinets for three weeks to settle fermentation and remove any excess moisture. The cigars are then graded according to color and then shade within a particular color category.

A trademark paper band is then put on by an *anillado*. A Dutchman, Gustave Bock, introduced the band last century to distinguish his cigars from other Havanas. Later, bands served to prevent gentlemen smokers from staining their white evening gloves.

Finally, the cigars are laid in pinewood boxes, with the lightest cigar on the right and the darkest on the left (cigars range from the very mild, greenish-brown *double claro* to the very strong, almost black *oscuro*). The boxes are then inspected for alignment and uniformity. A thin leaf of cedar wood is laid on top to maintain freshness, and the box is sealed with a green-and-white label guaranteeing the cigars are genuine Havanas, or *puros Habanos* (today *puro* is a synonym for cigar).

CIGAR BOX CRYPTOGRAPHY: READING THE CODE

On the underside of every box of cigars is a code, printed as a series of letters. If you know the code, it can tell you a fair amount about the cigars inside. Even if you're not attuned to every nuance of specific factories, you can still determine at least the provenance and date of cigars, which vary markedly.

The first two or three letters usually refer to the factory where the cigars were made (for example, FPG refers to the Partagás factory); the next four letters give the date of manufacture (OASC, for example, means 0699—June 1999—though the 0 in front of single-digit months is often omitted).

Newly created cigars will have a different code.

Date Code	Factory Code
1 - N	BM . . . . Romeo y Julieta (Briones Montolo)
2 - I	CB . . . . El Rey del Mundo (Carlos Balino)
3 - V	EL . . . . El Laguito
4 - E	FR . . . . La Corona (Fernández Rey)
5 - L	FPG . . . . Partagás (Francisco Pérez Germán)
6 - A	HM . . . . Heroes de Moncada
7 - C	JM . . . . H. Upmann (José Martí)
8 - U	PL . . . . Por Larrañaga (Juan Cano Sainz)
9 - S	
0 - O	

If its states only "Hecho en Cuba," they are assuredly machine-made.

In addition, there are styles, sizes, and brands of cigars that have not been made in Cuba since shortly after the Revolution. They're the most valuable. Connoisseurs opt for "cabinet cigars," which come in undecorated cedar boxes.

Cigars, when properly stored, continue to ferment and mature in their boxes—an aging process similar to that of good wines. Rules on the topic don't really exist, but many experts claim that prime cigars are those aged for six to eight years. Everyone agrees that a cigar should be smoked either within three months of manufacture or not for at least a year (the interim is known as a "period of sickness"). Fatter cigars—the choice of connoisseurs—are more fully flavored and smoke more smoothly and slowly than those with smaller ring gauges. As a rule, darker cigars are also more full-bodied and sweeter.

Several of Cuba's 42 factories might be producing any one brand *simultaneously,* so quality can vary markedly even though the label is the same. Experts consider cigars produced in Havana's La Corona, El Laguito, and Romeo y Julieta factories the best. The source is marked in code on the underside of the box. The year of production is also indicated there—remember that, as with fine wines, the quality of cigars varies from year to year.

The Cuban government permits you to export US$2,000 worth of cigars with documentation—you'll need receipts. If you don't have your receipts, Cuban customs permits only two boxes. As for the U.S. government: persons with licenses to trade with Cuba may purchase US$100 of Cuban cigars or other goods, but the cigars may only be purchased in Cuba.

Street Deals

Everywhere you walk in Havana, *jineteros* will offer you cigars at discount prices. You'll be tempted by what seems the deal of the century. Forget it! You might get lucky and get the real thing, but the vast majority are low-quality, machine-made cigars sold falsely as top-line cigars to unsuspecting tourists. Don't be taken in by the sealed counterfeit box, either.

You can buy inferior domestic cigars—called "torpedoes"—for about one peso (US$1) in bars and restaurants and on the street.

Where to Buy

Quality cigars can be bought at virtually every hotel and store that welcomes tourists. There are now more than two dozen Casas del Habano or Casas del Tabaco throughout the city, plus scores of other cigar outlets. Most shops have poorly informed and uninterested clerks who know little about *tabacos* (the Cuban term for Habanos). Your best bet is to buy at a serious outlet; those in the deluxe hotels are usually trustworthy. Prices can vary up to 20 percent from store to store, so shop around. If one store doesn't have what you desire, another surely will. You should inspect your cigars before committing to a purchase. Most shops don't allow this, but the best shops do.

The best shops offer a broad selection—everything from cedar boxes of 100 Hoyos de Monterrey Double Coronas to five-packs of Corona Lanceros. Most shops sell by the box only. Due to high demand, some cigars are often on back order—one major London cigar merchant told me that the Cubans hold back supply to raise prices.

Habana Vieja: La Casa del Habano, Industria #520, e/ Barcelona y Dragones, tel. 33-8060, in the Partagás factory, has a massive walk-in humidor. The store has a front room catering to the busloads of tourists; hidden away to the rear is a lounge with a narrow humidified walk-in cigar showcase for serious smokers. Open Mon.–Fri. 9 A.M.–7 P.M., Sat. 9 A.M.–5 P.M.

Palacio del Tabaco, Agramonte #106, e/ Colón y Refugio, tel. 33-8389, in the Fábrica La Corona, offers rare cigars such as figurados and double coronas. It has a small bar. Open Mon.–Fri. 9 A.M.–6 P.M.

La Casa del Habano, Mercaderes #120, esq.

Obrapía, tel. 861-5795, below the Museo de Tabaco, has a selection fairly limited in range but high in quality. There's no smoking on-site. Open 9 A.M.–5 P.M.

La Casa del Tabaco y Ron, Calle Obispo, e/ Monserrate y Bernaza, tel. 867-0817, is above La Floridita restaurant. The sales staff is knowledgeable and friendly, and prices are among the best in town. Open 9 A.M.–5 P.M.

La Casa del Habano, Calle Mercaderes #202, esq. Lamparilla, tel. 862-9682, in the Hostal Conde de Villanueva, lures serious smokers. It offers a large range of quality cigars and a sumptuous smoker's lounge with TV and plump leather seating. Open 10:30 A.M.–7 P.M.

La Casa del Tabaco Parque Central, Neptuno e/ Prado y Zulueta, tel. 66-6627, in the Hotel Golden Tulip Parque Central, has an excellent smoking lounge—Salón Cuaba (open 9 A.M.–9 P.M.)—popular with a Cuban intellectual crowd. Manager Emilio Amin Nasser oversees the friendly staff.

Vedado: La Casa del Habano, Calle O y 21, tel. 33-3562, in the Hotel Nacional, is well-stocked, as is **La Casa del Tabaco,** Calle L y 23, tel. 873-2307, outside the Hotel Habana Libre Tryp; and the **Casa del Tabaco,** tel. 873-2307, on Calle 23, e/ O y P.

El Corona, Paseo y 1ra, tel. 33-3636, in the Hotel Meliá Cohiba, has professional staff and a large stock. Open Mon.–Fri. 9 A.M.–8:30 P.M., Sat. 9 A.M.–2 P.M. Also try the **Casa del Tabaco,** tel. 33-4051, ext. 135, in the Hotel Riviera.

Playa (Miramar and Beyond): La Casa del Habano, 5ta Avenida, esq. 16, tel. 204-1185, is perhaps the flashiest place in town. This impressive colonial mansion boasts a vast humidor, executive rooms, bar and lounge, and good service. Manager Pedro Gonzalez will be happy to offer his recommendations. Open 9 A.M.–5 P.M.

La Casa del Habano, 5ta Avenida e/ 188 y 192, tel. 204-5700, is run by Enrique Mons, whom *Cigar Aficionado* magazine has termed "the maestro of cigar merchants in Havana," and who for most of the 1970s and '80s was in charge of quality control for the Cuban cigar industry. Open 9 A.M.–5 P.M.

Tabaco El Aljibe, 7ma Avenida, e/ 24 y 26, tel.

204-1012, is also well-stocked, as is **Tabaco La Giraldilla,** Calle 222 y Avenida37, La Coronela, tel. 33-1155 (both stores are open 9 A.M.–midnight); and **La Escogida,** 3ra Avenida, esq. 84, Miramar, tel. 204-7646, in the Hotel Comodoro (open Mon.–Sat. 10 A.M.–7:30 P.M., Sun. 10 A.M.–2 P.M.).

La Casa del Habano, 5ta Avenida y 248, tel. 204-1151, in Marina Hemingway in the Santa Fe district, has "a good selection of cabinet cigars" plus "helpful and friendly" young staff. No smoking on-site. Open 9 A.M.–5 P.M.

CLOTHING AND SHOES

Cuba isn't renowned for its fashions and offers little in the way of boutiques, although Benetton of Italy now has three stores, and various stores sell designer fashion labels.

Males might want to purchase a *guayabera,* Cuba's unique short-sleeved, embroidered shirt.

You can buy *guayaberas* at many ARTEX stores, and for pesos in the Cuban department stores along Calle San Rafael or Galiano; and also at **El Quitrín,** Calle Obispo #163, e/ San Ignacio y Mercaderes, tel. 862-0810, in Habana Vieja. El Quitrín also sells embroideries and lace, plus chic blouses, skirts, and other clothing. Most items are Cuban-made, but far above average quality. Items can be made to order. Open 9 A.M.–5 P.M.

La Bella Cubana, Calle Oficios, esq. Lamparilla, tel. 860-6524, on the west side of Plaza de San Francisco, specializes in wedding wear. Next door is a **United Colors of Benetton,** Calle Oficios, esq. Amargura, tel. 862-2480. Open Mon.–Sat. 10 A.M.–6:30 P.M., Sun. 10 A.M.–1 P.M. Benetton also has an outlet in **Harris Brothers,** Avenida de Bélgica #305, e/ O'Reilly y Progreso, Habana Vieja, tel. 862-6882, and the **Complejo Comercial Comodoro,** 3ra Avenida, esq. 84, Miramar, tel. 204-5551, adjoining the Hotel

THE GUAYABERA

The traditional *guayabera,* Cuba's all-purpose gift to sexy menswear, was created in Central Cuba more than 200 years ago and is the quintessential symbol of Latin masculinity. Despite the infusion of New York fashion, this four-pocket, straight-bottom shirt remains the essence of sartorial style. The *guayabera,* thought Kimberley Cihlar, "is possessed of all the sex appeal any Latin peacock could want." Nonetheless, younger *habaneros* shun the shirt as a symbol of someone who works for the government.

The *guayabera,* which comes short-sleeved or long, is made of light cotton to weather the tropical heat. In shape, it resembles a short-sleeved jacket or extended shirt and is worn draped outside the pants, usually as an outer garment with a T-shirt beneath . . . perfect for hiding a figure flaw. Thus it fulfills the needs of summertime dressing with the elegance of a jacket and the comfort of, well, a shirt. It is embellished with patterned embroidery running in parallel stripes down the front and is usually outfitted with enough pockets—with buttons—to stow *habanos* (cigars) for a small shop.

There are two tales about the origin of the *guayabera.* In one, the shirt was conceived by a wealthy landowner who had his wife sew a shirt of lightweight cotton (called *batista*), with multiple pockets to carry items he needed for work. His workers and neighbors soon copied the style. Supposedly, the shirt was originally called a *yayabera* after the nearby Yayabo River. This degenerated into "guayabera" for the *guayaba* (guava) trees under which workers would sit for lunch to avoid the strong midday Cuban sun. However, Cuban *guayabera* designer Ramone Puig, who fled Cuba in 1961 and went on to make *guayaberas* for such luminaries as former presidents Ronald Reagan and George Bush and actor Robert Duvall, claims that the shirt was conceived in Sancti Spíritus by cattle farmer José Gonzáles, who had his wife sew up such an embroidered shirt to his specifications.

Comodoro, which also has outlets for Givenchy, Versace, and Yves Saint-Laurent.

Sombreros Jipi Japa, Calle Obispo, esq. Compostela, is the place to go for hats of every shade. Alternately, try **Novator,** Calle Obispo #365, open Mon.–Sat. 10 A.M.–7 P.M., Sun. 10 A.M.–1 P.M.

In Vedado, **Galerías Amazonas,** Calle 12, e/ 23 y 25, tel. 66-2438, is a mall with several shops devoted to fashion; open Mon.–Sat. 10 A.M.–7 P.M., Sun. 10 A.M.–2 P.M. The best store for designer jeans like Calvin Klein and Levi's and men's fashions is **Tienda Brava,** which also sells leather goods. For quality imported shoes, try the gallery's **Peletería Claudia.**

You can buy quality homemade sandals at street markets, such as that on Calle 23 e/ M y N.

In Miramar, **La Maison,** Calle 16, esq. 7ma Avenida, tel. 204-1543, is a former colonial mansion known for its nightly fashion shows. The rooms have been converted into shops selling upscale imported clothing, shoes, and deluxe duty-free items such as perfumes and jewelry. **Exclusividades Verano,** Calle 18 #4106 e/ Calles 41 y 43, Miramar, tel. 203-7040, sells Cuban-designed clothes, including beautiful one-of-a-kind Verano dresses and straw hats; upstairs sells men's fashion, including shoes. Open Mon.–Sat. 10 A.M.–6 P.M., Sun. 9 A.M.–1 P.M. Likewise, *Le Select,* 5ta Avenida y 30, Miramar, tel. 204-7410, is a good place for both men's and women's fashion.

Sportswear

Most clothes stores sell sportswear, including sneakers and running shoes. The **Galería Comercial Habana Libre,** Calle L, esq. 25, on the south side of the Hotel Habana Libre, has a sports store, as does **Plaza Carlos III,** Avenida Salvador Allende, e/ Árbol Seco y Retiro, Centro Habana. Also try **Tienda Deportiva,** in the Edificio Manzana de Gómez, between Agramonte y Monserrate and Neptuno y O'Reilly. And **Adidas** has its own well-stocked branches at Calle Neptuno, e/ Campanario y Manrique, Centro Habana, tel. 862-5178 (open Mon.–Sat. 9:30 A.M.–7 P.M., Sun. 9:30 A.M.–1:30 P.M.); in the Galería Comercial Habana Libre, Calle 25, e/

L y M, Vedado; and in the Miramar Trade Center, 3ra Avenida, e/ 70 y 82, Miramar.

DEPARTMENT STORES, SHOPPING CENTERS, AND DIPLOTIENDAS

Department stores and shopping malls are opening with increasing regularity all over town and selling all manner of Western goods, from Nikes and Reeboks to Japanese electronics. (Er . . . what was that about the embargo?) The malls are a far cry from their North American or European counterparts, but they point the way of the future. Security is tight, and a guard at the door will usually search your bags and correlate the contents against your itemized receipt after purchase. Most often Cubans are lined up outside and let in one by one.

Most department stores and shopping centers are dispersed throughout Miramar, where they cater predominantly to the resident foreign community and Cuba's dollar-favored political elite. Once known as *diplotiendas,* the original dollars-only outlets were exclusively for diplomats and other foreign residents. Today, Cubans are also welcome—as long as they have dollars to spend.

If you need toiletries and general supplies, head for any of the smaller **Tiendas Panamericanas** that serve Cubans with dollars.

Harris Brothers, Avenida de Bélgica #305, e/ O'Reilly y Progreso, Habana Vieja, tel. 861-1644, is a Havana institution with four stories of separate stores that span fashions and children's items to toiletries. Open 9 A.M.–6 P.M.

La Época, Avenida de Italiana (Galiano), esq. Neptuno, Centro Habana, tel. 66-9414, dating back to the 1950s, is a good place for clothing, including kiddie items and designer fashions. Open Mon.–Sat. 9:30 A.M.–7 P.M., Sun. 9:30 A.M.–2 P.M. One block north, in a similar vein, is **Variedades Galiano,** Avenida de Italia esq. San Rafael, tel. 862-7717, the former Woolworth's—it still has its original lunch counter.

The **Plaza Carlos III,** Avenida Salvador Allende, e/ Árbol Seco y Retiro, tel. 873-6370, taking up an entire block, is intended for Cubans, not tourists. It was built in 1953 with parking for cars on each of five levels. Today it has an auto shop, furniture store, Adidas sporting goods store, perfume shop, and other stores, including a Cuban take on the original Woolworth's dime store . . . everything inside costs US$1.

In Vedado, the **Galería Comercial Habana Libre,** Calle L, esq. 25, on the south side of the Hotel Habana Libre, has a few small stores. A larger, more modern mall is the **Galerías de Paseo,** 1ra Calle, e/ Paseo y A, tel. 55-3475, at the foot of Paseo in Vedado. It even has a car show-room with new Fiats and Japanese cars—it serves a foreign clientele, as Cubans can't legally buy new vehicles. Open Mon.–Sat. 10 A.M.–6 P.M., Sun. 9 A.M.–1 P.M.

Miramar is known for its department stores housed in classical mansions. **Casa Blanca,** 1ra Avenida, esq. 36, Miramar, tel. 204-3914, is strong on electronics. Open Mon.–Sat. 10 A.M.–6 P.M., Sun. 9 A.M.–1 P.M. **La Maison,** Calle 16, esq. 7ma Avenida, tel. 204-1543, offers a collection of boutiques selling perfumes, jewelry, cigars, toys, and fashions. Open Mon.–Sat. 10 A.M.–6:45 P.M. **Le Select,** 5ta Avenida, esq. 30, Miramar, tel. 204-7410, with its ritzy chandeliers and marble statues, is as close as you'll come to Bond Street or Rodeo Drive. This little Harrods in the tropics even has a ground-floor delicatessen, plus an array of boutiques selling high-fashion, cosmetics, and the like. Heck! the staff will even park your car and carry your bags to your car. Open Mon.–Sat. 10 A.M.–8 P.M., Sun. 10 A.M.–2 P.M.

La Puntilla Centro Comercial, 1ra Avenida, esq. 0, tel. 204-7309, is one of the newest and ritziest of plazas, with four floors and stores covering electronics, furniture, clothing, and more.

Quinta y 42, 5ta Avenida y 42, Miramar, tel. 204-7070, is a shopping center that includes a sporting goods store, toy store, bakery, and general supermarket. Open Mon.–Sat. 10 A.M.–6 P.M., Sun. 9 A.M.–1 P.M. The **Complejo Comercial Comodoro,** 3ra Avenida, esq. 84, Miramar, tel. 204-5551, also has a small supermarket, fashion stores, and stores selling electronics and sports equipment.

The largest *diplotienda* is **Supermercado 70,** 3ra Avenida, e/ 62 y 70, Miramar, with all manner of imported foodstuffs. Nearby, **Centro de Negocios Miramar,** 3ra Avenida, e/ 76 y 80, tel. 204-4437, has clothing, jewelry, and electronic stores, open Mon.–Sat. 10 A.M.–6 P.M., Sun. 10 A.M.–1 P.M.

Further west, **Centro Comercial Náutico,** 5ta Avenida y 152, tel. 208-6212, in the Náutico district, has a electronics goods store, plus perfumery and small supermarket. And Marina Hemingway has its own small supermarket, **Centro Comerical La Vigía,** 5ta Avenida y 248, tel. 204-1151. Open Mon.–Sat. 10 A.M.–7 P.M., Sun. 10 A.M.–2 P.M.

ELECTRONICS

There's no shortage of high-tech stores selling at inflated prices to hard-pressed Cubans. No high-tech equipment, such as VCRs, microwaves, or the like, may be brought into the country, as the government wishes to suck dollars out of Cuban pockets. Yes, you can buy Panasonic, Sony, and other quality names, but much of the other stuff is schlock. Beware any items assembled in Cuba from imported parts. Computers are sold only to those very few Cubans with authority from the government.

For computer items head to **Tecún,** Avenida 42, esq. 7ma, Miramar, tel. 204-9364, which also has a repair service. Open Mon.–Fri. 9:30 A.M.–noon and 1–4:30 P.M. Likewise, **Dita,** Calle 23, e/ L y M, Vedado, tel. 55-3278; and Calle 84, e/ 7ma y 9na, tel. 204-5119, sells computer parts and offers a repair service. Open Mon.–Sat. 10 A.M.–6 P.M., Sun. 9 A.M.–1 P.M.

Centro Video, Calle 23, e/ L y M, Vedado, tel. 66-2321; 3ra Avenida, e/ 12 y 14, Miramar, tel. 204-2469; and 5ta Avenida, esq. 86, Miramar, tel. 204-4919, is well-stocked with electronics.

Alas, the only cameras to be bought are small instamatics. See the Film and Photography section, in the Information and Services chapter, for information on cameras.

FLOWERS

Looking to impress a date, or thank someone? Cubans adore flowers. Why then, you may ask, do most homes have *plastic* flowers instead of the live thing? Because flower arrangements were supposedly disdained after the Revolution as a petty bourgeois indulgence. Who knows? Anyway, these days one of the most charming aspects of life in Havana are the flower-sellers selling floral arrangements on the street and at major markets, notably **Cuatro Caminos,** Máximo Gómez y Cristina (Avenida de México), esq. Manglar Arroyo y Matadero, tel. 870-5934.

Jardín Wagner, Calle Mercaderes #113, e/ Obispo y Obrapía, Habana Vieja, tel. 66-9017, sells both domestically grown and imported flowers (it also handles Interflora delivery); open 9 A.M.–5 P.M. **Floralia,** 1ra Calle, e/ Paseo y A, Vedado, tel. 55-3266, in the Galerías Paseo, sells both natural and artificial flowers; open Mon.–Sat. 10 A.M.–6 P.M., Sun. 9 A.M.–1 P.M. **Tropiflora,** Calle 12 #156, e/ Calzada y Línea, Vedado, tel. 66-2332, is known for its fantastic floral arrangements; open Mon.–Sat. 8 A.M.–8 P.M.

MUSIC AND MUSICAL INSTRUMENTS

You'll find cassettes and CDs for sale at every turn, but at rates no cheaper than the United States and Western Europe. Few outlets offer bargains. Musicians in restaurants will offer to sell you cassette tapes of their music for US$5–15, but the quality is often iffy.

You can buy a quality guitar for US$200 or a full-size conga drum for US$100. But check that they're Cuban-made. Most instruments are made in the United States or Japan.

In Habana Vieja, **Longina,** Calle Obispo #360, tel. 862-8371, sells drums (a *bata*—set of three—costs about US$400), plus guitars, and even trombones (from China). It also features a large CD collection. Open Mon.–Sat. 10 A.M.–7 P.M., Sun. 10 A.M.–1 P.M. The **Museo de la Música,** Calle Capdevila #1, Habana Vieja, tel. 861-9846, also has a wide selection of CDs.

For the widest selection, head to the **Casa de la Música Egrem,** Calle 10 #309, Miramar, tel. 202-6900, the sales room of EGREM, the state recording agency. Also try the **Casa de la Música,**

Calle 20 #3309, e/ 33 y 35, Miramar, tel. 204-0447, with a huge collection of Cuban cassettes and CDs; instruments are sold upstairs. Open 10 A.M.–12:30 P.M.

Farther out, **Tienda Tecmusic,** 5ta Avenida, esq. 88, Miramar, tel. 204-8759, also sells instruments, CDs, and cassettes. Open Mon.–Sat. 9 A.M.–6 P.M. And **Imágenes S.A.,** 5ta Avenida #18008 esq. 182, Reparto Flores, Playa, tel. 33-6166, also has a large stock of CDs and cassettes, plus videos of live performances.

You can even buy musical instruments at their source . . . at **Industria de Instrumentos Musicales Fernando Ortíz,** Calle Pedroso #12, esq. Nueva, Cerro, tel. 879-3161, where guitars, drums, claves, and other instruments are made.

PHILATELY

Many of the sellers at the second-hand book market on Plaza de Armas have entire collections of Cuban stamps dating back decades. Most post offices sell collectors editions of contemporary issues.

The **Unidad de Filatélia,** Calle Obispo #518, Habana Vieja, and **Filatélia Especializada,** Calle 27, e/ L y M, specialize in stamps for collectors. They're both open until 7 P.M.

The **Federación Filatélica Cubana,** Calle San Martín #1172, e/ Infanta y Basarrata, Centro Habana, tel. 870-5144, hosts regular meetings where stamp aficionados trade and sell stamps. It's open Wednesdays and Saturdays 1–4 P.M., and 9 A.M.–1 P.M. Sundays.

POSTERS AND MOVIE-RELATED ITEMS

Posters make great souvenirs. For reproduction prints, head to **Galería Exposición,** Calle San Rafael #12, e/ Bélgica y Agramonte, tel. 863-8364, in the Manzana de Gómez building.

You can buy movie posters plus Cuban films on video at the **Centro Cultural Cinematográfico,** Calle 23 #1155, e/ 10 y 12, Vedado, tel. 833-6430, the Cuban Film Institute (ICAIC), which sells film posters and videos on the fourth floor. Open Mon.–Sat. 9 A.M.–5 P.M.

CUBAN POSTER ART

Cuba's strongest claim to artistic fame is surely its unique poster art, created in the service of political revolution. Cuban poster art has blossomed, thanks to state support—a situation comparable to the United States in the 1930s, when the government paid artists to produce individual work.

The three leading poster-producing agencies—the Organization of Solidarity with the Peoples of Africa, Asia and Latin America; the Cuban Film Institute (ICAIC); and the Editora Política, the propaganda arm of the Cuban Communist Party—have produced more than 10,000 posters since 1959. Different state bodies create works for different audiences: artists of the Cuban Film Institute, for example, design posters for movies from Charlie Chaplin comedies to John Wayne westerns; Editora Política produces posters covering everything from AIDS awareness, baseball games, and energy conservation to telling children to do their homework.

Cuba's most talented painters and photographers rejected Soviet realism and developed their own unique graphic style influenced by Latin culture and the country's geography. The vibrant colors and lush imagery are consistent with the physical and psychological makeup of the country, such as the poster urging participation in the harvest, dripping with psychedelic images of fruit and reminiscent of a 1960s Grateful Dead poster.

Cuban posters typically combine strong, simple concepts and sparse text with ingenious imagery and surprising sophistication. One poster, for example, warns of the dangers of smoking: a wisp of smoke curls upward to form a ghostlike skull.

The vast collection—acclaimed as "the single most focused, potent body of political graphics ever produced in this hemisphere"—provides a lasting visual commentary of the Revolution.

See *¡Revolucion! Cuban Poster Art,* by Lincoln Cushing, and the **Cuba Poster Project,** c/o Inkworks, 2827 7th St., Berkeley, CA 94710, 510/845-7111, fax 510/845-6753, inkworks@igc.org.

RUM AND LIQUORS

About one dozen distilleries operate in Cuba today, producing some 60 brands of rum. They vary widely—the worst can taste like paint thinner. Each brand generally has three types of rum: clear "white rum," labeled *Carta Blanca,* which is aged three years and costs less than US$5 a bottle; the more asserting "golden rum," labeled *Dorado* or *Carta Oro,* aged five years, and costing about US$6; and *"añejo,"* aged seven years and costing US$10 or more.

The best in all three categories are Havana Club's rums, topped only by Matusalem Añejo Superior, described by a panel of tasting experts as showing "a distinctive Scotch whisky-like character, with peaty and smoky aromas and flavors accented by orange-peel notes dry on the palate and long in the finish." A few limited production rums, such as Ron Santiago 45 Aniversario

(US$20) and the 15-year-old Havana Club Gran Reserva (US$80) approach the harmony and finesse of fine Cognacs.

Three rum stores in Habana Vieja offer tastings before you buy: **Casa del Ron,** Calle Obispo, e/ Monserrate y Bernaza, tel. 33-8911, above El Floridita restaurant (open daily 10 A.M.–8 P.M.); **Taberna del Galeón,** Calle Baratillo esq. Obispo, tel. 33-8476, off the southeast corner of Plaza de Armas (try the house special, *puñetazo,* a blend of rum, coffee, and mint); and the **Museo de Ron,** Avenida del Puerto #262, e/ Churruca y Sol, tel. 861-8051 (Open 10 A.M.–9 P.M.).

Fábrica de Ron Bocoy, Máximo Gómez #1417, e/ Patrio y Auditor, Cerro, tel. 877-5781, makes the disappointing Bocoy and Legendario rums, and has a bar for tasting the goods as a prelude to buying. Open Mon.–Sat. 9 A.M.–5 P.M., Sun. 9 A.M.–2 P.M.

the official "Alchemist of Old Havana," will make up a fragrance to order. Open 10 A.M.–6 P.M.

Farmacia Taquechel, Calle Obispo #155, e/ Mercaderes y San Ignacio, tel. 862-9286, sells face creams, lotions, and other natural products made in Cuba.

Most larger deluxe hotels have perfume stores, as do major department stores listed earlier in this chapter.

FOR CHILDREN AND THE CHILD WITHIN

There's a shortage of stores selling with children in mind.

In Vedado, the **Galería Comercial Habana Libre,** in the Hotel Habana Libre, has a children's store. Most of the toys are made in China and are of poor quality; avoid the bicycles, which will break within days!

Pinochín—Casa de Fiesta, Calle Reina #313, e/ Lealtad y Campanario, Centro Habana, tel. 863-3023, sells children's party items for birthdays and other events. Open Mon.–Sat. 10 A.M.–6 P.M., Sun. 10 A.M.–2 P.M.

Delicatessen, Calle 12, e/ 23 y 25, in Galerías Amazonas, sells handmade chocolates. Open Mon.–Sat. 10 A.M.–7 P.M., Sun. 10 A.M.–2 P.M.

Harris Brothers, Avenida de Bélgica #305, e/ O'Reilly y Progreso, Habana Vieja, tel. 861-1644, has a children's department on the third floor. You'll also find kid's outlets in most other stores listed in the Department Stores section.

La Isla del Tesoro rum

You can even buy a French-produced Cohiba Cognac for a whopping US$364 for 0.70 liter.

PERFUMES AND TOILETRIES

Havana 1791, Calle Mercaderes #156, esq. Obrapía, tel. 861-3525, sells locally made scents in exquisite engraved bottles with not entirely trustworthy cork tops (US$6–18), in an embossed linen bag. The twelve fragrances—*"aromas coloniales"*—include Rosa, Violeta, and a surprisingly un-cigar-like Tabaco. It also sells brand-name French perfumes at duty-free prices. And Yanelda,

Information and Services

Money

CURRENCY

Dollars

All prices in this book are quoted in U.S. dollars unless otherwise indicated, as virtually every transaction—from toothpaste and toilet paper to car rentals and your hotel bill—requires payment in U.S. dollars, sometimes called *moneda efectiva* or *divisa,* and colloquially known as *fula, guano, guaniquiqi, varo,* and *verde.* U.S. coins, however, are no longer accepted as legal tender . . . only paper currency.

Plans were annouced in 2003 to accept the Euro as legal currency in Havana if its introduction to Varadero in 2002 proves a successful experiment. Some Cuban hotels were quoting room rates in Euros, rather than dollars at last visit. Expect acceptance of the Euro to spread.

There is no limit to the amount of convertible currency you can bring into Cuba. However, Cuba does not permit more than US$5,000 to be exported; an exception is if you're bringing in more than that amount and anticipate leaving with more than US$5,000, in which case you must declare it upon arrival.

You can exchange foreign currency for U.S. dollars at banks and some hotel cash desks

post office, Plaza de la Catedral

(arriving, you can change money at the José Martí International Airport). Cuban banks buy foreign currency in exchange for U.S. dollars, not for pesos.

You should always try to have a wad of small bills, as change for larger bills is often hard to come by.

Counterfeit US$100 bills are in circulation (printed in Colombia, apparently), and Cubans are wary of these. You'll usually have to supply your passport number or other ID number, which will be recorded when paying with a US$100 bill (and sometimes with a US$50 bill). Supposedly, only post-1962 bills are now legal tender, but you'll find greenbacks going back to the 1930s still circulating.

Cuban Currency

The Cuban currency (*moneda nacional*) is the peso, which is designated "$" and should not be confused with the U.S. "$." To make matters worse, the dollar is sometimes colloquially called the peso. Bills are issued in denominations of one (olive), three (red), five (green), 10 (brown), 20 (blue), and 50 (purple) pesos; a one-peso coin is also issued. The peso is divided into 100 centavos, issued in coin denominations of one, two, five, 10, and 20 centavos (which are also called pesetas).

There is very little that you will need pesos for. Exceptions are if you want to travel on local trains and buses, hang out at local bars and restaurants not normally frequented by tourists, or buy *refrescos, batidos,* or other snacks from street stalls. Otherwise, spending pesos in Havana is nigh impossible.

The Cuban peso is not traded on international markets as a convertible currency. Nonetheless, the Cuban government likes to pretend that its value is at parity with the U.S. dollar. However, the *unofficial* exchange rate—the black market rate—is used by almost everyone (including the government) to set the peso's true value, and that of goods and services. When possession and spending of dollars was legalized for Cubans in 1993, the value of the peso plunged to 150 to the dollar before climbing back to 25 to one. The rate has remained rela-

tively stable ever since and in early 2003 was valued at 27 pesos to one U.S. dollar.

Exchanging Dollars for Pesos

Legally, foreign currency can be changed for pesos only at an official *buró de cambio* (exchange bureau) operated by **Cadeca, S.A.** (an acronym for *casa de cambio*), Avenida 26, esq. 45, Nuevo Vedado, tel. 55-5701. Cadeca operates exchange booths throughout Havana. Most are aimed at culling dollars from the local economy. Nonetheless, foreigners can exchange dollars for pesos here. You *cannot* change any unused pesos into dollars, however, even at the airport upon departure. Exchange only small amounts of dollars for pesos as pocket change. And spend all your local currency before leaving.

The creation of Cadeca has taken the wind out of the sails of *jineteros* who change cash illegally on the streets and face prison terms if caught. Many tourists are ripped off during the deal. Even muggings have been reported. *It ain't worth it!*

Tourist Currency

Although they're now being taken out of circulation, you may occasionally be given rainbow-colored notes and flimsy coins that look like Monopoly money. They're called *pesos convertibles* (convertible pesos), or "B Certificates," and the flimsy coins are stamped "INTUR." Bills are issued in the following denominations: one, two, five, 10, 20, 50, and 100 pesos, on a par with U.S. dollar denominations. They're valid in lieu of dollars for all transactions. You can exchange them for hard currency at the airport on the day of departure.

Receipts and Bills

Overcharging is a common practice, mainly at restaurants. Make a point of checking every receipt you receive in Cuba for accuracy, as items you never requested or those that you requested but which never arrived have a sneaky way of finding their way onto your bill. Service charges are often automatically added to your restaurant bill—the government pilfers the money rather than giving it to the staff, as intended. You can challenge these and have them waived if you are not happy with the meal or service.

BANKS

The state-run **Banco Financiero Internacional** is the main bank, with eight branches throughout Havana (open Mon.–Sat. 8 A.M.–3 P.M., but 8 A.M.–noon only on the last working day of each month). It has currency exchange services at free-market rates. Its outlet in the Hotel Habana Libre Tryp has a special cashiers' desk handling traveler's checks and credit card advances for foreigners (Mon.–Sat. 9 A.M.–7 P.M., Sun. 9 A.M.–2 P.M.). The state-run **Banco de Crédito y Comercio** is the main commercial bank. Its Vedado branches have foreign-exchange desks (open Mon.–Fri. 8:30 A.M.–3 P.M.). The **Banco Internacional de Comercio** and **Banco Metropolitano** also have services for foreigners. The **Banco Popular** primarily serves Cubans.

No foreign banks are present.

ATM CARDS

Automated teller machines (ATMs) at major bank locations dispense U.S. dollars to Cubans with cash cards either issued in Cuba (see Money Transfers later in this chapter) or sent from relatives abroad and used to cull money wired into accounts in Canada, Europe, or Latin America. Most ATMs are not yet linked to international systems such as Cirrus. Exceptions include ATMs at the **Hotel Golden Tulip Parque Central,** Neptuno, esq. Agramonte, Habana Vieja; **Plaza de Carlos III,** Avenida Salvador Allende, esq. Árbol Seco, Centro Habana; **Banco Internacional de Comercio,** 3ra Avenida, esq. 78, Miramar; and **Banco Metropolitano,** 5ta Avenida, esq. 113, Miramar, all of which dispense up to US$300 on foreign credit cards (but not MasterCard . . . nor U.S. credit cards). Other ATMs may also dispense cash by the time you read this.

CREDIT CARDS

Most hotels, car rental companies, and travel suppliers, as well as larger restaurants, will ac-

---

BANKS

Banco Financiero Internacional

Oficios, esq. Brasil, Habana Vieja, tel. 860-8371

Avenida Salvador Allende, e/ Andre Seco y Retiro, Centro Habana, tel. 873-6496

Hotel Habana Libre, Calle L, esq. 25, Vedado, tel. 55-4520

Línea, esq. O, Vedado, tel. 33-3423

5ta Avenida y 92, Miramar, tel. 267-5000

9na Avenida y 26, Miramar tel. 204-0276

Edificio Sierra Maestra, 1ra Avenida y 0, Miramar, tel. 203-9762

Banco de Crédito y Comercio

Amargura, esq. Mercaderes, Habana Vieja, tel. 863-8314

Amargura #158, Habana Vieja, tel. 33-8962

O'Reilly #402, Habana Vieja, tel. 863-1489

Avenida de Italia #452, Centro Habana, tel. 861-2385

Avenida Padre Varela #452, Centro Habana, tel. 870-3088

Línea #705, Vedado, tel. 830-1762

Calle 23 #74, e/ P y Infanta, Vedado, tel. 870-2684

Marino y Conill, Nuevo Vedado, tel. 53-2347

Calle 42 #2714, Miramar, tel. 202-7010

Banco Internacional de Comercio

Empredado y Aguiar, Habana Vieja, tel. 66-6408

3ra y 78, Miramar, tel. 204-3607

Banco Metropolitano

Línea y M, Vedado, tel. 55-3116

5ta Avenida y 111, Playa, tel. 204-9188

---

cept credit card payments as long as the cards are not issued by U.S. banks (blame Uncle Sam; the U.S. Treasury Department forbids U.S. banks to process transactions involving Cuba). The following credit cards are honored: Access, Banamex, Bancomer, Carnet, Diners Club International, JCB, MasterCard, and VISA International. British travelers should check that their cards can be used, as about 20 percent of British-issued cards—including those of Abbey National—are outsourced to a U.S. company that is barred from processing such transactions.

Don't rely entirely on credit cards, however, because often you may find that no vouchers are available to process transactions. And the centralized computer system often fails for hours at a time, affecting every credit card machine in the country.

You can use your non-U.S. credit card to obtain a cash advance up to US$5,000 (US$100 minimum) at branches of Banco Financiero Internacional (BFI).

If you have a problem with your card while in Cuba, contact **Fincimex,** in the Hotel Habana Libre, Calle L, e/ 23 y 25, Vedado, tel. 55-4466 or 55-4024, and at Calle 2 #302, esq. 3ra, Miramar, tel. 204-4823; open Mon.–Fri. 8:30 A.M.–noon and 1–4:30 P.M. It can contact your credit card company to have your card reactivated, or canceled in the event of theft.

U.S. Travelers

In general, U.S. citizens must travel on a cash-only basis. (However, Rex Limousines accepts U.S. MasterCard payment for car rentals; see their listing under Rental Companies in the Transportation chapter). Until recently, you could obtain a cash advance against a U.S.-issued MasterCard at two locations, but at last visit this was no longer the case. If you run out of money, you may have difficulty getting more money forwarded quickly and easily. However, U.S. citizens can use Tran$Card to forward money to Cuba.

If you have a foreign bank account you can obtain a credit card which can then be used in Cuba. You'll still be breaking U.S. laws, but the Cubans make no distinctions.

TRAVELER'S CHECKS

Traveler's checks (unless issued by U.S. banks) are accepted in most tourist restaurant and hotels, and in some foreign-goods stores, although with more hesitancy than credit cards. Traveler's checks can also be cashed at most hotel cashier desks, as well as at banks.

Traveler's checks issued by U.S. banks, including American Express, *can* be used to get cash at branches of BFI and through Asistur offices (see If Trouble Strikes, later in this chapter). Large denomination traveler's checks are best to speed along your transaction.

You should *not* enter the date or the place when signing your checks. It's a quirky Cuban requirement.

MONEY TRANSFERS

Western Union, 800/325-6000 in the US, www.westernunion.com, is licensed to handle wire transfers to Cuba, permitting anyone in the United States to send up to US$300 every three months, but not to Cuban officials or government entities. Only designated Western Union offices are permitted to handle such transactions, which in Cuba are handled by Fincimex at about a dozen or so locations in Havana.

U.S. citizens (and others) can use a **Tran$card** to send money to Cuba from 24 nations around the world. You can apply for a Tran$card online—www.cash2cuba.com—or while in Cuba through the Miramar office of **Fincimex,** Calle 2 #302, esq. 3ra, tel. 204-4823. The card enables

WESTERN UNION LOCATIONS

Avenida Simón Bolívar, Centro Habana, tel. 33-0118

Neptuno, esq. San Nicolás, Centro Habana, tel. 33-0120

Avenida Salvador Allende y Retiro, Centro Habana, tel. 33-0128

Neptuno y Ignacio Agramonte, Centro Habana, tel. 33-0122

Calle 17 #55, Vedado, tel. 33-0129

Avenida 26 y 23, Vedado, tel. 33-0286

Calle 8 #319, Miramar, tel. 204-2291

La Puntilla Centro Comercial, 1ra Avenida y 0, Miramar, tel. 204-8735

1ra Avenida y 36, Miramar, tel. 204-8738

1ra Avenida y 294, Playa, tel. 204-7869

you to transfer funds online or via snail mail, including from your Visa, MasterCard, or American Express account, to your Tran$card account. Funds sent from the US are credited to secure card accounts in Canada; c/o ICC, Corp, 905/305-7703 or 800/724-5685, csr@transcard inter.com. Recipients then use their Tran$card in Cuba for cash advances at banks and ATMs, or for purchases at more than 2,000 retail merchant locations using pre-paid credit. You simply swipe the card through a Point of Sale (POS) terminal and enter your Personal Identification Number (PIN). For further information, contact Tran$card at 1600 Steeles Ave., Suite 400, Concord, Ontario L4K 4M2, Canada, 537/862-9900, help@cash2cuba.com.

The same Canadian company also offers **Quickcash** money transfer service for those without a Tran$card, permitting transfers via your Visa or MasterCard account online through the Internet. Deliveries are made in U.S. dollar cash (or the currency of your choosing) in one to five days through banks in Havana; the processing is via the Canadian banking system, and transfers are settled on your account in Canadian dollars. Each transaction is limited to a maximum of CAN$450, but you can make as many transactions as you wish.

MoneyGram, 800/328-5678 (USA), www .moneygram.com, with 50,000 agents in 135 countries, also permits money transfers via Tran$card.

GO CUBAN!

I t's frighteningly easy to burn through money in Havana. Virtually everything is sold in dollars at inflated rates. You'll save heaps of money by "going Cuban," living cheap, as much as this is permitted. By using *pesos* (obtained at Cadeca outlets), you can get by for pennies. Fifteen cents for pizzas bought at street stalls and washed down by *refrescos* for US$.10, or *guarapos* (sugar cane juice) for US$.05. An *ensalada* (bowl) of delicious ice cream at Coppelia costs another US$.15. Alas, *peso* taxis are now barred from picking up foreigners, period. But you could get lucky. And there's always a public bus.

Non–U.S. citizens have several other options, including a wire transfer through the Banco Financiero Internacional. It's a good idea to carry full details of your home account with you in Cuba, including your home bank's telex number. The process can take several days.

In an emergency, you can also arrange money transfers or even a cash advance through Asistur (see If Trouble Strikes, later in this chapter). And **DHL,** www.dhl.com, is supposedly trustworthy for sending money in the form of traveler's checks, although nine days is about the average time for a DHL package to Cuba.

COSTS

The Cuban government—which enjoys a monopoly on all services—is guilty of gouging and in danger of overpricing itself in its greed to cull dollars at every turn. Without competition to regulate the market, the state has jacked up prices in recent years to often ridiculous levels. Many hotels and restaurants are far more expensive than they deserve to be.

If you get around on public transport, rent rooms with Cuban families, dine on the street at *paladares* (private restaurants) and peso snack bars, and keep your entertainment to nontouristy venues, then you may be able to survive on as little as US$40 a day, with your room taking the lion's share. However, by being so frugal, you'll have to rough it and be prepared for a basic food regimen. If you want at least a modicum of comforts, then budget *at least* US$60 a day.

Accommodation in Havana costs US$15–300 per night. Meals average US$5–15 with a beer; although lunch or dinner at a *good* restaurant will usually cost upward of US$20 per person. Entrance to a cabaret or disco will cost US$5–65, plus drinks. Day tours featuring sightseeing and meals average US$35–50. Taxis average about US$1.50 per mile. Budget $55 upwards per day for a rental car.

Be prepared, too, for lots of extra expenses for minor services that are provided free of charge in North America and most European nations. Communist it may be, but the Cuban government could teach some nasty tricks to those evil capitalists to the north, and at last visit it was so desperate for dollars that it was prepared to bite the hands that feed it. It gives nothing for free . . . not even the bread and butter that arrive with your meal without your asking.

Foreigners studying at the University of Havana and other institutions can get a student *carnet* good for discounts on museums, concerts, Astro bus tickets, and more.

Communications

The **Ministerio de Comunicaciones,** Avenida de Independencia y 19 de Mayo, Plaza de la Revolución, tel. 66-8000, controls all communications, including mail, telephone, and online services (open Mon.–Fri. 8 A.M.–5 P.M.).

POSTAL SERVICE

Correos de Cuba operates the Cuban postal service. Cuba's mail system is terminally slow, and delivery is never guaranteed. Most international mail is read by censors—*never* send cash, and avoid any and all politically sensitive comments or your mail will *not* be delivered.

International airmail (*correo aereo*) averages about one month each way (to save time, savvy Cubans usually hand their letters to foreigners to mail outside Cuba). When mailing from Cuba, it helps to write the country destination in Spanish: England is "Inglaterra" (use this for Wales and Scotland also, on the line below either country); France is "Francia;" Italy is "Italia;" Germany is "Alemania;" Spain is "España;" Switzerland is "Suiza;" and the United States is "Estados Unidos."

Most major tourist hotels have small *correos* (post offices) and philatelic bureaus, and will accept your mail for delivery. Havana is also well served by post offices, which are relatively efficient (stamps are called *sellos*—pronounced "say-yos"). Most are open weekdays 10 A.M.–5 P.M. and Saturday 8 A.M.–3 P.M.

Rates

Within Cuba, letters cost from 15 centavos (20 grams or less) to 2.05 pesos (up to 500 grams); postcards cost 10 centavos. An international postcard costs US$.50 to all destinations; letters cost US$.80.

Parcels

All parcels to be mailed from Cuba must be delivered to the post office *unwrapped* for inspection. It is far better to send packages through an express courier service, although the same regulation applies. (If mailing to the United States, don't try mailing Uncle Fred a box of Cohibas for Christmas. They'll go up in smoke all right—on the U.S. Customs 24-hour funeral pyre!)

Receiving Mail

You can receive mail in Havana by having letters and parcels addressed to you using your name as it appears on your passport or other ID for general delivery to: "c/o Espera [your name], Ministerio de Comunicaciones, Avenida Independencia and 19 de Mayo, Habana 6, Cuba." To collect mail *poste restante*, go to the **Correos de Cuba**, tel. 879-6824 or 879-8654, on Avenida Rancho Boyeros, one block north of the Plaza de la Revolución; open Mon.–Sat. 8 A.M.–6 P.M. for parcel pick-up. The names of people who have received mail are posted. Keep incoming mail simple—parcels are less likely to make it.

Express Mail Services

DHL Worldwide Express, 1ra Avenida, esq. Calle 26, Miramar, tel. 204-1578 or 204-1876, fax 204-0999 (open weekdays 8 A.M.–8 P.M., Saturday 8 A.M.–4 P.M.) also has offices at Calzada, e/ 2 y 4, Vedado, tel. 832-2112; and in the Hotel Habana Libre Tryp. DHL acts as a Customs broker and offers daily door-to-door pickup and delivery service at no charge. It offers four options: *Express,* for sending documents with no commercial value; *International,* for documents to anywhere in the world; *International Packages,* for commercial samples; and *National* for sending documents and packages between towns throughout Cuba. DHL guarantees delivery within Havana in less than 24 hours. However, DHL packages mailed to or from the United States typically take more than a week to arrive.

An express document to Canada, Mexico, or the United States costs a minimum US$39; to anywhere else, US$49 minimum. Rates are higher for packages. The minimum cost to send *to* Cuba is US$60. Within Cuba, documents up to three kilos cost US$4 within Havana, and US$.50 more for each additional kilo. Interprovincial rates cost US$8–10, depending on zone.

Cubapost, Calle 21 #10099, e/ 10 y 12, Vedado, tel. 33-0483, fax 33-6097, servicioalcliente@cuba post.colombus.cu, offers an international express mail service (EMS) to virtually every country in the world using TNT. Rates begin at US$20 (0.5 kg) to the Americas, and US$23 to Europe. Service within Havana costs US$4 for the first five kilograms, and delivery is guaranteed within 24 hours. Domestic service within Cuba costs US$5–9 (up to five kg) according to zone. Open Mon.–Fri. 8 A.M.–5 P.M., Sat. 8 A.M.–noon.

Cubapacks, Calle 22 #4115, e/ 41 y 47, Miramar, tel. 204-2134, fax 204-2226, cupacks @imagenes.get.cma.net, www.cubapacks.cu (open Mon.–Fri. 8:30 A.M.–noon and 1:30–5:30 P.M.) also offers express mail service.

U.S. Restrictions

Uncle Sam restricts what may be mailed to Cuba from the United States. Letters and literature can be mailed without restriction. Gift parcels can be "sent or carried by an authorized traveler" to an individual or religious or edu-cational organization if the domestic retail value does not exceed US$200. Only one parcel per month is allowed. And contents are limited to food, vitamins, seeds, medicines, medical supplies, clothing, personal hygiene items, and a few other categories. All other parcels are subject to seizure! Don't think you can skirt around this by sending by DHL. Your package will either be returned or seized.

Online Mail

Want your mail to be delivered within seconds? You can write online and send letters, postcards or telex to friends and family in Cuba using **E-scriba,** escriba@escriba.com, www.escriba.com or www.cubaweb.com. Content is printed and sent from an E-scriba distribution center. Letters cost US$2 for up to 800 words (80 lines). Telegrams cost US$4 per 10 words (one line). You can pay with Visa, MasterCard or American Express, or with bank draft or money order payable to E-scriba Inc., 1 Yonge Street #1801, Toronto, ON M3E 1E5, Canada. You must buy credit for a minimum of six cyberstamps (US$2 each) to be deducted from your account as you use them.

Alternately, Correos de Cuba, www.correos-decuba.com, offers an online service. It will deliver your email as a telegram (24 hours), letter (72 hours), or postcard (120 hours).

TELEPHONE SERVICE

Cuba's telephone system is the responsibility of the Empresa de Telecomunicaciones de Cuba (ETECSA), headquartered at Águila #565, esq. Dragones, Centro Habana, tel. 860-7511, www.etecsa.cu, and a joint venture with the Italian telecommunications company, ILTE. Much of the telephone network predates the Revolution (the AT&T system, installed long before the Revolution, was replaced in the 1960s by "fraternal Hungarian equipment"—Castro's words—and it was downhill from there). Fortunately, ETECSA has in the past few years managed to replace more than 50 percent of Havana's inept and derelict analog system with a digital system and fiber-optic network, with most of the rest slated for upgrading in coming years. Modern

---

SENDING FLOWERS TO CUBA

Want to surprise a Cuban friend or lover with a bouquet of flowers? Easily done through Swiss-based **Interflora,** info@fleurop.com, www.fleurop.com, which handles requests online and can deliver to Cuba within 48 hours from worldwide. A bouquet of 12 red roses costs €67-73, delivered to the addressee's door.

You can even send a bottle of perfume, or pretty much anything else for that matter, via **Cuba Gift Store,** 877/284-4387 (in the United States), www.cubagiftstore.com.

CALLING HAVANA

Outside Cuba, telephone and fax numbers need to be preceded by 53-7, the codes for Cuba and Havana respectively.

telephones are gradually replacing the antediluvian relics that perform like something from a Hitchcock movie.

Still, things aren't yet perfect. Getting a dial tone may be the first obstacle. You might get a busy signal (though this does not necessarily mean that the line is engaged) or a series of squeaks and squawks. You just have to keep trying. A telephone line that is working one minute may simply go dead the next. Some days are better than others.

Cubans usually answer the phone by saying either "*¡Oigo!*" (I'm listening!) or "*¡Dígame!*" (Speak to me!). It sounds abrupt, but they're not being rude.

Telephone Directories

ETECSA publishes four comprehensive regional directories, including "Ciudad de la Habana." The directory is also available in CD-Rom (however, my 2002 edition wouldn't load correctly in my computer), and online at www.etecsa.cu—it functions best with Microsoft Internet Explorer. A less authoritative online directory is at www.paginasamarillas.com.

You'll need some creativity, however, as many entries are listed in specific categories that often aren't logical. For example, a specific restaurant you're seeking might not be listed under "Restaurants" but under "Bars." (Private businesses, such as *paladares,* by law may not advertise and are therefore not listed.)

Unfortunately, telephone numbers change with exasperating regularity. Those in Havana have been in flux as ETECSA upgrades to a digital system. Moreover, trying to determine a correct number can be problematic because many entities have several numbers and rarely publish the same number twice. If you get a wrong number, a recorded message will say: "*Este número no existe.*" (This number doesn't exist.)

Call 113 for directory inquiries.

Online Calling

In 2002, ETECSA introduced an online calling service, at www.calls2cuba.com. You deposit US$20 (good for two five-minute calls) or US$40 (four seven-minute calls) using your credit card. You book the time of your calls from anywhere in the world through an operator.

Public Phone Booths

ETECSA operates modern, efficient, glass-enclosed light-blue telephone kiosks called *centros telefónicos* or *telecorreos,* where they combine postal services, located at key points throughout Havana. They utilize phone cards as well as U.S. coins. These telephone bureaus do not accept collect or incoming calls.

There is also no shortage of stand-alone public phones throughout the city (although there are relatively few in touristed areas). Avoid these if

public telephone

USEFUL TELEPHONE NUMBERS

Emergency

Ambulance (public)	tel. 114 or 879-5400
Fire	tel. 115 or 867-5555
Police	tel. 116 or 867-7777

Medical

Clínica Cira García (international clinic)	tel. 204-0330
Farmacia Internacional (24-hour pharmacy)	tel. 204-2051

Embassies

Canada	tel. 204-2516, emergency tel. 204-2516
France	tel. 204-2132
Germany	tel. 33-2569
Italy	tel. 33-3378
Spain	tel. 33-8029
United Kingdom	tel. 204-2086
United States (Interests Section)	tel. 33-3551 to 33-3559
emergency/after hours	tel. 33-3026

Transportation

Cubana de Aviación (Reservations: national)	tel. 55-1024
Cubana de Aviación (Reservations: international)	tel. 33-4446
José Martí International Airport (information: Terminal 1)	tel. 33-5753 or 33-5576
José Martí International Airport (information: Terminal 2)	tel. 33-5577
José Martí International Airport (information: Terminal 3)	tel. 33-5666 or 206-4644
Estación Central de Ferrocarril (Central railway station: information)	tel. 861-4259 or 861-3047
Estación Central de Ferrocarril (Central railway station: Ferrotur ticket office)	tel. 861-4259
Estación 19 de Noviembre	tel. 881-4431
Estación Cristina	tel. 863-2989
Terminal de Ómnibus Nacionales (bus terminal: information for Cubans)	tel. 879-2456 or 879-3769
Terminal de Ómnibus Nacionales (bus terminal: information for foreigners)	tel. 870-3397
Víazul Bus Terminal	tel. 881-1413
Panataxi	tel. 55-5555

possible; they tend to be on noisy street corners. Some are modern and take phone cards. Others are older and can only be used for local calls; they take five-centavo coins. When you hear the "time-up" signal (a short *blip*), you must *immediately* put in another coin to avoid being cut off. Newer public phones also take 20-centavo coins and can be used for long-distance calls—you get any change back when you hang up.

Prepaid Phone Cards

You can buy a phone card called *Propia,* sold in pesos (for calls within Cuba only) and in dollars (US$10 and US$25) for international calls; they're sold at tourist hotels, *centros telefónicos,* certain restaurants, and miscellaneous other outlets. All ETECSA *centros telefónicos* and an increasing number of streetside public phones take prepaid phone cards. You insert the card into the phone and it automatically deducts from the value of the card according to period of time of your conversation; you'll be able to see the diminishing value of the card displayed during your call. If it expires, you can replace it with a new one without interrupting your call by pushing button C and inserting a new card.

International Calls

When calling Cuba from abroad, dial 011 (the international dialing code), then 53 (the Cuba country code), followed by 7 (Havana's city code) and the number. For direct outbound international calls from Cuba, dial 119, then the country code (for example, 44 for the UK), followed by the area code and number. For the international operator, dial 0, wait for the tone, then dial 9. For operator-assisted calls from Havana to the United States, dial 66-1212. Using a Cuban telephone operator can be a Kafkaesque experience, as many do not speak English. In the United States, AT&T has a "language line" that will connect you with an interpreter, 800/843-8420; US$3.50 per minute.

Most upscale tourist hotels have direct-dial telephones in guest rooms for international calls. Others will connect you via the hotel operator. Or you can call from ETECSA's *centros telefónicos.* The main international telephone exchange is in Vedado in the lobby of the Hotel Habana Libre Tryp.

Cost per minute varies depending on time of day and location from which you're calling. Typical calls charged per minute are: US$2.65 to the United States, US$2.40 to Canada, US$3.40 to Central America and Caribbean countries, US$4.45 to South America, US$4.80 to France, Germany, Italy, and Spain, and US$5.30 to Europe and the rest of the world. Operator-assisted calls cost more. You can use calling cards for international calls. Rates are about 40 percent higher for operator-assisted calls.

In December 2000, the Cuban government reduced phone links to the United States in a political spat that made calls into and out of the country more difficult. Things had eased up somewhat at last visit, but service remains hostage to fickle whims. Sometimes you can call a dozen times and never get through, week after week, then presto! Calling out from Cuba is usually much easier than calling into the country.

Domestic Calls

For local calls in Havana, simply dial the number you wish to reach. To dial a number outside Havana, dial 0, wait for a tone, then dial the local city code and the number you wish to reach. For the local operator, dial 0, wait for a tone, then dial 0. Local calls in Havana cost approximately five centavos (about a quarter of a cent). Rates for calls beyond Havana range from 30 centavos to three pesos and 15 centavos for the first three minutes, depending on zone—tourist hotels and ETECSA booths charge in U.S. dollar equivalent.

Cellular Phones

Cubacel, Calle 28 #510, e/ 5 y 7, Miramar, tel. 880-2222, fax 880-0000, www.cubacel.com, provides cellular phone service; open Mon.–Fri. 8 A.M.–5 P.M., Sat. 8 A.M.–noon. It also has offices in the Miramar Trade Center, 3ra Avenida y 70, Miramar, tel. 880-0200, and at José Martí International Airport, tel. 880-0043 (Terminal 2), and tel. 880-0222 (Terminal 3).

Cubacel rents cellular phones for US$7 daily (plus a US$3 one-time activation fee). You also have to pay a US$410 security deposit, plus US$100 per day deposit for use. Air time costs US$.90 per minute in addition to relevant long-

ONLINE SERVICE IN CUBA

Cuba is behind the times in its application of online services, although many state entities now have websites and email connections. Computer communications are tightly controlled by the government, and access for the average citizen is severely restricted. Few individuals are permitted to own a computer or modem, and the cyber cafes (without the coffee) are mostly reserved for tourist use. Cubans are permitted to send and receive emails—there are about 60,000 email accounts in Cuba; most allocated to businesses—but are denied Web access except for a few privileged persons who, with rare exception, can only view select sites placed on government servers.

Several Cuban entities compete. **Etecsa** offers Internet service at many *telecorreos* and telephone kiosks (typically a prepaid card costs US$15 for five hours; some outlets charge US$.05 per minute additional). Many entities use the **Tu Isla** service, which also uses a prepaid *tarjeta* (typically US$4.50 for three hours); some Tu Isla outlets permit full Internet access, but most restrict use to an "intranet" of approved sites, and you'll need to set up a separate email account on the Tu Isla server.

Tourists are permitted to bring laptop computers, which must be declared and may not be left behind in Cuba—your carry-on luggage is run through an X-ray machine upon arrival at José Martí International Airport to search for laptops. *Bring a surge protector!*

Since Internet time in Cuba is expensive, you can save money on Internet time by typing emails in advance on your laptop and saving them to disk, which you can use to paste to an email composition at a cyber café.

Most upscale tourist hotels now have either cyber cafés or business centers with online access for guests. Most allow you to send and receive email using only the hotel's email address (the Meliá Habana permits you to use your personal email address). A few, such as the Hotel Parque Central, also feature modem outlets in guest rooms. You can call your Internet provider, although there are no local access numbers for AOL, Yahoo, and other non-Cuban ISPs. Yahoo works much better in Cuba than, say, Hotmail (if you want to use Hotmail, sign on using www.msn.com).

Note that in many circumstances, email may be read by Cuban staff, including security personnel reading directly off the server. Be cautious about what you write in your emails. Secret police have even been known to make house calls to check up on guests traveling with computers.

Online Locales

You can send and receive emails (but not surf the Internet) at most **Infotur** offices (US$1 per message). Incoming messages go to the Infotur account; an employee then phones you in Cuba to let you know you have a message.

About a dozen **post offices** (*correos*) now offer email and limited Internet service to the general public for US$4.50 for three hours. Foreigners can freely surf the Internet.

At last visit, Rumbos was planning on opening three dedicated cyber cafes.

---

distance charges (US$2.45 per minute to North America). Long-term service costs US$40 monthly (plus US$120 activation and US30-40 cents per minute air time). Cubacel also sells cellular phones at outrageous markups. Far better is to bring your own cellular phone into the country; Cubacel will activate it and provide you with a local line for US$12. However, its network uses the DAMP standard, which is not compatible with most European cell phone systems.

A new company, **C-Com** (Celulares de Cuba), 3ra Avenida #9402, Playa, tel. 204-1640, was founded in 2001 as a joint venture with Spain's Soluciones and uses the GSM standard commonly used in Europe and incompatible with U.S. handsets.

Habana Vieja: There are two cyber cafés in the **Capitolio** (US$2.50 for 30 minutes; US$5 per hour). The first is up the main staircase, where you take a number for a reservation at the "Cibercafé," which serves snacks. Open Mon.–Fri. 9 A.M.–7:30 P.M. The second is in the library on the left (south side) of the building. The wait can be up to one hour—upstairs you take a number; downstairs you must wait in line. The mezzanine business center at the **Hotel Golden Tulip Parque Central,** Neptuno e/ Prado y Agramonte, tel. 866-6627, charges US$17.50 per hour (open Mon.–Fri. 8 A.M.–8 P.M., and weekends 8 A.M.–4 P.M.). The **Hotel Telegrafo** and **Hotel Santa Isabel** both have cyber cafés.

Centro Habana: The **Correo Electrónico,** Salvador Allende, esq. Padre Varela, tel. 879-5795, offers email and Internet access (US$4.50 for three hours). It's open 24 hours.

Vedado: The sixth-floor business center in the **Hotel Nacional,** Calle O y 21, tel. 55-0294, charges US$10 per hour (open Mon.–Fri. 8:30 A.M.–6 P.M., 8:30 A.M.–4:30 P.M. weekends). The second-floor business center in the **Hotel Habana Libre,** Calles L, e/ 23 y 25, tel. 55-4011, offers full Internet service for US$3 for 15 minutes and US$10 per hour; it charges US$2 per email sent, and US$1 for each received (service is free for the hotel's guests); open daily 7 A.M.–11 P.M. The business center in the **Hotel Meliá Cohiba,** Paseo, e/ 1ra y 3ra, tel. 204-3636, charges US$15 per hour (open Mon.–Sat. 8 A.M.–8 P.M.). The business center on the 20th floor of the **Hotel Riviera,** Paseo, e/ Malecón y 1ra, tel. 33-4051, also has Internet service.

Correos de Cuba, Avenida Rancho Boyeros, tel. 66-8249, the main post office next to the Ministerio de Comunicaciones, on the northeast side of Plaza de la Revolución, has 24-hour Internet service; as does the **Telecorreo,** Línea, esq. Paseo, tel. 830-0809.

There are also Internet services at the Etecsa office in the **Centro de Prensa Internacional,** Calle 23 e/ N y O, in Vedado (US$15 for up to five hours); and at the **Víazul** bus station, Avenida 26 y Zoológica, Nuevo Vedado, tel. 881-6954, viazul@transnet.cu.

Students at the University of Havana have free Internet service in the Biblioteca Central—you can have your home email account forwarded to their telnet account—at the faculties of Artes y Letras, where you sign up for a slot the day before, and Filosofía y História, which operates on the *último* system, with long lines for use.

Miramar: The **Novotel Miramar,** 5ta Avenida, e/ 72 y 76, tel. 204-3584, charges US$6 for 30 minutes, US$10 per hour; as does the business center at the **Hotel Meliá Habana,** 3ra Avenida, Calles 84, tel. 204-8500, with a US$3 minimum (open daily 8 A.M.–8 P.M.). The **Hotel Kohly,** Avenida 49 y 36A, Reparto Kohly, tel. 204-0240, also has a cyber café.

Also in Miramar, **Columbus Conectividad,** Calle 20 #711, e/ 7ma y 9ma, charges US$4 per hour. Further west, in the Atabey district, the **Biomunid Center,** Calle 200 e/ 19 y 21, charges US$5 per hour.

If you need technical assistance or computer parts, try DITA, Calle 23 e/ L and M, tel. 55-3278.

TELEX, FAX, AND TELEGRAM

You can send telexes and faxes from most tourist hotels, and from most *centros telefónicos* (notably the main international telephone center in the Hotel Habana Libre Tryp), and at the Centro de Prensa Internacional. A fax to the United States and Canada typically costs US$6.50 minimum plus $1 per minute.

ETECSA offers 24-hour "telegram by telephone" service by calling (81) 8844 or going through its *telecorreo* offices. International telegraphic service is charged per word: 75 centavos to North America, 80 to Europe, 85 to the rest of world. Domestic rates are posted in *telecorreos.*

Media and Other Resources

Cuba imposes its own blockade . . . on information, which is strictly controlled.

NEWSPAPERS AND MAGAZINES

Foreign Newspapers and Magazines

Foreign magazines of whatever shade are sold only in tourist hotel lobbies. There are no newsagents or newsstands on the streets; they were seized and closed after the Revolution. Availability is hit or miss and limited to a small selection of leading international newspapers and magazines (including *Newsweek, Time, USA Today, New York Times, Le Figaro,* and *Der Spiegel,* plus carefully selected consumer magazines), though even these disappear from the shelves during times of international crisis, when the government attempts to suppress *all* access to independent news. Expect to pay up to three times what you'd pay at home.

Most foreign publications are distributed in Cuba through **World Services Publications,** 5ta Avenida #1808, Flores, tel. 33-3002, fax 33-3066, which can steer you in the right direction.

Cuban Publications

The Cuban government owns and controls all publishing houses. There is no independent press, and the few independent journalists that exist do so under constant surveillance and fear of touching a third rail.

The most important publication, and virtually the sole mouthpiece of international news, is *Granma,* the cheaply produced, badly inked official Communist Party propaganda piece published daily. It focuses on profiling a daily succession of victories in the building of socialism; "lingo sludge" and "a degradation of the act of reading" are among the accusations hurled at it. No negatives are reported about domestic affairs—a serial killer could be lose in Havana, but it would never be reported . . . thus, instead, *habaneros* rely for news on *radio bemba,* the inordinately accurate and fast-moving street gossip or

grapevine. *Granma* is essential reading if you want to get the Cuban take on international events—some of the unsigned editorials are written by Castro, whose colorful style, highlighted with subtle invective, is unmistakable—but its triumphalist tone can be a bit Alice-in-Wonderlandish, inspired by a determination to denigrate the United States at every turn. Facts get misrepresented and the truth turned on its head to present Uncle Sam as the bad guy, while socialist thugs like Zimbabwe's Robert Mugabe and Yugoslavia's Slobodan Milosevic are made out to be heroes, presumably on the premise that the enemy of my enemy is my friend. You can buy *Granma* at streetside kiosks, but they rapidly run out. Many Cubans—seriously—stand in line to take *Granma* home to use as toilet paper. A weekly edition published in Spanish, English, and French is sold at hotel gift stores, and at the editorial offices: Avenida General Suárez y Calle Territorial, Plaza de la Revolución, tel. 81-6265, fax 33-5176, informacion@granmai.cip.cu. You can also read it online at www.granma.cu.

Juventud Rebelde, same address as *Granma,* tel. 882-0267, www.jrebelde.cubaweb.cu, published Wednesday–Sunday, is the evening paper of the Communist Youth League. It echoes *Granma,* although it does have a strong arts section and tends to probe more questioningly into international and social affairs. *Opciones,* same address as *Granma,* tel. 881-8621, www.opciones.cubaweb.cu, is a weekly serving the business, commercial, and tourist sectors, aimed at foreign businesspeople in Cuba.

Similar mouthpieces include the less easily found *El Habanero* (Tuesday and Friday); *Tribuna de la Habana* (Sunday), www.tribuna.islagrande.cu; *Trabajadores,* www.trabajadores.cubaweb.cu, the newspaper of the workers syndicates (Monday); and *Mujeres,* Avenida de Italia #264, Centro Habana, tel. 862-5175, a monthly magazine for women.

Magazines focusing on the arts and culture include *Habanera,* a monthly magazine about Havana; *Prisma,* tel. 832-9353, an English-language, bimonthly magazine covering politics, economics, travel, and general subjects on Cuba and the Americas; the weekly *Bohemia,* Avenida de la Independencia #575, Plaza de la Revolución, tel. 881-1431; and *Revolución y Cultura,* Calle 4 #205, e/ Línea y 11, Vedado, tel. 832-3665.

RADIO AND TELEVISION

The state-owned **Instituto Cubano de Radio y Televisión,** tel. 832-9544, controls all broadcast media.

Television

Most tourist hotel rooms have satellite TVs showing international channels such as HBO, ESPN, Cinemax, CNN, VH1, and TV España. The Cuban government pirates foreign satellite signals using a dish mounted on the Hotel Habana Libre Tryp, then retransmits to other tourist hotels so that foreigners may go home without any sense of reality beyond the tourist hotels. *TV Taíno,* intended for tourists, airs 7–8 P.M. each Thursday. Watch, too, for screenings of "Walking in Havana," a guided tour with City Historian Eusebio Leal.

Ordinary Cubans are denied such access and must make do with the three national TV networks: *Canal 6: CubaVisión* and *Canal 2: Tele Rebelde,* plus *Universidad para todos* ("University for All"), introduced in October 2000. The local *CH-TV Habana* airs 6–7 P.M. with local news programming. Tele Rebelde features selections from *CNN España* international news coverage. Otherwise, no foreign TV station is permitted to sully the airwaves. No Cuban is permitted access to satellite TV, and the government goes to great lengths to prevent Cubans accessing foreign stations—although illegal, a few jerrybuilt satellite dishes festoon Havana's rooftops, risking the wrath of authorities. It also does a good job of blocking *TV Martí,* a U.S. government boondoggle broadcast into Cuba—the only folks who get to see it, however, work in the U.S. Interests Section.

Nonetheless, virtually every home has a TV, and Cubans are addicted to television, especially the immensely popular Latin American *telenovelas* (soap operas) that have adherents among all levels of society . . . you can walk through Havana when the *novela* is showing and follow the show as you walk (all the windows are sure to be open).

Programming is largely an organ of political education, dominated by dreary reports on socialist progress; Fidel's lengthy speeches (which always take precedence over all other programming); and the daily *mesa redonda* (round table) political discussions—wicked Uncle Sam is the most common topic—in which no one in his right mind dare ask a probing question.

Cuban television stations also have some very intelligent programming, emphasizing science and culture, sports, and foreign movies. Cartoons are heavily moralistic and aim to teach Cuban youth sound morals, and educational shows have a broadly internationalist focus. There are no advertisements, but five-minute educative slots teach citizens about good behavior and might, for example, inveigh against abortions (*"Aborción no es un método anticonceptivo"*), exhort Cubans to work hard, or call for their participation in important festivals. CubaVisión shows movies (usually recent Hollywood classics) every Saturday night.

The weekly tourist publication *Cartelera,* www.cartelera.cu, available free at hotel newsstands, lists television programming for the coming week.

Radio

Cuba has five national radio stations: *Radio Enciclopedia* (1290 AM and 94.1 FM) and *Radio Musical Nacional* (590 AM and 99.1 FM) offer classical music; *Radio Rebelde* (640 and 710 AM, and 96.7 FM) and *Radio Reloj* (950 AM and 101.5 FM) both report news; and *Radio Progreso* (640 AM and 90.3 FM) features traditional music. In addition, Havana is served by *Habana Radio* (106.9 FM), which specializes in cultural information; and *Cadena Habana* (1140 AM and 99.9 FM) and *Radio Metropolitana* (910 AM and 98.3 FM), both specializing in mostly traditional music and culture. *Radio Ciudad de la Habana* (820 AM and 94.9 FM), caters to a younger crowd. *Radio Taíno* (1290 AM and 93.3 FM) cater to tourists with programs in

EMBASSIES AND CONSULATES IN HAVANA

The following nations have embassies/consulates in Havana—additional countries can be found in the local telephone directory under *Embajadas*. Phone numbers and addresses change frequently. Call to confirm address and hours of operation.

Argentina: Calle 36 #511 e/ 5ta y 7ma, Miramar, tel. 204-2972, fax 204-2140

Austria: Calle 4 #101 esq. 1ra, Miramar, tel. 204-2825, fax 204-1235

Belgium: 5ta Avenida # 7408 esq. 76, Miramar, tel. 204-2410, fax 204-1318

Brazil: Lamparilla #2, Habana Vieja, tel. 66-9052

Canada: Calle 30 #518, esq. 7ma, Miramar, tel. 204-2516, emergency tel. 204-2516; fax 204-2044, havan@havan01.x400.gc.ca

Chile: Avenida 33 #1423, e/ 16 y 18, Miramar, tel. 204-1222, fax 204-1694

China, People's Republic of: Calle 13 #551 esq. C, Vedado, tel. 33-3005, fax 33-3092

Colombia: Calle 14 #515 e/ 5ta y 7ma, Miramar, tel. 204-1246, fax 204-1249

Costa Rica: 5ta Avenida #6604, Miramar, tel. 204-6938, fax 204-6937

Czech Republic: Avenida Kohly #259, Nuevo Vedado, tel. 33-3467, fax 33-3596

Denmark: Calle 66 #1511, Miramar, tel. 33-6238

Ecuador: 5ta Avenida #4407 e/ 44 y 46, Miramar, tel. 204-2034, fax 204-2868

Egypt: 5ta Avenida #1801, Miramar, tel. 204-2441

Finland: Calle 140 #2102 e/ 21 y 23, Miramar, tel./fax 204-0793

France: Calle 14 #312 e/ 3ra y 5ta, Miramar, tel. 204-2308, fax 204-1439

Germany: Calle 13 #652, esq. B, Vedado, tel. 33-2569, fax 33-1586

Greece: 5ta Avenida #7802 esq. 78, Miramar, tel. 204-2995, fax 204-1784

Hungary: Calle G #458, e/ 19 y 21, Vedado, tel. 33-3365, fax 33-3286

India: Calle 21 #202 esq. K, Vedado, tel. 33-3777, fax 33-3287

Italy: Paseo #606 e/ 25 y 27, Vedado, tel. 33-3378, fax 33-3416, ambitcub@ceniai.inf.cu

Jamaica: Calle 22 #503, e/ 5ta y 7ma, Miramar, tel. 204-2908, fax 204-2531

Japan: 3ra Avenida 7 70, Miramar, tel. 204-8904

English, French, and Spanish, daily 1–3 P.M. promotes Cuban culture and plays middle-of-the-road music.

The *BBC World Service* (5975, 6195, 15220, and 17840 mHz), www.bbc.co.uk/worldservice, beams into Cuba but you'll need a short-band radio. And many Cubans listen surreptitiously to the right-wing *Radio Martí,* beamed in from Miami and of a decidedly anti-Castroite bent. The risks of being caught actually listening to the station are such that it is known colloquially as *Radio Casualidad,* as in "I was tuning my radio and *por casualidad* [by chance] I came across this station." You may be able to tune in to other radio stations from southern Florida.

EMBASSIES AND CONSULATES

The **U.S. Interests Section** (USINT), Calzada (5ta Calle), e/ L y M, Vedado, tel. 33-3551 to 33-3559, emergency/after hours tel. 33-3026, fax 33-3700, ormhav@usia.gov or infousis@pd.state.gov, usembassy.state.gov/havana/is, is the equivalent of an embassy but lacking an ambassador. The Interests Section represents American citizens and the U.S. Government in Cuba, and operates under the legal protection of the Swiss government. USINT provides the full range of U.S. citizen and other consular services. Readers report that it has been helpful to Americans in distress, and that its staff is not

INFORMATION/SERVICES

Mexico: Calle 12 #518 e/ 5ta y 7ma, Miramar, tel. 204-2498, fax 204-2717
Netherlands: Calle 8 #307, e/ 3ra y 5ta, Miramar, tel. 204-2511, fax 204-2059
Nicaragua: Calle 20 #709, Miramar, tel. 204-1025, fax 204-6323
Norway: Calle 30 #315, Miramar, tel. 204-0696
Panama: Calle 26 #109, Miramar, tel. 204-1673, fax 204-1674
Peru: Calle 30 y 1ra, Miramar, tel. 204-2477, fax 204-2636
Poland: 5ta Avenida #4407, esq. 46, Miramar, tel./fax 204-1323
Portugal: 5ta Avenida #6604 e/ 66 y 68, Miramar, tel. 204-2871, fax 204-9101
Romania: Calle 21 #307, e/ H y I, Vedado, tel. 33-3325, fax 33-3324
Russia: 5ta Avenida #6402 e/ 62 y 66, Miramar, tel. 204-5269, fax 204-1038
Slovak Republic: Calle 66 #521, Miramar, tel. 204-1884
South Africa: 5ta Avenida #4203, Miramar, tel. 204-9778
Spain: Calle Cárcel #51 esq. Agramonte (Zulueta), Habana Vieja, tel. 33-8029, fax 33-8006
Sweden: Avenida 34 #510, Miramar, tel. 204-2831
Switzerland: 5ta Avenida #2005 e/ 20 y 22, Miramar, tel. 204-2611, fax 204-1148
Turkey: 5ta Avenida #3805, Miramar, tel. 204-2237
Ukraine: 5ta Avenida #4405, e/ 44 y 46, Miramar, tel. 204-2586, fax 204-2341
United Kingdom: Calle 34 #708, e/ 7ma y 17-A, Miramar, tel. 204-1286 or 204-1771, fax 204-8104
United States: (Interests Section) Calzada e/ L y M, Vedado, tel. 33-3551 to 33-3559, emergency/after hours tel. 33-3026, fax 33-3700, ormhav@usia.gov
Uruguay: Calle 14 #506 e/ 5ta y 7ma, Miramar, tel. 204-2311, fax 204-2246
Venezuela: 5ta Avenida #1601, Miramar, tel. 204-2662, fax 204-2773
Vietnam: 5ta Avenida #1802, esq. 18, Miramar, tel. 204-1042, fax 204-1041
Yugoslavia: Calle 42 #115, Miramar, tel. 204-2488, fax 204-2982
Zimbabwe: 3ra Avenida #1001, Miramar, tel. 204-2857, fax 204-2720

overly concerned about policing potential infractions of Treasury Department regulations (Mon.–Thurs. 8:30 A.M.–5:00 P.M., and Fri. 8:30 A.M.–4:00 P.M.).

Also see the Special Topic "Embassies and Consulates in Havana."

TRAVEL AGENCIES

There are no independent travel agencies familiar to the rest of the world; since Cubans can't freely travel, what's the need? Hotels' tour bureaus can make reservations for excursions, car rental, and flights, as can many Cuban state tour companies.

The best bet is **Cubalinda.com,** Edificio Someillán, piso 27, Calle O # 2 e/ Línea y 17, Vedado, tel. 55-3980 or 88-51538, info@cubalinda.com, www.cubalinda.com, a competent U.S.-owned entity with European staff.

A British company, **Tour & Marketing,** Hotel Jardín del Eden, Suite 6005, Marina Hemingway, tel. 204-6827, fax 204-3546, www.gocubaplus.com, has a full-service travel office.

San Cristóbal Travel, Calle Oficios #110, e/ Lamparilla y Amargura, tel. 860-9585, fax 860-9586, reservas@sancrist.get.tur.net (open Mon.–Sat. 9 A.M.–6 P.M. and Sun. 9:30 A.M.–1 P.M.) specializes in travel in and around Habana Vieja, including hotel reservations.

There is also information on organized excursions in the Transportation chapter.

TOURIST INFORMATION
Tourist Offices

Cuba's **Ministerio de Turismo,** Calle 19 #710, Vedado, Havana, tel. 33-4202 (tel. 33-0545 for international relations), www.cubatravel.cu, is in charge of tourism. It has representative offices in about one dozen countries; see the Special Topic, "Cuban Tourist Bureaus Abroad." There is no such office in the United States; however, the Canadian offices will provide information and mail literature to U.S. citizens.

Publicitur, Calle 19 #60, e/ M y N, Vedado, tel. 33-4333, fax 33-3422, public@public .mit.cma.net, is responsible for publishing and disseminating tourism literature.

You can get travel literature from various state-run Cuban tour operators' offices—see Organized Tours in the Transportation chapter for more information.

Cuba is a member of the **Caribbean Tourism Organization** (CTO), 80 Broad St., 32nd Floor, New York, NY 10004, 212/635-9530, www.doitcaribbean.com, which is a handy information source; and the **Caribbean Hotel Association** (CHA), 18 Marseilles St., Suite 2B, San Juan, PR 00907, tel. 809/725-9139, fax 809/725-9108, wpina@caribbeanhotels.org, www.carib beanhotels.org, both of which are barred under U.S. law from promoting tourism to Cuba in the United States. In Canada, the **Tourism Industry Association of Canada,** 1016-130 Albert St., Suite 1016, Ottawa, ON K1P 5G4, 613/238-3883, fax 613/238-3878, TIAC@resudox.net, suffers no such restraint. The CTO has a Canadian office at Taurus House, 512 Duplex Ave., Toronto, Ontario, Canada M4R 2E3,

---

CUBAN TOURIST BUREAUS ABROAD

Argentina: Marcelo T. De Alvear #928 (4to piso), C.F. Buenos Aires, tel. 11/4326-7995, fax 11/4326-3325, oturcuar@infovia.com.ar

Brazil: Edificio Zarvos #222, Rua da Consolação, São Paulo, tel. 11/2588166, fax 11/2583103, cubasitur@uol.com.br

Canada: 55 Queen St. E, Suite 705, Toronto, ON M5C 1R5, tel. 416/362-0700, fax 416/362-6799, info@gocuba.ca; 440 Blvd. René Lévesque Ouest, Bureau 1402, Montreal, PQ H2Z 1V7, tel. 514/875-8004, fax 514/875-8006, mintur@generation.net

France: 280 Boulevard Raspail, 75014 Paris, tel. 01/4538-9010, fax 01/4538-9930, ot.cuba@wanadoo.fr

Germany: Steinweg 2, 6000 Frankfurt Main 1, tel. 069/28-8322/23, fax 069/29-6664, gocuba@compuserve.com

Italy: Via General Fara 30, Terzo Piano, 20124 Milano, tel. 02/6698-1463, fax 02/6738-0725, minturitalia@infuturo.it

Mexico: Goethe #16, 3er piso, Colonia Anzures, México D.F., tel. 05/250-7974, fax 05/255-5866, otcumex@mail.internet.com.mx

Russia: Kutuzovski Porspekt, Dom 13 KB 40, 121248 Moscow, tel. 095/243-0383, fax 095/933-5986, cubaturismo@mtu-net.ru

Spain: Paseo de la Habana #54, 1ed 28036, Madrid, tel. 91/411-3097, fax 91/564-5804, otcuba@otcubaesp.com

Sweden: Karibergsvegen 26 B 113 27 Stockholm, tel. 831-5360, fax 831-5320, cuba .info@chello.se

United Kingdom: 154 Shaftesbury Avenue, London WC2 H8JT, tel. 020/7240-6655, fax 020/7836-9265, cubatouristboard.london@virgin.net

416/485-7827, fax 416/485-8256; and in the UK at 42 Westminister Palace Gardens, Artillery Row, London SWIP 1RR, tel. (0171) 222-4335, fax (0171) 222-4325.

Information Bureaus

Infotur: The government tourist information bureau, **Infotur** (Información Turística), tel. 33-3333, has several information centers in Havana, including in the arrivals lounge at José Martí International Airport, tel. 66-6101 (Terminal 3) or 55-8733 (Terminal 2). The headquarters is at Calle 28 #303 e/ 3ra y 5ta Avenidas, Miramar, tel. 204-0624 or 204-6635, fax 204-8164, oficturi@ofitur.mit.tur.cu, www.infotur.cu. Offices are open 8:30 A.M.–8:30 P.M.

Infotur has three offices in Habana Vieja: at Calle Obispo #360, e/ Bernazas y Villegas, tel. 33-3333 or 62-4586; at Calle Obispo, esq. San Ignacio, tel. 863-6884; and in the Terminal de Cruceros (Cruise Terminal). A fourth office is at 5ta Avenida, esq. Calle 112, Miramar, tel. 204-7036, fax 204-3977, infomire@teleda .get.cma.net. And it has two offices in Playas del Este: at Ave. Las Terrazas, e/ 11 y 12, tel. 97-1261, fax 96-1111; and 5ta-C Avenida, e/ 468 y 470, Guanabo, tel. 96-3841, fax 96-6868.

Staff can make reservations for car rentals, accommodations, and bus transfers, as well as selling prepaid telephone cards. Offices stock a limited range of tourist literature.

Other Bureaus: Virtually every hotel has a *buró de turismo* in the lobby. Most of the bureaus are geared to selling package excursions, and staffers are otherwise not particularly well-informed.

Habaguanex, Calle Oficios #110, e/ Lamparilla y Amargura, Habana Vieja, tel. 867-1039, fax 60-9761, gerencia.comercial@habaguanex.ohch.cu, www.habaguanex.cu, can provide information on hotels, restaurants, and other places under its umbrella in Habana Vieja.

Agencia de Información Nacional Calle 23 #358, esq. J, Vedado, tel. 66-2049, ain@teleda .tur.cu, www.ain.cubaweb.cu, dispenses information about virtually every aspect of Cuba, but serves primarily as a "news" (read "propaganda") bureau. The **Oficina Nacional de Estadísticas,** Paseo #60, e/ 3ra y 5ra, Vedado, tel. 66-2273 or 830-5021, provides all manner of statistics on Cuba, although foreigners are made to jump through hoops to gain access.

Tourist Guides and Publications

Cartelera and *Guía Cultural de la Habana* are free weekly tourist publications. Infotur's *La Habana* lists the addresses and telephone numbers of hotels, restaurants, bars, shopping centers, and services. You'll find all three in hotel lobbies.

Sol y Son, Calle 216-A #1506, e/ 15 y 17, Siboney, tel. 33-0577, fax 33-0583, gremping@ ceniai.inf.cu, is the slick in-flight magazine of Cubana Airlines, published in English and Spanish. It provides profiles and news information on destinations, culture, and the arts.

The *Directorio Turístico de Cuba* (Tourist Directory of Cuba, US$40) is published once per year and includes names, addresses, telephone and fax numbers for ministries, hotels, airports, and airline offices, plus maps and other information. You can order it from the U.S.–Cuba Trade & Economic Council, 30 Rockefeller Plaza, New York, NY 10112, 212/246-1444, fax 212/246-2345, council@cubatrade.org, www.cubatrade.org.

Travel agents are catered to by *Travel Trade Cuba,* Hotel Deauville #318, Galiano, esq. Malecón, Centro Habana, tel. 33-6268, fax 66-2398, ttccuba@ttccuba.com, www.ttccuba.cu, a public relations tool for Cuban travel companies, published in English and Spanish.

U.S.-Based Information Sources

The Center for Cuban Studies,124 W. 23rd St., New York, NY 10011, 212/242-0559, fax 212/242-1937, cubanctr@igc.org, www.cubaup date.org, maintains the **Lourdes Casal Library,** with more than 5,000 books on Cuba, plus back issues of *Granma, Bohemia,* and other Cuban journals. Open Mon.–Fri. 10 A.M.–6 P.M., Sat. by appointment. The Center publishes the quarterly *Cuba Update,* which covers arts, economics, politics, women's and race issues, and travel. Contributors include leading experts on Cuban issues, both in and outside Cuba. Subscriptions cost US$35 a year, or US$50 a year including membership in the left-leaning center.

The **U.S.–Cuba Trade and Economic Council's** website, www.cubatrade.org/eyeon.html, provides weekly economic updates on Cuba.

CubaNews, 611 Pennsylvania Ave. SE #341, Washington, D.C. 20003, 202/543-5076, fax 202/546-8929, jfeer@bellatlantic.net, primarily serves investors and claims to be the "authoritative guide to Cuban business, politics, and economic development." Subscriptions cost US$429 yearly.

La Alborada is a monthly newsletter published by the Cuban American Alliance Education Fund, 614 Maryland Ave. NE #2, Washington, D.C. 20002-5825, 202/543-6780, fax 202/543-6434, caaef@igc.org, www.cubamer.org, and representing the perspectives of moderate Cuban-Americans.

Cuban Daily News Digest, P.O. Box 30003, North Vancouver, B.C., Canada V7H 2Y8, 604/929-9694, fax 604/929-3694, jhitchie@direct.ca, is a daily compilation of news articles about Cuba from various news sources, available free online. The same organization also publishes *Cuban Investment Letter.*

Cuba: Consular Information Sheet is published on a regular updated basis by the U.S. State Department's Bureau of Consular Affairs (D.O.S. Publication #9232, D.C.A.). It's available from the Superintendent of Documents, U.S. Government Printing Office, Washington, D.C. 20402, 202/783-3283, and online at http://travel.state.gov/cuba.html.

Online Sources

There are dozens of websites on Cuba. All Cuban-hosted sites are state-owned and operated and regardless of theme, usually are strongly politicized in the ongoing "war" against Uncle Sam. The majority of sites are poorly designed and extremely dysfunctional, but things are improving.

A key portal is the Republic of Cuba's Havana-based **CubaWeb,** www.cubaweb.cu, with links to individual sites in the following categories: news, travel and tourism, politics and government, business and commerce, Internet and technology, health and science, culture and arts, and festivals and events. **Cuba Sí,** www.cubasi.cu, is also one of the better state-run generic portals. The Ministerio de Turismo's website, www.cubatravel.cu, is a good entrée for travel information.

CubaNews, www.cubanet.org, is a non-partisan site offering breaking news and news reports from the leading wire services. It's particularly good for hard-hitting info. Its **"Green Screen" Cuba Travel Bulletin Board,** an online discussion board, is an excellent resource for catching the latest happenings.

The U.S. government's **Office of Cuban Affairs,** 202/647-9273, cubanaffairs@state.gov, www.state.gov/p/wha/ci/c2461.htm, has a site with information on such themes as human rights, U.S. policy, and Cuba-related legislation.

The **Latin American Network Information Center,** www.lanic.utexas.edu, is a well-organized reference site with links to many Internet resources on Cuba.

California-based Boulevards News Media maintains a Havana site—www.lahabana.com—featuring updates on travel, arts, culture, and news.

General searches on Google, Yahoo!, Excite, and other major search engines will pull up hundreds of other sites related to Havana and Cuba.

Also see Internet Resources for a more complete list of websites and portals.

MAPS AND NAUTICAL CHARTS
Before You Go

A 1:250,000 topographical road maps produced by Kartografiai Vallalat, of Hungary, and a similar map by Freytag & Berndt are recommended; both feature street maps of Havana. Likewise, Cuba's own Ediciones Geo produces a splendid 1:25:000 *La Habana Tourist Map,* plus a 1:20,000 *Ciudad de la Habana* map.

You can buy these and other Cuba maps from **Omni Resources,** P.O. Box 2096, Burlington, NC 72160, 800/742-2677, fax 336/227-3748, www.omnimap.com, and **Treaty Oak,** P.O. Box 50295, Austin, TX 78763, 512/326-4141, fax 512/443-0973, www.treatyoak.com, which both have a wide variety of Havana and Cuba maps. Omni Resources also sells an out-of-print *Cuban Atlas* (1989; US$395), as well as complete topographic map sets (US$60 to US$450).

In Canada, **ITMB Publishing,** 530 W. Broadway, Vancouver BC V5Z 1E9, 604/879-3621, www.itmb.com, is the best resource.

In the UK, try **Stanford's,** 12-14 Long Acre, London WC2E 9LP, tel. 020/7836-1321, fax 020/7836-0189, www.stanfords.co.uk, and the **Ordnance Survey International,** Romsey Rd., Southampton SO16 4GU, tel. (08456) 050505, fax 023/8079-2615, outside the UK tel. 23-8079-2912, www.ordsvy.gov.uk.

In Australia, try **The Map Shop,** 6-10 Peel St., Adelaide, SA 5000, tel. 08/231-2033, www.mapshop.net.au; in New Zealand, try **Specialty Maps,** 58 Albert St., Auckland, tel. 09/307-2217, www.specialitymaps.co.nz.

In Havana

You'll find maps of Havana for sale at Infotur offices, hotel gift stores, souvenir stalls, and post offices. And **Tienda de las Navegantes,** Calle Mercaderes #115, e/ Obispo y Obrapía, Habana Vieja, tel. 861-3625, fax 33-2869, (for boaters, VHF channel 16 CMYP3050), has a wide range of tourist maps of Havana and provinces.

Look for *La Habana Antigua,* which contains detailed maps of Habana Vieja.

Detailed specialist maps are produced by the **Instituto de Planificación Física,** Lamparilla 65, Habana Vieja, tel. 862-9330, fax 861-9533, though they don't sell maps.

Health Issues

MEDICAL SERVICES

Sanitary standards in Havana are generally good. As long as you take appropriate precautions and use common sense, you're not likely to incur a serious illness or disease. Cuba's much-vaunted public health system is geared to preventative medicine and, says, Dr. Joycelyn Elders, former U.S. Surgeon General, is better at keeping people healthy than the U.S. system. Certain key health indices surpass those of the United States, and Cuba has one of the highest rates of child immunization in the world. Nonetheless, the system faces severe shortages of medicines and equipment and with few exceptions, facilities and standards are not up to those of North America or northern Europe (which, notes Elders, do a better job of caring for the sick).

Resources have increasingly been shifted from primary care toward turning Cuba's medical system into a profit-making enterprise catering to foreigners, notably in the surgical and advanced medicines fields. Dr. Hilda Molina, founder of Havana's International Center for Neurological Restoration and a former member of the Cuban National Assembly, claims that "foreigners are assigned the highest priority, followed by government functionaries and their families, followed by athletes with good records of performance, then dancers, and lastly, ordinary Cuban patients."

Foreigners are assured special treatment through **Cubanacán Turismo y Salud** (formerly Servimed), Calle 18 #4304, e/ 43 y 47, Miramar, tel. 204-2658, fax 204-2948, tsalud@sermed .cha.cyt.cu, which guarantees services generally unavailable to the average Cuban and offers everything from "stress breaks" to advanced treatments such as eye, open-heart, and plastic surgery. It is acknowledged as a world leader in orthopedics and the treatment of vitiligo and Parkinson's disease, Alzheimer's disease, multiple sclerosis, and epilepsy. However, Dr. Molina's report is highly critical of the medical standards applied (see *Cuba Brief,* Summer 1998, www.cubacenter.org).

The larger tourist hotels have nurses on duty. Other hotels will be able to request a doctor for in-house diagnosis and treatment for minor ailments.

U.S. citizens should note that even if visiting Cuba legally, payment for "nonemergency medical services" is prohibited. Developing an ingrown toenail? Sorry, buddy. Endure!

Hospitals

Tourists needing medical assistance are usually steered to the **Clínica Internacional Cira García,** Calle 20 #4101 and Avenida 41, Miramar, tel. 204-0330 or 204-2811, fax 204-2640 or 204-1633, ciragcu@infomed.sld.cu, a full-service hospital dedicated to serving foreigners. It is staffed by English-speaking doctors and nurses. You pay in dollars—credit cards are acceptable unless they're issued on a U.S. bank, in which case greenbacks are required. It gets relatively little business, so there's usually no waiting. Don't expect privacy, however, for your *historial* (your descriptive interview of your problem) may happen in front of a curious crowd of nurses and patients. If you have valid insurance, show it, as you may otherwise be billed for charges that your insurance covers.

The **Centro Internacional Oftalmológica Camilo Cienfuegos,** Calle L, e/ Línea y 13, Vedado, tel. 832-5554, fax 33-3536, cirpcc@ infomed.sid.cu, specializes in eye disorders but also offers a range of medical services running from optometry to odontology.

Hospital Hermanos Almeijeiras, Padre Varela, esq. San Lázaro, Centro Habana, tel. 877-6077 or 33-5361, one of dozens of hospitals for Cubans, offers medical consultations for foreigners Mon.–Fri. 8 A.M.–4 P.M. (US$25). Overnight stays cost US$75.

Specialist hospitals include the **Centro Internacional de Restauración Neurológica** (CIREN), Avenida 25 #15805, e/ 158 y 160, Cubanacán, tel. 271-6999, fax 33-2420, www.ciren.cuba web.cu, which offers treatments for Parkinson's disease, multiple sclerosis, and other diseases of the nervous system.

Other centers are dedicated to treating HIV/AIDS, hepatitis, alcoholism and drug dependency, or performing plastic surgery.

Pharmacies

Local Pharmacies: There are local pharmacies serving Cubans everywhere, though all are meagerly stocked only with a few locally produced medicines. *Turnos regulares* are open 8 A.M.–5 P.M.; *turnos permanentes* are open 24 hours. The best-stocked is **Farmacia Taquechel,** Calle Obispo #155, e/ Mercaderes y San Ignacio, Habana Vieja, tel. 862-9286; open daily 9 A.M.–6:30 P.M.

For alternative (homeopathic) remedies, try **Farmacia Ciren,** Calle 216, esq. 11B, Playa, tel. 271-5044, and **Farmacia las Praderas,** Calle 230, e/ 15A y 17, Siboney, tel. 33-7473.

For Foreigners: International pharmacies (*farmacias internacionales*) cater to foreigners and

are stocked with a full range of Western drugs and pharmaceuticals imported from Central America, Canada, and Europe. The service is for foreigners only, who pay in dollars at very high prices. You may be approached by Cubans outside tendering dollars and begging you to purchase desperately needed medicines on their behalf.

In Habana Vieja, the **Hotel Plaza,** Agramonte #267, esq. Neptuno, tel. 860-8583, has a small pharmacy on the rooftop; open 24 hours.

In Vedado, **Farmacia Internacional Camilo Cienfuegos,** Calle L, e/ Línea y 13, tel. 832-5554 or 33-3538, fax 33-3536, cirpcc@infomed .sid.cu, is open 8 A.M.–8 P.M. There's also a small international pharmacy in the **Galería Comercial Habana Libre,** Calle 25 y L, open Mon.–Sat. 9 A.M.–6 P.M.

In Miramar, **Clínica Internacional Cira García,** Calle 20 #4101 and Avenida 41, Miramar, tel. 204-0330 or 204-2811, fax 204-2640 or 204-1633, ciragcu@infomed.sld.cu, has a 24-hour pharmacy, tel. 204-2811, ext. 14; open 9 A.M.–9 P.M. The **Farmacia Internacional,** across the street on Avenida 41, tel. 204-2051, is also fully stocked; open Mon.–Fri. 9 A.M.– 5:45 P.M., Sat. 9 A.M.–noon. **Casa Bella,** 7ma Avenida #2603, e/ 26 y 28, tel. 204-2377, also contains a smaller international pharmacy, open 8 A.M.–8 P.M.

In Habana del Este, there's a **Farmacia Internacional** at Villa Panamericana, 7ma Avenida y Calle 78, tel. 95-1157.

Be wary of expiration dates, as shelf life of drugs may be shortened under tropical conditions.

Opticians

Óptica Miramar, Calle Neptuno #411, e/ San Nicolás y Manrique, Centro Habana, tel. 863-2161; and 7ma Avenida, e/ Calle 24 y 26, Miramar, tel. 204-2269, provides full-service optician and optometrist services, and sells imported products such as solutions for contact lenses. It also has outlets at Avenida 11 #14614, Playa, tel. 204-7320; and Apartotel Las Brisas, Ciudad Panamericano, tel. 95-1216.

Gyms and Massage

Specialized massages (US$8 for 45 minutes) are

offered by **Dulce María** in the Hostal Valencia, Calle Oficios, Habana Vieja, tel. 862-3801, and at her home on Calle San Ignacio #78, tel. 861-0412. She offers acupressure and reflexology using both Japanese *yumeiho* and Chinese techniques. "After an hour of massage you will feel like a teddy bear," she says.

Upscale hotels have tiny gyms and/or spas, though most are a letdown by international standards. The best are at the **Hotel Parque Central,** the **Hotel Nacional,** the **Hotel Melía Cohiba,** the **Hotel Meliá Habana** (see the Accommodations chapter for contact information). Full-treatment spas include the **Club Comodoro Spa,** 3ra Avenida y 84, tel. 204-5049; **Primavera,** Calle Línea #459, e/ E y F, Vedado, tel. 832-0159; and **Suchel,** Calzada #709, e/ A y B, Vedado, tel. 833-8332 (open 8:30 A.M.–8 P.M.).

Spa La Pradera, Calle 230, e/ 15 y 17, tel. 204-7473, fax 204-7198, comercia@pradera .cha.cyt.cu, in Siboney, is a spa-hotel specializing in health treatments. It has a sauna, gym, hydromassage, massages, paraffin and mud treatments, ozone therapy, and the like.

HEALTH PROBLEMS

Despite admirable health statistics, Cuba *is* a tropical country, and Havana is a dirty city, where molds and fungus in particular thrive. Even the slightest scratch can fester quickly in the tropics. Treat promptly and regularly with antiseptic and keep any wounds clean.

Intestinal Problems

Havana's tap water is questionable, especially after heavy storms, which may render water supplies unsafe. Play it safe and drink bottled mineral water (*agua mineral*), which is widely available. Remember, ice cubes are water, too, and don't brush your teeth using suspect water.

Food hygiene standards are very high. Milk is pasteurized, so you're not likely to encounter any problems normally associated with dairy products. Most tourists who suffer intestinal bouts do so after eating at streetside stalls. Be fastidious with personal hygiene: always wash your hands before eating.

Diarrhea: The change in diet—which can alter the bacteria that are normal and necessary in the bowel—may briefly cause diarrhea or constipation (in case of the latter, eat lots of fruit). Fortunately, the stomach usually builds up a resistance to unaccustomed foods. Most cases of diarrhea are caused by microbial bowel infections resulting from contaminated food. Common-sense precautions include not eating uncooked fish or shellfish (which collect cholera bugs), uncooked vegetables, unwashed salads, or unpeeled fruit (peel the fruit *yourself*). Diarrhea is usually temporary, and many doctors recommend letting it run its course. If that's not preferable, medicate with Lomotil or another antidiarrheal products. Treat diarrhea with rest and lots of liquid to replace the water and salts lost. Avoid alcohol and milk products. If conditions don't improve after three days, seek medical help.

Dysentery: Diarrhea accompanied by severe abdominal pain, blood in your stool, and fever is a sign of dysentery. Seek immediate medical diagnosis. Tetracycline or ampicillin is normally used to cure bacillary dysentery. More complex professional treatment is required for amoebic dysentery. The symptoms of both are similar.

Other Infections: Giardiasis, acquired from infected water, is another intestinal complaint. It causes diarrhea, bloating, persistent indigestion, and weight loss. Again, seek medical advice. Intestinal worms can be contracted by walking barefoot on infested beaches, grass, or earth.

Sunburn and Skin Problems

Don't underestimate the tropical sun. It's intense and can fry you in minutes. It can even burn you through light clothing or while you're lying in the shade. The midday sun is especially potent. Even if you consider yourself nicely tanned, use a suncream or sunblock of at least SPF 8. Zinc oxide provides almost 100 percent protection. Bring sunscreens with you; they're not always readily available in Havana, although most hotel stores sell them. If you're intent on a tan, have patience. Build up gradually, and use an aloe gel after sunbathing; it helps repair any skin damage. The tops of feet and backs of knees are particularly susceptible to burning when walking

Havana's streets. Consider wearing a wide-brimmed hat, too. Calamine lotion and aloe gel will soothe light burns; for more serious burns, use steroid creams.

Sun glare can cause conjunctivitis. Use sunglasses. "Prickly heat" is an itchy rash, normally caused by clothing that is too tight or in need of washing. This, and "athlete's foot," are best treated by airing out the body and washing your clothes.

Dehydration and Heat Problems

The tropical humidity and heat can sap your body fluids like blotting paper. You'll sweat profusely and steadily while exploring Havana. Leg cramps, exhaustion, dizziness, and headaches are possible signs of dehydration. Although your body may acclimatize to the heat gradually, at the same time, dehydration can develop slowly. And diarrhea will drain your body of fluids swiftly.

Drink water regularly to avoid dehydration. Avoid alcohol, which processes water in the body; the more alcohol you drink, the more water you'll need, too.

Excessive exposure to too much heat can cause heat stroke, a potentially fatal result of a failure in the body's heat-regulation mechanisms. Excessive sweating, extreme headaches, and disorientation leading to possible convulsions and delirium are typical symptoms. Emergency medical care is essential! If hospitalization is not possible, place the victim in the shade, cover with a wet cloth, and fan continually to cool the person down.

Don't be alarmed if your ankles and legs get puffy. It's the heat. When you rest, keep your feet higher than your head (a cold Epsom salts footbath also helps).

Many tourists come down with colds (*gripe*—pronounced GREE-pe—or *catarro Cubano*), often brought on by the debilitating effects of constantly shifting from icily air-conditioned restaurants and hotels to sultry outdoor heat. A more serious ailment is bronchitis, easily acquired in Cuba, which can be treated with antibiotics.

Insects and Arachnids

The most common bugs you'll see will be cockroaches, which are found virtually everywhere and are harmless, although they carry disease—you don't want them crawling over your food.

Mosquitoes: Although daytime breezes help keep mosquitoes at bay, as do irregular eradication campaigns, mosquitoes are plentiful in Havana. The waterfront region of Miramar is particularly noted for mosquitoes. Fortunately, malaria isn't present in Cuba. However, mosquitoes (particularly those active by day) *do* transmit dengue fever, which *is* present on the island—a sudden explosion in the incidence of dengue in Havana in 2000–2002 resulted in a massive eradication campaign. The illness can be fatal (death usually results from internal hemorrhaging). Its symptoms are similar to those for malaria, with severe headaches and high fever and (unlike malaria) additional severe pain in the joints and bones, for which it is sometimes called "breaking bones disease." Unlike malaria, it is not recurring. There is no cure. Dengue fever must run its course. In the unlikely event you contract it, have plenty of aspirin or other painkillers on hand. Drink lots of water.

The best mosquito repellents contain DEET (diethylmetatoluamide). DEET is quite toxic; avoid using it on small children, and avoid getting it on plastic or Lycra, which it will melt. A fan (*ventilador*) over your bed and mosquito coils (*espirales*) that smolder for up to eight hours also help keep mosquitoes at bay. Citronella candles may help, too.

Bites can easily become infected in the tropics, so avoid scratching. Treat with antiseptics or antibiotics. A baking-soda bath can help relieve itching if you're badly bitten, as can antihistamine tablets, and hydrocortisone and calamine lotion.

Scabies: Many *habaneros* live in poor hygienic conditions that are a perfect breeding ground for scabies (a microscopic mite) and lice. Fortunately, both are fairly rare in Cuba. Infestation is possible if you're sleeping in unhygienic conditions or engage in sex with people already infested. Scabies is treated by using a body shampoo containing gamma benzene hexachloride or one percent lindane solution (lindane is a highly toxic pesticide). At the same time, you must also wash all your clothing and bedding in very hot water—and throw out your underwear. Your sexual partner will need to do the same. The severe itching caused by scabies infestation appears after three or

CUBA'S WAR ON AIDS

Cuba has one of the world's most aggressive and successful campaigns against AIDS. The World Health Organization (WHO) and the Pan-American Health Organization have praised as exemplary Cuba's AIDS surveillance system and prevention program. The program (aided by Cuba's insularity over decades) has stemmed an epidemic that rages only 50 miles away in Haiti and kept the spread of the disease to a level that no other country in the Americas can equal. As of January 2003, Cuba had recorded 4,400 cases of HIV, and about 1,000 people had died of AIDS. Cuba has an adult prevalence rate of 0.3 percent, compared to four percent in the Bahamas, and nearly six percent in Haiti. Although in Cuba in the early years it was predominantly a heterosexual disease, today about 70 percent of AIDS sufferers are gay men.

Cuba's unique response to the worldwide epidemic that began in the early 1980s was to initiate mass testing of the population and a "mandatory quarantine" of everyone testing positive. By 1994, when the policy of mandatory testing was ended, about 98 percent of the adult population had been tested. Voluntary testing continues.

At first, the purpose was to keep the disease from spreading. Twelve AIDS sanatoriums were developed throughout the island, and in the early years anyone who tested HIV-positive was sent there. Cuba defended its sanatorium policy as a way of guaranteeing first-class health care for patients while protecting the rest of the population. "When you think about the amount of money they spend on each of us, and that we don't pay one cent!" an AIDS-positive hemophiliac told journalist Karen Wald, "and apart from that, we receive our complete salary. What other country in the world has done that? You're asking if the Revolution violates my rights by sending me to a sanatorium? I'm alive because of the Revolution!"

Mandatory confinement was ended in early 1994. Instead, an outpatient program was implemented so that sufferers could continue to lead a normal life. The new emphasis is on personal responsibility. Residents live in small houses or apartments, alone or as couples (straight or gay).

In 2001, Cuba's biogenetic engineering industry began manufacturing anti-retrovirals for the country's AIDS patients, alleviating a crisis in the shortage of medicines. And in November 2001, scientists from Havana's Center for Genetic Engineering and Biotechnology announced they plan to test an AIDS vaccine in HIV-positive volunteers.

The **Centro Nacional de Educación Sexual,** Calle 19 #851, Vedado, tel. 55-2529, offers safe-sex workshops. The **Centro Nacional de Educación de Salud,** Calle I #507, Vedado, tel. 832-1920, has an AIDS-information drop-in center.

The **Cuba AIDS Project,** 500 West Leota St., Ste. 200, P.O. Box 1289, North Platte, NE 69103-1289, 308/532-4700, cubaids@aol.com, www.cubaaidsproject.com, delivers medications to Cubans who suffer from HIV/AIDS on the islands. The Project also supports Cuba's first soup kitchen for AIDS victims (many of whom are homeless) every Thursday night at Havana's **Nuestra Señora de Montserrat** church. The Cuba Aids Project runs Cuba Relief Trips designed for people-to-people contact, and also needs individual travelers to help carry humanitarian supplies to Cuba at a time best suited for them. Donations and couriers are needed.

four weeks (it appears as little dots, often in lines and sometimes ending in blisters, especially around the genitals, elbows, wrists, lower abdomen, nipples, and on the head of the penis). A second bout of scabies usually shows itself within 48 hours of reinfestation. Treatment in the United States is by prescription only. However, you can obtain *Scabisan* in Cuba.

Scorpions: Though present, scorpions are rarely encountered. Still, it pays to be wary about putting your hands into crevices without first checking things out with a flashlight.

INFORMATION/SERVICES

Rabies: Though rare in Cuba, rabies can be contracted through the bite of an infected dog or other animal. It's always fatal unless treated.

Gynecological Problems

Travel, hot climates, and a change of diet or health regime can play havoc with your body, leading to yeast and other infections. A douche of diluted vinegar or lemon juice can help alleviate yeast infections. Loose, cotton underwear may help prevent infections such as Candida, typified by itching and a white, cheesy discharge. A foul-smelling discharge accompanied by a burning sensation may indicate Trichomoniasis, usually caught through intercourse but also by contact with unclean towels or other items.

AIDS and Sexually Transmitted Diseases

The risk of contracting AIDS in Cuba is comparatively minor. The rate of infection is among the world's lowest, and the Cuban government conducts an exemplary anti-AIDS campaign (Cuba even manufactures AIDS diagnostic kits as well as interferons for treatment). However, the incidence of AIDS has shown signs of rapid increase in recent years.

Cubans are promiscuous, and gonorrhea, syphilis, genital warts, and other sexually transmitted diseases are fairly common. Avoiding casual sexual contact is the best prevention. If you do succumb to the mating urge, use condoms (*preservativos*), which can be purchased at dollar stores, although the selection is limited. Far better is to come prepared with your own favorite brand. Practice safe sex!

Lineayuda, tel. 832-3156, is a helpline for people seeking information and counseling on sexual diseases, including AIDS; Mon.–Fri. 9 A.M.–9 P.M. Also see the Special Topic "Cuba's War On AIDS."

Safety and Related Issues

THEFT AND HUSTLING

All the negative media hype sponsored by Washington has left many people with a false impression that Havana is unsafe. Far from it. Few places in the world are as safe for visitors. The vast majority of Cubans are friendly and full of integrity. Says Stephen Foehr: "Whenever I met a knot of males of testosterone-charged age coming down the sidewalk, I never felt it necessary to avoid them, as I might in many U.S. cities. The knot of boys always untangled to let me through without an intimidating glare, thrown elbow, or challenging slur."

However, Havana's many charms can lull visitors into a false sense of security. The material hardships of Cubans combined with the influx of wealthy tourists during the 1990s to foster a resurgence of crime. Pickpockets (*carteristas*) and purse slashers began working the streets of Havana. Then muggings of tourists escalated. Even corruption and drug use—until very recently virtually unknown in revolutionary Cuba—

reared their ugly heads again. The Cuban government effectively nipped the problem in the bud in January 1999, when hundreds of policeman took to the streets and as many as 7,000 suspect Cubans were arrested.

Drug dealing, although minuscule by comparison with the US, still goes on; for example, a resident of Arroyo Naranjo was shot and killed in October 2002 during a deal gone wrong. In 2002, anti-narcotic canine patrols were introduced to the streets.

Jineterismo

The throngs of *jineteros* (hustlers) and *jineteras* (females who trade sex for dollars or invitations to dinner) that used to overwhelm visitors with propositions of cheap cigars and romantic adventures were briefly swept aside by the special police brigade, which still stand guard 24 hours.

Nonetheless, you'll still get hustled by *jineteros* trying to sell you cigars or touting places to stay or eat, or even a good time with their sisters for chump change. And *jineteras* still work the streets

DRUGS IN CUBA

Cuban law prohibits the possession, sale, or use of narcotic substances, including marijuana. Laws are strictly enforced, and Cuba vigorously prosecutes drug traffickers caught in Cuban territory. Whatever your personal beliefs on drug use, Cuba is no place to try to make a statement about rights. If you're caught, you will receive no special favors because you're foreign. A trial could take many months, in which case you'll be jailed on the premise that you're guilty until proven innocent. Be aware that if offered drugs on the street, you may be dealing with a plain-clothes policeman.

Drug use has been increasing in recent years with the blossoming of tourism and as Colombian drug lords take advantage of Cuba's remote, scattered cays to make transshipments en route to the United States. Still, few countries are so drug-free, and use is negligible among the Cuban populace. You may, rarely, come across homegrown marijuana, but serious drug use is unknown.

Rape and other violent crimes are virtually unknown throughout Cuban society. However, muggings do occur, and there have been several murders of tourists in recent years.

Local bars and street parties can get rowdy after the *aguardiente* (cheap rum) has been flowing a while. Drunkenness is a problem on the streets of non-touristed areas, especially on Friday and Saturday nights.

Where to Avoid?: Bad apples that prey on tourists (no Cuban is worth a mugger's time) hang out at major touristed haunts. Be wary around the Capitolio and Parque Central, the Paseo de Martí (Prado), and Plaza 13 de Marzo in front of the Museo de la Revolución, once a favorite spot for nocturnal muggings. Other areas that require special caution are the back streets of southern Habana Vieja and Centro Habana, and anywhere in the Cerro and other slum districts.

The **U.S. State Dept,** 202/647-5225, www.travel.state.gov/cuba.html, publishes travel advisories warning U.S. citizens of trouble spots. The **British Foreign & Commonwealth Office,** Travel Advice Unit, Consular Division, Foreign & Commonwealth Office, 1 Palace St, London SW1E 5HE, tel. 020/7008-0232, www.fco.gov.uk/travel/default.asp, has a similar service.

Common-Sense Precautions

Make photocopies of all important documents: your passport (showing photograph and visas, if applicable), airline ticket, credit cards, insurance policy, driver's license. Carry the photocopies with you, and leave the originals along with your other valuables in the hotel safe where possible. If this isn't possible, carry the originals with you in a secure inside pocket. Don't put all your eggs in one basket. Prepare an "emergency kit" that includes photocopies of your documents and an adequate sum of money to tide you over if your wallet gets stolen.

Never carry more cash than you need for the day. The rest should be kept in the hotel safe. If you don't trust the hotel or if it doesn't have a safe, try as best you can to hide your valuables and secure your room.

and discos, brazenly taking your arm or even grabbing hold of your crotch. When they're buzzing like hornets, a good line to use is *"Soy ruso, me llamo* [pronounced *yamo*] *Vladimir!"* ("I'm Russian. My name is Vladimir!"). Russians are considered skinflints. Hopefully the *jineteras* will leave you alone. The best defense, however, is to completely ignore them. Don't say a single word . . . don't look them in the eye. Just keep walking.

Crime

Walking Havana is as safe as virtually any city in the world. Still, caution is required, despite the policing: there exists a seedy underworld not far removed from Havana's soft tourist haunts. Be wary of darker back streets at night—very few streets have lights. Most crime is opportunistic snatch-and-grab. Crowded places are the happy hunting grounds of crafty crooks. If you sense yourself being squeezed or jostled, don't hold back—elbow your way out of there immediately. Better safe than sorry.

Theft from hotel rooms is also a problem, especially of items of clothing craftily sneaked away by your maid. And petty theft by *jineteras* is common.

POLICE STATIONS

Habana Vieja

Picota, e/ Leonor Pérez y San Isidro, tel.
867-0496

Zulueta y Muralla, tel. 862-0773

Centro Habana and Cerro

Zanja y Escobar, tel. 863-2441

Castillejo y Zanja, tel. 877-5276

Calzada de Infanta y Manglar, Cerro, tel.
877-5240

Vedado

L y Malecón, tel. 830-1817

Zapata, e/ B y C, tel. 55-2039

Playa (Miramar and Beyond)

7ma Avenida y 62, Miramar, tel. 209-1116

Avenida 31 y 108, Marianao, tel. 260-2242

Avenida 124 y 49, Marianao, tel. 267-1345

Surburbs

Regla, tel. 97-6130

Guanabacoa, tel. 97-0116

Alamar, tel. 65-3116

Cojímar, tel. 95-2522

Guanabo, tel. 96-4116

Never carry your wallet in your back pocket. Spread your money around your person. You might carry your bills in your front pocket, packed beneath a handkerchief. Carry any other money in an inside pocket, a "secret" pocket sewn into your pants or jacket, hidden in a body pouch or an elasticized wallet below the knee. Most practical is to wear a secure money belt, but make sure that the strap is threaded through the belt-hoops of your pants (Cuba's sneak thieves are adept at releasing the buckles and making off with your fanny-pack before you realize what's happening).

Leave your ego at home. Don't flaunt expensive jewelry or walk unescorted around Havana's many slum districts with a purse or a US$3,000

camera loosely slung over your shoulder. Wear an inexpensive digital watch. And be particularly wary after cashing money at a bank, or if doing a deal with a *jinetero*. Insist that credit card imprints are made in your presence. Make sure any imprints incorrectly completed are torn up. Don't take someone else's word that it will be done. Destroy the carbons yourself.

Never leave items unattended. Always keep a wary eye on your luggage on public transportation, especially backpacks—sneak thieves love their zippered compartments. Don't carry more luggage than you can adequately manage; limit your baggage to *one* suitcase or duffel. And have a lock for each luggage item. Purses should have a short strap (ideally, one with metal woven in) that fits tightly against the body and snaps closed or has a zipper. *Always* keep purses fully zipped and luggage locked, even in your hotel room.

Don't leave anything of value within reach of an open window. Never leave anything of value in your car, which should always be parked overnight in a secure area.

OTHER PROBLEMS

Traffic and Pedestrians

Traffic is perhaps the greatest danger, despite a relative paucity of vehicles on the road. Be especially wary when crossing the streets in Havana. Stand well away from the curb—especially on corners, where buses often mount the sidewalk. Cyclists are everywhere, making insouciant turns and weaving with a lackadaisical disdain for safety. Sidewalks are full of gaping potholes and tilted curbstones. Watch your step!

Drive cautiously. Cuba presents unique dangers, from treacherous potholes and wayward bicyclists to cattle and ox-drawn carts wandering across four-lane freeways.

Racial Discrimination

Despite Cuba's achievements in creating an almost color-blind society, racial discrimination still exists. Cubans of European descent have a much easier time of things. Non-white tourists can expect to be mistaken for Cubans and hassled on the streets by police requesting I.D. Likewise, tourists of non-European descent are more likely to be stopped at the entrances to hotel lobbies and other tourist venues where Cubans are barred, and asked to show I.D. Mixed-race couples can expect to draw unwanted attention from the police.

Beyond Havana, where an "apartheid" system is more strictly enforced, many state-run restaurants and other tourist facilities do not permit Cuban partners to share tables with foreigners, or will bar entry altogether, but notably if the Cuban is black.

IF TROUBLE STRIKES

If things turn dire, you should contact **Asistur,** Calle 4 #110, e/ 1ra y 3ra, Miramar, tel. 204-8835, fax 204-1613 or 204-8088, comercia@asistur.get.cma.net, www.asistur.cubaweb.cu, which exists to provide assistance to tourists in trouble. It can provide insurance, medical assistance, funeral repatriation, and legal and financial aid, including help obtaining new travel documents and locating lost luggage, and may even indemnify against loss (assuming you already have travelers' insurance). It has a 24-hour "alarm center" in the Casa de los Científicos at Prado #212, e/ Trocadero y Colón, Habana Vieja, tel. 33-8527 or 33-

8920, fax 33-8087, asisten@asisten.get.cma.net, open 365 days a year.

You should also contact your embassy or consulate. Consulate officials can't get you out of jail, but they can help you locate a lawyer, alleviate unhealthy conditions, or arrange for funds to be wired if you run short of money. They may even be able to authorize a reimbursable loan while you arrange for cash to be forwarded, or even lend you money to get home—the U.S. State Department hates to admit this.

If you're robbed, immediately file a police report with the **Policía Nacional Revolucionario** (PNR), Calle Picota, e/ Leonor Pérez y San Isidro, tel. 867-0496 or 862-0116. You'll need this to make an insurance claim. You'll receive a statement (*denuncia*) for insurance purposes (and to replace lost tourist cards or traveler's checks), which you should make sure is dated and stamped. Don't expect the Cuban police to bend over backwards, however. In fact, they tend to treat foreigners with disdain. And proceedings are slow. There is no special unit responsible for pursuing thefts from tourists.

If you're involved in a car accident, call the **Tránsitos** (transit police), tel. 862-0116.

If you are charged with a crime, you should request that a representative of your embassy be present, and that any deposition be made in front of an independent witness (*testigo*).

U.S. Citizens: Although the **U.S. Interests Section** (see the Special Topic "Embassies and Consulates in Havana") exists mainly for political reasons, reports from travelers suggest that it has a good record in helping U.S. citizens in need. The *Handbook of Consular Services,* Public Affairs Staff, Bureau of Consular Affairs, U.S. Department of State, Washington, D.C. 20520, provides details of such assistance. Friends and family can also call the Department of State's **Overseas Citizen Service,** 202/647-5225, to check on you if things go awry. However, the United States does not have full diplomatic representation in Cuba, and its tapestry of pullable strings is understandably threadbare. If arrested, U.S. citizens should ask Cuban authorities to notify the U.S. Interests Section. A U.S. consular officer will then try to arrange regular visits,

---

EMERGENCY HELP FOR UNITED STATES CITIZENS

In the event of an emergency, the following may be of help:

Overseas Citizens Services, U.S. State Department, 317/472-2328 (Mon.–Fri. 8 A.M.–8 P.M.) or 202/647-4000 for after hours emergencies, travel.state.gov/acs.html#emr.

International SOS Assistance, 8 Neshaminy Interplex, Suite 207, Trevose, PA 19053-6956, 215/244-1500, fax 215/244-2227, www.internationalsos.com.

International Legal Defense Counsel, 1429 Walnut St. Suite 800, Philadelphia, PA 19102, 215/977-9982, www.internationalrecoveryllc.com.

at the discretion of the Cuban government. Cuba does not recognize dual citizenship for Cuban citizens who are also U.S. citizens; Cuban-born citizens are thereby denied representation through the U.S. Interests Section in the event of arrest.

Legal Assistance: Asistur provides legal assistance. The **Consultoría Jurídica Internacional** (International Judicial Consultative Bureau), Calle 16 #314 e/ 3ra y 5ta, Miramar, tel. 204-2490, fax 204-2303, also provides legal advice and services regarding all aspects of Cuban law—from marriages and notarization to advising on the constitutionality of business ventures. It can assist travelers, including those who lose their passports or have them stolen. For U.S. citizens, Cuban officials can produce documents— US$175—that preclude needing to have a new U.S. passport issued in the U.S. via the U.S. Interests Section. Open Mon.–Fri. 8:30 A.M.–noon and 1:30–5:30 P.M.

Likewise, **ICC Corp.,** Desamparados #166, e/ Habana y Compostela, tel. 862-9900, help@icc-cuba.com, www.icc-cuba.com, in office #513, is a Canadian company that provides legal and consular services.

The **Equipo de Servicios de Traductores e Intérpretes** (ESCI), Línea #506, esq. D, tel. 832-7586, provides translators and interpreters; open Mon.–Fri. 8 A.M.–noon.

Medical Evacuation

Uncle Sam has deemed that even U.S. emergency evacuation services cannot fly to Cuba to evacuate U.S. citizens without a license from the Treasury Department. Of course, the rules keep changing, so it may be worth checking the latest situation with such companies as **Traveler's Emergency Network** (TEN), 5155 34th St. S., Box 146, St. Petersburg, FL 33711, 800/471-3695, www.tenweb.com; and **International SOS Assistance,** 2211 Norfolk St., Suite 624, Houston, TX 77098, 713/521-7611 or 800/523-8662, fax 215/244-0165, www.internationalsos.com, or in the UK, tel. 020/8762-8008, both of which provide worldwide ground and air evacuation as well as medical assistance.

The insurance packages sold by **Aseguradora del Turismo La Isla S.A.** (see Travel Insurance) include US$5,000 coverage for repatriation in the need of medical evacuation.

Practicalities

FILM AND PHOTOGRAPHY

Havana is a photographer's dream. Photographer John Kings, who accompanied James Michener to illustrate his book *Six Days in Havana,* called Havana "one of the most photogenic cities in the world. . . . It was captivating and challenging and for the next five days my finger barely left the shutter of my little German eye."

Equipment and Film

A 35mm SLR camera is most versatile and will give top-notch results, but an instamatic is fine.

Officially you're allowed to bring two cameras plus six rolls of film into Cuba (but I've never heard of it being enforced). Film is susceptible to damage by airport X-ray machines. Film below 400ASA can withstand numerous passes through a machine without harm, but the effect is cumulative. Cuban airport officials rarely permit hand inspection, but may do so for high-speed film.

Decide how much film you think you'll need to bring—then triple it. I recommend one roll per day as a minimum if you're even half-serious about your photography. Bring all the film you need with you, and keep it out of the sun. Pack both your virgin and exposed film in a Ziploc plastic bag with silica gel inside to protect against moisture. Always put used film in a plastic film container—the felt edging attracts dirt, which can leave a nasty scratch along the *entire* film when unrolled.

Film is sold at most tourist hotels and at **Foto Video** and **Photo Service** stores (the main Photo Service outlet is at Calle 23 and O, Vedado, tel. 832-6833). Usually only print film is available; very rarely will you find slide (transparency) film.

Often this is old, or has been exposed to heat for long periods of time. Check the expiration date; it may be outdated. If you want the best results, only buy film that is refrigerated or at least stored in an a/c room.

Keep your lenses clean and dry when not in use. Silica gel packs are essential to help protect your camera gear from moisture; use them if you carry your camera equipment inside a plastic bag.

Most Photo Service stores also sell a few instamatic cameras, as well as a meager stock of batteries and small digital cameras. However, there are *no* camera stores as we know them in North America or Europe. At last visit, 35mm SLRs, lenses, flash units, filters, and other camera equipment were entirely unavailable. **Foto Prado,** Prado, esq. Virtudes, Habana Vieja, tel. 863-4186 (open Mon.–Sat. 9 A.M.–7 P.M., Sun. 9 A.M.–11 P.M.) and **Fotografía Luz Habana,** Calle Tacón #22, e/ O'Reilly y Empredado, Habana Vieja, tel. 863-4263, sell instamatic cameras.

Never turn your back on your camera gear in Havana. Watch it at all times! And guard against snatch and grab of expensive cameras from your shoulders.

Film Processing

Most Foto Video and Photo Service stores offer processing services (film processing US$2, slide processing US$5, slide framing US$.20 per slide) and passport photos (six for US$3). They also make color prints and copies up to 50 by 60 inches. However, Cuba faces a chemical shortage, and there is no guarantee that the processing chemicals are clean. For this reason, you should consider waiting until you get home. Avoid taking film with prepaid processing (rolls that come with a self-mailer), as the chances that your film will be seized by Cuban authorities is very high.

Video Cameras

Video cameras for tourist purposes are not restricted. However, you may have to declare it, and be sure to take it out with you. Camcorder batteries can be found at Foto Video and Photo Service outlets, but it is wise to bring some spares. Blank tapes are in short supply.

Camera Fees

You will normally be charged extra for photography inside museums. These charges are noted in the listings in the individual sightseeing chapters, such as "cameras US$2."

Photo Etiquette

Cubans love to ham for your camera and will generally cooperate willingly. However, never assume an automatic right to take a personal photograph. If you come across individuals who don't want to be photographed, honor their wishes. It's a common courtesy, too, to ask permission to photograph what might be considered private situations.

Many children will request money for being photographed, as will the mulattas dressed in traditional costume in the plazas of Habana Vieja (the latter are officially sanctioned to do so). Whether you pay is a matter of conscience. If they insist on being paid and you don't want to pay, don't take the shot. It is considered a courtesy to buy a small trinket in markets from vendors you wish to photograph. Don't forget to send photographs to anyone you promise to send to, as few Cuban own cameras and they cherish being gifted highly treasured photos.

Warning: Several foreigners have been arrested and deported in recent years for filming "pornography." The Cuban government defines it fairly broadly (nude photography is forbidden) and keeps a strict watch for such illicit use of cameras. Don't attempt to photograph members of the police or military—they are under strict instructions not to allow themselves to be photographed. Military installations are also taboo.

BUSINESS HOURS

Banks are usually open Monday–Friday 8:30 A.M.–noon and 1:30–3 P.M., Saturday 8:30-10:30 A.M.. Offices are usually open Monday–Friday 8:30 A.M.–12:30 P.M. and 1:30–5:30 P.M. and every second Saturday 8:30 A.M.–noon. Pharmacies generally open daily 8 A.M.–8 P.M. (*turnos*

INDEPENDENT LIBRARIES IN HAVANA

Everyone has the right to freedom of opinion and expression; this right includes freedom to hold opinions without interference and to seek, receive and impart information and ideas through any media and regardless of frontiers.

United Nations Universal Declaration of Human Rights

The past few years have seen a sudden blossoming of independent libraries in Cuba, consisting of small collections of books housed in private homes. The Project for Independent Libraries has the goal of providing access to literature that cannot be purchased in Cuba or borrowed from public libraries. By 2002 the initiative had grown to more than 100 libraries nationwide. The libraries have proved extremely popular with Cubans.

The government, however, considers them illegal and counter-revolutionary. According to Amnesty International, independent librarians have been subject to intense persecution. The movement's founders, Berta Mexidor Vázquez and her husband, Dr. Ramón Humberto Colas Castillo, who in April 1998 established the Biblioteca Félix Varela, were fired from their jobs and then evicted from their home by the government—Amnesty International adopted Colas as a Prisoner of Conscience. Other librarians have been imprisoned and/or received beatings, and their books and magazines were confiscated. Ironically, prohibited material includes copies of the United Nations Universal Declaration of Human Rights.

The libraries are entirely dependent on donations from abroad. Books, magazines, and videotapes on all subjects and from all perspectives are needed (Spanish language materials are preferred, but not essential).

For further information and to arrange donations, contact **Friends of Cuban Libraries,** 474 48th Ave., #3-C, Long Island City, NY 11109, 718/340-8494, rkent20551@cs.com, www.friendsofcubanlibraries.org, which provides stockpiled books to people traveling to Cuba for delivery to the libraries.

Centro Habana and Cerro

Biblioteca 24 de Febrero: Campanario #564, e/ Dragones y Salud, Centro Habana. Specialty: Children's books. (Director: Leonardo Miguel Bruzón Ávila.)

Biblioteca Félix Varela: Campanario #354 (1ra piso), e/ San Miguel y San Rafael, Centro Habana. Specialty: Children's books. (Director: Roberto de Miranda Hernández.)

Biblioteca Fernando Ortiz: Calle Espada # 404, e/ San Rafael y San Miguel, Centro Habana. (Director: Vicente Escobal Rabeiro.)

Biblioteca Francisco de Arango y Parreño: San Nícolas #206 (bajos), e/ Virtudes y Concordia, Centro Habana. Specialty: Political science. (Director: Lázaro Jaime Martínez.)

Biblioteca Gertrudis Gómez de Avellaneda: 20 de mayo #531 Apt. B 14, e/ Marta Abreu y Línea, Cerro. (Director: Julia Cecilia Delgado.)

Biblioteca José Lezama Lima: Jovellar #1, Apto. 83, (8vo piso), e/ Marina y Soledad, Centro Habana. (Director: Gladys González.)

Biblioteca José Lezama Lima: Francos #10, Apt. 53, e/ Salvador Allende y Estrella, Centro Habana. Specialties: Children's books, journalism and art. (Director: Beatriz del Carmen Pedroso.)

Biblioteca Juana Alonso: Rodríguez I. Falguera #324 (altos), e/ San Pedro y Domínguez, Cerro. (Director: Rogelio Travieso.)

Biblioteca Manuel Sanguily: Cuchillo de Zanja #19 (1ra piso), e/ Rayo y San Nicolás, Centro Habana. (Director: Estrella García.)

Biblioteca Miguel Ángel Ponce de León: San Miguel #655 (2do piso), e/ Lucena y Marquez González, Centro Habana. (Director: Richard Rosell.)

Vedado

Biblioteca Dulce María Loynaz: Calle 25 #866, Apto. 3, e/ A y B, Vedado. (Director: Gisela Delgado; current director of the library movement.)

Biblioteca Frederick Remington: Este #805-07, Apto. B-3, Esquina a Conill, Nuevo Vedado. (Director: Irene Martínez.)

Playa

Biblioteca Jorge Mañach: Calle 86 #719, e/ 7ma y 9na, Playa. (Director: Ricardo González Alfonso.)

Suburban Havana

Biblioteca 30 de Noviembre Frank País: Figueroa #352 1/2, Apto. 10, e/ San Mariano y Vista Alegre, Víbora. (Director: Caridad González.)

Biblioteca Benjamín Franklin: Calle 486 #7806, e/ 7ma y 9na, Guanabo, Habana del Este. (Director: Reynaldo Cosano Alén.)

Biblioteca Elena Mederos: Sofía #330, e/ Carlos y María Luisa, Párraga, Arroyo Naranjo. (Director: Yolanda Triana.)

Biblioteca Helen Martínez: 5ta B Avenida #47812, e/ 478 y 480, Guanabo, Habana del Este. Specialty: Children's books. (Director: María Elena Mir.)

Biblioteca Grito de Baire: Calle 186 #40914, e/ 409 y 411, Santiago de las Vegas, Boyeros. (Director: Rolando Monteagudo Pérez.)

Biblioteca Ignacio Agramonte Loynaz: Calle Martí #264-C (interior), e/ Mártires de Girón y Enrique Hart, Habana del Este. Specialty: Children's books. (Director: Nereyda Rodríguez.)

Biblioteca Martin Luther King: María Luisa #64, e/ Estela y Sofía, Párraga, Arroyo Naranjo. Specialty: social sciences and politics. (Director: Carlos Alberto Domínguez.)

Biblioteca Pedro R. Someillán: Avenida 19 #30833, Playa Santa Fe, Playa.

Biblioteca Union Lucista: Vía Blanca #511, e/ Mendoza y General Lee, Santos Suárez. Specialties: History, philosophy, and theology. (Director: Rafael Barrios.)

Biblioteca Vaclav Havel: Calle 180 #37907, e/ 383 y Final, Reparto Guadalupe, Boyeros. Specialties: Ecology and agriculture. (Director: Adoracián Tulimia.)

Havana Province

Biblioteca General Juan Bruno Zayas: Calle 28 #2719, e/ 27 y 29, Quivicán, (Director: José Miguel Martínez Hernández.)

Biblioteca Rafael María Mendive: Edificio 56, Apto. 7, Reparto Los Cocos, Baracoa, (Director: Pablo Silva Cabrera.)

Biblioteca José González Curbelo: Calle 2 #327, Complejo Agroindustrial "Abraham Lincoln," Artemisa, Provincia Habana. (Director: María Elena Iturralde Bello.)

permanentes stay open 24 hours). Post offices are usually open Monday–Saturday 8 A.M.–10 P.M., Sunday 8 A.M.–6 P.M. Shops are usually open Monday–Saturday 8:30 A.M.–5:30 P.M., although many remain open later, including all day Sunday. Museums vary widely (and change frequently), although most are closed on Monday; typically they open Tuesday–Saturday 9 A.M.–5 P.M., and Sunday 8 A.M.–noon.

Most banks, businesses, and government offices close during national holidays.

Many Cubans still honor the *merienda,* coffee breaks taken usually at about 10 A.M. and 3 P.M.

Habaneros like to dine late. Hence, many restaurants are open until midnight, and some stay open 24 hours. However, local eateries serving Cubans often run out of food by mid-evening—don't leave dining too late.

Unless otherwise stated, the establishments listed in this book are open daily.

ELECTRICITY

Cuba operates on 110-volt AC (60-cycle) nationwide, although a few newer hotels operate on 220 volts. Most outlets use U.S. plugs: flat, parallel two-pins, and three rectangular pins. A two-prong adapter is a good idea (take one with you; they're impossible to come by in Cuba).

Although things have improved of late, Havana still suffers regular electricity blackouts (*apagones*). Take a flashlight and spare batteries. A couple of long-lasting candles are also a good idea. Don't forget the matches or a lighter. Since blackouts strike different areas at different times, many *habaneros* have managed to avoid the effects of the *apagones* by rigging *tendederas,* or extension wires, between two adjacent buildings that lie across the dividing lines of areas affected by *apagones*. Thus, neither house goes without electricity. Often, the *tendederas* extend for blocks around.

HAIRCUTS

There's no shortage of *peluquerías* (hairdressers) and *salones de belleza* (beauty parlors). A reader has recommended Papito, at Aguiar #10, e/ Peña Pobre y Avenida de los Misiones, Habana

Vieja, tel. 861-0202. He charges $3. Also try **Barbería Plaza de Armas,** tel. 863-0943, on Calle Obispo in Habana Vieja near the Palacio de Capitanes Generales.

LAUNDRY

In Habana Vieja, **Lavandería El Guerrillero,** Máximo Gómez #521, e/ San Nicolás y Indio, tel. 863-7585, offers a wash and dry service for 3 pesos; open daily 6 A.M.–6 P.M. Another small laundrette is at the corner of Villegas and Lamparilla. You drop off your clothes and, presto, they're usually ready a few hours later, crisp and folded, for US$3 a load.

In Miramar, **Aster Lavandería,** Calle 34 #314, e/ 3ra y 5ta, Miramar, tel. 204-1622, also has a self-day wash-and-dry service (US$3 per load for wash-and-dry) and dry-cleaning (US$2 for pants, US$1.50 for shirts). Open Mon.–Fri. 8 A.M.–5 P.M., Sat. 8 A.M.–2 P.M.

Most upscale hotels offer dry-cleaning and laundry service. It's expensive and usually takes two days, and the results can be questionable. Many locals are willing to wash your clothes for a few dollars, but be prepared to have your clothes stretched, beaten, and faded.

The telephone directory lists several dozen other laundries under the heading "Tintorerías y Lavanderías."

LIBRARIES

Cuba's many libraries (*bibliotecas*) have been neglected since the Revolution and are poorly stocked and in a sadly deteriorated condition. Books—most of which are in tatterdemalion condition—are stocked in closed areas, while library access is limited to a few privileged Cubans who are granted special permits: the **International Federation of Library Associations & Institutions,** Birketinget 6, 6th floor, DK-2300 Copenhagen S, Denmark, tel. 32/58-70-77, ext. 532, fax 32/84-02-01, susanne.seidelin@ifla.org, even reports monitoring of borrowers by the state. Many books by internationally respected authors are banned and are not represented. And access for foreigners is difficult to obtain.

Cuba's official librarians' association is known as **ASCUBI,** ascubi@fcom.uh.cu.

The main library is the **Biblioteca Nacional,** Avenida de la Independencia, esq. 20 de Mayo, tel. 55-5442, fax 81-6224, fernando@jm.lib.cult.cu or aponce@jm.lib.cult.cu, 169.158.120.135/bnjm/ espanol/index_no.asp, on the east side of Plaza de la Revolución. It has about 500,000 texts, plus a 100,000 photo archive. Getting access, however, is another matter. Five categories of individuals are permitted to use the library, including students and professionals, but not your lay citizen. Foreigners can obtain a library card (valid for one year; US$3) if they have a letter from a sponsoring Cuban government agency and/or I.D. establishing academic credentials, plus two photographs and a passport, which you need to hand over whenever you wish to consult books. The dilapidated file system is totally antiquated, making research a Kafkaesque experience. There is no open access to books. Instead, individuals must request a specific work, which is then brought to you: your passport or (for Cubans) personal I.D. is recorded along with the purpose of your request. Big Brother at work! Open Mon.–Fri. 8 A.M.– 9 P.M., Sat. 8 A.M.–6 P.M.

The University of Havana has several libraries, including the **Biblioteca Central,** tel. 878-5573 or 878-3951, ranero@dict.uh.cu, on the campus at Calle San Lázaro and Ronda, in Vedado.

The **Biblioteca Provincial de la Habana,** Calle Obispo, Plaza de Armas, tel. 862-9035, is a meagerly stocked affair with a modest supply of mostly out-of-date encyclopedias and texts, mostly from the 1960s. It has a small magazine room and musical library. Open Mon.–Fri. 8:10 A.M.–9 P.M., Sat. 9 A.M.–5:30 P.M.; closed first Mon. of each month.

The **Biblioteca del Instituto de Literatura y Lingüística,** Avenida Salvador Allende #710, e/ Castillejo y Soledad, tel. 878-5405, has novels and foreign-language texts (open Mon.–Fri. 8 A.M.–4 P.M., Sat. 8 A.M.–1:30 P.M.); and the **Biblioteca de Medicinas,** Calle 23, esq. N, tel. 832-4317, offers medical texts (open Mon.–Sat. 7:45 A.M.–7:45 P.M.). The **Biblioteca Nacional**

de Ciencias and Tecnología, in the Academy of Sciences at the Capitolio, Prado, e/ Dargones y San Martín, Habana Vieja, tel. 860-3411, ext. 1329, has books on sciences and technology. Open Mon.–Sat. 8 A.M.–5 P.M.

TIME

Cuban time is equivalent to U.S. eastern standard time: five hours behind Greenwich mean time, the same as New York and Miami, and three hours ahead of the U.S. West Coast. There is little seasonal variation in dawn. Cuba has daylight savings time May–October.

TOILETS

The only modern public toilet to Western standards is on Calle Mercaderes, e/ Brasil y Amargura. Otherwise, public toilets are a rarity. The few that exist are disgustingly foul.

Most hotels and restaurants will let you use their facilities, though most lack toilet paper, which gets stolen. An attendant usually sits outside the door, dispensing a few pieces of toilet paper (usually for US$.50 or US$1). Toilet paper is difficult to find, even in dollar stores. Many Cubans resort to using soap and water (though there are no sponges in toilets) after visiting the loo.

WEIGHTS AND MEASURES

Cuba operates on the metric system. Liquids are sold in liters, fruits and vegetables by the kilo. Distances are given in meters and kilometers. See the chart at the back of the book for metric conversions.

Vestiges of the U.S. system and old Spanish systems remain, however, such as the *pulgada* (2.54 cm, or one inch), *cordel* (20.35 meters, or 22.26 yards), or more commonly, the *caballería* (about 324 square *cordeles,* deemed sufficient to support a mounted soldier and his family). Old units of weight still heard include the *onza* (about one ounce), *libra* (about one pound), *saco* (a measure of coffee), and *quintal.*

OF LOVE AND SHADOWS

We rode back to Vedado and spent the late afternoon hours making love. Juanita loved well and industriously, perhaps because she took no other pleasure from life, and her sad face eventually drove me away.

"Let's go see a movie," she said, stirring briefly. Cine Riviera was showing an adaptation of Of Love and Shadows, *Isabel Allende's tragic tale of two people prepared to risk everything for the sake of justice and truth amid the terror and violence of Pinochet's Chile, a country of arbitrary arrests, sudden disappearances, and summary executions.*

Afterwards, back in bed, I asked Juanita if she saw any parallels to contemporary Cuba. Her raven hair was cut page-boy fashion and I found most fetching her habit of blowing the fringe out of her eyes. Now she blew upward in a puff of disdain and shot me an angry look for good measure.

"It's not like that here. In Batista's day, yes. But not now."

I told her that I had recently witnessed a disturbing "disappearance" in Miramar, when an unmarked van had screeched to a halt and a young man walking a few yards ahead of me had been hustled inside by four men.

"I don't believe you," she replied, raising her head off my shoulder. Perspiration glistened on her tobacco-colored skin.

Something about Juanita made me uneasy. Seeking to get to the root of things, I asked her point-blank what she thought of Fidel.

"He's a good man," she replied as we lay naked together on the bed and let the downdraft of the ceiling fan cool the sweat on our bodies. She had been fearful to date me and still seemed nervous. My questions began to unnerve her.

"Do you think the government knows I'm here, in this house?"

"Most likely."

"Do you think they know that you're here with me?"

"Sí," she replied, turning her face away from me slightly and piercing me sideways with her cold eyes.

"How?"

She shrugged, then pursed her lips and let out another puff of air. "The government knows you are here and where you go. Cristóbal, I don't want to talk of this."

I wasn't sure I could trust her. Still, I confided in her perhaps more than was prudent, saying that I was unsure to what degree to reveal the darker side of Cuban realities in my guidebook. I told her about Francisco's admonition to tell the truth:

"¡No mentiras!"

"¡No!" *she exclaimed.*

Juanita grew agitated as I told her of the restrictions that I felt MINREX and Publicitur had wanted to place on my travel.

"What kind of restrictions?"

"They wanted me to be accompanied. I think to keep tabs on me. After all, I'm a journalist."

"¡Ay! ¡Madre de dios!" she exclaimed. "You will make my life a misery."

Her fears sparked my own paranoia. Perhaps she's a Mata Hari. *Why not? G2, Cuba's KGB, often used shapely agents. "If you belong to G2 and are young and female and beautiful you can become a delectable detector of enemies of the party," wrote Guillermo Cabrera Infante, "You see, they can perform cover and uncover jobs."*

Cubans were always warning me to be careful. "Anyone can be an informer," "Don't talk to strangers," and my favorite, "Beware the H.P.s," for hijos de putas, literally "sons of whores" but one of many names used for informers, people in cahoots with the government.

Next day I introduced Juanita to a trusted friend, a woman whose opinions I valued. After Juanita departed, my friend raised her forefinger and tapped the end of her nose.

"What does that mean?" I asked.

"She's an embori siciñanga."

"What's that?"

"Untrustworthy. A fidelista."

"How do you know?"

"I can tell."

Juanita called me daily, but I kept her at arm's length. Her presence made me nervous. I wondered if I was being followed on the streets. Sometimes I peered at the reflections in store front windows, trying to identify anyone who might be tailing me. Finally, I became paranoid that MININT agents might search my room and seize my notebooks. So I hid them. Whatever else happened, I couldn't afford to lose those.

Christopher P. Baker, Mi Moto Fidel: Motorcycling Through Castro's Cuba

Special Notes

NOTES FOR MEN

What do men want to know about? Women! It doesn't take the average male visitor long to discover that Cuban woman are hot-blooded. True, they like being romanced but they're also much more aggressive than most foreign men are used to, displaying little equivocation and a keen interest in foreign males. They often call foreign men timid: "They touch you like you're crystal!"

See the Sidebar "Permissive, and Then Some!" and the Sex and Gender section in the Introduction chapter.

Most women count themselves lucky to have found a foreigner's acceptance and are happy to accept whatever comes their way. However, Cuba is not free of the kind of scams pulled by good-time girls in other countries and such liaisons require prudence. Petty robbery (your paramour steals your sunglasses or rifles your wallet while you take a shower) is common. Muggings by male accomplices are a rare possibility, and even drugging and robbery occurs—in 2002, a ring of high-class hookers was robbing tourists by drugging their drinks, according to police.

Men in "sensitive" occupations (journalists and government employees) should be aware that the femme fatale who sweeps you off your feet may be in the employ of Cuba's state security.

NOTES FOR WOMEN

Most women stress the enjoyment of traveling in Cuba. With few exceptions, Cuban men treat women with great respect and, for the most part, as equals. True, Cuba remains a macho society, but post-revolutionary political correctness is everywhere. Sexual assault of women is unheard of. It is hard to imagine a safer place for women to travel.

If you do welcome the amorous overtures of men, Havana is heaven. Many Stellas travel to Cuba to get their groove back with Cuban men, who see foreign women as the ultimate prize. The art of gentle seduction is to Cuban men a kind of national pastime—a sport and a trial of manhood. They will hiss in appreciation from a distance like serpents, and call out *piropos*—affectionate and lyrical epithets that, in general, Cuban women encourage. See Feminism and Machismo in the Introduction chapter.

Take effusions of love with a grain of salt; while swearing eternal devotion, your Don Juan may conveniently forget to mention he's married. Be aware, too, that while the affection may be genuine, you are assuredly the moneybags in the relationship. Plenty of Cuban men earn their living giving pleasure to foreign women looking for love beneath the palms.

If you're not interested in love in the tropics, simply pretend not to notice advances and avoid eye contact; a longing stare is part of the game. You can help prevent these overtures by dressing modestly.

Resources

Women Travel: Adventures, Advice, and Experience, by Niktania Jansz and Miranda Davies (Rough Guides), offers practical advice for women travelers, as does *Gutsy Women,* by Mary-Beth Bond (Travelers' Tales), a small-format guide with travel tips for women on the road. Likewise, the following magazines may be useful: quarterly *Journeywoman,* 50 Prince Arthur Ave. #1703, Toronto, Canada M5R 1B5, 416/929-7654, editor@journeywoman.com, www.journeywoman.com; the quarterly *Maiden Voyages,* 109 Minna St. #240, San Francisco, CA 94105, 800/528-8425, info@maiden-voyages.com; and the monthly *Travelin' Woman,* 855 Moraga Dr. #14, Los Angeles, CA 90049, 800/871-6409, traveliw@aol.com.

The **Federation of Women's Travel Organizations,** P.O. Box 466, Avenida Palma de Mallorca 15, Spain, tel. 95/205-7060, fax 95/205-8418, www.ifwto.org; in the United States, IFWTO, Enterprise, AL 36330, 334/393-4431, fax 530/686-8891, hedegolyers@earthlink.net, is a useful resource.

In Cuba, a good resource is the **Federación de**

Mujeres Cubanas (FMC), Cuban Women's Federation, Paseo #260, Vedado, Havana, tel. 55-2771, which sponsors forums and acts to promote the interests of women. *Revista Mujeres,* Galiano #264, e/ Neptuno y Concordia, Centro Habana, mujeres@teleda.get.tur.cu, www.mujeres.cubaweb.cu, is dedicated to women's issues.

Tours

The **Center for Cuban Studies,** 124 W. 23rd St., New York, NY 10011, 212/242-0559, fax 212/242-1937, cubanctr@igc.org, www.cubaupdate.org, and **Global Exchange,** 2017 Mission St. #303, San Francisco, CA 94110, 415/255-7296, fax 415/255-7498, info@globalexchange.org, www.globalexchange.org, lead women's study tours, as do the international women's rights organizations **MADRE,** 121 West 237th St. #301, New York, NY 10001, 212/627-0444, fax 212/675-3704, madre@madre.org, www.madre.org, and **Women's International League for Peace and Freedom,** 12-13 Race St., Philadelphia, PA 19107, 215/563-7110, fax 215/563-5527, www.wilpf.org.

NOTES FOR GAY AND LESBIAN TRAVELERS

Cuba is schizophrenic when it comes to homosexuality. Following the Revolution, homosexuals were treated harshly. In the past decade the Cuban government has attempted to make amends. Things have never been so open, although the situation blows hot and cold and significant discrimination still exists. Nonetheless, the gay community is fairly overt in Havana; the lesbian scene is much less evolved and remains largely hidden—Cuban machismo is still so strongly entrenched that it is inconceivable to many that lesbianism actually exists. Gays—especially *jineteros*—who befriend foreigners often fall afoul of the law of *peligrosidad,* which declares as "dangerous" anyone who acts in an antisocial manner and against the norms of socialist morality.

See Homosexuality, in the Sex and Gender section, in the Introduction chapter. Also see the Sidebar "The Gay Scene" in the Entertainment and Recreation chapter for meeting places in Havana.

Resources

Useful resources include the **International Gay and Lesbian Association,** 208 West 13th St., New York, NY 10011, 212/620-7310 or 800/421-1220, info@gaycenter.org, www.gaycenter.org; the **International Gay & Lesbian Travel Association,** 4431 N. Federal Hwy. #304, Fort Lauderdale, FL 33308, 954/776-2626 or 800/448-8550, fax 954/776-3303, iglta@iglta.org, www.iglta.org; and **Odysseus: The International Gay Travel Planner,** P.O. Box 1548, Port Washington, NY 11050, 516/944-5330 or 800/257-5344, fax 516/944-7540, odyusa@odyusa.com, www.odyusa.com.

In Cuba, gay organizations are illegal. The first gay men's group on the island, called Cubans in the Struggle Against AIDS, and the Cuban Association of Gays & Lesbians, founded in 1994, were broken up in 1997 and their members arrested. The **Centro Nacional de Educación Sexual,** Calle 10 #460, Vedado, Havana, tel. 55-5529, may be of assistance.

Two websites of interest are those of **Gay Cuba,** www.gay-cuba.com, and **Black On White,** www.blacklightonline.com/cuba.html.

Tours

The **Center for Cuban Studies,** 124 W. 23rd St., New York, NY 10011, 212/242-0559, fax 212/242-1937, cubanctr@igc.org, www.cubaupdate.org, offers occasional study tours of lesbian and gay issues in Cuba. It requests donations of condoms, safe sex materials, literature, and medicines for distribution in Cuba. **Gayjet Travel,** 584 Castro St. #834, San Francisco CA 94114, gayjet.com, offers licensed "study" tours to Cuba for gays.

NOTES FOR STUDENTS AND YOUTH TRAVELERS

Cuban students receive discounts for entry to many museums and other sights, as do foreign students with the **International Student Identity**

KEY ORGANIZATIONS TO KNOW

IN THE UNITED STATES

Center for a Free Cuba, 1320 19th Street NW, Suite 201, Washington, D.C. 20036, 202/463-8430, fax 202/463-8412, www.cubacenter.org, is an anti-Castro organization that defines itself as "an independent, non-partisan institution dedicated to promoting human rights and a transition to democracy and the rule of law on the island."

Center for Cuban Studies, 124 W. 23rd St., New York, NY 10011, 212/242-0559, fax 212/242-1937, cubanctr@igc.org, www.cubaupdate.org. This "solidarity" organization sponsors educational forums on Cuba, publishes the quarterly *Cuba Update,* organizes study tours, and sells books and videos on Cuba. It has an art gallery and the largest research library on Cuba in North America.

Conchord Cayo Hueso, P.O. Box 2306, Key West, FL 33045, tel./fax 305/294-0205, jitters@aol.com, www.geocities.com/conchordcayohueso, carries humanitarian aid to Cuba using registered private vessels. It also organizes athletic, cultural, religious, and other exchanges.

Cuba Policy Foundation, 2300 M Street NW, Washington, D.C. 20037, 202/835-0200, fax 202/835-0291, www.cubapolicyfoundation.org. This influential, nonpartisan, centrist organization works to end the U.S. ban on travel to Cuba, lift the U.S. embargo against Cuba, and foster democratic change in Cuba. It is led by former senior diplomats in Republican administrations.

Cuban American Alliance Education Fund, 614 Maryland Ave. NE #2, Washington, D.C. 20002-5825, 202/543-6780, fax 202/543-6434, caaef@igc.org, www.cubamer.org, represents moderate Cuban-Americans who wish for dialogue with Cuba. It sponsors efforts at family reunification and an end to travel restrictions. It also has a program to assist in the physical rehabilitation needs of children at the Julito Díaz Hospital—donations of medicines and medical equipment are needed.

Cuban American National Foundation, 1312 SW 27th St., Miami, FL 33145, 305/592-7768, fax 305/592-7889, hq@canf.org, www.canfnet.org. An ultra-conservative lobbying group dedicated to the overthrow of Fidel Castro and replacement by a self-appointed government formed of CANF leaders. It effectively shapes White House policy towards Cuba.

Cuban Liberty Council, P.O. Box 352735, Miami, FL 33135, 305/642-0610, fax 305/642-0410, www.cubanlibertycouncil.org. An anti-Castro organization representing Cuban-Americans in exile dedicated to a democratic government through "free and fair elections."

Global Exchange, 2017 Mission St. #303, San Francisco, CA 94110, 415/255-7296, fax 415/255-7498, info@globalexchange.org, www.globalexchange.org, organizes monthly "solidarity" study tours to Cuba on an eclectic range of themes, and works to end the embargo.

IFCO/Pastors for Peace, 620 West 28th St, Minneapolis, MN 55408, 612/670-7121 or 612/378-0062, fax 612/870-7109 or 612/378-0134, p4p@igc.apc.org, www.ifconews.org, organizes the U.S.–Cuba Friendshipment Caravans, challenging the embargo by traveling with vehicles filled with donations of humanitarian aid. Also has study tours and organizes work brigades to assist in community projects in Cuba. IFCO stands for Interreligious Foundation for Community Organization.

U.S.–Cuba Medical Project, c/o: MADRE, 121 West 27th St. #301, New York, NY 10001, 212/627-0444, madre@madre.org, www.madre.org, provides medical and humanitarian aid to Cuba, working through the Cuban Red Cross. Leads caravans that deliver medical supplies to hospitals in Cuba.

U.S.–Cuba Sister City Association, 320 Lowenhill St., Pittsburgh, PA 15216, 412/563-1519, fax 412/563-1945, uscsca@aol.com, www.USCSCA.org, exists to foster ties between U.S. and Cuban cities. Typically this involves regular exchanges of delegations, including scholars, artists, religious figures, musicians, and local politicians.

U.S.–Cuba Trade and Economic Council, 30 Rockefeller Plaza, New York, NY 10112, 212/246-1444, fax 212/246-2345, council@cubatrade.org, www.cubatrade.org. This nonpartisan business organization provides accurate, up-to-the-minute information on every aspect regarding U.S.–Cuban commercial relations. John Kavulich, president of the U.S.–Cuba Trade and Economic Council, is a foremost authority on doing business in Cuba. It publishes the newsletter *Economic Eye on Cuba.*

U.S. Engage, 1625 K St. NW, Washington, D.C. 20006, 202/887-0278, ext. 115, www.usaengage.org, is a broad-based coalition representing American business and agriculture interests that lobby for an end to the embargo and for open trade with Cuba.

OUTSIDE THE UNITED STATES

The following "solidarity" organizations work to support Cuban socialism.

Australia

Australia-Cuba Friendship Society, P.O. Box 1051, Collingwood, Victoria 3066, tel. 03/9857-9249, fax 03/9857-6598.

Canada

Canadian–Cuba Friendship Association, P.O. Box 743, Station F, Toronto M4Y 2N6, 414/742-6931 or tel. 406/654-5585, fax 416/744-6143. Promotes "friendship, understanding, and cooperation" between the peoples of Canada and Cuba. It offers cultural exchanges, lectures, and cultural events, plus sends medicinal and material aid to Cuba, as well as publishing the *Amistad* newsletter.

France

Association Cuba Si, 20 Rue Denis-Papin, 94200 Ivry-sur-Seine, tel. 01/4515-1143, fax 01/4515-1144.

Italy

Associazione di Amicizia Italia-Cuba, Visa Foscolo 3, 20121 Milano, tel. 02/8646-3493, web.tiscali.it/ItaliaCuba.

New Zealand

Cuban Friendship Society, 3 Oakdale St., Christchurch, tel./fax 03/365-6055, 100250.1511@compuserve.com.

United Kingdom

Cuba Solidarity Campaign, c/o Red Rose Club, 129 Seven Sisters Rd., London N7 7QG, tel. 020/7263-6452, fax 020/7561-0191, www.cuba-solidarity.org.uk.

Card (ISIC) or similar student I.D. The card entitles students 12 years and older to discounts on transportation, entrances to museums, and more. When purchased in the United States (US$20; 800/GET-AN-ID), ISIC even includes emergency medical coverage (although this won't apply in Cuba) and access to a 24-hour emergency hotline. Students can obtain ISICs at any student union. Alternately, in the United States, contact the **Council on International Educational Exchange** (CIEE), 212/882-2600 or 888/268-6245, fax 212/822-2699, info@ciee.org, www.ciee.org. In Canada, cards (C$13) can be obtained through **Travel Cuts,** 416/614-2887 or 800/667-2887 in Toronto, 604/717-7800 in Vancouver, www .travelcuts.com. In the UK, students can obtain an ISIC from any student union.

Transitions Abroad, P.O. Box 1300, Amherst, MA 01004-1300, 413/256-3414 or 800/293-0373, fax 413/256-0373, info@Transitions Abroad.com, www.transitionsabroad.com, provides information for students wishing to study abroad; as does **Studyabroad.com,** 1450 Edgmont Ave., Suite 140, Chester, PA 19013, 610/499-9200, fax 610/499-9205, www.study abroad.com; **Study Abroad Directory,** 8 East First Ave., Suite 102, Denver, CO 80203, 720/570-1702, fax 720/570-1703, www.study abroaddirectory.com; and **CIEE's Work Abroad Department,** 205 E. 42nd St., New York, NY 10017, 212/661-1414, ext. 1130, www.council exchanges.org, with offices throughout Europe and Asia.

The **Federación Estudiantil Universitario,** Calle 23, esq. H, tel. 832-4646, is Cuba's national student federation.

The U.S. government permits academic exchanges with Cuba, and students can enroll at Cuban universities. See the Special Topic "Studying In Cuba" in the Planning Your Trip chapter.

NOTES FOR SENIORS

Cuba treats its senior citizens with honor, and discounts are offered for entry to museums and other attractions. Again, this may apply to foreign seniors in a few instances.

Resources

Useful resources include the **American Association of Retired Persons** (AARP), 601 E. St. West, Washington, D.C. 20049, 202/434-2277 or 800/424-3410, member@aarp.org, www.aarp.or, whose benefits include a "Purchase Privilege Program" offering discounts on airfares that you may be able to use for flights to a third country en route to Cuba.

Another handy resource is *The International Health Guide for Senior Citizen Travelers,* by Robert Lange, M.D. (New York: Pilot Books).

Tours

Canadian company **ElderTreks,** 597 Markham St., Toronto, Ontario M6G 2L7, 416/588-5000 or 800/741-7956, fax 416/588-9839, www.elder treks.com, offers 14-day trips to Cuba. **Elderhostel,** 11 Avenue de Lafayette, Boston, MA 02111, 978/323-4141 or 877/426-8056, fax 617/426-0701, www.elderhostel.org, did not offer trips to Cuba at press time, but may be a useful resource.

Global Exchange, 2017 Mission St. #303, San Francisco, CA 94110, 415/255-7296, fax 415/255-7498, info@globalexchange.org, www .globalexchange.org, occasionally offers an "Elders in Cuba" study tour.

NOTES FOR TRAVELERS WITH DISABILITIES

Cubans go out of their way to assist travelers with disabilities. However, you'll need to plan your vacation carefully—few allowances have been made in infrastructure.

Resources

The **Asociación Cubana de Limitados Físicos y Motores** (Cuban Association for Physically-Motor Disabled People, ACLIFIM), Ermita #213, e/ San Pedro y Lombillo, Plaza de la Revolución, CP 10600, Havana, tel. 881-0911, fax 204-3787, aclifim@informed.sld.cu, can be of assistance.

In the United States, the **Society for Accessible Travel & Hospitality,** 347 5th Ave. #610, New York, NY 10016, 212/447-7284, fax 212/725-8253, sathtravel@aol.com, www.sath.org; and

BITE YOUR TONGUE!

Many foreigners are fearful because Cuba is a Communist country. Fear not!

That said, Cuba is a paranoid nation that zealously guards against threats to the state's integrity. It is disconcerting to see the degree to which "Big Brother" keeps a close eye on Cubans, although this constant surveillance isn't very obvious to first time visitors.

Fear of Informers

As Pico Iyer wrote in *Cuba and the Night:* "The whole city is a circle of informers." *Habaneros* are a paranoid people, never sure who might be a *chivato,* a finger-man for the CDR or MININT, the much-loathed Ministry of the Interior. In this regard, Havana doesn't seem to have changed much since the 1930s, when Hemingway told Arnold Samuelson, "Don't trust anybody. That fellow might have been a government spy trying to get you in bad. You can never tell who they are."

Many visitors take the fact that you never hear a bad word about the system or the Bearded One expressed in public as a tacit expression that Cubans overwhelmingly support their government. In fact, no one in his or her right mind would dare to criticize the government or Fidel Castro in public. Irreverence (*desacato,* or criticism of the government) is defined as "anti-social behavior" and a crime against the Revolution and is punishable by law, as is *peligrosidad* (dangerousness), a general term that encompasses whatever the government wishes. Dissenting or being considered unsupportive risks being labeled a "counter-revolutionary," with all the consequences of loss of privileges, such as employment, or even jail, however trivial the infraction. With so many people employed as informers, there is a culture of mistrust summed up in the Cuban saying: "You can swim safely if you keep your mouth closed." Even in private conversations, *habaneros* size people up to gauge whether someone is trustworthy before risking mouthing their inner feelings. Sometimes a diatribe against the government (usually offered in hushed tones) will end in mid-stream as the speaker taps his two forefingers on his opposite shoulder, signifying the presence of a member of State Security. Hence, Cubans have developed a cryptic, elliptical way of talking where nuance and meaning is hidden from casual tourists.

Many Cubans are even afraid to be seen with tourists. Government snoops, for example, routinely question the neighbors of Cubans slated to travel abroad, merely to ensure they are not tainted by foreign contacts—a foreign lover is out of the question for a contender for a Cuban national sports team, for example.

Feeling Like James Bond

Even foreigners are not above surreptitious surveillance; those in sensitive occupations, such as embassy staff, are *muy bien acompañada* (well accompanied) by agents of State Security . . . sometimes identifiable by their imitation Lacoste shirts or *guayaberas,* pressed pants or stonewashed jeans, mirrored glasses, and well-groomed moustaches. Journalists may even be assigned specific hotel rooms—which may be bugged or otherwise kept an eye on—be wary, for example, of the beautiful *cubana* or *cubano* too eager to be your lover. Says Stephen Smith: "The [security services] represented, at a conservative estimate, a substantial proportion of Cuba's productive capacity . . . and the spies had to find *something* to do all day."

Fortunately, you, the average tourist, are free to roam wherever you wish without hindrance or a need to look over your shoulder. That said, you can be sure that nay-saying the Revolution or you-know-who in public can swiftly land you in trouble. Cuban authorities have zero tolerance for foreigners who become involved in political activity, especially with known dissidents. Be circumspect about what you say, especially to anyone you do not implicitly trust.

Avoid making inflammatory or derogatory comments; otherwise you could well find yourself on the next plane home.

the **American Foundation for the Blind,** 11 Penn Plaza No 300, New York, NY 10001, 212/502-7600 or 800/232-5463, afbinfo@afb .org, www.afb.org, are good resources.

Tours

In the United States, **Marazul Tours,** Tower Plaza Mall, 4100 Park Ave., Weehawken, NJ 07087, 201/840-6711 or 800/223-5334, info@ marazultours.com, www.marazultours.com and www.marazulcharters.com, arranges trips to the Cuban conferences on disabled people's rights.

NOTES FOR TRAVELERS WITH CHILDREN

Cubans adore children and will dote on yours.

Children under the age of two travel free on airlines; children between two and 12 are offered special discounts (check with individual airlines). Children under 16 usually stay free with parents at hotels, although an extra-bed rate may be charged. And children under 12 are normally given free (or half-price) entry to museums. Cuban TV features a few children's programs, and you can find kiddies' books in Spanish at leading bookstores.

There are few sanitary or health problems to worry about. However, the heat can be a problem. There are few public toilets. And children's items such as diapers (nappies) and baby foods are very difficult to obtain in Cuba. Bring cotton swabs, diapers, Band-Aids, and a small first-aid kit with any necessary medicines for your child. If you plan on driving around, bring your own children's car seat—they're not offered in rental cars. (See For Children and the Child Within, in the Shopping chapter, for shops catering to children's needs.)

Havana has seven children's hospitals, including the **Pediátrico Centro Habana,** Benjumeda y Morales, Centro Habana, tel. 877-5540.

The equivalent of the Boy and Girl Scouts and Girl Guides is the **Pioneros José Martí,** Calle F #352, Vedado, Havana, tel. 832-5292, which has chapters throughout the country. Its main focus is instilling youth with revolutionary correctness and civil responsibility. Having your children interact would be a fascinating education.

Great Vacations with Your Kids (E.P. Dutton), by Dorothy Jordan and Marjorie Cohen, is a handy reference guide to planning a trip with children, as is *Travel with Children,* by Cathy Lanigan (Lonely Planet).

PERSONAL CONDUCT

Cubans are immensely respectful and courteous, with a deep sense of integrity and exemplary morals. Politeness is greatly appreciated, and you can ease your way considerably by being both courteous and patient. Always greet your host with *"¡Buenos días!"* (good morning) or *"¡Buenas tardes!"* (good afternoon). And never neglect to say, *"Gracias."*

You may find yourself becoming frustrated far more than you're used to, even to the point of anger, due to Cuba's insufferable bureaucracy, the state's subtle injustices against its own people (such as racist harassment by police), and/or the trials of daily life. Cubans are stoically inured. Getting angry is guaranteed to get you nowhere . . . and usually will only make matters worse. Cuba is the opposite of a service-oriented society. Difficult as it may be, you may just have to grin and bear it.

Topless and nude bathing are neither allowed nor accepted, except at key tourist resorts.

Cubans are extremely hygienic and have an understandable natural prejudice against anyone who ignores personal hygiene, for which the Russians—*bolos*—were despised.

Respect the natural environment. Take only photographs, leave only footprints.

Transportation

Arriving in Havana

José Martí International Airport (switchboard tel. 206-4644 or 33-5753) is 25 kilometers southwest of downtown Havana, in the Wajay district. It has four terminals spaced well apart and accessed by different roads—they are not linked by a connecting bus service.

Terminal One: This terminal serves domestic flights.

Terminal Two: Charter flights originating in Los Angeles, Miami, and New York arrive at Terminal Two, tel. 33-5576 or 33-5577, carrying passengers with OFAC licenses. Occasionally other flights pull in here, although the outbound flight from Havana will invariably depart from Terminal Three. There's an Infotur information booth, tel. 55-8733, plus car rental outlets.

Terminal Three: All international flights (except USA–Havana charters) now arrive at the ritzy new Terminal Three, at Wajay, on the north side of the airport. For information on arrivals and departures, call tel. 266-4133 or 33-5666.

Terminal Four: This currently serves the military.

Terminal Five: AeroCaribbean and AeroTaxi flights arrive here.

IMMIGRATION AND CUSTOMS

Anticipate a long delay in clearing immigration, as proceedings are slow. The usually sour-faced officials are assiduous, and not a little paranoid in their duties.

Personal carry-on baggage is X-rayed upon arrival. Havana's airport has the international two-zone system: Red for items to declare and green for

coches (taxis), Parque de la Fraternidad

nothing to declare. Visitors to Cuba are permitted 20 kilos of personal effects plus "other articles and equipment depending on their profession," all of which must be re-exported. In addition, up to 10 kilos of medicines, 200 cigarettes, 50 cigars, 250 grams of pipe tobacco, and three liters of wine and alcohol, plus US$50 of additional goods are permitted tax-free, as are a reasonable quantity of items deemed for personal use. An additional US$200 of "objects and articles for noncommercial use" can be imported, subject to a tax equal to 100 percent of the declared value—you must fill out a Customs form and use the red zone—but this applies mostly to Cubans and returning foreign residents bringing in electrical goods. Most electrical goods are banned, including videocassette recorders. Laptops must be declared; you will need to fill out a customs declaration, and the laptop *must* depart Cuba with you. "Obscene and pornographic" literature is also banned—the definition of "obscene" includes politically unacceptable tracts considered critical—or implicitly so—of the Castro regime.

Travelers arriving without prebooked accommodations are usually made to book—and pay for—at least two nights' hotel stay before being granted entry. You'll be escorted to a tour desk where representatives sell hotel rooms at full price.

For further information, contact the **Aduana** (Customs), Calle 6, esq. 39, Plaza de la Revolución, tel. 55-5466, fax 33-5222, adm@agr.adu ana.cu, www.aduana.islagrande.com. The main Customs office is on Avenida San Pedro, opposite the Iglesia San Francisco de Asís.

INFORMATION AND SERVICES

There's an **Infotur,** tel. 66-6101, tourist information office immediately on the left after exiting the Customs lounge. It's poorly stocked with information and maps, but is staffed 24 hours. You should check in here if you have prepaid vouchers for accommodations or transfers into town.

There's a foreign exchange counter in the baggage claim area, but this serves mostly to change other foreign currency into U.S. dollars. You'll not need Cuban pesos.

Getting into Town

There is no public bus service from either of the international terminals. A **public bus** marked "Aeropuerto" departs from Terminal 1 (domestic flights) for Vedado and Parque Central about 15 minutes after the arrival of domestic flights (one peso). The bus is intended for Cubans, and foreigners may be refused. It only runs about once every two hours.

Alternately, you can catch a "camel bus" (no. M2 originating in Santiago de las Vegas) or Omnibus no. 480 from the east side of Avenida de la Independencia, about a 20-minute walk east of the terminal—no fun with baggage. The bus goes to Parque de la Fraternidad on the edge of Habana Vieja. The journey takes about one hour, but the wait can be just as long; the bus gets incredibly crowded, and is renowned for pickpockets. You'll need 20 pesos for the fare.

Taxis are plentiful outside the arrivals lounges. You'll be charged about US$10–12 by Cubataxi

(yellow-and-black Ladas) and US$12–20 by tourist taxis to downtown hotels. Some taxi drivers will want to not use their meter and may ask you how much you're prepared to pay (they reset their meter at a discount rate and pocket the difference) . . . in which case always quote below the fares given here. You can also take a private (albeit illegal) taxi for a negotiable fee (usually about US$8); touts will approach you if there are no police around.

Most people arriving on package tours will have been issued prepaid vouchers for a shuttle. Often they're also happy to act as a shuttle service for individual travelers, too.

Car Rental

The following have booths at Terminal 3: **Havanautos,** tel. 33-5197; **Micar,** tel. 33-0333; **Panautos,** tel. 33-0307; **Rex,** tel. 66-6074; and **Transauto,** tel. 33-5765. The following have booths at Terminal 2: **Cubacar,** tel. 33-5546; **Havanautos,** tel. 33-5215; **Panautos,** tel. 33-0306, and **Transauto,** tel. 33-5764.

The cars are poorly maintained. Check your car thoroughly before driving away. If you find a problem later on and want to exchange cars, you'll have to return to the airport office. I recommend you wait and rent a car downtown.

Getting Around Havana

ON FOOT

Havana is a walker's city, easily and best explored on foot. Only when traveling between districts will you need transport.

Except in Habana Vieja, sidewalks are in atrocious repair. Beware potholes and dog excrement underfoot. And be wary of walking beneath corroded *porticos,* which frequently collapse, killing pedestrians. Watch where *habaneros* are walking; if they're avoiding certain arcades to walk in the street, so should you.

BY BUS
Tourist Buses

The **Tren Turística Bella Época,** tel. 66-2476, departs from the Terminal Sierra Maestra, on the east side of Plaza de San Francisco, daily 10 A.M.–1 P.M. (US$1). This motorized "train" (it's a jeep dressed up as a train) has shaded open-air carriages and takes in major sights in Habana Vieja, the Malecón, and Vedado, where it ends at the Hotel Meliá Cohiba.

Rumbos, S.A., Línea #60, esq. M, Vedado, tel. 66-2113 or 204-9626, fax 33-3110, previously operated a minibus service for tourists: the Vaivén Bus Turístico. It was suspended at last visit.

Public Bus

Havana's public buses, or *guaguas* (pronounced WAH-wahs), are for stoics. *Habaneros* are inured and would rather take a bus than walk under almost all circumstances, even if this means traveling like sardines in a can. No buses operate within Habana Vieja except along the major peripheral thoroughfares. Fares are cheap, but buses are usually packed to the gills (exiting has been compared to being birthed), especially during rush hours—7–10 A.M. and 3–6 P.M. Be wary of pickpockets.

In the early 1990s, the bus system ground to a virtual halt. At last visit, things were back to normal, aided by the introduction of modern (albeit "pre-owned") Mercedes and Volvo buses from Europe. That said, many buses are either pass-me-down Yankee school buses imported via Canada or Mexico; horribly uncomfortable Hungarian buses that belch out black fumes; poorly made and equally uncomfy Cuban Giróns; or *tren buses* (also called *camellos*—camels), which are lengthy, truck-pulled passenger cars that sag in the middle, like the rolling stock on U.S. railways. See the Sidebar "Camels in Cuba?"

Expect a long wait in line. Cuban lines (*colas*) are always fluid but tend to re-form when the bus appears, so you should follow the Cubans' example and identify the last person in line ahead of you by asking for *el último?* It's like a game of tag. You're now *el último* until the next person arrives. Thus you don't have to stand in line, but can wander off to find some shade and then simply follow the person ahead of you onto the bus. Cubans have zero tolerance for folks who abuse the *el último* system . . . so pay attention! You'll undoubtedly be the only foreigner aboard and may find yourself being offered a seat as an honored guest.

Buses stop frequently, but when full, the driver may stop only when requested to do so. Bus stops—*paradas*—are usually well marked. Shout *Pare!* (Stop!), or bash the box above the door in Cuban fashion. You'll need to elbow your way to the door well in advance (don't stand near the door, however, as you may literally be popped out onto your face). Don't dally, as the bus driver is likely to hit the gas when you're only halfway out.

Bus service is the responsibility of three agencies: **Asociación de Transportes de Servicios de Ómnibus** (Astro), **Transmetro,** and **Ómnibus Metropolitano.**

TRANSPORTATION

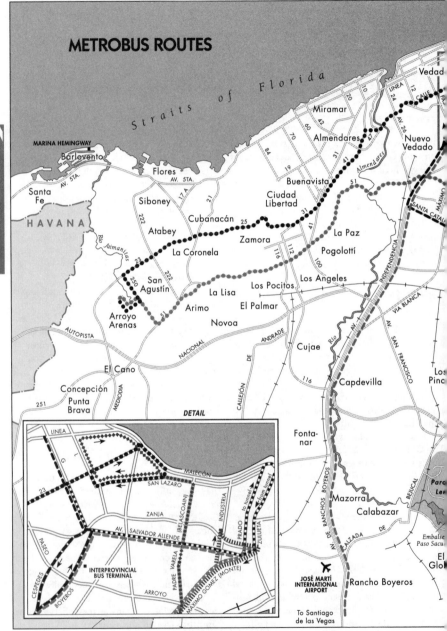

METROBUS ROUTES

Straits of Florida

MARINA HEMINGWAY
Barlovento

HAVANA

Santa Fe

AV. 5TA.

Flores
AV. 5TA.

Siboney

Atabey

La Coronela

San Agustín

Arroyo Arenas

Cubanacán

Miramar

Almendares

Buenavista

Ciudad Libertad

Zamora

Arimo

Novoa

La Lisa

Los Pocitos

El Palmar

Los Angeles

La Paz

Pogolotti

Vedado

Nuevo Vedado

AUTOPISTA

El Cano

Concepción Punta Brava

NACIONAL

MEDIODIA

CALLEJÓN DE

ANDRADE

Cujae

Capdevilla

Fontanar

José Martí International Airport

Rancho Boyeros

To Santiago de las Vegas

Mazorra

Calabazar

VIA BLANCA

AV. SAN FRANCISCO

AV. DE RANCHOS BOYEROS

CALZADA DE BEJUCAL

Los Pino

Para Len

Embalse Paso Sacu

El Glo

DETAIL

LINEA

MALECÓN

SAN LAZARO

ZANJA

AV. SALVADOR ALLENDE

INTERPROVINCIAL BUS TERMINAL

ARROYO

PASEO

CESPEDES

BOYEROS

PADRE VARELA

BELASCOAIN

MAXIMO GOMEZ (MONTE)

INDUSTRIA

PRADO

ZULUETA

To tunnel

From tunnel

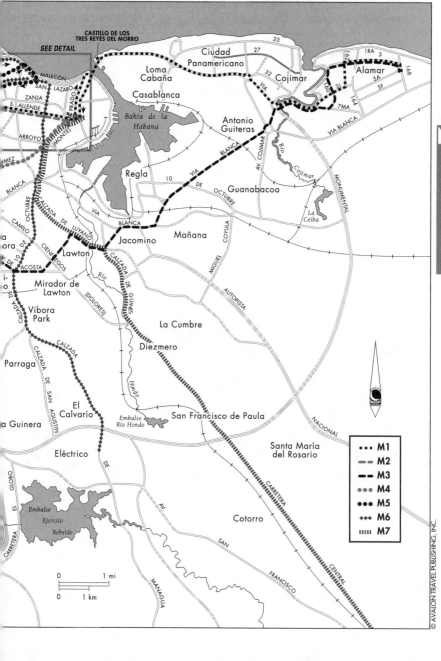

TRANSPORTATION

M

CAMELS IN CUBA?

Yes, camels roam the streets of Havana. These giant buses—*camellos*—were designed locally to save the day during the gasoline crisis, when ingenious engineers added bodies to articulated flatbed trucks. They're so named for the shape of the coach: sagging in between two humps like a bactrian camel.

About half of the one million trips that *habaneros* make daily are aboard the rumbling behemoths, which carry the "M" designation (for Metro-bus) on bus routes. The "camel" is a warehouse on wheels: officially a *supertrenbus*. Designed to carry 220 people, they are usually stuffed with more than 300, so many that the true number can't be untangled. As a popular Cuban joke goes, the always-packed and chaotic *camellos* are like the Saturday night film on state TV, "because they contain sex, violence, and swear words!" Adds one young *habanera:* "You don't want to get on one with your purse, your wallet, your panties, or anything else you value. It's not just that you can't stop the hands moving over you, you can't even locate their owners."

More than 200 camels roam the streets of Havana. They were made in a factory in Havana and weigh more than 20 tons. Of course, the Mack trucks that pull them weren't designed for stop and start work, so maintenance is an ongoing problem. At last visit, many were on their last legs.

Most camels originate from Parque de la Fraternidad. Seven routes span Havana and the most distant suburbs. Two key "camel" routes to know are the M1 (Parque de la Fraternidad to Habana del Este) and M2 (Parque de la Fraternidad to Santiago de las Vegas via the international airport).

Most begin operation at 4 A.M. with the last departure at 10 or 11 P.M. A standard 20 centavo fare applies.

© CHRISTOPHER P. BAKER

Note that public transportation often comes to a halt on May 1 and other days of major political celebrations, as buses are redirected to transporting the masses to the demonstrations.

Schedules and Fares: Most *guaguas* run 24 hours, at least hourly during the day but on reduced schedules 11 P.M.–5 A.M. The standard fare for any journey throughout the city is 20 centavos, or 40 centavos on smaller buses called *ómnibuses ruteros,* which have the benefit of being uncrowded. *Taxibuses*—buses that ply a fixed, non-stop route to the airport and bus and train stations—charge one peso. You deposit the money in the box beside the driver.

Routes and Route Maps: Many buses follow a loop route, traveling to and from destinations along

M1—Alamar to Vedado

Route: Calle 168 (e/ 5taE y 7taF) - 5ta Ave. - Calle 168 - 3ra Ave. - Calle 162 - Ave. Los Cocos - 7ma Ave. - Vía Monumental - Tunnel - Agramonte - Máximo Gómez (Monte) - Simón Bolívar (Reina) - Salvador Allende - Calle G

M2—Santiago de las Vegas (Boyeros) to Parque de la Fraternidad

Route: Avenida 349 (y Final) - Calle 17 - Calle 2 - Avenida Boyeros - Salvador Allende - Simón Bolívar (Reina)

M3—Alamar to Ciudad Deportiva

Route: Calle 168 (e/ 5taE y 7taF) - 5ta Ave. - Calle 168 - 3ra Ave. - Calle 160 - 7ma Ave. - Ave. Cojímar - Vía Blanca - Calzada de Guanabacoa - Lindero - Calzada de Luyanó - Porvenir - Acosta - Mayía Rodríguez - Santa Catalina - Avenida Boyeros

M4—San Agustín (Lisa) to Parque de la Fraternidad

Route: Calle 270 (e/ 25 y 27) - Ave. 27 - Calle 264 - Ave 31 - Calle 250 - Ave. 51 - Calzada de Puentes Grandes - Calzada de Cerro - Máximo Gómez (Monte) - Prado (return to Monte via Dragones and Zulueta)

M5—San Agustín (Lisa) to Vedado

Route: Calle 270 (e/ 25 y 27) - Ave. 27 - Calle 264 - Ave. 31 - Calle 250 - Ave. 23 - Ave. 26 - Ave. 31 - Ave. 41 - Calle 28 - Calle 23 - Malecón - Marina (return to Calle 23 via San Lázaro and Calle L)

M6—Calvario (Arroyo Naranjo) to Vedado

Route: Calzada de Managua (e/ Camilo Cienfuegos y 1ra) - 10 de Octubre - Cristina - Belascosín - San Lázaro - Calle L (return to San Lázaro via Calle L, Línea, Malecón and Marina)

M7—Alberro (Cotorro) to Parque de la Fraternidad

Route: Ave. 99 (y Final) - Carretera de Alberro - Ave. 101 - Calzada de Güines - Lindero - Calzada de Luyanó - 10 de Octubre - Cristina - Máximo Gómez (Monte) - Industria (return to Monte via Dragones and Prado)

TRANSPORTATION

different streets. Most buses display the bus number and destination above the front window. If in doubt, ask. Many buses arrive and depart from Parque Central and Parque de la Fraternidad in Habana Vieja and La Rampa (Calle 23) in Vedado, especially at Calle L and at Calzada de Infanta.

Few routes are a circle. If you find yourself going in the wrong direction, don't assume that you'll eventually come around to where you want to get to. You'll more likely end up in the boondocks.

BY TRAIN

Intracity service is provided to a limited number of suburban destinations on commuter trains from the following stations.

ferro-ómnibus, Cristina station

Estación 19 de Noviembre: Local service aboard a commuter train (*ferro-ómnibus*) operates to ExpoCuba and the provincial town of San Antonio de los Baños from Estación 19 de Noviembre (also called Estación Tulipán), Calle Tulipán and Hidalgo, tel. 881-4431 or 881-3642, south of Plaza de la Revolución.

Trains depart for San Antonio (US$1.10) at 6:30 and 9:40 A.M., and 12, 4:15, 6:10, and 8 P.M. Departures from San Antonio are at 5:37, 8:45, and 11:40 A.M., and 1:50, 6:38, and 8:24 P.M.

The *Servicio ExpoCuba* departs Estación 19 de Noviembre at 9:20 A.M. via Víbora (50 minutes). Return trains depart ExpoCuba Wed.–Sun. at 5:15 P.M. (one peso).

Estación Cristina: This suburban station, at Avenida de México (Cristina), esq. Manglar Arroyo, tel. 863-2989 or 879-3546, in southwest Habana Vieja, serves Artemisa in Havana province (40 centavos). Trains depart at 5:45 A.M. and 5:05 P.M. Return trains depart Artemisa for Cristina at 9:25 A.M. and 10:30 P.M. Trains also run from here to Guanabo, in Playas del Este, in July–August only (1 peso) at 8:45 A.M. (return trains depart Guanabo at 6:30 P.M.).

TAXI

Havana has a superb taxi system. Hundreds of taxis—including top-class Mercedes—serve both the tourist trade and the local population. However, lousy maintenance is an issue . . . many taxis lack seat-belts (they've been stolen) or are in a bad state of repair.

Dollar Taxis

Turistaxis are operated by state organizations and charge in dollars. Rates vary slightly between companies and, often, the size of the car. Taxis are metered and usually begin at US$1. You will rarely pay more than US$10 or so for any journey within town. Expect to pay about US$5 between Habana Vieja and the Hotel Habana Libre. Nighttime fares cost about 20 percent more. About 50 percent of the time, your driver will use the meter. But, as with everything in Cuba, the *taxistas* have their own *trampas* or *estafas* (swindles) and you can expect the driver to reset his (or her) meter to record a much lower mileage, then charge you the going rate for the journey, or slightly lower. Taxi drivers are paid in near worthless pesos, so don't get uppity . . . so long as you aren't being ripped off. They pocket the difference. Since his dispatcher records the destination, mile for mile, usually a dollar per mile, the taxi driver splits the excess with the dispatcher. Most taxi drivers are scrupulously honest with passengers. Often they'll ask you in advance for permission. If you think you're being gouged, contest the fee. Take any statement such as "it's my child's birthday today" with a grain of salt; normally the driver is hoping to extract some extra generosity on your part.

Tourist taxis hang around outside tourist hotels but can also be radio dispatched.

Panataxi, tel. 55-5555, panataxi@transnet.cu, provides efficient radio-dispatched taxi service using Peugeots. It's rare to have to wait more than 15 minutes for a taxi to arrive. It charges US$1 at flag drop, then US$.45 a kilometer.

The following companies operate tourist taxis: **Fénix,** tel. 863-9720; **Habanataxi,** tel. 204-9600 or 53-9085; **Taxis-OK,** tel. 204-0000 or 204-9518; **Transgaviota,** tel. 267-1626; and **Transtur Taxi,** tel. 208-6666, fax 33-5535, taxiweb@trans tur.tur.cu, www.transturtaxi.com.

Classic Cars: Fancy tootling around in a 1950 Studebaker or 1959 Buick Invicta convertible? **Gran Car,** Vía Blanca and Palatino, Cerro, tel. 57-7338, fax 33-5647, grancarDP@transnet.cu, rents classic-car taxis for US$15 per hour (20 km limit the first hour, with shorter limits per extra hour). Day rates decline from US$90 for one day to US$70 daily for five days (120 km daily limit). Set prices apply for provincial touring. They can usually be found outside the major hotels, notably the Hotels Inglaterra, Nacional, and Melía Cohiba.

Minivans: You can rent Mitsubishi minivans through **Panataxi,** tel. 33-2020; and through **Micar,** tel. 204-2444, which offers minibuses on a sliding scale (US$40 four hours, US$70 eight hours, US$90 10 hours), plus US$.85 per km for the first 50 km (US$.70 per km thereafter).

Peso Taxis

Peso-only taxis serve Cubans and although they were not supposed to give rides to foreigners, many did so, especially for a dollar gratuity. In spring 2002, however, the official word went out and police began to crack down. Nonetheless, many drivers will still risk huge fines to pick up foreigners for dollars in the absence of police—expect to be asked to slink down out of sight. Expect to pay about half the fare you'd pay in a turistaxi; you should negotiate the price. With luck, you'll be able to pay in pesos—you should change dollars for pesos beforehand.

Cubataxi, officially the Empresa Provincial de Taxi, has the cheapest taxis. It uses Ladas, the Russian-made Fiat described (by Martha Gellhorn) as "tough as a Land Rover, with iron-hard upholstery and, judging by sensation, no springs." They're painted black-and-yellow with a strange Hebrew-type logo on the sides. A light lit up above the cab signifies if the taxi is *libre* (free). The base fare is one peso for the first km, and 25 centavos per km thereafter (35 centavos at night). If you get lucky and are given a ride, you'll be charged in dollars; few drivers will use the meter but will ask you how much you want to pay, or will charge you about the same rate as Panataxi. You can't call for one, but must wave one down on the street—they're deprecatingly called *los incapturables*—the uncatchables—by Cubans.

The workhorses of the taxi system for Cubans are the privately-owned *colectivos* or *coches* (shared cabs that pick up anyone who flags them down, often until they're packed to the gills), sometimes called *botes* (boats) or simply *máquinas* (machines). They run along fixed routes, much like buses, and charge 10 or 50 pesos for a ride anywhere along the route. Most are old Yankee jalopies. Look for a *Pasaje* ("passenger") sign in the window, or even a hand-written "Taxi" sign. Even if it doesn't have markings, follow the local example—wave down any large Yankee behemoth coming your way.

The south side of Parque de la Fraternidad and Paseo, opposite the Capitolio, is their preferred starting point for set routes throughout the city.

Reader Bridget Murphy offers this advice: "To avoid getting scolded [by the *chofer*], 'No tire la puerta.'" Don't slam the door!

"Gypsy" Cabs

Illegal "gypsy" cabs driven by freelance chauffeurs are usually beat-up Ladas or American jalopies.

TRANSPORTATION

You'll find freelance driver-guides outside the largest tourist hotels and outside discos late at night. Educate yourself about *turistaxi* fares to your destination beforehand, as many drivers attempt to gouge you and you may end up paying more than you would in a tourist taxi. Beware scams.

Jineteros work on commission and will approach you and whisper under their breath, "Hey, friend—taxi?"

Ciclotaxis

Hundreds of homespun tricycle taxis with shade canopies ply the streets of Habana Vieja and Vedado. They offer a cheap (albeit bumpy) way of sightseeing and getting around if you're in no hurry. You can go the full length of the Malecón, from Habana Vieja to Vedado, for US$3 or so—not much less than a taxi ride, but would *you* want to pedal two passengers in the sweltering heat? You can hire them by the hour for about US$10.

Some *ciclotaxis* are only licensed to take Cubans (who pay pesos). The owners are happy to take you—you've got dollars!—but may take circuitous routes to avoid police.

Cocotaxis

Toys R Us doesn't yet have an outlet in Cuba, but you'd never know it. These bright yellow motorized tricycles housed in a bright yellow fiberglass hemisphere look like scooped-out Easter eggs on wheels, or something out of a children's picture book. You'll find them outside major hotels and cruising the tourists zones. They're irresistibly cute for an open-air ride . . . except when it's raining! They charge about 20 percent less than tourist taxis. It's illegal for Cubans to take one.

Calezas

Horsedrawn *calezas* (open-air coaches) offer a popular way of exploring the Malecón and Old Havana, although the buggies are barred from entering the pedestrian-only quarter. They're operated by **San Cristóbal Travel,** Calles Oficios #110 e/ Lamparilla y Amargura, tel. 860-9585. Their official starting point is the junction of Empedrado and Tacón, but you can hail them wherever you see them. Others can be hailed outside the Hotel Inglaterra, on Parque Central. Expect to pay US$3 per person per hour in low season, US$5 in high season (Oct.–April).

© CHRISTOPHER P. BAKER

cocotaxi

BY RENTAL CAR

I recommend renting a car only if you anticipate exploring the suburbs, are staying in Miramar, or if you intend touring beyond Havana. In Havana, there are no traffic jams—Havana is probably the only Latin American city without rush-hour traffic. Traffic signage is very good. And most of the traffic lights work—and are even obeyed. However, Havana's streets are badly deteriorated.

A four-lane freeway—the **Autopista Circular** (route Calle 100 or *Circunvalación*)—encircles southern and eastern Havana, linking the arterial highways. Be careful! It has treacherous potholes, mainly at the equally dangerous intersections.

Traffic Regulations

To drive in Cuba, you must be 21 years or older and hold either an International Drivers' License (IDL) or a valid national driver's license. You must also have at least one year's driving experience. Traffic drives on the right, as in the United States. The speed limit is 100 kph (62 mph) on freeways, 90 kph (56 mph) on highways, 60 kph (37 mph) on rural roads, 50 kph (31 mph) on urban roads, and 40 kph (25 mph) in children's zones. Speed limits are vigorously enforced.

The ubiquitous, over-zealous traffic police (*tránsitos*) like to pull innocent drivers over for the slightest reason and issue *multas* (fines) on a whim. If you receive a traffic fine, it will be deducted from the deposit for your rental (there's a space for fines provided on the rental-car papers). The *tráfico* cannot levy a fine on the spot. Occasionally, however, Cuban police attempt to extract a subtle bribe. If you suspect any such irregularity, ask for the policeman's name and where you can fight the ticket—this usually results in you being waved on your way.

Rental Companies

You can't book Avis or Hertz in Cuba and must make do with the badly managed Cuban car rental agencies. All tourist hotels have a car rental bureau on-site, and there are plenty more throughout the city. Demand sometimes exceeds supply, so you may need to hunt around, particularly for the smaller models or a 4WD jeep. Expect all kinds of promises: a car will be ready in one hour, or we'll have a car for you this afternoon. Yeah . . . and the moon is made of cheese! In high season it's best to make a reservation before arriving in Cuba, which can only be done within 15 days or arrival, and is no guarantee that your reservation will be honored. You can rent a car at the airport upon arrival. If you're tired or jetlagged, this is not a good idea: relax for a day or two, then rent your car.

Expect to pay about US$45–125 per day plus insurance, depending on the size of the vehicle. Rates vary between agencies. The companies accept payment by credit cards (except those issued by U.S. banks; see Rex Limousines in the Rental Companies section later in this chapter for an exception), as well as in cash and traveler's checks. You will normally be required to pay a deposit of US$200–500.

Don't accept a car without thoroughly inspecting it, including a test drive. Insist on this. Most Cuban car rental agencies fail to budget for adequate maintenance and let their cars go to ruin quickly—often dangerously so!

Havanautos, tel. 203-9658 fax 204-0648, reshautos@cimex.com.cu, www.havanautos.cu, offers a range of Japanese cars in all categories, from a small Daewoo Tico (US$55 per day with unlimited mileage; less for seven days or more, on a sliding scale) to a five-passenger Nissan Sentra for US$80 daily, a Suzuki Vitara jeep for US$65 daily, and a Hyundai Trajet minivan for US$125 daily.

Micar, tel. 204-2444, fax 33-6476, micar @columbus.cu, rents five models of Fiats.

Panautos, tel. 55-3256, fax 55-5657, pan autos@transnet.cu, rents a broad range of makes, from a VW Polo to E-series Mercedes-Benz.

Rex Limousine Service, Avenida de Rancho Boyeros y Calzada de Bejucal, Plaza de la Revolución, tel. 33-9160, fax 33-9159; and Línea y Malecón, Vedado, tel. 33-7788, fax 33-7789, reservas@rex.transnet.cu, rents Audis and Volvo sedans, plus the Audi TT sports car. Rates at last visit started at US$110 per day for an Audi A4, plus US$20 insurance; and US$150 for a Volvo plus insurance (US$25 daily). It also has chauffeured Volvo limousines (hourly rentals are available). The company is a Cuba-Danish joint venture and cars are better maintained and the service more trustworthy than any of the other companies. *U.S. travelers can pay using a MasterCard issued by U.S. institutions . . . a major plus!*

Other car rental agencies include **Cubacar,** Avenida 5ta y 84, Miramar, tel. 204-2104, fax 33-0760; **Transtur,** Calle 19 #210, e/ J y K, Vedado, tel. 55-3252, www.transtur.cu, and Paseo, esq. 3ra Calle, Vedado, tel. 66-2164; and **Vía Rent-a-Car,** Avenida del Puerto #102, e/ Obrapía y Justíz, tel. 260-4455, 207-1710, or 66-6777, fax 33-2780, rentvia@teleda.get.cma.cu, www.gaviota-grupo.com.

Insurance

If you rent a car you will be responsible for any damage or theft. Hence you should purchase insurance offered by the rental agency. You have two choices. Option A (US$10–15 daily depending on vehicle; with a deductible of US$200–500 or so) covers accidents, but not theft. Option B (US$15–20) offers fully comprehensive coverage, except for the radio and spare tire. Inspect your car thoroughly for damage and marks before setting off; otherwise, you may be charged for the slightest dent when you return. On the diagram you'll be given to sign, note even the most innocuous marks. Don't forget the inside, as well as the radio antenna. Don't assume the car rental agency has taken care of tire pressures or fluids. Check them yourself before you set off.

If you have your own vehicle, the state-run organization **ESEN,** Calle 18, e/ 5ra y 7ma, Miramar, Havana, tel. 832-2508 or 832-5510, insures automobiles and has special packages for foreigners. It offers a choice of all risks, including theft, roll-overs, "catastrophes," and "partial theft."

Gasoline

Gasoline *(petról)* and diesel *(gasolina)* are sold at **Cupet** and **Oro Negro** stations *(servicentros),* with several dozen outlets throughout Havana; some are open 24 hours. There are no self-service stations. "Regular" and "Superior" *(especial)* grades are available, but not unleaded. Some gas attendants may insist that as a tourist you are

permitted to buy only *especial,* but I've bought *regular* without any problems. Gasoline costs US$.90 per liter—about US$3.40 a gallon. Payment is in U.S. dollars only.

Local gas stations *(bombas)* charge in pesos and serve *regular* only to the hoi polloi, who need special vouchers to buy.

It's wise to not let your gas tank get below half-full unless you'll soon be returning the car, especially since occasional electrical blackouts shut the pumps down. If you run out of gas, there's sure to be someone willing to sell from private stock, but be forewarned that it may be watered down.

Scams

Most car agencies pull scams as a matter of course. Swindles include renting cars with partially filled gas tanks, attempts to charge for damage you didn't cause, "not returning the car on time," or failing to service the car—this scam is often used if the odometer passes a significant mileage, such as 10,000 km, during your journey. The government itself is involved: rental agencies charge upfront for a full tank of gas when you sign on for the car, and then require you to return the car with an empty tank (no refunds are given). Thus the agency pockets the gas that's left in the tank.

Parking

A capital city without parking meters? Imagine! Parking meters were detested during the Batista era, mostly because they were a source of *botellas* (skimming) for corrupt officials. After the Revolution, *habaneros* rampaged through the city smashing the meters.

Finding parking is rarely a problem, except in Habana Vieja. No-parking zones are well marked. Avoid these like the plague, especially if it's an officials-only zone, in which case a policeman will usually be on hand to dispense a *multa* (fine) and have you towed. You can pay your parking ticket through your car rental agency—and be sure to do so before leaving the country.

Theft is a serious problem. As such, follow the local example and park in *parqueos,* designated parking lots with a *custodio* to guard against thieves 24 hours. Expect to pay about US$2 overnight. *Always* use a car park with a *custodio,* or hire someone to guard your car.

In central Vedado, the Hotel Habana Libre Tryp has an underground car park (US$.80 for one hour, US$.50 each additional hour; US$4 maximum for 24 hours).

Accidents and Breakdowns

One of the most common sights in Cuba is to see a car stalled in the road with females sitting stoically to the side while the males toil to jury-rig a repair. If your car breaks down, there will be no shortage of Cubans willing to offer advice and consummate fix-it skills. If the problem is minor, fine. However, rental car agencies usually have a clause to protect against likely damage to the car from unwarranted repairs. For major problems, call the rental agency; it will arrange a tow or send a mechanic.

You should also call the agency in the event of an accident. After an accident, *never* move the vehicles until the police arrive. Get the names, license plate numbers, and *cédulas* (legal identification numbers) of any witnesses. Make a sketch of the accident. Then call the **Tránsitos** (transit police), tel. 882-0116. In case of injury, call for an **Ambulance** tel. 114.

Do *not* offer statements to anyone other than the police. Try not to leave the accident scene, or at least keep an eye on your car; the other party may tamper with the evidence. And don't let honking traffic pressure you into moving the cars.

The *tráficos* (or *tránsitos*) traffic police usually treat foreigners with a certain disdain and, as you have deep pockets, the blame might be assigned to you in the event that in cannot be proved otherwise. Don't expect much help from locals. Cubans are loath to involve themselves where the police are concerned. Show the police your license and car rental documents, but make sure you get them back. If you suspect the other driver has been drinking, ask the policeman to administer a Breathalyzer test—an *alcolemia.* If someone is seriously injured or killed and you are blamed, you should immediately contact your embassy

for legal assistance. **Asistur,** Prado #212, between Trocadero and Colón, in Habana Vieja, tel. 33-8527 or 33-8920, fax 33-8087, asisten@asisten.get.cma.net, can also offer legal and other assistance.

Your car rental company can arrange repairs. However, if you need emergency treatment, **Oro Negro,** 5ta Avenida, esq. 120, Miramar, tel. 208-6149; Calle 2, esq. 7ma, Miramar, tel. 204-5760; and Avenida 13, esq. 84, Playa, tel. 204-1938, has *servicentros* open Monday–Saturday 8 A.M.–7 P.M.

You can arrange a tow through **Agencia Peugeot,** tel. 57-7533 or 879-3854, which charges US$.75 per km outbound and US$1 per km for the tow.

BY SCOOTER

Renta de Motos, 3ra Avenida, e/ 28 y 30, Miramar, tel. 204-5491, rents scooters for US$10 one hour, US$15 three hours, or US$24 per day (US$21 per day for rentals of 3–10 days). It does not offer insurance. Open 9 A.M.–9 P.M.

If you're staying in Cuba any length of time, consider buying a scooter (US$1,300 to US$2,500) from **Agencia Vedado,** Calle 23 #753, e/ B y C, Vedado, tel. 33-3994, fax 33-3994, ventas23@23c.automotriz.cubalse.cu.

BY BICYCLE

Almost one million bicyclists wheel through the streets of the Cuban capital—so why not you? Bicycling offers a chance to explore the city alongside the Cubans themselves, although the roads are a bit dodgy, with bullying trucks and buses pumping out fumes, plus potholes and other obstacles to contend with. An average of two cyclists every three days are killed in traffic accidents in Havana, so a helmet is a wise investment.

Bring your own bike if you plan on spending any time here; for the city, you'll need a mountain bike or hybrid. Airlines generally allow bicycles to be checked free of charge (properly packaged) with one piece of luggage. Otherwise, a small charge may apply.

Scores of Cubans now make a living repairing

THE BICYCLE REVOLUTION

I n 1991, when the first shipment of Flying Pigeon bicycles arrived from China, there were only an estimated 30,000 bicycles in Havana, a city of two million people. The visitor arriving in Havana today could be forgiven for imagining he or she had arrived in Ho Chi Minh City. Bicycles are everywhere, outnumbering cars, trucks, and buses 20 to 1. The story is the same across the island.

Cynics have dubbed Cuba's wholesale switch to bicycles since the collapse of the Soviet bloc as a socialist failing, a symbol of the nation's backwardness. Others acclaim it an astounding achievement, a two-wheel triumph over an overnight loss of gasoline and adversity. *Granma,* the Cuban newspaper, christened it the "bicycle revolution."

American cars had flooded the island for half a century. Then came the U.S. trade embargo. The 1960s saw the arrival of the first sober-looking Lada and Moskovitch sedans, imported in the ensuing decades by the tens of thousands from the Soviet Union, along with Hungarian and Czech buses, which provided an efficient transport network. The Eastern bloc buses were notorious for their lack of comfort, as were the stunted Girón buses that Cuba began producing in 1967. But they carried millions of Cubans for years despite their defects, most notably their low gas mileage.

Professor Maurice Halperin, who taught at the University of Havana, does not "recall seeing a single adult Cuban on a bicycle in Havana during the entire period of my residence in the city, from 1962 to 1968."

Goodbye to Gas

The collapse of the Soviet Union severed the nation's gasoline pipeline. Transportation virtually ground to a halt, along with the rest of the Cuban economy.

In November 1990, the Cuban government launched sweeping energy-saving measures

that called for a "widespread substitution of oxen for farm machinery and hundreds of thousands of bicycles for gasoline-consuming vehicles." Cuba's program of massive importation, domestic production, and mass distribution was launched as a "militant and defensive campaign," embodied on May 1, 1991, when the armed forces appeared on bicycles in the May Day parade.

The government contracted with China to purchase 1.2 million bicycles, and by the end of 1991, 530,000 single-gear Chinese bicycles were in use on the streets of Havana.

Cuba: Bicycle Capital of the Americas

Overnight, Cuba transformed itself into the bicycle capital of the Americas. "The comprehensiveness and speed of implementation of this program," said a 1994 World Bank report, "is unprecedented in the history of transportation." The report noted that about two million bicycles were in use islandwide.

"Today, we can say that the bicycle is as much a part of the Cuban scenario as the palm tree," says Narciso Hernández, director of Empresa Claudio Arugelles Fábrica de Bicicletas in Havana. Hernández's factory is one of five established in 1991 by the Cuban government to supplement the Chinese imports. The government's goal was to produce half a million domestic two-wheelers within five years. Each of the factories produces a different model. Cuba imports parts such as small bolts, chains, spindles, and brakes, but makes the frames, forks, and handlebars.

The bicycles are disbursed through MINCIN (Ministerio de Comercial Interior), which parcels them out to schools, factories, and workers' associations. Others are sold at special stores. Lucky recipients can purchase their bicycles outright or pay for them in monthly installments. Workers pay 125 pesos—equivalent to about half the average monthly salary—while students pay 65 pesos. Cuba still can't produce enough bicycles to satisfy the demand, and a thriving black market has arisen.

The Chinese bicycles were cumbersome, hard-to-pump beasts—true antediluvian pachyderms with only one gear. Worse, they weighed 48 pounds. The Cubans redesigned the chunky models with smaller frames, thereby lopping off 15 pounds. Other Cuban innovations include a tricycle for disabled people, and a *"bicibus,"* a Dr. Seuss-worthy contraption made of two bicycles with rows of seats—and pedals—for 12 people in between. "One day soon, Cuba hopes to begin exporting bikes," comments Hernández. Not likely any time soon. The new bikes are made of poor quality parts and, like more modern Chinese bicycles sold at dollars stores throughout Havana, are basically junk . . . "after two days, the screws are already falling off," says Linda Nauman, director of **Bicycles Crossing Borders,** 416/364-7295 or 416/934-9243, a Canadian cooperative that sends new and used bikes to Cuba. The organization's bikes are sold to Cubans for US$30–55, one-third of what they would cost on the black market. Bicycles Crossing Borders also trains Cuban men and women to be mechanics and has set up a bike repair workshop in Habana Vieja.

Cubans manage to coax great speed from their sturdy steeds. Young men zigzag through the streets, disdainful of all other traffic, while old men and women pedal painstakingly down the middle of the road with leisurely sovereignty, like holy cattle. During the early phase of the bicycle revolution, hospital emergency rooms were flooded with victims. Most Cubans had never ridden bicycles before. They teetered en masse through the potholed streets, often with passengers, even whole families, hanging onto jury-rigged seats and rear-hub extenders. Due to the paucity of cars, cyclists rode the wrong way down major boulevards, which they crisscrossed at will. Few *bicis* had rear reflectors, and the brakes on the Chinese-made models barely worked. Handlebar warning bells chirp incessantly.

Cuban planners like Gina Rey, of the Group for the Integral Development of the Capital, were challenged to reorganize Havana's transportation network to prevent turmoil on the streets. The plan called for many colonial streets in Habana Vieja to be closed to motorized traffic. Bicycle lanes were created. The city government initiated classes in bicycle safety. Bicycle parking lots were created throughout the city. Ferry boats threading their way across Havana harbor were equipped for bicycles. And special buses (*Ciclobuses*) were detailed to carry cyclists through the tunnel beneath the bay.

"We've entered the bicycle era," Castro has noted. "But after this Special Period disappears we mustn't abandon this wonderful custom." Bicycles would solve many of the country's energy quandaries—and pollution and health problems, too. "With bicycles, we will improve the quality of life in our society," Castro claims. Anyone who has seen Hungarian buses coughing fitfully through the streets of Cuba, belching thick black clouds, would agree.

poncheras (punctures) and mechanical problems. Nonetheless, bring spares.

Also see the Bicycling section in the Entertainment and Recreation chapter.

Renting Bicycles

You can rent 21-speed hybrid Peugeot and Norco bicycles from **Cubalinda,** Edificio Someillán, piso 27, Calle O # 2 e/ Línea y 17, Vedado, tel. 55-3980 or 88-51538, mari@cubalinda.com, which charges US$11 per day (less for longer periods, declining to US$7 per day for 15-day rentals). A US$250 deposit is required.

BY FERRY

Tiny ferries (standing room only—no seats) bob across the harbor between the Havana waterfront and Regla (on the east side of the bay) and Casablanca (on the north side of the bay). The ferries leave on a constant yet irregular basis, 24 hours, from a wharf called Muelle Luz on Avenida San Pedro at the foot of Calle Santa Clara in Havana Vieja, tel. 97-7473 (in Regla); 10 centavos; five minutes.

ORGANIZED EXCURSIONS

City Tours

Hotel tour bureaus offer guided city tours, usually aboard a/c buses. **Tours & Travel,** Calle 23, esq. M, Vedado, tel. 66-2077 or 66-4082, fax 66-4084, and Avenida 1ra e/ Calles 0 y 2, Miramar, tel. 204-0993, for example, offers a city tour, plus excursions to places like Finca Vigía, and ExpoCuba and Jardín Botánico. However, most tours, including guided walking tours, provide only a cursory and poorly informed experience, often with an obligatory anti-imperialist jibe or two.

Agencia San Cristóbal, Calles Oficios #110 e/ Lamparilla y Amargura, tel. 860-9585, fax 860-9586, reservas@sancrist.get.tur.cu, offers guided walking tours of Habana Vieja. Open Mon.–Sat. 8:30 A.M.–6 P.M., Sun. 8:30 A.M.–4 P.M. **Infotur,** Calle Obispo #358, esq. San Ignacio, Habana Vieja, tel. 33-3333, offers four-hour guided walking tours (US$15).

Gaviotatours, tel. 204-7963, fax 204-9470, gavitour@gavitur.gav.cma.cu; or Avenida del Puerto, Edificio la Marina, Habana Vieja, tel.

Muelle Luz ferry terminal

66-9668, fax 33-9061, dtor_av@gaviota.gav .tur.cu, offers tours over Havana by Soviet-made ex-military helicopters (US$39).

Private Guides

Hotel tour bureaus and tour agencies can arrange personal guided tours. They're bilingual and usually versed in history, albeit with a heavily politicized twist.

Cubatur, Calle 23, esq. L, Vedado, tel. 33-4120, 55-4736 or 33-4135, fax 33-3142, offers guides for US$25 per day (up to 12 hours) in Havana, US$30 (US$200 weekly) outside Havana. Tours & Travel, Calle 23, esq. M, Vedado, tel. 66-2077 or 66-4082, fax 66-4084, and Avenida 1ra e/ Calles 0 y 2, Miramar, tel. 204-0993, and Agencia San Cristóbal, Calles Oficios #110 e/ Lamparilla y Amargura, tel. 860-9585, fax 860-9586, reservas@sancrist.get.tur.cu, also arrange guides.

Jineteros (hustlers) will offer to be your guide. Although great for showing you the off-beat scene that most tourists miss, they're usually pretty useless as sightseeing guides.

English-speaking professional tour guide José "Pepe" Alvarez, Lazada Norte I #182, Santa Catalina, Havana, tel. 41-1209, fax 33-3921, americuba@yahoo.com, is recommended for walking and other tours. He charges from US$25 per day for one person to US$15 per person for larger groups.

Long-term Cuba resident and U.S. citizen Olivia King Canter, Calle 21 #5015, e/ 50 y 52 Miramar, tel. 204-0414, oliviakingcanter@ yahoo.com, is a useful and helpful resource. She welcomes calls and will be happy to assist you.

Harbor Cruises

The *Havana Princess* sails from the small wharf by the Fuente de Neptuno (Neptune Fountain), Avenida Carlos M. de Céspedes, at the foot of Empedrado; the two-hour cruises depart at 7 P.M., with disco to follow until 5 A.M. (Mon.–Thurs. US$10, Fri.–Sat. US$15). Alas, no Cubans are allowed on board . . . ostensibly so that the boat isn't hijacked.

Cubanacán, 5ta Avenida 7 #248, tel. 204-6848, fax 204-5280, comercial@prto.mh .cyt.cu, offers "seafaris" from Marina Hemingway, including a coastal tour, and a snorkeling tour that includes lunch in the marina. Also see Marina Puertosol Tarará, in the Playas del Este section of the Exploring Suburban Havana chapter.

Exploring Beyond Havana

Moon Handbooks Cuba (Avalon Travel Publishing, 2003) offers complete information for exploring the island.

BY AIR

Most of Havana Province's main cities have an airport, and virtually every major tourism destination is within a two-hour drive of an airport. Domestic flights depart Terminal 1 at José Martí International Airport.

Cuba's poorly managed, state-owned national airlines have a monopoly, alas. Cubana, Calle Infanta, esq. Humbolt, Havana, tel. 55-1024 or 55-1036, the largest carrier, has service between all the major airports. Its fares are 25 percent cheaper if booked in conjunction with an international Cubana flight. Its safety record is appalling, however. The domestic ticket office (open Mon.–Fri. 8:15 A.M.–4 P.M., Sat. 8 A.M.–1 P.M.) gets horrendously crowded. Far better is to book through Cubana's Sol y Son Travel Agency, Calle 23 #64, e/ Infanta y O, tel. 33-3162 or 33-3647, fax 33-5150, gerencia@solyson.avia net.cu (open Mon.–Fri. 8:30 A.M.–7 P.M. and Sat. 8:30 A.M.–noon).

Aero Caribbean, Calle 23 #64, Vedado, tel. 33-5636 or 897-7524, fax 33-5016, aero-carvpcre@iacc3.get.cma.net, operates charter flights from Havana to Cayo Coco, Holguín, Santiago, Trinidad, and Varadero. AeroTaxi, Calle 27 #102, e/ M y N, Vedado, Havana, tel. 832-4460 or 33-4064, utilizes 12-passenger biplanes, mostly for excursion flights. Aero

Gaviota, Avenida 47 #2814 e/ 28 y 34, Reparto Kohly, tel. 203-0668, fax 204-2621, offers charter flights in 30-passenger Yak-40s and 38-passenger Antonov-26s, as well as "executive" service in eight-seat helicopters. Flights depart from **Aeropuerto Baracoa** airstrip on the Autopista Habana-Mariel, about two miles west of Havana's Marina Hemingway in Santa Fe.

Reservations: Flights are frequently fully booked, especially in the August–December peak season, when Cubans take their holidays. The most solidly booked routes are Havana–Santiago, Havana–Trinidad, Santa Lucía–Trinidad, and Varadero–Cayo Largo. Fortunately, foreigners with dollars are usually given priority on waiting lists. Reservations usually must be paid in advance and are normally nonrefundable. Forego telephone reservations: make your booking in person at the airline office or through one of the major tour agencies.

Arrive on time for check-in, otherwise your seat will likely be given away. If that happens, don't expect a refund, and you may not even be able to get a seat on the next plane out. Delays, flight cancellations, and schedule changes are common—you'll never complain about U.S. or European airlines again. And don't expect luxury—be happy if you get a Spam-and-cheese sandwich. More likely, since flights are short, you'll receive a boiled sweet.

BY BUS
Tourist Buses
Víazul, Avenida 26, esq. Zoológico, Nuevo Vedado, tel. 881-1413, fax 66-6092, viazul@transnet.cu, www.viazul.cu, operates bus services for foreigners to key places on the tourist circuit using modern a/c Volvo and Mercedes buses. After departing Terminal Víazul (city bus no. 27

VÍAZUL BUS SCHEDULE

Havana–Varadero . . . . .8 A.M., 8:30 A.M., and 4 P.M. (2 hr. 45 min.) . . . . . . US$10
Varadero–Havana . . . . .8 A.M., 4 P.M., and 6 P.M.
   Stops are made at Matanzas (US$7) and
   Aeropuerto de Varadero (US$12, by request)

Havana–Viñales . . . . .9 A.M. (3 hr. 15 min.) . . . . US$12
Viñales–Havana . . . . .1:30 P.M.
   A stop is made in Pinar del Río (US$11)

Havana–Trinidad . . . . .8:15 A.M. and 1 P.M. (5 hr. 35 min.) . . . . US$25
Trinidad–Havana . . . . .8 A.M. and 3 P.M.
   Stops are made at Entronque de Jagüey (US$12),
   Aguada de Pasajeros (US$13), Yaguarama (US$14),
   Rodas (US$15), and Cienfuegos (US$20).

Havana–Santiago . . . . .3 P.M. and 8 P.M. (13 hr. 50 min.) . . . . US$51
Santiago–Havana . . . . .5:30 P.M.
   Stops are made at Entronque de Jagüey (US$12),
   Santa Clara (US$18), Sancti Spíritus (US$23),
   Ciego de Ávila (US$27), Camagüey (US$33),
   Las Tunas (US$39), Holguín (US$44), and Bayamo (US$44).

Havana–Cayo Coco . . . . . . .7:45 A.M. (11 hr. 30 min.), Dec.–April . . . . US$44
Cayo Coco–Havana . . . . . . .7:30 A.M.

ASTRO BUS SERVICE FROM HAVANA

Destination	Regular Fare	*Especial* Fare
Baracoa	US$43.50	US$53
Bayamo	US$30	US$36
Camagüey	US$22.50	US$27
Cardenas	US$6	US$7
Cayo Coco	US$44	
Ciego de Ávila	US$18.50	US$22.50
Cienfuegos	US$14	US$17
Guantánamo	US$38	US$46
Holguín	US$30	US$36
Las Tunas	US$27	US$33
Manzanillo	US$32.50	US$39
Matanzas	US$4	US$5
Morón	US$19.50	US$24
Pinar del Río	US$7	US$8
Playa Girón	US$10.50	US$13
Remedios	US$14	US$17
Sancti Spíritus	US$15.50	US$19
Santa Clara	US$12	US$15
Santiago de Cuba	US$35	US$42
Trinidad	US$17	US$21
Varadero	US$5.50	US$6
Viñales	US$8	US$10

Destination	Depart	Return
Cayo Coco	7:45 A.M.	7:30 A.M.

via Jagüey Grande, Cienfuegos, Trinidad, Sancti Spíritus, Jatibónico, Ciego de Ávila, Morón

Santiago de Cuba	8:15 A.M.	7 P.M.

via Jagüey Grande, Santa Clara, Sancti Spíritus, Ciego de Ávila, Las Tunas, Bayamo, Holguín

Trinidad	8:15 A.M. and 1 A.M.	8 A.M. and 3 P.M.

via Jagüey Grande and Cienfuegos

Varadero	8 A.M., 8:30 A.M., and 4 P.M.	8 A.M., 4 P.M., and 6 P.M.

Viñales	9 A.M.	1:30 P.M.

via Pinar del Río

connects the Víazul terminal to Vedado and Centro Habana), buses make a 10-minute stop at the public bus terminal, where you can also buy a ticket just prior to the bus's arrival. Terminal Víazul has a café and a/c waiting room, and free luggage storage. Children travel at half price. See the Víazul Bus Schedule chart for details.

Havanatur, Calle 6 #117, e/ 1ra y 3ra, Miramar, Havana, tel. 204-2406 or 204-0908, **Veracuba,** Calle 162 #317, esq. 3ra, Playa, tel. 33-0600, fax 33-6619, vaccomer1@cbcan.cyt.cu, and other Cuban tour agencies offer transfer seats on tour buses serving Varadero, Trinidad, and other key destinations.

The tour buses that park in Plazuela de la Maestranza, at Calle Cuba and Peña Pobre, in Habana Vieja, reportedly will take you to Varadero and possibly other destinations. Ask the drivers, who pocket the fare (expect to pay US$10–20 to Varadero).

Take a sweater; tourist buses are overly air-conditioned.

Public Buses

Public buses serve almost every nook and cranny of the island. Virtually the entire population relies on the bus system for travel within and between cities, although they sometimes must wait *weeks* to get a seat. Demand so exceeds supply that there is often a waiting list in excess of one month for the most popular long-distance routes. Hence, Cuban bus stations have been called "citadels of desperation." Reservations are essential; do *not* expect to show up at the station and simply board a bus.

Astro (Empresa Ómnibuses Nacionales), tel. 870-6155, operates all interprovincial services. Buses to destinations throughout the country leave from the **Terminal de Ómnibuses Nacionales** (Terminal de Ómnibuses Interprovinciales), Avenida Independencia #101, esq. Calle 19 de Mayo, tel. 879-2456 or 879-3769, two blocks north of Plaza de la Revolución. The terminal is served by local bus no. 47 from the Prado (at Calle Ánimas) in Habana Vieja; by bus no. 265 from the east side of Parque Central; and by buses no. 67 and 84 from La Rampa in Vedado. Facilities include a post office and snack

bars, and an information booth, tel. 870-9401 or 879-2456, downstairs. Buses to towns throughout Habana province depart from Calle Apodaca #53, e/ Agramonte y Avenida de Bélgica. You pay in pesos, but expect very long lines.

There are two classes of buses for long-distance travel: a/c *especiales* are faster, air-conditioned, and more comfortable than *regulares*. Fortunately, upscale Mercedes and Volvo buses are gradually being added to the service, but on many routes you may find yourself on a noisy, rickety old Hungarian-made bus with ass-numbing seats.

For Dollars: Foreigners pay in dollars—*especial* fares are about 20 percent less than Víazul—and receive preferential seating. The ticket office (*venta de boletines US$*), tel. 870-3397, is to the right of the entrance and has an air-conditioned lounge with TV (open daily 7 A.M.–9 P.M.). The ticket agent will most likely not sell you a ticket until your specific bus departure is confirmed, as buses are frequently delayed or canceled. Only one-way tickets are available; you'll need to book any return trip once you arrive in your destination. On the day of travel, arrive at the terminal at least one hour ahead of departure, otherwise your seat may be issued to people on the waiting list.

For Pesos: Foreigners who try to travel like a Cuban and pay dollars are usually shooed away to the dollars-only counter. If you want to try the peso route, make your reservation as early as possible, either at the bus terminal, tel. 870-0939, or at the **Agencia Reservaciones de Pasaje,** Factor y Tulipán, Nuevo Vedado, tel. 881-5931 or 55-5537. Your name will be scrawled on a decrepit pile of parchment and added to the scores of names ahead of you. Ask to see the sheets for the destination you want so that you can gauge how many days' delay is likely.

If you don't have a reservation or miss your departure, you can try getting on the standby list (*lista de espera*) at **Terminal La Coubre,** tel. 872-3726, on Avenida del Puerto at the foot of Avenida de Bélgica (Egido) in southwest Habana Vieja. Interprovincial buses that have unfilled seats call in here after departing the Terminal de Ómnibus Nacionales to pick up folks on the standby list. The *lista de espera* service is at the western end of the terminal. Expect a Kafkaesque experience. *Lista de espera,* a Cuban movie based on Arturo Arango's short story of that name by Carlos Tabío, mocks the anguishing waiting list as his protagonists wait for a bus to Manzanillo. So long is the wait that people fall in and out of friendships, make love, marry, and die.

Baggage: Passengers are granted a 22 kg baggage limit plus one piece of hand luggage, although it seems not to be strictly enforced. Some buses have room for storage below; others do not, in which case luggage space will be limited to overhead racks. *Travel light!*

Miscellaneous: Conditions can be very cramped and—if the air-conditioning isn't working—very hot; the back tends to get the hottest (and often smelliest—from exhaust fumes). Take water, but don't drink too much coffee or other liquids—toilet stops can be few and far between. Bring snacks. Long-distance buses make food stops, but often there isn't sufficient food for everyone. Likewise, Cubans will rush to the bathroom, where a long line may develop.

BY TRAIN

One main rail axis spans the country connecting all the major cities, with major ports and secondary cities linked by branch lines. Service has improved markedly in recent years, aided in 2001 when Cuba took delivery of 44 stainless steel, air-conditioned former Trans-Europe-Express coaches to be used for long-distance service from Havana. The equipment included dining cars . . . which Cuba had not had in years. Alas, no one has thought to clean them; the interiors are filthy!

Departure times change often. The schedule is in no way firm, so double-check days and times given in this book. Also check the arrival time at your destination carefully and plan accordingly, as many trains arrive (and depart) in the wee hours of the morning. Few trains run on time.

Bicycles are allowed on most trains. You usually pay (in pesos) at the end of the journey.

Railway Stations

Estación Central de Ferrocarril: The most important station is the Central Railway Station,

Avenida de Bélgica (Egido), esq. Arsenal, Habana Vieja, tel. 861-4259 or 861-3047. Trains depart here for most major cities, including Pinar del Río, Cienfuegos, Santa Clara, Sancti Spíritus, Ciego de Ávila, Camagüey, Las Tunas, Santiago and Guantánamo, and Bayamo and Manzanillo.

Two services operate between Havana and Santiago de Cuba. The fast *especial* (train #01) takes 12.5 hours for the 860 kilometer journey. It stops at Santa Clara and Camagüey en route but is not particularly good for sightseeing as most of the journey takes place at night. Take your pick of *clase primera* (first class) with comfy recliner seats, or *clase segunda* (second class), with smaller, non-reclining seats. Both classes have bone-chilling air-conditioning and TVs showing movies. The train has a poorly stocked *cafetería* wagon, plus *ferromoza* (rail hostess) service. Fares (first-class/second-class) were US$18/22 to Santa Clara, US$33/41 to Camagüey, and US$51.50/63 to Santiago de Cuba (fares includes a sandwich and drink).

Slower *regular* trains (colloquially called the *lechero,* or "milkman," because it makes frequent stops) also depart daily. Some *regular* services are *clase segunda* (second class) only and best suited to hardy travelers—the trains are typically dirty and overcrowded, with uncushioned wooden seats. *Clase primera* (first class) is marginally better, with padded seats, though still crowded and hardly comfortable. Take snacks and drinks.

The state agency **FerroCuba,** Calle Arsenal, e/ Cienfuegos y Apontes, tel. 861-4259, on the north side of the station, handles ticket sales and reservations for foreigners, who pay in dollars for a guaranteed seat (open daily 8 A.M.– 8 P.M.). Tickets can be purchased up to 30 minutes prior to departure, but you must purchase your ticket before 8 P.M. for a nighttime departure. You may be able to buy tickets in pesos in the main station, but you'll usually need to book days, or weeks, in advance.

Terminal La Coubre, tel. 862-1012, on Avenida del Puerto, 100 meters south of the main railway station, offers service to Matanzas, Morón, Cienfuegos, and Santiago de Cuba.

Estación Casablanca: An electric train—the famous **Hershey Train**—operates to Matanzas

A SUGAR OF A JOURNEY

Rail journeys hold a particular magic, none more so in Cuba than the Hershey Train, which runs lazily between Casablanca and Matanzas year-round, four times a day. This fascinating electric railway has its origin in a chocolate bar.

In its heyday, before the Revolution, the Hershey estates belonging to the Pennsylvania-based chocolate company occupied 69 square miles of lush cane fields around a modern sugar-factory town (now called Camilo Cienfuegos), with a baseball field, movie theater, and amusements, and a hotel and bungalows for rent next to the mill.

At its peak, the estate had 19 steam locomotives. Their sparks, however, constituted a serious fire hazard, so they were replaced with seven 60-ton electric locomotives built especially for the Her-

© CHRISTOPHER P. BAKER

from a harborfront station, tel. 862-4888, at Casablanca on the north side of Havana harbor. See the Special Topic "A Sugar of a Journey."

There is more information about other train stations in the Getting Around Havana section earlier in this chapter.

Tourist Trains

Transnico Train Tours, Lonja del Comercio, Piso 6, Plaza San Francisco de Asís, Habana Vieja, tel. 66-9954, fax 66-9908, trans@mail.info com.etecsa.cu, offers 7-day luxury train trips on the "Cuba & Caribe Express," departing Cristina station weekly and traveling as far as Santiago de Cuba, round-trip. In the UK, contact Rob Dick-

inson, 5, Ash Lane, Monmouth, NP5 4FJ, tel./fax (01600) 713405, steam@dial.pipex.com; in Belgium contact **Transnico,** Avenue Montjoie, 114-1180 Brussels, R.C. 579074, tel. 02/344-4690, fax 02/346-5665, www.transnico.com.

Trains Unlimited Tours, P.O. Box 1997, Portola, California 96122, 530/836-1745 or 800/359-4870, fax 530/836-1748, www.trainsun limitedtours.com, offers a 14-day "Cuban Rail Historian Tour."

BY TAXI

Most taxi companies offer chauffeured taxi excursions by car or minivan, usually limited to

shey-Cuban Railroad. Milton Hershey also introduced a three-car passenger train service between Havana and Matanzas every hour, stopping at Hershey. Alas, the diminutive vermilion MU-train locomotive that looked like it could have fallen from the pages of a story about Thomas, the little "live" engine, was replaced in 1998 with a spiffy fleet of more comfortable, antique Spanish cars.

The train departs the Estación de Casablanca, Carretera de los Cocos, tel. 862-4888, on the north side of Havana harbor, and stops at Guanabacoa and dozens of little way-stations en route to Matanzas. Two minutes before departure, the conductor gives a toot on the horn and a mad rush ensues. The train shudders and begins to thread its way along the narrow main street that parallels the waterfront of Casablanca. The rattle of the rails soon gathers rhythm, with the windows remaining wide open, providing plenty of breeze.

The train winds in and out among the palm-studded hills, speeds along the coast within sight of the Atlantic, then slips between palms, past broad swathes of sugarcane, and through the Yumurí Valley. Two hours into the journey, you'll arrive at a blue station still bearing the Hershey sign. You are now in the heart of the old Hershey sugar factory, where the train pauses sufficiently for you to get down and capture the scene for posterity. Bring some snacks to share with locals, who willingly share from their meager packages unfolded on laps.

After a mesmerizing four-hour journey, you finally arrive at the sky-blue Matanzas station. The train—which makes about 40 stops en route—departs Casablanca at 4:10 and 8:32 A.M. and 9 P.M., arriving Matanzas 3.5 hours later (the 8:32 A.M. departure is an express and takes only about 2.5 hours). Tickets cost US$2.80 to Matanzas and go on sale one hour in advance. Kids ride half-price. Passengers are assigned seat numbers. Ask for a window seat.

Two additional return journeys depart Havana's Estación La Coubre, Avenida de Bélgica, esq. Desamparados, tel. 862-1006, at 12:05 and 4:30 P.M., avoiding the need for boat travel to and from Casablanca. These are diesel-hauled to/from the electrified line; the route takes you through the dock area and associated freight yards, and the service is subject to considerable delay. The trains avoid Casablanca, but travel directly to Matanzas. Tickets cost $3 and must be bought from the Ferrotur ticket office, Calle Arsenal, esq. Cienfuegos, tel. 861-4259, on the north side of the main railway station, 400 yards north of La Coubre.

You can order a 60-minute VHS video, **Hershey Electric: Adios to the Brills,** from Canadian Caboose Press, Box 844, Skookumchuck, BC V0B 2EO, Canada (CAN/US$29.95).

places within a 150-mile radius of Havana. Alternately, they offer special long-distance and hourly rates. However, touring far from Havana by taxi can be inordinately expensive unless several people are sharing the cost. You're probably better off renting a car.

Typical round-trip prices are: to Varadero (US$180), Soroa (US$85); Bay of Pigs (Playa Girón, US$320), and Viñales (US$250). Hourly rates for a chauffeured taxi are on a sliding scale, from about US$15 the first hour (20-km limit) to US$80 for eight hours (125-km limit), typically with US$.70 per km for extra distance.

See the Getting Around Havana section earlier in this chapter for a list of taxi companies.

Far cheaper is **Cubataxi,** tel. 870-1326 or 879-0443, which offers service by Lada. Taxis depart from next to the bus station at Calle 19 de Mayo, esq. Avenida Independencia, in Plaza de la Revolución. Typical fares (at US$0.35 per kilometer) are Cienfuegos (US$90), Pinar del Río (US$55), Santa Clara (US$75), Trinidad (US$100), and Varadero (US$45).

Freelance Cabs

Don't mind the possibility of breaking down in the boonies? Many Cubans with classic cars from the heyday of Detroit treat their prized possessions as exotic cash cows—they rent them out (mostly illegally) for guided tours. Says Cristina

TRAIN SCHEDULES AND FARES

From Havana

No.	Origin Station	Destination	Depart	Arrive
13	Estación Central	Bayamo/Manzanillo	8:20 P.M.	10:10 A.M./11:35 A.M.
21	Terminal La Coubre	Cienfuegos	7:30 A.M.	5:50 P.M.
29	Terminal La Coubre	Cienfuegos	3:20 P.M.	8:02 P.M.
15	Estación Central	Holguín	9:30 P.M.	11:30 A.M.
27	Terminal La Coubre	Morón	1:40 P.M.	7:28 P.M.
03	Estación Central	Morón	5 P.M.	11:15 P.M.
905	Terminal La Coubre	Matanzas	12:05 P.M.	4:41 P.M.
907	Terminal La Coubre	Matanzas	4:03 P.M.	7:40 P.M.
23	Estación Central	Pinar del Río	10:35 P.M.	4:20 A.M.
17	Estación Central	Sancti Spíritus	00:15 A.M.	8 A.M.
19	Terminal La Coubre	Santiago	8:45 A.M.	8:35 P.M.
01	Estación Central	Santiago (*Especial*)	6:05 P.M.	6:25 A.M.
11	Estación Central	Santiago/Guantánamo	2:55 P.M.	4:05 A.M./6:05 A.M.

To Havana

No.	Origin Station	Destination	Depart	Arrive
29	Cienfuegos	Terminal La Coubre	5:50 A.M.	10:15 A.M.
22	Cienfuegos	Terminal La Coubre	7 A.M.	4:55 P.M.
12	Guantánamo/Santiago	Estación Central	3:55 P.M./9:15 P.M.	11:35 A.M.
16	Holguín	Estación Central	3:30 P.M.	5:40 A.M.
14	Manzanillo/Bayamo	Estación Central	3:50 P.M./4:35 P.M.	5:40 A.M.
902	Matanzas	Terminal La Coubre	8:30 A.M.	11:31 A.M.
904	Matanzas	Terminal La Coubre	12:30 P.M.	4:05 P.M.
04	Morón	Estación Central	6:15 A.M.	12:30 P.M.

García, "Twenty dollars buys gas enough for a decent spin. Seventy dollars gets you a day in a top-of-the-line Cadillac convertible with fins so big they block the rear-view mirror. Forget about renting from Hertz or Avis ever again."

Alas, in 2001 peso taxis were banned from taking foreigners under any conditions. Still, in a country desperate for dollars (and where everybody breaks the rules), there are still freelancers who'll take the risk of whopping fines . . . but expect to be asked to slink down out of sight in the back seat whenever you pass a policeman.

Negotiate your fare and agree on it *before* getting in. Make sure you know whether this is one-way or round-trip. It's possible to hire a car and driver for as little as US$30 for a full day, plus gasoline—a common courtesy is also to buy your driver his or her lunch—but much depends on the quality of the car.

Penny-pinchers might try finding a *colectivo* taxi at Parque de la Fraternidad or near the central railway station, where drivers are used to making long-distance runs to Playas del Este or even Pinar del Río and Viñales. Alternately, you

No.	Origin Station	Destination	Depart	Arrive
28	Morón	Terminal La Coubre	7:10 A.M.	12:55 P.M.
24	Pinar del Río	Estación Central	10:15 A.M.	4 P.M.
18	Sancti Spíritus	Estación Central	9:30 P.M.	5:20 A.M.
02	Santiago (*Especial*)	Estación Central	6 P.M.	6:55 A.M.
20	Santiago de Cuba	Terminal La Coubre	8:51 A.M.	8:39 P.M.

Destination	Fare (Regular)
Cacocum (Holguín)	US$26
Camagüey	US$19
Ciego de Ávila	US$15.50
Cienfuegos	US$9.50
Colón	US$6
Florida	US$17.50
Guantánamo	US$32
Holguín	US$26.50
Jatibónico	US$14
Jovellanos	US$5
Las Tunas	US$23
Matanzas	US$3
Morón	US$24
Pinar del Río	US$6.50
Placetas	US$11.50
Sancti Spíritus	US$13.50
Santa Clara	US$10
Santiago de Cuba	US$30

can try the *máquinas,* the intercity taxis (usually old Yankee cars) that gather outside railway and bus terminals. Often they won't depart until they fill up with passengers. Count on traveling about three km per peso.

BY RENTAL CAR

For lengthy exploring outside Havana, it's best to rent a car.

You'll want the *Moon Handbooks Cuba* (Avalon Travel Publishing, 2003), which has complete information for exploring Cuba, plus the *Guía de Carreteras,* a complete atlas in booklet form that can be purchased in Cuba from tour desks and souvenir outlets.

See the Getting Around Havana section earlier in this chapter for car rental companies, plus further details on car rentals.

Fly-Drive Packages

Viajes Horizontes, Calle 23, e/ N y O, tel. 33-0395, 33-4585, or 66-2160, fax 33-4361, crh@ horizontes.hor.cma.net, www.horizont.cu, offers

DISTANCES FROM HAVANA

All figures represent kilometers.

Baracoa	1,069
Bayamo	842
Camagüey	570
Cárdenas	152
Ciego de Ávila	461
Cienfuegos	336
Guantánamo	971
Holguín	771
Isla de la Juventud	138
Las Tunas	694
Matanzas	101
Pinar del Río	176
Rancho Boyeros	17
Sancti Spíritus	386
Santa Clara	300
Santiago de Cuba	876
Soroa	95
Surgidero de Batabanó	56
Trinidad	454
Varadero	140
Viñales	188

a "Flexi Fly & Drive" prepurchased package combining car rental and hotel vouchers. You simply pick up your car at the airport in Havana and hit the road armed with vouchers good at any of Horizontes' 70-plus hotels islandwide.

Campervans

A joint Italian-Cuban venture—**Cubamar Campertour,** 3ra Calle, esq. Malecón, tel. 880-1542, or Calle 15 #752, esq. Paseo, tel. 880-6874; in Italy, **Yorkitalia Tours,** Via Ghibellina 178/R, 501222 Firenze, tel. 055/264-5553, fax 055/264-5545, york@yorkitaliatours.com, www.yorkitaliatours.com, rents Mercedes Benz BRIG 670s, which sleep six people. The vehicles are powered by Mercedes turbodiesel engines and contain all the services of a small apartment: bathroom with flush toilet and shower, kitchen with fridge and three-burner stove, wardrobes, and even a security box. Prices range from US$155 for up to three days, to US$130 daily for 15 days or more (plus US$20 per diem insurance). Twenty "camp" sites are designated islandwide.

BY WHATEVER MOVES!

Beyond Havana, Cuba's meager transportation system is so dysfunctional that the populace relies on anything that moves. So many Cubans rely on hitching that there are official state-run *botellas* (literally bottles, but colloquially used to signify hitchhiking posts) on the edge of Havana and provincial towns. Officials of the Inspección Estatal, wearing mustard-colored uniforms and therefore termed *coges amarillas,* or yellow jackets, wave down virtually anything that moves and allocate seats.

The Cubans will be honored and delighted by the presence of a foreigner and may usher you to the front of the line. Early morning is easiest for hitching, when there's more traffic.

Sticking out your thumb won't do it. Do things the Cuban way: try to wave down the vehicle—whether it be a tractor, a truck, or a motorcycle. If it moves in Cuba, it's fair game. Open-bed trucks are the most common vehicles. Often there are no seats, and the local "bus" might be a converted cattle truck or a flatbed pulled by a tractor, with passengers crammed in and standing like cows (even less fun if it rains). If you're hitchhiking, this is for you.

ORGANIZED TOURS AND EXCURSIONS

If your time is limited and you like the idea of a smooth-running itinerary, book an excursion with one of the national tour agencies, available through tour desks in the lobbies of tourist hotels.

Popular one-day excursions include to Cayo Coco (about US$145), Cayo Largo (US$110), Soroa (US$30), Varadero (US$35), and Valle de Viñales (US$45). Typical overnight trips include to Trinidad (US$195) and Viñales (US$80).

U.S. owned **Cubalinda,** Edificio Someillán,

JET KAT EXPRESS

The **Cubanacán Jet Kat Express II** links Havana and Varadero. The high-speed, 380-passenger catamaran leaves the Terminal de Cruceros, San Pedro #1, tel. 862-1925 or 33-6566, fax 66-9688, cubanacanjet@ip.etecsa.cu, at 8:30 A.M. on Mondays, Wednesdays, and Fridays (US$45 per person) and whips along at 35 knots. The journey takes about three hours, providing precious views of the coast. You can "jet" down to Varadero in the morning, spend the afternoon on the beach, and sail back at 4 P.M., arriving back in Havana with plenty of time to eat and party. The catamaran has a bar with fine music, plus a sundeck.

Hotel pickups are provided.

piso 27, Calle O #2, e/ Línea y 17, Vedado, tel. 55-3980, fax 55-3686, info@cubalinda.com, www.cubalinda.com, offers a full travel agency service, including tours nationwide. Belgium-owned **Transnico,** Lonja del Comercio #6D, Habana Vieja, tel. 66-9954, fax 66-9908, trans @ip.etecsa.cu, www.transnico.com, offers similar services, but specializes in special-interest tours, including bicycle tours, music and dance programs, and train trips.

The following state-owned companies also offer excursion tours: **Cubanacán Viajes Tour,** Calle 46, esq. 9na, Playa, tel. 208-6044, fax 208-6702, tra40@viajes.cha.cyt.cu; **Cubatur,** Calle F #157, Vedado, tel. 33-4037, or Calle L, seq. 23, Vedado, tel. 33-3142; **Gaviota Tours,** tel. 204-7963, fax 204-9470, gavitour@gavitur .gav.cma.cu; **Rumbos, S.A.,** Línea #60, esq. M, Vedado, tel. 66-2113 or 204-9626, fax 33-3110; **Sol y Son,** Calle 23 #64, e/ Infanta y O, tel. 33-3162 or 33-3647, fax 33-5150, gerencia@solyson.avianet.cu; **Tours & Travel,** Calle 23, esq. M, Vedado, tel. 66-2077 or 66-4082, fax 66-4084, and Avenida 1ra e/ Calles 0 y 2, Miramar, tel. 204-0993; **Transtur,** Calle 19 #210, e/ J y K, Vedado, tel. 55-3252, www .transtur.cu; **Veracuba,** Calle 162 #317, esq. 3ra, Playa, tel. 33-0600, fax 33-6619, vacco mer1@cbcan.cyt.cu; and **Viajes Horizontes,** Calle 23, e/ N y O, tel. 33-0395, 33-4585, or 66-2160, fax 33-4361, crh@horizontes.hor .cma.net, www.horizont.cu.

EcoTur S.A., 5ra Avenida #9802, esq. 98, Playa, tel. 204-5195, fax 204-7520, offers eco-oriented tours and excursions.

Paradiso: Promotora de Viajes Culturales, Calle 19 #560 esq. C, Vedado, tel. 832-6928, fax 33-3921, paradis@turcult.get.cma.net, www.ceniai.inf.cu/paradiso, specializes in cultural tours.

Foreign Pastures: If you want to combine Cuba with a visit to one or more neighboring countries, **Cubanacán Viajes Tour,** Calle 46, esq. 9na, Playa, tel. 208-6044, fax 208-6702, tra40@viajes.cha.cyt.cu, and **Havanatur,** Calle 6 #117, e/ 1ra y 3ra, Miramar, Havana, tel. 204-2406 or 204-0908, promote multi-destination packages combining excursions in Cuba with a choice of destinations in the Bahamas, Costa Rica, Jamaica, Mexico, Panama, Guatemala, and other destinations.

Departing Cuba

BY AIR

The international airlines are linked by computer to their reservations headquarters abroad. However, computer links "go down" frequently. Confirming and changing reservations may be more time-consuming than you're probably used to. Don't leave things until the last minute.

The **Cubana** office, Calle 23 #64, e/ P y Infanta, tel. 33-4446/7/8/9, is always horrendously crowded. Double-check departure times, which change frequently and at short notice. Reconfirm your flight at least 72 hours before departure, as Cubana is notorious for canceling the reservations of those who don't reconfirm on time.

Tickets for Cubana charter flights must be purchased through Havanatur's **Tours & Travel,** Calle 23, esq. M, Vedado, tel. 66-2077 or 66-4082, fax 66-4084. You may be able to purchase tickets at the airport, but don't count on it. If you miss your flight and want to buy another ticket, you will have to go to a Tours & Travel office.

José Martí International Airport
The airport, 25 kilometers southwest of downtown Havana, is accessed by Avenida de la Independencia (Avenida Rancho Boyeros). The airport has four terminals spaced well apart from each other and accessed by different roads—they are not linked by a connecting bus service.

INTERNATIONAL AIRLINE OFFICES

The following have offices in the Hotel Habana Libre, Calle L e/ 23 y 25, Vedado:
Aeropostal, tel. 55-4000, fax 55-4128
Air Europa, tel. 66-6918
Grupo Taca, tel. 33-3114, fax 33-3728 (airport tel. 66-6040)

The following have offices at Calle 23 #64, e/ Calles P y Infanta, Vedado:
Aero Caribe, tel. 33-3621, fax 33-3871
Aeroflot, tel. 33-3200, fax 33-3288 (airport tel. 33-5432 or 45-1022)
ALM Antillean Airlines, tel. 33-3730, fax 33-3729
AOM, tel. 33-4098 or 33-39997
COPA, tel. 33-1503 or 33-1504 (airport tel. 266-4668)
Cubana, tel. 33-4446/7/8/9
Iberia, tel. 33-5041, fax 33-5061 (airport tel. 33-5234 or 66-6095)
LTU, tel. 33-3524, fax 33-3590
Mexicana, tel. 33-3531 or 33-3532, fax 33-3077 (airport tel. 33-5051)
TAAG, tel. 33-3527, fax 33-3049
Tame, tel. 33-4949, fax 33-4126

The following also have offices in Havana:
Air Europe, La Lonja del Comercio, Plaza de San Francisco, Habana Vieja, tel. 66-6745, fax 66-6744 (airport tel. 33-0111)
Air France, Calle 23, e/ L y M, Vedado, tel. 66-9709
Air Jamaica, 1ra Calle, e/ Paseo y 2, Vedado, tel. 66-2447, fax 66-2449 (airport tel. 33-0212)
Martinair, Calle 23, esq. E, Vedado, tel. 833-3729, fax 833-3732, martinair@enet.cu

Make sure you arrive at the correct terminal for your departure.

Terminals: Domestic flights leave from **Terminal 1,** Avenida Van Troi, off Avenida Rancho Boyeros, Rancho Boyeros, tel. 33-5753 or 33-5777 (or tel. 33-5576 for flight information). The terminal has a snack bar and restaurant. **Terminal 2** (Terminal Nacional, tel. 33-5577), on the north side of the runway, handles U.S. charter flights.

Terminal 3 (switchboard tel. 206-4644 or 33-5753, tel. 33-5666 for flight information), at Wajay, about one km west of Terminal 2, handles all international flights. The departure tax (US$25) must be paid at a separate counter after you've checked in with the airline. The foreign exchange bank refuses to accept Cuban pesos, so you should spend these in Havana or give them to a needy Cuban before leaving for the airport. **Restaurante Paradiso,** tel. 55-8864, adjoining Terminal 3, is recommended if you have an interminable wait for your flight. It serves a wide range of fare, including grilled fish, lobster, even beef, served with chips and a vegetable (US$3–35). Open 11 A.M.–11 P.M.

Terminal 4, currently used by the military, awaits expansion as a second international terminal. **Terminal 5** (also called Terminal Caribbean), about two miles west of the international terminal, at the northwest corner of the airport, handles small-plane flights (mostly domestic) offered by Aero Caribbean and AeroTaxi.

Getting to the Airport: No buses serve the international terminals. A taxi to the airport will cost about US$10–16 from Havana. You can also arrange a shuttle through one of the tour agencies (US$10–15).

A green-and-white bus marked "Aeropuerto" operates to Terminal One—the domestic terminal—from the east side of Parque Central in Habana Vieja. The *cola* begins near the José Martí statue. Note that there are two lines: one for people wishing to be seated (*sentados*) and one for those willing to stand (*de pie*). The journey costs one peso, takes about one hour, and is very unreliable (departures are about every two hours). Allow plenty of time. You can also catch bus or Omnibus no. 480 or Metrobus M-2 from the west side of Parque de la Fraternidad—you can also get the M-2 near the University on Avenida Salvador Allende. Both go to Santiago de las Vegas via the domestic terminal.

CUSTOMS REGULATIONS WHEN RETURNING HOME
Returning to the United States

U.S. citizens who have traveled *legally* to Cuba are allowed to bring back no more than US$100 of Cuban goods as accompanied baggage, plus up to US$10,000 of artwork and an unlimited amount of literature, posters, and other informational materials protected under the First Amendment of the Constitution. Sculpture created by Cubans may be licensed for importation provided it is lower than $25,000 in value. Uncle Sam's quixotic rules also state that if you are legally permitted to visit Cuba, you are also allowed to bring back Cuban cigars—as long as you purchased them in Cuba—but quirkily forbids you to bring cigars back if bought anywhere else. Be sure to get a receipt, even if you buy from a street seller. No goods of Cuban origin may be imported to the United States unaccompanied, either directly or through third countries, such as Canada or Mexico.

All other U.S. citizens are liable to have any Cuban goods confiscated, however innocuous and however acquired. Don't tempt fate by flaunting your Cuban T-shirt or shaking your Cuban maracas.

Restrictions on importing Cuban-made goods to the United States apply to citizens of *any* country arriving from any other country, including in-transit passengers.

The **Office of Foreign Assets Controls,** U.S. Department of the Treasury, 1500 Pennsylvania Avenue NW, Washington, D.C. 20220, 202/622-2520, fax-on-demand 202/622-0077, www.treas.gov/ofac, publishes a pamphlet, *What You Need to Know about the U.S. Embargo.* Alternately, contact the U.S. Customs Service, 1300 Pennsylvania Avenue NW, Washington, D.C. 20229.

Returning to Canada

Canadian citizens are allowed an "exemption" of C$500 annually (or C$100 per quarter) for goods purchased abroad, plus 1.1 liters of spirits and 200 cigarettes or 50 cigars.

Returning to the UK

UK citizens are permitted to import goods worth up to £200, plus 200 cigarettes, 50 cigars, and two liters of spirits.

Returning to Australia and New Zealand

Australian citizens may import A$400 of goods, plus 250 cigarettes or 50 cigars, and 1.125 liters of spirits. New Zealand citizens can import NZ$700 worth of goods, 200 cigarettes or 50 cigars, and 1.125 liters of spirits.

Exploring Suburban Havana

Boyeros

Boyeros is a vast, mostly undeveloped area that encompasses large tracts of countryside.

RANCHO BOYEROS

The region is most easily accessed from downtown Havana via Avenida de la Independencia, a fast-paced (albeit denuded) four-lane freeway that runs south through the industrial area of Rancho Boyeros to the José Martí International Airport. The Circunvalación—the poorly maintained four-lane freeway—leads east from Avenida de la Independencia and encircles Havana.

An agricultural show comes to town each last weekend of August, when a real rodeo—complete with roping, bull riding, and horse competitions—is held at the **Fería Agropecuaria,** Avenida de la Independencia #31108, tel. 06/83-4536, opposite the Escuela Técnico Industrial Julia A. Mella, immediately north of the junction for Terminal 1, at José Martí Airport.

Parque Zoológico Nacional

Cuba's national zoo, Avenida Zoo-Lenin (Avenida 8), esq. Avenida Soto, tel. 44-7613, fax 204-0852, pzn@ceniai.inf.cu, is 400 meters east of Avenida de la Independencia. It covers 340 hectares, and contains about 1,000 animals and more than 100 species. You can drive your own car through the park. A walk-through section houses a leopard, tiger, chimps, monkeys, and birds, but the cages are small and bare—there are no natural habitats—many of the animals look woefully neglected, and the conditions are deplorable. The zoo also reproduces more than 30 endangered species and includes a

narrow-gauge railway, Parque Lenin

SUBURBAN HAVANA

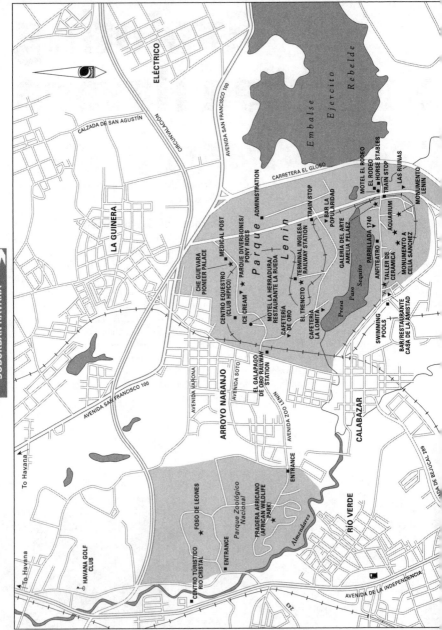

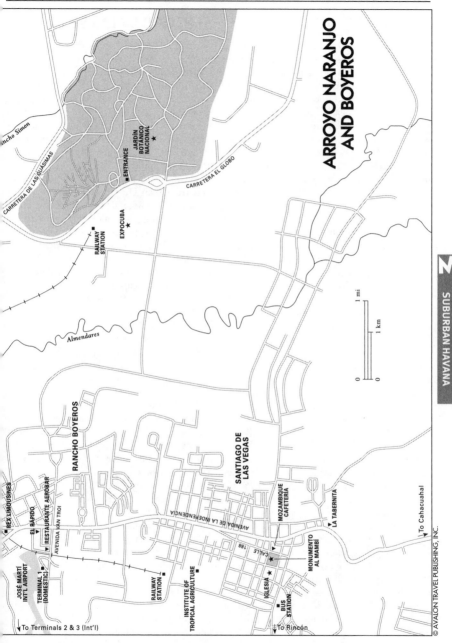

ARROYO NARANJO
AND BOYEROS

SUBURBAN HAVANA

© AVALON TRAVEL PUBLISHING, INC.

taxidermist's laboratory. A children's area provides pony rides.

Tour buses (0.40 centavos) depart the parking lot about every 30 minutes and run through the African wildlife park—**Pradera Africano**—and lion's den. The guided bus trip is the highlight, taking you through an expansive area not unlike the savanna of east Africa. Elephants come to the bus and stick their trunks in through the window to glean tidbits handed out by tourists. There are rhinos, two species of zebra, wildebeests, ostriches, and two hippos that spend most of their daylight hours wallowing in a deep pool. Gawkers gather at the low wall, where they can simply reach over and stroke the elephants. Amazingly, there's no security fence nor moat, and you sense that the animals could simply leap or step over the four-foot-high wall any time they wanted. Scary! No park staff are on hand, so visitors feed the animals all manner of junk food.

The lion pit—**Foso de Leones**—is a deep quarry on the north side of the park. The bus makes a quick loop through the pit, but you can also sit atop the cliff on a viewing platform and look down upon the lions fornicating—which is all they seem to do when they're not snoozing; 30 times a day for the males is an average performance, explains the guide.

A map of the zoo is posted at the main entrance gate, where there's a snack bar.

It's open Wednesday–Sunday 9:30 A.M.–3:30 P.M. Entrance costs US$3 per person (US$2 per child, US$5 for a vehicle).

Getting There: To get to the main entrance, take Avenida de la Independencia to Avenida San Francisco (the Parque is signed at the junction) which merges with the Circunvalacíon. Take the first exit to the right and follow Calzada de Bejucal south. Turn right onto Avenida Zoo-Lenin (signed). A second entrance is at Carretera de Vento, about one kilometer south from the Circunvalación (the turn-off from the latter is 200 meters east of Avenida de la Independencia).

Buses no. 31, 73, and 88 operate between La Víbora and Arroyo Naranjo. A taxi will cost about US$12 each way.

SANTIAGO DE LAS VEGAS

South of the airport, Avenida de la Independencia becomes Avenida de los Mártires, which continues to Santiago de las Vegas, a colonial-era rural town in the midst of the country, about three kilometers south of the airport and 20 kilometers south of Havana. This small provincial town has a certain bucolic charm. Santiago's streets are horrendously potholed with huge troughs big enough to swallow Cuba's hefty homegrown cattle.

The tiny main square is pinned by the **Monumento a Juan Delgado Gonzáles,** a marble statue of a local Mambí hero who led a regiment of Mambí (insurgent nationalist troops) during the Wars of Independence. A quaint whitewashed church, **Iglesia Parroquial de Santiago de las Vegas,** Calle 190, e/ 409 y 411, tel. 683-3233, stands on the west side of the plaza. It dates from 1694, though the cupola was only added in 1944. Open Tues.–Fri. 9:30 A.M.–1 P.M. and 7–8:30 P.M., and Sunday 10:30 A.M.–1 P.M. Mass is Tues.–Fri. at 7:30 A.M., and Sunday at 11 A.M.

Vívero de Begonia, Calle 188, esq. 413, tel. (0683) 2184, is a three-hectare nursery that grows ornamentals for sale in Havana. Open daily 7 A.M.–5 P.M.

El Cacahual

Avenida de los Mártires rises abruptly south of Santiago de las Vegas, passes through pine forests (the area contains several military camps), and deposits you at **Mausoleo de General Antonio Maceo Grajables,** about two kilometers south of Santiago de las Vegas. Here, Maceo (1845–96)—the black general and hero of the Wars of Independence—slumbers in a mausoleum in a circular park the size of a football field. The mausoleum also contains the tomb of Capitán Ayudante (Captain Adjutant) Francisco Gómez Toro (1876–1896), General Máximo Gómez's son, who gave his life alongside Maceo at the Battle of San Pedro on December 7, 1896. The granite tombs are engraved in the style of Mexican artist Diego Rivera. An adjacent pavilion features a small exhibit with photos and maps showing the black general's route during the war.

The park forms a giant traffic circle, on the east side of which stands another monument—this one in bronze—to Coronel (Colonel) Juan Delgado, chief of the Santiago de las Vegas regiment, who recovered Maceo's body. The tiny hamlet of **Cacahual** lies hidden from sight no more than 200 yards east, behind the pine trees.

Food: The nicest place is **La Tabernita,** tel. (0683) 2033, Doble Vía Cacahual, a thatched restaurant on the main road to Cacahual, one km south of town. It serves *criollo* fare and is popular with Cuban families on weekends. In a similar vein is **Rincón Criollo,** tel. (0683) 2083, about one kilometer south of town, amid pine trees.

In town, try the **Mozambique Cafetería,** on the northeast corner of the plaza.

Getting There and Away

Bus M2 runs from Parque de la Fraternidad in Havana. Ómnibus no. 480 also serves Santiago de las Vegas from Havana's main bus terminal, Avenida Independencia #101, Plaza de la Revolución, tel. 879-2456. The *terminal de ómnibus,* Calle al Rincón #43, tel. (0683) 3159, is on the southwest side of town, on the road to Rincón.

RINCÓN

This small crossroads village, three kilometers southwest of Santiago de las Vegas, is provincial Cuban at its quintessential best. The streets resound to the clip-clop of hooves as cowboys in shade hats ride past time-worn wooden homes with aged red-tile roofs.

The town is most famous, however, as the setting for Cuba's most important pilgrimage.

Sanctuario de San Lázaro

Cuba's most important pilgrimage site is the Sanctuary of San Lázaro, Carretera de San Antonio de los Baños, tel. (0683) 2396, half a kilometer west of Rincón. The well-maintained complex comprises a graceful church with a gray marble floor and various altars (the main one is a popular roosting site for local birdlife).

On any given day, the **Iglesia de San Lázaro** is busy with mendicants, especially on Sunday,

when Cubans come in droves to have their children baptized, while others fill bottles with holy water from a fountain behind the church. San Lázaro (in *santería,* his avatar is Babalú Ayé) is the patron saint of the sick, and is an immensely popular figure throughout Cuba. His symbol is the crutch. His stooped figure is usually covered in sores, and in effigy he goes about attended by his two dogs.

A procession to the sanctuary takes place each 17th of the month. Plus, the annual **Procesión de los Milagros** (Procession of the Miracles) takes place December 17, when thousands of pilgrims—up to 50,000 in some years—make their way to the sanctuary to give thanks to the saint for miracles they believe she granted. The villagers of Rincón do a thriving business selling votive candles and flowers to churchgoers. Limbless beggars, lepers, and other mendicants crowd at the gates and plead for a charitable donation, while penitents crawl on their backs and knees, and others walk ahead of them and sweep the road ahead with palm fronds. "A man inched along painfully on his back, with cinder blocks tied to his feet," wrote Andrei Codrescu in *Ay Cuba!* "I asked the man coiling and uncoiling on his back with the cinder blocks tied to his feet what he was going to ask San Lázaro. 'To help me walk,' the man replied."

It's open daily 7 A.M.–6 P.M. Entry is free. You'll be hit up for donations, however, by any number of limbless and infirm.

Behind the church is a leprosy and AIDS sanatorium: **Los Cocos,** Cuba's first sanatorium built to house patients infected with HIV. Both Pope John II and President Jimmy Carter visited, in 1998 and 2002, respectively.

Getting There

If driving, follow Carretera al Rincón, which begins at the bus station on the southwest edge of town.

A three-car train for San Antonio de los Baños departs Estación 19 de Noviembre (Tulipán), Calle Tulipán, Nuevo Vedado, tel. 881-4431, at 6:30 A.M. and 9:30 A.M. and noon, 4:15 P.M., 6:10 P.M., and 8 P.M., stopping at Rincón (US$.80 one-way).

Arroyo Naranjo

The *municipio* of Arroyo Naranjo lies due south of Havana.

PARQUE LENIN

Parque Lenin, Calle 100 y Carretera de la Presa, tel. 44-2721 or 44-3026, southeast of the village of Arroyo Naranjo, about 16 kilometers south of central Havana, was created from a former hacienda and landscaped mostly by volunteer labor from the city. Today it is maintained by inmates from a nearby psychiatric hospital. The vast complex features wide rolling pastures and small lakes surrounded by forests and pockets of bamboo, ficus, and flamboyants, or *güira,* from which maracas are made. What Lenin Park lacks in grandeur and stateliness, it makes up for in scale. You'll need a long study to get an idea of the full scope of the park, which is laid out around a large dam, **Presa Paso Sequito,** with a huge reservoir—**Ejército Rebelde**—to the east. Cuban families flock to the park on weekends for the children's park, with carousels and fairground

pleasures, horseback riding, rodeos, and all the fun of the fair. And each September 1, the park is packed for a day of special activities.

All the following venues are open Tuesday–Sunday 9 A.M.–5 P.M. **Casa de la Popularidad** is an information center with a small bar and restaurant. It's just off Calle Cortina at the junction with the loop road that leads along the north shore of the lake from Calzada de Bejucal.

Sights, Galleries, and Museums

The **Galería del Arte Amelia Peláez,** at the south end of Calle Cortina, displays works by the noted Cuban ceramist Amelia Peláez (she was responsible for the ceramic mural on the facia of the Hotel Habana Libre, in Vedado) along with changing exhibitions of other artists. Behind the gallery is a series of bronze busts inset in rock.

A short distance to the west is the **Monumento Lenin,** a huge granite visage of the communist leader and thinker in Soviet-realist style, carved by Soviet sculpture I. E. Kerbel. Further west, you'll pass an **aquarium** displaying freshwater fish and

pony ride, Parque Lenin

turtles, including the antediluvian garfish (*mari-juarí*) and a couple of Cuban crocodiles, Pepe and Rosita, in lagoons and tanks; entry costs US$1.

About 400 meters farther west is the **Monumento a Celia Sánchez.** Here, a trail follows a wide apse of large natural slabs to a broad amphitheater lined with ferns. At its center is a bronze figure of Sánchez ("the most beautiful and endemic flower of the Revolution"), inset in a huge rock. Sánchez set up the secret system that supplied arms to Castro's Rebel Army in the Sierra Maestra. She was Castro's secretary, lover, and most intimate advisor, and played a steadying influence on the fickle Cuban leader until her death from cancer in 1980. A small museum exhibits portraits of the heroine alongside her personal items.

Also worth a visit are the **Taller Cerámica** (ceramic workshop), on the southwest corner of the park; and, on the north side, the **Palacio de Pioneros Che Guevara,** displaying stainless-steel sculptures of the revolutionary hero.

Activities, Recreation, and Entertainment

Horseback Riding: There's an equestrian center—**Centro Ecuestre** (often called Club Hípico), tel. 44-1058, immediately east of the entrance off Calzada de Bejucal. It offers riding lessons (a course of 10 one-hour riding lessons costs US$100), one-hour horseback trips (US$15), and you can rent horses. The riding club covers 20 hectares and has stables for 30 horses, a training racetrack and paddock, several dressage paddocks, a smithy, veterinary clinic, changing rooms, showers, and even sauna and massage facilities. Open daily 9 A.M.–5 P.M. (June–Aug.), and Wed.–Sun. 9 A.M.–5 P.M. (Sept.–July). Horseback riding is also offered at **El Rodeo,** tel. 57-8893; and at the *parque de diversiones* (described later in this chapter) for 60 pesos for one hour, or five pesos for a *revuelta* (a circuit).

Rodeo: El Rodeo offers *rodeo cubano* in the national rodeo arena (entry costs three pesos) every Sunday, with "Rodeo Pionero" (for youth) at noon, "torneo campesino" at 1 P.M., and competitive adult rodeo at 3 P.M. (admission is three pesos adults, one peso children). The **Feria de Rodeo** (National Championships) is held each August 25.

Train Rides: A narrow-gauge railway circles the park, stopping at four stages. The old steam train dates from 1870 and operates daily 10 A.M.–4 P.M. (four pesos), departing Estación Galapagos de Oro and taking 25 minutes to circle the park. Another old steam train dating from 1915 is preserved under a red-tiled canopy in front of the disused **Terminal Inglesa.**

Bicycle and Rowboat Rental: You can rent aquatic bicycles and rowboats on the lake at El Rodeo (five pesos for 30 minutes).

For Children: A *parque de diversiones* (amusement park) located in the northwest quarter includes carousels, a miniature "big dipper," and pony rides.

Cabaret, Theater, and Music: Classical and other concerts are held at the **Anfiteatro,** a half-moon amphitheater hollowed from natural rock on the south side of the lake. The bands play on a floating stage. **El Rodeo** has a cabaret, plus a bar with mechanical bull!

Swimming Pools: There are swimming pools in the **Palacio de Pioneros Che Guevara** and east of the community of Calabazar, on the south side of the park (five pesos), tel. 57-8154.

Accommodations

Motel La Herradura, tel. 44-1058 or 44-2819, on the south side of the Centro Ecuestre, offers five a/c rooms with TV (local stations only), mini-fridges, and utilitarian decor for US$17 s/d. It caters mostly to Cubans, for whom it serves as a *posada* . . . a "love" motel.

Motel Rodeo Nacional, tel. 44-3026, ext. 242, near the rodeo, has four very simple rooms for US$10 s/d nightly. It, too, serves principally as a place of coital convenience for Cubans; foreigners are charged US$5 for four hours of hanky-panky.

Food

Las Ruinas, Calle 100 y Cortina de la Presa, tel. 44-3336 or 57-8286, looks like something Frank Lloyd Wright might have conceived. Designed in concrete, it encases the ruins of an old sugar mill, with remnant free-standing walls overgrown with epiphytes and mosses. Downstairs is a bar and restaurant where a pianist plays and tables are lit by

Tiffany lamps. Upstairs features stained-glass panels, with louvered wooden French windows—beware the dangerous lip at the top of the stairs, which have no guard rails. The decor is elegant, with linens, silverware, classical urns full of flowers, and dozens of crystal chandeliers. It serves continental cuisine (lobster bellevue—US$20—is a specialty) described by readers as both "reminiscent of school dinners" and "the best in Havana." It offers a tasty shrimp enchilada (US$12). Other dishes include pizza (US$4.50), blue cheese soup (US$2), shrimp brochette (US$12), and grilled fish *uruguayo* (US$11). Open Tues.–Sun. noon–9 P.M.

Restaurante Herradura at the Centro Ecuestre offers a pleasant ambience and serves garlic shrimp, pizzas, lobster, and *criollo* dishes for US$4–20. Abutting it is an outdoor grill—**La Rueda Parrillada**—with a pleasant patio.

There are several snack bars serving *bocaditos,* fried chicken, and the like.

Las Majaguas Cafetería, Carretera el Globo y Carretera a las Guásimas, is a pleasant thatched roadside bar and restaurant, open 24 hours.

Getting There

See Parque Zoológico Nacional, earlier in this chapter, for instruction on getting there by car. The park is bounded by the Circunvalación to the north and Calzada de Bejucal to the west; there is an entrance off Calzada de Bejucal. A second road—Calle Cortina de la Presa—enters from the Circunvalación and runs down the center of the park. Calle Cortina is linked to Calzada de Bejucal by a loop road.

Buses no. 31, 73, and 88 operate between La Víbora and the park entrance. A taxi will cost about US$15 each way.

In past years, a train has operated from the Estación Station in Havana to Galápago de Oro station on the northwest side of the park; it was not operating at last visit.

OTHER SIGHTS

ExpoCuba

ExpoCuba, on the Carretera del Globo (the official address is Carretera del Rocío Km 3.5, Arroyo Naranjo), tel. 54-9111 or 66-4419, houses a permanent exhibition of Cuban industry, technology, sports, and culture touting the achievements of socialism. It's a popular venue for school field trips and conventions.

The facility covers 588,000 square meters and is a museum, trade expo, world's fair, and entertainment hall rolled into one. It has 34 pavilions, including booths that display the crafts, products, music, and dance of each of Cuba's provinces. It holds plenty of other attractions, too. Railroad buffs might check out the vintage rolling stock (including turn-of-the-century carriages) on the entrance forecourt. Booth #9—the maritime booth—displays an armored motor launch, among other vessels. Booth #25 exhibits old carriages and cars.

Open Jan.–Aug., Tues.–Sun. 9 A.M.–5 P.M. (closed Sept.–Dec.). Entrance costs US$1.

There's an information office at the main entrance, plus a *buró de cambio* and bank.

Getting There: ExpoCuba is three kilometers south of Parque Lenin. Take the Calle Cortina de la Presa south through Parque Lenin and continue past the village of El Globo. ExpoCuba is on your left, down the hill.

Buses no. 88 and 113 leave for ExpoCuba (and the Jardín Botánico) from the north side of Havana's main railway station weekends at 10 A.M., noon, and 3 P.M., and from Havana's Terminal de Ómnibus at 9 A.M., 11 A.M., and 4 P.M. Bus no. 80 also serves the park from Lawton.

A three-car train runs to ExpoCuba, opposite the garden, from the 19 de Noviembre (Tulipán) station on Calle Tulipán, Nuevo Vedado, tel. 881-4431, Wed.–Sun. at 9:20 A.M.; it departs ExpoCuba at 5:15 P.M. (US$1 one-way).

Jardín Botánico Nacional

This massive (600-hectare) botanical garden, Carretera del Rocío Km 3.5, Arroyo Naranjo, tel. 54-9170 or 54-9159, directly opposite ExpoCuba, doesn't have the fine-trimmed herbaceous borders of Kew or Butchart, but nonetheless is worth the drive for enthusiasts. Thirty-five kilometers of roads lead through the park, which was laid out between 1969 and 1984.

The expansive garden consists mostly of wide pastures planted with copses divided by Cuban ecosystems (from coastal thicket to Oriental humid forest) and by regions of the tropical world. More than 100 gardeners tenderly prune and mulch such oddities as the *satchicha* tree, with pendulous pods that certain African tribeswomen rub on their nipples in the belief that it will give them large breasts.

The geographic center contains a fascinating variety of palm trees from around the world. There is even an "archaic forest" containing species such as *Microcyca calocom,* Cuba's cork palm, from the antediluvian dawn. The highlight is the **Japanese garden,** beautifully landscaped with tiered cascades, fountains, and a jade-green lake full of koi. It was donated by the Japanese government for the 30th anniversary of the Revolution.

Be sure to walk through the **Invernáculo Rincón Eckman,** a massive greenhouse (*invernáculo*) named after Erik Leonard Eckman (1883–1931), who documented Cuban flora between 1914 and 1924. The greenhouse is laid out as a triptych: a cactus house; a room full of epiphytes, bromeliads, ferns, and insectivorous plants; and a room containing tropical mountain plants, a small cascade, and a pool.

The greenhouse (which has wheelchair access) boasts a souvenir stall and café, plus toilets. And the **Bambú Restaurant,** which overlooks the Japanese garden, serves some of the best vegetarian food in Havana.

Open daily 8:30 A.M.–4:30 P.M. (last entry is at 3:30 P.M.). Entrance costs US$1 per person, or US$3 with a guide. Private vehicles are allowed through the park with a guide (US$3). You can buy a tourist map of the garden for US$1.

Food

There are several restaurants and cafés at Ex-poCuba. The best is the elegant **Don Cuba Restaurant,** with neoclassical Roman-cum-Arabic architecture. Musicians perform in the courtyard. It offers a tasty grilled fish with rice and spiced vegetables for US$8.

The **Bambú Restaurant,** tel. 54-4106l, overlooks the Japanese garden in the botanical garden. It bills itself as an *"eco-restorán,"* and functions to educate Cubans on healthier eating habits. The vegetables—beetroot, cassava, pumpkin, spinach, taro, and others—are all grown right there in the garden. I recommend the *fufo* (mashed boiled banana with garlic), and eggplant cooked in cheese sauce. You're permitted free refills. Locals, and foreign students with ID, are charged 40 pesos, including *jugo natural* and *helado* (ice cream); other foreigners pay US$10. Be prepared for a long wait, as the restaurant is often booked solid. You can reserve a table by calling ahead, tel. 54-7278, fax 54-4184. Sometimes they run out of food. They serve lunch only; open Wed.–Sun. noon–5 P.M.

San Miguel del Padrón and Cotorro

The *municipio* of San Miguel del Padrón, which extends south of the Bahía de La Habana, is mostly residential, with ugly modern factory areas in the lowlands by the harbor and time-worn colonial housing on the hills south of town.

The region is accessed from the Vía Blanca or (parallel to it) Calzada de Luyano via the Carretera Central (Calzada de Güines). En route, you pass through the suburb of **Luyano.**

LUYANO

Luyano is home to Manuel Mendive Hoyo, a famous artist whose works derive from African roots. He is the champion of popular culture

hereabouts and is most known for his live performances using completely nude women with painted bodies. He's easy to spot on the streets in his traditional Yoruban costume, strolling around with a cane.

The **Fuente de la Virgen del Camino,** at the junction of Calzada de Luyano and Carretera Central, is noteworthy. This fountain of the Virgin of the Way, by acclaimed sculptor Rita Longa, draws Cubans who come to throw coins in the pool; the money goes to pay for the indigent. Two blocks east is the **Monumento a Doña Leonor Pérez,** Calle Balear, esq. Leonor Pérez, dedicated to José Martí's mother. The patinated bronze figure sits in a dignified pose atop a marble pedestal, book in hand, and shaded by trees. Bas-reliefs depict key moments in Martí's life, including riding to his fate in 1895 at the Battle of Dos Ríos.

Immediately south, Calzada de Güines rises through the near-derelict Juanelo district, known for its community of papier mâché artists . . . an artform introduced to the local school in 1970 by artist Antonia Eiriz. The artform took hold and is now an integral part of local culture, with production of masks, dolls, mobiles, and a creative miscellany of papier mâché—including furniture—centered on the **Trabajo Comunitario del Reparto Juanel Silvia Fernández Rodríguez,** Pasaje 2 #5, e/ Piedra y Soto, tel. 91-6752, a tiny alley one block west of Calzada de Güines.

SAN FRANCISCO DE PAULA

Eventually you arrive at San Francisco de Paula, on the city's outskirts, 12.5 kilometers south of Habana Vieja. This community of small wooden houses of colonial vintage moves at a bucolic pace. Rising above the village, but hidden from view, is Ernest Hemingway's former home, Finca Vigía.

Museo Ernesto Hemingway

In 1939, Hemingway's third wife, Martha Gellhorn, was struck by Finca Vigía (Lookout Farm), Calle Vigía y Steinhart, a one-story Spanish-colonial house built in 1887 and boasting a wonderful view of Havana. They rented it for US$100 a month. When Hemingway's first royalty check from *For Whom the Bell Tolls* arrived in 1940, he bought the house for US$18,500 because, like his character Ole Anderson in "The Killers," he had tired of roaming from one place to another. In August 1961, his widow, Mary Welsh, was forced to sign papers handing over the home to the Castro government, along with its contents (see the Special Topic "Ernest Hemingway and Havana").

On July 21, 1994, on the 95th anniversary of Papa's birthday, Finca Vigía reopened its doors as a museum, Calle Vigía, tel. 91-0809, following nearly two years of repairs and remodeling. The house is preserved in suspended animation, just the way the great writer left it. His presence seems to haunt the large, simple home.

Bougainvilleas frame the gateway to the 20-acre hilltop estate. Mango trees and sumptuous

Finca Vigía

jacarandas line the driveway leading up to the gleaming white house. No one is allowed inside—reasonably so, since every room can be viewed through the wide-open windows, and the temptation to pilfer priceless trinkets is thus reduced. (Two years after Hemingway died, someone offered $80,000 for his famous Royal typewriter which sits on a shelf beside his workroom desk; today, you can buy it for $7—inscribed in gray on a T-shirt that reads "Museo Ernesto Hemingway, Finca Vigía, Cuba").

Through the large windows, you can see trophies, firearms, bottles of spirits, old issues of *The Field, Spectator,* and *Sports Afield* strewn about, and more than 8,000 books, arranged the way he supposedly liked them, with no concern for authors or subjects. The dining-room table is set with cut crystal, as if guests were expected.

It is eerie being followed by countless eyes—those of the guides (one to each room) and those of the beasts that had found themselves in the crosshairs of Hemingway's hunting scope. "Don't know how a writer could write surrounded by so many dead animals," Graham Greene commented when he visited. There are bulls, too, everywhere bulls, including paintings by Joan Miró and Paul Klee; photographs and posters of bullfighting scenes; and a chalk plate of a bull's head, a gift from Picasso.

Here is where Hemingway wrote *Islands in the Stream, Across the River and into the Trees, A Moveable Feast,* and *The Old Man and the Sea.* The four-story tower next to the house was built at his fourth wife's prompting so that he could write undisturbed. Hemingway disliked the tower and continued writing amid the comings and goings of the house, surrounded by papers, shirtless, in Bermuda shorts, with any of 50 cats at his feet as he stood barefoot on the hide of a kudu.

Beside his toilet is a penciled diary with entries recording his morning weight, one of the few fights he continually lost.

Finca Vigía's sprawling grounds are equally evocative. Hemingway's legendary cabin cruiser, the *Pilar,* is poised loftily beneath a wooden pavilion on the former tennis court, shaded by bamboo and royal palms. Nearby are the swimming pool where Ava Gardner swam naked, and the graves of four of the novelist's favorite dogs.

The museum, headed by a trained curator, offers free tours. Open Mon.–Sat. 9 A.M.–4 P.M., Sun. 9 A.M.–12:30 P.M. Closed Tuesday and rainy days. Entrance costs US$3. A gift shop sells portraits, T-shirts, and other souvenirs.

Getting There: Metrobus no. 7 (the M-7 *camello*) departs from Industria, e/ Dragones y Avenida Simón Bolívar, Parque de la Fraternidad, in Habana Vieja. Omnibus no. 404 departs from Avenida de Bélgica (Monserrate) and Dragones. Both travel via San Francisco de Paula en route to Cotorro and Havana.

Trains run from the Cristina station at Avenida de México (Cristina), esq. Manglar Arroyo, tel. 879-0354. Take the train for Cotorro (four times daily) via San Francisco de Paula.

Paradiso: Promotora de Viajes Culturales and **Cubanacán,** Calle 19 #560 esq. C, Vedado, tel. 832-6928, fax 33-3921, paradis@turcult .get.cma.net, www.ceniai.inf.cu/paradiso, offer excursions from Havana.

COTORRO

This *municipio* lies south of San Miguel del Padrón, from which it is divided by the Circunvalación, the dangerous four-lane freeway that forms a ring around southern and eastern Havana.

Sites of interest are clustered in and around **Santa María del Rosario,** a charming colonial village surrounded by palm-studded farmland about five kilometers southeast of San Francisco de Paula. (From San Francisco de Paula head south one km to the Circunvalación; head east on the Circunvalación to the first junction; turn south on Carretera a Santa María del Rosario.) The village was founded in 1732 by José Bayona y Chacón, the Conde (Count) de Casa Bayona, who formed the subject of the movie *La última cena* (*The Last Supper;* 1976), by Tomás Gutiérrez Alea. The town boasts a number of 18th- and 19th-century buildings, many of which were restored by a wealthy patron in the years preceding the Revolution.

The village is centered on **Plaza Mayor,** the main square, fronted by the **Casa del Conde**

ERNEST HEMINGWAY AND HAVANA

Ernest Hemingway first set out from Key West to wrestle marlin in the wide streaming currents off the Cuban coast in April 1932. Years later, he was to sail the Key West–Havana route dozens of times. The blue waters of the Gulf Stream, chock-full of billfish, brought him closer and closer until, eventually, "succumbing to the other charms of Cuba, different from and more difficult to explain than the big fish in September," he settled on this irresistibly charismatic isle.

Hemingway loved Cuba and lived there for nearly 20 years. It was more alluring, more fulfilling, than Venice, Sun Valley, or the green hills of Africa. Once, when Hemingway was away from Cuba, he was asked what he worried about in his sleep. "My house in Cuba," he replied, referring to Finca Vigía, in the suburb of San Francisco de Paula, 15 kilometers southeast of Havana.

Hemingway's ghost haunts you wherever you go in Havana. His bronze bust looks down from its pedestal in El Floridita, his favorite watering hole where he supped with such illustrious guests as Jean-Peal Sartre, Marlene Dietrich, and Ava Gardner.

Hemingway's life in Cuba was filled with adventures that would find their way into novels. In *Papa: A Personal Memory,* Hemingway's son Gregory recalls how while driving "at a snail's pace through the crowded, narrow back streets . . . shots rang out and a man came running toward us with a submachine gun." The assassin ran up to the car and handed the gun to Juan, the chauffeur, saying "'Hold this for me, will you please? I have to run.' Juan was too surprised to do anything else; but papa, who was sitting next to him in the open Lincoln convertible, cursed at him under his breath. 'You've got your prints all over it now, you bloody fool. Wipe it off and drop it, and let's get the hell out of here.'"

Walking the streets you can still feel Hemingway's presence. In a way, Papa never left. It was—and is—easy to imagine the sun-bronzed writer driving in his brand new Chrysler New Yorker DeLuxe convertible, white mane and beard haloed in tropical light, hoary chest showing beneath khaki shirt, en route for his daily sugarless double daiquirí with his friends.

The Cult of Hemingway

Havana's city fathers have leased Papa's spirit to lend ambience to and put a polish on his favorite haunts. Havana's marina is named for the prize-winning novelist. A special rum, "El Ron Vigía," was even introduced to coincide with the author's 95th birthday, on July 21, 1994. Hemingway's room in the Hotel Ambos Mundos and Finca Vigía are preserved as museums. His name is attached to fishing tournaments and sugar-free daiquirís, and his likeness adorns T-shirts and billboards.

The novelist's works are required reading in Cuban schools. His books are bestsellers. "We admire Hemingway because he understood the Cuban people; he supported us," a friend told me. "He was very simple. His friends were fishermen, jai alai players, bullfighters. He never related to high society," adds Evelio González, one of the guides at Finca Vigía, although an A-list of international notables—actors, actresses, novelists, philosophers, royalty—were constant guests.

The Cuban understanding of Hemingway's "Cuban novels" is that they support a core tenet of Communist ideology—that humans are only fulfilled acting in a "socialist" context for a moral purpose, not individualistically. Many of Hemingway's novels appear to condemn economic and political injustices. "All the works of Hemingway are a defense of human rights," claims Castro, who knows Papa's novels "in depth" and once claimed that *For Whom the Bell Tolls,* Hemingway's fictional account of the Spanish Civil War, inspired his guerrilla tactics. Castro has said the reason he admires Hemingway so much is that he envies the adventures he had.

The two headstrong fellows met only once, during the Tenth Annual Ernest Hemingway Billfish Tournament in May 1960. As sponsor and judge of the competition, Hemingway invited

Cuba's youthful new leader as his guest of honor. Castro was to present the winner's trophy; instead, he hooked the biggest marlin and won the prize for himself. Hemingway surrendered the trophy to a beaming Castro. They would never meet again. One year later, the great writer committed suicide in Idaho.

After Hemingway's death, Finca Vigía (including its precious artworks) was seized by the Castro government, though the writer had willed the property to his fourth wife, Mary Welsh. When Cuban officials arrived with papers for her to sign, she replied: "I'm not sure I wish to give you our *finca.*" She had no choice, of course. The Cuban government allowed Mary Hemingway to remove 200 pounds of papers, but insisted that most of their home's contents remain untouched, including 3,000 letters and documents, 3,000 photographs, and 9,000 books . . . all kept secret in the humid basement, where they have since been allowed to deteriorate to the point of near ruin. Only in 2002 was this invaluable, uncharted resource opened to scholars.

Somehow Hemingway's sleek black 1955 Chrysler New Yorker escaped and apparently passed into the hands of Augustin Nuñez Gutiérrez, a Cuban policeman, according to writer Joann Biondi. Later, Nuñez hid the car and hopped on a raft for Miami. Popular legend says the car's whereabouts are still a mystery and that the Chrysler still awaits discovery as some incredibly fortunate collector's dream.

Papa and the Revolution

There has been a great deal of speculation about Hemingway's attitude toward the Cuban Revolution. Cuba, of course, attempts to portray him as sympathetic (Gabriel García Márquez refers to "Our Hemingway" in the prologue to exiled Cuban novelist Noberto Fuente's *Hemingway in Cuba*).

Hemingway's Cuban novels are full of images of prerevolutionary terror and destitution. "There is an absolutely murderous tyranny that extends over every little village in the country," he wrote in *Islands in the Stream.*

In 1960, Hemingway wrote to a friend, "I believe completely in the historical necessity of the Cuban revolution." Hemingway's widow, Mary, told the journalist Luís Báez that "Hemingway was always in favor of the Revolution." Another writer, Lisandro Otero, records Hemingway as saying, "Had I been a few years younger, I would have climbed the Sierra Maestra with Fidel Castro." Papa was away from Cuba all of 1959, but he returned in 1960, recorded *New York Times* correspondent Herbert Matthews, "to show his sympathy and support for the Castro Revolution." Papa even used his legendary 38-foot sportfishing boat, the *Pilar,* to run arms for the rebel army, claimed Gregorio Fuentes, the weatherbeaten sailor-guardian of the *Pilar* for 23 years. Mary Welsh claims however to have been on board when Hemingway dumped his stash of sporting guns and ammunition into the sea so that neither side would get them.

The truth of these comments, alas, can't be validated.

With the Cold War and the United States' break with Cuba, Hemingway had to choose. Not being able to return to Cuba contributed to Hemingway's depression, says his son Patrick: "He really loved Cuba, and I think it was a great shock to him at his age to have to choose between his country, which was the United States, and his home, which was Cuba."

Hemingway's enigmatic farewell comment as he departed the island in 1960 is illuminating. "*Vamos a ganar. Nosotros los cubanos vamos a ganar.* [We are going to win. We Cubans are going to win.] I'm not a Yankee, you know." Before leaving Cuba, however, Hemingway expressed hope that the revolution would not become Communist, claims writer Claudia Lightfoot. Prophetically, in *Islands in the Stream,* a character says: "The Cubans . . . double cross each other. They sell each other out. They got what they deserve. The hell with their revolutions." What would he have made of the outcome?

Bayona, Calle 33 #2404, esq. 24, the count's former home, comprising three adjacent structures complete with coach house. Part of the home is now occupied by a bar with snacks (tel. 682-3510; open daily noon–10 P.M.

Adjacent, and commanding the plaza, is a large baroque **Iglesia de Santa María del Rosario,** Calle 24, e/ 31 y 33, tel. 682-2183, one of the nation's finest churches. This national monument is colloquially called the Catedral del Campo de Cuba (Cathedral of the Fields of Cuba). Highlights include a resplendent carved ceiling of *jigüi* (indigo); a wooden baroque altar dripping with gold leaf; plus four priceless art pieces by José Nicolás de Escalera. One such shows the Count with his family and an old slave who, reportedly, cured his master of rheumatism using healing waters. Open Tues.–Sat. 8 A.M.–noon, and Sun. 3:30–7 P.M. Mass is Thursday at 8 A.M. and Sunday at 5 P.M.

The curative waters have been tapped at **Balneario de Santa María del Rosario,** Calle 30, esq. Final, tel. 682-2734, a mineral spa within a copse. Open Mon.–Fri. 8 A.M.–4 P.M. Behind it rises **Loma La Cruz** (Hill of the Cross), named for the large cross erected by the Count to honor those killed in a slave rebellion. You have a fine view of the countryside from the hillcrest.

The **Casa de la Cultura,** Calle 33 #202, esq. 24, tel. 682-4259, hosts a *peña* with local musicians each Sunday at 8:30 P.M. Note the intriguing mural by artist Manuel Mendive.

Santa María is served by no. 97 bus from Guanabacoa.

Regla and Guanabacoa

These contiguous townships extend inland from the eastern shore of Havana harbor.

REGLA

Regla evolved in the 16th century as a fishing village and eventually became Havana's foremost warehousing and slaving center. It also developed into a smugglers' port in colonial days, a reputation it maintained until recent days, when pirates (who made their living stealing off American yachts anchored in the harbor) were known as *terribles reglanos.* It was also the setting for Havana's bullfights. Today, the town is a somewhat forlorn port town and center of industry. The main electricity-generating plant for Havana is here, along with petrochemical works, both of which pour bilious, foul-smelling plumes over town.

The marvelous restoration project of Habana Vieja has finally crossed the waters, and the first efforts are being made to save those edifices with the most obvious touristic potential.

Slaves were brought in large numbers in colonial days, infusing the town with a profound African heritage still extant today. Regla is a center of *santería;* while walking its streets, you may note tiny shrines outside many houses. Calle Calixto García has many fine examples. Check out #116, with a small madonna enclosed in glass in the wall, with fresh flowers by its side; and #114, whose large altar in the middle of the house is easily seen from the street.

See the *Santería* section, in the Introduction chapter, for more information, including *babalawos* in Regla.

A **Fiesta de los Orishas,** a quasi-religious ceremony featuring Afro-Cuban music and dance, has been held in the past but was not offered at press time.

Iglesia de Nuestra Señora de Regla

The harborfront hermitage of Our Lady of Regla, Calle Sanctuario #11, e/ Máximo Gómez y Litoral, tel. 97-6228, built in 1810, is one of Havana's loveliest churches. The ocher-colored church is well preserved. Its inner beauty—a blaze of white and sky blue lit by incandescent light pouring in through the huge studded wooden doors—is highlighted by a fabulous gilt altar beneath an arched ceiling. On holy days, the altar is sumptuously lit with votive candles. Dwelling in alcoves in the wall are figurines of miscellaneous saints, which devotees reach up

Regla street scene

to touch while reciting silent prayers. Check out the vaulted niche on the left side of the nave, which contains a statue of St. Anthony leading a wooden suckling pig wearing a dog collar and a large blue ribbon. Devout *habaneros* flock to pay homage to the black Virgen de Regla, patron saint of sailors and Catholic counterpart to Yemayá, the African goddess of the sea in the Yoruba religion. She is shown holding a white baby Jesus in her arms.

If you can, time your visit for the seventh of each month, when large masses are held—or, better yet, September 8, when a pilgrimage draws the devout of Catholicism and *santería* and the Virgin is taken down from her altar and paraded through town. The church is open Tuesday–Sunday 7:30 A.M.–5:30 P.M. Masses are held Tuesday and Sunday at 8 and 9 A.M.

Outside, 20 meters to the east and presiding over her own private chapel, is another statue of the Virgin de Regla, with a second statue of the Virgen de la Caridad del Cobre, Cuba's patron saint, enveloped in a robe adorned with embroidered roses. The altar is in a private home. Syncretized as the *orisha* Ochún, the Virgen de la Caridad del Cobre also draws adherents of *santería*.

Other Sights

From the harborfront plaza, the tidy, well-preserved main street (Calle Martí) leads two blocks east past a small plaza to the **Museo Municipal de Regla,** Calle Martí #158, e/ Facciolo y La Piedra, tel. 94-6989. The museum tells the tale of the Virgin of Regla and of the city's participation in revolutionary struggles. It also presents an intriguing exhibit on Regla's *santería* associations. An astronomical observatory was added on the roof in 1921; it fell into disuse following the Revolution, but was slated to be restored as part of an expansion that will gift the museum additional storage space for art exhibitions. Open Tues. 9 A.M.–6 P.M., Wed. 1–9 P.M., Thurs.–Sat. 9 A.M.–6 P.M., and Sun. 9 A.M.–1 P.M. Entrance costs US$2. The museum hosts cultural activities such as poetry recitals.

Around the corner, betwixt the church and the museum is a small triangular plaza. The colonial home on the northeast corner is **Galería-Taller de Antonio Canet Hernández,** Calle Eduardo Facciola #167, the studio-gallery of the eponymous artist who specializes in woodcuts. The home's original owner, Eduardo Facciola y Alba, was garroted in 1862 at the age of 23 for

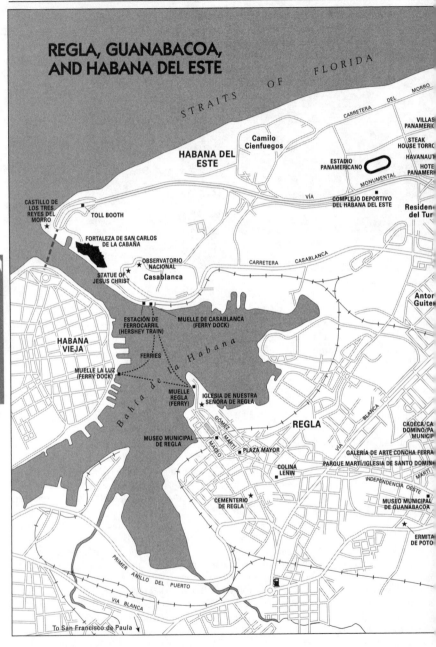

REGLA, GUANABACOA, AND HABANA DEL ESTE

STRAITS OF FLORIDA

CARRETERA DEL MORRO

VILLAS PANAMERIC

Camilo Cienfuegos

STEAK HOUSE TORRO

HABANA DEL ESTE

ESTADIO PANAMERICANO

HAVANAUT

HOTE PANAMER

MONUMENTAL

VÍA

COMPLEJO DEPORTIVO DEL HABANA DEL ESTE

Residen del Tur

CASTILLO DE LOS TRES REYES DEL MORRO ★

TOLL BOOTH

FORTALEZA DE SAN CARLOS DE LA CABAÑA

OBSERVATORIO NACIONAL

CARRETERA CASABLANCA

STATUE OF JESUS CHRIST

Casablanca

Anton Guite

HABANA VIEJA

ESTACIÓN DE FERROCARRIL (HERSHEY TRAIN)

MUELLE DE CASABLANCA (FERRY DOCK)

FERRIES

MUELLE LA LUZ (FERRY DOCK)

Bahía de la Habana

MUELLE REGLA (FERRY)

IGLESIA DE NUESTRA SEÑORA DE REGLA ★

REGLA

VÍA BLANCA

CADECA/CA DOMINO/PA MUNICI

MUSEO MUNICIPAL DE REGLA

GOMEZ MARTI

PLAZA MAYOR

MACEO

GALERÍA DE ARTE CONCHA FERRA

PARQUE MARTÍ/IGLESIA DE SANTO DOMIN

COLINA LENIN

INDEPENDENCIA OESTE

MARTI

CEMENTERIO DE REGLA ★

MUSEO MUNICIPAL DE GUANABACOA

★

ERMITA DE POTO

PRIMER ANILLO DEL PUERTO

VIA BLANCA

To San Francisco de Paula ↓

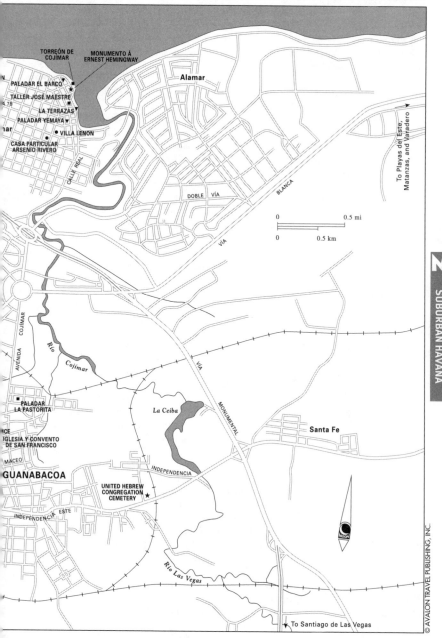

TORREÓN DE COJIMAR
MONUMENTO Á ERNEST HEMINGWAY
Alamar
PALADAR EL BARCO
TALLER JOSÉ MAESTRE
LA TERRAZAS
PALADAR YEMAYÁ
VILLA LENÓN
CASA PARTICULAR ARSENIO RIVERO
CALLE REAL
DOBLE VÍA
VÍA BLANCA
To Playas del Este, Matanzas, and Varadero

0   0.5 mi
0   0.5 km

VÍA MONUMENTAL

AVENIDA COJIMAR
Río Cojimar
PALADAR LA PASTORITA
La Ceiba
Santa Fe
IGLESIA Y CONVENTO DE SAN FRANCISCO
MACEO
GUANABACOA
INDEPENDENCIA
UNITED HEBREW CONGREGATION CEMETERY
INDEPENDENCIA ESTE
Río Las Vegas
MOON
To Santiago de Las Vegas

SUBURBAN HAVANA

editing the pro-independent *La voz del pueblo cubano* (The Voice of the Cuban People).

Continuing east, you'll reach **Parque Guaycanamar,** Calle Martí, e/ Arangura y Céspedes, the main plaza fronting a splendidly preserved town hall in Georgian style, with columns and, on the east, side the somewhat dilapidated **Teatro Céspedes.** The Guaracheros de Regla, a renowned *comparsa* (African-derived dance troupe), often practice here.

From here, Calle Martí continues east about one kilometer to **Cementerio de Regla,** at the junction with 10 de Octubre. The cemetery contains many fascinating tombs and headstones dating back over a century.

About 400 meters north of the cemetery, steps lead uphill to **Colina de Lenin** (Lenin Hill), Calle Vieja e/ Enlase y Rotaria, where a three-meter-tall bronze face of the Communist leader is carved into the cliff face, with a dozen life-size figures (in cement) cheering him from below. More cement figures attend an olive tree dedicated to Lenin's memory that grows above the cliff. A small and rather pitiful museum, tel. 97-6899, atop the hill is dedicated to the life of Lenin and various martyrs of the Cuban revolution; open Tues.–Sat. 9 A.M.–6 P.M. It's a good vantage point from which to survey the town. (Bus no. 29 will also take you there from the ferry). The Colina is more directly reached from Parque Guaycanamar via Calle Alberquerque and 24 de Febrero; you'll reach an unmistakable metal staircase that leads to the park.

Food

There are several basic eateries on Calle Martí. Two pleasant restaurants sit on the southwest corner of Parque Guaycanamar, where an ice cream shop can help you beat the heat. **Pizzeria Puerto Bello** is on the southeast corner.

Services

There's a **Banco de Crédito,** Calle Martí #372, e/ 27 de Noviembre y Arangura, tel. 97-3031, and a **Cadeca,** directly opposite. The **police station** is at the east end of Martí at the corner of Juan Gualberto Gómez.

Getting There

The little Regla ferries, tel. 97-9130 (in Regla), bobbing like green corks, are magic carpets across Havana harbor. The ferries run constantly between Regla and the wharf on Avenida San Pedro at the foot of Santa Clara; it's a five-minute crossing (10 centavos). Other ferries depart Regla's wharf for Casablanca.

Bus no. 6 departs from Agramonte (Zulueta) and Genios for Regla; bus no. 106 departs from Agramonte and Refugio.

GUANABACOA

Guanabacoa, about three kilometers east of Regla, was founded in 1607 and developed in colonial days as the major trading center for slaves for more than a century. Thus, an Afro-Cuban culture evolved here, expressed not least in a strong musical heritage. Many of the leading families of songsters and musicians hail from Guanabacoa, and you're sure to come across *rumberos* playing while you walk the streets. Guanabacoa also remains Cuba's most important center of *santería*. So strong is the association that all over Cuba, folks facing extreme adversity will say "I'm going to have to go to Guanabacoa," implying that only the power of a *babalawo* can fix the problem. The town is nicknamed El Pueblo Embrujado— "enchanted village." Guanabacoa was also a major ecclesiastical venue during throughout the colonial epoch and boasts several important religious sites.

It is a popular pilgrimage site for *habaneros,* but its various touristic attractions await restoration. It is currently of interest only to those with a serious interest in *santería,* a bent for ecclesiastical history, or a fascination for traditional Afro-Cuban music.

A recently established **Zona Franca** (Free Trade Zone), Carretera de Berroa, Km 1, Municipio del Este, AP 6965, tel. 95-9636, is three kilometers east of Guanabacoa. It is hoped that the zone will become a major center for foreign-owned industry.

Parque Martí

The sprawling town is centered on a small tree-shaded square at Calles Martí, División Pepe Antonio, y Adolfo del Castillo Cadenas. Parque Martí is dominated by the recently restored **Iglesia Nuestra Señora de la Asunción** (commonly called the Parroquial Mayor, or Parish Church), Calle División #331, e/ Martí y Cadenas, tel. 97-7368. The church was completed in 1748. It features pink walls and a lofty *mudéjar*-inspired wooden roof painted sky blue, plus a beautiful baroque gilt altar dripping with gold. Lateral altars line the nave. Note the 14 carved and painted Stations of the Cross. It's normally closed, but you can try the side entrance on Calle Enrique Guiral. Open Mon.–Fri. 8:30 A.M.–noon, and Sun. 8:30-11:30 A.M. Mass is Tuesday–Thursday at 8 A.M., and Sunday at 9:15 A.M.

On the west side of the church sits the **Museo Histórico de Guanabacoa** (Historical Museum of Guanabacoa), Calle Martí #108, e/ Valenzuela (Versalles) y Quintín Bandera, tel. 97-9117, which tells the tale of Guanabacoa's development. The 33-room museum outlines the evolution of Afro-Cuban culture, with emphasis on the slave days and *santería*. However, the latter are displayed in a separate section that's sometimes closed. Open Mon. and Wed.–Sat. 10 A.M.–6 P.M., and Sun. 9 A.M.–1 P.M. (US$2 entrance). If the museum is closed, try the **Bazar de Reproducciones Artísticas** down the road at Calle Martí 175, with a shrine to Yemayá and rooms brimming with *santería* regalia. It's open Monday–Saturday 10 A.M.–6 P.M.

The **Galería de Arte Concha Ferrant,** Calle Martí #8A, tel. 97-9804, on the north side of the church, is open Tuesday–Saturday 9 A.M.–5 P.M., and Sundays 10 A.M.–2 P.M.

Facing the church on the east side is the **Casa de Domino de Guanabacoa,** where adherents of dominoes slap down their pieces; and the columned **Palacio Municipal,** or town hall.

Walk north 50 meters and you pass **Teatro Carral,** Calle Pepe Antonio, esq. Rafael de Cadena, fronted by a grand Moorish arch.

Other Sights

The list of religious sites is long. Notable is the **Convento de Santo Domingo,** Calle Santo Domingo #407, esq. Rafael de Cadena (Lebredo), tel. 97-7376. This impressive convent,

with its neo-baroque facade, was designed in 1728 and constructed by artisans from the Canary Islands. Its church, the **Iglesia de Nuestra Señora de la Candelaria,** boasts a magnificent blue-and-gilt baroque altar plus one of the most complicated *alfarjes* (intricately pieced, Moorish-inspired ceilings layered with geometric and star patterns) in Cuba, comprising thousands of fitted wooden pieces adjoined without nails. Open Tues.–Fri. 9–11:30 A.M. and 3:30–5 P.M. (ring the bell in the doorway to the left of the main entrance). Mass is Tues.–Fri. at 8 A.M. and Sunday at 10:30 A.M.

Convento y Iglesia de San Antonio (sometimes called "Los Escolapios"—"the scholars"—for its dedication to education), Calle Máximo Gómez, esq. San Antonio, tel. 97-7241, was begun in 1720 and completed in 1806. It boasts an exquisitely decorated *alfarje* ceiling. Mass is Tuesday–Sunday at 5 P.M.

The tiny, red-tiled hilltop **Ermita de Potosí** (Potosí Hermitage), Calzada Vieja Guanabacoa, esq. Calle Potosí, tel. 97-9867 (information), and its overgrown cemetery are in a sad state of neglect. The hermitage dates back to 1644, and is thereby the oldest religious structure still standing in Cuba. It contains two tombstones, one dating from 1747 with the remains of Captain Don Juan de Acosta. His self-penned epitaph reads: "Traveler, you who step on me today, reflect that you will one day be turned to ashes like me." Open Mon.–Sat. 8 A.M.–noon, and Sun. 8–10 A.M. Mass is on Sunday at 8:30 A.M. The cemetery is open daily 8 A.M.–5 P.M.

At the corner of San Juan Bosco and San Joaquín is a small shrine to San Lázaro beneath a fulsome bougainvillea bower. Pilgrims flock here each December 17, bearing flowers and *promesas* (pledges).

Guanabacoa also boasts two Jewish cemeteries. The **Cementerio de la Comunidad Religiosa Ebrea Adath Israel** (also known as the United Hebrew Congregation Cemetery), Avenida de la Independencia Este, e/ Obelisco y Puente, tel. 97-6644, on the eastern outskirts of town, is for Ashkenazi. It dates from 1912 and is entered by an ocher-colored Spanish-colonial frontispiece with a Star of David. A

Holocaust memorial (immediately to the left of the gate upon entering) stands in somber memory of the millions who lost their lives to the Nazis, with emotionally stirring text: "Buried in this place are several cakes of soap made from Hebrew human fat, a fraction of the six million victims of Nazi savagery in the 20th century. May their remains rest in peace." Open Mon.–Fri. 8–11 A.M. and 2–5 P.M.

Behind the Ashkenazi cemetery is the **Cementerio de la Unión Hebrea Chevet Ahim,** Calle G, e/ 5ta y Final, tel. 97-5866, opened in 1942 for Sephardic Jews. It too has a memorial to the Holocaust victims. Turn north off Avenida de la Independencia Este at Avenida de los Mártires (4ta) to reach it. Open daily 7 A.M.–5 P.M.

The **Centro Gráfico de Reproducciones Para el Turismo,** Calles San Juan Bosco y Barreto, displays ceramics and other artwork.

Food and Entertainment

Try **Pizzería Bambino,** Calle Martí y División, tel. 97-7490, on the northwest corner of the main plaza, where there're also **Coppelia** and **Helado Tropical** for ice cream.

Paladar La Pastorita, Calle 18 #21, esq. 6ta, tel. 97-3732, in Reparto Guiteras (also known as the Bahía district) of northern Guanabacoa, serves *criollo* dishes in huge portions.

The **Casa de la Trova,** Calle Martí #111, e/ San Antonio y Versalles, tel. 97-7687, hosts performances of Afro-Cuban music and dance. Open Tues.–Sun. 9 A.M.–11 P.M. (one peso).

Services

There's a tourist information bureau at Calle Albuquerque y Martí, tel. 97-0297. The **Dirección Municipal de Cultura,** at the juncture of San Andres and Martí, can offer information on the town's culture. An **Etecsa Telecorreo** post office and phone booth is Calle Adolfo del Castillo Cadenas, on the south side of Plaza Martí.

Banco de Crédito y Comercio is at Calle Martí #66, tel. 97-0316.

Getting There

Bus no. 3 departs for Guanabacoa from Máximo Gómez and Aponte, on the south side of Parque de la Fraternidad, in Habana Vieja; and bus no. 95 from the corner of Corrales and Agramonte (Zulueta). From Vedado, you can take bus no. 195; from the Plaza de la Revolución, take bus no. 5.

It's a 40-minute uphill hike from Regla if walking.

Habana del Este

Beyond the tunnel under Havana harbor, you pass through a heavily-policed toll booth (no toll is charged), beyond which the six-lane Vía Monumental four-lane freeway leads east to Ciudad Panaméricano and Cojímar. One km east of the second (easternmost) turnoff for Cojímar, Vía Monumental splits awkwardly. Take the narrow Vía Blanca exit to the left to reach Playas del Este; the main Vía Monumental swings south (you'll end up circling Havana on the Circunvalación).

Warning: The tunnel is monitored by cameras; fines are dispensed to tourists for the slightest transgression . . . often imagined. *Keep your speed down to the posted limits!* Motorcycles are *not* allowed through the harbor tunnel; if you're on two wheels, you'll have to take the Vía Blanca, which skirts around the bay. Motorcycles with sidecars are permitted, as are pedestrians.

CIUDAD CAMILO CIENFUEGOS

About one kilometer after exiting the tunnel you'll pass the Reparto Braulio Coroneaux and Camilo Cienfuegos districts, on your right. The former is a heavily guarded military base that includes the **Hospital General Luis Diaz Soto** (formerly known as the Hospital Naval), Carretera el Dique, tel. 862-6825, where Fidel Castro apparently receives his medical care. More controversially, attached to it is **"La Fabriquita"**—the "Little Factory"—officially known as Fábrica de Pienso Animal, where the U.S.

government claims Cuba undertakes super-secret biological and chemical warfare research.

Ciudad Camilo Cienfuegos is the first of the residential complexes thrown up in haste after the Revolution. The apartment block had received fresh coats of paint at last visit, but first views are often deceiving . . . I found the elevators trashed, and the hallways littered with dog feces and detritus.

The hospital and Camilo Cienfuegos are accessed via Carretera el Dique; the southern fork leads downhill to Casablanca. On the north side of Camilo Cienfuegos is the lonesome **Fuerte No. 1,** a fortress built in 1897 during the last phase of the War of Independence. Its squat construction is bored through with elaborate trenches and tunnels.

CIUDAD PANAMERICANO

Three kilometers east of Havana, you'll pass the Ciudad Panamericano complex, built at great cost in 1991 for the Pan-American Games, which Cuba won convincingly. A high-rise village (to the east of the sports complex) was built to ac-commodate the athletes, spectators, and press. Today, it is a residential community for Cubans. Built in the hurried, jerry-rigged style of postrevolutionary years and but a decade old, it already betrays its third-rate construction techniques. Crumbling concrete, rusting metal door frames, and other decay hint that it's on its way to becoming a slum.

Ciudad Panamericano is pushed prominently in tourist literature, but offers nothing but regret for tourists. Many budget tour operators use the hotels here. Don't fall for the marketing hype.

Avenida 78 (Paseo Panamericano) is the main boulevard, sloping down toward the shore. All the main services can be found along here.

The night spot of choice is the disco of the Hotel Panamericano (open 10 P.M. until 6 A.M.).

Accommodations

Hotel Panamericano Resort, Calle 5A, esq. Avenida 78, tel. 95-1010, fax 95-3913, features a hotel and two apartment complexes. The hotel's unappetizing lobby, full of dowdy utility furniture, is your first hint that a reservation here is a grave error. At last visit the rooms likewise cried

Ciudad Panamericano complex

out for refurbishment. Telephone and satellite TV are standard. The hotel has a large swimming pool popular with Cubans on weekends. There's also a large gym plus sauna, car and moped rental, and tourism bureau. Rates are US$45 s, US$59 d low season; US$54 s, US$71 d high season. (Horizontes.)

Apartotel Panamericano Resort, opposite the hotel, offers 421 meagerly furnished two- and three-bedroom apartments popular with budget European charter groups. The minimal facilities include a small bar and basic restaurant. Rates are US$48 low season, US$55 high season two-bedroom; US$58 low season, US$68 high season three-bedroom. (Horizontes.)

Food

Several modest restaurants line the main street. The best is **Steak House Toro,** Avenida 78, e/ 5A y 5B, tel. 33-8545, offering clean, modern, a/c surroundings. It serves rib steak, filet mignon, T-bone steak, and other meats, and has an all-you-can-eat roast beef special for US$10. **Restaurante Allegro,** Avenida 78, e/ 5C y 5D, serves pizzas and Italian dishes. The village's other eateries are all dreary affairs, if not in decor, then in their menus.

A **coffee shop** one block west of the hotel has a patio.

Services

The **Banco de Crédito y Comercio,** Avenida 78, esq. 5, tel. 95-1303, is open Monday–Friday 8:30 A.M.–3 P.M., Saturday 8:30–11 A.M. **Cadeca,** Avenida 78 y 5D, can change dollars into pesos. The **post office,** Avenida 78, e/ 5 y 3, is open Monday–Friday 8 A.M.–noon and 2–6 P.M., Saturday 8 A.M.–noon. You can make calls from the **telecorreo,** Avenida 78 y 5C.

There's a pharmacy and **Óptica Miramar,** Avenida 78, e/ 7 y 5D, tel. 95-1216. The **medical center** is on Avenida 80, esq. 5D.

Getting There and Around

From the Vía Monumental heading east, take the first exit to the right—marked Cójimar—which will take you back over the freeway into the Pan-American complex and the Hotel Panamericano.

Metrobus (*camello*) M-1 departs the Prado, opposite the Capitolio, in Habana Vieja; and also from the corner of Avenida de los Presidentes y 27 in Vedado. It runs along the Vía Monumental; the third stop is for Ciudad Panamericano. Bus no. 195 and 265 also run to Ciudad Panamericano, where they arrive and depart the Hotel Panamericano.

A free shuttle departs the Hotel Panamericano for Havana four times daily.

Havanautos, tel. 95-1093, outside the Hotel Panamericano, rents cars and scooters (scooters cost US$24 per day; US$21 per day for eight days or longer). A US$50 deposit is required. **Transauto** also has an office in Villa Panamericana, tel. 33-8802.

The Hotel Panamericano offers a Hemingway Tour.

COJÍMAR

Cojímar is a forlorn fishing village adjoining and immediately east of Ciudad Panamericano. The waterfront is lined with weather-beaten, red-tile-roofed cottages with shady verandas. Whitecaps are often whipped up in the bay, making the Cuban flag flutter above **Fuerte de Cojímar** (locally called El Torreón), the pocket-size fortress guarding the cove's entrance. It was here in 1762 that the English put ashore their invasion army and marched on Havana to capture Cuba for King George III. The fortress, built in the 1760s to forestall another fiasco, is still in military hands, and you will be shooed away from its steps if you get too close.

Cojímar is best known as the place where Ernest Hemingway berthed his legendary sport-fishing boat, the *Pilar.* When Hemingway died, every fisherman in the village apparently donated a brass fitting from his boat. The collection was melted down to create the bust of the author—**Monumento Ernest Hemingway**—that has stared out to sea since 1962 from atop a large limestone block within a columned rotunda at the base of El Torreón. A plaque reads: "Parque Ernest Hemingway. In grateful memory from the population of Cojímar to the immortal author of *Old Man and the Sea,* inaugurated July 21

uerte de Cojímar and Monumento Ernest Hemingway

962, on the 63rd anniversary of his birth." The rass bust occasionally receives a spit and pol-sh, and the classical rotunda was recently reno-ated. It is a stirring site, and the royal blue sky nd hard windy silence make for a profound ex-erience as you commune alone with Papa.

After exploring, appease your hunger with sherman's soup and paella at Hemingway's fa-orite restaurant, **La Terraza** (described later in his chapter), on the main street 200 meters outh of El Torreón. After Hemingway's death, he restaurant went into decline. Apparently, Castro, passing through in 1970, was dismayed to earn of its condition and ordered it restored. he gleaming mahogany bar at the front, ac-epting dollars only, gets few locals—a pity; what hangout it could be. You sense that Papa could troll in at any moment. His favorite corner table s still there. He is there, too, patinated in bronze top a pedestal, and adorning the walls in black nd white, sharing a laugh with Castro.

Cojímar was most famous as the residence of Gregorio Fuentes, Hemingway's old pal and skip-er after whom the novelist modeled the proud sherman in *The Old Man and the Sea*. Travelers ame from far and wide to hear Fuentes recall his adventures at his home at Calle Pesuela #209, esq. 3D, where his grandson, Rafael Valdés, charged visitors $50 for 15-minute "consulta-tions." The old man could often be found re-galing travelers in La Terraza (his former home is five blocks uphill from the restaurant), where you can toast to his memory with a turquoise cocktail—Coctel Fuentes. See the Sidebar "The Old Man: Gregorio Fuentes."

Taller El Viejo y El Mar, opposite La Ter-raza, is an artists' studio representing various local artists.

Accommodations

Villa Lennon, Calle Los Pinos #3E02, e/ 27 y 28, Cojímar, tel. 65-0557, is a handsome house where hosts Sonia and Joaquín have an independent apartment with a small lounge and kitchen, plus private bath with hot water (US$20). You can use the family's well-lit TV lounge.

Casa Particular Arsenio Rivas, Calle 27 (Es-partero) #98, e/ Maceo y Los Pinos, tel. 65-2962, cater-corner to Villa Lennon, also has a pleas-ing, cross-ventilated, a/c upstairs apartment with modern furnishings, a small kitchen, and large

THE OLD MAN: GREGORIO FUENTES

Gregorio Fuentes, born in 1897, died in 2002 at the grand old age of 104. His memory remained keen to the end, particularly when it came to his old fishing companion, Ernest Hemingway. "His absence is still painful for me," said Fuentes, who from 1938 until Hemingway's death was in charge of the writer's sportfishing boat, the *Pilar.*

Fuentes was the model for "Antonio" in *Islands in the Stream,* and is considered by many—albeit more contentiously—to be the model for Santiago, the fisherman cursed by *salao* (the worst form of bad luck) in *The Old Man and the Sea,* a simple and profound novel that won Hemingway the Nobel Prize for Literature. Hemingway—who claimed that the "Santiago" in the novella was partly modeled after another Cuban fisherman, Anselmo Hernández—looked the part: "The old man was thin and gaunt with deep wrinkles in the back of his neck. The brown blotches of the benevolent skin cancer the sun brings from its reflections on the tropic sea were on his cheeks. . . . Everything about him was old except his eyes and they were the same color as the sea and were cheerful and undefeated."

Fuentes started his sea life on Lanzarote, in the Canary Islands, when he was four years old. He came to Cuba at age 10 and met Hemingway in 1931 on Tortuga, in the Bahamas, when the two men were sheltering from a storm—Fuentes was captain of a smack. The two men were virtually inseparable from 1935 to 1960. During World War II, they patrolled the coast for German U-boats. Years later, says Fuentes, he and Hemingway patrolled the same coast to assist Castro's rebel army. Their birthdays were 11 days apart and, reports Tom Miller, the two would celebrate each together with a bottle of whiskey. Fuentes kept the tradition alive after Hemingway's death by pouring a whiskey over the latter's bust down by the harbor.

The old skipper dined daily at Las Terrazas, where his meals had been free since 1993, courtesy of Castro, who named him a national treasure and gifted him a color TV and a doubling of his pension. Cojímar's venerable homegrown hero is venerated by Cubans.

modern bathroom with hot water (but no toilet seat), and a terrace shaded by an arbor (US$20).

Food

At **La Terraza,** Calle Real #161, esq. Candelaria, tel. 55-9232, Ernest Hemingway's old haunt, the food is good, with a wide-ranging menu that includes paella (US$7–15), pickled shrimp (US$6.50), oyster cocktail (US$2.95), and sautéed calamari (US$6.15). The paella is inconsistent—from sublime to fair. Open 10:30 A.M.–11 P.M. **Paladar El Barco,** Calle Moré #2, e/ A y Malecón, tel. 65-6710, serves *criollo* fare for the impecunious; open noon–midnight. **Restaurante Yemayá,** Calle Pezuela #226, Cojímar, is a *paladar* in the hills.

Getting There

By car, the exit from the Vía Monumental is well marked—coming from Havana, take the *second* exit marked Cojímar.

Buses no. 58, 116, 195, 215, and 217 depart from the bottom of the Prado, at the junction with Avenida de los Estudiantes (10 centavos); bus no. 58 departs Avenida Rancho Boyeros and Bruzón, Plaza de la Revolución. It departs Cojímar from Calle 99 y 3A.

Hotels in Havana offer excursions to Cojímar through their tour desks. **Paradiso: Promotora de Viajes Culturales** includes Cojímar on a five-hour guided excursion called "Hemingway: The Mystery of a Footprint" (Calle 19 #560 esq. C, Vedado, tel. 832-6928, fax 33-3921, paradis@ turcult.get.cma.net, www.ceniai.inf.cu/paradiso).

ALAMAR AND CELIMAR

Immediately east of Cojímar, you'll pass a dormitory city long prized by the Cuban government as an example of the achievements of socialism. Alamar (pop. 100,000) is a sea of concrete high-rise complexes—what Martha Gellhorn considered "white rectangular factories"—jerry-built with shoddy materials by microbrigades of untrained "volunteer" workers borrowed from their normal jobs and taught on-site. Alamar sprawls east to its sister city, Celimar.

In April 1959, Alamar emerged on the drawing board as the first revolutionary housing scheme in postrevolutionary Cuba. The initial plan for 10,000 people in four- to 11-story prefabricated concrete apartment blocks was to be fully self-contained in self-sufficient "superblocks." These were partly inspired by the British postwar models for fixed-rent, low-cost housing run by the state, already discredited in Europe.

Castro was a regular visitor during the early years of construction: Alamar was a matter of pride and joy for him. He touted the project as a model for future revolutionary housing schemes. Later, Cuban planners came to acknowledge its isolating nature and overwhelming deficiencies—the plumbing came from the Soviet Union, the wiring from China, the stoves from North Korea; there were no spare parts budgeted for upkeep. Nonetheless, Alamar was vastly expanded beginning in 1976 and today covers four square miles. Today, the city wears a patina of mildew and grime, and, by any standards, is a virtual slum. Refuse litters the potholed roads, and the roadside parks are untended. And Castro never gets to see the dead rats and dog feces that go uncleaned in the hallways. There are no jobs here, either, and few stores. Nor proper transportation. And no logic to the maze of streets, or to the addresses of buildings, so that finding your way around is a study in frustration.

Perhaps because there are no social facilities, Alamar has evolved its own artistic, predominantly alternative, culture. It's Havana's center of hip-hop and rap, and hosts a rap concert each mid-August. Tattoo festivals are also held here.

The singular redeeming feature is **Playa Bacuranao,** a small horseshoe cove with a white-sand beach backed by seagrape and palms at the east end of Alamar. It's popular on weekends with locals escaping city life for a day by the sea in the sun. The Spanish built a watchtower here (still extant), where they could watch for pirate ships and signal to Havana with smoke fires. Later, it was used as a lookout station to signal contraband boats at sea, letting them know whenever the *rurales* (soldiers on horseback) were around by hanging out clothes on the clothesline. Hemingway also used to berth his *Pilar* here, and it was here that his fishermen in *To Have* *and Have Not* had squeezed "the Chink's" throat until it cracked.

The area is good for **scuba diving.** The wreck of an 18th-century galleon lies just off the tiny beach. Another wreck farther out is a popular playpen for turtles. Coral grows abundantly on both sides of the bay, so if you have **snorkeling** gear, bring it.

Getting There

The M1 *camello* serves Alamar. Buses no. 62 and 162 pass by Bacuranao, departing from Parque Central in Havana.

Most residents hitch. The junctions of the two major access roads off the Vía Blanca are major *botellas* (hitching points).

Playas del Este

"A sense of the island's racial history and diversity wasn't to be culled from the telephone directory," wrote Carlo Gébler in *Driving Through Cuba,* "but was to be seen at first hand on the sand by the edge of the sea." Cubans are great beachgoers, and nowhere on the island proves the case more than the Playas del Este. On hot summer weekends all of Havana seems to come down to the beach. The beaches of Playas del Este are temples of ritual narcissism: young Cubans congregate here to meet friends, tan their bodies, play soccer or volleyball, and flirt.

The beaches of Playas del Este stretch unbroken for six kilometers east-west. They are divided by name.

A nearly constant tropical breeze is usually strong enough to conjure surf from the warm turquoise seas—a perfect scenario for lazing, with occasional breaks for grilled fish or fried chicken from thatch-roofed *ranchitas,* where you can eat practically with your feet in the water.

Playas del Este is pushed as a hot destination for foreign tourists and, in the mid-1990s, enjoyed some success, bringing tourists (predominantly Italian and male) and Cubans (predominantly young and female) together for rendezvous under *palapas* and palms. The westernmost beaches were considered by *jineteras* to be a great place to find single Italian males, for whom the resort has become a virtual colony. When a ban was placed on Cuban women in hotel rooms, private room rentals rocketed in the easterly residential section of Guanabo. The beach resort has also long been popular with Cuban couples seeking to rent private rooms by the hour as places of coital convenience. Then a police crackdown initiated in early 1999 knocked the wind clear out of Playas del Este's sails. Young *cubanas* were arrested and began to stay away. As a result, Italians canceled their vacation plans in droves. At last visit, Cuban females (whether they're *jineteras* or not) remained wary of the heavy police presence and were reticent to interact with foreigners.

By international standards, it's a nonstarter other than for a day visit. This isn't Cancún or even Negril. Although upscale villas are available, the hotels are disappointing. The nightlife and services are desultory. And other than the marvelous beaches, forget any other hopes of aesthetic appeal.

Avoid swimming in springtime, when the seas are full of microorganisms that cause raised welts on your skin; locals call it *agua mala.* The beaches also get terribly littered . . . ugh! Care should always be taken when swimming: the waves can be powerful and rip currents are common.

TARARÁ

East of Alamar, you'll cross the Río Tarará and pass by Tarará, hidden down the hill to the north. Tarará is a villa resort at the far western end of Playas del Este. Before the Special Period, it was used by Cuban schoolchildren, who combined study with beachside pleasures and stayed at Tarará's **José Martí Pioneer City,** replete with soccer pitch, cinema, and other services. Here, too, several thousand young victims of the Chernobyl nuclear disaster in the Ukraine in 1988 have been treated free of charge, as they still are; blonde, blue-eyed children still abound. About 20,000 Ukrainian children have been treated for free, using shark cartilage and human placenta to cure many skin problems and other ills ranging

TOURIST INFORMATION OFFICES

nfotur, tel. 33-3333, oficturi@ofitur.mit.tur.cu, www.infotur.cu, the government tourist information bureau, has offices at Ave. Las Terrazas e/ 10 y12, Playa Santa María, tel. 97-1261, fax 96-1111, infoeste@teleda.get.cma.net; and 5ta-C Avenida, e/ 468 y 470, Guanabo, tel. 96-3841, fax 96-6868.

from thyroid disorders to tumors. About 60 percent of arrivals are treated as outpatients; others are hospitalized and stay an average of nine months to a year.

It was here, too, that Castro operated his secret government in the early stage of the Revolution. Che Guevara was convalescing here after his debilitating years of guerrilla warfare in the Sierra Maestra, and the location away from Havana proved perfect for secret meetings to shape Cuba's future while Castro played puppeteer to the weak and demoralized official democratic government of President Urrutia.

The villa complex fell on hard times following the Soviet collapse, but most of the villas have recently been refurbished, promising to bring life back to Tarará as a tourist resort (Servimed, tel. 204-2377, operates a portion of Tarará as a health tourism facility). Services are fairly limited, but Tarará has two splendid beaches. To the west is a delightful pocket-size beach that forms a spit at the rivermouth; it features a volleyball court and shady *palapas*. The main beach—**Playa Mégano**—lies further east and forms the westernmost of the Playas del Este. It, too, has a sand volleyball court, shade umbrellas, and lounge chairs.

The rivermouth channel is renowned for its coral, large groupers, and schools of snappers—great for snorkeling and scuba diving.

Entry is free, but you must show ID—bring your passport in case the occasionally mule-minded *custodios* get a case of *burro-cracia*.

Marina Puertosol Tarará

Marina Puertosol Tarará, tel. 97-1510 or 97-462, fax 97-1499, channel VHF 77 or 108, marina@mit.tur.cu, at the rivermouth, has 50 berths with water and electricity hookups, plus diesel and gas. It also has a dry dock.

Boat Rental: You can rent **yachts** for US$200 for nine hours. **Pedal boats** are available for forays along the river estuary (US$9 per hour).

Scuba Diving: Trips cost US$30 (one dive) or US$45 (two dives). A certification program costs US$300. Initiation dives (three hours) are also offered, as is equipment rental.

Sportfishing: You can charter a boat for four hours' sportfishing for US$200–250, depending on the vessel (one to four people). Each July, the marina hosts the "Old Man and the Sea Fishing Tournament;" registration costs US$450 for up to three anglers. The marina also hosts the "La Hispanidad Fishing Tournament" in October.

Snorkeling: Three-hour snorkeling excursions at 9:30 A.M. (US$20–30 based on a minimum of four people per boat).

Yacht Cruises: Excursions include six-hour "seafaris" at 9:30 A.M., featuring fishing, snorkeling, and lunch, (US$55 based on a minimum of four passengers). A three-hour nocturnal cruise costs US$15 with dinner on board, plus music and dancing.

Accommodations

Villas Tarará offers a range of villas—*casas confort*—for rent, with from one to four bedrooms. Those at the east end belong to Cubanacán, Calle 9na, esq. 14, Villa Tarará, tel. 97-1616, fax 97-1619, reservas@vtarara.cha.cyt.cu, which has 172 attractive air-conditioned units, all with TV, radio, security box, kitchen with fridge, and private parking. Facilities include a swimming pool, pharmacy, rental car agency, shop, gym and massage. Rates are US$30/50/75/96/115 one-/two-/three-/four-/five-bedrooms low season, US$35/60/72/98/115 high season. Units near the beach cost US$35/65/86/112/135 low season, and US$40/75/111/135/150 high season.

Villas to the west belong to **Puertosol,** tel. 97-1462, fax 96-1333, www.puertosol.net, which rents out to Cubans and tourists alike. Each villa has a radio, satellite TV, telephone, and private parking. Nonregistered guests are strictly

PLAYAS DEL ESTE

proscribed—none may stay overnight without authority of the management, which even requires a list of guests attending "a social gathering." A grocery, laundry service, and restaurants are on-site. Rates are US$58/82/104/123/141 two-/three-/four-/five-/six-bedrooms low season, US$72/103/130/154/176 high season. Deluxe units cost US$115/164/208 two-/three-/four-bedroom low season, US$144/205/250 high season; deluxe units with swimming pools cost US$139/188/232 low season, US$174/235/290 high season.

Food

Restaurante Cojímar is next to the marina office and serves basic *criollo* fare, as does a handsome, thatched restaurant immediately west of the swimming pool near the marina. A juice bar serves the east end of the beach, where there's also a restaurant 100 meters inland.

Services and Entertainment

The **Discoteca La Sirena,** near the marina, is open 9 P.M.–4 A.M. A *parque de diversiones* (amusement park) on the west side of the Río

Tarará offers carousels and other rides; access is by a separate exit from the Vía Monumental west o the river.

Getting There

Tarará is at Vía Blanca Km 17, 27 kilometer: east of Havana. It is signed off the Vía Blanca. A taxi will cost about US$17.

SANTA MARÍA DEL MAR

Playa Mégano extends east from Tarará an merges into **Playa Santa María del Mar,** th broadest and most beautiful swathe, with light golden sand shelving into stunning aquamarine and turquoise waters. The beaches are palm shaded and studded with plentiful thatched shad umbrellas. Most tourist facilities are here, in cluding bars and water sports, plus a fistful o tourist hotels. There is no residential commu nity. The village of Santa María Loma, one kilo meter inland, atop the hill that parallels the shore offers modest rental units, plus homes for for eign employees permanently residing in Cuba.

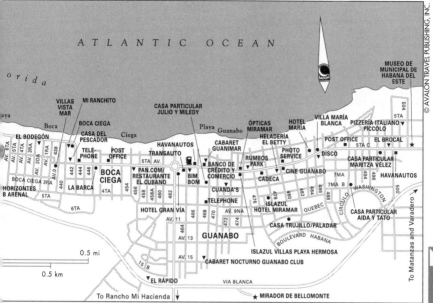

SUBURBAN HAVANA

Playa Santa María runs east for about three kilometers to the mouth of the Río Itabo—a popular bathing spot for Cuban families. A large mangrove swamp centered on **Laguna Itabo** extends inland from the mouth of the river, where egrets, herons, and other waterfowl can be admired. The system is an important nursery for all manner of marine life.

Accommodations

Horizontes runs the show in Santa María.

Under US$50: The **Aparthotel Horizontes Atlántico,** Avenida de las Terrazas, tel. 97-1494, fax 97-1203, carpeta@hatlan.hor.tur.cu, offers 52 pleasantly furnished a/c one-, two-, or three-bedroom apartments with satellite TV, telephone, and safety deposit box. Facilities include a restaurant, swimming pool with bar, scooter rental, tour desk, tennis courts, and entertainment. Its pool draws Cubans on hot days, when it gets lively. Rates are US$30/40/52 one-/two-/three-bedroom apartments low season, US$30/48/60 high season. (Horizontes.)

Villas Mirador del Mar, Avenida de las Banderas, tel. 97-1354, fax 97-1262, carpeta@mira dor.hor.tur.cu, is a hilltop option a 15-minute walk from the beach. Most guests are Cuban. It has one- to five-bedroom air-conditioned units with cable TV. There's a hilltop swimming pool, restaurant, and medical service. Rates are US$20 s, US$28 d low season; US$22 s, US$30 d high season for one-bedroom units. (Islazul.)

US$50–100: The **Hotel Horizontes Mégano,** Avenida de las Terrazas, tel. 97-1610, fax 97-1624, vmegano@hor.tur.cu, at the far west end of Playas del Este, is a 10-minute walk from the beach. The ambience and decor of the a/c cabins is simple yet appealing, with tile floors, bamboo furnishings, tiny satellite TV, small tiled bath with showers, and plate-glass doors opening to verandas. Posted rates are US$57 s, US$74 d low season; US$65 s, US$90 d high season. However, at last visit over-the-counter rates were US$32 s, US$45 d low season US$38 s, US$54 d high season. (Horizontes.)

Aparthotel Las Terrazas, Avenida Las Terrazas, e/ 10 y Rotunda, tel. 97-1344, fax 97-1316, fronts the shore. It has 83 one-, two-, and three-bedroom a/c apartments with kitchen, TV, radio, and telephone. Facilities include a swimming pool. Rates are US$36/54/63 one-/two-/three-bedroom units low season, US$50/75/88 high season. (Horizontes.)

Hotel Tropicoco, Avenida de las Terrazas, e/ Calles 5 y 7, tel. 97-1371, fax 97-1389, recepcion@htropicoco.hor.tur.cu, operated by Horizontes, is the most popular place in town. The uninspired five-story building was recently reopened after a complete renovation, but no amount of tinkering can improve the unwelcoming lobby. Still, it remains popular with budget-minded Canadian tour companies (but, one suspects, not their clientele). It has 188 a/c rooms with simple yet adequate decor and bamboo furniture, plus telephone, and radio, and modern bathrooms. Services include a pleasing restaurant, plus bar, tour desk, shops, post office, and car rental. Rates are US$50 s, US$75 d low season, US$60 s, US$85 d high season. (Horizontes.)

US$100–150: The **Hotel Horizontes Club Arenal,** Lago de Boca Ciega, tel. 97-1272, fax 97-1287, reservas@arenal.get.cma.net, in the midst of the lagoon between Playas Santa María del Mar and Boca Ciega, is much nicer. It relies mostly on European charters. It has 166 a/c rooms in three categories. Rooms are spacious and offer eye-pleasing decor and furnishings. The red-tile-roofed units surround a massive pool and lush lawns with thatched restaurant and bar. However, this all-inclusive property doesn't quite live up to the images presented in the slick brochure. It has a few shops, and the staff try hard to keep guests amused with canned *animación* (entertainment). Rates are US$85/130 s/d standard, US$105/150 s/d suite low season; US$95/150 s/d standard, US$125/190 suite high season. (Horizontes.)

Club Atlántico, Avenida de las Terrazas, esq. Calle 11, tel. 97-1085, is a beachfront all-inclusive. It's a bit dreary and lowly by international standards and is meager in its public amenities. It has 92 a/c rooms with satellite TV, radio, and minibar. Facilities include a restaurant and snack bar, swimming pool, tiny gym, tennis court, and shop. Entertainment staff try to put a bit of pep

into the scene. Rates (including meals and drinks) were US$65 s, US$100 d low season, US$75 s US$120 d high season. (Gran Caribe.)

US$150–250: The **Villas los Pinos,** Avenida Las Terrazas y Calle 4, tel. 97-1361, fax 97-1524, recepcion@pinos.gca.cma.net, offers the most elegant option, with 26 two-, three-, and four-bedroom villas. Some appear a bit fuddy-duddy; others are impressive and up to international standards and have their own private pools. Villa #35 even has its own squash court They all have TV, VCR, radio, telephone, and kitchen. Rates are US$128–244 low season US$200–425 high season, including housemaid service. (Gran Caribe.)

Food

Several thatched bars and eateries can be found on the beach. One of the best is **Club Mégano** tel. 97-1404, at the west end of Playa E Mégano, with a thatched bar and grill serving burgers (US$2), chicken, and seafood including lobster (US$15). I recommend the grilled fish (US$8). Nearby, but less appealing, is the **D'Prisa Centro Turístico.**

Mi Casita de Coral, 100 meters east of the Hotel Tropicoco, serves *criollo* fare 24 hours daily and has some appealing seafood, including grilled fillet of fish (US$5) plus spicy lobster enchilada (US$8). Likewise, **Casa Club Atlántico** has a snack bar offering seafood, *criollo* dishes, and spaghetti (US$3.50), plus a chicken *oferta especia* (lunch special) for US$2.

Parrillada Costarenas, Avenida Norte, esq Avenida de las Terrazas, tel. 97-1361, serves in expensive grilled fare and offers seaviews from it air-conditioned beachside diner. It serves half chicken (US$3.25), steaks (US$2–4), smoked pork loin (US$4.60), and a house special: por with orange and rum sauce (US$4). Dishes however, run to an outrageous US$22.50 fo lobster. It has a pool table upstairs. Open noon–6 P.M.

Pizzería Mi Rinconcito, toward the west en of Avenida de las Terrazas, offers slices of pizz from US$1. Also catering to Italian tastes i **Pizzería Yara,** Avenida las Terrazas, esq. Call 10, with its own swimming pool. **Café Pinomar**

Avenida Sur, esq. Calle 5, also serves pizzas and burgers, and is open 24 hours.

Restaurante Mi Cayito, Avenida las Terrazas, tel. 97-1339, is a pleasant thatched restaurant on a small island overhanging the mangroves of Laguna Itabo. It has the usual fare: grilled fish, shrimp, and lobster, but is overpriced (US$10–26). Open daily 10 A.M.–10 P.M. July–Aug., and 10 A.M.–6 P.M. Sept.–June.

Recreation
Several outlets on the beach rent **jet skis** (US$15 for 15 minutes) and **Hobie-Cats** (US$20 per hour), including **Club Mégano,** where you can also rent shade umbrellas (US$3 per day) and beach chairs and lounge chairs (US$2 per day). **Mi Cayito,** Avenida las Terrazas, tel. 97-1339, a small island with restaurant just west of the Río Itabo, rents kayaks and water-bikes on the lagoon; you can rent beach umbrellas and chairs here, from the outlet on the beach side of the road.

Horses can be rented on the beach in front of Hotel Tropicoco.

Scuba diving is available from the watersport stand on the beach in front of the Hotel Tropicoco. A coral reef runs offshore at a depth of no more than 20 feet, with lots of brain, elkhorn, and staghorn formations.

Entertainment
The liveliest nightspot is the **Disco Bananarama,** a thatched bar-cum-disco on Playa Santa María. **Hotel Tropicoco** also has a disco (entrance free to hotel guests, US$2 to others). **Aparthotel Atlántico** offers afternoon theme entertainment, including an Afro-Cuban show. The **Casa Club Atlántico** has a pool hall and dance club upstairs with a bar, TV, and karaoke (open 2 P.M.–2 A.M.), plus *cabaret espectáculo* on weekends.

Services
There's an **Infotur,** Ave. Las Terrazas, e/ 11 y 12, tel. 97-1261, fax 96-1111, tourist information office near Club Atlántico.

You can purchase postage stamps and make international calls at the Hotel Tropicoco. There's also a **post office,** Avenida de las Terrazas, e/ 10 y 11, in Edificio Los Corales, open 8 A.M.–1 P.M. There are plenty of phone booths.

The **Clínica Internacional,** Avenida de las Terrazas, e/ 8 y 9, tel. 97-1032, 100 yards east of Hotel Tropicoco, is open 24 hours. A visit costs US$25 (US$30 at night). The doctor also makes hotel visits if needed (US$50). It has a pharmacy, clinical laboratory, and ambulance.

The **Tropical Travel Agency,** Avenida de las Terrazas at Calle 11, Edificio Los Corales, can advise on and make travel arrangements.

Photo Service has two small stores in the Hotel Tropicoco, and on Avenida 5ta y Calle 480.

Getting There and Around
See Boca Ciega and Guanabo section for information on getting to Playa Santa María.

Havanautos has a car-rental office in the parking lot of Hotel Tropicoco. It also rents scooters for US$10 per hour, US$24 per day (with a US$50 deposit). **Transauto** has an office outside the Aparthotel Atlántico; it also rents scooters. **Micar,** tel. 96-6895, fax 96-1532, reserva@complejo.gca.tur.cu, has an outlet at Club Atlántico; and **Via Rent-a-Car,** 5ta Avenida, e/ 10 y 11, tel. 96-1152, is nearby.

Cubatur and Havanatur, in Hotel Tropicoco, offers excursions.

BOCA CIEGA AND GUANABO

Playa Boca Ciega begins east of the Río Itabo estuary and is another beautiful beach backed by dunes. It is particularly popular with Cuban families, many of whom choose to rent simple bungalows in the residential and rental complex called Boca Ciega, built in the 1960s for use by the masses.

Playa Boca Ciega merges eastward into **Playa Guanabo,** the least-attractive beach, but running for several km along the shorefront of Guanabo, a Cuban village with many plantation-style wooden homes. Local Cubans use it for recreation, including old men looking like salty characters from a Hemingway novel standing bare-chested, reeling in silvery fish from the surf. It has gradually been accruing tourist facilities and is the only place with a sense of active community.

Playa Guanabao ends at the mouth of the Río Guanabo. The rivermouth estuary is slated to become an ecological park—**Rincón de Guanabo**—although at last visit no effort had been made to bring this to fruition.

The **Museo de Municipal de Habana del Este,** Calle 504 #5B12, esq. 5C, Guanabo, tel. 96-4184, is housed in a charming little yellow *casa,* and has motley displays tracing the history of the area. A tank displays saltwater fishes. Open Mon.–Fri. 9 A.M.–4 P.M., Sat. 9 A.M.–noon. **Iglesia Nuestra Señora de Carmen,** one block east, may be of interest to those with an ecclesiastical or architectural bent.

For grand views up and down the beaches, head inland of Guanabo to **Mirador de Bellomonte,** Vía Blanca km 24.5, tel. 96-3431, where a café and bar atop the Altura Bellomonte hill offers fine vistas. Open daily 2 P.M.–2 A.M. There's a 17th-century mansion nearby.

Accommodations

This section of Playas del Este has traditionally been the spot of choice for *habaneros* on weekends and during summer holidays. They are catered to with simple bungalows that don't meet international standards. This has led to a growing trade in private room rentals. The entire complex is divided into *zonas,* each with a *carpeta* for rental units. Islazul runs the entire show.

By the way, don't mistake **Motel Rosita** for somewhere to lay your head. Instead it's a place to get laid. Sure, it's location a block from the beach is appealing, but this is a "love motel" that charges couples in pesos.

Casas Particulares: One of the best options is **Casa de Julio y Miledy,** Calle 468 #512, e/ 5ta y 7ma, Guanabo, tel. 96-0100. Set in a beautiful garden, this a/c apartment is equipped for the handicapped and has a security box, large lounge with antiques, an open kitchen, and a small and simply furnished bedroom for US420. A small swimming pool was planned. The owners are a delight.

Casa Maritza Vélez, Calle 5D #49610, e/ 496 y 498, Guanabo, tel. 96-4389, is a handsome 1950s house with a beautiful interior in a well-maintained garden. It has two a/c rooms

with modern furnishings, old metal-frame beds, soothing pastel colors, and modern tiled bathrooms (but no toilet seats) for US$30.

Casa Trujillo, Avenida Quebec #55, e/ Calle 478 y 482, Guanabo, tel. 96-3325, mail@cubanasol.com, www.cubanasol.com/casatrujillo.htm, is a two-story family unit with one spacious a/c bedroom, a TV lounge, and a modern kitchen to which guests have access. Meals are prepared on request. Miriam Trujillo and Alberto Mendes, your hosts, are fluent in Spanish, French and English. Alberto can arrange water sports and fishing trips. Room rates are US$25.

Miriam and Alberto act as agents for a number of neighborhood *casas particulares,* each charging US$25 and each with its own page: see www.cubanasol.com. For example, **Casa Campimar,** Avenida Quebec, is another charming two-story home with clean, modestly furnished room with private entrance and lots of wicker. Guests get use of a kitchen, lounge, and patio with rockers. José, the owner, offers scuba diving. **Casa Daisy,** Avenue Mexico #156, has particularly pleasing decor. **Casa Armada,** Avenue A #50025, e/ Calle 500 and the beach, has a handsome bathroom.

Rental Villas: The *carpeta* (office) called **Boca Ciega,** 1ra Avenida, tel. 96-2771, has 13 simple houses for rent for US$25 s/d one-bedroom, US$26 two-bedroom, US$35 three-bedroom, and US$38 four-bedroom. (Islazul.)

Hotel Gran Vía, 5ta Avenida, esq. 462, tel. 96-2271, offers five rooms for Cubans and five for foreigners at US$21 s/d low season, US$26 d high season. It has an a/c restaurant adjacent. (Islazul.)

Food

Paladar Italiano Piccolo, 5ta Avenida, e/ 502 y 504, tel. 96-4300, run by Greek owners, offers colorful colonial ambience near the shore. It offers surprisingly tasty Italian fare served with hearty salads at low prices (US$5–10). It grows its own produce in the garden. Open noon–midnight.

Paladar Maeda, Avenida Quebec #55, e/ Calle 478 y 482, Guanabo, tel. 96-3325, is a clean and pleasant place where *criollo* meals are cooked in a wood-fired brick oven. It has indoor and patio dining, and a large wine bar. **Paladar Don**

edro, 5ta Avenida y 482, also serves pizza and sagne *horno a leña* from a wood-fired oven.

El Cubano, 5ta Avenida, esq. 454, is a modern ean eatery serving *criollo* dishes. Next door is an.Com, which offers a wide range of sandich (from US$1.50), plus omelets, burgers JS$2.50), tortillas (US$1), yogurts, fruit juices, *atidos* (milk shakes), and cappuccinos. Open A.M.–3 A.M.

El Bodegón, on 1ra Avenida in Boca Ciega, is simple seafront restaurant with *criollo* fare served n a breeze-swept patio. Two blocks east is the andsome, thatched Los Caneyes, open 24 hours d also serving *criollo* dishes.

The most atmospheric place in Boca Ciega is asa del Pescador, 5ta Avenida #44005, esq. alle 442, tel. 96-3653, a Spanish-style *bodega* ith fishing nets hanging from the ceiling. The enu is huge. Fish dishes average US$7, and rimp and lobster start at US$8. The house spealty is *escabeche* (US$3.50). Open noon–11 P.M.

El Brocal, Avenida 5C, esq. 498, tel. 96-2892, a 1930s red-tile-roofed cottage in eastern Guaabo, offers rustic ambience (the wooden tables are lexican) and simple *criollo* fare such as roast pork d grilled fish (US$7.50); plus quasi-Mexican re such as tacos (US$1.50) served with that rary of Cuban rarities . . . bottles of tongue-lashg salsa. Better yet, cocktails and beers cost less an US$1. Open noon–midnight.

For ice cream, head to Bim-Bom, a clean, odern, well-run operation serving various sunes and 32 flavors of ice cream along the lines of askin-Robbins. Heladería El Betty, 5ta venida, esq. Calle 480, serves ice cream cones for e peso. There's a bakery next door.

ntertainment

abaret Guanimar, 3ra Avenida and Calle 468, as a simple *cabaret espectáculo* followed by a isco. Open Thurs.–Sun. 9 P.M.–2 A.M. (US$3). draws an unsophisticated local crowd, as do e Centro Nocturno Habana Club, Calle 10 e/ y 3ra, and Cabaret Nocturno Guanabo Club, alle 468 #1302 y Avenida 15, tel. 96-2884.

Films dubbed in Spanish are shown at Cine uanabo, 5ta Avenida y Calle 480, tel. 96-2440 ne peso).

There's a basic children's playground—parque de diversiones—on 5ta Avenida and Calle 470.

Services

There's an Infotur, 5ta-C Avenida e/ 468 y 470, Guanabo, tel. 96-3841, fax 96-6868, tourist information office one block east of the traffic circle.

There's a Banco de Crédito y Comercio, 5ta Avenida, e/ 468 y 470, tel. 96-3320, with a Cadeca exchange booth adjacent.

There's a post office, 5ta Avenida and Calle 448, in Boca Ciega; and at 5ta-C Avenida y 492 in Guanabo.

Getting There and Away

Buses no. 62, 162, and 262 serve Playas del Este from Parque Central; bus no. 219 departs from the main bus terminal. Bus no. 400 serves Guanabo and departs from Parque Taya Piedra, at the junction of Manglar Arroyo and Almanbique, in the Atarés neighborhood; you may be able to get on at the junction of Agramonte and Gloria, near the main railway station (five pesos).

Tourist taxis cost about US$20 one way. Although *máquinas* (shared or *colectivo* taxis) are barred from picking up tourists, you can try your luck; they depart from the Prado near Parque de la Fraternidad.

A train runs daily to Guanabo (July–Aug. only) from Estación Cristina, Avenida de México and Arroyo, Habana Vieja, tel. 879-0354, departing at 8:45 P.M. The station is at Agromar, about two kilometers inland from Guanabo; trains depart for Estación Cristina at 6:30 P.M.

Getting Around

Havanautos, 5ta Avenida y Calle 464, tel. 96-3858, and Calle 500-A e/ 5ta y 7ma, tel. 96-3845, has two offices; as does Transautos, 5ta Avenida y 464, tel. 96-4161, and Calle 478, e/ 7ma y 9ta, tel. 96-2917.

There's a Cupet gas station on Avenida 5ta y Calle 462 in Guanabo.

MINAS

This sleepy rural community, about four km inland from Guanabo, is the setting for two *fincas de recreo* (dude ranches): **Finca de Recreo Guanabito,** Calzada de Jústiz Km 3.5, Guanabo, tel. 96-4610 (open daily 9 A.M.–6 P.M.); and just up the road, **Rancho Mi Hacienda Guanabito,** Calzada de Jústiz, Km 4, Guanabo, tel. 96-4711 (open daily 9 A.M.–9 P.M.). Rancho Mi Hacienda, the more developed of the two, is a 13-hectare *finca* that raises animals and vegetables used in the ranch's restaurant. It offers horseback riding, as well as boat rides on a lake. Take your camera to record the flurry of feathers during ferocious yet bloodless cockfights—fortunately, in deference to tourist politically correct modern tastes, the bird's spurs are covered to prevent them from seriously hurting each other. Rancho Mi Hacienda hosts an Afro-Cuban cultural show once a week. Accommodation is provided in six handsome albeit rustic cabins connected by suspension bridges on the banks of the Río Itabo, plus three rooms in what was once a posh mansion. Each a/c unit has a telephone, satellite TV, and minibar. There's a dining hall and swimming pool amid lush gardens.

Resources

Cuban Spanish

Learning the basics of Spanish will aid your travels considerably. In key tourist destinations, however, you should be able to get along fine without it. Most Cubans are well educated, English is widely spoken in Havana, and the number of English speakers is growing rapidly. For example, English is now required of all university students and hotel staff. Most larger hotels have bilingual desk staffs, and English is spoken by the staff of car rental agencies and tour companies. Cubans are exceedingly keen to practice their English and you will be approached often by such individuals. Many Cubans know at least the basics of one other European language—a surprising number are fluent in French and, of course, Russian. Away from the tourist path, far fewer people speak English.

Use that as an excuse to learn some Spanish. Cubans warm quickly to those who make an effort to speak their language. Don't be bashful. Use what Spanish you know and you'll be surprised how quickly you become familiar with the language.

Ediciones Universal, P.O. Box 450353, Miami, FL 33145, publishes a *Diccionario de Cubanismos,* www.ediciones.com, but in Spanish only.

Pronunciation

Castilian Spanish, with its lisping "c"s and "z"s, is the Spanish of Spain, not Latin America. Cubans do not lisp their "c"s and "z"s; they pronounce the letters more like an "s," as do Andalusian Spaniards and most other Latin Americans. In its literary form, Cuban Spanish is pure, classical Castilian. Alas, in its spoken form Cuban Spanish is the most difficult to understand in all of Latin America. Cubans have lent their own renditions to the Spanish sound: like a zebra that is not quite a horse, Cuban Spanish is white but with black stripes.

Cubans speak more briskly than other Latin Americans, blurring their rapid-fire words together. The diction of Cuba is lazy and unclear.

Thought Richard Henry Dana, Jr., in 1859: "it strikes me that the tendency here is to enfeeble the language, and take from it the openness of the vowels and the strength of the consonants." The letter "s," for example, is usually swallowed altogether, especially in plurals. Thus, the typical greeting *¿Cómo estás?* is usually pronounced Como-tah. The swallowed "s"s are apparently accumulated for use in restaurants, where they are released to get the server's attention—*"S-s-s-s-s-st!"* Because of this, a restaurant with bad service can sound like a pit full of snakes. The final consonants of words are also often deleted, as are intervocalic consonants such as "d" and, often, the entire last syllable of words—"If they dropped any more syllables, they would be speechless," suggests author Tom Miller. Regional variants exist, too. I find the Spanish of the Oriente a bit slower and less confusing. Around Baracoa, the idiom of the Indians endures.

Cubanisms to Know

Cubans are long-winded and full of flowery, passionate, rhetorical flourishes. Fidel Castro didn't inherit his penchant for long speeches from dour, taciturn Galicia—it's a purely Cuban characteristic. Cubans also spice up the language with little affectations and teasing endearments—*piropos*—given and taken among themselves without offense.

Many English (or "American") words have found their way into Cuban diction. Cubans go to *béisbol* (and use Cubanized American terms at the game) and eat *hamburguesas*. Like the English, Cubans are clever in their use of words, imbuing their language with double entendres and their own lexicon of similes. Cubans are also great cussers. The two most common cuss words are *cojones* (balls) and *coño* (cunt), while one of the more common colloquialisms is *ojalá*, which loosely translated means "I wish" or "if only!" but is most commonly used to mean "Some hope!"

Formal courtesies are rarely used when greeting someone. Since the Revolution, everyone is *compañero* or *compañera* (*señor* and *señora* are considered too bourgeois). Confusingly, *ciao!* used as a long-term goodbye, and spelled "chao" in Cuba) is also used as a greeting in casual passing—the equivalent of "Hi!" You will also be asked ¿*Como anda?* ("How goes it?"), while younger Cubans prefer ¿*Que bola?* (the Cuban equivalent of "Wassup?") rather than the traditional ¿*Qué pasa?* ("What's happening?").

Cubans speak to each other directly, no holds barred. Even conversations with strangers are laced with "*¡Ay, muchacha!"* ("Hey, girl!"), "*¡Mira, chica!"* ("Look, girl!"), and "*¡Hombre!"* ("Listen, man!") when there is a disagreement. Cubans refer to one another in straightforward terms, often playing on their physical or racial characteristics: *El chino, la mulata, el nose hairs, la plucked eyebrows.* Black people with kinky hair are called *negros de pasas* (Negroes with raisins); those with straight hair are *negros de pelo.* Cubans do not refer to themselves with a single definition of "white" or "black." There are a zillion gradations of skin-color and features, from *negro azul trompudo* (blue-black and thick-lipped) and *muy negro* (very black), for example, to *leche con una gota de café* (milk with a drop of coffee). Whites, too, come in shades. *Un blanco* is a blond- or light-haired person with blue, green, or gray eyes. *Un blanquito* is a "white" with dark hair and dark eyes.

Bárbaro is often used to attribute a positive quality to someone, as in *él es un bárbaro* ("he's a great person"). It can also be used to express appreciation of something, as can *está en talla!* ("this is excellent"). The opposite would be *está en llamas* (literally, "on fire") figuratively used to express a negative opinion of something, as in "that's awful." *Está en candela* ("a flame") is its equivalent, but more commonly used to describe an alarming or complicated situation, or excess, as in something that's "hot" (such as a promiscuous person); or to signify "I'm broke!" Young Cubans fortunate to have some money might slap the pocket of their jeans and say *tengo guano* ("I've got some palm leaf").

Marinovia defines a live-in girlfriend (from *marido,* for spouse, and *novia,* for girlfriend). An *asére* is one's close friend, though the street term is considered a low-class word, especially common with blacks. A *flojo* (literally, "loose guy") is a lounger who pretends to work. Cubans also have no shortage of terms referring to spies, informers, and untrustworthy souls. For example, *embori* refers to an informer in cahoots with the government. *Fronterizo* is a half-mad person. *Chispa* ("spark") is someone with vitality. To become "Cubanized" is to be *aplatanado.*

Cuban Spanish

Spanish Phrasebook

Pronunciation Guide

Spanish pronunciation is much more regular than that of English, but there are still occasional variations.

Consonants

c — as 'c' in "cat," before 'a', 'o', or 'u'; like 's' before 'e' or 'i'

d — as 'd' in "dog," except between vowels, then like 'th' in "that"

g — before 'e' or 'i,' like the 'ch' in Scottish "loch"; elsewhere like 'g' in "get"

h — always silent

j — like the English 'h' in "hotel," but stronger

ll — like the 'y' in "yellow"

ñ — like the 'ni' in "onion"

r — trilled at the beginning of words; in between vowels pronounced like 'tt' in "butter."

rr — trilled 'r'

v — similar to the 'b' in "boy" (not as English 'v')

y — similar to English, but with a slight 'j' sound. When standing alone it's pronounced like the 'e' in "me."

z — like 's' in "same"

b, f, k, l, m, n, p, q, s, t, w, x — as in English

Vowels

a — as in "father," but shorter

e — pronounced like a long 'a,' as in "same"

i — as in "machine"

o — as in "phone"

u — usually as in "rule;" when it follows a 'q' the 'u' is silent; when it follows an 'h' or 'g', it's pronounced like 'w,' except when it comes between 'g' and 'e' or 'i', when it's also silent (unless it has an umlaut, when it again is pronounced as English 'w')

Stress

Native English speakers frequently make errors of pronunciation by ignoring stress. All vowels—a, e, i, o, and u—may carry accents that determine which syllable of a word gets emphasis. Often, stress seems unnatural to nonnative speakers—the surname Chávez, for instance, is stressed on the first syllable—but failure to observe this rule may mean that native speakers may not understand you. There is a rule for when written accents appear, but it's generally too complicated for nonnative speakers to understand at first. Your best bet is to listen to the speakers around you and imitate where they stress their words.

Numbers

0 - cero
1 - uno (masculine)
1 - una (feminine)
2 - dos
3 - tres
4 - cuatro
5 - cinco
6 - seis
7 - siete
8 - ocho
9 - nueve
10 - diez
11 - once
12 - doce
13 - trece
14 - catorce
15 - quince
16 - dieciseis
17 - diecisiete
18 - dieciocho
19 - diecinueve
20 - veinte
21 - veintiuno
30 - treinta
40 - cuarenta
50 - cincuenta
60 - sesenta
70 - setenta
80 - ochenta

)0 - noventa
100 - cien
101 - ciento y uno
200 - doscientos
1,000 - mil
10,000 - diez mil
1,000,000 - un millón

Days of the Week

Sunday - domingo
Monday - lunes
Tuesday - martes
Wednesday - miércoles
Thursday - jueves
Friday - viernes
Saturday - sábado

Time

While Latin Americans mostly use the 12-hour clock, in some instances, usually associated with plane or bus schedules, they may use the 24-hour military clock. Under the 24-hour clock, for example, *las nueve de la noche* (9 P.M.) would be *las 21 horas* (2100 hours).

What time is it? - ¿Qué hora es?
It's one o'clock - Es la una.
It's two o'clock - Son las dos.
At two o'clock - A las dos.
It's ten to three - Son las tres menos diez.
It's ten past three - Son las tres y diez.
It's three fifteen - Son las tres y cuarto.
It's two forty five - Son las tres menos cuarto.
It's two thirty - Son las dos y media.
It's six A.M. - Son las seis de la mañana.
It's six P.M. - Son las seis de la tarde.
It's ten P.M. - Son las diez de la noche.
Today - hoy
Tomorrow - mañana
Morning - mañana
Tomorrow morning - mañana por la mañana
Yesterday - ayer
Week - semana
Month - mes
Year - año
Last night - anoche
The next day - el día siguiente

Useful Words and Phrases

Spanish-speaking people consider formalities important. Whenever approaching anyone for information or some other reason, do not forget the appropriate salutation—good morning, good evening, etc. Standing alone, the greeting *hola* (hello) can sound brusque.

Hello. - Hola.
Good morning. - Buenos días.
Good afternoon. - Buenas tardes.
Good evening. - Buenas noches.
How are you? - ¿Cómo está?
Fine. - Muy bien.
And you? - ¿Y usted?
So-so. - Más o menos.
Thank you. - Gracias.
Thank you very much. - Muchas gracias.
You're very kind. - Muy amable.
You're welcome - De nada (literally, "It's nothing.")
Yes - sí
No - no
I don't know. - No sé.
It's fine; okay - Está bien.
Good; okay - Bueno.
Please - Por favor
Pleased to meet you. - Mucho gusto.
Excuse me (physical) - Perdóneme.
Excuse me (speech) - Discúlpeme.
I'm sorry. - Lo siento.
Goodbye - adiós
See you later - hasta luego (literally, "until later")
More - más
Less - menos
Better - mejor
Much, a lot - mucho
A little - un poco
Large - grande
Small - pequeño, chico
Quick, fast - rápido
Slowly - despacio
Bad - malo
Difficult - difícil
Easy - fácil
He/She/It is gone; as in "She left," "He's gone" - Ya se fue.

I don't speak Spanish well. - No hablo bien el español.

I don't understand. - No entiendo.

How do you say. . . in Spanish? - ¿Cómo se dice. . . en español?

Do you understand English? - ¿Entiende el inglés?

Is English spoken here? (Does anyone here speak English?) - ¿Se habla inglés aquí?

Terms of Address

When in doubt, use the formal *usted* (you) as a form of address. If you wish to dispense with formality and feel that the desire is mutual, you can say *Me puedes tutear* (you can call me "tú").

I - yo

You (formal) - usted

you (familiar) - tú

He/him - él

She/her - ella

We/us - nosotros

You (plural) - ustedes

They/them (all males or mixed gender) - ellos

They/them (all females) - ellas

Mr., sir - señor

Mrs., madam - señora

Miss, young lady - señorita

Wife - esposa

Husband - marido or esposo

Friend - amigo (male), amiga (female)

Sweetheart - novio (male), novia (female)

Son, daughter - hijo, hija

Brother, sister - hermano, hermana

Father, mother - padre, madre

Grandfather, grandmother - abuelo, abuela

Getting Around

Where is. . . ? - ¿Dónde está. . . ?

How far is it to. . . ? - ¿A cuanto está. . . ?

from. . . to. . . - de. . . a. . .

Highway - la carretera

Road - el camino

Street - la calle

Block - la cuadra

Kilometer - kilómetro

North - norte

South - sur

West - oeste; poniente

East - este; oriente

Straight ahead - derecho; adelante

To the right - a la derecha

To the left - a la izquierda

Accommodation

Is there a room? - ¿Hay cuarto?

May I (we) see it? - ¿Puedo (podemos) verlo?

What is the rate? - ¿Cuál es el precio?

Is that your best rate? - ¿Es su mejor precio?

Is there something cheaper? - ¿Hay algo más económico?

Single room - un sencillo

Double room - un doble

Room for a couple - matrimonial

Key - llave

With private bath - con baño

With shared bath - con baño general; con baño compartido

Hot water - agua caliente

Cold water - agua fría

Shower - ducha

Electric shower - ducha eléctrica

Towel - toalla

Soap - jabón

Toilet paper - papel higiénico

Air conditioning - aire acondicionado

Fan - abanico; ventilador

Blanket - frazada; manta

Sheets - sábanas

Public Transport

Bus stop - la parada

Bus terminal - terminal de buses

Airport - el aeropuerto

Launch - lancha; tiburonera

Dock - muelle

I want a ticket to. . . - Quiero un pasaje a. . .

I want to get off at. . . - Quiero bajar en. . .

Here, please. - Aquí, por favor.

Where is this bus going? - ¿Adónde va este autobús?

Round-trip - ida y vuelta

What do I owe? - ¿Cuánto le debo?

Food

Menu - la carta, el menú
Glass - taza
Fork - tenedor
Knife - cuchillo
Spoon - cuchara
Napkin - servilleta
Soft drink - agua fresca
Coffee - café
Cream - crema
Tea - té
Sugar - azúcar
Drinking water - agua pura, agua potable
Bottled carbonated water - agua mineral
    con gas
Bottled uncarbonated water - agua sin gas
Beer - cerveza
Wine - vino
Milk - leche
Juice - jugo
Eggs - huevos
Bread - pan
Watermelon - sandía
Banana - banano
Plantain - plátano
Apple - manzana
Orange - naranja
Meat (without) - carne (sin)
Beef - carne de res
Chicken - pollo; gallina
Fish - pescado
Shellfish - mariscos
Shrimp - camarones
Fried - frito
Roasted - asado

Barbecued - a la parrilla
Breakfast - desayuno
Lunch - almuerzo
Dinner (often eaten in late
    afternoon) - comida
Dinner, or a late night snack - cena
The check, or bill - la cuenta

Making Purchases

I need. . . - Necesito. . .
I want. . . - Deseo. . . or Quiero. . .
I would like. . . (more polite) - Quisiera. . .
How much does it cost? - ¿Cuánto cuesta?
What's the exchange rate? - ¿Cuál es el tipo de
    cambio?
May I see. . . ? - ¿Puedo ver. . . ?
This one - Ésta/Éste
Expensive - caro
Cheap - barato
Cheaper - más barato
Too much - demasiado

Health

Help me please. - Ayúdeme por favor.
I am ill. - Estoy enfermo.
Pain - dolor
Fever - fiebre
Stomach ache - dolor de estómago
Vomiting - vomitar
Diarrhea - diarrea
Drugstore - farmacia
Medicine - medicina
Pill, tablet - pastilla
Birth control pills - pastillas anticonceptivas
Condom - condón, preservativo

Suggested Reading

For a complete range of texts on Cuba, visit www.cubabooks.com, which also offers most of the books listed here online at a discount.

Books About Havana

Coffee Table

Aguilar Cabello, Juan Carlos (photographs by Alberto Fernández Miranda). *Tropicana de Cuba.* Havana: Visual América, 1998. The story, in Spanish, of Havana's showiest nightclub, from its beginnings in 1939 to the present day, lavishly illustrated in full color.

Barclay, Juliet (photographs by Martin Charles). *Havana: Portrait of a City.* London: Cassell, 1993. A well-researched and abundantly illustrated coffee table volume especially emphasizing the city's history. Written in a lively, readable style.

Edinger, Claudio. *Old Havana.* New York: Distributed Art Publishers, 1998. Gritty, sorrowful life in Habana Vieja is portrayed in evocative and dramatic fashion by this noted photographer. Introductions by Guillermo Cabrera Infante and Humbert Wernerck provide equally powerful statements.

Graetz, Rick. *Havana: The City, The People.* Helena, MT: American Geographic Publishing, 1991. A tribute to Havana in full color photography that captures the spirit of the 500-year-old city. Minimal text.

Leal, Eusebio. *Challenge of a Utopia: A Comprehensive Strategy to Manage the Safeguarding of Old Havana.* Havana: Office of the City Historian, 2002. Notwithstanding its lengthy title, this lavishly illustrated, well-designed book provides a light-hearted yet in-depth profile on the restoration of the ancient city.

Lobo Montalvo, María Luisa. *Havana: History & Architecture of a Romantic City.* New York: Monacelli Press, 2001. This sumptuous volume documents the city's architectural patrimony, from fortified colonial outpost to thriving 1950s capital.

Michener, James, and John Kings. *Six Days in Havana.* Austin, TX: University of Texas Press, 1989. A wonderful read regaling the noted novelist's brief but emotionally touching week in Havana. Beautifully illustrated.

Polidori, Robert. *Havana.* Göttingen, Germany: Steidl, 2001. An emotive and evocative large-format volume of fabulous photos that catalog Havana's tragic urban decay. Highly recommended.

Sapieha, Nicolas. *Old Havana, Cuba.* London: Tauris Parke Books, 1990. A small yet beautifully illustrated coffee table book accompanied by lively text.

Stout, Nancy, and Jorge Rigau. *Havana.* New York: Rizzoli, 1994. A stunning coffee table book that captures the mood of the city in color and black-and-white photography; superb text and essays add to the photographic perspectives on Havana's cultural and architectural history.

Walker, Evans. *Havana.* New York: Pantheon, 1989. A reissue of the classic collection of black-and-white photographs depicting life in Cuba in the 1930s, first published in 1933.

Fiction

Cabrera Infante, Guillermo. *Three Trapped Tigers.* New York: Avon, 1985. A poignant and comic novel, described as "a vernacular, elegiac masterpiece," that captures the essence of life in Havana before the ascendance of Castro. Written by an "enemy of the state" who has lived in embittered exile since 1962.

Chavarria, Daniel. *Adios Muchachos.* New York: Akashic Books, 2002. Cuban *noir* at its best. Darkly erotic, this brutally funny romp through the back streets of Havana, a city full of petty hustlers, beautiful prostitutes, and international hucksters whose lives combine in a series of slapstick misadventures. The ending, alas, is a let-down.

Greene, Graham. *Our Man in Havana.* New York: Penguin, 1971. The story of Wormold, a conservative British vacuum-cleaner salesman in prerevolutionary Havana. Recruited by British intelligence, Wormold finds little information to pass on, and so invents it. Full of the sensuality of Havana and the tensions of Batista's last days.

Gutiérrez, Pedro Juan. *Dirty Havana Trilogy.* New York: Farrar, Straus & Giroux, 2001. A bawdy, hilarious, and depressing semi-biographical take on the gritty life of Havana's underclass—begging, whoring, escaping hardship through sex and *santería*—during the harshest years of the Special Period.

Smith, Martin Cruz. *Havana Bay.* New York: Random House, 1999. Arkady Renko returns, this time to Havana, to solve a murder mystery that eventually leads to discovery of a plot to assassinate Fidel.

Villaverde, Cirilo. *Cecilia Valdés.* Havana: Ediciones Cátedra, 2001. A marvelous Spanish-language story of a lovely mulatta girl's ill-fated attempt to climb the social ladder of colonial society through a love affair with a wealthy *criollo* seducer whom neither knows is her half-brother. A wonderful source of information about all aspects of life in 19th-century Havana, this novel addresses many social and racial issues and was a call for abolition of slavery. It is considered Cuba's greatest contribution to literature.

Travel Guides

Cramer, Mark. *Culture Shock! Havana.* Portland, OR: Graphic Arts Center Publishing, 2000. Part guidebook, part personal account of living and vacationing in the Caribbean's greatest city. Sympathetic to the culture to the point of being yawningly anti-American and depicting the Revolution and Cuba as socialist paradise.

Lightfoot, Claudia. *Havana: A Cultural and Literary Companion.* Northampton, MA: Interlink Publishing, 2001. A marvelous work in which the author leads you through Havana past and present using literary quotations and allusions to add dimension to the sights and experiences.

Rodríguez, Eduardo Luis. *The Havana Guide.* New York: Princeton Architectural Press, 2000. A marvelous guide to individual structures—homes, churches, theaters, government buildings—representing the best of modern architecture (1925–65) throughout Havana.

Segre, Roberto, Mario Coyula, and Joseph L. Scarpaci. *Havana: Two Faces of the Antillean Metropolis.* New York: John Wiley & Sons, 1997. Aimed at both the academic and lay reader, this informative and accessible volume written by two architects and an urban geographer profiles the urbanization of Havana over its 500-year history.

Other

Miller, John, and Susannah Clark, eds. *Chronicles Abroad: Havana.* San Francisco: Chronicle Books, 1996. Short essays and extracts on Havana and other places in Cuba by such authors as Richard Henry Dana, Graham Greene, Ernest Hemingway, Mario Puzo, and Fidel Castro. A marvelous read.

Tattlin, Isadora. *Cuba Diaries: An American Housewife in Havana.* Chapel Hill, NC: Algonquin Books, 2002. A fascinating and marvelous account of four years in Havana spent raising two children, entertaining her husband's clients (including Fidel), and contending with chronic shortages. A must read.

Books About Cuba

Coffee Table

Baker, Christopher P. *Island Classics: Cars of Cuba.* London: Macmillan Caribbean, 2003. This visually stunning coffee table book offers more than 200 images of American classics—chrome-laden DeSotos, corpulent Buicks, stylish Plymouth Furies—in settings that evoke the time-warp appeal of the island.

Beytout, Olivier, and François Missen. *Memories of Cuba.* New York: Thunder's Mouth Press, 1997. Spanning the country, two French photographers capture the spirit and sadness and, above all, the surrealism of Cuba in this small book of images backed by snippets of text from well-known Cubans.

Carley, Rachel (photography by Andrea Brizzi). *Cuba: 400 Years of Architectural Heritage.* New York: Whitney Library of Design, 1997. A beautiful large-format work that spans the island and ages, tracing the evolution of architectural styles from the earliest colonial influences to the contemporary edifices and influences.

Evans, Walker. *Walker Evans: Cuba.* New York: Getty Publications, 2001. Recorded in 1933, these 60 beautiful black and white images capture the "eternal Cuba" in Evans' portraits, which portray in stark clarity the misery and hardships of life in the era. Andrei Codrescu wrote an accompanying essay.

García, Cristina, and Joshua Greene. *Cars of Cuba.* New York: Harry N. Abrams, 1995. A splendid little book with color photographs of 53 lovingly maintained beauties from the heyday of Detroit.

Giovan, Tria. *Cuba: The Elusive Island.* New York: Abrams, 1996. More than 100 images capture the richness of Cuba in all its complex and enigmatic forms, with textual extracts from a wide range of contemporary and historical sources.

Harvey, David Alan and Elizabeth Newhouse. *Cuba.* Washington, D.C.: National Geographic Society, 1999. A lavishly illustrated coffee table book that shows Cuba's diverse beauty with stunning visual imagery. The accompanying text provides a lucid synopsis of the historical and contemporary setting.

Kohli, Eddy. *Cuba.* New York: Rizzoli, 1997. A luxurious large-format book in which the sharp-eyed photographer captures the spirit of the people and land in dreamy imagery.

Kufeld, Adam. *Cuba.* New York: W.W. Norton, 1994. A photographic portrait of Cuba depicting all aspects of life. The book is enhanced by Tom Miller's introduction, which says in part that "Kufeld has achieved that rare perspective of looking at Cuba from the inside out, and in doing so he has given us a gentle look at a hard place."

Núñez Jiménez, Antonio. *The Journey of the Havana Cigar.* Havana: Empresa Cubana del Tabaco, 1995. A voluminous treatise on the history of Cuban cigars lavishly illustrated with glossy photos.

Smith, Wayne (photographs by Michael Reagan). *Portrait of Cuba.* Atlanta, GA: Turner Publishing, 1991. A succinct, lucid, and entertaining profile on contemporary Cuba told by a noted expert. This splendid coffee table book is superbly illustrated.

Stout, Nancy. *Habanos: The Story of the Havana Cigar.* New York: Rizzoli, 1997. Stout explores the history and culture of Cuba in depth to tell the tale of the Havana cigar. The large-format book is lavishly illustrated with the author's own photography.

Williams, Stephen. *Cuba: The Land, The History, The People, The Culture.* Philadelphia, PA: Running Press Books, 1994. A richly evocative, lavishly illustrated coffee table book with a concise and enlivened text.

Art and Culture

Behar, Ruth, ed. *Bridges to Cuba/Puentes a Cuba.* Ann Arbor, MI: University of Michigan Press, 1995. An evocative anthology of essays, poetry, and fiction providing perspectives on contemporary Cuba from within the country and throughout the Cuban diaspora.

Camnitzer, Luís. *New Art of Cuba.* Austin, TX: University of Texas Press, 1994. Profiles the work of 40 young Cubans who formed part of the first generation of postrevolutionary artists.

Carpentier, Alejo. *Music in Cuba.* Minneapolis: University of Minnesota Press, 2001. The definitive study of the rich musical tradition of Cuba by one of the early giants of modern Latin American literature.

Foehr, Stephen. *Waking up in Cuba.* London: Sanctuary Publishing, 2001. A marvelous and sympathetic personal portrait of Cuba's social and music scene recounted by an author who, though politically naïve, expresses a solid grounding in music.

Geldof, Lynn. *Cubans: Voices of Change.* New York: St. Martin's Press, 1991. Interviews with Cubans representing the spectrum of viewpoints and backgrounds.

Stubbs, Jean, and Pedro Pérez Sarduy, eds. *AfroCuba: An Anthology of Cuban Writing on Race, Politics and Culture.* New York: Ocean Press/Center for Cuban Studies, 1993. An anthology of black Cuban writing on aspects of "Afrocuba," including essays, poetry, and extracts from novels.

Sweeney, Philip. *The Rough Guide to Cuban Music.* London: Rough Guides, 2001. A pocket-size compendium that is a perfect handbook to the island's various music traditions, telling the story from the era of slavery to the contemporary scene.

Fiction

Correa, Arnaldo. *Spy's Fate.* New York: Akashic Books, 2002. This captivating spy thriller from within Cuba is a fascinating, light-footed tale of the intrigues of Cuba's intelligence community and the culture of the Miami exile community against which it is pitted.

García, Cristina. *Dreaming in Cuban.* New York: Ballantine Books, 1992. A brilliant, poignant, languid, and sensual tale of a family divided politically and geographically by the Cuban revolution and the generational fissures that open on each side.

Hemingway, Ernest. *Islands in the Stream.* New York: Harper Collins, 1970. An exciting triptych. The second and third parts are set in Cuba during the war and draw heavily on the author's own experience hunting Nazi U-boats at sea.

Hemingway, Ernest. *The Old Man and the Sea.* New York: Scribner's, 1952. The simple yet profound story of an unlucky Cuban fisherman. The slim novel won the author the Nobel Prize for Literature.

Hemingway, Ernest. *To Have and Have Not.* New York: Macmillan Publishing, 1937. The dramatic, brutal tale of running contraband between Havana and Key West.

Iyer, Pico. *Cuba in the Night.* New York: Alfred A. Knopf, 1995. A slow-moving story of a love affair between a globetrotting photojournalist and a young Cuban woman. Set in Cuba during the Special Period, the author stresses the atmosphere of suspicion and negativity.

Leonard, Elmore. *Cuba Libre.* New York: Delacorte Press, 1998. Set on the eve of the Spanish-

American War, this explosive mix of adventure and history makes exciting reading.

History and Politics

Benjamin, Jules R. *The United States and the Origins of the Cuban Revolution.* Princeton, NJ: Princeton University Press, 1990. A study explaining how Cuba and the United States arrived at the traumatic rupture in their relations.

Bonachea, Rolando, and Nelson Valdés. *Cuba in Revolution.* New York: Anchor Books, 1972. A collection of essays by noted academics, providing a comprehensive, many-sided overview of the Cuban Revolution and the issues it raises.

Eckstein, Susan. *Back from the Future: Cuba under Castro.* Princeton, NJ: Princeton University Press, 1994. A well-reasoned and balanced attempt to provide a broad overview of Castro's Cuba. Eckstein contends that Cuba is less rigidly Marxist than presented and that a revisionist view is needed.

Fernández, Damián J. *Cuba and the Politics of Passion.* Austin, TX: University of Texas Press, 2001. An academic study that explores the emotions and affections that have affected political attitudes in Cuba.

Johnson, Haynes. *The Bay of Pigs.* New York: Norton, 1964. Writing in collaboration with leaders of the Brigade, Haynes provides both perspectives in this masterful, encyclopedic work.

Kennedy, Robert F. *Thirteen Days: A Memoir of the Cuban Missile Crisis.* New York: Norton, 1969. A gripping portrait from inside the White House reveals the stress of crisis and how the various characters ultimately brought the world back from the brink of disaster.

Luis, Julio García, ed. *Cuban Revolution Reader: A Documentary History.* New York: Ocean Press, 2001. Documents four decades of Revolution focusing on 40 decisive moments, including the Bay of Pigs, Fidel Castro at the United Nations, and the 1990s economic crisis. The essays are from a leftist perspective.

Martí, José. *Inside the Monster: Writings on the United States and American Imperialism.* New York: Monthly Review Press, 1975 (Phillip S. Fosner, ed.). Essential prose works of the late 19th century activist, literary man, and national hero, who has exercised a lasting influence on the politics of 20th-century Cuba.

Meyer, Karl E., and Tad Szulc. *The Cuban Invasion.* New York: Praeger, 1962. A shrewd and fascinating interpretation of the Bay of Pigs.

Murray, Mary. *Cruel and Unusual Punishment: The U.S. Blockade Against Cuba.* Melbourne: Ocean Press, 1992. Details the U.S. embargo from its inception in 1960 to today from the official Cuban perspective.

Ortíz, Fernando. *Cuban Counterpoint: Tobacco and Sugar.* New York: Alfred A. Knopf, 1947. A seminal work on the decisiveness of tobacco and sugar in Cuban history.

Pérez, Louis A. *Cuba: Between Reform and Revolution.* New York: Oxford University Press, 1988. Spanning Cuba from pre-Columbian times to the present, Perez examines the island's political and economic development within the context of its ongoing struggle for self-determination.

Pérez-Stable, Marifeli. *The Cuban Revolution: Origins, Course, and Legacy.* New York: Oxford University Press, 1993. A negative review of the past four decades. It closes with a polemic offering a damning accusation of a revolution betrayed.

Smith, Wayne. *The Closest of Enemies.* New York: W.W. Norton, 1987. Essential reading, this personal account of the author's years serving as President Carter's man in Havana during the 1970s is a moving and entertaining account providing key insights into the complexities that haunt U.S. relations with Cuba.

Thomas, Hugh. *Cuba: The Pursuit of Freedom, 1726–1969.* New York: Harper & Row, 1971. A seminal work—called a "magisterial conspectus of Cuban history"—tracing the evolution of conditions that eventually engendered the Revolution.

Thomas, Hugh. *The Cuban Revolution.* London: Weidenfeld and Nicolson, 1986. The definitive work on the Revolution, offering a brilliant analysis of all aspects of the country's diverse and tragic history.

Wyden, Peter. *Bay of Pigs: The Untold Story.* New York: Simon and Schuster, 1979. An in-depth and riveting exposé of the CIA's ill-conceived mission to topple Castro.

Personalities

Anderson, John. *Che Guevara: A Revolutionary Life.* New York: Grove Press, 1997. The definitive biography on Guevara, revealing an astonishing profile of this fascinating, controversial, and charismatic figure.

Castro, Fidel. *Che: A Memoir by Fidel Castro,* Melbourne: Ocean Press, 1983. Fidel's account of his relationship with Che Guevara documents the man, the revolutionary, the thinker, and the Argentine-born doctor's extraordinary bond with Cuba.

Cruz, Mary. *Cuba and Hemingway on the Great Blue River.* Havana: Editorial José Martí, 1994. A critical study of Hemingway's writings in which the author presents the theory that Hemingway's works reflect core tenets of Cuban ideology.

Franqui, Carlos. *Family Portrait with Fidel.* New York: Vintage Books, 1985. An insider's look

at how the Sovietization of the Cuban Revolution occurred and precisely what goals Fidel Castro had in mind.

Fuentes, Norberto. *Hemingway in Cuba.* Secaucus, NY: Lyle Stuart, 1984. The seminal, lavishly illustrated study of the Nobel Prize winner's years in Cuba.

Geyer, Georgie Anne. *Guerrilla Prince: The Untold Story of Fidel Castro.* Boston: Little, Brown & Company, 1991. An extraordinary biography that reveals the Machiavellianism of Fidel Castro as the author attempts to explain the mysticism of the meticulously secretive Cuban leader.

Gray, Richard Butler. *José Martí, Cuban Patriot.* Gainesville, FL: University of Florida Press, 1962.

Halperin, Maurice. *The Taming of Fidel Castro.* Berkeley, CA: University of California Press, 1981.

Hemingway, Gregory. *Papa, A Personal Memory.* New York: Pocket Books, 1976. A funny, serious, and touching account of the author's childhood, including a long period in Cuba with his father, Ernest Hemingway.

Lockwood, Lee. *Castro's Cuba, Cuba's Fidel.* Boulder, CO: Westview Press, 1990.

Oppenheimer, Andres. *Castro's Final Hour.* New York: Simon & Schuster, 1992. A sobering, in-depth exposé of the darker side of both Fidel Castro and the state system, including controversial topics such as drug trading.

Quirk, Robert E. *Fidel Castro.* New York: W.W. Norton, 1993. A detailed, balanced, disturbing, and none too complimentary profile of the Cuban leader.

Szulc, Tad. *Fidel: A Critical Portrait.* New York: Morrow, 1986. A riveting profile of the astounding life of this larger-than-life figure. A marvelous read and among the best of the biographies on Castro.

Travel Literature

Baker, Christopher P. *Mi Moto Fidel: Motorcycling Through Castro's Cuba.* Washington, D.C.: National Geographic Adventure Press, 2001. Winner of the Lowell Thomas Award 2002 Travel Book of the Year, this erotically-charged tale of the author's 7,000-mile adventure by motorcycle through Cuba, offers an insightful, bittersweet look at the last Marxist "utopia." The first book from National Geographic in which the sex isn't just between monkeys.

Codrescu, Andrei. *Ay, Cuba!* New York: St. Martin's Press, 1999. A no holds barred, barefisted account of the Rumanian author's 12-day sojourn in Havana during the Pope's visit in January 1998. Combining trenchant social criticism, Codrescu explores the sensual culture while skewering you-know-who at every turn.

Gébler, Carlo. *Driving Through Cuba.* New York: Simon & Schuster, 1988. The tale of a three-month sojourn through Cuba by car.

Hungry Wolf, Adolf. *Letters from Cuba.* Skookumchuck, BC: Candian Caboose Press, 1996. This collection of "letters home" provides a tender and sympathetic account of the author's journeys through Cuba in fulfillment of his passion for steam trains.

Jenkins, John, ed. *Travelers' Tales of Old Cuba.* New York: Ocean Press, 2002. An engaging collection of 18 essays painting personal accounts of Cuba spanning the late 17th-century to today.

Miller, Tom, ed. *Travelers' Tales: Cuba.* San Francisco: Travelers' Tales, 2001. Extracts from the contemporary works of 38 authors provide a lively and entertainment account of Cuba that is at times hilarious, cautionary, and inspiring.

Miller, Tom. *Trading with the Enemy: A Yankee Travels Through Castro's Cuba.* New York: Atheneum, 1992. Thoughtful, engaging, insightful, compassionate, and told in rich narrative, this travelogue adopts a non-controversial tone.

Ryan, Alan, ed. *The Reader's Companion to Cuba.* New York: Harcourt Brace & Company, 1997. This anthology offers two dozen eyewitness "reports" spanning two centuries, from mob lawyer Frank Ragano's recollections of the Mafia in Havana to Tommy Lasorda's remembrances of his years playing in the Cuban leagues.

Ripley, Peter C. *Conversations with Cuba.* Athens, GA: University of Georgia Press, 1999. An eloquent, sympathetic look at contemporary Cuba, Ripley's account is rich with intelligence and insight expressed through interviews with a cross-section of Cubans.

Samuelson, Arnold. *With Hemingway: A Year in Key West and Cuba.* Maine: Thorndike Press, 1984. Recollections of a year accompanying "E.H." on fishing excursions around Key West and Cuba, showing Hemingway "off-guard and all-too-human."

Schaefer, Dave. *Sailing to Hemingway's Cuba.* Dobbs Ferry, NY: Sheridan House, 2000. An at first drifting, firsthand account of a Yankee sailor's time spent cruising around the forbidden isle. Once the skipper finally arrives, the reader is treated to some well-researched insights.

Smith, Stephen. *The Land of Miracles.* London: Abacus, 1997. An engaging and intelligent account of the author's time exploring Cuba in the mid-1990s.

Travel Guidebooks

Baker, Christopher P. *Moon Handbooks Cuba.* Emeryville, CA: Avalon Travel Publishing, 2003. The definitive guidebook to Cuba, this tome spans the island end to end, with dozens of maps and photographs. Complete coverage leaves no stone unturned.

Baker, Christopher P. *National Geographic Traveler's Cuba.* Washington, D.C.: National Geographic Society, 2002. A perfect companion to *Moon Handbooks Cuba,* this lavishly illustrated guide offers a series of recommended walks and drives, plus succinct practical information.

Other

Agee, Philip. *Inside the Company: CIA Diary.* New York: Bantam Books, 1975. This sobering work details the mission to discredit Cuba, including dirty tricks employed by the CIA against Latin America leftists. Told by a CIA "deep-cover" agent who eventually resigned and today lives in Havana, purportedly having subsequently been employed by Cuba's own spy service.

Benjamin, Medea, and Peter Rosset. *The Greening of the Revolution.* Melbourne: Ocean Press, 1994. A detailed account of Cuba's turn to a system of organic agriculture by two noted authorities on the subject.

Cabrera Infante, Guillermo. *¡Mea Cuba!* New York: Farrar, Straus & Giroux, 1994. An acerbic, indignant, raw, wistful, and brilliant set of essays in which the author pours out his bile at the Castro regime.

Calder, Simon, and Emily Hatchwell. *Cuba: A Guide to the People, Politics and Culture.* London: Latin America Bureau, 1995. A slender yet thoughtful and insightful overview of Cuba.

Halperin, Maurice. *Return to Havana.* Nashville, TN: Vanderbilt University Press, 1994. An engaging and scathing personal essay on contemporary Cuba by a professor who taught in Havana and worked for Cuba's Ministry of Foreign Trade in the 1960s.

Howard, Christopher. *Living and Investing in the New Cuba.* Miami: Costa Rica Books, 1999. A guide to living, making money, and the good life in Cuba.

LaFray, Joyce. *¡Cuba Cocina!* New York: Hearst Books, 1994. A compilation of Cuban recipes, both classic and *nuevo cubano,* from Floridian Cuban restaurants and such famous Havana restaurants as La Bodeguita del Medio.

Moses, Catherine. *Real Life in Castro's Cuba.* Wilmington, DE: Scholarly Resources, 2000. This brutally candid report on life in contemporary Cuba is told by a former employee at the U.S. Interests Section in Havana. While scathing in its take on the state system, Moses expresses a deep warmth for the Cuban people.

Padula, Alfred, and Lois Smith. *Sex and Revolution: Women in Socialist Cuba.* New York: Oxford University Press, 1996. An examination of Cuba's attempt to conceptualize, prioritize, and implement sexual equality.

Randall, Margaret. *Women in Cuba: Twenty Years Later.* Union City, NY: Smyrna Press, 1981. An important book for an understanding of Cuban society and the goals of the Revolution, full of examples of how a society can marshal its resources to undermine centuries of female subjugation.

Schwartz, Rosalie. *Pleasure Island: Tourism & Temptation in Cuba.* Lincoln, NE: University of Nebraska Press, 1997. An engaging review of tourism development in Cuba and how it has shaped the face of Havana.

Timerman, Jacobo. *Cuba: A Journey.* New York: Knopf, 1990. A passionate, provocative, and sometimes scathing report of a journey through Cuba by a man who suffered torture at the hands of right-wing Argentinian extremists and who formerly idealized Cuba as a model socialist state.

Suggested Viewing

Videos

Arroz con Frijoles: The Budget Traveler's Guide to Cuba. A 60-minute review geared to the impecunious, no-frills traveler. Copies cost US$39.95 from Fej Films, P.O. Box 24062, Lansing, MI 48909-4062 (indicate PAL or NTSC).

Classic American Cars of Cuba. This 42-minute video follows a procession of classic American autos on a procession from Havana to the colonial city of Trinidad. Copies are available for US$75 including donation to WLIW21 public television, P.O. Box 21, Plainview, NY 11803.

Cuba Va: The Challenge of the Next Generation. This 60-minute documentary released in 1993 captures the vigor and diversity of Cuban youth, who express their divergent perspectives on the Revolution and the future. Cuba Va Video Project, 12 Liberty St., San Francisco, CA 94110, 415/282-1812, fax 415/282-1798.

Gay Cuba. This one-hour documentary takes a candid look at one of Cuba's most controversial human rights issues: the treatment of the gay and lesbian people in Cuba since the Revolution. Frameline, 346 Ninth St., San Francisco, CA 94103, 415/703-8654, fax 415/861-1404, distribution@frameline.org, www.frameline.org.

Havana Nagila: The Jews of Cuba. An hour-long look at the history of Jews in Cuba during five centuries. Copies can be ordered from Schnitzki & Stone, 819 W. Roseburg Ave. #240, Modesto, CA 95350, 209/575-1775, fax 209/575-1404.

Trains of Cuba. This two-hour video is a delight for serious antique train buffs, with dozens of puffing billies shown at work. Copies cost US$39.95 plus shipping. Order from Canadian Caboose Press, Box 844, Skookumchuck BC V0B 2EO, Canada, 250/342-1421.

Movies

Before Night Falls. Fine Line Features, 2000. A potent and poignant adaptation of Reinaldo Arenas's autobiography, in which the Cuban novelist and poet recounts his life first in Castro's Cuba and then in exile, in the United States. Says film-critic Lucas Hilderbrand, "Its power is two-fold: it's an intoxicating, intensely erotic account of sexual discovery and liberation, and a devastating record of the artist's persecution under the Castro regime."

Bitter Sugar. Azucar Films, 1996. This bittersweet portrait of contemporary Cuba charts the journey of an idealistic young Marxist scholar whose plans to attend the University of Prague go awry when he falls for a dancer who abhors the Revolution and plans to escape to Florida. Gradually his ideals dissolve in the face of corruption, poverty, and repression that leave him bitter and hollow.

Buena Vista Social Club. Artisan Entertainment, 1999. A magnificent, adorable documentary look at the reemergence from obscurity of veteran performers Rubén González, Omara Portuondo, Ibrahim Ferrer, Eliades Ochoa and Compay Segundo culminating in their sell-out concert at Carnegie Hall. The performers tell their stories directly to the camera as they wander the decayed streets of Havana and gather to record and perform.

Death of a Bureaucrat. New Yorker Films, 1966. Tomás Gutiérrez Alea's questioning portrait of the absurdities of the Cuban bureaucratic system and people's propensity to conform to absurd Kremlin-style directives that cause misery to others.

Guantanamera. New Yorker Films, 1997. A road movie with a twist, this rueful romantic comedy by Tomás Gutiérrez Alea and Juan Carlos Tabio begins to unfold after an elderly dame dies from an excess of sexual stimulation. The farce of returning her body to Havana for proper burial provides the vehicle for a cutting yet comic parody of an overly-bureaucratic contemporary Cuba, and a lighthearted admonishment to live for the moment.

Libertad. Bougainvillea Films, 1999. A profoundly disturbing true-life tale about a young Cuban artist's failed attempt to escape Cuba in search of freedom on a raft. Caught in the act, he is sent to prison and tortured but eventually departs Cuba with friends and reaches Florida after a harrowing sea journey that claims the lives of his family. Shot in stark black and white.

Memories of Underdevelopment. New Yorker Films, 1968. Director Tomás Gutiérrez Alea's intellectual and sensual, wide-ranging, stream of consciousness masterpiece revolves around an erotically charged, intellectual "playboy" existence in early '60s Cuba, pinned by the tragedy of the central character's alienation from the "underdeveloped" people around him and his own inability to attain a more fulfilled state.

Paradise Under the Stars. Vanguard Cinema, 1999. Set around a star-struck woman's dream of singing at the Tropicana nightclub, this buoyantly witty comedy (winner of the Audience Award at the Havana Film Festival) combines exuberant musical numbers, bedroom farce, and some light-hearted satiric jabs at Cuban machismo.

Strawberry and Chocolate. Miramax, 1995. Legendary Cuban director Tomás Gutiérrez Alea's famous skit about the evolving friendship between a gay man and an ardent revolutionary is a classic comedic drama and the first Cuban film to be nominated for an Oscar (Best Foreign Language Film). David, the young Communist, is selected by Diego, an artist, as a potential target for seduction. The tale that unfolds in derelict Havana is an indictment of the treatment of homosexuals in Cuba.

Soy Cuba! Milestone Films, 1964. Filmed by great Russian director Mikhail Kalatozov, "I Am Cuba" is a brilliant, melodramatic, agit-prop black and white, anti-American epic to Communist kitsch that exposes the grinding poverty, oppression, and decadence of Batista's Havana, told in four didactic tales.

Thirteen Days. New Line Studios, 2001. A riveting, intense, and thought-provoking dramatic study of leadership under pressure, this movie takes a fascinating look at the machinations that went on in the highest circles of power in Washington during the nerve-wracking Cuban Missile Crisis as John F. Kennedy (Bruce Greenwood) and Robert F. Kennedy (Steven Culp) maneuver to negotiate a peaceful settlement with Russia.

Internet Resources

Note: many Cuban sites are offered in Spanish only (most are configured for Microsoft Explorer) and regardless of theme, usually reflect the political flavor of the month.

This directory is *not* a comprehensive listing; see individual chapters for additional sites.

GENERAL INFORMATION

Books
Cuba Books
www.cubabooks.com

More General Information Sources
AfroCuba Web
www.afrocubaweb.com

Cubanet
www.cubanet.org

Cubanos.org
www.cubanos.org

Latin American Network Information Center
www.lanic.utexas.edu

Cuban Portals
Cubaweb
www.cubaweb.cu

Cubasi
www.cubasi.cu

Infocom
www.infocom.etecsa.cu

Isla Grande
www.islagrande.cu

Paginas Amarillas
www.paginasamarillas.cu

Havana-Specific
Havana Supersite
www.lahabana.com

**Innovaciones en La Habana
(Innovations in Havana)**
www.anirch.islagrande.cu

Mi Habana
www.mihabana.islagrande.cu

Tribuna de La Habana (News)
www.tribuna.islagrande.cu

CULTURE

1,2,3 . . . y (Music)
www.123y.islagrande.cu

Artcuba
www.artcuba.com

Ballet Nacional de Cuba
www.balletcuba.cu

Casa de las Américas
www.casa.cult.cu

Cubacine
www.cubacine.cu

Cuba Fine Art
www.artecubano.com

Discuba (music shop)
www.discuba.com

Fondo Cubano de Bienes Culturales
www.infocex.cu/fcbc

Fundación del Nuevo Cine Latinoamericano
www.fncl.cult.cu

Instituto Cubano del Libro
www.cubaliteraria.com

Instituto de Cinematográfía
www.havanafilmfestival.com

La Jiribilla Revista Cultural
www.lajiribilla.cubaweb.cu

Oficina del Historiador de la Ciudad Habana (Office of the City Historian)
www.ohch.cu

Radio/TV Martí
www.martinoticias.com

Soy Cubano
www.soycubano.com

Timba (Music)
www.timba.com/index.asp

UNEAC
www.uneac.cult.cu

TOURISM

General Information
1click2click Journeys to Cuba
www.1click2cuba.com

Alma de Cuba (Italian)
www.almadecuba.cu

Bienvenidos: Guía del Ocio y la Cultura
www.bienvenidoscuba.com

Caribbean Hotel Association
www.caribbeanhotels.org

Caribbean Tourist Organization
www.doitcaribbean.com

Infotur
www.infotur.cu

Ministry of Tourism (Ministerio de Turismo)
www.cubatravel.cu

Tourism Directory of Cuba (Directorio Turístico de Cuba)
www.dtcuba.com

Airlines: Domestic
Cubana de Aviación
www.cubana.cu

Airlines: International
Aerocaribe
www.aerocaribe.com

Aeroflot
www.aeroflot.ru

Aeropostal
www.aeropostal.com

Air Canada
www.aircanada.ca

Air Europa
www.aireuropa.com

Air Europe
www.aireurope.it

Air France
www.airfrance.com.fr

Air Jamaica
www.airjamaica.com

Air Transat
www.airtransatholidays.com

AOM
www.air-liberte.fr

British Airways
www.britishairways.co.uk

Condor
www.condor.com

Internet Resources

Copa Air
www.copaair.com

Grupo Taca
www.grupotaca.com

Iberia
www.iberia.com

JAL
www.jal.co.jp

KLM
www.klm.com

LanChile
www.lanchile.com

Lauda Air
www.laudaair.it

LTU
www.ltu.de

Martinair
www.martinair.com

Mexicana
www.mexicana.com

Spanair
www.spanair.com

Tame
www.tame.com.ec

Licensed Travel Service Providers (TSPs)
Cuba Travel Services
www.cubatravelservices.com

Gulfstream
www.gulfstreamair.com

Marazul Charters
www.marazulcharters.com

Marazul Tours
www.marazultours.com

Tico Travel
www.destinationcuba.com

Car Rental Companies and Taxis
Cubacar
www.cubacar.cubanacan.cu

Gran Car
www.cuba.cu/turismo/panatrans/grancar.htm

Havanautos
www.havanautos.cu

Panautos
www.cuba.cu/turismo/panatrans/panautos

Rex Limousines
www.rex-rentacar.com

Transtur Rent-a-Car
www.transtur.cu
www.transturtaxi.com

Vía Rent-a-Car
www.gaviota-grupo.com

Cruise Companies
Aida Cruises
www.aida.de

Festival Cruises
www.festivalcruises.com

Fred Olsen Cruise Lines
www.fredolsencruises.co.uk

Hamburg-Süd Reiseagentur GMBH
www.hamburg-sued-reiseagentur.de

Hapag-Lloyd
www.hapag-lloyd.com

Sun Cruises
www.suncruises.co.uk

Hotel Groups

Cubanacán
www.cubanacan.cu

Gaviota
www.gaviota-grupo.com

Gran Caribe
www.grancaribe.cubaweb.cu or
www.grancaribe.cu

Horizontes
www.horizontes.cu

Hoteles Habaguanex
www.habaguanex.cu

Islazul
www.islazul.cubaweb.cu

Sol Meliá (Spain)
www.solmeliacuba.com

Hotels

(See the hotel group listed under individual
hotels, in the Accommodations chapter.)

Hostal Las Frailes
www.hostalosfrailes.cu

Hostal Valencia
www.hostalvalencia.cu

Hotel Ambos Mundos
www.hotelambosmundos.com

Hotel Conde de Villanueva
www.hostalcondevillanueva.cu

Hotel Florida
www.hotelflorida.cu

Hotel Golden Tulip Parque Central
www.goldentuliphotels.nl

Hotel Palco
www.cubaweb.cu/palco

Hotel San Miguel
www.hostalsanmiguel.com

Hotel del Tejadillo
www.hostaldeltejadillo.cu

Online Booking Agents

Blue Ocean Tours
www.blueoceantour.com

Casaparticular.com
www.casaparticular.com

Cubalinda
www.cubalinda.com

E-travelcuba
www.e-travelcuba.com

Go Cuba
www.gocubaplus.com

Havana Flying Club
www.havanaflyingclub.com

Travelnet (Cuban)
www.travelnet.cu

Vacacionar (Cuban)
www.vacacionartravel.com

Sights

Acuario Nacional (National Aquarium)
www.acuarionacional.cu

Museo Nacional de Bellas Artes
www.museonacional.cult.cu

Palacio de los Convenciones
www.cubaweb.cu/palco

Universidad de la Habana
www.uh.cu

Tour Companies: Cuban

Cubatur
www.cubatur.cu

Gaviota Tours
www.gaviota-grupo.com

Grupo Cubanacán
www.cubanacan.cu

Havanatur
www.havanatur.cu

Paradiso
www.ceniai.inf.cu/paradiso

Rumbos
www.cubaonline.cu/rumbos

Transtur
www.transtur.cu

Viajes Horizontes
www.horizont.cu

Tour Companies: U.S.
Cross-Cultural Journeys
www.crossculturaljourneys.com

Cuba Cultural Travel
www.cubaculturaltravel.com

Cuba Now
www.cubanow.org

Cuba Travel USA
www.cubatravelusa.com

Gayjet Travel
www.gayjet.com

Island Travel & Tours
www.islandtraveltours.com

Last Frontier Expeditions
www.cubatravelexperts.com

Marazul Tours
www.marazultours.com

National Geographic Expeditions
www.nationalgeographic.com

Plaza Cuba
www.plazacuba.com

Tico Travel
www.destinationcuba.com

Trains Unlimited Tours
www.trainsunlimitedtours.com

Worldguest
www.worldguest.com

Tour Companies: International
Airtours (UK)
www.airtours.co.uk

Active Journeys (Canada)
www.activejourneys.com

Canadian Universities Travel Service (Canada)
www.travelcuts.com

Captivating Cuba (UK)
www.captivating-cuba.co.uk

Caribbean Bound (Australia)
www.caribbean.com.au

Caribbean Expressions (UK)
www.expressionsholidays.co.uk

Caribic Vacations (Jamaica)
www.caribicvacations.com

**Council on International
Educational Exchange**
www.ciee.org or www.counciltravel.com

Cuba Connect (UK)
www.cubaconnect.co.uk

Cuba Connection (Turks & Caicos)
www.cuba.tc

Cuba Holidays 4 Less (UK)
www.cuba-holidays4less.co.uk

ElderTreks (Canada)
www.eldertreks.com

Explore Worldwide (UK)
www.explore.co.uk

Friendship Tours (Canada)
www.cubafriendship.com

Interchange (UK)
www.interchange.uk.com

Journey Latin America (UK)
www.journeylatinamerica.co.uk

Kubareisen (Germany)
www.ccc-tours.de

Kuoni (UK)
www.kuoni.co.uk

MacQueen's Adventures Tours (Canada)
www.macqueens.com

Niagara Safaris (Canada)
www.niagarasafari.com

Ocean Travel
www.cubatravel.com.au

Regent Holidays (UK)
www.cheapflights.co.uk

San Cristobal Travel (Canada)
www.sancristobaltravel.com

Scuba Cuba (Canada)
www.diving-cuba.com

STA Travel
www.statravel.co and www.statravel.co.uk

Taíno Tours (Mexico)
www.pceditores.com/taino

Trailfinders (UK)
www.trailfinders.com

Transnico (Belgium)
www.transnico.com

Tropical Tours (Jamaica)
www.marzouca.com

Voyage Culture Cuba (Canada)
www.culturecuba.com

Miscellaneous
American Foundation for the Blind
www.afb.org

American Friends Service Committee
www.afsc.org

Center for Creative Education
www.ccedrums.org

Interlocken International Camp
www.interlocken.org

International Gay & Lesbian Travel Association
www.iglta.org

Society for Accessible Travel & Hospitality
www.sath.org

Volunteers for Peace
www.vfp.org

Víazul (tourist buses)
www.viazul.cu

NEWS ORGANIZATIONS AND PUBLICATIONS

Bohemia
www.cuba.cu/bohemia

Cubanet
www.cubanet.org

Granma (international edition)
www.granma.cu

Information Services Latin America (ISLA)
www.igc.org/isla

Juventud Rebelde
www.jrebelde.cubaweb.cu

Latin American News Syndicate
www.latam-news.com

Opciones
www.opciones.cubaweb.cu

Prensa Latina
www.prensa-latina.org

Radio Metropolitana
www.metropolitana.islagrande.cu

Radio Reloj
www.radioreloj.cu

Revista Mujeres
www.mujeres.cubaweb.cu

Trabajadores
www.trabajadores.cubaweb.cu

Travel Trade Cuba
www.ttcuba.com

Tribuna de la Habana
www.tribuna.islagrande.cu

GOVERNMENT-RELATED AND NGO'S

Cuban Government
Academy of Sciences (Academía de Ciencias)
www.cuba.cu/ciencia/acc/index0.htm

Aduana (Customs)
www.aduana.islagrande.com

Agencia de Información Naciónal
www.ain.cubaweb.cu

Chamber of Commerce (Cámara de Comercio)
www.camaracuba.com

Consultória Jurídica Internacional
www.cji.cubaweb.cu

Correos de Cuba (postal service)
www.correosdecuba.com

Cuban government (official site)
www.cubagob.cu

Cuba (enterprises)
www.nuevaempresa.cu

Cuba (industry)
www.cubaindustria.cu

Cuba (medical sciences)
www.infomed.sld.cu

Cuba (science)
www.cubaciencia.cu

Cuban Embassy (Canada)
www.embacu.ca

Cuban Embassy (China)
www.embonline.net/cuba

Cuban Embassy (Germany)
www.cubaifno.de

Cuban Embassy (Mexico)
www.embacuba.com.mx

Cuban Interests Section (Washington, D.C.)
www.geocities.com/cubainte

Ministry of Foreign Relations (MINREX)
www.cubaminrex.cu

Internet Resources

Ministry of Superior Education
www.mes.edu.cu

U.S. Government
U.S. Government Health Advisories
www.cdc.gov

U.S. State Department
www.state.gov

U.S. State Department (Office of Cuban Affairs)
www.state.gov/r/pa/ei/bgn/2886.htm

U.S. State Department (Overseas Citizens Services)
http://travel.state.gov/acs.html#emr

U.S. State Department (Travel Advisories)
www.travel.state.gov/cuba.html

U.S. Treasury Department (OFAC)
www.treas.gov/ofac

Non-Governmental Organizations (NGO's)
Center for Cuban Studies
www.cubaupdate.com

Centre for a Free Cuba
www.cubacenter.org

Conchord Cayo Hueso
www.geocities.com/conchordcayohueso

Cuba AIDS Project
www.cubaonline.org

Cuban American National Foundation
www.canfnet.org

Cuban American Alliance Education Fund
www.cubamer.org

Cuban Solidarity Campaign
www.cuba-solidarity.org.uk

Cuba Policy Foundation
www.cubapolicyfoundation.org

Food First
www.foodfirst.org/cuba

Friendship Force
www.friendship-force.org

Global Exchange
www.globalexchange.com

Jewish Solidarity
www.jewishcuba.org/solidarity

MADRE
www.madre.org

Pastors for Peace
www.ifconews.org

People to People Ambassadors
www.ambassadorprograms.org

Servas
www.servas.org

U.S.–Cuba Sister City Association
www.USCSCA.org

U.S.–Cuba Trade & Economic Council
www.cubatrade.org

U.S.–Latin American Medical Aid Foundation
www.medaid.org

USA*ENGAGE
www.usaengage.org

Venceremos Brigade
www.venceremosbrigade.org

Witness for Peace
www.witnessforpeace.org

**Women's International League for Peace
and Freedom**
www.wilpf.org

MISCELLANEOUS

Banco Metropolitano
www.banco-metropolitano.com

Bluewater Books & Charts
www.bluewaterweb.com

Bridge for Historic Preservation
www.connect2cuba.org

British Foreign & Commonwealth Office
www.fco.gov.uk/travel/default.asp

Buró de Convenciones
www.buroconv.cubaweb.cu

Caledonia Languages Abroad
www.caledonialanguages.co.uk

**Centro de Ingeniería Genética
y Biotecnología**
www.cigb.edu.cu

**Centro Internacional de
Restauración Neurologica**
www.ciren.cubaweb.cu

Clínica Central Cira García
www.sld.cu/webs/cirag/index.html

Coral Container Lines
www.coral.cubaweb.cu

Cubacel (cellular telephones)
www.cubacel.com

Cuba Gift Store
www.cubagiftstore.com

Cubapacks (express delivery)
www.cubapacks.com

DHL
www.dhl.com

Elián González
www.elian.cu/elian0.htm

E-scriba
www.e-scriba.com

Etecsa (Cuban telephone company)
www.etecsa.cu

Friends of Cuban Libraries
www.friendsofcubanlibraries.org

Fundación del Nuevo Cine Latinamericano
www.fncl.cult.cu

Gay Cuba
www.gay-cuba.com

Habanos, S.A. (cigars)
www.infocex.cu/habanos/index.htm

Interflora
www.fleurop.com

International Gay and Lesbian Association
www.gaycenter.org

**Joven Club de Creadores (Computer
Youth Club)**
www.jcce.org.cu/jovenclub

Marinas Puertosol
www.puertosol.net

Moneygram
www.moneygram.com

**National Oceanic &
Atmospheric Administration**
www.chartmaker.ncd.noaa.gov

Páginas Amarillas de Cuba (Yellow Pages)
www.paginasamarillas.cu

Send a Piana to Havana
www.sendapiana.com

Tran$card
www.cash2cuba.com

Union de Periodistas (Journalists' Union)
www.upec.cu

Western Union
www.westernunion.com

Zona Franca Ciudad Habana
(Free Trade Zone)
www.zonafrancach.cu

Insurance
AFTA
www.afta.com.au

American Express
www.americanexpress.com

Aseguradora del Turismo La Isla
www.cuba.cu/laisla

Association of British Insurers
www.abi.org.uk

Council on International Education
Exchange (CIEE)
www.ciee.org

Endsleigh Insurance
www.endsleigh.co.uk

ESEN
www.esen.com.cu

STA Travel
www.sta.com

Travelers
www.travelers.com

TravelGuard International
www.travelguard.com

Travel Insurance on the Net
www.travelinsurance.com.au

Jewish Organizations
Cuba–America Jewish Mission
www.thecajm.org

Jewish Solidarity
www.jewishcuba.org

Sephardic Friendship Committee
www.sephardicfriends.com

Legal, Financial, Medical Assistance
Asistur
www.asistur.cubaweb.cu

Assist-Card
www.assist-card.com

Cuba Directo
www.directocuba.com

International Association for Medical
Assistance to Travellers
www.iamat.org

International Legal Defense Counsel
www.internationalrecoveryllc.com

International SOS Assistance
www.internationalsos.com

Traveler's Emergency Network
www.tenweb.com

Weather
www.intellicast.com

Index

Acknowledgments

Heartfelt thanks are due to those individuals who in sundry ways assisted my research for this edition.

I especially appreciate the support of Juan Carlos Aguilar Cabello, of Tropicana; Michael Sykes, of Cuba Cultural Travel; Manuel Estefanía Seoane, vice president of Gran Caribe; Alicia Pérez Casanova of Horizontes; Ralph Martell; plus Carl G. Finstrom; Katharine Kinney; Eugenio O'Hallarans; Bridget Murphy; Iain Neighbour; and all others who through my forgetfulness have not been acknowledged.

Special acknowledgement must go to Jorge Coalla Potts and his wife, Marisel, and Julio Muñoz and his wife, Rosita.

Special words of appreciation and affection go to Damaris Bencomo Nay; Mercedes Martínez Crespo; Maryolis "Yoli" Bernal; and Lourdes Mulen Duarte, of the Consultoría Jurídica Internacional.

Last, and above all, I offer my deepest affection, gratitude, and a lifelong *abrazo* to Daisy Prometa Bartolomé, whose gaiety, love, and affection filled my time in Havana with boundless joy. Cuba will never be the same without her.

U.S. ~ Metric Conversion

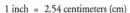

1 inch	=	2.54 centimeters (cm)
1 foot	=	.304 meters (m)
1 yard	=	0.914 meters
1 mile	=	1.6093 kilometers (km)
1 km	=	.6214 miles
1 fathom	=	1.8288 m
1 chain	=	20.1168 m
1 furlong	=	201.168 m
1 acre	=	.4047 hectares
1 sq km	=	100 hectares
1 sq mile	=	2.59 square km
1 ounce	=	28.35 grams
1 pound	=	.4536 kilograms
1 short ton	=	.90718 metric ton
1 short ton	=	2000 pounds
1 long ton	=	1.016 metric tons
1 long ton	=	2240 pounds
1 metric ton	=	1000 kilograms
1 quart	=	.94635 liters
1 US gallon	=	3.7854 liters
1 Imperial gallon	=	4.5459 liters
1 nautical mile	=	1.852 km

To compute Celsius temperatures, subtract 32 from Fahrenheit and divide by 1.8. To go the other way, multiply Celsius by 1.8 and add 32.

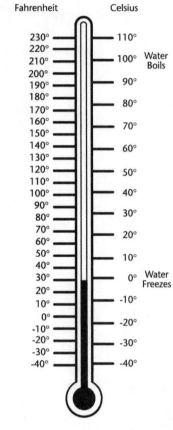

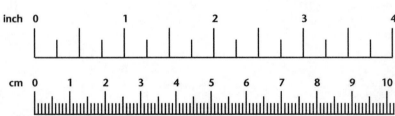

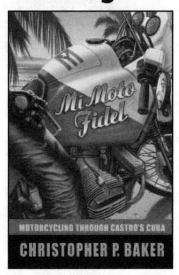

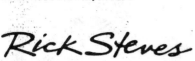